SPLENDID SERVICE

SPLENDID SERVICE

The Montana National Guard, 1867–2006

Edited by Orlan J. Svingen

WSU PRESS

Washington State University Press
Pullman, Washington

WASHINGTON STATE UNIVERSITY

Washington State University Press
PO Box 645910
Pullman, Washington 99164-5910
Phone: 800-354-7360
Fax: 509-335-8568
E-mail: wsupress@wsu.edu
Web site: wsupress.wsu.edu

First printing 2010

Library of Congress Cataloging-in-Publication Data

Splendid service: the Montana National Guard, 1867-2006 / edited by
Orlan J. Svingen.
p. cm.
Includes bibliographical references and index.
ISBN 0-87422-286-9 (alk. paper)
1. Montana. National Guard—History. I. Svingen, Orlan J.
UA300.S66 2006
355.3'709786--dc22

2006001975

WSU PRESS
Fine Quality Books from the Pacific Northwest

MIX
Paper from responsible sources
FSC www.fsc.org FSC® C015906

Table of Contents

Foreword

Brigadier General Bill Yeager, MTARNG (Retired)

When I was asked to review *Splendid Service*, I did so with some trepidation, not really sure that I was up to the task. When I received my draft, I was astounded by the excellent research and writing of so many historians, concerning an organization that I thought I knew so well. I joined the guard and was assigned as a cook in 1956 when Maj. Gen. S.H. Mitchell was adjutant general and completed my career 39 years later when Maj. Gen. John E. Prendergast held the top job. Because I was involved during those years, I felt I was pretty familiar with that portion of the guard's history. But I learned a great deal about that period, as well as the history before and after it.

As a longtime broadcast newsman, I especially appreciated the historians telling the whole story, or, as we used to say, "warts and all." Everyone is reluctant to let the skeletons out of the closet when it comes to talking about family or the organizations they belong to, and there was the wish by many that only the "good" stuff be made known. However, the good becomes even more impressive with the backdrop of the "not so good." When I was questioned about news stories where this subject came up, I explained that jewelers display diamonds on black velvet because they look much more brilliant that way.

This book does a splendid job in describing the great things done by the Montana National Guard and the sacrifice and dedication of so many of its soldiers and airmen. That's the way it should be. There is much for us to be proud of in the guard's struggles in peacetime just to exist and of the brave and dedicated service in numerous wars and state emergencies.

However, there are many things that we would just as soon forget: instances of bad judgment, mistakes, and even unlawful activities. My heart aches for the Indian women and children who died needlessly in the Big Hole. I find little comfort in Gen. Meagher's solo decision to call out the militia without doing so legally, and running up a tab that he expected taxpayers to cover. And there were others. One finds fascinating reading about the good—and the bad—in this superb history.

One last thing. The book was built upon archive materials that many of us were unaware existed and upon the 1976 monograph, *The Montana Militia*, by Spec. Richard H. Lacey. I'm especially aware of the background for that publication. For a time, I commanded the guard's 103rd Public Affairs Detachment and Rick was a member. Our workspace held many boxes of old papers, ledgers, and the like. I went through them and found several bits of guard history that I did up as features in the newspaper, which we then published quarterly. I was increasingly concerned that someone would toss out those old materials before they could be examined.

Enter Spec. Lacey. He owned a registered angus cattle ranch near Drummond. Feeding cattle made it really tough for him to get to drill in the winter, so he came up with a plan: he'd receive equivalent training for the winter drills and come to Helena for an equal number of days in the spring to research and write the history. Rick also received great help from another unit member, Spec. Raymond Bell, who made his print shop available for Rick to do the layout.

When Rick had finished that part, the adjutant general, Maj. Gen. John J. Womack, who owned the newspaper in Dillon, made the facility available to Spec. Lacey after hours to print the publication. Most writers are reluctant to have someone else edit their work, and Rick was no different. The history was published before anyone had a chance to review it. Despite obvious errors, the bottom line was this: a lot of interesting history of the Montana National Guard was captured and preserved in a usable form.

I feel that in this book, Montana will have a history of her militia and guard that will be equal or superior to that of any other state or territory. I am pleased and proud of this great publication and of the opportunity that I have had to be part of the editorial process.

Foreword

Hal Stearns
Brigadier General MTARNG (Retired)

History is really story. It has drama, tragedy, highlights, miscues, heroes, leaders and followers, individuals who have dreams and aspirations. It is life itself. Military history, on the other hand, is "for keeps." It is the story of men and women who leave home, train hard, and put their very lives on the line for a cause. Some volunteer, some are conscripted, but all share in common a love and devotion to country. I taught history for many years, always with the firm belief that we need to understand the past in order to deal with the present and future. At one time in my military career, I commanded a Public Affairs Detachment. In addition to sharing the story of the Montana Army National Guard with our fellow troops and the public, unit members were diligent about giving the background of the stories produced. The past was very much a part of the unit. Wonderful soldiers like Sgts. Kermit Edmonds, Lyle Gillette, Howard Anderson, Milo McLeod, and Orlan Svingen had rich military records. They began to capture the story of the Montana Guard. Colonel Ray Read and countless others shared the same enthusiasm for piecing together the history of the guard.

When Orlan Svingen went to Washington State University, the story really began to be gathered. His graduate seminars and diligent students worked so tirelessly researching and writing and melding *Splendid Service* into a marvelous tale of the Montana Guard.

Anyone who has ever served has a special relationship with every other soldier. History ties the bond together. *Splendid Service* is the Montana Guard story. It is a wonderful and vital piece of the jigsaw puzzle that is Montana's past.

Introduction and Acknowledgments

This volume, *Splendid Service, The Montana National Guard, 1867–2006,* had its beginnings as a spring 1998 public history seminar in the History Department at Washington State University in Pullman, Washington. So often, people are curious about the field of public history and how it differs from "history." At its simplest, perhaps, public history is applied history—history used, applied, or presented outside academic circles. Someone reading an interpretive sign on the Lewis and Clark Trail or watching the most recent Ken Burns film presentation is reading or viewing the handiwork of a public historian. Local, state, regional, and national archives and museums are filled with "public historians" who provide an array of scholarly expertise, services, and interpretation for the public. They produce television documentaries, interpretive panels, oral histories, historic preservation projects, cultural resource assessments, records management plans, public policy studies, contract histories, any number of archival and museum services. Public history professors at colleges and universities train undergraduate and graduate students for these endeavors. Public historians—either as individuals or more commonly as team members—are also collaborators who work toward a common goal with other specialists, and they frequently produce work products for a variety of private sector, local, state, regional, and nationally based clients.

When I arrived at Washington State University in 1989, I was hired to head the History Department's public history track. As I considered how I might organize its curriculum, I decided to use, in part, what I had learned in my tenure at Historical Research Associates (HRA), a private research firm in Missoula, Montana. Among other things, I learned how to work with a research team to produce a scholarly manuscript or product in accordance with a contract negotiated between the firm and the client. Each project involved extensive planning, budgeting, deadlines, and ultimately producing what the firm called a "client deliverable." As a direct outcome of my time with HRA, I decided to use the HRA model (as I came to refer to it) as one of the central components to my public history graduate students' training. If an essential goal of the public history curriculum was to train graduate students to work effectively with agencies outside the academy, then incorporating a private sector model inside the public history seminar seemed an ideal approach.

My first opportunity came quickly because I used my first public history seminar at WSU as a training ground for researching, writing, and editing a draft manuscript detailing the history of the Idaho National Guard. Ten M.A. and Ph.D. students in that 1990 seminar researched and wrote the chapters that formed that volume. After editing and subsequently publishing my students' chapters in *The History of the Idaho National Guard* in 1995, I had discussions with officials in the Montana National Guard who indicated their interest in a similar effort for Montana. Our mutual interest in such a project gelled over the next year or so, and finally preparations for the extramurally supported seminar began in Pullman during the fall semester of 1997. We addressed class readings, project chapter assignments, and made preparations for a project research trip to Montana to conduct research and collect historical materials for researching and writing the history of the Montana National Guard. The "primary course objective" in the seminar syllabus read as follows:

> In response to a request from the Montana National Guard [MT-ARNG] of Helena, Montana, this public history seminar will devote itself to researching and writing a history of the Montana National Guard, beginning with the establishment of Montana Territory in 1864 until the present. A funded contract exists between Washington State University and MT-ARNG which supports certain activities and costs involved in the researching and writing phases of the work. The professor and the graduate students will act in the capacity of paid consultants [employees] to the MT-ARNG [employer]. This will involve working within the guidelines outlined in the contract, meeting time schedules and providing draft and final "deliverables" to the client–MT-ARNG. Accordingly, each graduate student will research, write, submit, and revise a chapter length paper for this seminar.

During the week of February 16, 1998, the seminar participants traveled to Helena, Montana, first checking into a local motel that afternoon and then attending a welcoming dinner at Fort Harrison, just outside of Helena. Colonel Raymond Read, the lead MT-ARNG representative throughout the project, greeted us and then introduced SFC Kermit Edmonds, who gave a slide presentation on the history of the Montana National Guard. The next morning, we visited the State Area Command (STARC) Headquarters in Helena, where Adjutant General John E. Prendergast addressed the students and offered his support for the project. Next the class attended a welcome and orientation at the Montana Historical Society. For the remainder of the week, students conducted research at STARC, the Montana State Library, the Montana Historical Society, and the Montana Military History Museum at Fort Harrison. Each evening that week, the seminar met for a one hour "roundtable discussion," addressing the day's findings and other pertinent research concerns. Several students made research trips outside of Helena—one to Butte and another to Great Falls—and other state repositories were consulted, such as the university libraries at the University of Montana in Missoula, and Montana State University in Bozeman. Later that spring, I took several seminar students to conduct research at the National Archives in Washington, D.C., and in College Park, Maryland. We also completed valuable research in the National Guard Memorial Library collections housed in the National Guard Memorial Building, the headquarters for the National Guard Association of the United States.

The M.A. and Ph.D. students in the seminar used these research materials from Montana and Washington, D.C., to write their individual chapters, and subsequently drafts were forwarded to a variety of readers for comments. Eventually, four M.A. students expanded their chapter drafts into M.A. theses, and one Ph.D. student, Richard Hines, published an abridged version of his chapter in *Montana, The Magazine of Western History*. As the edited manuscript progressed, we obtained a publishing contract with the Washington State University Press in 2004. That sparked more research into locating, retrieving copies, and obtaining permission to use approximately 75 photographs in the book.

Few of my seminar students had any formal background in military history, much less National Guard history, and this required them to "get up to speed" on a new topic. Pursuing a graduate field in public history means that students will probably conduct research and write on a topic at some point in their careers that is unfamiliar to them, and training such as this serves them well as they enter the field. It is typical work for those in public history to apply historical methodology, research, and writing techniques to what may be to them a new and somewhat foreign field of study. Non-public historians often focus their entire careers on specific, narrow topics, perhaps occasionally getting outside of their specialties when teaching a survey history class, for example. Public historians, on the other hand, might work on a National Guard project such as this one, an American Indian federal recognition initiative, the history of a state's wine industry, a national park cultural resource assessment, or maybe the beginning stages of proposing a new national park. Reading and working in a variety of public history subfields and conducting research and writing on diverse topics prepares public history students to accept challenging projects. Collaborating with other specialists in or outside the history discipline and producing deliverables in accordance with project proposals, budgets, deadlines, and client-related expectations distinguishes the public historian from the non-public historian.

Acknowledging the encouragement, assistance, and efforts of all the people connected to a project of this magnitude is daunting, for there are so many to thank. But let me begin by thanking each one of the M.A. and Ph.D. students whose diligent work the readers will encounter as they page through this volume. Their dedication to careful and thorough research, writing, and rewriting as well as their acceptance of ongoing editorial criticism made this challenging graduate student project a valued training ground for future historians.

Colonel Raymond Read, Retired, has been the ballast for this project. His unflagging enthusiasm, commitment, and optimism, plus his willingness to make historical resources available throughout the project, enabled this volume to become a reality. Most people connected to our work will agree that without Colonel Read, this project could not have been completed. As a longtime Public

Affairs Officer for the Montana National Guard, he understood the operations and the structural underpinnings of the organization, and he knew almost everyone there was to know who needed to be contacted. When the project was first conceived, Colonel Read briefed Adjutant General John E. "Gene" Prendergast and persuaded him of its merits. It is my hope that General Prendergast will consider this volume as one of the many achievements in his 46-year career in the Montana National Guard, 12 of which he served as Adjutant General. John B. Wheeler, the Administrator of the Army Environmental Program, was instrumental early in the project, helping to procure project funding, and reading and commenting on early chapter drafts. Kermit Edmonds is well known in Montana as an interpreter of Montana National Guard history and material culture. His many displays of armaments, uniforms, and flags have brought clarity, understanding, and interest in the Montana National Guard. Edmonds read each manuscript chapter with great care, offering an array of technical advice on many levels. His assistance to Colonel Read, my graduate students, and to me throughout the project was an act of kindness and friendship. Milo McLeod also read several chapters and offered valuable editorial remarks, corrections, and elaborations. Montana artist Robert F. "Bob" Morgan, CW3, Retired, of Helena graciously read several chapters and offered kind, thoughtful advice and suggestions that improved the manuscript. Brigadier General Harold J. "Hal" Stearns offered valuable support as well, endorsing the project, and reading and commenting on chapter drafts.

Other members of the National Guard have offered important support and encouragement. My association with Major General Bruce Jacobs, Army National Guard, Retired, was one that has reminded me over the years about the central role the National Guard has occupied in the military history of the United States. General Jacobs values the role of every state and territorial National Guard organization in the United States, and he has labored to promote its role to the nation. Similarly, Brigadier General Leonid Kondratiuk, the former Chief of Historical Services at the National Guard Bureau in Washington, D.C., spent his years as chief overseeing that office's responsibilities in promoting the National Guard's history, heraldry, and museums. He was most helpful to me in his work coordinating the Army National Guard Field History Program and working with state command historians, museum curators, and military history detachment commanders. John Listman, W2, Retired, has long been helpful to National Guard researchers, especially in the field of historic photos. Finally, I want to acknowledge LTC Leonard Krenk, Retired, my commanding officer in the Nebraska National Guard, and Doug Hartman, my former student and friend. Thank you to LTC Loren Call, my commanding officer in the Idaho National Guard. Their friendship and encouragement over the years have been a wellspring of support.

When my students descended upon the Montana Historical Society in Helena, Montana, some years back, they were met by consummate professionals dedicated to providing first-rate historical services to their patrons. Thank you to former Montana State Archivist Kathryn D. Otto, Society Librarian Robert M. Clark, the current State Archivist Jodie Foley, Library Manager Brian Shovers, Photograph Archives Manager Lory Morrow, and Library Reference Technician Angie Murray. Thank you to Ellen Crain, Manager of the Archives Department at the Butte-Silver Bow Public Archives, for her assistance on early twentieth century research materials in Butte, and to Kenneth W. Karsmizki, Associate Curator of Historical Archaeology at the Museum of the Rockies in Bozeman, Montana, for his help on the early history of Fort Ellis.

Another significant partner in this project is Roger Schlesinger, Professor Emeritus and former WSU History Department Chair, for his departmental support and for approving a generous publication subvention from the Washington State University History Department's Margaret Pettyjohn Endowment. Those funds, coupled with the equally generous subvention from the Montana National Guard Thrift Shop, made this Washington State University Press publication possible.

And finally, much gratitude is owed to Washington State University Press for accepting the manuscript for publication, for providing editorial guidance and encouragement, and steering the book through production and marketing. Their patience and effort in shepherding this book to completion has been monumental. Editor-in-chief Glen Lindeman provided much careful attention to historical detail, supplied refinements and maps, and filled in historical holes that occasionally occurred. His extensive knowledge of American history and historical research was inestimable, and his own military experience supplied him a valuable framework of knowledge for this subject. Thanks to Charles Mutschler, archivist at Eastern Washington University Library, who thoughtfully reviewed the manuscript for the Press. Mary Read, Director of the WSU Press, has proven instrumental in wrapping up the final details, and deserves credit for her role in seeing *Splendid Service* make it to press. Great appreciation is extended to all who have touched these chapters in some way, in draft or final form!

Orlan J. Svingen

Contributors

Janet Creighton received her bachelor and master degrees from the University of Washington, and a doctorate in American/public history from Washington State University in 2004. She is a member of the board of directors for the Burke Museum of Natural History and Culture and the Archaeological Conservancy. She is also a part of the WSU Advisory Council for the College of Liberal Arts and the University of Washington Press Development Advisory Board.

Michael H. Evans is a master's student in history at Washington State University, writing his thesis on the Oregon National Guard during the Spanish American War.

Matthew Godfrey earned a bachelor's degree in history from Brigham Young University, a master's degree in history from Utah State University, and a doctorate in American/public history from Washington State University in 2001. He is the co-owner and president of Historical Research Associates Inc., a consulting firm in Missoula, Montana. Godfrey is the author of *Religion, Politics, and Sugar: The Mormon Church, the Federal Government, and the Utah-Idaho Sugar Company, 1907-1921* (Utah State University Press, 2007), which won the 2007 Mormon History Association's Best First Book on Mormon History.

Carol Scally Grigas earned her doctorate from Washington State University in 2004. She is teaching at Embry-Riddle Aeronautical University in Daytona, Florida.

Richard K. Hines earned his master's degree in 1996 and his doctorate in 2001 from Washington State University, where he is an instructor in the general education program.

Suzanne Julin received her doctorate from Washington State University in 2001. She lives in Missoula, Montana, and works as a public historian for local, state, and national organizations. She specializes in twentieth-century South Dakota and western history.

Mari Hillestad Knirck, who earned a master's degree in 2000 from Washington State University, is a librarian at Brooks Library, Central Washington University, in Ellensburg, Washington.

Diane L. Krahe earned her doctorate in 2005 from Washington State University. She is an assistant research professor in the Department of History at the University of Montana. Krahe also conducts research and consults for the National Park Service.

Dwayne A. Mack, who received his doctorate in 2002 from Washington State University, is an associate professor in the Department of History and the Carter G. Woodson Chair in African American History at Berea College in Kentucky.

John W.W. Mann earned a bachelor's degree from Bowdoin in 1992 and a master's degree (1997) and doctorate (2001) from Washington State University. He is an associate professor of history at the University of Wisconsin, Eau Claire where he teaches public and American history. He has research interests in American Indian history.

Susan Paras earned her master's degree in 2000 from Washington State University. She was a museum specialist with the Bureau of Reclamation and later worked for the Boise Public Library. She currently resides in Boise, Idaho.

Jennifer Ross-Nazzal received her doctorate from Washington State University in 2004. She currently serves as the historian at the NASA Johnson Space Center in Houston, Texas. She also teaches classes in U.S. and women's history for the University of Maryland University College and the American Public University System.

Shirley Stephens received her master's degree in 1996 and her doctorate in 2008 from Washington State University. She has taught at Central Washington University and Yakima Valley Community College and currently lives in Pullman, Washington.

Michelle Tabit, an assistant professor of history at Defiance College in Ohio, received her master's degree in 2000 and her doctorate in 2004 from Washington State University.

1
Stampede! The Montana Territorial Volunteers of 1867

John W.W. Mann

Meagher, in Montana, is a stampeder, and can always with a fair show of truth raise a clamor.—William T. Sherman, May 4, 1867.

Montana's first militia was organized in 1867 in response to a probably unjustified, but nevertheless genuinely felt, fear of impending Great Plains tribal incursions into western Montana, and because of the machinations of the acting territorial governor, Thomas Francis Meagher. The Montana volunteers established defensive positions, but their overall performance proved to be a mixed record, or even a fiasco in a few instances.

Historian Robert Athearn, with some hyperbole, has characterized this as a case study of how "an Indian war which never materialized, despite the efforts of the [militia] troops to produce it, cost the federal government a half million dollars and complicated the job of the regular troops by exciting the native tribes."[1] Aside from being costly to both the federal government and the territory's citizens, the campaign was marred by some desertion and mutiny among the more unruly militia elements. Most settlers in Montana, however, believed they were well served by the militia's defensive operations and supported its actions.

The fear that Indians would drive whites from western Montana stemmed from the fact that settlement was not yet firmly entrenched in the region. After the visit by Lewis and Clark's Corps of Discovery in 1805–1806, profits from furs had lured trappers over the Continental Divide in following decades. Father Pierre DeSmet and other Catholic missionaries also came to the Bitterroot and Clark Fork country in the 1830s and 1840s, hoping to convert the Flathead and Pend Oreille tribes to Christianity. In 1850, John Owen established a trading post in the Bitterroot Valley, drawing other whites to Montana and creating a base for future agricultural settlement.

As prospectors fanned out from southeast Idaho's Fort Hall, an important supply point on the Oregon Trail, rumors of gold in Montana's creeks began to circulate, but the region remained too remote for exploitation and the early discoveries attracted little attention. Yet new routes soon made Montana more accessible. The first steamboat reached Fort Benton, the head of Missouri navigation, in the spring of 1860, and the Mullan Road linking Fort Benton with Fort Walla Walla near the Columbia River became usable by 1860 and was completed in 1863. Moreover, in the early 1860s, as gold fields in California, Nevada, Colorado, British Columbia, Washington, Oregon, and Idaho were worked out or became overcrowded, the potential of finding wealth in Montana became attractive to prospectors from all across the West.[2]

The first boom came with the discovery of color in July 1862 at Grasshopper Creek, a tributary of the Beaverhead River in southwest Montana. The influx of miners resulted in the founding and rapid growth of Bannack City. In the next spring, gold was found at Alder Gulch and Virginia City was born. In July 1864, Helena arose in the Prickly Pear Valley after a discovery at Last Chance Gulch.

By then, John Bozeman and John M. Jacobs had pioneered a new route into Montana, a northerly offshoot from the Oregon Trail linking Fort Laramie to the Yellowstone and Gallatin valleys. Passing through important Indian hunting grounds, the Bozeman Trail became a favorite, if dangerous, route across the western Plains via the Powder River country to the Montana gold fields.[3]

The miners, merchants, and other immigrants sweeping into the western part of Montana impacted the traditional lifeways of local Indian people, particularly the Flathead, Pend Oreille, and Shoshone, though a strained peace held. On the Great Plains, however, Indian hostility toward the whites prevailed, thwarting settlement in most areas east of the Rockies. The Teton Sioux, under Red Cloud and Young-Man-Afraid-of-His-Horses, were particularly determined to retain their hunting grounds in the Powder River country. For years they had fought hard to wrest this region from the Crow tribe, now largely becoming allied with the U.S. Army. Bands of Arapahoe and Cheyenne, harried by the U.S. Army and territorial militia in Colorado and Nebraska, meanwhile had moved north to the southern tributaries of the Yellowstone River. These movements put added pressure on their traditional enemies farther west and northwest in Montana—the Crow and Blackfeet. In the mid 1860s, the white population in the western mountains and valleys perceived the formidable Plains tribes as a growing threat.[4]

Aware that the widely scattered units of the U.S. Army might not provide timely assistance or protection, territorial officials looked to organizing their own citizenry for self-defense. The first such effort came in 1865. In May, Blackfeet Indians killed 10 men near Fort Benton at the Marias-Missouri confluence, disrupting shipping and sending the territory into alarm. Governor Sydney Edgerton contacted the Secretary of War, requesting troops and supplies, while also informing Washington, D.C., that he was raising a volunteer force.

James Stuart, one of the first to find gold in Montana and who subsequently served in the territorial legislature, was commissioned as a lieutenant colonel by Edgerton. Stuart was charged with raising a militia of 500 men. Recruitment efforts met with little success.[5] "We had more Generals and Colonels…than there were in the Army of the Potomac, trying, with beat of drum, a great display of flags, and a most melancholy waste of cheap whisky, to raise 500 men," one witness remembered. After a two-week recruiting effort, "the company numbered about 30, and broke up in disgust."[6]

Hopes of establishing a militia, however, were rekindled after the arrival of Thomas Francis Meagher, a flamboyant Irish-American. At age 42, Meagher had already led a life full of adventure and danger. As a young man before coming to America, he played a prominent role in a failed uprising in Ireland in 1848. He and other leaders of the Young Ireland movement were arrested, tried, and found guilty of treason and sedition by British authorities. Despite a recommendation for mercy due to his youth and a show of remorse, the court sentenced Meagher to death by hanging, followed by decapitation and quartering. The following summer, however, the sentence was commuted to banishment to Tasmania.

Upon reaching Tasmania, he settled down, married, and began farming. But boredom and word that the United States offered sanctuary eventually prompted Meagher to escape from exile. He stowed away on a fishing boat that took him to a small island off the coast of Australia. From there, he traveled to Pernambuco, Brazil, and gained passage to New York. Meagher received a hero's welcome among the city's Irish population, and thereafter busied himself giving lectures and meeting dignitaries.

With the outbreak of the Civil War, Meagher was appointed commander of New York's Irish Brigade. His soldiers won accolades for valor during the war—particularly for charging up Marye's Heights at Fredericksburg in December 1862, but the battle cost all but 280 of the 1,200 men in his command. By 1863, Meagher's brigade numbered only 520, and he lost a fifth of these at Chancellorsville. With no real force to command, he tendered his resignation, which was accepted on May 14.

Although reinstated in 1864, he was not given charge of a fighting force. A lack of enthusiasm for mundane tasks, coupled with a growing alcohol addiction, rendered him ineffectual. He was forced to resign before the war's end. Meagher then staked hopes on a political career in the West, and inquired about gaining the Idaho Territory governorship. Instead, in August 1865 came an offer to serve as secretary of Montana Territory. He accepted and arrived to assume his position in September.[7]

Meagher hoped this would serve as a launching pad for a political career, thus bringing him back into the national limelight. In an 1865 letter to an Irish American friend, he noted that, if eventually attaining the position of territorial governor, it "would enable me, after a little, to enter Congress." Once there, he bragged, "I have no fear but that I should make myself Master of the Situation—to my own credit, to the gratification of my friends, to the confusion and mortification of my enemies, and to the honour of our race."[8]

The new secretary quickly found himself in the center of a political struggle. Democrats held a firm majority in Montana's territorial assembly, but the appointed territorial officials were Republicans. Governor Sydney Edgerton had vetoed an apportionment bill passed by the Democratic legislature that would have provided for the election of the next legislature, which certainly would be won by the Democrats. Furthermore, the provisions of the territory's organic act had expired. Edgerton felt compelled to travel to Washington, D.C., and sort out the controversy, even if it meant leaving a neophyte, Meagher, in charge.

With Edgerton gone, the Democrats expected that Meagher, who had been a strong northern Democrat before the war, would support them in the election of a new legislature. The Republicans, on the other hand—knowing that Montana's Democrats would win a majority as they had in 1864—thought that Meagher, as a Republican Administration appointee, would support their position and expect the Republican dominated U.S. Congress to establish a legislature in their favor.[9]

If the acting governor was uncertain about how to deal with political turmoil, military affairs offered a welcome diversion. The Plains Indian hostilities of the mid 1860s brought out the soldier in Meagher, and he began demanding the presence of regular army troops as well as raising a volunteer force. In late 1865, shortly after arriving in Montana, he wrote to General William T. Sherman, commander of the Division of the Missouri, requesting a cavalry regiment. Sherman responded by saying he could not possibly fulfill the request, as only one cavalry regiment was at his disposal.[10]

Even before receiving Sherman's answer, the acting governor began raising a territorial militia in response to a statement of grievances submitted by a citizens' group. The petition tabulated the lives and property lost due to Indian depredations in the Plains border region next to Montana's settlements. Meagher issued certificates of commission, but the excitement, along with recruiting efforts, faded before much of anything was accomplished.

By March 1866, petitions again demanded protection, inducing Meagher to try again. He asked the territorial legislature to pass an appropriation to raise a force of 100 men for protecting Fort Benton and Fort Union on the Missouri. Due to opposition from the War Department, however, the legislature refused to grant the request.[11]

Meanwhile, the Sioux were opposed to whites traveling on the Bozeman Trail, which cut through their buffalo hunting grounds in what is now northern Wyoming and south-central Montana Territory. In 1865, warriors also had been incensed by a provocative Powder River campaign led by the U.S. Army's General Patrick Conner. Nonetheless, in June 1866, Red Cloud and other chiefs agreed to meet with a treaty commission headed by E.B. Taylor at Fort Laramie on the Platte River. During the negotiations, however, Col. Henry B. Carrington arrived with a battalion of regular infantry, plus cavalry, en route to constructing forts along the Bozeman Trail to protect Montana travelers. Shortly, Red Cloud defiantly withdrew from the negotiations, vowing to prevent further incursions into the Powder River country.

Throughout the summer, large numbers of Sioux, Cheyenne, and Arapahoe warriors attacked or skirmished with travelers. Meanwhile, Carrington's troops constructed three forts on the Bozeman Trail north from Fort Fetterman and the North Platte River. Positioned along the east side of the Bighorn Mountains, these included Fort Reno on the Powder River and Fort Phil Kearny on Piney Creek (both in Wyoming), and Fort C.F. Smith on the Bighorn River (in southern Montana). Throughout the winter of 1866–1867, tribesmen laid siege to and harassed these posts. In December, Sioux decoys led by Crazy Horse managed to lure a large detachment from Fort Phil Kearny into a trap. Captain William J. Fetterman and all 80 men under his command died in the ambush.[12]

While the Fetterman Massacre provoked debate over federal Indian policy in Washington, D.C., it threw western Montana into alarm. Rumors circulated that springtime would bring an attack by Red Cloud's warriors aimed at driving whites from Montana Territory. The *Montana Post* on February 9, 1867, claimed receiving "well-founded reports of an alliance of Indian tribes—for the purpose of carrying the war into the settlements." The *Post* urged the formation of volunteer defenses.[13]

In March, word reached Virginia City that Red Cloud and 5,400 Sioux and their allies were encamped near Fort C.F. Smith with plans to attack the U.S. Army as soon as weather allowed. The *Montana Post* reported that the garrison did not expect to be able to repel such an assault. Later that month, John Bozeman wrote to Meagher from the Gallatin Valley, warning that the "immanent danger" of Indian attack was driving settlers from that locality, which was closest to the Bozeman Trail hostilities. The *Montana Post* published the letter on April 16 and called again for organizing a militia.[14]

By this time Meagher had set wheels in motion. He commissioned Martin Beem as a captain in the militia, instructing him to oversee recruitment and organization. On April 4, "Adjutant General" Beem issued General Order Number 1—instructing Colonel Walter DeLacey, as "engineer-in-chief," and Capt. Isaac Evans, "Assistant Quartermaster," to report to "Brigadier-General Thomas Thoroughman, commanding forces in the field," at Bozeman City.[15]

On April 9, Meagher telegraphed General Ulysses S. Grant regarding the danger to the Gallatin Valley—"The most populous and prosperous portion of our Territory….threatened by the Sioux. The greatest alarm reasonably prevails," the acting governor reported. "Danger is imminent and will overpower unless measures for defense are immediately taken." He requested permission to raise 1,000 volunteers at government expense.[16]

The War Department was reluctant to give authorization. On May 3, Secretary of War Edwin M. Stanton wrote to Sherman, informing the general that he had conferred with Grant and they both were of the opinion that giving Meagher authority to form a militia was ill-advised. "Very serious evils besides enormous expenditure," Stanton wrote, "always attend to conferring such authority on territorial governors, unless controlled by the supervision and authority of discreet military officers." Nonetheless, Stanton granted Sherman the authority to recognize a Montana territorial militia if the general thought it necessary.[17]

Montana's predicament was particularly delicate in light of the recent Doolittle Committee's report, sent to Congress on January 26, 1867. The Doolittle commission had convened in 1865 to investigate overall conditions among the tribes and the manner in which native peoples were being treated by civilian and military authorities. The study revealed that Indian populations were rapidly diminishing due to disease, war, and the loss of lands to white settlers. Moreover, the report blamed "the aggression of lawless whites" for starting many of the hostilities. Another special committee appointed to investigate the Fetterman Massacre echoed the Doolittle findings.[18]

If such criticism caused Sherman's reluctance to authorize the formation of a militia, the thought of Meagher leading it made him even more wary. In response to Stanton, Sherman noted, "Meagher, in Montana, is a stampeder, and can always with a fair show of truth raise a clamor."[19]

On April 16, the famous trailblazer John Bozeman was killed by Blackfeet while traveling toward Fort C.F. Smith with Thomas Cover to negotiate a government flour contract. Cover arrived in Bozeman City with the news on April 21. The report of Bozeman's death, together with recent rumors that a confederation of Bloods, Piegan, and Blackfeet were preparing to attack the Gallatin Valley, launched fears of an impending Indian uprising to a new level.[20]

News of Bozeman's death proved "too much for the military blood pressure of the acting governor." On April 24, Meagher again publicly called for volunteers.[21] On April 27, he and Chief Justice H.L. Hosmer telegraphed Stanton: "Our Territory in serious danger from the Indians. Positive evidence of general attack from Yellowstone and Wind River Mountains. Richest portion already invaded, citizens murdered. Troops within Territory no use whatever. Forts Phil Kearny and Smith inaccessible…People of Montana thrown upon themselves. Ask therefore authority from War Department to organize eight hundred (800) men for military duty in the field until relieved by regulars…Not an hour to be lost."[22]

Meagher's reference to the unavailability of federal troops was based on a request for aid sent to Maj. William Clinton on April 9, the same day the acting governor telegraphed Grant. Clinton commanded several companies of the 13th Infantry at Camp Cooke, situated at the confluence of the Judith and Missouri rivers. Clinton informed Meagher that he lacked the authority to dispatch troops, and cited the Fetterman Massacre when noting he thought it unwise to divide his force.

Clinton's letter was reprinted in the *Montana Post* on April 27, accompanied by an editorial criticizing the major for "guarding a grove of cottonwood trees against the attack of the 'badlands,' hundreds of miles in extent, over which the whippoorwill has to carry rations on his aerial voyage, and where an Indian is never seen." For all the U.S. Army cared, the article suggested, "the Gallatin may be depopulated; its people murdered and ravished; their towns laid waste, and the finest valley in all this north be the camping grounds of Indians." Clinton's letter, the editorial continued, "shows clearly the spirit that animates its writer, and the less military protection our frontiers have of that kind the better they are off."[23]

As if to confirm that aid from the regular army was unnecessary, the *Post* printed a story from the Helena *Tri-Weekly Republican,* extolling the success of Meagher's recruiting efforts, then well underway. "The streets…resembled more the stirring times of '61 than anything we have seen since. The Jefferson House was opened as a recruiting office; a huge placard, 'Headquarters Montana Militia,' posted over the door." The article also proclaimed: "The merchants have responded liberally, offering all the necessary supplies not furnished by the people of the Gallatin."[24]

Despite this optimism, recruitment started faltering, and merchants curtailed their generosity when it became evident that government funding for the militia might not be coming.[25] Under these circumstances, Meagher and Chief Justice Hosmer redoubled their efforts to gain authorization for a Montana militia. Hosmer attempted to bypass the War Department, appealing directly to President Andrew Johnson in a telegram sent May 3. But Johnson deferred to Stanton, who referred it to Grant, who replied that there was no law authorizing Hosmer's request. In the event that it became necessary for the acting governor to form a militia in self-defense, Grant explained, then territorial officials could petition Congress for reimbursement afterward. Yet Hosmer also was informed by the War Department that General Sherman had the authority to "call out, organize, officer, arm and subsist such a militia force in Montana as he deems necessary."[26]

Meanwhile, Sherman had discussed the matter with Sydney Edgerton's recent successor as Montana territorial governor, Green Clay Smith, who yet remained in the East. Sherman agreed to ship 2,500 muskets up the Missouri to arm a volunteer force.[27] By now, Meagher also learned from Stanton that General Sherman had the authority to sanction a militia force. Consequently, Meagher contacted Sherman again seeking authorization. On May 7, Sherman replied by telegram, specifying: "If Indians *enter* the valley of the Gallatin organize eight hundred volunteers and drive them out." Yet when Sherman's telegram was reprinted in the *Montana Post,* it read: "If Indians *threaten* the valley of the Gallatin, organize (800) eight hundred volunteers, and drive them out"[28]

Recruitment in Montana was well underway. As further enticement for men to join without any guarantee of federal funding, the *Montana Post* in early May proclaimed that volunteers could keep any plunder they captured. One announcement went so far as to offer $10 for every scalp taken.[29] Convincing merchants to provide supplies without a guarantee of reimbursement proved more difficult. Sherman's authorization of May 7, contrived as it was in the *Montana Post*, offered no such guarantee.

On May 11, however, the *Post* reprinted official correspondence in support of the bold affirmation: "The Government Authorizes the Organization of the Militia On a Sure Footing at Last." The *Post* assured citizens that a dispatch from Sherman to Mayor J.M. Castner of Virginia City, in response to the latter's request to raise a militia force, provided "sufficient authorization for raising troops, and obviates, in a great measure, the difficulties of procuring equipments."

But Sherman's letter, which appeared above the article, noted that "official reports from that quarter do not justify such extreme alarm." Moreover, Sherman advised: "There is no necessity of mustering you in for three months. You should render this service in self-defense...without the formality of muster in or muster out." The letter offered no actual suggestion that the government would assume the costs incurred by the territory in its self-defense.[30]

Meanwhile, editor James Fisk of the *Helena Herald* also warned of impending danger, while wildly exaggerating the number of hostile warriors. "In our judgment, nothing can avert or change the fixed purpose of these savages—now numbering full 30,000 fighting men—to strike a terrible and final blow at the aggressive whites before yielding to the inevitable demand which the march of civilization makes upon them." In Fisk's interpretation, Sherman's dispatches, which were reprinted in Montana newspapers, amounted to more than authorization to raise a militia. They constituted a mandate: "The U.S. War Department, through Lieut-General Sherman, has commanded us to muster, arm, equip, and place in the field at once, 800 efficient citizen soldiery."[31]

Despite the best efforts of the editors to convince merchants that they would be fairly reimbursed, equipping the militia remained problematic. In Virginia City, the *Montana Post* reported with disgust: "Rifles and carbines that two weeks ago were selling at from $10 to $40 are now held at $75 to $100, and holders of them are very indifferent about selling them." The resulting delay, the *Post* noted, "is dangerous, costly, and discreditable."[32] In Helena, a volunteer force being raised for defending the Gallatin Valley was disbanded due to a lack of horses. "If the dispatches from the Secretary of War and the Adjutant General had arrived a day or two earlier," a newspaper article lamented, "the movement would have undoubtedly resulted in a success."[33]

Despite some faltering steps, a militia force had materialized. By April 29, several companies were enrolled in Bozeman and ready for service under General Thomas Thoroughman. In Helena, volunteers under Capt. Lyons, numbering 55 privates and 3 commissioned officers, were mustered in as Company A by May 14, and left for the Gallatin Valley on May 19. Recruitment continued in Helena, with two or three other companies being organized; by May 25, a company of 30 scouts was raised and departed for the Gallatin. Virginia City also contributed to the defense of the Gallatin Valley, sending a company of 50 cavalrymen, plus 25 special scouts.[34]

On May 6, the day before he had telegraphed Meagher with conditional authorization to raise a militia, Sherman had contacted General Christopher C. Augur, commander of the Department of the Platte. Auger was asked to move U.S. forces north toward the Yellowstone.

On May 9, another telegram from Meagher had increased Sherman's conviction that the acting governor was a "stampeder," and it prompted the general to verbally curb the acting governor. Meagher had wired Sherman asking that muskets and saddles be sent to Montana from Salt Lake City. Sherman, clearly tired of the pestering (he made a point of asking Meagher to quit sending telegrams collect), replied in the negative. "If the danger is so great that not an hour is to be lost," Sherman noted, "how can you wait for saddles from Utah?"

Sherman contacted General Augur the same day, asking him to dispatch an officer to investigate the Montana situation and to lead a volunteer force in the event its existence proved necessary. Augur selected Lt. Col. William H. Lewis, commander at Camp Douglas, Salt Lake City, for the task, ordering him to proceed without delay.[35]

Lewis arrived in Virginia City on May 19 to begin the investigation. Just as he was getting underway, however, Lewis received a telegram from Sherman, authorizing him to "muster in a battalion of eight hundred men at the cost of the United States, for three months." Sherman specified that the militia should be equipped to the best extent possible until the arms sent up the Missouri reached Fort Benton. A pay rate of 40¢ per day was authorized, and the volunteers were required to furnish their own horses. The order also directed that rations be acquired on contract. Lewis was to lead the troops as quickly as possible to the "threatened point."

Lewis's investigation was the subject of much local attention, since considerable doubt yet lingered as to whether the acting governor had the authority to raise a militia. Lewis seems to have enjoyed being the focus of this interest. Upon receiving the telegram from Sherman, he reportedly posted it in the window of A. Hanan & Co., a Virginia City bank, stating: "There, gentlemen, is the authority for you; that is sufficient."[36]

With Lewis's seeming guarantee of government reimbursement, the reluctance of Montana merchants evaporated and they began supplying the troops, but often at inflated prices. A later investigation revealed that much of the arms, saddles, riding equipment, and supplies were overcharged by 30 to 40 percent. For example, the average reasonable price for a horse was $80, yet the average cost when sold to the militia was $201. Firewood, normally $6.25 to $7.50 per cord, went up to $16 or $20, while oats and barley, previously costing 8¢ to 11¢ per pound, increased to 14½¢ a pound. The official authorization and promise of militia pay (though meager), improved recruiting and the militia took final shape.[37]

The U.S. Army's Lt. Col. Lewis did not participate in the raising of troops, however, nor would he lead them. Moreover, Sherman later specified that the orders Lewis posted at the Virginia City bank were provisional, subject to the findings of Lewis's investigation.[38] A May 29 telegram from Sherman to Lewis supported this contention. "I hear of no facts that warrant a war in Montana," Sherman said, "so be over prudent in your office, don't involve us in expense unless the safety of the settlements absolutely demands it. A stampede now will be a public crime."[39]

Soon after, Lewis received another telegram from Sherman asking for a report on Indian depredations on civilians. At the time, the only verifiable incident that Lewis could provide was the death of John Bozeman. Consequently, Lewis was ordered to cancel any efforts to recruit volunteers and to return to Salt Lake City. He did so without bothering to inform anyone that the U.S. Army had not sanctioned, or agreed to finance, the raising of a militia.[40]

Meanwhile, rumors of Indian activity continued to circulate, and "in an ironical twist of events," volunteers would soon march to Fort C.F. Smith with the purpose of assisting federal troops. On May 17, the *Helena Herald* printed a letter from an unidentified Fort C.F. Smith soldier, seemingly confirming earlier rumors that warriors "burning with insatiable hatred to the white man" were heavily armed and preparing to besiege the fort, where a shortage of supplies threatened starvation.

The report gained further credence when the fort commander, Brevet Lt. Col. Nathaniel C. Kinney, sent a request to the Gallatin Valley for provisions. A supply train with 42 volunteers set out from the Gallatin Valley under Lt. Col. Walter DeLacey. When arriving at the fort on June 10, however, the only Indians they saw were some friendly Crow families. Nonetheless, they were kept "under strict surveillance."[41]

No trace of a rumored large hostile force appeared at this time. However, less than two months later, on August 1, 1867, more than 500 Sioux and Cheyenne attacked a hay cutting party of 12 civilians and 20 soldiers near the fort. In the "Hayfield Fight," the warriors finally were repulsed after six hours when army reinforcements arrived from the post. The next day, August 2, at Fort Phil Kearny, a similar engagement, the "Wagon Box Fight," occurred with a similar result. Despite these setbacks, tribesmen continued to effectively harass the army posts and the Bozeman Trail in the summer of 1867.

In western Montana throughout June, the recruitment of volunteers continued as units were assigned duties, including patrolling on the Plains. One wag observed that enough officers were commissioned "to staff an army of 8,000 rather than 800." As troops assembled or arrived in the Gallatin Valley—the focus and base of the campaign—they erected a stockade to protect Bozeman

City. They then began work on Camp Elizabeth Meagher, named in honor of the acting governor's wife. Colonel DeLacey, chief engineer for the volunteers, selected the site, eight miles east of Bozeman City at the mouth of Rock Creek.

On June 13, work also began on a post located 35 miles east of Bozeman City near the confluence of the Shields and Yellowstone rivers in the upper Plains country. From this position east of the Bridger Range, volunteers could provide protection for the settlements. Named Camp Ida Thoroughman in honor of the daughter of militia commander General Thomas Thoroughman, it was completed by July 13 and manned by three companies from Helena, Deer Lodge, and Virginia City. Late in June, a company under Capt. William Matlock also established a camp at the forks of the Musselshell River; this became Fort Howie. Also in July, the U.S. Army began constructing Fort Ellis in the Gallatin Valley near Camp Elizabeth Meagher.[42]

Thomas H. Leforge was one of the volunteers assigned to Camp Ida Thoroughman on the Yellowstone. Leforge's family had left Ohio for the Montana gold fields in 1864 and settled in the Gallatin Valley in 1865. He met recruitment officers at Bozeman City in June 1867 and was accepted into the militia despite being only 17 years old. According to Leforge, the unit he joined "was composed largely of ex-ruffians of the Missouri-Kansas border," who were an "utterly unruly" group of men. Leforge's company mutinied two days after he joined, refusing to leave camp on an expedition to the Yellowstone. Meagher had the company assembled before him, under the guard of Virginia City and Bannack City companies.

As the acting governor began to berate Leforge's unit, men in the companies that supposedly were guarding them provided the mutinous troops with rifles. At this point a "man known as 'Chris,' a tough, but good-hearted, Mormon, leveled a rifle at the governor" and informed him that such criticism was not appreciated, whereupon the men in the other companies offered encouragement, shouting "We are with you, boys." Meagher somehow managed to diffuse the situation. "Settled in a way acceptable to all," the mutineers soon departed for the Yellowstone.

There appears to have been other incidents of insubordination. If Leforge's reminiscences (recorded and published late in his life, 1928) are correct, he claimed one company responded to its captain's efforts to instill discipline by putting a rope around his neck and then dragging him behind a horse, back and forth across the Shields River until he died. Captain Hart, of yet another company, was shot to death by one of his men. "Desertion," Leforge explained, "was a matter to be determined merely by personal inclination." Leforge's own company later disintegrated after their captain deserted, and only Leforge and a handful of others stayed around long enough to receive formal discharge papers.[43]

A number of the officers were former vigilantes, accustomed to dealing with tough characters, dispensing justice, and maintaining order without formal sanction. J.X. Beidler, one of the more famous Montana vigilantes, was known simply as "X." As one contemporary observer noted, this was "a letter of the alphabet having singular terrors for all evil-doers in Montana, being calculated to awaken the idea of crime committed and punishment to follow, more than all the rest of the alphabet, even if the enumeration were followed by the repetition of the Ten Commandments."[44] As a colonel in the volunteers, X. Beidler—together with Capt. Robert Hereford of Company I, Brig. Gen. Charles D. Curtis commanding the first military district of Montana, Maj. A.M.S. Carpenter, the chief ordnance officer for the Montana militia, and other vigilantes—brought their frontier brand of firmness to the volunteers' campaign.[45]

Neil Howie, who would eventually assume command of the volunteer force in the field, also had made a name for himself as a vigilante. A Scottish immigrant, Howie arrived in Montana in 1863 seeking gold, and in January 1864 single-handedly captured the notorious highwayman "Dutch John" Wagner. Thereafter, he climbed the political ladder from vigilante to respected officer of the law. By spring 1864, he was appointed deputy sheriff, and in the summer became the first popularly elected sheriff of Madison County. When Montana became a territory, Howie served as the first U.S. deputy marshal, and he later replaced George M. Pinney as U.S. marshal.[46]

Meanwhile, the federal government's effort to provide weapons, ammunition, a half-section of mountain howitzers, and other accoutrements had materialized at the St. Louis Arsenal. On Sherman's orders, the shipment was not to be sent up the Missouri by riverboat unless accompanied by a sizeable contingent of regular army officers and soldiers. Otherwise the costly ordnance stores might be vulnerable to theft.

Notification reached Meagher that the shipment was on its way. Accordingly, in late June 1867 he led an expedition to Fort Benton to take possession of the arms. After the party arrived on July 1, Meagher spent the day visiting with friends at a store owned by I.G. Baker, before retiring for the night aboard the docked *G.A. Thompson,* a Missouri River paddle wheeler piloted by an old acquaintance, Johnny Doran. Around 10 or 11 o'clock in the evening, a night watchman heard a noise and then saw a white figure moving on deck at the boat's stern. He did not think much of it until hearing a splash. The watchman sounded an alarm for man overboard, and life preservers were thrown into the water. Soon, men searched from rowboats and along the river banks. But the Missouri was running high and swift, and Thomas Francis Meagher was never seen again.

Much speculation surrounds Meagher's death. He had consumed considerable blackberry wine earlier in the day with friends, and, due to his past reputation, it was widely assumed he fell overboard in a stupor. Other rumors labeled his death a suicide, but offered no plausible explanations for why Meagher might take his own life. More convincing to some were suggestions that an enemy pushed him into the water. The political struggle in the territory certainly created adversaries, and that same day Meagher apparently accused certain individuals at Fort Benton of conspiring to murder him. Moreover, before going to bed in his cabin, the acting governor expressed fears to Doran of being murdered. Doran left only after Meagher insisted he be provided with two revolvers for self-defense. There is, however, no more than circumstantial evidence to support this latter version of his death.

Perhaps Meagher fell off the boat when disoriented from a combination of sleepiness and drink and due to his unfamiliarity with the surroundings. The cabin opened onto a narrow strip of deck "quite favorable for an accidental fall." Meagher's biographer, historian Robert Athearn, contends that an unintentional fall was likely and argues that the acting governor was more ill than drunk on the last night of his life.[47] Meagher had served in the territorial government a little less than two years.

The newly appointed governor, Green Clay Smith, arriving in Montana from the East to assume his position in June, took command of the militia immediately after Meagher's death. Smith issued a special order on July 3 calling for three days of mourning, "in token of the high esteem in which the deceased was held as a true soldier and gentleman, and as evidence of the deep sorrow felt for the loss of one who has endeared himself to the hearts of the soldiers and citizens...by his manly virtues and gallant conduct."[48]

Smith pursued the defensive campaign against the Plains Indians with enthusiasm. Yet, while he continued recruitment, he also sought to overhaul the militia, introducing needed discipline and fiscal responsibility. The ink on the order declaring a mourning period for Meagher scarcely had dried before the governor issued a flurry of directives. On July 4, a second special order was released from militia headquarters in Helena, calling upon Assistant Quartermaster James Fisk at Helena to inventory all supplies under his authority, while also detailing the prices at which they were purchased and from whom.

In other special orders issued over the next few days, Smith authorized the continued recruitment of a company of 100 men at Helena, specifying that the proper authorities be notified and the muster rolls forwarded when the task was completed. He appointed George Pinney with the rank of captain as aide-de-camp and as ordnance officer for the District of Helena. Smith also directed Brig. Gen. Neil Howie, the District of Helena commander, to oversee construction of a powder magazine to store the ordnance coming from Fort Benton, which arrived on July 7. On July 6, Smith's General Orders No. 1 required all militia officers to provide written receipts for special and general orders received, and stipulated that Thomas Thoroughman, the overall militia commander, would see to it that all orders were carried out.[49]

As Smith established his grip over the militia, troops in the Gallatin Valley became involved in two incidents with neighboring Montana Indians. The historical evidence for these incidents, if entirely true, is sparse. In early July, a band of Flathead traveling to the buffalo grounds east of the Bridger Range encountered a rancher, who was wounded in an ensuing altercation. After proceeding over Flathead Pass to the Shields River, the Flathead were intercepted by a militia force at the mouth of Brackett Creek. The troops demanded that the individual responsible for injuring the rancher be turned over. The Flathead refused to give up the intended person, but offered another in his stead. Not willing to negotiate, the militia seized the man believed to be responsible and, in vigilante style, hanged him from a cottonwood tree. The band was permitted to continue on its way, but the militia followed to guard against retaliation for the execution.[50]

Also in early July, a Crow horse-raiding party of about 150 individuals established a camp in the Gallatin Valley. Three men from this band stole a herd of cattle and horses. While attempting to elude pursuing citizens, they happened to encounter Company A of the Helena Battalion, under Capt. Robert Hughes. With the benefit of surprise, the militia recaptured all but one of the horses, and shot and killed two Crow in the process. Hughes then gathered 35 of his men and proceeded to the Crow camp to reclaim the last stolen horse, which was turned over to him. Still not satisfied that justice was served, Hughes demanded that the third member of the raiding party surrender. The leader of the band conceded. The third horse raider stepped forward, whereupon he was lassoed around the neck, dragged to a tree, and hanged, again in vigilante fashion.[51]

Governor Smith's full reorganization of the militia came with another General Orders No. 1 on July 14. The directive reduced the number of officers, demoted others to less inflated ranks, and reorganized the militia into nine companies. Thomas Thoroughman remained as overall commander, but demoted from brigadier general to colonel. The nine reorganized companies of the First Regiment of Montana Volunteers included: Company A, under Capt. L.K. Lyda; Company B, Capt. Robert Hughes; Company C, Capt. Charles J.D. Curtis; Company D, Capt. J.H. Evans; Company E, Capt. Cornelius Campbell; Company F, Capt. John A. Nelson; Company G, Capt. A.F. Weston; Company I, Capt. Robert Hereford; and Company K, Capt. William Deasey.

The orders also listed the governor's staff. Martin Beem remained adjutant general with the rank of colonel, and Walter DeLacey continued in the role of chief engineer as a major. George M. Pinney and James K. Duke, aides-de-camp, held ranks of major and captain respectively. Smith also appointed Col. Hamilton Cummings as quartermaster general and Col. J.J. Hull as commissary general.

Smith's orders specified that "all commissions issued by the late Governor Meagher, other than those mentioned in this order, with their rank, will be held as complimentary." He also required officers in the field to send weekly reports to headquarters detailing their troop rolls, the number of men absent with and without leave, and the names of deserters. Officers also were expected to summarize the status of supplies and ammunition in their weekly reports. "It is hoped," the orders concluded, "that the troops in the field will perform their duty with alacrity, and teach the hostile Indians that if they prefer war, we know how to carry it on—their policy shall be ours."[52]

Not surprisingly, Smith's reorganization was unpopular among a number of militia officers and some tendered their resignations. But Smith was determined to see his reforms completed. Upon receiving word of the resignation of Aide-De-Camp George Pinney, Smith responded, "I intend the military moves in this Territory to be a success, and have my orders to [do so] approved by Gen'ls Terry, Sherman, and the War Department." Smith expressed disappointment over Pinney's resignation, but nonetheless accepted it. Thomas Thoroughman likewise resigned, refusing to lead the militia with the mere rank of colonel. Smith accepted this, too, and appointed Col. Neil Howie as commander of the troops in the field. X. Beidler, the noted vigilante, also was among the officers resigning.[53]

The *Montana Post* gave the reorganization a "hearty endorsal," while publishing General Orders No. 1 in its July 20 edition. "It was necessary," an accompanying editorial declared. "There were evils to correct, abuses to be remedied, and order had to be evoked from the realm of chaos, or the movement rest under a dead weight that was crushing out its vitality and bringing it into contempt."[54]

But General Orders No. 1 failed to correct all problems. Having received reports of continued desertion and theft in the ranks, Smith redoubled his reform efforts. General Order No. 9, issued August 13, warned that any deserter attempting to sell government property would be "arrested anywhere in the United States and tried for his offense and punished by imprisonment in the penitentiary."

In a later special order, Smith outlined further strict regulations for officers to enforce: roll call would be conducted at 6:00 a.m. and 5:00 p.m.; squad drill would occur from 5:00–5:30 p.m. and company drill, including inspection, would follow from 5:30–6:00 p.m.; men found absent from roll call without permission three times in succession were to be reported to headquarters as deserters "and dealt with accordingly"; men were not "allowed to leave camp at a distance of more than one mile without a written pass from the sergeant commanding, nor for a longer time than twenty-four hours without a pass"; and "men caught selling, or disposing of any government property whatsoever," were to be "charged on his muster roll in double the amount of the original cost to the government" for those articles.[55]

As Smith endeavored to reform the militia, he deployed troops in response to reported hostile sightings.[56] Newspaper reports from "the Front" kept Montana citizens up to date regarding volunteer activities. The *Montana Post* of June 27, for example, described the Camp Ida Thoroughman fortifications at the Shields-Yellowstone confluence. The report declared: "That we have hostile Indians down here in innumerable numbers, there is no doubt, and our people [i.e., Montana's citizens], I opine, have been wondering why we have not engaged them before, and have probably grown impatient at our apparent inactivity." The writer explained the need to "prepare a base for all future operations," and that a chronic lack of arms had restricted offensive forays, but the volunteers were on the verge of launching an "active campaign."[57]

Despite the optimism reflected in the report, the volunteers were rather dissatisfied with their equipment, rations, and pay, and indeed were restless for action. The arrival of Col. Neil Howie on August 10, with news of Governor Smith's order for a six-month reenlistment, lifted their spirits. Howie furloughed one quarter of his force, sending them to Virginia City and Helena to recruit additional men to meet Smith's directive to fill the 800-man militia roster.[58]

A clash of arms soon came. On August 27, prospectors William J. Weston and T.H. Mann arrived at Camp Ida Thoroughman, reporting they had just escaped from a hostile attack near the Stillwater River, about 50 miles to the east. Two members of their party, A.F. Weston and a man they met in the area named Frank Hodges, were left surrounded by warriors. A.F. Weston had formerly served as Company G's commander and was the father of one of the just arrived prospectors. In response, Col. Howie immediately departed eastward with 75 men and a 12-pounder mountain howitzer on a prairie carriage with its ammunition limber.[59]

The following day, Howie's force encountered warriors at the nearby Boulder River. Seeing Howie's troops, the warriors sought cover in timber and underbrush on the opposite side of the stream, occupying strategic positions above and below the ford. Reluctant to charge across the stream in these circumstances, Howie drove the Indians from the timber with the howitzer, then divided his force and sent them in pursuit. When the troops emerged from the trees and onto the prairie, the Indians had a two-mile lead. The volunteers could not close this distance, after following for eight miles.[60]

While Howie's men failed to apprehend the hostiles, they did succeed in fortuitously rescuing three messengers from Fort C.F. Smith who happened to be engaged in a skirmish with the Indians when the volunteers arrived. The missing prospectors, Capt. A.F. Weston and Frank Hodges, were not so fortunate. The volunteers found some of their equipment in a nearby abandoned Indian camp, and Weston's stolen horse was shot out from under a warrior in the fighting with the Fort C.F. Smith men. "Everything found in their deserted camp," Howie reported, "goes to prove that these Indians were…a 'war party' of Crows, Cheyenne & Sioux."[61]

In preparing to leave the next day, the volunteers killed an Indian found near the river, who was identified by Company A men as a Crow who served as their guide in the past. Eager for greater retribution, Howie took 50 men and departed east toward the Stillwater River that night, in order to "overtake and chastise the war party of savages."

On the 30th, they reached the place where Weston and Hodges were last seen and discovered the remains of both men. After burying the bodies and erecting crude markers, the volunteers proceeded to the Stillwater. Finding no trace of the Indians, they turned back. Howie arrived back at the Boulder River on September 1, meeting John A. Nelson with a reinforcement of 80 men. Howie sent Nelson on a scouting foray, while he continued with his own force, now short of rations, back toward Fort T.F. Meagher (Camp Ida Thoroughman was renamed to honor the former acting governor). Nelson's scouting column soon rejoined Howie because the country was too rocky for their unshod horses. The combined group returned to Fort Meagher without incident.[62]

During Howie's absence, the volunteer force had increased through recruitment. Howie now ordered the troops to build fortifications at a new location, providing better protection from attack and improved quarters for the coming winter months. Though the men were eager for continued action, Howie reported they undertook the task with enthusiasm. Six-month reenlistment meant that the volunteers would have food and shelter provided through the winter. Many of the men planned to prospect or settle in the locality when their enlistment expired. Spirits were further lifted by the governor's directive to prepare for a long-awaited offensive. With a new fort site selected up the Yellowstone River and with work underway, Howie departed for Virginia City to acquire the supplies needed for the coming expedition, leaving Capt. Nelson in command during his absence.[63]

Upon arriving in Virginia City, Howie received important news. The U.S. Army's General Alfred H. Terry had arrived in Montana Territory and ordered the territorial government to disband the militia. No doubt disappointed, Howie returned to the Yellowstone to carry out the directive, arriving during a "dress parade" on the evening of September 23. The news, Howie later reported, "fell harshly on the ears of all," because the men "had been positively promised to be kept in the service a full six months from date of enlistment." He added: "They had no pay, nor but little clothing, the working season was about closed, the long winter staring them in the face, and with the large majority...the situation was indeed discouraging and almost desperate."

Howie attempted to assuage the disappointment. He assured the men that after their equipment was accounted for when mustering out, it would be redistributed to them as compensation for their service. The offer proved hardly satisfactory to many of the volunteers. They asked instead that Howie lead them, or at least allow them to go, on a three-week prospecting trip so they might have some means of earning cash for the winter. All government property, the men promised, would be returned at the end of the venture. Howie rejected the plan.[64]

The independent-mined volunteers took matters into their own hands. Under the lead of Capt. Robert Hughes of Company B, the majority mutinied and "stealthily availed themselves of most of the revolvers and other improved arms, as well as the best and all surplus animals." The mutineers then seized the commissary and quartermaster buildings, and "profusely supplied and equipped themselves for their trip." "Those who did not openly engage in open mutiny,"

Howie later reported, "strongly sympathized with, and virtually countenanced it by refusing to assist me in an endeavor to quell it."[65]

Having lost control at the fort, Howie rode to Bozeman with the volunteers not joining the mutiny, arriving on September 26. He sent the Virginia City men home to muster-out under the command of John Nelson. Before Howie departed for Helena with the remainder of his volunteers, he was joined by Company H under Capt. William Mattock. Company H had been en route from the Musselshell River to rendezvous with Howie "at the front." Mattock's troops, Howie surmised, "were not tainted with 'rebellion,'" and might provide him with an opportunity to regain control on the Yellowstone. But when calling upon them to return to deal with the mutineers, only 26 agreed, and then only on the condition that they be allowed to keep the supplies they could recapture. Defeated, Howie returned to Helena, where he received orders to sell the government property remaining in his possession, and use the proceeds to pay off and muster out his troops.[66]

Meanwhile, on September 28, Governor Smith issued General Order Number 12 announcing General Terry's directive that "the Montana Volunteers were no longer required." Fearful of further mutiny, Smith ordered the mustering out process to be done with "the utmost good order and decorum." The volunteers' "conduct as citizens again," Smith hoped, "will be exemplary and not such as will tarnish their record as soldiers." The governor also called upon Montana's citizens to join him in extending "our heartfelt thanks and gratitude" to those who had served responsibly.[67]

Local newspapers heeded the governor's call by publishing editorials thanking the volunteers for their service. The *Montana Post,* for example, declared, "it is but right that we should accord the volunteers the credit they well deserve. Their presence on the Yellowstone preserved this Territory." "It is not their fault," the editorial continued, "that their victory has been almost bloodless. They have not been permitted or prepared to make any advance on the Indians, but have stood a wall of fixed, determined and brave men between the settler's home and the savage scalping knife, warding off the blow that fell on Kansas, Colorado, and Nebraska."[68] Other newspapers were more critical of the volunteers, condemning the mutiny under Capt. Hughes.[69] The *Montana Post*, however, managed to put a positive spin on this, characterizing the revolt as "an easy method of ridding Montana of a large number of the worst characters in the Territory, at a comparatively trifling expense, and less formality."[70]

While many Montanans lauded the volunteers for thwarting hostile Indian intentions, the U.S. Army believed the militia's activities worsened relations with the tribes. General Sherman maintained that the Indian threat to western Montana had been negligible. He accused Meagher of raising troops "in spite of the decision to the contrary by the rightful department of government," and also implicated Governor Smith, charging that he "also has retained in service these volunteers, and has brought about a conflict with the Crows and other Indians outside the settled limits of the Territory, when he knew that the government desired very much to retain peaceful relations with them."[71]

The *Omaha Herald* shared Sherman's concern over the volunteers undermining peaceful relations with the Crow. By now, reports about events in Montana Territory had reached Nebraska. The *Herald* declared it "an outrage" that a "murderous attack upon the Crows" by a force of 600 volunteers had occurred. The *Herald* called for a "searching and severe" investigation and predicted the removal of Governor Smith.

Montana newspapers reprinted the article, with reassurance from Smith that the *Omaha Herald*'s report was inaccurate and the result of a "grand mistake." An accompanying editorial in one of the newspapers defended the volunteers, noting they "have never made an offensive movement, but, on the contrary, have acted on the defense all the while."[72]

Indeed, the shame of desertion and mutiny stained the record of many in the campaign. In a letter enclosed with the orders to muster out the volunteers, Adjutant General Beem advised Col. Howie to find consolation in the fact that he had done his duty. "Unfortunately," Beem lamented, "we have not the power of seeing into the future vouchsafed to us poor mortals—or we might have averted the calamity that has befallen our campaign." Beem counseled Howie to move beyond the past because it could not be changed, and offered words of wisdom in Latin, "ne quid nimis"—be wisely moderate.[73]

In the following months, as the merchants and individuals who provided supplies to the militia attempted to redeem their vouchers, the cost of the campaign became staggeringly apparent, amounting to nearly a purported $1 million. The Montana legislature asked the U.S. Congress to pass an appropriation to cover the debt. Meanwhile, individual clients hired lawyers to press their claims. The War Department referred the claims to General Sherman. He was displeased to find that the government was being held responsible for costs arising from a volunteer force that he insisted was not authorized by him. Meagher, he noted in a terse response to an inquiry about the redemption of vouchers, "had no authority from me, but such authority was emphatically withheld; the so-called troops were never mustered into the service of the United States, and no department of government is liable for the debts created or the vouchers issued."[74]

Lawyers for claimants contested the general's denial by sending copies of telegrams sent by Sherman and others to Meagher that ostensibly authorized the Montana militia. The War Department referred the matter to the Senate Committee on Territories. On February 9, 1870, the committee issued a report to Congress favorable to the claimants. Consequently, Congress passed an act authorizing an investigation into the validity of the claims, which was approved by the president on July 15.[75]

On August 31, 1870, the War Department appointed Col. James A. Hardie, the inspector general for the Military Division of the Missouri, to conduct the complicated investigation. Hardie submitted a preliminary report to the Committee on Military Affairs on February 4, 1871. The voucher claims, he reported, totaled an aggregate of $980,313.11. His investigation, however, also revealed "fictitious vouchers, where no property of any kind was delivered, overstated deliveries...suspected transactions which may fail of establishment to an extent justifying payment in full, and exorbitant charges."

In light of these findings, Hardie determined that "the sum of $513,343.10 will discharge all the equitable obligations that the United States has seen fit to assume," and he recommended Congress appropriate that amount.[76] Hardie then undertook the time-consuming task of determining the disposition of each of 743 vouchers—a task further complicated when his completed claims list, along with the documentary evidence it was based on, were destroyed in the Chicago fire of October 9, 1871. Nonetheless, he was able to reconstruct the list and submit it by early 1872.[77]

Meanwhile, the Committee on Military Affairs had considered Hardie's report. It concluded that the threat of Indian depredations was significant enough to "alarm persons of ordinary prudence, and that the battalion placed in service may have been instrumental in preventing much more extended hostile incursions by the Indians." While the committee believed that the "actions of the civil authorities was hasty and injudicious," it nonetheless granted that there was "ostensible recognition" of the troops, even if they were not legitimately mustered into the service of the government. The committee therefore declared that "repudiation of reasonable indemnity for property furnished in good faith by individuals would fall far short of that equity and justice which the Government so generally extends to all her decisions." Consequently, the committee recommended that the $513,343.10 specified by Hardie be appropriated.[78]

The government's assumption of financial responsibility was welcomed by those who had provided goods and equipment, but it did not eliminate all the monetary hardships they had experienced. The claimants deemed eligible for full or partial payment had waited five years for the investigation to run its course. Also, the federal government retained full authority in calculating the fair price for the goods issued, and did not include interest in making payments to the voucher holders. The claimants whose vouchers were rejected as illegitimate were left to absorb their losses

Not long after the militia disbanded in late 1867, Red Cloud's War finally ended, with the Sioux, Cheyenne, and Arapahoe achieving their goal of forcing the U.S. Army to abandon the Powder River country. According to the terms of the 1868 Fort Laramie Treaty, troops vacated the Bozeman Trail forts. Warriors then burned the abandoned posts to the ground. An unsteady peace with the Sioux would hold for eight years, until 1876, when a major gold rush in South Dakota's Black Hills sparked a resurgence of hostilities across the northern Plains.

Meanwhile, the Bozeman Trail had declined in economic importance as a link to Montana. With the Central Pacific/Union Pacific transcontinental railway nearing completion in 1869, other wagon roads connecting to railroad supply points to the south became more important to Montana commerce. This fact, along with concerns raised by congressional groups, such as the Doolittle Committee, also influenced the federal government in bringing Red Cloud's War to a conclusion.

Retrospectively, it appears that Red Cloud's warriors probably had little intention of making incursions into western Montana. The militia effort focused on preparing defenses for assaults that never materialized, and the few engagements that did occur were minor skirmishes. Unfortunately, some incidents, such as the Boulder River encounters, were blown out of proportion by some persons outside of Montana Territory, giving rise to rumors that have persisted. The question of whether or not the militia indeed served as a deterrent, preventing the warring Plains tribes from attacking outlying settlements in Montana, remains a matter of some speculation.

Notes

1. Robert Athearn, "The Montana Volunteers of 1867," *Pacific Historical Review* 19 (2) (May 1950): 136. The costs accrued were closer to $1 million, though Congress eventually appropriated about half of that amount.
2. Clark C. Spence, *Territorial Politics and Government in Montana, 1864–89* (Urbana: University of Illinois Press, 1975), 4–19; Granville Stuart, *Forty Years on the Frontier*, ed. Paul C. Phillips (Cleveland: Arthur C. Clark, 1925), 1: 133–40.
3. Spence, *Territorial Politics and Government*, 4–19.
4. Francis Paul Prucha, *The Great Father: The United States Government and the American Indians,* abridged ed. (Lincoln: University of Nebraska Press, 1984), 143–51; Stuart, *Forty Years on the Frontier* 2: 59–61; Robert Utley, *The Indian Frontier of the American West, 1846–1890* (Albuquerque: University of New Mexico Press, 1984), 99–102.
5. Spence, *Territorial Politics and Government*, 33; Granville Stuart, "A Memoir of the Life of James Stuart," *Contributions to the Historical Society of Montana* 1: 59–60.
6. Chief Justice H.L. Hosmer to Samuel Hauser, June 24, 1865, Hauser MSS, Montana Historical Society, Helena, Montana, quoted in Spence, *Territorial Politics and Government*, 33.
7. Robert Athearn, "Thomas Francis Meagher: An Irish Revolutionary in America," *University of Colorado Studies* 1 (Boulder: University of Colorado Press, December 1949). See also Michael Cavanaugh, *Memoirs of Thomas Francis Meagher* (Worcester: Messinger Press, 1892).
8. Brig. Gen. Thomas Francis Meagher to Capt. James R. O'Beirne, April 30, 1865, "Some Letters of General T.F. Meagher," *The Journal of the American Irish Historical Society* 30 (1932): 85–86.

9. James Thane Jr., "An Active Acting Governor: Thomas Francis Meagher's Administration in Montana Territory," *Journal of the West* 9 (4) (October 1970): 537–51.
10. Athearn, "The Montana Volunteers of 1867," 128.
11. Michael A. Leeson, *History of Montana, 1739–1885* (Chicago: Warner, Beers, 1885), 118–19.
12. Utley, *The Indian Frontier of the American West*, 99–105; Robert M. Utley, *Frontier Regulars: The United States Army and the Indians, 1866–1891* (New York: Macmillan, 1973), 100–7.
13. Quoted in James L. Thane Jr., "The Montana 'Indian War' of 1867," *Arizona and the West* 10 (2) (Summer 1968): 154.
14. Ibid., 155–56.
15. This was the first of three versions of a General Orders "No. 1" that would be issued in 1867. Leeson, *History of Montana*, 119.
16. Meagher to Grant, April 9, 1867, "Special Files" of Headquarters, Division of the Missouri, Relating to Military Operations and Administration, 1863–1885, National Archives Microfilm M-1495 (Roll 7), Records of the United States Army Continental Commands, Record Group 93, National Archives [hereafter cited as Special Files, M-1495 (Roll 7), USACC, RG 393, NA].
17. Stanton to Sherman, May 3, 1867, Special Files, M-1495 (Roll 7), USACC, RG 393, NA.
18. Prucha, *The Great Father*, 154–55.
19. Sherman to Stanton, May 4, 1867, Special Files, M-1495 (Roll 7), USACC, RG 393, NA. Meagher was not particularly fond of Sherman either, and in an article published in 1861, entitled "The Last Days of the 69th in Virginia," he criticized Sherman for causing the 69th undue suffering by providing them with only a single ambulance, and referred to Sherman as "a rude and envenomed martinet." See Athearn, "Thomas Francis Meagher," 96.
20. Stuart, *Forty Years on the Frontier* 2: 62–64.
21. Athearn, "The Montana Volunteers of 1867," 129.
22. Meagher and H.L. Hosmer to E.M. Stanton, April 27, 1867, Special Files, M-1495 (Roll 7), USACC, RG 393, NA.
23. *Montana Post*, April 27, 1867.
24. Ibid., quoted in Athearn, "The Montana Volunteers of 1867," 130.
25. "Report on the Montana Indian War Claims of 1867," May 24, 1872, Testimony of Inspector General James Hardie, Appendix, House Report 82, 42d Congress, 2d Session (Serial 1542) (Washington, D.C.: U.S. Government Printing Office, 1872) [hereafter cited as Hardie Report, HRpt 82].
26. Hosmer to Johnson, May 2, 1867; Grant to Hosmer, May 3, 1867; Stanton to Sherman, May 3, 1867; E.A. Townsend to Hosmer, May 4, 1867 (reprinted in *Montana Post*, May 11, 1867), Special Files, M-1495 (Roll 7), USACC, RG 393, NA.
27. Thane, "The Montana 'Indian War' of 1867," 159.
28. Italic added to emphasize the difference in implied meaning. Athearn, "The Montana Volunteers of 1867," 130–31.
29. Thane, "The Montana 'Indian War' of 1867," 162.
30. *Montana Post*, May 11, 1867.
31. *Helena Herald*, May 14, 1867. Three days later, Fisk was appointed assistant quartermaster general of the Montana Territorial Militia by Quartermaster General H.C. Cummings. See Leeson, *History of Montana*, 120.
32. *Montana Post*, May 11, 1867.
33. Ibid., May 18, 1867, quoting the Helena *Tri-Weekly Republican*. The dispatches referred to are probably those that appeared in the *Montana Post* on May 11.

34. Leeson, *History of Montana*, 119–20.
35. Sherman to Augur, May 4, 1867; Sherman to Meagher, May 9, 1867; Sherman to Augur, May 9, 1867; Special Order 85, Department of the Platte, May 10, 1867, Special Files, M-1495 (Roll 7), USACC, RG 393, NA.
36. Testimony of M.H. Insley, May 18, 1872, "Testimony in Relation to Indian War Claims of the Territory of Montana," House Miscellaneous Document 215, 42d Congress, 2d Session (Serial 1527) (Washington, D.C.: U.S. Government Printing Office, 1872), 2–4.
37. Hardie Report, HRpt 82, 5, 21.
38. Ibid., 13–14.
39. Sherman to Lewis, May 29, 1867, Record Series (RS) 250, Montana Secretary of State Office Records, Box 1, Folder 1-21, Military Affairs [including Little Prickly Pear petition for arms] 1868, Correspondence, Legal Documents, Circulars, Montana Historical Society [hereafter cites as MHS], Helena, Montana.
40. When later asked if he had expressed any disapproval to the proper territorial authorities, or conveyed to them that the government did not sanction the militia, Lewis replied: "I was not called upon to approve or disapprove anything they had done. I had nothing to do with the territorial authorities, or what they had done." Hardie Report, HRpt 82, 13.
41. Thane, "The Montana 'Indian War' of 1867," 162–63; Stuart, *Forty Years on the Frontier* 2: 65.
42. Athearn, "The Montana Volunteers of 1867," 132; Leeson, *History of Montana*, 205; Thane, "The Montana 'Indian War' of 1867," 164; Vertical File: Fort (Camp) Elizabeth Meagher, MHS, Helena, Montana. Camp Ida Thoroughman was later converted to a fort, and renamed Fort T.F. Meagher.
43. "Chris" later murdered a fellow volunteer in a fight in Bozeman after a drinking bout. He was court martialed and acquitted after "a scanty inquiry." Thomas H. Leforge, *Memoirs of a White Crow Indian*, as told by Thomas B. Marquis (Lincoln: University of Nebraska Press, 1974 [1928]), 3–18.
44. Thomas J. Dimsdale, *The Vigilantes of Montana or Popular Justice in the Rocky Mountains* (Norman: University of Nebraska Press, [1866] 1953), 245–46.
45. Leeson, *History of Montana*, 119–20, 265–66.
46. Vertical File, Neil Howie, MHS, Helena, Montana.
47. Athearn, "Thomas Francis Meagher," 164–66; Excerpt of "Bradley Manuscript," "Account of the Drowning of Gen. Thoman Francis Meagher, Authority: I.G. Baker, St. Louis," in *Contributions to the Historical Society of Montana* 8 (1917): 131–33; Thane, "The Montana 'Indian War' of 1867," 164–65.
48. Special Order No. 1, July 3, 1867, Folder 2/6, General Correspondence, 1867, General and Special Orders of Territorial Headquarters and the District of Helena, RS 162, Montana Volunteer Records, MHS, Helena, Montana.
49. An expanded and revised version of General Orders No. 1 was issued July 14. Special Orders Nos. 2–5, July 4, 1867, and General Orders No. 1, July 6, 1867, Folder 2/6, General Correspondence, 1867, General and Special Orders of Territorial Headquarters and the District of Helena, RS 162, Montana Volunteers Records, MHS, Helena, Montana.
50. Leforge, *Memoirs of a White Crow Indian*, 18–19.
51. It must be pointed out that there is some contradiction and uncertainty in the sources describing these events. James Thane Jr. in "The Montana 'Indian War' of 1867" (1968), 166, identifies the men killed by Company A as Blackfeet, but he cites Michael A. Leeson, *History of Montana*, 120, who claims they were Crow. Thane does not mention the earlier incident with the Flathead. Richard H. Lacey in *The Montana Militia* (1976), 10, mentions

encounters in early July with both the Flathead and Crow; presumably, the incident with the Flathead that he mentions is the same one described by Thomas H. Leforge in *Memoirs of a White Crow Indian*, cited above, but Lacey does not mention a hanging—he merely says that the Flathead were "subdued." Moreover, Lacey places Capt. Nelson, rather than Hughes, in command of the troops that met the Crow raiding party, and in his version only two died—both hanged. Lacey seems to cite Dorothy M. Johnson's *The Bloody Bozeman* (1971), 296, in support of his Flathead account. Johnson draws on Leforge for her description of the first incident, and does not mention the second. Moreover, she does not identify any Indian group by name.

52. General Orders No. 1, July 14, 1867, Vertical File, Montana Volunteers, 1867, MHS, Helena, Montana.
53. Smith accepted Pinney's resignation on August 5, and appointed W.S. Scribner in his place. Green Clay Smith to George M. Pinney, July 24, 1867, Folder 1/6, General Correspondence, 1867, May–November Misc., see also General Order No. 8, August 5, 1867, Folder 2/6, RS 162, Montana Volunteer Records, MHS, Helena, Montana; Leeson, *History of Montana*, 123.
54. *Montana Post*, July 20, 1867.
55. General Orders No. 9, August 13, 1867, and Special Order No. 9, undated, folder 2/6, General Correspondence, 1867, General and Special Orders of Territorial Headquarters and the District of Helena, RS 162, Montana Volunteer Records, MHS, Helena, Montana.
56. See for example Green Clay Smith to George M. Pinney, July 16, 1867, Folder 1/6, General Correspondence, 1867, May–November Misc., RS 162, Montana Volunteer Records, MHS, Helena, Montana; Special Order No. 2, July 14, 1867, Special Order No. 12, July 17, 1867, and Special Order No. 6, July 31, 1867, Folder 2/6, General Correspondence, 1867, General and Special Orders of Territorial Headquarters and the District of Helena, RS 162, Montana Volunteer Records, MHS, Helena, Montana.
57. "From the Front," *Montana Post*, July 27, 1867.
58. Howie to Beem, November 10, 1867, Folder 5/6, Reports, Reports of Commanding Officer Neil Howie, RS 162, Montana Volunteer Records, MHS, Helena, Montana.
59. Ibid.; Leeson, *History of Montana*, 123.
60. Howie to Capt. N.L. Turner, A.A. General, Montana Volunteers, August 29, 1867, Folder 5/6, Reports, Reports of Commanding Officer Neil Howie, RS 162, Montana Volunteers Records, MHS, Helena, Montana.
61. Ibid.
62. Howie to Turner, September 1867, Folder 5/6, Reports, Reports of Commanding Officer Neil Howie, RS 162, Montana Volunteer Records, MHS, Helena, Montana.
63. Howie to Beem, November 10, 1867, Folder 5/6, Reports, Reports of Commanding Officer Neil Howie, RS 162, Montana Volunteer Records, MHS, Helena, Montana.
64. Ibid.
65. Ibid.
66. Ibid.
67. General Order No. 12, September 28, 1867, Folder 2/6, General Correspondence, 1867, General and Special Orders of the Territorial Headquarters and the District of Helena, RS 162, Montana Volunteer Records, MHS, Helena, Montana.
68. *Montana Post*, September 28, 1867.
69. Athearn, "The Montana Volunteers of 1867," 135.
70. *Montana Post*, November 9, 1867.

71. "Annual Report of Lieutenant General Sherman to the Secretary of War," October 1, 1867, excerpted in "Letter from the Secretary of War in answer to the request of the Committee on Military Affairs, transmitting report upon the Montana Territorial militia," February 7, 1870, House Executive Document No. 121, 41st Congress, 2d Session (Serial 1417) (Washington, D.C.: U.S. Government Printing Office, 1870), 4.
72. Unidentified newspaper article, October 5, 1867, Vertical File, "Montana Volunteers, 1867," MHS, Helena, Montana.
73. Martin Beem, Adjutant General to Capt. W.S. Scribner, Aide-de-Camp, Montana Volunteers, September 30, 1867, Folder 1/6, General Correspondence, May–November Misc., RS 162, MHS, Helena, Montana. Governor Smith in his 1867 message to the territorial legislature agreed with Beem that Howie was blameless for the mutiny. The mutiny, he maintained, had erupted suddenly, and Howie "could not prevent the action of so large and well organized a band." See the *Montana Post*, November 9, 1867.
74. House Exec. Doc. No. 121, February 7, 1870, 2.
75. Ibid., 2–3; "Joint Memorial of the Legislative Assembly of Montana," February 26, 1872, House Misc. Doc. No. 99, 42d Congress, 2d Session (Serial 1525) (Washington, D.C.: U.S. Government Printing Office, 1872), 1–2.
76. "Letter from the Secretary of War transmitting 'A Report upon the Montana War Claims of 1867,'" February 4, 1871, House Exec. Doc. No. 98, 41st Congress, 3d Session (Serial 1458) (Washington, D.C.: U.S. Government Printing Office, 1872), 1–3; Hardie Report, HRpt 82, 36.
77. Hardie Report, HRpt 82.
78. Ibid., 3–4, 6.

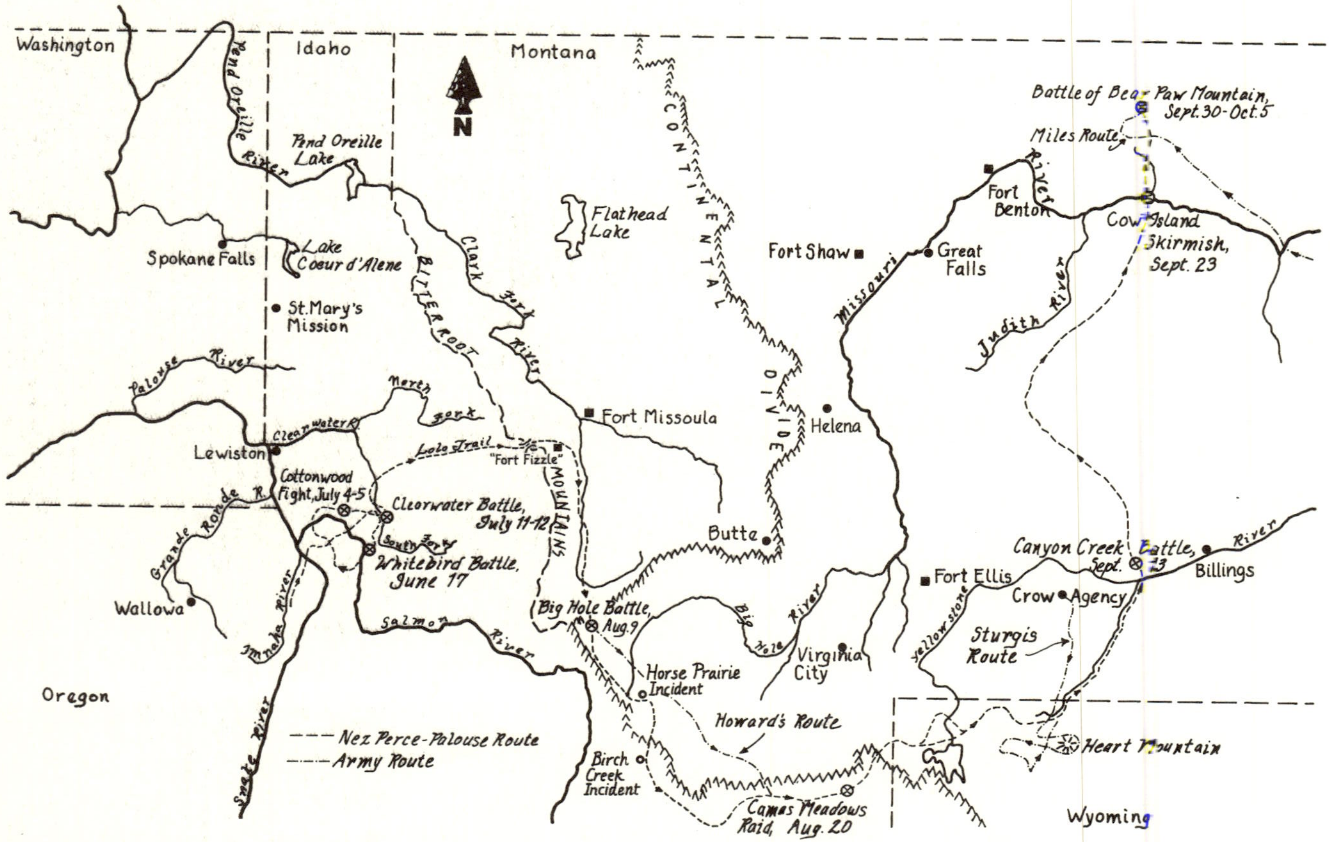

Route of the Nez Perce and Palouse bands, 1877. Modified from Clifford E. Trafzer and Richard D. Scheuerman, *Renegade Tribe* (WSU Press, 1986).

2

Men, Do Your Duty: Montana Territory, 1876–1889

Janet Creighton

We need help and it must be soon or it will be too late. Send everybody that can be armed.—Helena *Independent Extra*, July 28, 1877.

Here me my chiefs! I am tired. My heart is sick and sad. From where the sun now stands I will fight no more forever.—Chief Joseph, October 5, 1877.

For many Montanans, Red Cloud's War enhanced a distrust of the federal government's ability to provide effective assistance in protecting Montana Territory. Charges and countercharges also had flown back and forth between the territorial capitol at Virginia City and Washington, D.C., over payment of expenses accrued during the militia's operations in 1867. The latter dispute, however, did not diminish Montana Territory's willingness to rely on a home-guard, although the militia concept remained rather latent for several years.[1]

The old Montana vigilante motto, "Do Your Duty,"[2] and the willingness to take up arms to protect home and community remained strong. As independent-minded pioneers, Montana residents felt they had the right to determine most of their own destiny, and they sometimes resisted federal control.[3] Their support in the U.S. Congress came from territorial and state rights politicians who opposed the lessening of local authority.[4]

Also, as a practical matter, the vast geographical expanses of the West could hinder the U.S. Army in acting effectively for territorial security, whereas a militia could mobilize quickly in a locality familiar to them. For many Montanans, Washington, D.C., seemed a far-off place—in distance and understanding. Thus, the idea of a home guard in Montana remained strong, and the tradition of the citizen volunteering for service would prevail.

Against this backdrop, General Alfred Terry's column, with Lt. Col. George Armstrong Custer and the 7th Cavalry, left Fort Abraham Lincoln, Dakota Territory, in the early summer of 1876. Entering eastern Montana, the army intended to wage a punitive campaign against Sioux, Cheyenne, and Arapaho warriors, who were alarmed over a new gold rush in the Black Hills. When news of Custer's subsequent defeat at the Little Big Horn reached Territorial Governor Benjamin Potts on July 5, 1876, he immediately recognized the urgency of re-establishing the territorial militia.[5]

On July 6, Potts wired a proposal to General William Tecumseh Sherman requesting approval for a volunteer call up. Sherman, a personal friend and Civil War associate of Potts, replied on July 12, stating that the War Department could not justify approval, but that Montanans were free to protect their communities. Thus, Sherman did not discourage mustering in a militia, however, no federal funds were available. In the meantime, Potts already issued a call in Montana newspapers for volunteers.

Governor Potts again appealed for federal support through the introduction of a bill in Congress allowing President Ulysses S. Grant to accept the service of Montana volunteers, but the legislation died in committee. Potts then requested that forts be constructed on the Yellowstone and Musselshell rivers, which Congress did authorize in mid-July 1876.[6]

The territory's store of arms consisted of sixty Model 1861 contract Springfield .58 caliber rifled-muskets in Helena and another 1,200 in Virginia City, which had been sent in the federal shipment of 1867. Territorial authorities had at hand a 12-pound mountain howitzer mounted on a deteriorating prairie carriage in Virginia City. Potts also tried to collect the Model 1868 .50 caliber Springfield breech-loading rifles sent to Montana's territorial arsenal in 1872 and issued from time to time to citizens on a consignment basis, but met with little success. After the authorities gathered what Springfields they could, Potts requested "2,000 new breech-loaders from the War Department," but at the same time he assured the local populace that the "1,200 muskets currently in the territory's possession would be sufficient."[7]

The War Department eventually issued 500 weapons, which the governor signed for while personally guaranteeing that the territorial government would pay the freight bill.[8] Meanwhile, as Virginia City organized its volunteers in early August, and Butte residents scheduled a meeting for August 27 in the town schoolhouse for the same purpose, the Indian threat diminished and fears eased. By then, large numbers of federal troops were campaigning against the Sioux. As a result, Butte residents voted instead to form a volunteer fire department.[9]

In an address on January 9, 1877, Governor Potts asked the Tenth Montana Legislature to assume the financial obligations he had personally incurred. In response, the territorial legislature allocated money for paying the freight for the 500 rifles and rifled-muskets. Also, House Bill Number 24 provided funds for repairing the mountain howitzer carriage.[10]

Meanwhile, a Montana Territory financial claim dating from Red Cloud's War was finalized by federal legislation on March 3, 1873. However, it remained unpaid because federal funds were exhausted. Finally, on February 6, 1877, Secretary of War J.D. Cameron authorized an appropriation for the claims.[11]

Hardly had the Sioux War subsided and the "people of western Montana ceased to shudder over the details of the massacre of Custer and his command," when word suddenly came from west of the Bitterroots that Nez Perce bands were in revolt in Idaho Territory.[12] This kindled fears of an Indian uprising spreading across the Northwest.

The origin of the 1877 Nez Perce War dated from the previous decade. Due to a gold rush on native lands in Idaho in the early 1860s, the federal government had renegotiated the 1855 Nez Perce Treaty, thereby greatly reducing the size of the original tribal reservation in a new 1863 treaty. Generally, those Nez Perce bands that traditionally resided within the reduced reservation tract in Idaho signed the document, but bands outside of the new boundaries—in southeast Washington and northeast Oregon, as well as portions of Idaho—refused to do so. This split the tribe into a sizeable "non-treaty" faction and a somewhat larger "treaty" group.

In 1875, the government opened portions of the "non-treaty" Nez Perce lands to white settlement, creating pressure on a people long prudently peaceful toward whites. Land surveyors began working in the Wallowa Valley of northeast Oregon where a semi-migratory group of non-treaty Nez Perce, led by Chief Joseph, normally resided in the summer and autumn months. Joseph attempted to remain friendly, though the Wallowa band was determined to hold on to the extensive grassy valley surrounded by forested hills and mountain crags, where their ancestors were buried.[13] Nearby to the east, along the Snake and Salmon rivers, non-treaty bands under White Bird, Toohoolhoolzote, and other headmen also were allied with Joseph's people and their cause. Joseph told the whites that his father had not signed the 1863 treaty to give up the Wallowa Valley and it still belonged to his people. White homesteaders in the Wallowa country had a different view, and felt they had the government's permission to stake claims.

Groups of Nez Perce had traditionally migrated each spring from their Columbia Plateau homeland over the Lolo Trail and other mountain routes into the Bitterroot Valley and continued on to the Great Plains. Seeking hides for tepees and meat for the winter, these buffalo-hunting bands regularly traveled without incident through Montana's settled valleys while trading with local merchants and settlers. But with reports of an uprising in June 1877, Montana farmers and townspeople, who had known the Nez Perce as a friendly tribe, nevertheless began fearing that hostilities might spread to Montana's tribes, such as the Flathead.[14]

The armed conflict in Idaho Territory occurred after the Bureau of Indian Affairs, backed by the U.S. Army, finally sought to force the Wallowa band and other non-treaty groups to cease their seasonal migrations and to settle on the much-reduced reservation with the treaty bands. Brigadier General Oliver Otis Howard, the Department of the Columbia commander, had set June 14, 1877, as the date for their removal to the Clearwater River reserve.[15]

Just before a 30-day deadline ended, the revengeful actions of a few young tribal men precipitated a series of raids on local settlers. Full scale warfare quickly erupted. In late June and most of July 1877, after checking U.S. Army and volunteer forces in several large clashes, Joseph, Looking Glass, White Bird, and other Nez Perce leaders with about 800 followers from five separate non-treaty bands, including some neighboring Palouse, turned eastward via the Lolo Trail toward Montana, where they believed a more benign treatment of Indians prevailed.[16] Meanwhile, General Howard and the army set out in pursuit, unable to close with the fast moving Nez Perce and their large horse herd.

At first, ambiguous reports about the Nez Perce revolt drifted to Missoula and the Bitterroot Valley, Deer Lodge, and the Silver Bow country. In preparedness should the Nez Perce come eastward, Montanans in the Bitterroot Valley hastily constructed fortifications.[17] A mile northwest of Stevensville, settlers strengthened a bastion and some of the adobe walls of the 1850s' trading post, Fort Owen. With typical citizen waggery, they called it "Fort Brave." South of Fort Owen, on the northern outskirts of Corvallis, an earthen redoubt of sod was built, whimsically named "Fort Gunnybags." East of the little hamlet of Grantsdale, south of Corvallis, stood a hastily constructed defensive structure on Skalkaho Creek known as "Fort Skeedaddle."[18] In Missoula, a few structures were designated as defensive strong points and retrofitted to serve as protection for citizens and fortifications for posting armed volunteers.

As early as June 29, it was reported that most of the women and children of the Bitterroot country could be protected at Fort Owen.[19] Meanwhile, miners from Deer Lodge County voiced their readiness to respond as volunteer militia,[20] and other volunteers were organizing in Missoula, the Bitterroot Valley, Helena, Butte, Virginia City, and the mining camps.

In the latter part of July, when definite word came that the warring Nez Perce were traveling eastward, companies A and I of the 7th U.S. Infantry halted work in constructing two-week old Fort Missoula. A hasty defensive surround was thrown up on the post grounds—using construction materials and the garrison's baggage and boxed equipment—for the protection of dependents and others. On July 24, half of the men, commanded by Capt. Charles Rawn and assisted by Capt. Logan, moved south in the Bitterroot Valley and then west a short distance along Lolo Creek to block the Nez Perce coming east. Eventually joining them were about a hundred local volunteers, as well as volunteers from other parts of Montana and some friendly Flathead Indians.[21]

Four miles up Lolo Canyon, they hastily built what soon came to be called "Fort Fizzle," a rough, open triangle of earth and timber breastworks, including rifle pits.[22] Under federal orders to treat all Indians coming from Idaho as hostile, Capt. Rawn had placed his command squarely across the Lolo Trail leading into the Bitterroot Valley.[23] The Nez Perce would be approaching very shortly.

Governor Potts briefly visited the breastworks twice, giving official sanction to the territorial volunteers. Potts also earlier had contacted Capt. James H. Mills, editor of the *New North-West* in Deer Lodge, appointing him as adjutant general of the Montana militia that was forming to resist the Nez Perce.[24] Potts responded quickly to Capt. Rawn's request for further volunteer assistance.[25] On his return to Helena, the governor issued a proclamation calling up all of the organized companies.[26] Montana Territory was being invaded by hostile Indians from Idaho, he warned, with less than fifty federal soldiers available to oppose them. As commander-in-chief of the Montana militia, Potts ordered the volunteer forces in Missoula and Deer Lodge counties to report immediately to Missoula. Potts admitted he had no authority to issue supplies, but promised to use every effort in his power to secure payment for any used.

Meanwhile, panic-provoked stories appeared in the local newspapers, typically proclaiming: "We need help and it must be soon or it will be too late. Send everybody that can be armed."[27] Both alarm and a sense of adventure motivated the volunteers.[28]

When news of Potts's edict[29] reached Capt. W.A. Clark at Deer Lodge, Clark rode off to Butte to raise more volunteers.[30] Clark quickly organized the 1st Battalion of the Montana Volunteer Militia[31]—with Capt. Joseph A. Talbout commanding Company A; Capt. John Noyes, Company B; and Capt. William Wilson, Company C.[32] Altogether, 25 men from Deer Lodge and 69 from Butte left for duty on July 29.[33] Excitement filled the air as the Butte volunteers pledged an oath of allegiance to serve honestly and faithfully, and to obey the orders of the governor and their commanding officers.[34] Oblivious to red tape or official commissioning letters, they quickly marched off toward Missoula [35]

Other volunteer units included Capt. Thomas Stuart's Deer Lodge Company,[36] Capt. James E. Callaway's Virginia City Company, Capt. Thomas P. Fuller's Helena Cavalry, and Capt. Charles Curtis's Helena Light Artillery.[37] Volunteers also came from other communities and mining districts, including Phillipsburg, Beartown, Pioneer City, Silver Bow, Flint Creek, Granite, Henderson Gulch, and Georgetown.[38]

Earlier, on July 6, the *Weekly Missoulian* had outlined the local volunteer organizations in the Bitterroot locality. Missoula's Company A was led by Civil War veteran Capt. E.A. Kenny, a former regular army sergeant,[39] along with 1st Lt. W.J. Stephens and 2nd Lt. Thomas Andrews. Forty-four Model 1868 .50 caliber breechloading Springfield rifles were issued to these men. Stevensville's B Company was commanded by Capt. Robert W. Martin, assisted by 1st Lt. Anderson Buker and 2nd Lt. Decatur Buker, with a total of 38 enlisted volunteers and 30 rifles. Stevensville's Company C included Capt. J.A. Landram, 1st Lt. John

Chatfield, and 2nd Lt. W.N. Smith, with 32 men receiving only 20 rifles. Frenchtown's Company of 34 men, under Capt. P.J. Kline, 1st Lt. George Henault, 2nd Lt. Albert Milton, and Orderly Sergeant O.H. McCormick, remained partially armed. John B. Catlin at Skalkaho and J.L. Humble in Corvallis also were organizing companies while awaiting supplies and orders.[40]

All of the companies as yet had no official authorization from the federal government.[41] After initially calling for volunteers, Governor Potts had contacted the War Department for permission to muster a force of 300 men for 30 days. On August 2, however, Potts would receive dispatches from both Secretary of War George McCrary and Adjutant General E.D. Townsend stating that it was unnecessary to call out volunteers to intercept the Indians, as General Philip Sheridan and General Alfred Terry would meet the threat with federal troops under their command.[42] The military establishment had little faith in independent, untrained, volunteer forces.[43] As a result, Sheridan's headquarters in Chicago telegraphed John Gibbon, commander of the Montana District and colonel of the U.S. 7th Infantry at Fort Shaw, to provide protection for the western Montana settlements.[44] Colonel Gibbon with 100 men from Camp Baker, Fort Benton, and Fort Shaw, all east of the Rockies, would soon arrive in Missoula.[45] Another company of 7th Infantry soldiers, plus 8 troopers of the 2nd U.S. Cavalry, traveled directly from Fort Ellis near Bozeman to Fort Missoula.

By now, the volunteers had fully responded and were in motion. Though the governor had no authority to commit the territory to paying expenses, almost every man brought his own horse or borrowed one. Meanwhile, the citizens of Deer Lodge raised $1,750 to purchase supplies.[46]

The Nez Perce believed that once they crossed the mountains into the Bitterroot Valley, leaving General Howard's command behind in Idaho, their troubles would end. The warriors not only brought along their families, they were driving 2,000 horses with them. When coming over the Bitterroots in late July, and when barely in Montana, the Nez Perce discovered that the Lolo Trail was blocked by Capt. Rawn's hastily built fortification, manned by regulars and volunteers. The warriors encamped, awaiting Joseph to come up to join in conference with the tribe's main war chief, Looking Glass, and other headmen in regard to their next move.

The Nez Perce deployed their caravan casually, including the women and children, to suggest nothing of an aggressive nature. They went into camp on "Woodman Flats," about four miles above the barricade. Looking Glass, meanwhile, rode forward to explain to Capt. Rawn that the Nez Perce had no quarrel with them; they simply wanted freedom of passage. Rawn demanded that the Nez Perce dismount and disarm themselves, and then they would be allowed to pass. These terms, of course, were unacceptable to the Nez Perce. For a couple days, they delayed.[47]

In the meantime some local volunteers saw no reason for exposing their families and property to danger by refusing to accept a truce proposed by the Nez Perce. These men felt prompted to withdraw.[48] A group of Phillipsburg volunteers, when arriving in the area, actually passed peacefully through the Nez Perce lines.[49] While other volunteers were moving at a quick pace toward the Bitterroot Valley, the Nez Perce outmaneuvered Capt. Rawn. On July 28, the Indians took to the high surrounding ridges and drainages to the north—thought impassable by some whites—and bypassed Rawn's fortifications. The blocking force of regulars and volunteers could only watch as the Nez Perce trailed off eastward toward the Bitterroot Valley.[50]

Rawn ordered volunteers under Lt. Stevens to follow the Nez Perce, already disappearing over a wooded slope. When the pursuers approached, Looking Glass came forward and assured the volunteers that if the Nez Perce were not attacked, no one in Montana would suffer at the hands of his people.[51] As a result of the Nez Perce maneuvering, Rawn and his soldiers soon abandoned the log and earth fortification, shortly called "Fort Fizzle."[52] Many of the volunteers and the Flatheads returned home, while Rawn marched back to Missoula's embryonic post to await Col. Gibbon's arrival.

The Nez Perce proceeded south through the Bitterroot Valley.[53] Under Looking Glass's supervision, they stopped in the Stevensville vicinity for two days, where merchants and others—some looking for profit, others attempting to avoid retaliation if they did not open their doors for business, and all recognizing that there was a kind of truce—sold flour, sugar, coffee, and tobacco to the Indians for gold dust or currency. Farther down the valley, a number of unoccupied homes were entered. In one incident, a few young Nez Perce pilfered through the unoccupied cabin of Bitterroot volunteer Myron Lockwood and stole some of his horses along with household goods and clothing.

Still believing they had left General Howard and the war behind in Idaho, the Nez Perce continued their march over the Continental Divide to the Big Hole Valley. On August 7, they reached the level prairie of the North Fork Big Hole River, at the junction of Trail and Ruby creeks, where they paused in sparsely inhabited country and prepared for the next leg of the journey to the Great Plains.[54]

Confirmation that the Nez Perce had left southward eased local tensions, but it did not affect Col. John Gibbon's orders. After arriving at Fort Missoula from Fort Shaw, Gibbon added Rawn's and Logan's companies of regulars to his own plus the Fort Ellis detachments, and sent a messenger back up the Lolo Trail to inform Howard's column that he was pursuing the Nez Perce. Gibbon then proceeded up the Bitterroot Valley, with his infantry and supply wagons driven by a civilian contractor and local settlers. At Corvallis he met volunteers wanting to join him. However, the militia's Capt. J.L. Humble, who opposed pursuit of the now peaceful tribesmen, only agreed to accompany his volunteers for a short time, leaving the column at Ross Hole.

When news of Gibbon's advance reached Skalkaho, volunteers there persuaded their reluctant Capt., John B. Catlin,[55] to lead them in joining Gibbon.[56] Confident in the ability of the nearly 170 regulars under his command, Gibbon was annoyed that the volunteers believed he needed their assistance. After grudgingly accepting Capt. Catlin's services, Gibbon allowed the Skalkaho volunteers to join the chase. Catlin, however, had mixed feelings about pursuing Indians who just a few days before had peacefully interacted with Bitterroot settlers.[57] A number of other citizens felt conflicted in the same way and had not joined in the pursuit.

Eventually, after Humble left, Catlin would lead all of the volunteers that did not turn back, finally numbering approximately 37 men.[58] They were typical Montana settlers, including Myron Lockwood, who had come to the Bitterroot in 1873 to farm and raise livestock; Missouri natives Millard Sherrill and his brother Thomas were ranchers;[59] Riley B. Cooper had immigrated from Marshall, Arkansas;[60] the Chaffins came to Montana in 1864 from Tennessee and Missouri;[61] Amos Buck, an Ohioan, was a Stevensville merchant; Virginian Oscar Clark had manufactured shingles at Alder Gulch before ranching in the Bitterroot; the Wilkerson brothers, Austin and Barnett, were the sons of a Bitterroot mountain man and his Spanish wife;[62] and brothers Alexander and Campbell Mitchell, and Luther Johnson, were miners.[63] These men were armed with .50 caliber Model 1868 Springfield rifles provided by Governor Potts.[64] The motives of these volunteers, who now were joining the military column after allowing the Nez Perce to peacefully pass through the Bitterroot Valley, caused some controversy with the regulars, who were contemptuous of volunteer citizenry anyway.[65]

Col. Gibbon nevertheless welcomed these volunteers knowing they were familiar with the local terrain. Accordingly, he sent Catlin and his men ahead to scout. After determining that the Nez Perce had crossed the Continental Divide, they camped that evening on the summit.[66] Next, Catlin's mounted volunteers and 30 mounted regulars started through the woods and creek bottoms searching for the Indian camp.[67] In the early hours of August 8, 1st Lt. James H. Bradley climbed a tree and in the distance spotted the Nez Perce tepees in a meadow at the foot of the mountains. They then waited through the day for the main column to come up.

When Gibbon arrived that evening, he quickly ordered the wagon train, a mountain howitzer, and most of the horses, supplies, and equipment off the trail into defensive positions. Here, the men rested. No fires were allowed, and the infantry shed their heavier accoutrements. At 11 p.m., the command set out for a distance of five miles, with orders to take a position at the base of the mountain near the sleeping camp, wait for the first lifting of darkness, and then to advance stealthily on the unsuspecting village.

Meanwhile in the Indian camp, the Nez Perce were lax in sending out scouts, unlike when in Idaho and on the Lolo Trail. Looking Glass insisted, "The war is now quit." Thus the stage was set for the two-day Battle of the Big Hole, August 9–10, 1877.[68]

After advancing to near the Indian encampment late in the night, Gibbon ordered the final assault. The men slowly proceeded down a grass and sagebrush covered slope to the creek bottom, then silently picked their way among willows and ponds in the meadow. At dawn's first light, as the troopers approached the tepees, an elderly Palouse headman on horseback emerged from the camp to check on the horse herd.[69] Unknowingly, he advanced toward the volunteers and Lt. Bradley's regulars, on the extreme left flank of Gibbon's line of battle.[70]

Volunteers Oscar Clark, Alexander Mitchell, Amos Buck, and one of the Sherrill brothers opened fire prematurely, sparking the attack. The advancing line of shouting soldiers and volunteers, some wading waist-deep in water, shot into the encampment. The assault was withering. Astonished Nez Perce families fled, or dashed to cover along the creek banks or in hollows out in the grassy prairie. Some hid among their dead and wounded. The warriors, however, had sufficient time to seize their arms.[71]

Lt. Bradley, leading his men toward the Indian camp, fell in the first moments. Consequently the men of Gibbon's left flank were leaderless and lay immobilized along the stream bank near the tepees. Alvin Lockwood, a volunteer, fell soon after. David Morrow was killed next, and several soldiers also lay dead. Other volunteers, John Armstrong and Lynde Catlin Elliott, also would die.[72] All along the line, a number of troopers and volunteers were wounded. Injured volunteer Campbell Mitchell feigned death, but was discovered by the Indians and then killed.[73] Colonel Gibbon and his adjutant, Lt. Charles A. Woodruff, received wounds.

Looking Glass, White Bird, Joseph, and other leaders shouted encouragement to the warriors, urging them to join the fight around the tepees. With disorder and panic now beginning to spread among the troops, Gibbon was forced to react to the warriors' determined counterattack. He ordered a retreat toward a slightly elevated alluvial bench at the base of the mountain. There, the men began digging entrenchments among downed logs, some timber, and a few boulders.

When volunteer Capt. Catlin[74] reached this defensive point, he noted its sparse stand of trees and the higher ground to the west. Realizing the terrain favored the Indians, he asked who had ordered the halt. When told it was Gibbon, he snapped, "I don't give a damn. It's a hell of a place to camp."[75] Some laughs percolated among the regulars. While the men dug in, the Nez Perce extended a firing line around Gibbon's men, isolating them.[76]

Around noon, not far above the entrenched position, Nez Perce warriors also routed Gibbon's small detachment of artillerymen. They had just arrived and had time to fire only twice—apparently spherical shell shot—into the Indian camp.

The Indians captured the howitzer and a mule carrying 2,000 rounds of rifle ammunition and subsequently dismantled the howitzer.[77]

As warriors pinned down Gibbon's men, Joseph organized the horse herd and the Indian camp, now wailing in mourning. More than fifty tribal members had died, including a number of women, children, and the elderly, accidentally or intentionally shot in the confusion of the soldiers' crossfire. Others were wounded, some severely. Joseph and White Bird hastily led the caravan southward along the western edge of the Big Hole Valley, while a number of warriors continued to hold Gibbon's command in check.

The siege continued throughout the day, with casualties on both sides. Several Nez Perce tried to burn out the troops by setting fires, but the green grass failed to ignite. The soldiers began running out of water and could do little to quench the dreadful thirst of the wounded. Further complicating their plight, Gibbon's command had no surgeon or medical supplies, and few blankets for the coming cold evening. A now diminished number of Nez Perce continued firing into the shallow trenches throughout the night, though some soldiers were able to elude the warriors in the dark and return with filled canteens.

Gibbon managed to send out a messenger toward Deer Lodge. Volunteer William H. "Billy" Edwards eluded the Nez Perce and then traveled for two days, going without sleep or food.[78] He proceeded 40 miles on foot to French Gulch where he acquired a horse and finally reached Deer Lodge, bringing the first news of the battle.[79]

The command remained pinned down throughout the night of August 9, suffering from hunger and cold until daybreak. In the morning, after firing a parting volley at the troops, the remaining Nez Perce warriors rounded up the last of their pony herd and rode off. Gibbon dispatched some men to intercept, but the warriors evaded them. The last Nez Perce disappeared over the bluffs to the south.

The Nez Perce lost 12 of their best men and leaders; Poker Joe, a half-breed, now assumed leadership. He had joined the Nez Perce in the Bitterroot Valley and had extensive knowledge of Montana's mountain trails. Some Nez Perce were critical of Looking Glass, who they blamed for encouraging the band to linger too slow in their march. They felt he had not listened to the cautionary advice of others.

As they moved out of the Big Hole to Horse Prairie, Nez Perce warriors killed five ranchers and drove off livestock. Having abandoned tepees and other possessions at the Big Hole camp, the Nez Perce ransacked ranch homes for provisions and bandages. Though burdened with their wounded, they quickly moved westward across Bannock Pass and into Idaho.

Meanwhile, General Howard arrived at the Big Hole and assumed overall command, determined to continue pursuing the Nez Perce.[80] The uninjured men of Gibbon's command were added to Howard's large column. Colonel Gibbon, suffering from a gun shot wound, was in no condition to proceed. One-third of his command were casualties—29 men, including 2 officers and 5 volunteers, lay dead, and 40 were wounded, 2 of them mortally. Bitterroot settler Otto Leifer's wound was caused by the accidental discharge of a weapon, and Myron Lockwood had been shot in the hip.[81] Both survived, though they would be hobbled for life. At this time, Catlin and his battered Bitterroot Valley volunteers marched home.

When the news reached Deer Lodge, Helena, and Butte, citizens quickly arranged light wagons, provisions, and surgeons to send to the Big Hole to care for the wounded and transport them to a Deer Lodge hospital.[82] The militia's Capt. W.A. Clark and Lt. T.M. Lowry organized an ambulance corps and a guard of 35 men from Butte. Lieutenant James W. Wheelock and Doctor O.B. Whitford were the attending surgeons.[83] From Helena, Dr. Reese likewise joined Clark's group; Helena's citizens also raised $2,000 to cover expenses. Capt. Thomas Stuart's relief company of 60 volunteers, mainly from the Deer Lodge Valley, also included physicians, Dr. Mitchell and Dr. Steele.

The new volunteers reached Howard's column and announced they were joining in the pursuit.[84] As the sense of urgency subsided, however, a number of these volunteers from Helena, Butte, and Deer Lodge returned home. The remaining volunteers were sent ahead as scouts. They reached Junction Station to the south with exhausted horses on August 17, only to find poor grazing and no firewood. There they encountered 55 additional volunteers from Virginia City, commanded by Col. James B. Callaway, awaiting Howard's arrival.[85]

The Nez Perce in the meantime had left the upper Salmon drainage and turned east, proceeding toward the lava plains of southeast Idaho, with intentions of eventually entering Yellowstone National Park (recently established in 1872). Idaho settlers organized defensive postures similar to those of Bitterroot residents.[86]

When resuming the march, Howard succumbed to pressure from settlers, who wanted him to follow a less direct stagecoach road to the east in order to boost morale in the settlements of that locality.[87] Meanwhile, the Nez Perce had moved on toward Camas Meadows, following a traditional route to the Yellowstone country.[88] For many years, groups of Nez Perce visited these Idaho meadows each summer to harvest onion-shaped roots of the blue-flowered camas, a dietary staple. Rendezvousing here, on open plains with lush fodder for horses, was always a key social event among the bands.

On August 19, General Howard's column reached the broad grassy meadows. Nearby stood a slightly elevated lava plateau; all around were miles of undulating lava knolls and hollows.[89] Howard bivouacked in the bottom at a camp site abandoned that very morning by the Nez Perce.[90] Here, Col. James Callaway's volunteers joined them. Callaway requested that his men be allowed to camp on the east side of a branch of Camas Creek where they might better provide for their horses. For security of the herd, Howard assigned men in position to guard approaches to the camp.[91]

Despite the army's precautions, Nez Perce warriors surprised the encampment under the cover of night. Howard's camp was thrown into confusion while Callaway and his volunteers tried to recover their horses, which were stampeding in the darkness. The warriors intended to run off the command's horses, but instead captured nearly 200 army mules, though they did eventually seize a number of the volunteers' scattered mounts.

After daylight, three U.S. Cavalry companies went in pursuit, following the raiding party's tracks. Shortly they engaged the Nez Perce in a lengthy fight across the rugged lava fields. The Battle of Camas Meadows cost Howard one killed and seven wounded, and again he failed to capture or defeat the Nez Perce.

Callaway and his volunteers returned to Virginia City with Howard's wounded. A number were on foot, but they had suffered no casualties.[92] As the Nez Perce escaped northeastward, further distancing themselves from Montana and Idaho's population centers, the role of the citizen volunteer diminished.[93]

Thomas Baker, a volunteer and special correspondent for Montana's *Madisonian*, enlivened his campaign reporting with doggerel, "Our Volunteers."

Lay low boys, it is a general attack
Down in the creek or you'll get shot in the back
I pledge you my word I wish I hadn't come
And I'll bet you ten to one we'll have to foot it home.

Oh, I am one of the volunteers,
Who marched right home on the tramp, the tramp,
When Joseph set the boys a foot,
At the battle of Callaway's camp.[94]

By now the infantry and cavalry were bedraggled, tired, and short of supplies. Howard faced increasing pressure from the national press, which was critical of the army's performance or actually sympathizing with the non-treaty Nez Perce's plight. Frustrated, Howard rode to Virginia City where he purchased mules and wired General Sherman, noting that his "command was worn by overfatigue and jaded animals that could not be pushed much further." Sherman's reply did not inspire confidence. "If you are tired," he responded, "give the command to some young, energetic officer."

Howard rethought the situation and chose to continue. He wired Sherman with assurance there was no need to doubt his pluck and energy. Howard resumed the pursuit.[95] By then, the Nez Perce had passed into Yellowstone Park and proceeded toward the Plains, eluding all the military commands pursuing them, including Col. S.D. Sturgis of the 7th cavalry. Howard sent a courier to

Col. Nelson A. Miles at Fort Keogh on the Tongue River, asking Miles to try to overtake the Indians from the east.

On September 5, in a dispatch to Washington, D.C., Howard reported the names of the Montana volunteers who fought at the Big Hole. He requested that some provision be made in regard to pay, allowances, and pensions similar to those of regular soldiers.[96] Meanwhile, Col. Miles in far eastern Montana prepared to lead a combined infantry and cavalry column on a diagonal march northwest to intercept the Nez Perce.[97]

When moving east through Yellowstone Park, the Nez Perce killed some whites, including tourists, and captured and later released others.[98] When entering the Great Plains, the help that the Nez Perce expected from their long-time friends, the Crow, never materialized. At this time the Crow were closely allied with the U.S. Army in the continuing hostilities against the Sioux. The Crow, as well as Snake and Cheyenne tribesmen, began skirmishing with the Nez Perce while opportunistically stealing horses.

The Nez Perce now were proceeding north over the Plains. They planned to join the Sioux in Canada, where Sitting Bull had sought refuge due to the U.S. Army's intensive year-long campaign following Custer's defeat. On September 13, after fording the Yellowstone River near modern-day Laurel, the Nez Perce thwarted a 7th Cavalry attack at Canyon Creek.

Proceeding farther north, they crossed the Missouri River at Cow Island, the location of a steamboat landing and secondary military freight depot, where supplies recently were unloaded during the Missouri's low-water season. The Indians ran off the few soldiers, took what they needed, burned the rest, and moved northward again, between the Bears Paw Mountains and the Little Rockies.[99]

When news of the raid reached Fort Benton farther up the Missouri, a company of the 7th Infantry under Maj. Guido Illges set out for Cow Island on horseback, accompanied by 36 mounted volunteers. On September 25, Illges found the Nez Perce's trail. Encountering warriors in the Judith River area, a two-hour fight left one citizen-volunteer dead before Illges' command returned to Fort Benton.[100]

In late September, the Nez Perce reinstated Looking Glass as leader and he slackened the pace. Unaware of Col. Miles coming from the east, and thinking that the open prairie allowed for good visual detection of any pursuers, the Nez Perce stopped four miles north of the Bears Paw Mountains, and only 40 miles and an easy day's march from the Canadian border. In a situation rather similar to the Big Hole, the Indians again camped in a grassy hollow beside a small stream, adjacent to higher ridgeland.[101]

Low hanging clouds and mist concealed Miles' command, rapidly pushing forward to intercept the Nez Perce. On September 30, when belatedly becoming aware of the approaching column, warriors rushed to take up positions and dig rifle pits. They opened fire on the charging U.S. troopers with deadly accuracy, deliberately trying to pick off officers and noncommissioned officers. Heavy casualties blunted the thunderous frontal assault by the 7th cavalry, forcing a withdrawal. Miles then laid siege around the Nez Perce camp with infantry and dismounted cavalry.

In the following six-day battle, mainly sustained by sharpshooters on either side, some Nez Perce left under cover of night, making their way to Canada and seeking assistance from Sitting Bull's warriors, but none was forthcoming.[102] The Nez Perce continued to hold their ground while suffering a heavy toll in the fighting. Among the dead were Toohoolhoolzote, Ollokot (Joseph's brother), Poker Joe, Looking Glass, and other leaders. Meanwhile, Chief White Bird along with more than 200 Nez Perce managed to slip through the soldiers' lines, escaping to Canada and joining the Sioux. Of the principal chiefs, only Joseph remained alive and active in the Indian camp.

Miles, an ambitious but capable officer, had two concerns—the prospect of Sitting Bull sending warriors south to assist the Nez Perce, and General Howard's expected arrival to assume command and thus share credit for victory. On the first day of the battle, rain turned into snow, causing suffering for both sides. The next day Miles displayed a white flag, and though Joseph decided to meet with him (over the objections of the remaining headmen), he refused to surrender.

As the siege continued for four more days and after the death of so many of his people, Joseph accepted the inevitable. He believed Col. Miles' promise that the Nez Perce, now numbering just over 400 people, could return to their homeland with whatever livestock remained in their possession. (After the battle, however, the Nez Perce were eventually sent to Oklahoma. They would not be allowed to return to the Northwest until 1885.[103])

On October 5, advancing to meet Miles as well as the recently arrived General Howard, Joseph through an interpreter gave an eloquent surrender speech, which in following weeks appeared in newspapers across the nation. Joseph stated his wish to end the fighting, noting that the head chiefs were dead and it was the young men now saying "yes" and "no." Children were freezing, and some of his people were hiding in the hills without blankets or food. He wished to search for his family to see if they were among the living or dead. "Here me my chiefs! I am tired. My heart is sick and sad. From where the sun now stands I will fight no more forever."[104]

In the same year as the Nez Perce War, a home guard was organized in Great Falls in response to the continuing threat from Sitting Bull's followers in Canada. Though having no official designation or recognition, the volunteers conducted drills at frequent intervals. In 1879, the Sioux attempted to return to their former hunting grounds in the United States, but were driven back by troops under

Nelson A. Miles. The Sioux suffered severely during the wintertime in Canada, where game was depleted.

Small raiding parties occasionally crossed the border, primarily to steal horses. Residents of this part of Montana remained in an anxious state, but large-scale Indian warfare never again materialized. Sitting Bull finally surrendered, and eventually resided on the Standing Rock Reservation in South Dakota.[105]

On October 5, 1881, exactly four years after Chief Joseph's surrender, Congress authorized payment of $6,879 to 442 Montana volunteers recognized on War Department rosters as enlisting in the hastily-created Montana Territorial Militia for the Nez Perce War.[106] This concluded the federal-militia relationship for that conflict, but it also afforded federal recognition of the role played by volunteers in supplementing U.S. troops in the campaign.[107]

Despite the end of the Indian wars, militia activity continued. Across America, in fact, there was a resurgence of public interest and support for citizen soldiery. It was becoming fashionable to join militia organizations, and Montanans were no exception. In March 1883, Capt. Samuel J. Reynolds and Lt. Mitchell formed the Union Guard in Butte.[108] In Deer Lodge County, a group of leading citizens called for a meeting on April 9, 1883,[109] at the Fireman's Hall, for the purpose of establishing a military company.[110] The Helena Light Guard completed its organization on January 2, 1884, by the appointment of non-commissioned officers, including corporals W.H. Trowbridge, Frank L. Sizer, W.D. Wheeler, and D.P. Pateneaud.

In Butte, the Emmet Guards formed on June 21, 1884, with 20 men under the command of Capt. John Brannagan, 1st Lt. James Murphy, 2nd lts. D.T. Hester and J.L. Sullivan, and sergeants P.S. Harrington, Harry Cassidy, Peter Byrne, and Thomas Hayes. Drills were held Monday evenings at the courthouse hall.[111] On February 7, 1887, the Parnell Rifles also organized in Butte.

In return for an allowance from the Territory, company commanders were required to complete monthly reports regarding drills. Payments also were based on the results of annual inspections and the percentage of men attending drills.[112]

The flurry of forming Montana militia units might at first glance seem out of step with the times since there was no military need, but it was due to several notable factors. These included Montana's vigilante heritage,[113] the camaraderie of men donning uniforms to the tune of martial airs, rivalries between communities, and the growing national popularity of serving in militia organizations. Perhaps, too, it occurred because of concerns over labor union unrest in the rapidly expanding timber, railroading, and mining industries. At the time, however, mine workers in Montana earned comparatively high wages and usually refrained from strikes and confrontations. The expanding presence of organized labor, nevertheless, undoubtedly gave pause to mine owners and the business establishment. Indeed, in a few years deep rifts would develop between management and workers.

March 10, 1885, proved to be a momentous occasion for the territorial militia. On that date the Montana legislature passed House Bill No. 20, creating the Montana National Guard.[114] According to the act, companies, batteries, and regiments would be organized with the governor's authorization, and five or more companies would form a regimental organization. The governor also had authorization to appoint an adjutant general's staff, with the adjutant general issuing orders under the governor's authority. The legislation provided directives for enlistment oaths, officers' duties, and unit activation, as well as rules for drills, compensation, rations, uniforms, discipline, inspections, and public parades.[115] Companies could be organized with a minimum of 30 and a maximum of 100 men.

This initial legislation allowed the territorial government to flex its authority in centralizing control of the militia. Two years later, the legislature passed another bill requiring that the Montana National Guard's organization and equipment conform to the standards of federal troops.[116] Existing militia groups were absorbed under the new arrangements. The only Montana military organization to remain independent was the Parnell Rifles of Butte, formed in early 1887 with a membership of 90, mostly Irish miners. They declined to be mustered into the territorial troops, and retained their grey uniforms with green facing rather than adopting U.S. Army uniforms.[117]

By 1888, C.W. Turner of Helena served as Governor Preston H. Leslie's adjutant general. C.W. Hoffman of Bozeman was the quarter-master general. The territorial militia included nine active units:[118]

Company B (Emmet Guard), Butte City
Company C (Meagher Guard), Helena
Company D, Virginia City
Company E, Dillon
Company F (Montana Rifles), Butte City
Company H (Webb Guard), Billings
Cavalry Troop A (Capital Guard), Helena
Cavalry Troop B (Gallatin Valley Guard), Bozeman
Artillery Battery A, Helena

The adjutant general's first biennial report on December 1, 1888, recommended that a board of officers convene to examine the ordnance stores and prepare recommendations regarding the disposal of unserviceable weapons and equipment. A number of muzzle-loading weapons, still in the territory's possession since 1867, were obsolete.

The guard's membership numbered over 500 uniformed and equipped officers and men, though the two cavalry troops did not have carbines or revolvers.[119] In an overall assessment, the units appeared prepared for any call to action.[120]

On August 21, 1888, the National Guard of Montana Territory assembled for its first annual encampment, a three-day affair, at the Helena fairgrounds with all nine companies present.[121] Most of the men arrived by train. Thirty-nine men from Virginia City's Company D came by wagon. Sixty tents purchased with funds raised by Helena's citizens were pitched on the in-field at the fairgrounds racetrack.

Adjutant General Turner, however, reported that the weather was "too hot to exercise the troops in company and battalion drill, and that they had neither ammunition supplies nor targets for rifle practice."[122] The military spectacle, though, appealed to visitors coming to the fairgrounds.[123] The adjutant general noted the men's good enthusiasm, and made several recommendations for the next encampment, including providing at least two cooks. Turner also recommended placing future camps on higher ground near water, and extending the training period to one week.

Regarding other matters, the adjutant general requested that an arsenal be built in Helena. He also recommended that officers and enlisted men should be subject to court martial when warranted, that as many guardsmen as possible should attend the annual encampment, and the governor should be allowed to disband unauthorized units and muster out inefficient ones. He also reaffirmed that the National Guard should be organized along regular army lines, with commissions issued by the governor through the adjutant general.

With these goals on the horizon, the guard looked forward to added responsibilities and increased support as Montana achieved statehood. By the will of Congress, Montana entered the Union on November 8, 1889, as the 41st state.

Notes

1. Early English settlers brought the militia tradition with them to the New World. John K. Mahon, *The American Militia: A Decade of Decision, 1789–1800* (Gainesville: University of Florida Press, 1960), 1.
2. "Do Your Duty" was a slogan adopted from the Montana vigilance committee of the 1860s; it was the command given to hang a rustler or murderer before effective law and order came to Montana. Thomas J. Dimsdale, *The Vigilantes of Montana or Popular Justice in the Rocky Mountains* (Helena, [1866] 1915), 124.
3. Populism always has been evident in Montana politics and society. Michael P. Malone, Richard B. Roeder, and William L. Lang, *Montana: A History of Two Centuries* (Seattle: University of Washington Press, 1976), 218.
4. Clark C. Spence, "James M. Ashley, Spoilsman in Montana," in Michael P. Malone and Richard B. Roeder, eds., *Montana's Past: Selected Essays* (Missoula: University of Montana Publications in History, 1973), 161–64.
5. Benjamin Potts, a native of Ohio, was appointed Governor of Montana Territory by President Ulysses S. Grant on July 13, 1870, and served for 13 years. He had been a Civil War officer, achieving the rank of brigadier general.

6. Vertical File, Early Attempts to Organize National Guard, Montana Historical Society, Helena [Montana Historical Society hereafter cited as MHS]; Extract of Annual Report of December 24, 1877, Nez Perce Campaign, RS250, Box 5, Folder 5-25, MHS.
7. In 1875, the territorial capitol was moved from Virginia City to Helena. Richard H. Lacey, *The Montana Militia: A History of Montana's Volunteer Forces, 1867–1976* (Dillon, Montana: Dillon Tribune-Examiner Press, 1976), 13; Malone and Roeder, *Montana's Past*; Appendix I, 519; Governor Potts to J.H. Mills, July 17, 1877, Early Attempts to Organize Montana National Guard, Folder Misc., Drawer 2, MMHM, LA, Bldg. T-15, Fort Harrison.
8. Lacey, *Montana Militia*, 13.
9. Ibid.
10. Ibid.
11. Secretary of War J.D. Cameron to Governor Potts, *House Executive Document* 34, 44 Congress, 2nd Session (Serial Set 1542).
12. Arthur L. Stone, *Following Old Trails* (Missoula, Montana: Morton John Elrod, 1913), 55; David Lavender, *Let Me Be Free: The Nez Perce Tragedy* (New York: Harper Collins, 1992), 238; Col. J.B. Catlin, "The Battle of the Big Hole," Montana Volunteers Nez Perce War, Drawer 2, Montana Military History Museum, Library Archives, Building T-15, Fort William H. Harrison, Helena, Montana [hereafter cited as MMHM, LA, Bldg. T-15, Fort Harrison].
13. According to Chief Joseph: "A man who would not love his father's grave is worse than a wild animal." Alvin M. Josephy Jr., *The Nez Perce Indians and the Opening of the Northwest* (New York: Houghton Mifflin, 1965), 450. In addition to Josephy, cited here, other overviews of the 1877 Nez Perce conflict include: Merrill D. Beal, *"I Will Fight No More Forever": Chief Joseph and the Nez Perce War* (Seattle: University of Washington Press, 1963); Mark H. Brown, *The Flight of the Nez Perce* (New York: G.P. Putnam's Sons, 1967); Jerome T. Greene, *Nez Perce Summer, 1877: The U.S. Army and the Nee-Me-Poo Crisis* (Helena: Montana Historical Society Press, 2000); and Bruce Hampton, *Children of Grace: The Nez Perce War of 1877* (New York: Henry Holt, 1994).
14. Josephy, *The Nez Perce Indians*, 563.
15. Howard was a Civil War hero with strong—some thought fanatic—religious beliefs.
16. S.L.A. Marshall, *Crimsoned Prairie...* (New York: Scribner, 1972), 185–86.
17. Josephy, *The Nez Perce Indians*, 563–65; Stone, *Following Old Trails* 55; W.B. Harlan, "The Fiasco at Fort Fizzle," *Journal of the West* 3 (October 1964): 503–7; Merrill G. Burlingame, "The Mining Frontier in Montana," in Michael P. Malone and Richard B. Roeder, eds., *The Montana Past: An Anthology* (Missoula: University of Montana Publications in History, 1969), 62, 86; Will Cave, *Nez Perce Indian War of 1877 and Battle of the Big Hole* (Missoula, Montana: Missoulian, ca. 1926), 9–10.
18. Today, all three of these sites are preserved, protected, or physically marked.
19. Stone, *Following Old Trails*, 59.
20. Lacey, *Montana Militia*, 14–15.
21. Included among their number at Fort Fizzle were A.S. Blake, John Chatfield, Frank C. Eves, Thomas Fruen, Simon Greenfield, Frank Tudor, William Turnage, and W.R. Woodmancy, all members of Company No. 7, serving under Capt. John A. Landram. Joseph M. Putman, a member of Catlin's Company No. 1, also was present. John Landram was born in Pike County, Missouri, fought for the Confederacy during the Civil War, and eventually became a leader in the Montana Democratic Party. He had come to the Bitterroot in 1875 and was chosen Capt. of the company formed at Stevensville. Landram died in

1903 at age 61, with the funeral held under the auspices of the Odd Fellow and Workmen lodges. Montana Militia, Pre-National Guard, 1880s, Drawer 2, MMHM, LA, Bldg. T-15, Fort Harrison; "John Catlin," *Missoulian*, June 1917, File 010, Big Hole National Battlefield, Wisdom, Montana.

22. Rawn began construction of the barricade on July 25, and the Nez Perce diverted around the position on July 28. Josephy, *The Nez Perce Indians,* 569; Amos Buck, Montana Volunteer Citizen, Drawer 5, MMHM, LA, Bldg. T-15, Fort Harrison.
23. Col. John Gibbon to Governor Potts, Missoula, August 2, 1877, Nez Perce Campaign, RS250, Box 5, Folder 5-25, MHS; Maj. Gen. McDowell to Governor Potts, San Francisco, July 23, 1877, National Guard Association of the United States Library, One Massachusetts Avenue, Washington, D.C. [hereafter cited as NGAUS].
24. J.H. Mills to Governor Potts, Montana Volunteers, Nez Perce War 1877, Drawer 2, MMHM, LA, Bldg. T-15, Fort Harrison; General Order No.1, Territory of Montana Executive Department, SMF Roll 6—Records of Montana Territory and State Papers Relative to the Indian Excitement of 1877, MHS.
25. John Barsness, "Impassable Garrison Gave Chief Joseph Little Trouble," Vertical File, Fort Fizzle, MHS.
26. "A Proclamation," Helena *Independent Extra*, July 29, 1877, Vertical File I, Nez Perce 1877, MHS.
27. Helena *Independent Extra*, July 28, 1877, Vertical File I, Nez Perce 1877, MHS.
28. Organizing a militia command was consuming valuable time. On July 13, Potts had received a letter from newly appointed Adjutant General Mills, requesting forms for the oath of enlistment and muster rolls, and to designate who should be the mustering officers. J.H. Mills to Governor Potts, Deer Lodge, Montana, July 13, 1877, Montana Volunteers, Nez Perce War 1877, Drawer 2, MMHM, LA, Bldg. T-15, Fort Harrison.
29. On July 31, even as the Nez Perce were traveling through the Bitterroot Valley, Potts would appoint as staff officers R.H. Mason, chief of ordnance, Peter Valston, chief quarter master, S.E. Larabee, chief of commissary, and A.H. Mitchell, surgeon general. M.A. Leeson, *History of Montana: 1739–1885* (Chicago: Warner, Beers, 1885), 138.
30. William Andrews Clark became famous as one of Montana's "Copper Kings," and later, U.S. Senator from Montana. He was born in 1839 in Pennsylvania, and in the spring of 1863, while working his way west, heard of the gold discovery at Grasshopper Creek. He secured a placer claim on Horse Prairie, earning his first $1,000. In 1877, Clark was elected Grand Master of the Masons in Montana, and in 1878 received a commission from the governor as a major in the Butte Battalion of volunteers.
31. Leeson, *History of Montana*, 1326.
32. This organization has the distinction of being the first federally recognized military body in Montana. Montana Militia, Pre-National Guard, 1880s, Drawer 2, MMHM, LA, Bldg. T-15, Fort Harrison.
33. Vertical File I, Nez Perce 1877, MHS.
34. Governor Potts also had sent word that the Flatheads were cooperating with Capt. Rawn's forces. Letter from Potts, Helena *Independent Extra*, Vertical File I, Nez Perce 1877, MHS.
35. Lacey, *Montana Militia*, 15.
36. Capt. Stuart's company of 32 volunteers marched 94 miles from Deer Lodge to Missoula in under 26 hours. Lacey, *Montana Militia*, 16; Vertical File, Montana National Guard, MHS; Leeson, *History of Montana,* 141.
37. Ibid.

38. Kermit Edmonds, *Montana Militiaman* 26 (Summer 1988); Montana Volunteers, Nez Perce War, Drawer 2, MMHM, LA, Bldg. T-15, Fort Harrison.
39. Cave, *Nez Perce Indian War of 1877*, 9.
40. Samuel Lloyd Cappious, "A History of the Bitter Root Valley to 1914" (MA thesis, University of Washington, 1939), 36; *Weekly Missoulian*, July 6, 1877, 2; James H. Mills to Governor Potts, Deer Lodge, July 8, 1877, Relating to Nez Perce War, Nez Perce Campaign 1877–1878, RS250, Box 5, MHS.
41. Eventually, 442 volunteers from different localities were recognized on War Department rosters as serving in the Montana militia in the 1877 war. Robert Vaughan, *Then and Now; or Thirty-Six Years in the Rockies* (Minneapolis: Tribune Printing, 1900), 349.
42. Early Attempts to Organize Montana National Guard, 1870s–1880s, Folder Misc., Drawer 2, MMHM, LA, Bldg. T-15, Fort Harrison; Vertical File I, Nez Perce 1877, MHS; Adjutant General E.D. Townsend to Governor Potts, Washington, D.C., August 1, 1877, Relating to Volunteer Call-up, RS250, Box 5, Folder 5-25, MHS; Secretary of War George W. McCrary to Governor Potts, Washington, D.C., August 2, 1877; Brig. Gen. Terry to Lt. Gen. Sheridan, St. Paul, August 2, 1877, NGAUS.
43. Kermit Edmonds, *Montana Militiaman*, 26 (Summer 1988); Montana Volunteers Nez Perce War, Drawer 2, MMHM, LA, Bldg. T-15, Fort Harrison; Vertical File I, Nez Perce 1877, MHS.
44. Josephy, *The Nez Perce Indians*, 561.
45. On August 3, the Butte Battalion encountered a courier from Missoula bearing letters from Brig. Gen. O.O. Howard, written while en route on Lolo Pass. The messages explained that Capt. Rawn had marched his command up the Bitterroot Valley to block the eastern entrance to the Lolo Trail, and that Gibbon's command was proceeding to Missoula. Montana Volunteers Nez Perce War 1877, Drawer 2, MMHM, LA, Bldg. T-15, Fort Harrison; Vertical File I, Nez Perce 1877, MHS.
46. Ibid.
47. Nichols, "The Short, Useless Life of Fort Fizzle," in Vertical File, Fort Fizzle, MHS.
48. Marshall, *Crimsoned Prairie*, 194.
49. Lacey, *Montana Militia*, 16; "Capt. Rawn on the Lolo," *Idaho Tri-Weekly Statesman*, August 21, 1877; Jerome Greene Collection, Lolo Folder 8, Nez Perce National Historical Park, Spalding, Idaho. In addition to the Jerome Greene Collection cited here, see Jerome T. Greene, *Nez Perce Summer, 1877: The U.S. Army and the Nee-Me-Poo Crisis* (Helena: Montana Historical Society Press, 2000).
50. Vertical File, Fort Fizzle, MHS.
51. Leeson, *History of Montana*, 141; Lucullus V. McWhorter, *Hear Me, My Chiefs! Nez Perce History and Legend* (Caldwell: Caxton, 1952), 350–52. In the early decades of the 20th century, Lucullus V. McWhorter of Yakima, Washington, a white rancher and farmer, became a spokesman and historian for the then elderly Nez Perce veterans of the 1877 war. McWhorter presented the "non-treaty" Nez Perce point of view in two classic accounts: *Hear Me, My Chiefs!*, cited above, and *Yellow Wolf: His Own Story* (1940). For a definitive biography, see Steven Ross Evans, *Voice of the Old Wolf: Lucullus Virgil McWhorter and the Nez Perce Indians* (Pullman: Washington State University Press, 1996).
52. The fortification's remains were consumed in a brush and timber fire in 1934. A partial reconstruction has been built in recent times at the site's roadside park.
53. About 150 volunteers withdrew from Rawn's command after realizing the Nez Perce's peaceful intentions. The men from Philipsburg and Deer Lodge left the Bitterroot Valley via Missoula. Harlan "The Fiasco at Fort Fizzle," 505; O.O. Howard to Lt. Joseph Sladen,

Department of the Columbia, August 8, 1877, RG 393, Entry 897, Part III, 1877, Box 1, National Archives; Jerome Green Collection, Big Hole, folder 8, Nez Perce National Historical Park, Spalding, Idaho.

54. Josephy, *The Nez Perce Indians*, 574–78.
55. Capt. John B. Catlin, who had marched back up the Bitterroot Valley from Fort Fizzle, was a Civil War veteran and local homesteader. Born on June 21, 1837, in Cleveland, Ohio, he grew up in Indiana. When the Civil War began, Catlin joined Company H of the 87th Indiana Regiment in August 1862, enlisting as a private. Repeatedly promoted for bravery—to commissary sergeant, and eventually Capt.—Catlin was given command of Company I of the 87th Indiana. He held that position until the end of the war, participating in Sherman's March to the Sea through the Deep South. In 1866, Catlin and a young friend traveled west, hiring themselves out in Nebraska City as bullwhackers on a wagon train bound for Montana Territory. Once there, he settled in the Bitterroot Valley and began farming. In 1895, Catlin was a member of the Territorial Constitutional Convention.
56. Josephy, *The Nez Perce Indians,* 579; Cave, *Nez Perce Indian War of 1877,* 13; Leeson, *History of Montana,* 1301.
57. Montana Militia Pre-National Guard, 1880s, Drawer 2, MMHM, LA, Bldg. T-15, Fort Harrison; John B. Catlin, 1877 Montana Territorial Volunteer, File 010, Big Hole National Battlefield, Wisdom, Montana.
58. Included among these volunteers were John Armstrong, Jacob Baker, Amos Buck, Vincent Burch, John B. Catlin, Anthony Chaffin, John S. Chaffin, Newt Chaffin, Samuel O. Chaffin, Oscar Clark, Riley Buchanon Cooper, Isaac Newton Davis, Sam Dunham, William "Billy" Edwards, Linde Catlin Elliot, Charles B. Hart, Fred Heldt, Joe Hull, Luther Johnson, Otto Leifer, Eugene Lent, Alvin Lockwood, Myron Lockwood, Samuel Squire Madding, Alexander Mitchell, Campbell Mitchell, David Morrow, William "Billy" Ryan, Millard Fillmore "Bunch" Sherrill, Thomas Crittenden Sherrill, John Shinn, George Wade, Jerry Wallace, Austin A. Wilkerson, Barnett Wilkerson, Harrison Wilson, and Mike Wright.
59. Years later, Tom Sherrill became a U.S. Forest Service employee stationed at the Big Hole Battle historical site. Austin A. Wilkerson, Montana Citizen Volunteer 1877, Drawer 5, MMHM, LA, Bldg. T-15, Fort Harrison.
60. Riley B. Cooper enlisted at Corvallis under Capt. J.L. Humble, then served in John B. Catlin's Skalkaho Guards. Cooper carried a brass-framed Model 1860 .44 Henry rifle into battle. Riley Buchanan Cooper, Montana Citizen Volunteer 1877, Drawer 5, MMHM, LA, Bldg. T-15, Fort Harrison.
61. Samuel Chaffin was born on August 18, 1859, in Green County, Missouri, and came to Montana at age six. He passed away on January 19, 1916, at Corvallis, Montana. Samuel O. Chaffin, 1877 Montana Territorial Volunteer, File 010, Big Hole National Battlefield, Wisdom, Montana.
62. Just 19 years old, Barnett Wilkerson offered his services to the army and was accepted as a paid scout, while Austin Wilkerson remained with the civilian volunteers, undertaking pack- and wagon-train duties. Barnett died in Missoula in March 1939, at age 80. Austin spent his remaining years in the Hamilton area, passing away in 1940. Austin A. Wilkerson, Montana Citizen Volunteer, 1877, Drawer 5, MMHM, LA, Bldg. T-15, Fort Harrison.
63. On July 8, 1877, Cameron and Alexander Mitchell along with Luther Johnson had left their Idaho mining camp and set out for the Bitterroot Valley. They first volunteered at

Corvallis to serve under J.L. Humble, were with Capt. Rawn on Lolo Creek, and then proceeded to Ross Hole, where they joined John B. Catlin's Company No. 2. At the Battle of the Big Hole, Cameron Mitchell was killed in action, close by his brother Alexander's side. Alexander Mitchell, Montana Citizen Volunteer 1877, Drawer 5, MMHM, LA, Bldg. T-15, Fort Harrison.

64. Arms from the Virginia City arsenal were sent to Butte and Missoula to furnish the volunteer companies. Montana Volunteers Nez Perce, and, Arsenals and Armories, Virginia City, 1867–1920, Drawer 2, MMHM, LA, Bldg. T-15, Fort Harrison; J.B. Catlin, "The Battle of the Big Hole Reminisience," SC520, MHS.
65. Lavender, *Let Me Be Free*, 254; Leeson, *History of Montana*, 146, 1301, 1302, 1316.
66. Volunteer Otto Leifer later recorded a somewhat erroneous account of the scouting duties, embroidering his role. Born in Germany, Leifer was wounded in the fighting at the Big Hole, disabling him as a farmer and stockman. Otto Leifer, Montana Citizen Volunteer 1877, Pension Records, MMHM, LA, Bldg. T-15, Fort Harrison; "Tom and Bunch Sherrill Reminiscence" (1916), SC737, MHS.
67. Ibid.; Cave, *Nez Perce Indian War of 1877*, 14–15.
68. Montana Volunteers, Nez Perce War, Drawer 2, MMHM, LA, Bldg. T-15, Fort Harrison. For a comprehensive overview of the Battle of the Big Hole, see Aubrey L. Haines, *An Illusive Victory: The Battle of the Big Hole* (West Glacier, Montana: Glacier Natural History Association, 1991).
69. Wilkerson, 1877 Montana Territorial Volunteer, File 042, Big Hole National Battlefield, Wisdom, Montana,
70. Amos Buck, a Stevensville resident, was born in Sandusky, Ohio, on February 26, 1844. He served with Capt. John Landram's volunteers at Lolo Creek, then under Capt. J.B. Catlin. Amos Buck, Montana Citizen Volunteer, Drawer 5, MMHM, LA, Bldg. T-15, Fort Harrison.
71. Catlin felt they lost valuable time when trying to burn the lodges. Josephy, *The Nez Perce Indians*, 581–82; "John B. Catlin Marks Eightieth Year Today," *Missoulian* article, File 010, Big Hole National Battlefield, Wisdom, Montana; Amos Buck, Montana Citizen Volunteer, Drawer 5, MMHM, LA, Bldg. T-15, Fort Harrison; Catlin, "The Battle of the Big Hole," Montana Volunteers, Nez Perce War, Drawer 2, MMHM, LA, Bldg. T-15, Fort Harrison.
72. Lynde Catlin Elliott was related to Capt. Catlin. In 1883, his widow married a Hamilton rancher, Charles B. Hart, who worked on Elliot's ranch. Hart also was one of the Bitterroot volunteers at the Big Hole. Lynde Catlin Elliott, Montana Citizen Volunteer, Drawer 5, Ibid.
73. Campbell Mitchell was killed among the lodges near the upper part of the Indian camp. "Tom Sherrill Reminiscence," Jerome Greene Collection, Big Hole, File 6, Nez Perce National Historical Park, Spalding, Idaho.
74. Catlin later felt that Gibbon's report to the War Department failed to give the volunteers just praise. The volunteers had fired the first shot, one carried dispatches to Deer Lodge, and they had fought through both days. Nonetheless, Gibbon failed to make special mention of them. John B. Catlin, "The Battle of the Big Hole," Montana Volunteers, Nez Perce War, Drawer 2, MMHM, LA, Bldg. T-15, Fort Harrison; Leeson, *History of Montana*, 142.
75. Ibid.; Josephy, *The Nez Perce Indians*, 583.
76. Lt. W.L. English died of wounds in the Sisters of Charity Hospital at Deer Lodge, on August 19, 1877. In Capt. Catlin's company, the five volunteers killed were John

Armstrong, L.C. Elliott, Alvin Lockwood, Campbell Mitchell, and David Morrow. Otto Leifer and Myron Lockwood were severely wounded, and Jacob Baker, Fred Heldt, and William "Billy" Ryan were slightly injured; Billy Ryan of Skalkaho was wounded in the groin. Amos Buck, "Review of the Big Hole," from speech delivered at Hamilton, August 9, 1908, at the first reunion of the settlers that engaged in the battle, MMHM, LA, Bldg. T-15, Fort Harrison; Leeson, *History of Montana,* 142; Deer Lodge *New North-West,* August 17, 1877, Jerome Greene Collection, HOC 488, File 8, Nez Perce National Historical Park, Spalding, Idaho.

77. Douglas D. Scott, *A Sharp Little Affair: The Archeology of the Big Hole Battlefield* (Lincoln, Nebraska: J and L Reprint, 1994), 19.
78. Billy Edwards, born in England, had arrived in the Montana gold camps in 1865. In 1867, he was defeated in an election for the Deer Lodge seat in the territorial legislature. He mined in western Montana, worked on the Bitterroot wagon road in 1882–1883, owned a ranch and hotel in Ross Hole, and in 1885 prospected at the Big Hole. Edwards was murdered in 1890; his body was found floating in the Bitterroot River near Riverside, and buried in the Grantsdale cemetery. Billy Edwards, Montana Citizen Volunteer, MMHM, LA, Bldg. T-15, Fort Harrison; Billy Edward, 1877 Montana Territorial Volunteer, File 012, Big Hole National Battlefield, Wisdom, Montana.
79. Reportedly, Gibbon dispatched another messenger, who disappeared and never was heard from again. Billy Edwards, Montana Citizen Volunteer, Drawer 2, MMHM, LA, Bldg. T-15, Fort Harrison.
80. Josephy, *The Nez Perce Indians*, 590–91.
81. Myron Lockwood, taken to the Deer Lodge hospital with a shattered hip joint, was not expected to live. After seven months of recovery, however, he returned to his Skalkaho ranch. Kermit Edmonds, *Montana Militia* 26 (Summer 1988); Montana Volunteers, Nez Perce War, Drawer 2, MMHM, LA, Bldg. T-15, Fort Harrison.
82. One of the original wagons used in the ambulance train is preserved at the Grant-Kohrs Ranch National Historic Site near Deer Lodge. "Fight on the Big Hole," Deer Lodge *New North-West*, August 17, 1877, Jerome Greene Collection, Big Hole, Folder 8, Nez Perce National Historical Park, Spalding, Idaho.
83. Leeson, *History of Montana*, 142–43.
84. Ibid., 143.
85. Callaway had served with distinction as an officer in the 21st Illinois Infantry during the Civil War. Brig. Gen. O.O. Howard, *Nez Perce Joseph...* (Boston: Lee and Shepard, 1881), 216, 219.
86. Thomas Farrell, owner of a large ranch, furnished horses to the volunteers and for pulling the mess wagons and gun carriages. Colonel Callaway's volunteers included Samuel Word, a lawyer and future politician, Simeon R. Buford, a merchant and future state senator, and Tom Baker, a future editor. *Husbandman* 65 (35) (September 4, 1941): 5. For an overview of the campaign during this period, see Helen Addison Howard, with Dan L. McGrath, *War Chief Joseph* (Caldwell, Idaho: Caxton, 1941); for a later revised version by the same author properly relegating Joseph to a lesser role among the Nez Perce war chiefs, see Helen Addison Howard, *Saga of Chief Joseph* (Caldwell, Idaho: Caxton, 1965).
87. McWhorter, *Hear Me, My Chiefs!*, 412. In order to maintain pressure on the Nez Perce, General Howard dispatched Lt. George Bacon and a contingent of troops ahead to Henrys Lake and Targhee Pass, along a main trail leading into Yellowstone Park. Supposedly, Bacon's force would block passage, allowing Howard's command coming from behind to catch up with the Nez Perce. Bacon and his party, however, would see no

Indians at Henrys Lake and Targhee Pass, and they turned back. The Nez Perce later hurriedly passed through that same area into Yellowstone Park.

88. Josephy, *The Nez Perce Indians*, 594; Howard and McGrath, *War Chief Joseph*, 216.
89. Waldevar Lindgren, *A Geological Reconnaissance across the Bitterroot Range and Clearwater Mountains in Montana and Idaho* (Washington, D.C., 1904), 61.
90. Robert M. Utley, *Frontier Regulars: The United States Army and the Indian, 1866–1891* (New York: Macmillan, 1973), 308.
91. According to Callaway's son, "General Howard was glad to have the assistance" of Col. Callaway and his volunteers. Lew L. Callaway to L.V. McWhorter, May 1, 1931, Lucullus V. McWhorter Papers, Washington State University, Pullman.
92. Howard, *Nez Perce Joseph,* 223, 234; Marshall, *Crimsoned Prairie,* 209; Utley, *Frontier Regulars*, 308; Howard and McGrath, *War Chief Joseph*, 228, 232.
93. Kermit Edmonds, "Territorial Militia to State National Guard," *Montana Militia* 26 (Summer 1988); Drawer 2, MMHM, LA, Bldg. T-15, Fort Harrison; Jerome Greene Collection, Camas Meadows, Folder 8, Nez Perce National Historical Park, Spalding, Idaho.
94. Tom Baker, "At Callaway's Camp," Helena *Daily Independent*, Jerome Greene Collection, Camas Meadows, Folder 8, Nez Perce National Historical Park, Spalding, Idaho.
95. Marshall, *Crimsoned Prairie,* 211; Utley, *Frontier Regulars*, 309; Lavender, *Let Me Be Free*, 295; McWhorter, *Hear Me My Chiefs!*, 431–32.
96. "For relief of citizens of Montana who served with the United States troops in war with Nez Perce and for the relief of heirs of such killed in said service," *Senate Report 646,* 45 Congress, 3 Session (Serial A4736); *Senate Report 827,* 46 Congress, 3 Session (Serial A4736), 1948.
97. Malone and Roeder, *Montana's Past,* 138; Howard and McGrath, *War Chief Joseph*, 267.
98. Ironically, General Sherman had just visited Yellowstone Park while on an inspection tour of western army posts. He had left for Helena shortly before the Nez Perce arrived in the park. Howard and McGrath, *War Chief Joseph*, 233.
99. Ibid., 265–67.
100. Ibid., 267.
101. Marshall, *Crimsoned Prairie*, 216.
102. Utley, *Frontier Regulars*, 312.
103. The captured Nez Perce were taken to Fort Leavenworth, Kansas, and held there for a time, before finally being sent to Indian Territory (Oklahoma). They remained for seven years, before being sent back to the Northwest, either to the Nez Perce Reservation in Idaho Territory or the Colville Reservation in Washington Territory. Joseph died of natural causes in 1904, about 64 years of age.
104. Three days later, Col. Gibbon notified Governor Potts of the Nez Perce surrender. Leeson, *History of Montana*, 145.
105. Gladys Robinson, "Great Falls Men Organize Guards to Battle Sioux," *Great Falls Tribune*, March 22, 1931, Vertical File II, Nez Perce, MHS.
106. "For relief of citizens of Montana who served…in war with Nez Perce," *Senate Report 85,* 46 Congress, 3 Session (Serial A4736), 2612.
107. Kermit Edmonds, "Territorial Militia to State National Guard," *Montana Militiaman* 26 (Summer 1988); Leeson, *History of Montana*, 145–46.
108. Ibid., 944.
109. Ibid.
110. Leeson, *History of Montana,* 565, 748; Montana Militia Pre-National Guard, 1880s, Drawer 2, MMHM, LA, Bldg. T-15, Fort Harrison.

111. *Butte Daily*, January 1, 1886, Montana Militia Pre-National Guard, 1880s, Drawer 2, MMHM, LA, Bldg. T-15, Fort Harrison.
112. Leeson, *History of Montana*, 748.
113. An unusual legacy of the vigilante era is the survival of their recognition signal, 3-7-77, on the shoulder patches of Montana state highway patrol officers. Malone, Roeder, and Lang, *Montana: A History of Two Centuries*, 81.
114. Robert E. Fisk, *Laws, Resolutions and Memorials of the Territory of Montana, Passed at the Fourteenth Regular Session of the Legislative Assembly* (Helena, 1885), 95–100; Ref 345.12M76, MHS.
115. Lacey, *Montana Militia*, 19.
116. *Compiled Statutes of Montana, Enacted at the Regular Session of the Fifteenth Legislative Assemble of Montana* (Helena, 1888), Montana National Guard, 1887–1889, Drawer 2, MMHM, LA, Bldg. T-15, Fort Harrison.
117. Montana Militia Pre-National Guard, 1880s, Drawer 2, Ibid.
118. A.W. Ide, Publisher, *Ide's Helena City Directory*; Montana National Guard, 1887–1889, and *Butte Daily Miner* (1887–1888), Montana National Guard, Drawer 2, MMHM, LA, Bldg. T-15, Fort Harrison.
119. C.W. Turner, *Biennial Report of the Adjutant General of the Territory of Montana, December 1, 1888* (Helena: Independent Publishing, 1888).
120. Ibid.
121. Ibid.
122. Lacey, *Montana Militia*, 21.
123. *Helena Herald*, August 21, 1888.

A soldier of Company G, 1st Montana Infantry, taken by a Butte photographer in the mid-1890s. *Jerome Greene Collection, #357 Montana Military History Museum, Fort Harrison [MMHM]*

3

From Territorial Militia to State National Guard, 1889–1897

Michael H. Evans

Montana has enormous mining interests and a more or less migratory class of employed men who may at times, if we learn anything by contemporaneous history, become turbulent, and to meet any possible feeling of insecurity, a reasonable observance of constitutional provisions in sustaining a National Guard would not be inappropriate.—Captain William H. Bisbee, 4th U.S. Infantry, 1892.

We are not organizing, equipping, or drilling a Guard for the purpose of suppressing riots amongst our citizens.—Colonel Hiram Allen, Adjutant General, Kansas National Guard, 1897.

The final decade of the 19th century found the National Guard in America searching for its identity. Some of its riot- and strike-breaking duties during this time gave it a reputation as an extension of the constabulary. While these activities brought the National Guard to the attention of the greater populace—in both negative and positive aspects—many within the guard believed they would not become a viable reserve force for the regular army unless distancing themselves from a strike-breaker reputation. In the years leading up to the 1898 Spanish-American War, many guard units across the nation strived to increase professionalism, bringing a more positive emphasis to their military training and skills.

Montana's organization experienced these same problems. The militia already was designated the "National Guard" before Montana became a state in 1889. From then until the war with Spain, the Montana guard transformed itself from a loose confederation of distinct companies to a tighter, centrally controlled organization more uniformly trained and equipped.

Low funding remained a constant concern and hindrance, compromising training and the ability to purchase arms and equipment. With the absence of foreign or domestic wars during this period, the Montana National Guard garnered its active duty experience only when policing civil unrest. When the Montana guard left for service in the Philippines during the Spanish-American War, however, it undoubtedly was a superior organization compared to nine years earlier.

Even prior to statehood, the Montana guard took steps in this direction. In 1888, Adjutant General C.W. Turner reported that despite the problem of being under-supplied, several positive moves were taken to build a firm base of professionalism. Although arms and uniforms often were paid for by individual enlistees, Montana received an annual apportionment of $2,764 from the federal government for expenses. This helped enable the guard to hold its first annual encampment at the Helena fairgrounds, August 21–23, 1888. Though General Turner admitted some logistical difficulties, he maintained that the encampment successfully fostered esprit de corps among the men.[1]

Budgetary restraints kept most guard units lesser equipped compared to regular army units. Turner nonetheless reported that "infantry and cavalry companies are armed, respectively, with rifles and carbines of the patterns now issued to the army."[2] Apparently, the Montana men were rather better equipped than most other National Guard organizations, which failed to keep pace with the regular army regarding modern firearms. But the latter situation seems to have been somewhat the case in Montana, too, despite Turner's statement.

At the time, the regular army used Springfield breech-loading, single-shot, .45 caliber rifles and carbines, whereas many guard units still were assigned Civil War era, muzzle-loading arms.[3] In 1888, Montana's chief of ordnance, Harry L. Luke, reported that the Helena arsenal held 73 breech-loading .50 caliber rifles, whereas the bulk of weapons, 337 of them, were .58 caliber muzzle-loading rifled muskets. The Virginia City arsenal had another 217 muzzle-loading rifled muskets.[4] The muzzle-loaders were remnants of 2,500 Springfield contract rifled muskets sent to Montana Territory in 1867, along with six 12-pound Model 1841 mountain howitzers.[5] Thus, the 1888 ordnance report suggests that not all of Montana's troops had modern firearms similar to those of the regular army.

On October 1, 1889, Montana's citizens resoundingly approved a state constitution and on November 8, 1889, President Harrison officially admitted Montana as the 41st state. The first year of statehood, however, was marked with partisan debates over election results. While Montana voters largely united over accepting the new constitution, the same October election reflected a populace evenly split between Democrats and Republicans. Democrat Joseph K. Toole became governor by less than a 1,000-vote margin, while Republican Thomas Carter won the congressional seat in Washington, D.C., by less than 2,000 votes.

Montana's legislature was just as divided. The senate consisted of eight Democrats and eight Republicans, with a Republican lieutenant governor serving as the tiebreaker. The Montana House of Representatives faced an even more deadlocked situation. Seats were evenly divided between the two parties, with 25 apiece, but both parties contested 5 seats from Silver Bow County, each accusing the other of manipulating the vote count. Due to the electoral wrangling,

Republican and Democratic legislators met separately during the entire congressional session from November 23, 1889, to February 20, 1890. The first legislative session accomplished little.[6]

These early political difficulties affected the Montana guard, which was in need of funding to bring its companies up to regular army standards. The guard managed to hold a summer encampment again in 1889, but political turmoil caused the state's appropriations for annual encampments to vanish.[7] The next encampment was not organized until 1894—a five year hiatus.

Initially the guard did not have adequate storage facilities for equipment and weapons; thus in 1889 the territorial governor received authorization to build an arsenal in Helena. A contract was issued to a local builder in October 1889, and the arsenal opened in May 1890. The building's design was similar to that of other armories erected in the late 19th century. Because of labor and social unrest during this period, armories often were built with their defense in mind, both in an actual and symbolic sense. The Helena arsenal design was typical, resembling a medieval castle incorporating firing ports, towers, cupolas, and crenellations. The second story remained uncompleted, however, since the state failed to allocate sufficient financing. The guard needed to borrow funds to complete the work, but the job was never entirely finished. Lack of maintenance money also allowed some deterioration over the years.[8]

While the annual encampment was missed in the early 1890s, the companies still participated in their own self-regulated target practice sessions. This was deemed unproductive, however, and on March 18, 1892, the Montana Military Board resolved that an officer should be detailed to take charge of target practice for all the guard. An officer was not designated for the position in that year, but the guard did manage to organize a target competition between the companies. Also participating were five men from the military department at the College of Montana, Deer Lodge. All of the infantry companies, except Company B of Butte, were represented at the competition in Helena on October 17–20, 1892. Adjutant General H.S. Howell judged the event a success, claiming the marksmanship as "very satisfactory."[9]

This competition was indicative of the great interest in precision marksmanship then sweeping through most guard organizations in the country. New York guardsmen had been instrumental in founding the National Rifle Association (NRA) in 1871. In its early incarnation, the NRA focused largely on improving marksmanship in guard units through "scientific riflery."[10] The NRA also encouraged marksmanship programs among the general populace in order to prepare citizens called upon as volunteers in the event of war.[11]

Montana's guard experienced an organizational restructuring from 1891 to 1892. The Military Code of 1889 had allowed for ten companies of infantry, two troops of cavalry, and one artillery battery, and this had been achieved. By 1892, however, the organization was reduced slightly to nine infantry companies, one cavalry troop, and the artillery battery. Company H of Billings had mustered out when its term of service expired, and the governor disbanded Missoula's Company I for not meeting requirements regarding uniforms, equipment, and discipline. Troop B of Bozeman also had given up its cavalry troop designation, but was reorganized as Company H (infantry).

The cavalry was trimmed to one troop because of a shortage of adequate facilities and funds for maintaining horses. Actually the cavalry troops largely existed in name only; most of their training was on foot, instead of in the saddle. Adjutant General Howell reasoned that with the tightening of the budget, the state could afford only one cavalry troop.[12]

Meanwhile, a greater degree of cooperation between the National Guard and the U.S. Army developed. During the 1880s, the regular army began sending officers to observe guard units during summer encampments. More importantly, by the early 1890s the War Department assigned regular army officers to serve three- to four-year rotations with state military headquarters. By the late 1890s, more than 40 officers nationwide were involved with state and territorial forces in this capacity. Many others participated in the encampments, inspecting National Guard troops.[13]

In September 1892, Capt. William H. Bisbee of the 4th U.S. Infantry assessed Montana's guard units. The nine infantry companies, one cavalry troop, and one artillery battery represented the recent restructuring:[14]

Company A, 1st Montana Infantry, Great Falls.
Company B, 1st Montana Infantry, Butte.
Company C, 1st Montana Infantry, Helena.
Company D, 1st Montana Infantry, Virginia City.

Company D, 1st Montana Infantry, in Virginia City. Dress uniforms are militia variant of regular Army pattern. The drummer's coat has non-regulation chest ornamentation, and the men wear non-regulation pillbox caps. *MMHM*

Company E, 1st Montana Infantry, Dillon.
Company F, 1st Montana Infantry, Butte.
Company G, 1st Montana Infantry, Butte.
Company H, 1st Montana Infantry, Bozeman.
Company K, 1st Montana Infantry, Anaconda.
Troop A, Cavalry, Helena.
Battery A, Light Artillery, Helena.

All units received favorable remarks, with the exception of Company C of Helena. Company C's members declined to drill in Bisbee's presence, and he found order and discipline wanting. For the Montana guard as a whole, Bisbee noted in his report that all soldiers were equipped with .45 caliber Springfield rifles and carbines—the same as issued to the regular army. Guardsmen had the same field dress as the regular army, but were deficient in belts, knapsacks, canteens, and other field gear.[15] Capt. Bisbee's inspection was generally positive. More often than not, Bisbee attributed deficiencies to the lack of state funding, rather than to the guard organization itself. As a result of such inspections, the companies improved their record keeping methods.

Meanwhile, Governor Joseph K. Toole stressed the continuing need to hone marksmanship, while he also attempted to convince the legislature of the importance of funding summer encampments. For the time being, though, no additional allocations were forthcoming.[16]

Budgetary restraints affected the men's pay. Federal statute required that guardsmen receive $1.50 per day and $1.50 per night when called up for duty, but Adjutant General Howell made the point that no state paid that amount. Howell suggested, however, that pay should be based on rank. He reasoned that a graded pay scale would motivate men to perform their duties more efficiently in the hopes of receiving a promotion with pay increase.[17]

A change in the top command structure occurred in 1893. On January 2, Adjutant General Howell resigned. He was replaced by C.F. Lloyd, promoted from colonel to brigadier general. On January 18, Lloyd announced that he was instructed by Governor Toole to relocate the guard's headquarters from Helena to Butte.[18] No explanation was given. The shift likely mirrored the uncertainty over where the new state's capital ought to be located.

Since achieving statehood, Helena had remained the temporary capital. In the general election of November 8, 1892, Montana citizens voted for a permanent site. Seven locations were proposed—Anaconda, Boulder, Bozeman, Butte, Deer Lodge, Great Falls, and Helena. No community, however, received a majority vote. Accordingly by statute, a choice would be made two years later between the two locations receiving the most votes—Helena and Anaconda. Thus it was clear that the capital would be located in western Montana, which had a greater population, wealth, and influence than other parts of the state. After two years of political infighting between communities, the issue came up for a vote in the November 6, 1894, general election, with Helena winning by a slim majority.[19]

The capital decision, favoring western Montana, reflected a trend also apparent in the home locations of guard units. They were preponderantly located in the western part of the state. After Company H in Billings had mustered out in 1892, no guard unit was assigned east of the Rockies for five years, except at Great Falls. Not until 1897 would Cavalry Troop A be reestablished in Billings.

In 1892, Capt. Bisbee had observed: "Montana has enormous mining interests and a more or less migratory class of employed men who may at times, if we learn anything by contemporaneous history, become turbulent, and to meet any possible feeling of insecurity, a reasonable observance of constitutional provisions in sustaining a National Guard would not be inappropriate."[20] Bisbee's remarks reveal his bias in viewing the National Guard as an extension of the constabulary, aligning himself with those approving of troops as strikebreakers and policemen. To these people, the assigning of guard units in key western Montana towns made sense.

In 1893, other organizational changes came. Owing to Company C's poor showing during Capt. Bisbee's recent inspection, the Helena unit mustered out on March 17. Difficulties in securing and maintaining horses continued. With no funding forthcoming, Troop A of Helena became an infantry unit (the new Company C), also on March 17. A week later, a Helena unit previously given permission to organize was admitted as Company I.[21]

The guard continued to make significant strides to professionalize. On April 12, the new governor, J.E. Rickards, directed Col. Harry Clay Kessler to organize officer and non-commissioned officer schools to serve all state units. An officer selected from each company would serve as instructors. Col. Kessler oversaw implementation of uniform lesson plans; he also required instructors to submit progress reports on a monthly basis. At this time the 1st Regiment was organized into three battalions:

First Battalion, Col. H.C. Kessler, Commanding—
Companies B, F, G – Butte
Company K – Anaconda

Second Battalion, Lt. Col. C.S. Shoemaker, Commanding—
Company A – Great Falls
Companies C, I – Helena

Third Battalion, Maj. Henry Elling, Commanding—
Company D – Virginia City
Company E – Dillon
Company H – Bozeman

Battalion commanders were instructed to visit their assigned companies at least twice a month, and to hold at least one battalion drill each month, weather permitting.[22]

Col. Kessler was one of the driving forces for professionalism. Born in Philadelphia on March 18, 1844, he had joined the 104th Pennsylvania Volunteers with the rank of 2nd Lt. in 1861. Mustered out near the end of the Civil War as a 1st Lt., he went into business in Philadelphia. He came to Montana in 1875, establishing the *Butte Miner* newspaper in 1876 and remained involved in mining and politics. He joined the militia with the rank of captain in 1887.[23]

In 1893, the Montana legislature finally appropriated sufficient funds to allow planning for an annual encampment. The U.S. Army had vacated Fort Ellis, outside of Bozeman, in 1886, and the guard intended to use the grounds and remaining structures for training purposes, just as the territorial militia had done earlier. Just at this juncture, however, a severe financial crisis struck America and Europe. The Panic of 1893 halted the state's ability to provide funds. On August 29, a disappointed Adjutant General Lloyd informed his officers of the encampment's postponement.[24]

1st Montana Infantry Regiment during summer training, circa mid-1890s, at Fort Ellis near Bozeman. Abandoned by the U.S. Army in 1886, the post later became the training site for Montana's National Guard into the early 20th century. *Arthur Canning photo, Montana Historical Society [MHS] collection, #947-250 MMHM*

Meanwhile, the officer and NCO schools established in April by Col. Kessler proved helpful in professionalizing the leadership and ranks. To assist Kessler, the guard requested that a regular army officer be assigned to the governor's general staff. On April 2, 1894, Capt. Charles L. Hodges of the 25th U.S. Infantry reported to the governor, receiving an appointment as assistant inspector general with the rank of colonel. Hodges' new assignment found him working closely with Kessler in providing military instruction and supervising drills.[25]

Soon after Hodges' arrival, the Montana guard was called to duty in response to the Coxeyite protest sweeping the nation. Jacob Coxey, a wealthy quarry operator from Massillon, Ohio, was a Populist reformer. He had lobbied Congress in 1892, hoping that funding for public works and the adoption of silver coinage would solve the nation's unemployment problem. The severe effects of the Panic of 1893 further prompted Coxey's emergence as a champion of the downtrodden and unfortunate. Senator William A. Peffer, a Kansas Populist, introduced public works legislation in Congress on March 14, 1894. Meanwhile, hoping to influence Congress, Coxey called for the formation of an "army" of the unemployed, organizing in all parts of the nation and descending on Washington, D.C. He intended to lead them in the march up to the Capitol.[26]

The Panic of 1893 had severely impacted western Montana. Silver prices plummeted, mines shut down, banks closed, and businesses dependent on the mines failed. The economic downturn left 20,000 unemployed. Hearing of Coxey's proposed march on Washington, D.C., an unemployed Butte miner named William Hogan began organizing other workers in early April 1894, intending to lead them east as a part of Coxey's army descending on the capital. Hogan's men gathered and camped outside of a Northern Pacific rail yard in Butte. They tried to convince railroad workers to join their cause, but the two sides failed to reach an agreement. Determined to go to Washington, D.C., Hogan and his followers stole a locomotive and several railroad cars at 2 a.m. on April 24, and headed east.[27]

Guard officers were monitoring the confrontation in Butte and prepared for deployment should Governor Rickards deem it necessary. Two days before, guardsmen were ordered to report to the armories. When Hogan's group absconded with the train, however, these units were not immediately called out. Federal Marshall William McDermott, who had deputized a group of citizens to confront Hogan, was handling the situation. On April 25, McDermott's men caught up with Hogan's train in Billings, where a large crowd had turned out to welcome the Coxeyites. As McDermott's deputies stepped forward, they were thwarted when gunfire erupted and the crowd took weapons from the deputies and broke them into pieces. A Billings man died and several deputies and miners were wounded.

The same day, by order of Governor Rickards, several guard companies boarded trains, intending to pursue Hogan. Before departing, however, the operation was called off. That evening, President Cleveland ordered federal troops from Fort Keogh to board trains at Miles City and proceed west to stop Hogan and his men. When the Coxeyites were found camped in Forsyth, Hogan and most of his followers were arrested. With the situation under control, Governor Rickards discharged the activated guard companies on April 26.[28]

Coxey, indeed, had left Ohio by foot, on March 25, 1894, with approximately 100 followers. When reaching Washington, D.C., on May 1, the group numbered about 500, significantly less than the 100,000 he had hoped for. Coxey was arrested for violating an ordinance against walking on the grass. The bills died in Congress, and the "army" eventually dispersed and returned home.

Later in 1894, the guard was called upon again, this time to suppress a riot in Butte. In anticipation of an upcoming July 4 celebration, saloon owners decorated their establishments in the usual patriotic manner. Some added their own unique expression of patriotism by festooning windows with the letters "APA"—the American Protective Association, noted for its anti-Catholic and anti-immigrant stance, which was a hot-button issue in America in this era. A significant portion of Butte's miners and other workers were immigrant Catholics. Spectators gathered and heated exchanges followed. In the early morning hours of July 4, an unidentified person detonated a bomb outside one of the saloons, damaging a wall and glass window. Crowds continued to gather on the streets during the day, as Catholics and anti-Catholics argued and scuffled.

The mayor appealed for calm, while also asking the saloon owners to remove the offending letters. One saloon keeper complied, but the others held their ground. Around 6:30 p.m., a fight broke out between two men on a crowded street. Policemen moved in to separate them, but shots rang out, leaving an officer dead and five men wounded. Soon after, a fire broke out in a gambling house and Butte firefighters moved in to extinguish the flames. Quickly dousing the blaze, the firemen turned their hose on the saloon where the proprietor had removed the APA letters from the windows, and began hosing away the rest of the decorations and filling the saloon with water. After the owner threatened to shoot the firefighters, they moved down the street and began hosing other saloons decorated with APA letters. Gunfire erupted from several of these establishments. At 7:15 p.m., 30 guardsmen led by Col. Kessler marched down the street with fixed bayonets. The crowd dispersed and the guardsmen secured the street.[29] They maintained their position until 9 a.m. on July 5, on the alert in case further disturbances arose, but none did.[30]

More change in the guard's organizational structure came in 1894. A Signal Corps was added in July, based in Helena and comprising 14 men. Meanwhile, Battery A from Helena was mustered out of service that

Corporal John Baker, Company D, 1st Montana Infantry, Virginia City. Coat is a militia variant of the Federal pattern from the early 1880s to 1902; rifled musket a contract manufacture pattern of 1861 from the store of arms at the Virginia City territorial arsenal; sling, belt, cartridge box, and belt from the same store of ordnance at the arsenal; button probably embossed with Montana coat-of-arms. *MMHM*

summer, having faced the same difficulties in securing and maintaining horses as the cavalry. Horses were required to pull the carriages, limbers, and caissons. Furthermore, the Model 1861 3-inch ordnance allotted to Battery A was far outdated. With no funding to upgrade equipment, it was decided to disband Battery A.[31]

The most positive event that year was a summer encampment, finally held at Fort Ellis, August 20–27, 1894. Reportedly a great success, it was named "Camp Rickards" in honor of Montana's governor. The men earned $3 per day.[32] Kessler and Hodges were accomplishing their goal of promoting improved military studies and drilling. While still lacking some of the necessary field gear, the Montana guard's arms and uniforms matched those of the regular army.

On October 26, 1894, 2nd Lt. Robert Bruce Wallace of the 2nd U.S. Cavalry reported for duty with the Montana National Guard. Over the following 3½ years, Wallace proved to be instrumental in further elevating overall training and effectiveness. Born in Chicago on February 7, 1869, Wallace had moved to Helena with his family when 10 years old, though maintaining contacts in the Midwest during the years that followed. Wallace graduated from the U.S. Military Academy in 1890, 15th in a class of 54. He was assigned to the 2nd U.S. Cavalry at Fort Huachuca, Arizona, and while stationed there participated in operations against the Apaches.[33] When arriving in Montana, Wallace was well educated and experienced, and put his considerable talents to good use.

Promoted to lieutenant colonel while assigned to the guard, Wallace first inspected the First Battalion in the spring of 1895.[34] From April 15 to June 1, he observed Companies B, F, and G of Butte, as well as Anaconda's Company K. Wallace's intense scrutiny was evident in observing the officers: "During the ceremonies in several instances, swords were drawn and returned by officers without first unhooking the scabbard; this is quite unmilitary." Referring to the First Battalion's marching skills, Wallace remarked that "the command bore more resemblance to a mob."[35]

Clearly, here was an officer refusing to settle for a loose interpretation of the accepted military protocol of the day. Wallace carefully noted uniform infractions he found unacceptable, and chided officers for not being more thorough in their reporting. Acknowledging funding problems, Wallace suggested abolishing dress uniforms, because keeping both dress and fatigue clothing in serviceable condition was impractical. "Let efficiency, not show, be the criterion," Wallace explained. For all of his criticisms, Wallace was quick to praise the First Battalion for what it had accomplished, and he reserved highest praise for Col. Kessler, the commanding officer.[36]

Wallace spent the remainder of the summer visiting other units. During June, he inspected companies C and I at Helena, and Company A in Great Falls. Company H at Bozeman and Company E in Dillon were visited during July, but Virginia City's Company D was missed because costly travel expenses would

After 1895, U.S. Army units occupied newly established Fort Harrison west of Helena with the closing of Montana's smaller camps and forts of the Indian Wars period. In time, the grounds to the north became the Montana National Guard training site, primitive at first. *MMHM*

be incurred in going there. Wallace noted that most companies were proficient in close order drill, though with some minor defects. With the exception of companies A and C, Wallace criticized the remaining units for failing to use the proper cadence when executing the manual of arms. Wallace also admonished the officers, charging that they were lax in disciplining the men. He judged drill attendance as adequate, except for Company I, which Wallace suggested be mustered out if attendance did not improve. On a positive note, Wallace singled out Company A from Great Falls, "for its excellent appearance, good drill, and fine discipline."[37]

In the spring of 1895, the federal government began constructing Fort Harrison near Helena to house regular army units. The post officially was dedicated on September 26, 1895, and troops of the 22nd U.S. Infantry from Fort Assiniboine were assigned there. During the next two years, men of the 2nd U.S. Infantry and 25th U.S. Infantry also arrived at Fort Harrison. (By 1898, the Montana National Guard also began using the installation, particularly as a mustering site for troops during the Spanish-American War.)[38]

The annual encampment on August 9–16, 1895, again held at Fort Ellis, was named "Camp Lloyd" in honor of the adjutant general. Overall attendance stood at 81.5 percent. Apparently, Wallace's suggestion of doing away with full dress uniforms was heeded because the companies arrived with only their fatigues. This year, the companies had managed to purchase campaign hats and leggings to complement their uniforms. Wallace judged, however, that too little care was shown for the men's firearms, and he suggested that screwdrivers and shell extractors be made available to the troops.

With the rifle range ready for use on August 12, Bozeman's Company H won what became known as the "State Trophy" by achieving the highest marks during the encampment's marksmanship competition. However, Wallace proscribed changes when warning: "I consider the range as used this year very dangerous; and that travelers on the road and members of the Guard were not killed or wounded as a matter of good luck."[39]

Wallace and Kessler both mentioned a recurring activity referred to as "Kangarooing." Kessler complained: "'Kangarooing,' and the organization of burlesque secret societies was carried to such an extent as to become dangerous." Neither Wallace nor Kessler offered any details regarding exactly what "Kangarooing" or the "burlesque secret societies" actually entailed, leaving this open to speculation.[40]

Wallace made special note of the Signal Corps, praising its commander, Col. Miller, and stating that the unit required little improvement.[41] To inspire competition, the "Kessler Banner" also was introduced, and awarded to the company demonstrating the highest proficiency in drill and discipline during the encampment. (Three years later when Montana's 1st Infantry Regiment began organizing, equipping, and training for service in the Philippines, this blue-silk, gold-fringed banner with an embroidered state seal in the center became the regimental standard. A Helena seamstress added an embroidered title—1st Montana Infantry, U.S.V.—in a gentle arch above the state seal. The banner survived the year-long war in the tropics and came back with the regiment. When the state government began considering an appropriate state flag, the banner, minus the top embroidered name of the regiment, was chosen. It remains the design for Montana's flag today, now with the addition of "Montana" in bold block letters.)

Throughout 1895, the only activation of the Montana guard occurred on November 6 when 2 non-commissioned officers and 13 enlisted men assembled at the Butte armory to protect public property if necessary. The election of county officers that day had become heated, prompting some to fear that a mob might form to break into the armory. No outbreak of violence occurred.[42]

More organizational changes came in 1896. Undermanned Company I from Helena mustered out on March 17, having been a part of the Montana National Guard for only three years. Helena's Company C likewise was terminated on April 8 (Company C had been former Cavalry Troop A, reorganized as an infantry company in 1893). With the dissolution of both of these units, Helena ceased to have a guard company for a short time.

Two new Montana guard units, however, were organized later in 1896. On May 6, Cavalry Troop A in Billings was mustered into service, while in Helena on October 29, the Company A Cadets were formed, comprised of Wesleyan University students who received military instruction at that institution. Owing to the meager budget, the Montana guard proved unable to issue equipment to the cadets; they were expected to provision themselves. Dillon's Company E had experienced a marked decline in membership at the time of its annual inspection on May 30. Due to its previous proficiency, however, it was allowed to maintain company status, since the drop in membership was thought to be temporary.[43]

Col. Wallace inspected the Butte companies on May 30, 1896. With the benefit of a year to enact Wallace's recommendations, there was notable improvement in appearance, discipline, and drilling. Wallace criticized the condition of the firearms, while noting other improvements over the previous year. He also reported minor problems regarding how the officers issued drill commands, but found no glaring errors. Regarding some questions over the accounting of money and property, Wallace recommended a thorough inventorying at the company level, with any deviations included in the quarterly reports sent to the adjutant general.[44]

NCOs and other men in camp near Helena, 1898. *MMHM*

The 1896 encampment, July 15–22, again was designated for Fort Ellis, and this time was named "Camp W.W.H. Davis," in honor of Brevet Brig. Gen. W.W.H. Davis, a former colonel of the 104th Regiment of Pennsylvania Volunteers. Attendance had dropped from the previous year to about 71 percent, largely attributable to Dillon's Company E, whose strength had finally fallen to an unacceptable low.

Guardsmen still lacked some necessary accoutrements for field service, such as canteens, haversacks, tents, knapsacks, and Dutch ovens. Target practice was scaled back from previous years, essentially being limited to the State Trophy competition. Since the companies practiced marksmanship at their own ranges during the year, the encampment training could place greater emphasis on drills, exercises, and instruction. Wallace and Kessler both complained about mess hall conditions at Camp Davis. During previous encampments, officers ate separately from the enlisted men, but at Camp Davis officers and enlisted men dined together. Wallace questioned whether a combined mess was conducive to good discipline. Kessler also noted that a separate mess afforded officers the opportunity to discuss matters among themselves, and afforded them an opportunity for social interaction not possible during the year.[45]

Although Wallace had a sharp eye for deficiencies, he was quick to give praise where merited. He particularly was impressed with the Signal Corps and Cavalry Troop A. Regarding the Signal Corps, he said, "a more efficient signal corps does not exist; and if the entire Guard were in the same efficient state as this corps further instruction would be unnecessary." In focusing on Troop A, he stated that it was "composed of first class material," and "their horsemanship is beyond criticism." Wallace praised all of the Montana guard's units in their quest to win the coveted Kessler Flag. He also remarked that Montana's troops could easily stand alongside National Guard units in other states that had existed for longer periods of time.[46]

Some reorganization came again in early 1897. Bozeman's Company H became Cavalry Troop B, and an artillery unit was revived by mustering in Light Battery A at Helena. Allowing the unit to furnish its own horses dodged the old expense problem regarding horses. However, Light Battery A's equipment—a Gatling gun and 3-inch Model 1861 cannon—were largely unchanged from what the battery had been assigned when mustered out in 1894. Though the ordnance was outdated, Wallace suggested it could prove useful depending on circumstances.[47]

An 1897 encampment was not funded by the state legislature and thus cancelled. Wallace took this opportunity to inspect all of the Montana guard. Overall, the units were in excellent status. Even the two new units, Light Battery A and Cavalry Troop B, had made excellent progress. In regard to the Anaconda unit, however, Company K's Capt. John Durkin had left the country in the fall of 1896, absconding with all the company's funds. The men had to make personal donations to pay for the unit's expenses. Due to these factors, Company K's performance had dropped from previous levels, but it was hoped that a new commander would revive it. Cavalry Troop A had been a shining example to other units in the previous year, but this time Wallace's inspection found their carbines dirty, the horses ungroomed, and commands improperly executed.[48]

The guard's basic firearm, the breech-loading, Model 1879 .45 caliber Springfield rifle, continued to be the mainstay. Meanwhile, in 1892–1894, the U.S. Army had begun adoption of the Krag-Jorgensen .30 caliber five-shot repeater. The Krags were not black powder weapons like the Springfields, and thus did not produce a puff of revealing smoke each time a rifle was fired. The Krags' range and rate of fire were superior. When the Montana guard fought alongside the

U.S. Army in the Philippines, the differences between these weapons became apparent.[49]

By the end of 1897, the Montana National Guard had been in existence for thirteen years. Inadequate funding had dogged the organization—a constant theme. Some annual encampments were cancelled, and some equipment was either sub-par or lacking. Nevertheless, this period was important in marking the development of the Montana guard as a reserve arm of the U.S. Army. Under Kessler and Wallace's guidance, vast improvements were accomplished. When the Spanish-American War began, the Montana guard was poised for action, demonstrating its preparedness for duty beyond the role of curbing riots and disturbances.

In 1897, the Adjutant General of the State of Kansas pertinently observed: "We are not organizing, equipping, or drilling a Guard for the purpose of suppressing riots amongst our citizens."[50] The soldiers of the Montana guard would have agreed. They had come to epitomize the volunteer soldier—a tradition in American military history.

Notes

1. C.W. Turner, *Biennial Report of the Adjutant General of the Territory of Montana, December 1, 1888* (Helena: Independent Publishing, 1888), 4, 7–8.
2. Ibid., 4.
3. Kohn K. Mahon, *History of the Militia and National Guard* (New York: Macmillan, 1983), 120.
4. Turner, *Biennial Report, December 1, 1888*, 27.
5. A.B. Dyer, Chief of Ordnance, War Department, to Green Clay Smith, Governor, Montana Territory, April 1, 1867, RS40, Montana Territorial Governor's Correspondence, Montana Historical Society, Helena; see also Kermit M. Edmonds, "The History of the Montana Territorial Arsenals," private manuscript, Missoula, Montana.
6. Michael P. Malone and Richard B. Roeder, *Montana: A History of Two Centuries* (Seattle: University of Washington Press, 1976), 150–51.
7. H.S. Howell, *Biennial Report, 1891–1892* (Helena: C.K. Wells, 1892), 6.
8. Kermit Edmonds, "'From Brick to Concrete': The Fate of Helena's Old Arsenal," *Montana Militiaman* 27 (3) (Fall 1989): 10–11.
9. Howell, *Biennial Report, 1891–1892*, 7–8, 54.
10. Jerry Cooper, *The Rise of the National Guard: The Evolution of the American Militia, 1865–1920* (Lincoln: University of Nebraska Press, 1997), 85, 87–88.
11. Jerry Cooper, *The Militia and National Guard in America Since Colonial Times: A Research Guide* (Westport: Greenwood Press, 1993), 83–84.
12. Howell, *Biennial Report, 1891–1892*, 3–5.
13. Cooper, *Rise of the National Guard*, 89–90.
14. Howell, *Biennial Report, 1891–1892*, 19–28.
15. Ibid., 33.
16. Richard H. Lacey, *The Montana Militia: A History of Montana's Volunteer Forces, 1867–1976* (Dillon, Montana: Dillon Tribune-Examiner Press, 1976), 23.
17. Howell, *Biennial Report, 1891–1892*, 9.

18. C.F. Lloyd, *Report of the Adjutant General of the State of Montana, 1893–1894* (Butte: Inter Mountain Publishing, 1894), 31, 33. Lloyd's name did not appear in the officer's role from the previous adjutant general's report, so it is likely he was appointed from outside of the Montana National Guard.
19. William L. Lang, "Spoils of Statehood: Montana Communities in Conflict, 1888–1894," *Montana: The Magazine of Western History* (Autumn 1987): 38–39, 45.
20. Howell, *Biennial Report, 1891–1892*, 36.
21. Lloyd, *Report of the Adjutant General, 1893–1894*, 5–7.
22. Ibid., 6, 34–35.
23. Lt. Alexander Laist, "Official History of the Operations of the First Montana Infantry, U.S.V. in the Campaign in the Philippine Islands," in Karl Irving Faust, *Campaigning in the Philippines* (San Francisco: Hicks-Judd, 1899), 39.
24. Lloyd, *Report of the Adjutant General, 1893–1894*, 7–9.
25. Ibid., 7, 10.
26. Thomas A. Clinch, "Coxey's Army in Montana," *Montana: The Magazine of Western History* 15 (4) (October 1965): 2–4.
27. Ibid., 5–7.
28. "Hard Lines for the Army," Butte *Daily Inter-Mountain*, April 23, 1894; Clinch, "Coxey's Army in Montana," 7–8; "The Militia," *Daily Inter-Mountain*, April 26, 1894, 2; "Get Marching Orders," *Anaconda Standard*, April 26, 1894; "Under Arms," *Dillon Tribune*, April 26, 1894.
29. "Butte's Big Riot," *Butte Weekly Miner*, July 5, 1894; "It Ended Most Sadly," Helena *Daily Independent*, July 6, 1894.
30. The Montana National Guard's deployment during the 1894 civil disturbances linked them to National Guard units around the country used in a similar fashion. Historians such as William H. Riker argue that it was this role as strikebreaker that largely contributed to the rise of the National Guard in the latter decades of the 19th century. Other scholars, such as Jerry Cooper, maintain that the National Guard's growth was founded on a more complex basis, pointing out that the guard flourished in states where no industrial or civil strife occurred. Ultimately, most scholars agree that guard troops were deployed most often in the late 19th century for putting down citizen uprisings. William H. Riker, *Soldiers of the States: The Role of the National Guard in American Democracy* (Washington, D.C.: Public Affairs Press, 1957), 47–50; Cooper, *Militia and the National Guard in America*, 85–87.
31. Lloyd, *Report of the Adjutant General, 1893–1894*, 6, 79, 118.
32. Ibid., 61–73. It appears that former Adjutant General Howell's suggestion in 1892 for a graded pay scale never took effect or was rescinded before the 1894 encampment.
33. "Comrade Tells Tale of Colonel Wallace," *Billings Gazette*, June 23, 1940.
34. Ibid.
35. C.F. Lloyd, *Report of the Adjutant General of the State of Montana, 1895–1896* (Helena: State Publishing, 1897), 65, 78.
36. Ibid., 78–80
37. Ibid., 65–66.
38. The information in this paragraph was derived from notes available at the Montana National Guard Museum at Fort Harrison. The notes were written by Sgt. Maj. William E. Morrow and were based on information from William C. Campbell's *From the Quarries of Last Chance Gulch*, Vol. II (Helena: Montana Record Publishing, ca. 1951–64). The notes are in a box with folders that cover late 19th and early 20th century Montana National Guard history. The folder containing Morrow's notes covers topics from 1867 to 1898. Museum Storage Building, National Guard Museum, Fort Harrison, Helena, Montana.

39. Lloyd, *Report of the Adjutant General, 1895–1896*, 66–70.
40. Ibid., 68, 116.
41. Ibid., 71, 116.
42. Ibid., 114.
43. Ibid., 160.
44. Ibid., 81–84.
45. Ibid., 56–58, 60, 62, 118–19.
46. Ibid., 60, 64.
47. Charles F. English, Report of the Adjutant General of the State of Montana for the Years 1897–98 (Helena: Independent Publishing, 1899), 12, 14.
48. Ibid., 6, 12–13.
49. Ibid., 13; Mahon, *History of the Militia and the National Guard*, 120.
50. Riker, *Soldiers of the States*, 61, 63.

The 1st Montana's tattered colors after the battle hardened troops returned to the Presidio, 1899—(left) the regimental flag, and (right) the 1895 "Kessler Banner," originally presented to the best company at the conclusion of summer training at Fort Ellis. In 1905, the Kessler Banner served as the pattern for Montana's state flag. *MHS, MMHM*

4

Spanish-American War and the Philippine-American War, 1898–1899

Richard K. Hines

Montana, in proportion to her population, sent forth to fight the battle of free institutions a greater number of her sons than any other state of the American union.—Helena *Daily Independent*, April 15, 1899.

The sinking of the U.S.S. *Maine* in Havana Harbor on February 15, 1898, precipitated the Spanish-American War and America's gradual emergence as a world power. The Montana militia had never served the nation outside of the Northwest, but this changed with a call to federal duty in the spring of 1898.

In response to a depressed economy, Congress in 1897 had authorized the U.S. Army to maintain a strength of 25,000 officers and men, which was insufficient when hostilities with Spain broke out. More troops were needed, but initially federal law seemed ill prepared for the mobilization of National Guard units. Some politicians questioned the legality of using the National Guard overseas, while others argued over what role the militia should play. While some insisted that the guard's duty rested solely in dealing with state emergencies, the National Guard Association had contended in 1897 that the state militias should augment the U.S. Army as a reserve force. The Spanish-American War provided the National Guard with an opportunity to assume just such a role.[1]

The U.S. Navy prior to the Spanish-American War had adopted an active policy toward protecting overseas interests, which necessitated the build-up of naval forces. The U.S. government was helping to promote foreign markets, seen by many as essential for national prosperity. Consequently in the 1880s, a "new" American naval revival had resulted in a shift from wood-hull to steel-clad steam-powered vessels. Between 1883 and 1889, Congress appropriated funds to construct 33 steel-hulled warships, including the battleship *Maine.*

In 1890, Captain Alfred T. Mahan's *The Influence of Sea Power upon History* further invigorated the nation's commitment to the U.S. Navy and a new, expanding manifest destiny. In his highly influential book, Mahan argued that sea power historically defined a nation's greatness, and that warships and commercial fleets required refueling stations worldwide. The increase of American economic involvement in Latin America and the Pacific eventually necessitated an active role for the new navy, and the army as well, in protecting those interests.[2]

In Cuba as early as 1868 and continuing into the early 1870s, antigovernment activity became chronic as revolutionaries fought for independence from Spain. With a renewal of hostilities in 1895, some American politicians suggested intervention, but President Grover Cleveland adhered to neutrality. The rebellion proved so threatening that Spain appointed Valeriano y Nicolau Weyler as the new Governor-General of Cuba. Weyler divided Cuba into districts and in a *reconcentrado* policy imprisoned almost a half million Cubans. Unsanitary conditions, disease, and inadequate food supplies resulted in nearly 200,000 deaths. Weyler's troops also killed livestock and burned fields in an effort to starve the insurgents into submission. The Spanish campaign against the rebels, combined with the insurgent's own destructive actions in burning sugarcane fields and destroying railways, left the Cuban economy in shambles.[3]

Prompted in part by the 1893 depression, American businessmen had invested heavily in foreign markets, including an estimated $50 million in the Cuban sugar industry. The revolution, however, produced a sharp decline in sugar production, endangering American investments. Additionally, the brutality of Weyler's *reconcentrado* policy produced outcries from the American press. The "yellow journalism" of the times embellished stories of Spanish atrocities and invented others. In 1896, the U.S. Congress passed concurrent resolutions proposing the granting of belligerent status to Cuban insurgents and strongly urging Spain to recognize Cuban independence. President Cleveland ignored the resolutions, deciding instead to bequeath the Cuban problem to the incoming administration.

When taking office in 1897, President William McKinley's political platform called for a resolution of the crisis in Cuba. In July, McKinley demanded that Spain end the fighting and give autonomy to the rebels. In response, Madrid recalled Weyler and granted a degree of self-government, but the Cuban revolutionary junta refused to lay down arms and demanded full independence. As tensions mounted in Cuba, McKinley ordered the battleship *Maine* to Havana on January 24, 1898.[4]

On February 9, 1898, the State Department intercepted a copy of a letter written by Enrique Dupuy de Lôme, the Spanish Minister to the United States. In this confidential correspondence meant only for Spanish officials, the minister labeled McKinley as "weak," and a "would-be politician who tries to leave the door open behind himself while keeping on good terms with the jingoes in his party." Printed in the *New York Journal*, de Lôme's remarks infuriated the American public. When McKinley protested, Spain acquiesced. The president accepted Spain's apology and de Lôme was recalled. However, any hopes for a diplomatic solution in Cuba ended on February 15, 1898, when an explosion tore through the *Maine* in Havana Harbor, killing 266 officers and crew.[5]

The destruction of the *Maine* remains shrouded in mystery. Recent forensic studies still cannot determine if the explosion began internally as a result of a fire in the coal bunkers igniting a powder magazine, or whether an external mine sank the vessel. At the time, a naval investigating commission appointed by President McKinley issued a report on March 25, claiming that the ship sank because of an external explosion, although the report did not indicate who was responsible.

Americans, stimulated by journalistic sensationalism, blamed the Spanish. In response, McKinley issued several ultimatums to Spain—an immediate armistice, the termination of the *reconcentrado* policy, arbitration of Cuban-Spanish peace negotiations by McKinley if there was no settlement by October 1898, relief aid to the Cubans, and Cuban independence under United States supervision. McKinley's demands had little chance of acceptance. Spanish national pride precluded acceptance of American arbitration and Cuban independence, even though Madrid already had ended the *reconcentrado* system and appeared willing to begin reforms and accept an armistice, provided the rebels started the process.[6]

On April 11, McKinley sent a message to Congress requesting authorization to "empower the President to take measures to secure a full and final termination of hostilities between the government of Spain and the people of Cuba, and to insure in the island the establishment of a stable government." Invoking memory of the *Maine*, the president further insisted that the conflict in Cuba represented a "very serious injury to the commerce, trade, and business of our people, and the wanton destruction of property."[7]

Within days the House passed a resolution granting McKinley's request, but the Senate, against the chief executive's wishes, sought immediate recognition of the rebels. McKinley remained convinced that the Cubans were ill prepared for self-government without American tutelage. Meanwhile, anti-imperialist politicians were opposed to what they saw as the expansion of an American empire. After endorsing the Teller Amendment, which disclaimed any intent at annexation, Congress narrowly passed a joint resolution calling for Cuban independence without recognizing the Cuban junta. Furthermore, the April 19 proclamation demanded that Spain vacate the island, and authorized the president to use whatever force necessary to achieve that end.[8]

McKinley signed the resolution on the following day. Spain responded by breaking off diplomatic relations on April 21. On April 22, McKinley ordered American warships to blockade the north coast of Cuba between Cardenas and Bahia Honda as well as the port of Cienfuegos on the south coast. In response to the naval blockade, Spain declared war on April 24, 1898.

The next morning McKinley sent a message to Congress: "The Government of Spain...responds by treating the reasonable demands of this Government as measures of hostility." The president continued: the "instant and complete severance of relations by" Spain meant "by the usage of nations" that there is "an existent state of war between sovereign nations." The president concluded with a request that Congress adopt a joint resolution, "declaring that a state of war exists between the United States of America and the Kingdom of Spain." After receiving word that the House had passed resolution 10086, the Senate unanimously agreed, declaring that war had existed with Spain since April 21.[9]

Well before the declaration of war, nationalistic emotion swept across the country. For over a year, "yellow press" newspapers such as William Randolph Hearst's *New York Journal*, Joseph Pulitzer's *New York World*, and James Gordon Bennett Jr.'s *New York Herald* sensationalized events in Cuba. Montana journalists, although not to the extent as their eastern seaboard counterparts, had begun discussing the "Cuban question" as early as January 1898, apprising Montanans of the growing crisis. On January 24, the Helena *Evening Herald* noted that the *Maine* was being sent to Cuba to protect American citizens and it was "not there on dress parade."[10] On February 16, the *Evening Herald* announced the sinking of the *Maine* with the headline: "Down to a Watery Grave…While Slumbering Death Stepped In."[11]

On the morning after the *Maine* sinking, President McKinley urged the nation to suspend any judgment about the nature of the tragedy until a board of inquiry could determine cause. For the first day, major newspapers adhered to the president's request. But on February 17, the *New York Journal* claimed that the Spaniards intentionally directed the *Maine* to be anchored over a mine in the harbor. Later that week, the *Journal* insisted that the *Maine* was intentionally sunk by the Spanish.[12] In the days to follow, the *Helena Herald* embraced the same sort of sensationalism, announcing on April 8 that "War cannot be averted."[13]

As diplomacy between Spain and the United States eroded, Montanans reacted with the same patriotic fervor as the rest of the nation. Well before the president issued a call for troops and Congress declared war, letters poured into Governor Robert B. Smith's office requesting permission to organize regiments throughout Montana. Just days after the sinking of the *Maine*, Captain John C. Bond from Billings sent a telegram to the governor: "Troop A await your orders and ready to go."[14] On the same day, the governor answered Bond. "I fully appreciate the spirit which inspires such sentiments in you and your troop and am proud to learn that Montana has sons so ready to respond in case their country needs them." Smith continued, "but I sincerely hope that there will be no war or other reason for calling your troop to arms."[15]

Other units of the National Guard sent the governor notice that they stood ready. Each time the governor responded much the same. "I do not anticipate that the present conditions confronting the government will culminate in war," he wrote to Col. Charles F. Lloyd of Butte.[16]

Letters also poured into Smith's office from men aspiring to be officers. On April 2, the governor responded to one such request from Emmett Callahan of Silver Bow County. "I am afraid from present indications that, should we have war and a call for volunteer troops be necessary in Montana, all Montana soldiers will have to be officers," Smith wrote. "I have had about five hundred applications; we may need a few privates."[17]

Ten days later, Tom Cooney from Helena wrote to the governor: "I am informed from the most unreliable sources that you have not less than 2,000 applications for commissions in the army to be raised in Montana." Cooney continued: "While the duty will be somewhat arduous...I shall, nevertheless, if accepted, endeavor to do my duty, and will doubtless have the distinguished honor of being the only Private in the army of Montana."[18]

On April 20, Montana's Adjutant General James W. Drennan wired the governor: "[Lt. Col. Harry Clay] Kessler desires to volunteer service of first infantry to federal government. I would suggest that you tender service of entire guard."[19] At the time, however, no effective method of mobilization existed in the United States. If the Civil War had taught the military anything, it was that the mobilization of volunteer units created chaos. State troops frequently reported for duty ill equipped and untrained. Following the Civil War, numerous regular army officers wrote reports, articles, and books advocating a new system. General Emory Upton, in *The Military Policy of the United States*, became the most outspoken of the army reformers. Upton advocated a federal reserve force controlled by professionally trained officers, and avidly disavowed the traditional use of often unprepared state militias.

With the possibility of war, some reform-minded politicians attempted to pass a bill sponsored by Congressman John A.T. Hull. The legislation would result in the bypassing of the state militia system and centralize all power of organization in the regular army. Such congressmen, however, failed to take the states' opposition into full account, which was fueled by local patriotism and a desire to maintain the organizational integrity of their own volunteer units. Congress discarded the Hull bill, and on April 22 passed a new Mobilization Act that allowed the National Guard units to volunteer.[20]

The day before passage of the Mobilization Act, Governor Smith cabled Montana's U.S. Senator Thomas H. Carter, stating there was concern in Montana that any call for volunteers might not include artillery batteries and cavalry. Senator Carter responded: "Under provisions of the pending bill...a company troop battery battalion or regiment of organized militia may enlist in the volunteer army in a body." Carter continued: "The president contemplates calling for one hundred thousand volunteers of which number the Montana quota will be four hundred and nineteen...Montana will be called upon to furnish one battalion of cavalry." Carter noted that "this arrangement is deemed wise by the secretary of war because of the great abundance of splendid saddle horses in that state."[21]

In its final form, the Mobilization Act proscribed that each volunteer regiment include one surgeon, two assistant surgeons, and a chaplain, and that the state governors should appoint all company and regimental officers. Furthermore, the act provided that both regular and volunteer organizations should consist of three or more regiments in a brigade, with three brigades in a division, and three divisions in each army corps. Section 13 of the act also allowed state governors to appoint regular army officers as field grade officers in the volunteer army, but only one regular army officer was authorized per volunteer regiment.[22] Section 13 proved to be invaluable to the Montana National Guard in the person of Lt. Robert B. Wallace, the regular army officer assigned as military secretary to Montana's governor.

Born in Chicago in 1869, Robert Wallace moved to Helena with his family at the age of 10. He attended Helena public schools and spent summers on his father's sheep ranch in the Judith Basin. At age 15, Wallace found employment in a Helena store while preparing to take the entrance examination for the U.S. Military Academy. Successful in this endeavor, Wallace graduated in 1890.[23]

Lt. Col. R.B. Wallace of the 1st Montana Infantry Regiment, Helena, 1898. A graduate of West Point and then assigned to the 2nd U.S. Cavalry Regiment, Lt. Wallace transferred to the 1st Montana as a regular Army advisor in 1894, and eventually was elevated to lieutenant colonel with activation of Montana troops for the Spanish-American War. Being second in command, he brought a trained professional eye to Montana's citizen soldiers during training, and then during combat in the Philippines. *MMHM*

Upon leaving West Point, Wallace joined the 2nd U.S. Cavalry stationed at Fort Huachuca, Arizona. After four years of activities against the Apache Indians, Wallace was assigned as the military secretary to Montana's governor in November 1894. His duties included training the Montana National Guard and organizing its military instruction system, and developing military laws for the state. In many respects, Wallace proved instrumental in preparing the Montana guard for duty in the Philippines.

In the *Report of the Adjutant General of the State of Montana*, issued on November 30, 1898, Brig. Gen. Charles F. English noted Wallace's contributions: "The personnel of the Guard was excellent. Under the efficient instruction of Lieutenant R.B. Wallace, U.S.A., the work of the past two years has been devoted in perfecting the organization in drill and discipline of the troops." English further noted that the militia "under his supervision has made marked progress in every direction."[24]

When Congress declared war on April 25, 1898, Wallace asked to be reassigned from Montana to rejoin the 2nd U.S. Cavalry in the Southwest. Wallace had pneumonia at the time, however, causing the U.S. Army's adjutant general to temporarily deny the request. When Governor Smith learned that Montana might be allowed to raise a squadron of cavalry, he visited Wallace at his bedside, offering him command. However, the U.S. Army's acceptance of a full regiment of Montana infantry—which Wallace had painstakingly trained for four years—soon proved to be of more importance than organizing cavalry. Wallace would remain in Montana, mustering the 1st Montana into federal service.[25]

Under Section 13 of the 1898 Mobilization Act, Governor Smith promoted Robert Wallace as lieutenant colonel of the 1st Montana Infantry. On June 23, Wallace sent a dispatch to the 2nd U.S. Cavalry, informing the regimental adjutant of his Montana volunteer affiliation. "I have the honor to inform you that on May 7th, 1898, I took advantage of leave of absence granted me in Special Order No. 105, dated 'H.Q.A. Adjutant General's Office, Washington, May 5, 1898,' and on that date assumed my duties as Lieut. Col. of the First Montana Volunteer Infantry, and my address," Wallace advised, "will be care of this organization."[26]

Word of the 1st Montana Regiment's mobilization generated a rising interest among young men in enlisting. W.M. Leighton, a law student at the State University of Minnesota and a member of the Crow tribe, wrote the governor offering to help raise a company of 100 Crow Indians. In the letter, Leighton noted this would have a beneficial effect on "young Indians," as well as allowing the tribe to demonstrate its loyalty to the government.[27] In response, the governor questioned the legality of enlisting American Indians: "The fact that the Crow Indians are wards of the government in its charge on a reservation might raise the question of their right to join a state organization."[28]

In an unusual request, Mrs. M.F. Sherman wrote to the governor suggesting that convicts be recruited from the state prison at Deer Lodge. "Why not take them as soldiers," Mrs. Sherman inquired. "By doing so you would remove an onerous tax on the people of Montana."[29] Governor Smith described Mrs. Sherman's suggestion as "abhorrent," and insisted that institutions such as the Deer Lodge prison were necessary to protect the people of the state.[30]

In addition to the many requests for commissions or authorizations to raise additional companies of infantry, the governor received appeals from women inquiring about service as nurses. One group of Great Falls women, admitting they had no medical experience, nevertheless petitioned the governor for permission to go to the front with Company A. Smith politely reminded the petitioners that the present call for troops did not allow for nurses.[31]

Montana's volunteer quota out of the president's call for 125,000 men initially numbered only 419. But Wallace's organizational accomplishments over the past few years prompted Russell Alexander Alger, the Secretary of War, to authorize calling up an entire regiment from the state. On the same day that Congress declared war, Secretary Alger telegraphed Governor Smith: "The number of troops from your state under the call of the president dated April 23, 1898, will be one regiment of infantry." Alger continued: "It is the wish of the President that the regiments of the National Guard or state militia shall be used as far as their numbers will permit for the reason that they are armed, equipped and drilled[;] please wire as early as possible what equipments amunition [sic] arms blankets, tents etc. you have and what additional you will require."[32]

On April 26, Smith wired Alger, inquiring as to how many companies would make up a regiment and the number of men required for each company. The following day, Army Adjutant General Henry C. Corbin telegraphed a response: "Regim[ent] not less than ten nor more than twelve companies[,] battal[ion] not less than three companies[,] each company not more than eighty four officers and men and not less than eighty."[33]

Over the next few days, Governor Smith requested additional information from Washington, D.C., about the mobilization. Senator Carter indicated the regiment should rendezvous in Helena and the governor could utilize Fort Harrison if necessary. In response to the telegram, Smith asked permission to use the unoccupied buildings at the fort, but Adjutant General Corbin denied the request.[34]

On April 28, Col. Harry Clay Kessler ordered his Montana guard units to report for duty at their respective armories. Prior to the war, there were nine companies of infantry, but all fell well below the minimum 80-man requirement. These included: Company A, Great Falls; B, F, and G, Butte; D, Virginia City; E, Dillon; H, Kalispell; I, Lewistown; and K, Anaconda. To bring the regiment up to 12 companies, Cavalry Troop B from Bozeman and the Helena Light Battery joined to form Company C. Additionally, Anaconda organized Company M. Also, at a meeting held in the Helena Auditorium on the evening of April 27, the "Queen City" signed up 105 men for Company L. After listening to rousing speeches delivered by Governor Smith, Attorney General Cornelius B. Nolan, Wilbur Fisk Sanders, and others, the new recruits—accompanied by Civil War veterans representing 34 separate regiments—paraded through the town led by a drum corps.[35]

On May 4, the companies left their respective towns and cities to rendezvous in Helena. The new Helena company, already present at the Fort Harrison reservation, mustered in on May 5. Virginia City's Company D mustered in the following day. The three Butte companies, reaching Helena on May 5, also mustered in on May 6. Company E from Dillon, as well as companies M and K from Anaconda, arrived at Fort Harrison on May 6 and mustered in on May 8 along with Company A from Great Falls. The last three companies to reach the encampment came from Kalispell, Lewistown, Bozeman, and Helena, mustering in on May 9. Lt. George P. Ahern, detached from the 25th U.S. Infantry to replace Wallace as military secretary, mustered in all of the companies.[36]

The regimental area set aside near Fort Harrison became known as Camp Robert B. Smith, in honor of the governor. Located near the Broadwater Hotel, the site also was called "Camp Mud" due to the unbearable conditions. Six hours of daily drill in melting snow turned the grounds into a bog and it became increasingly difficult for the recruits to remain dry. Illness spread through the camp. By May 16, the intolerable conditions necessitated moving the troops to a more hospitable site closer to town, on Henderson Avenue near the present-day fairgrounds.[37]

Not all of the men volunteering for service were accepted. Some did not meet the age requirements designated by the Secretary of War, stipulating that recruits must be between 18 and 45. On the day before Col. Kessler called up the regiment, Adjutant General Henry Corbin telegraphed the governor: "An army surgeon has been designated to conduct physicial [sic] examination for volunteers at each state rendezvous. The secretary of war requests," Corbin continued, "that you appoint two civil Physicians to constitute with the army surgeon a board for carrying out the above provision."[38]

Physical requirements during the Civil War consisted of simply having recruits run the length of a parade ground, but the rules became much more rigid after 1889. Now volunteers needed to pass a thorough physical examination and complete an extensive questionnaire. Age limitations and physical exams reduced the original 106 enlistees in Helena's company down to the required 84.[39]

On May 9, after the companies formed up to complete the regiment, the U.S. Army's Adjutant General Corbin telegraphed Governor Smith: "If equipped and ready…it is desired to order them to San Francisco for service in expedition that may leave the coast in the not distant future." If the regiment was not fully equipped, Corbin advised, the governor should notify the Secretary of War regarding the supplies required.[40] Smith responded with a specific list of needs—"680 blouses, 680 trousers, 800 pairs leggings, 800 campaign hats, 170 canvas wall tents complete, and 600 rifles Cal 45, and necessary ammunition." The governor went on to suggest that the "regiment can easily travel to San Francisco and be fully equipped and armed there."[41]

Budget restraints in 1897 had forced the Montana guard to forego the annual encampment and inspections during that summer indicated units lacked some necessary equipment. In his report to the state adjutant general on June 7, 1897, Lt. Wallace noted the shortage of uniforms: "The supply of clothing now in the possession of the companies shows wear, and in several organizations there are not sufficient blouses and trousers and leggings on hand to fully uniform its men."[42] Furthermore, there was an insufficient number of rifles to completely arm the troops.

An inspection by the Office of the Chief of Ordnance, U.S. Army, in December 1897 accounted for 427 Springfield .45 caliber model 1873 rifles. However, another 67 were unaccounted for. On May 27, 1898—with the mustering of the regiment—the army's chief of ordnance insisted that the Montana guard account for the missing weapons. Since the rifles disappeared during the previous gubernatorial administration, Governor Smith had to establish a line of communication between himself and former Governor John E. Rickards, as well as Rickards' adjutant general, Charles F. Lloyd.

After weeks of corresponding, it was determined that some of the missing rifles simply had worn out, but the majority had been destroyed during the Coxieite unrest. As Rickards noted in a July 26 letter to Governor Smith: "The Coxieites as you will remember had stolen a train. Deputy U.S. Marshalls went in pursuit of them armed with rifles, loaned them by the National Guard." Rickards further explained: "Overtaking the Coxieites at Billings, there was some gun play made, the Coxieites overpowering the Marshalls, taking their guns from them and breaking them over the railroad track."[43]

Equipping and clothing the nation's volunteer regiments proved a major task for the U.S. Army's Quartermaster Department. In the years following the Civil War, the department was radically reduced to only 57 serving officers. Complicating matters, Brig. Gen. Marshall I. Ludington became the new quartermaster general only days before the sinking of the *Maine*. Ludington's unfamiliarity with his position illustrated just one of numerous aspects in which the nation was unprepared for war. Secretary of War Alger later explained the main reason for these inadequacies. The U.S. Army "had, during thirty years, been called upon only to plan for and meet the requirements of the regular army in time of peace, and naturally enough had become quite fixed in the narrow grooves of peace."[44]

The Montana guard's field uniforms, as well as those of the regular army, consisted of wool textile—sky blue for trousers and dark blue for blouses—continuing the American tradition initiated well before the Civil War. For years, cavalry troops stationed in the Southwest lobbied unsuccessfully for a summer uniform. With the president's April 23 proclamation calling for 125,000 volunteers, Ludington suddenly was confronted with outfitting many additional thousands of soldiers for tropical duty. To meet the demand, the linings from existing wool uniforms were removed, and new summer underwear was distributed. The army also contracted for khaki-colored canvas uniforms, just as uncomfortable as wool.

For the Montana guard, there would prove to be sufficient time for the issuance of clothing before shipping out from San Francisco. In addition to a regulation wool uniform, each volunteer received nankeen underclothing, gingham shirts, a white drill suit, and light cotton socks. Fortunately for the Montana troops, Chief Quartermaster James W. Pope also later managed to purchase lightweight khaki and white uniforms in Manila.[45]

At Helena, however, the government issued blankets to the volunteers, but little else. The insufficient number of rifles necessitated that the manual of arms be practiced in shifts. Although the regiment lacked adequate clothing and arms, it never suffered a deficiency in spirit, or support from Montana's citizens. As a number of the companies departed from their home communities to muster in at Helena, local citizens presented them with silk flags.

Helena women also presented the regimental flag to the 1st Montana just days before the regiment left for San Francisco. The "Kessler Banner" had been in the guard's possession since 1895, awarded to the most efficient and exemplary company at the conclusion of the annual summer encampment. Recently, the banner had been in the hands of an accomplished embroiderer, who added "1st Montana Infantry, U.S.V." in an arched pattern over the state seal. This flag was taken to the Philippines in preference to a standard eagle-and-scroll infantry flag. The Kessler Banner was not only sentimentally important to the regiment's men, but after its return from the Philippines, the design, without the embroidered unit designation, served as the basis for Montana's state flag adopted after the turn of the century.

As one newspaper reported, "the flag was received with all the pomp and ceremony usually attending such presentations." The account mentioned that "Miss Sarepta Sanders presented the flag through color sergeant Charles R. Sutton, of Company L, to Col. Harry C. Kessler,"[46] in view of the entire regiment and more than 5,000 spectators. The Helena *Weekly Herald* also noted: "Such a flag is a constant reminder to the boys that wherever they are, what ever they are fighting or enduring, the 'fireside brigade' is waiting to applaud their courage and fortitude."[47]

Two days after the flag presentation, Helena's citizens also gave the regiment a mascot. "A magnificent specimen of the American [sic; golden] eagle, very much alive—with a screech fierce enough to pierce the air from vale to mountaintops for miles about—will be the mascot of the Montana First," reported the *Weekly Herald*.[48] Donated by the Wadsworth Post No. 3 of the Grand Army of the Republic, the eagle, appropriately named "Commodore Dewey," came from Helena's Central Park. Following the presentation, Col. Kessler placed the eagle under the care of Private Andrew McGinnis of Company L, a Civil War veteran who served with the Army of the Potomac. Less than enamored with this duty, the survivor of 32 Civil War battles was quoted by the *Avant Courier* as saying, "he ain't goin' to carry no aigle when the Spaniards is a shootin' at him."[49]

"Commodore Dewey," presented to the 1st Regiment by Montana's Civil War veterans, 1898. At the close of training at the Presidio, it was determined that a golden eagle would not fare well in the tropics. Dewey was given to a zoo; there is no record of his subsequent history. *103rd PAD collection, MMHM*

On May 24, during final preparations for departure, Col. Kessler announced that no passes would be allowed. That same day, the men stood for the governor's review. "To those who may never see the whole regiment together again, the memory of...[the] review of the troops by the governor and his staff will never be forgotten," the *Helena Independent* reported. "The regiment, the regimental band, 'Admiral Dewey,' the regimental eagle and the staff of the governor were on their best behavior."[50]

Taps sounded early that night. Reveille came at 4 a.m. the next morning. After finishing breakfast by 4:30 a.m., the men hastily broke camp, stood again for review, visited the fort's hospital to have vaccinations checked, and then marched through Helena to the railway station, boarding trains for San Francisco.

The Great Northern and Northern Pacific railroads were contracted to transport the regiment. Leaving Helena at 8:40 a.m., two Northern Pacific trains took that line's route over MacDonald Pass to Garrison and then south to Silver Bow. Shortly after the departure of the Northern Pacific specials, two Great Northern trains headed south toward Clancy, where they joined up as a 15-car "double header." Proceeding to Butte at 1:45 p.m., the Great Northern special switched tracks to the Oregon Short Line, and rolled off to rendezvous with the Northern Pacific trains in Silver Bow. There the trains consolidated into two sections and headed for San Francisco at 3 p.m.[51]

Anxious to see the departing soldiers, citizens of Butte and Anaconda boarded special trains of the Butte, Anaconda and Pacific Railroad for the short journey to Silver Bow. "The First regiment was given a rousing welcome in Silver Bow upon its arrival," the *Anaconda Standard* reported later that day. "There were several thousand Butte and Anaconda friends of the soldiers present, and all were kindly remembered with huge boxes of delicacies and presents."[52]

Two weeks before the 1st Montana Infantry Regiment boarded trains for California, four troops of cavalry also had begun to be mustered into the 3rd Regiment U.S. Volunteer Cavalry. Early on during the preparations for war, Senator Thomas Carter had informed the governor that a cavalry battalion would be called up from Montana. This was not accomplished, however, until Adjutant General James W. Drennan received a telegram from Carter informing him of the possibility of securing a place for the state's cavalry in three special volunteer regiments being formed by the War Department. In response, Governor Smith telegraphed the senator on the following day: "Squadron of four good troops of cavalry anxious to tender their services to special organizations."[53]

Smith had assumed that the existing cavalry troops from Great Falls, Missoula, Billings, and Miles City would be the units accepted into service. But on May 4, the governor received a telegram from senators Carter and Mantle informing him that a Butte unit had been substituted for the Great Falls troop.[54]

A troubled governor telegraphed the Secretary of War: "I am advised by Senators Carter and Mantle that the best drilled and the best equipped cavalry troop in our state, the one that today carries the state prize has been set aside and a new and untried and unequipped and unorganized crowd at Butte substituted." Governor Smith concluded, "I do not know why this change but it is a great wrong and should be corrected."[55]

The following day, Senator Carter wired the governor, hoping to appease him. Carter indicated it was only natural to accept a troop from the most populous city in the state, and he assured the governor that efforts were being undertaken to organize additional cavalry regiments. Later that same afternoon, the governor also received a telegram from Senator Mantle assuring him that the Butte troop would "give a good account of themselves," and that the disposition of cavalry troops, unlike that of the infantry, rested with the Secretary of War and not the governor.[56]

Lt. Col. Charles F. Lloyd of Butte commanded the squadron of Montana cavalry that would be assigned to "Grigsby's Roughriders" of the 3rd U.S. Volunteer Cavalry Regiment. The troop from Butte, redesignated Company A, mustered into service on May 10, 1898. Company F from Missoula, Troop I of Miles City, and Troop M from Billings mustered in three days later. The squadron totaled 13 officers and 291 enlisted men. Each troop had at least one trumpeter, a wagoner, and a farrier. Additionally, each troop, except Company M, had its own blacksmith.[57]

The 3rd U.S. Cavalry Regiment rendezvoused at Camp George A. Thomas on the Chickamauga Battlefield Park in northern Georgia. Established as one of 12 mobilization sites by the Secretary of War, Camp Thomas covered 11 square miles of woodland just south of Chattanooga, Tennessee, and offered good rail connections to the Gulf coast. Several years earlier, the Cleveland administration had designated this site as a training ground for the U.S. Army and the National Guard. Prior to the mobilization, Chickamauga Park consisted of little more than a train station and a few homes, but within a short time the site bristled with new buildings, tents, and thousands of soldiers.[58]

On May 15, the War Department issued orders for all volunteer forces to concentrate at various camps. As part of the order, 42 troops of cavalry, 53 infantry regiments, and 11 field batteries were assigned to Chickamauga. Within five days, 35,000 volunteers had reached Camp Thomas. One provision of the April 22 Mobilization Act called for 3,000 volunteers to be recruited directly by the federal government and not counted against state quotas. These troops included three cavalry regiments organized in the western states and commanded by Theodore Roosevelt, Melvin Grigsby, and Col. Torrey.

By early June, the number of troops at Chickamauga mushroomed to 60,000, designated for the First and Third Army Corps. Consequently, the men from Montana became assigned as the 3rd Regiment, Third Division, First Army

Corps, initially commanded by Maj. Gen. John R. Brooke. The 3rd Regiment—composed of troops from Fort Meade and Sioux Falls, South Dakota; Missoula, Miles City, Butte, and Billings, Montana; Fargo, North Dakota; and Lincoln, Nebraska—arrived at Chickamauga Park on May 23, 1898.[59]

Though originally considered an ideal location for mobilization, Camp Thomas quickly proved unsuitable for such a large body of soldiers. Because sewage runoff had contaminated the local water supply, potable water was hauled from six miles away and never came in sufficient quantities. As a result, guards were posted around contaminated pools of standing water to prevent men from drinking it.[60]

Living conditions at the camp were worsened by insufficient clothing and supplies. The Quartermaster Corps sent trainloads of food, clothing, and equipment to the mobilization sites, but the overwhelmed supply depots still could not adequately fulfill the massive need for tents, uniforms, rifles, and other equipment. A Kentucky regiment arrived at Camp Thomas "with lots of whisky and fine horses but no arms or clothing."[61] Food spoilage also was a problem, and ammunition was so scarce that rifle practice was uncommon. A subsequent investigation revealed that supplies sent from St. Louis to Chickamauga frequently took over two weeks to travel less than 300 miles.[62]

Meanwhile, the war in Cuba proceeded at a quick pace after 16,000 American troops landed on June 22. Following just four weeks of fighting, the Spaniards sued for peace on July 18. Secretary of War Alger meanwhile assigned General Nelson Miles to command an expeditionary force against Spanish troops in Puerto Rico. Realizing that the fighting had ended in Cuba, Montana's Senator Mantle petitioned the Secretary of War to have Grigsby's Roughriders assigned to the Puerto Rico expedition. Senator Carter wired the same request to Alger on July 29.[63] Aware that an armistice was imminent, Carter made one last ditch effort on the Montana squadron's behalf. "If possible," Carter implored, "send Grigsby's cavalry to Porto [sic] Rico or Cuba. They want to get into or near a fight."[64]

On August 12, 1898, Spain and the United States signed a peace agreement. Within 12 days, the units in Grigsby's Roughriders received orders to return to their states of origin. The Montana squadron mustered out of federal service on September 8. Although the 3rd U.S. Cavalry never saw action, a number of troopers succumbed to disease. A report issued in 1902 listed 9 deaths from illness in the 3rd Regiment. Reports regarding the 2nd Nebraska, however, counted 26 dead. A list of casualties of Montana volunteers issued in 1903 reported that privates Charles Connors, Clarence Langley, and William Sweet from Butte's Company A, and Private Patrick Egan from Billings' Troop M, as having died at Camp Thomas. In total, Chickamauga Park led all mobilization centers with 352 deaths, with most of the reported cases due to typhoid fever.[65]

On May 10, 1898, in addition to the special cavalry units, Congress also authorized recruitment of 3,500 men as U.S. Volunteer Engineers. On June 30, F.J. Mills from Salt Lake City, Utah, arrived in Butte to recruit skilled mechanics for the 2nd Regiment of Volunteer Engineers. Within a few short days, Mills managed to enlist a full compliment of 28 men to make up Company K. On July 4, these soldiers left Butte for Salt Lake City and mustered in at Fort Douglas.

Other units in the regiment came from California, Colorado, Illinois, Indiana, Minnesota, Nebraska, Ohio, Oregon, and Utah. After a few days in Utah, the company was ordered to San Francisco. Lt. Tom Cooney, former chief of the Northern Pacific Land Department, who three months before had written the governor requesting "the distinguished honor of being the only Private in the army of Montana," left Helena for San Francisco to command Company K. On August 5, the regiment boarded the transports *Charles Nelson* and *Lachne* for Honolulu, Hawaii.[66]

The men of Company K hoped they would be sent to the Philippines. During their brief period in San Francisco, the regiment was armed and trained as infantrymen, and they left for Honolulu with the understanding that the regiment would be sent to the front. After months in the Hawaiian Islands, however, it became apparent that the 2nd Regiment of Volunteer Engineers would never see the Philippines. Lt. Cooney noted this created some discontent, though never affecting the work at hand. "Although the men were deprived of the excitement of an active campaign in an enemy's country," Cooney explained, "they did their duty and did it well."[67]

During the stay in Hawaii, the regiment produced a topographic survey of Pearl Harbor, where the U.S. Navy later built a naval station. Other work at Camp McKinley, three miles from Honolulu, consisted of constructing five barracks, each 36 by 156 feet to house 800 soldiers. In addition, the regiment remodeled other barracks formerly used by the Hawaiian government and constructed roads and water works for the post.[68]

The regiment left Honolulu on the steamship *Australia* on August 6, 1899, arriving in San Francisco eight days later. Many of the Montana men were enchanted with Hawaii and a few would return. After being mustered out of service, Cooney, who had been promoted to captain, returned to Helena for a week before going home to Afton, Minnesota. Although conditions at Hawaii's Camp McKinley were much better than those experienced by the 3rd U.S. Cavalry at Chickamauga Park, Cooney reported five deaths in his unit. In total, the 2nd Regiment of Volunteer Engineers recorded 13 deaths and 22 desertions. Only two men from the Third Battalion, which included Company K, deserted; Captain Cooney described them as the "scrubs of the Battalion."[69]

Although Company K never reached the Philippines, another 15 Montana men in a special unit commanded by Lt. George H. Tilly, assigned to the Volunteer Signal Corps, eventually saw action there. One week after Congress authorized the enlistment of 3,500 men as engineers and 10,000 U.S. Volunteer infantrymen, it created the Volunteer Signal Corps. According to this directive, each division would have 8 officers and 55 enlisted men designated as signalmen. By July 5, 1898, Lt. Tilly completed his recruiting effort. Briefly stationed at Fort Harrison, all of Tilly's men, except one electrician and two cooks, were experienced telegraphers. As for Lt. Tilly, he had been a longtime member of the Montana National Guard Signal Corps, organized earlier by Maj. John R. Miller.[70]

After promotion to captain, Tilly was assigned to General Marcus P. Miller's staff. In the Philippines, General Miller commanded the Visayan Military District, where Captain Tilly headed the signal corps. On January 25, 1899, Tilly wrote to a friend in Helena stating the climate apparently agreed with him and his health had improved. By March 10, the Helena *Daily Independent* received a dispatch indicating that Captain Tilly had gone to Negros Island with a California battalion to establish communications from that locality to the rest of the Philippines.[71]

By this time, native Filipinos not willing to trade one colonial power for another had started fighting the Americans in what eventually became known as the Philippine Insurrection, or later, as the Philippine-American War. In late May 1899, Tilly requested permission to assist a company laying cable by ship from Iloilo, Panay, around the northern end of Negros to Cebu Island. After laying cable for most of a day, the ship proceeded to Escalante, arriving on the morning of May 27. Captain Tilly, accompanied by the ship's captain, the second officer, and several crewmen, took a launch to shore, where they were warmly greeted by some local residents. As Tilly and the others walked toward town, however, Filipino insurgents ambushed them. Tilly and several men fled to the river, apparently intending to swim to safety on the other side. Tilly went unaccounted for.

On May 28, Maj. Richard E. Thompson, the Chief Signal Officer of the Department of the Pacific and Eighth Army Corps, telegrammed Washington, D.C.: "Captain Tilly, one of a party landed at Escalante, Negros, cable work, treacherously attacked by insurgents. Tilly missing. Worst feared."[72]

The following day, General Jacob H. Smith and a force of 75 men boarded a gunboat to search for Tilly at Escalante. On May 30, Maj. Gen. Elwell S. Otis cabled the War Department regarding Smith's findings. "He reports this morning that body Captain Tilly found floating in river; marks of violence on head; body sent to Iloilo."[73] In a message sent to Maj. Thompson, 2nd Lt. Alfred Clifton speculated that Tilly probably was killed in the river. The insurgents then dragged him ashore, looted his body, and sank it in the river. When the detachment found

Tilly, his body had a stone tied around the waist.[74] General Smith remained on the island a few days, located the insurgents, and "severely punished" them.[75]

On May 30, 1899, Captain Tilly was buried with full military honors in Iloilo, Negros, in a British cemetery. Helena's Lt. William B. Hanna of the 1st Montana Infantry, recently promoted from sergeant and an old friend of Tilly's, attended the funeral. In a letter sent to Signal Corps authorities in Washington, D.C., Maj. Thompson noted that all of those present at the funeral did "honor to the remains of one of the most efficient, upright, and lovable of men; who laid down his life in the service of his country as truly as though he had met death on the battle line."[76] Of the 1,457 officers and enlisted men of the Signal Corps during the Spanish-American War, Captain Tilly was the only one listed as killed in action.[77]

After a three-day train journey to San Francisco, the 1st Montana Infantry Regiment arrived on the morning of May 28, 1898. Women of the San Francisco Red Cross treated the regiment to a lavish breakfast, as they did for all arriving units. The troops then boarded a ferry for the Presidio. Living conditions at their destination, Camp Merritt, were decidedly better than at some other mobilization camps, but the bivouac still had its share of problems.

Five blocks from Golden Gate Park, the regiment pitched tents in the sand dunes. Winds from the Pacific Ocean blew in a nightly fog dampening everything, causing pneumonia and other illness among the men. A limited number of latrines resulted in unsanitary conditions and an outbreak of typhoid fever. In these sandy conditions, recruits initially lined the tents with straw, but General Wesley Merritt, the overall commander of troops at San Francisco, issued a directive forbidding this practice as unsanitary. Afterward, troops slept on the sand and fleas became a nuisance that none escaped. Bathing provided the only relief, but the nearest shower was a two-mile march away.[78]

Despite adverse conditions, the Montana regiment settled into a routine under the new brigade commander, General Arthur MacArthur (the father of General Douglas MacArthur, later of WWII fame). Along with units from California, South Dakota, and Wyoming, the 1st Montana drilled daily. On June 4, the regiment received uniforms and old model Springfield rifles, outfitting the entire force. When MacArthur left for the Philippines on June 21, Col. Kessler, as the ranking volunteer officer, became the acting brigade commander. Noting that the 1st Montana had mustered in first, senators Carter and Mantle urged the president to promote Kessler to brigadier general. However, Brig. Gen. Harrison Gray Otis assumed command of the brigade within a few weeks and Kessler returned to take over lead of the 1st Montana from Lt. Col. Wallace.[79]

Throughout the early summer, other units continued to arrive at San Francisco. Designated as the Eighth Corps, the regimental elements came from

The 1st Montana Infantry, U.S.V., after receiving uniform issue in San Francisco prior to shipping out to the Philippines, 1898. *MMHM*

California, Colorado, Idaho, Kansas, Montana, Nebraska, North and South Dakota, Oregon, Pennsylvania, Utah, and Wyoming. General Merritt had hoped to send units to the Philippines by May 21, but transportation shortages prevented this; the army lacked sufficient shipping capabilities.

To remedy the situation, the army chartered commercial vessels, refitting them to carry troops. On May 25, an expeditionary force of the 1st California, 2nd Oregon, and five companies of the 14th U.S. Infantry, under the command of Brig. Gen. Thomas M. Anderson, got underway. A second force, commanded by Brig. Gen. Francis V. Greene, departed on June 15 consisting of the 10th Pennsylvania, 1st Colorado, 1st Nebraska, four companies of the 18th U.S. Infantry, and four from the 23rd U.S. Infantry.[80]

Jack Onarheim of Company M wrote home about the event. "They received a great cheering as they marched downtown yesterday and to-day. San Francisco is wild over the soldiers, and she ought to be, as they have all brought money here with them and will have more after getting paid."[81] On June 21, General Merritt departed with the 1st North Dakota, 13th Minnesota, 1st Iowa, 1st Wyoming, and four companies each from the 18th and 23rd U.S. infantry.[82]

Not assigned to the first three convoys, the 1st Montana men despaired that they might miss the fourth call. Tension eased when the regiment had the opportunity to participate in a sham battle for Oakland's citizens. On the morning of July 4, the regiment boarded the ferry *Garden City* for the trip to Oakland, where they paraded through town. Red Cross women served lunch at Adam's Point. A correspondent for the *Anaconda Standard* reported: "It took 300 gallons of coffee and 10,000 sandwiches and fruit no end to check the advance of that hungry horde," and "when they beat retreat they had no words but those of praise for the generosity of their hostesses."[83]

With lunch finished, seven companies under Lt. Col. Robert Wallace's direction attacked the "Spaniards," represented by Maj. Robert Miller's five companies. With over 25,000 people watching, "volley after volley poured across the narrow valley."[84] As those previously designated as wounded fell and were carried off the battlefield, Maj. Miller's command made a valiant stand, but eventually gave way to the superior force. The mock battle lasted nearly two hours and afterwards the citizens of Oakland presented the Montanans with yet another regimental flag.[85]

Two days after the "Battle of Oakland," the Montana men suffered their first fatality. Private Robert Lennington, who enlisted in Anaconda's Company K and recently transferred to the U.S. Army Hospital Corps, died from typhoid pneumonia. Lennington entered the French Hospital ten days before his death. The 1st Montana, along with the regimental band, escorted Lennington's body to the gates of the Presidio. Ten days later, Private Frank A. Camp of Company C became the second Montanan to die from disease.[86]

After weeks of waiting, Col. Kessler finally received orders for his command to ship out for the Philippines. On the morning of July 18, 1898, the 1st Montana broke camp and boarded the transport *Pennsylvania*. Built in 1873, the *Pennsylvania* recently rounded Cape Horn from New York to take part in the booming Klondike gold rush trade. When the ship arrived in San Francisco, however, the government chartered it for service in the Philippines. Only 300 feet long, the vessel could reasonably carry 700 passengers. But when departing, the transport held the 1st Montana, plus 303 soldiers from the 1st California, totaling more than 1,400 men. Compounding the overcrowding, the ship held fresh water for only 700. Meanwhile, the regiment's eagle mascot, Commodore Dewey, remained at San Francisco in the care of zoo keepers.

Though it was expected that Spain would sign an armistice at any time due to defeats at sea and on land in Cuba and the Philippines, the War Department had continued shipping out as many troops as possible. Attempts were being made to fulfill General Merrritt's request for 20,000 men in the Philippines.[87]

A *Pennsylvania* crew member warned that the narrow beam caused the vessel to roll. "She is a strong, safe boat, but the worst thing afloat to roll. She would roll if she was on the dry dock." Not long after leaving port, the ship encountered a 12-hour-long gale. The men below deck were thrown about until battered and bruised. No one seemed to escape seasickness and the stench in the living quarters became nearly unbearable. It took days for the men to recover. Captain James F. Keown, Company C, particularly having hard time of it, later remarked that if the United States ever wanted him to fight a "foreign foe" again it would have be in the Gallatin Valley.[88]

A scarcity of provisions was another difficulty. Although some complained that food was inadequately cooked, the main issue was a shortage at mealtimes. Due to the overcrowding, the cooks were not preparing enough food to feed the men. The troops called for a mass meeting, hoping to meet with Col. Kessler, who did not appear. Lt. Col. Wallace and Maj. Miller, however, assessed the situation and took charge of distribution. Col. Kessler ordered the cooks to give the men all they wanted, adding that if this exceeded the regular allowance, he would pay for it personally.[89]

As the *Pennsylvania* neared Honolulu, Col. Kessler gave an interview to a correspondent from the *Anaconda Standard.* "It is against my wish to have so many men on this ship," he explained. "I protested in San Francisco against taking more than the Montana regiment aboard, but my wishes were not regarded." Kessler continued, "I am going to try to get rid of some of them at Honolulu. If General Otis is at that point when we arrive I feel sure that he will sanction a change. If he is not there I will take the responsibility myself of leaving the California men behind."[90] Later at Honolulu, indeed, the men of the 1st California would be transferred to the *Rio de Janeiro,* giving the Montana men sufficient room.

As the *Pennsylvania* neared the Hawaiian Islands, Molokai was sighted at 4:30 p.m. on July 27. To avoid arriving at night, the ship slowed speed, finally docking at the Pacific Mail wharf in Honolulu at 7:30 the next morning. When the vessel rounded the lighthouse, a Hawaiian band played "The Star-Spangled Banner." The Montana regimental band responded with the same tune, and the two bands continued alternating songs until the ship docked. The local citizenry crowded the wharf and threw bananas, oranges, and pineapples to the soldiers. The regiment remained at Honolulu for only a week—long enough for most of the men to become enamored with the island. The locals provided dinner for the entire regiment in a garden at the Queen Liliuokalani palace. Letters home spoke of Hawaii as an "earthly paradise," and "a place as lovers dream of."[91]

On the morning of August 3, the *Pennsylvania*, accompanied by the *Rio de Janeiro*, and with General H.G. Otis along, embarked for the Philippines. After three weeks of poor food, hot weather, stormy seas, and still cramped quarters, the expedition reached Cavite in the Philippines on August 24. Some experienced anxiety over the possibility of a Spanish gunboat attack, but as the ships entered the harbor, word reached the men that the Spanish had surrendered in the Philippines on August 13. Some feared the *Pennsylvania* would turn around and head for home.

Their anxiety lessened, however, when the First and Second battalions went ashore early that evening aboard a small side-wheeler captured from the Spanish. Sgt. Asa F. Fisk, a musician from Helena's Company L, remained on board with the Third Battalion, writing of his view from the ship. "To our stern we could see the lights of Manila and the war vessels of the different nations, German, French, Chinese, Japanese and English, though at present there is only one of the latter here as the rest have gone to China on account of trouble between England and Russia."[92] Early the next morning, the remainder of the regiment disembarked.

Though disappointed at missing the action, the 1st Montana nevertheless learned that American troops probably would remain in the Philippines until the Spanish raised a $150 million indemnity. On hearing this news, Sgt. Fisk remarked: "I imagine [this] means that we may spend the rest of our natural lives in this part of the country."[93]

Assigned to the First Brigade in the First Division of the Eighth Army Corps, the regiment moved into old Spanish barracks. With 15- to 24-feet-thick walls on the seaward side and 6-feet walls facing a parade ground, the 1st Montana men thought themselves lucky to have the best sleeping quarters available in this tropical area. During the first nights, men from the regiment guarded wreckage of the Spanish fleet in the harbor to discourage scavenging Filipinos. Dillon's Company E under Captain Andrew Jensen was assigned guard duty the first night. They killed two Filipinos and wounded three others. The next morning, regular army personnel commended Company E, noting that units from California and Oregon had been on guard duty for the past few weeks and thieves ravaged the wrecks nightly. On August 25, a board of inquiry investigated the killing of the Filipinos by Company E and found the circumstances justifiable. According to a statement of one of the prisoners, they did not understand the English expression to surrender.[94]

The Philippines situation had changed considerably since the start of the conflict. On April 24, one day before the United States declared war on Spain, Commodore George Dewey received orders to sail to the Philippines. Dewey's seven ships arrived in Manila Bay on the night of April 30. The following morning, his warships destroyed the seven outmoded vessels of the Spanish fleet. Unable to take Manila with the 1,700 troops accompanying his squadron, Dewey sought the aid of the long-time Filipino revolutionary leader, Emilio Aguinaldo, in pinning down the Spanish in Manila. Aguinaldo's Filipino army, meanwhile, was in the process of conquering the rest of Luzon from Spanish garrisons. For the next two months, as additional U.S. troops began arriving in the Philippines, Dewey's forces and Aguinaldo's soldiers kept the Spaniards at bay. Finally, by late July, General Wesley Merritt with an American force growing to 15,000 joined the Filipinos in laying siege around Manila.[95]

Aware of the hopelessness of the situation, Spain ordered its troops to offer token, but honorable, resistance before surrendering. On the morning of August 13, the Eighth Corps advanced through entrenchments toward the Spanish lines. By prior secret arrangement, the Spanish were expected to surrender only to the Americans, and not to the Filipino army. However, unidentified personnel—perhaps Filipino—began firing into the Spanish lines. Token resistance suddenly erupted into a pitched battle. The Eighth Corps commanders eventually brought the melee under control, but 17 Americans were killed and 105 wounded.

The formal surrender of the garrison came two days after Madrid's agreeing to an armistice with the United States. Just four days earlier, Aguinaldo, who envisioned an independent Philippines, petitioned various foreign governments for recognition.[96] While the United States and Spain negotiated a final peace treaty, Aguinaldo became increasingly suspicious of American intentions and established a provisional government at Malolos, 20 miles north of Manila.

For the next two months, the newly arrived 1st Montana occupied Cavite, south of Manila, and guarded Spanish prisoners of war. The quarters in the Spanish fort, initially considered the best in the vicinity, began to pose problems. As tropical rains saturated Luzon, the fort's dampened walls caused illnesses. A Great Falls artificer in Company A, John C. Adams, died of typhoid fever on September 1, followed by Private Cary A. Sayler four days later; Private William C. O'Leary of Company I succumbed to spinal meningitis the same day as Sayler's death. By the end of October, Private Daniel McElliott of Company A and Private Walter J. McLean of Company L also passed away. In addition, 1st Lt. Edgar S. Paxson from Company C, the noted Montana artist, became so ill that he

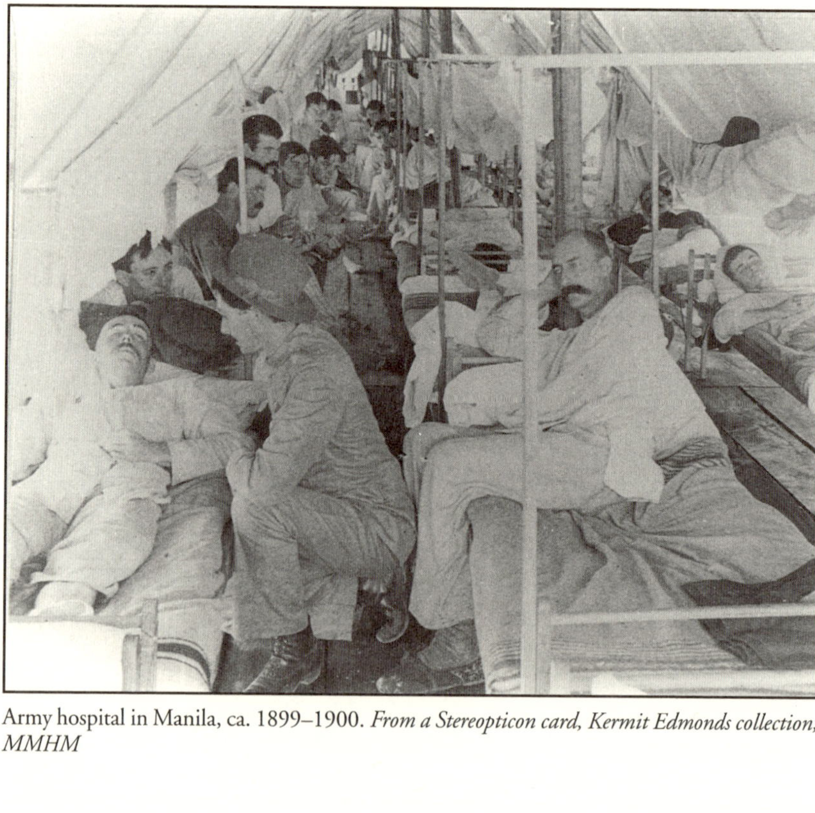

Army hospital in Manila, ca. 1899–1900. *From a Stereopticon card, Kermit Edmonds collection, MMHM*

was forced to return to the states on October 15, and was mustered out of the service.[97]

As tensions between U.S. and Filipino forces mounted on the outskirts of Manila, General Merritt ordered the 1st Montana into the city. With the entire regiment reassigned to the Second Division, the First and Second battalions transferred to Manila on October 24 (the Third Battalion later joined them on February 4, 1899). Fourteen days later, the 1st Montana assumed its place in the American line on the outskirts of the city, facing entrenched Filipino forces. To the regiment's left, next to Manila Bay to the north, stood the 20th Kansas and the 3rd U.S. Artillery. To the Montana men's right, the 10th Pennsylvania, 1st South Dakota, 1st Colorado, and 1st Nebraska extended to the Pasig River. Continuing across the river, the 1st Washington, 1st Idaho, 1st California, 14th U.S. Infantry, and 1st North Dakota maintained defensive positions stretching to the bay south of Manila.[98]

> **Patron Obligations**
>
> Frequently disparaged by American soldiers, the Filipinos nevertheless could be able fighters, though they often were under-armed. Initially for many Filipinos, however, their participation in the insurgency was largely due to their societal obligations as servants and followers of the oligarchs, big landowners, and tribal chieftains of the country's complex, traditional, patron system. Consequently, most commoners would not go so far as to adhere to a fight-to-the-last tradition for their more determined leaders. Under these circumstances, American combat forces could apply direct frontal attacks to good effect.
>
> For most individual Filipino fighters, their loyalty to a local community and affiliation with one of a myriad of tribes was paramount. A widespread sense of a "national" Philippines consciousness, on the other hand, was only in a seminal stage at this time.

Little happened over the coming weeks, other than the insurgents shouting epithets at the American in the trenches. Then, after the signing of a final peace treaty by Spain and the United States on December 10, 1898, word that America purchased the Philippines for $20 million infuriated the Filipino forces. General Otis, now in overall command of the American army, expressed a growing concern when he wired Adjutant General Henry Corbin on January 11, 1899. "Insurgent forces have increased in number, still threaten attack, and rising," he warned.[99] At this early stage in the insurgency, the Filipino forces, utilizing weapons confiscated from the Spanish, were somewhat better armed than American troops, though this changed later on.

Two days later, the 1st Montana confronted Filipinos advancing with their rifles leveled toward Company E's position. This kind of bravado was traditional in Filipino tribal and patron/servant societal affairs. Commands to halt went unheeded. A squad of Americans, posted 150 yards in advance of the regiment's line, fell back since they had orders not to fire. Within a half hour, General Otis and members of MacArthur's staff met with the Filipino commander and restored order.[100]

Nevertheless, by now the long monotony of guard duty and inaction had taken hold. Many 1st Montana men wondered whether their time would be better spent if they returned home. On January 2, Quartermaster Sgt. Charles R. Sutton from Helena had written to the governor: "I have the honor to inclose [sic] herewith a partition [sic] circulated throughout the Montana Regt. in the past two days."[101] Claiming that 80 percent of the regiment signed the petition, Sutton requested that the governor use his influence to bring the 1st Montana back to the United States.

By the time Sutton's letter reached Governor Smith's desk, however, the Philippine Insurrection, or Philippine-American War (1899–1902), began with the Battle of Manila, the first and largest engagement of the conflict. On the night of February 2, Filipinos positioned in front of the 1st Montana fired two shots at Company B sentries. The regiment immediately deployed skirmishers from companies B and G, then on duty, but the night ended without incident. "There has been a great deal of friction along the lines in the past two days," General Otis reported to Admiral Dewey, "and we will be unable to tamely submit to the insulting conduct and threatening demonstrations of these insurgents much longer."[102]

On the night of February 4, companies M and I, with Captain John Hallahan in command, were on duty in the lines. At approximately 8:20 p.m., Hallahan heard shots in the distance and reported this to the officer of the day (a 10th Pennsylvania soldier). Initially both officers believed it might be firecrackers. Actually, Private William W. Grayson on patrol in front of the 1st Nebraska had shot the first insurgent of the outbreak. Moments later, Filipino bugles blared as gunfire spread along the line.

Sgt. Michael Henry, a sentry on the 1st Regiment's left flank, was the first Montana soldier to be fired upon by the insurgents, and the first to return fire. As companies M and I became engaged, they withdrew slowly. As the only Montana companies currently assigned to the line, they maintained contact on both sides—with the 3rd U.S. Artillery on the left and the 10th Pennsylvania to the right—but their line was spread thin. The two companies reached a cemetery and held off a tenacious Filipino advance until reinforcements arrived. The cemetery offered good protection as companies L and C joined the fighting. Meanwhile, on the far-left flank of the American line near Manila Bay, Company G fought alongside the 20th Kansas. Despite the piecemeal attacks throughout the night, the 1st Montana suffered no casualties.[103]

At daybreak on February 5, General MacArthur received permission to take the initiative with big gun support from Dewey's fleet in the bay. In the Montana sector, Captain James Keown and a squad from Company C moved out in advance of the line to torch several huts shielding the enemy. As companies M and I advanced 1,000 yards, Captain William L. Hill and a squad from Company F reconnoitered on the extreme left. Earlier that morning, the Nebraska,

Colorado, and South Dakota volunteers had advanced on the right with little resistance. Movement on the left, however, became more difficult; facing the 1st Montana and the 10th Pennsylvania was steep-sloped La Loma Hill, on which stood a Chinese cemetery and the La Loma Church surrounded by a rock wall. The Filipinos entrenched there had several muzzle-loading cannon aimed at the American lines.[104]

American artillery bombarded the hill for a half-hour, after which the 3rd U.S. Artillery, 1st Montana, and the 10th Pennsylvania made an advance. Well entrenched, the Filipinos poured devastating fire into the Pennsylvania troops. The 3rd Artillery and the Montana regiment suffered casualties, but they managed to take the hill. In total, the 1st Montana had six wounded, two of them dying later. Company G, which fought the night before with the 20th Kansas, remained with that regiment and advanced through the jungle nearly two miles.

"We are still driving enemy and think we shall punish him severely," General Otis wired Washington, D.C., later that evening. "Troops enthusiastic and acting fearlessly."[105] The first engagement of the Philippine Insurrection had proved that the Eighth Corps' volunteer units could withstand a frontal assault. In the eyes of their regular army commanders, the excellent marksmanship of troops from the West gave them an edge when confronting the enemy.[106]

Over the next few days, units of the Eighth Corps moved slowly forward with little opposition. However, the situation soon became much more heated. At this time, Harry Paxson, a 17-year-old bugler with Company G and the son

A 1st Montana battalion advances across an open field in Luzon, Philippine Islands, 1899. *From a Stereopticon card, Kermit Edmonds collection, MMHM*

of artist Edgar S. Paxson, was fighting alongside the 20th Kansas. He wrote to his parents: "We have been 66 hours on the battlefield up to just now, 15 of them under continuous fire." Paxson added: "War to us is a picnic. By the help of God, we are brave."[107]

During the night of February 9, the Filipinos attacked the 1st Montana on the outskirts of the town of Caloocan. "The woods came down in front of us pretty close to our line," wrote Private Edward Harvey of Company F, and "we sent volley after volley crashing into these woods." The attack began at 9 p.m., and by daybreak, Harvey noted, "my shoulder was sore from shooting, and I was cramped from lying in the rifle pit."[108]

An all-out assault on Caloocan began on the morning of February 10 after a heavy barrage from Dewey's fleet. As soon as the U.S. Navy finished, the 1st Montana fired three volleys and advanced on the Filipino line. "As we climbed over our trenches, everybody put down his head and went like the very devil," Private Harvey wrote. "Down inclines, up again, through gulches and thick brush, across the railroad track and back again and on to the enemy's line."[109] At intervals in the advance, the regiment dropped to the ground and fired volleys into the Filipino defenses. About 75 yards from the enemy, Lt. Col. Wallace fell. Shot in the chest, the bullet passed through his left lung and out his back, but he survived.[110]

Before the regiment launched the assault, each soldier was issued 250 rounds of ammunition. Knowing they would be running in the attack, the troops had discarded everything they could, except their rifles and extra cartridges. Bayonets and scabbards were left behind, which caught in the brush or jammed into a man's side as he hit the ground. "From the sprinting abilities of the natives too," Sgt. Fisk later bantered, "the men concluded they wouldn't need bayonets anyway, and I guess they were about right."[111]

As the 1st Montana approached the insurgent line, the enemy fell back. "Three cheers for the Montanans," a Utah battery shouted.[112] As the Filipino retreat became complete, companies B, F, K, and L, which had been stationed in the rear as the reserve, joined the full regiment in the charge. At this point, General MacArthur's aide approached Col. Kessler. "The general's compliments, but your regiment is in advance of the firing line and it is supposed

Harry Slack, Tom Anderson, and Asa Fisk (l. to r.) occupy earth breastworks adjacent to their tent bivouac in a rice paddy, 1899. *MHS, MMHM*

to be in the reserve," he explained. "My compliments to the general," replied Col. Kessler, "and tell him to bring up the firing line."[113]

The retreating Filipinos set Caloocan ablaze, but the heat from the burning houses failed to slow the onrushing regiment. After pursuing the Filipinos for nearly two miles, the 1st Montana returned to Caloocan. Remarkably, the only Montanan killed was Private Fred Hall of Company I. In an initial report, General H.G. Otis listed 14 men wounded from the 1st Montana, but he amended his report on the following day to 21 wounded.[114]

The 1st Montana remained in the line on the outskirts of Caloocan for nearly 1½ months. The duty proved tedious and dangerous; tents had to be pitched in the trenches because Filipino snipers shot into the American lines from the rear as well as in front. Sniper fire over the next few weeks claimed the life of Private Henry Beecher of Company C and wounded 19 others. Eleven of these casualties occurred the day before the regiment resumed its advance toward Malolos.

Private Tommy Dunn. *MMHM*

Among the wounded were 1st Lt. Philip Greenan, who later became Montana's adjutant general, and Private "Tommy" Dunn. A Mauser bullet struck Dunn between the left eye and ear, passed through his skull, and exited between the right ear and eye. Just minutes after Tommy was shot, his brother, Private John Dunn from Company C, came to his aid. While tending to Tommy, he too was wounded in the hand and leg. Miraculously, Tommy Dunn survived the gunshot through his brain, remaining unconscious for only a few minutes. However, he lost sight in one eye and never was the same mentally. The injury required his return to the United States. For reasons not clearly understood, Dunn spent several months in a San Francisco guardhouse, but arrived in Helena on July 17, 1899, to a hero's welcome.[115]

On February 23, Filipinos slipped through the American lines and attacked Manila. In response, units from various commands were sent back to locate and neutralize the attackers. A Company L squad, commanded by Lt. Eugene S. French, came upon some insurgents, who raised a white flag of truce. French ordered his men to cease firing. He approached the rebels, assuring them of safety, when one of them raised a rifle and fired, killing French instantly. The lieutenant had been a prominent member of the Helena community and the "exalted ruler" of the local Elks Lodge. The night before the 1st Montana departed for San Francisco, French had addressed the Helena Elks. His remarks proved to be grimly prophetic when warning, "some of us may never return."[116]

On the night of March 24, the 1st Montana, now with a combined strength of 42 officers and 796 enlisted men, set out to help capture the Filipino army's provisional capital at Malolos. Miraculously, Lt. Col. Wallace, shot through the lungs at Caloocan in the previous month, was hospitalized for only nine days. He now returned, leading companies C, H, and K advancing on the left flank. Wallace remained with the regiment through the rest of its tour, but he struggled with labored breathing from the wound to his chest. The enemy was positioned in bamboo thickets along the banks of the Tuliahan River. Despite intense fire from the Filipinos, the regiment managed to ford the river and take the enemy works, where they rested until the next day. Losses in that action totaled 5 dead and 16 wounded. Among the injured was Private Thomas Rickards of Company D, the son of the former governor.[117]

The regiment resumed its march the next morning northward toward Polo. In the distance, smoke rose from villages set afire by retreating Filipinos. Throughout this day's march, the 1st Montana had little contact with the enemy, save an occasional sniper's bullet. Maj. Francis J. Adams, the regimental surgeon, was the victim of a Filipino sharpshooter when he fell wounded while attending to a soldier. More than anything, the men suffered from the intense heat. By nightfall, the Montanans reached the outskirts of Polo where they camped for the night in trenches deserted by the Filipinos.

Company L (Helena) firing a volley at Filipino insurrectionists at Bataan—"So much firing the Springfields got hot clear through." Smoke from black powder cartridges was detrimental to any effort in position concealment. *MMHM*

On March 27, General H.G. Otis assigned the 1st Montana to the reserve, while the 3rd U.S. Artillery took the lead. After another day of marching in the heat, the regiment reached the Marilao River only to find the bridge destroyed. Throughout the night, Montana troops under the direction of the Corps of Engineers constructed a pontoon bridge, enabling the Americans to cross the river the next morning and proceed on toward Malolos. Approaching the town by March 30 proved costly. Despite performing reserve duty, the 1st Montana suffered 1 killed and 16 wounded.[118]

MacArthur and Otis anticipated that the Filipino army would mount a strong defense of their capital, thus the generals ordered an artillery barrage for the next morning. Following the bombardment, the division advanced with the 20th Kansas on the right, the 1st Montana in the center, and the 3rd U.S. Artillery to the left. Overwhelmed during weeks of continuous American assaults, the Filipinos were demoralized. As the Second Brigade approached Malolos, the natives fled after setting the town ablaze. "The boys just rushed those trenches and flopped through those swamps in magnificent style," wrote Corporal Wilmer Brinton to his parents, "while the fire of the insurgents was as poor as could be."[119]

Since the Montanans were nearest Malolos, General Otis ordered them to occupy the town. "A Montana man was the first to raise the glorious Stars and Stripes over the domed capital," remarked Brinton.[120] The flag was from Company G. Facing only slight resistance, the entire division's losses for the day consisted of 1 killed and 15 wounded, with the 1st Montana taking no casualties. Otis later noted the gallant conduct of Col. Kessler.[121]

In an attempt to ascertain the direction of the insurgents' retreat, MacArthur issued new instructions to the 1st Montana. Strengthened by two 3.2 field pieces and a 1-inch Colt automatic gun borrowed from the U.S.S. *Helena* and manned by Lt. Cleland Davis, U.S.N., the regiment undertook a reconnaissance of the Bagbag River locality. The Montanans encountered strong resistance near the stream, prompting MacArthur to order them back to Malolos where they remained a couple of weeks.

The time spent in Malolos soon became tedious and the regiment longed for more action. Their spirits were raised with issuance of the Norwegian-designed Krag-Jorgensen .30 caliber, five-shot magazine rifle. Only 25 of these new weapons were assigned to each company, but they significantly increased the regiment's firepower and range.[122]

On the morning of April 24, the 20th Kansas and the 1st Montana renewed the advance toward the Bagbag River. By following railroad tracks, the attackers were backed by an armored railroad car with Gatling guns and four cannon. The Second Brigade dislodged the enemy fairly easily, but a river crossing was delayed until the engineers repaired a bridge. The next morning, the brigade approached the Rio Grande de Pampanga River. Here, the main body of the Filipino army, after crossing over and destroying a bridge, lay in wait on the other side.[123]

On the morning of April 27, two men handpicked by Col. Frederick Funston of the 20th Kansas swam the Rio Grande and secured a rope to the opposite bank. Col. Funston and 43 men then crossed the river and established an enfilading fire on the enemy. Heroic efforts by this small band of 20th Kansas soldiers pushed the enemy back far enough to allow the 1st Montana to cross the stream on the destroyed bridge's framework. Once over, they drove the enemy from Apalit Station, taking up a position there for a week. On May 4, the men next took the town of Santo Tomas and marched into San Fernando two days later.[124]

Stationed on the west end of the city for several weeks, the 1st Montana fended off minor attacks on its outposts. Writing in his diary, Private Alexander Robertson from Lewistown's Company I seemed more concerned about mosquitoes than the enemy. Things changed dramatically, however, on the morning of May 24. During the night, the enemy completely surrounded San Fernando. "Everything was very quiet last night till about 6:30 this morning," wrote Robertson, "when we were suddenly attacked by the natives, they advanced on our outpost but were eventually driven back."[125] At the sound of rifle fire, Col. Kessler alerted the entire regiment. A company led by Lt. Col. Wallace and seven companies from the 20th Kansas outflanked the enemy and pursued the Filipinos for some distance. Sporadic firing on the American outposts continued, but the insurgents did not mount an all-out attack again for three weeks.[126]

At daybreak on June 16, the 1st Montana awoke to the sound of artillery shells crashing into camp as the enemy attacked on all sides of San Fernando. "I tell you," Private Robertson penned, "we were in a hot-place for awhile amidst shell and bullets galore."[127] After about an hour of intense action, the insurgent fire weakened as American artillery began to take a toll. Following the assault, General MacArthur instructed his troops to gather the Filipino dead in the center of town, where the corpses were displayed at the cemetery for the locals to see.[128]

At this juncture, after more than five months of combat, the campaign was ending for the 1st Montana. The regiment was nearing the end of its enlistment period and would be replaced by other units. The regiment returned to Cavite, where it began making preparations for departure from the Philippines.

The fighting in the Philippines, however, did not cease, and continued until July 1902. By early 1900, with the defeat of the Filipino army in the field, the conflict took a darker turn as a guerilla war, with a subsequent rise in harsher tactics and retributions among the combatants. An American victory and the lessening of tensions eventually came about for several reasons—the concentration of Filipino civilians in large camps, the cutting of the rebels' supply system, relentless pursuit of insurgents by "flying columns" of U.S. troops, effective assistance by America's Filipino allies, and the U.S. Navy's control of the coasts.

The 1st Montana Infantry Canteen (at right), on San Miguel Street, Manila. *MMHM*

Long-term resolution also was due to non-military developments, particularly the establishment of community, education, and health services for the population, the redistribution of land, and the incorporation of the Filipino mercantile classes into the colony's new economic, social, and political order, along with a mutual U.S.-Filipino goal of eventually allowing national independence.

Armed clashes, retributions, and especially cholera and other diseases had taken a staggering toll on the population—over 200,000 deaths. Some scattered guerilla outbreaks continued into 1913 involving revolutionaries and religious cults. Resistance especially continued in the southern islands, where the Muslim Moros opposed the American banning of slavery and abduction of women.

After the summer of 1899, some Montana soldiers wished to remain in the Philippines to continue campaigning. Consequently, a number of officers and 62 enlisted men signed up with new "U.S. Volunteer" regiments. Eventually, over 40 such regiments were formed by the U.S. Army. Promoted to the rank of colonel, Robert Wallace assumed command of the 37th U.S. Volunteer Infantry. Montana officers transferring with Wallace to the 37th included captains William B. Hanna, Albert J. Erickson, and John E. Moran, and lieutenants Daniel T. Bowman and Ernest V.D. Murphy. Both Erickson and Murphy had risen through the ranks to become officers, and Captain Moran went on to win the Medal of Honor. The 37th U.S. Volunteer Infantry and other veteran volunteer regiments were strictly federal and not affiliated with any state. This arrangement reflected the long simmering dissatisfaction of the War Department and the regular army over individual states and their governors traditionally having jurisdiction over militia and National Guard units. By the formation of "U.S. Volunteer" regiments, control of these volunteer soldiers shifted strictly to federal direction.

Robert Wallace, still suffering from the chest wound received at Caloocan, soon became too ill to serve and eventually returned to the United States to recuperate. On the way to Fort Huachuca, Arizona, Wallace's condition worsened. He died on March 13, 1900, and his body was sent to Helena for a city-wide public funeral. His imposing tombstone remains today in the Evergreen Cemetery. The army listed the cause of death as acute bronchitis and stenosis of the left bronchus associated with the gunshot wound sustained in action on February 10, 1899. At the time of his death, Wallace reportedly was the youngest colonel in the army.

In addition to the officers who joined the 37th U.S. Volunteer Infantry, Captain Frank Green signed on with the 11th U.S. Volunteer Cavalry, and captains Charles W. Mead and Charles French transferred into the 36th U.S. Volunteer Infantry. Ninety other enlisted men and two officers received their discharges in Manila so they could remain in the Philippines. Nine remained because they were too sick to travel.[129]

As the Montana men prepared to embark for home, Maj. James W. Drennan languished in a hospital at Malate. Drennan had been serving as Montana's adjutant general prior to the war and resigned that position to serve in the Philippines with the 1st Montana Infantry. After the Caloocan battle, Drennan contracted

Wallace funeral procession in Helena, with the coffin resting on a caisson provided by Helena's Battery A, March 25, 1900. Both National Guard and U.S. Army troops from Fort Harrison marched in commemoration of Col. Robert B. Wallace, who succumbed to a combat wound that would not heal. *MMHM*

Bright's disease. Doctors in the Philippines urged him to return to the United States to recuperate, but Drennan refused, insisting he would "go home with the regiment or die."[130] On June 24, two months before the regiment left the Philippines, Maj. Drennan passed away.

The transports *Valencia* and *Zealandia* arrived on August 8, 1899, to carry the 1st Montana back to the United States after a full year of service in the Philippines. The regiment boarded on August 18, but a typhoon delayed departure. On August 23, the two ships finally left port. The *Zealandia* carried 16 officers and 324 enlisted men of companies D, E, G, H, K, and M. Companies A, B, C, F, I, and L—24 officers and 339 enlisted men—sailed on the *Valencia*. After refueling and refitting stops at Nagasaki and Yokohama, Japan, the 1st Montana arrived in San Francisco on September 22.[131]

While the 1st Montana steamed toward home, a Montana woman in the Bay area, Mabel Pace, wrote to Governor Smith inquiring if he intended to meet the men on their return. "San Francisco patriotism and enthusiasm is going to be at a low ebb," Pace wrote, "and I don't know what two forlorn Montana women can do by their lone selves to make a welcome."[132] Smith did his duty. Before the regiment disembarked from their San Francisco docking, Governor Smith and his staff, accompanied by former Governor Rickards, Senator Carter, and other prominent Montanans, boarded the *Valencia* and *Zealandia* to welcome the men home. The 1st Montana also received word that Col. Kessler had been promoted to brevet brigadier general.[133]

The 1st Montana mustered out at San Francisco on October 17, and two days later the regiment boarded trains for the trip home. On October 23, the men arrived in Butte to an enthusiastic welcome. The 1st Montana marched through town, passing under an Arch of Triumph designed by Western artist E.S. Paxson, the former Company C officer who fell ill in Manila and was mustered out. At the juncture of Main and Granite streets, the 48-foot-high double arch of painted canvas and wood extended across the entire intersection. On top stood a 14-foot-high Statue of Peace holding a wreath in one hand and an olive branch in the other. Illumination was

The Arch of Triumph in Butte, erected in celebration of returning Montana soldiers, October 1899. *MMHM*

provided by 800 red, white, and blue light bulbs. At the conclusion of the parade, the 1st Montana Volunteer Regiment stood in formation for the last time. The governor then presented each soldier with a ribboned, silver-plated, medal bearing the inscription, "First to respond to their country's call."[134]

Earlier in the year, on April 15, Lt. Eugene French's remains had arrived in Helena and lay in state at the city's auditorium. That same afternoon, the *Daily Independent* paid homage to French, shot under a flag of truce, and to the other 1st Montana men who at that time still manned firing lines in the Philippines.

"Montana, in proportion to her population," the *Daily Independent* explained, "sent forth to fight the battle of free institutions a greater number of her sons than any other state of the American union."[135]

After the declaration of war on April 25, 1898, the Montana National Guard had been one of the first state militias to offer its service to the nation. In the Philippines fighting, the 1st Montana suffered 1 officer killed, 9 officers wounded, and 1 officer dying from disease. Among the enlisted ranks, 12 died in action, 111 were wounded, 8 died from wounds, 14 succumbed to disease, and 1 drowned.

Prior to the Spanish-American War, many politicians and regular army theorists questioned the National Guard's ability to serve efficiently as reserve troops for the U.S. Army. America's first large-scale overseas military operations had proven that the guard could respond in force and act effectively. Over two-thirds of the nation's soldiers participating in the conflict came from state militias. Altogether, nearly 125,000 Americans served in the Philippines alone. Problems had emerged with mobilization and equipping this force, but these disruptions largely originated with an unprepared War Department crippled by a long-term lack of federal funds and support. With lessons now learned, the U.S. military and Congress began considering reforms to insure military preparedness in the early 20th century.

Indeed, the citizens of the state had unselfishly responded to their nation's call, and many more offered their services than could be accommodated. A number of the veterans of the 1st Montana Volunteer Regiment now returned to the state militia ranks. With the experience gained in the Philippines, these veterans sought to reinvigorate the Montana National Guard as it entered a new phase of development.[136]

Notes

1. Graham A. Cosmas, *An Army for Empire: The United States Army in the Spanish-American War* (Columbia: University of Missouri Press, 1971), 12; William H. Riker, *Soldiers of the States: The Role of the National Guard in American Democracy* (Washington, D.C.: Public

Affairs Press, 1957), 63; Jerry Cooper, *The Rise of the National Guard: The Evolution of the American Militia, 1865–1920* (Lincoln: University of Nebraska Press, 1997), 96–97.

2. Michael H. Hunt, *Ideology and U.S. Foreign Policy* (New Haven: Yale University Press, 1987), 36–37; Center of Military History [hereafter cited as CMH], *American Military History* (Washington, D.C.: Center of Military History, U.S. Army, 1989), 319.
3. Ibid.
4. Ibid., 321; William Thaddeus Sexton, *Soldiers in the Sun: An Adventure in Imperialism* (Freeport, New York: Books for Libraries Press, 1939), 17; Murat Halstead, *Full Official History of the War with Spain* (Chicago: W.S. Reeve Publishing, 1899), 210–13; Lewis L. Gould, *The Spanish-American War and President McKinley* (Lawrence: University of Kansas Press, 1980). Often criticized at the time by political opponents and fervent imperialists as an indecisive, irresolute individual frequently controlled by big-money interests, President McKinley has gained new favor among modern historians as a master of diplomacy seeking expansion without war.
5. CMH, *American Military History,* 321; Cosmas, *An Army for Empire*, 72.
6. CMH, *American Military History*, 322.
7. *Congressional Record*, 55th Congress, 2nd Sess, April 11, 1898, 3699–3702.
8. Halstead, *History of the War with Spain*, 244–45; Hunt, *Ideology and U.S. Foreign Policy*, 37–41.
9. *Congressional Record*, 55th Cong, 2nd Sess, 4228–4229, 4244.
10. Helena *Evening Herald*, January 24, 1898.
11. Ibid., February 16, 1898.
12. Charles H. Brown, *The Correspondents' War: Journalists in the Spanish-American War* (New York: Charles Scribner's Sons, 1967), 122–23.
13. Helena *Evening Herald*, April 8, 1898.
14. Captain J.C. Bond to Governor Robert B. Smith [telegram], February 21, 1898, Box 26, Folder 12, Governor Robert B. Smith Papers, Manuscript Collection 35a, Montana Historical Society, Helena, Montana [hereafter cited as Smith Papers, MC 35a, MHS].
15. Governor Robert B. Smith to Captain J.C. Bond, February 21, 1989, Box 26, Folder 12, Smith Papers, MC 35a, MHS.
16. Governor Robert B. Smith to Col. C.F. Lloyd, February 21, 1898, Box 26, Folder 12, Smith Papers, MC 35a, MHS.
17. Governor Robert B. Smith to Emmett Callahan, April 2, 1898, Box 26, Folder 13, Smith Papers, MC 35a, MHS.
18. Tom D. Cooney to Governor Robert B. Smith, April 12, 1898, Box 26, Folder 13, Smith Papers, MC 35a, MHS.
19. Adjutant General James W. Drennan to Governor Robert B. Smith, April 20, 1898, Box 26, Folder 13, Smith Papers, MC 35a, MHS.
20. Cooper, *Rise of the National Guard,* 91–92, 98; Frederick Louis Huidekoper, *The Military Unpreparedness of the United States: A History of Land Forces from Colonial Times until June 1, 1915* (New York: MacMillan, 1915), xi; Jerry Cooper and Glenn Smith, *Citizens as Soldiers: A History of the North Dakota National Guard* (Fargo: North Dakota Institute for Regional Studies, North Dakota State University, 1986), 36–37; *U.S. Statutes at Large* 30:361–63.
21. Governor Robert B. Smith to Senator Thomas H. Carter, April 21, 1898, Senator Thomas H. Carter to Governor Robert B. Smith, April 21, 1898, Box 26, Folder 13, Smith Papers, MC 35a, MHS.
22. *U.S. Statutes at Large* 30:361–63.

23. *Billings Gazette*, June 23, 1940.
24. *Report of the Adjutant General, 1897–1898*, 6.
25. *Billings Gazette*, June 23, 1940.
26. 1st Lt. R.B. Wallace to Regimental Adjutant, Second U.S. Cavalry, June 23, 1898, Drawer 2, Lt. Robert Bruce Wallace Papers, Montana Military History Museum, Library Archives, Building T-15, Fort William H. Harrison, Helena, Montana [hereafter cited as MMHM, LA, Bldg. T-15, Fort Harrison].
27. W.M. Leighton to Governor Smith, April 23, 1898, Box 26, Folder 14, Smith Papers, MC 35a, MHS.
28. Governor Smith to W.M. Leighton, April 27, 1898, Box 26, Folder 14, Smith Papers, MC 35a, MHS.
29. The major part of Mrs. Sherman's concern related to the luxurious lifestyle of the prison warden, and her belief that emptying the prison would put him out of a job. Mrs. M.F. Sherman to Governor Smith, April 19, 1898, Box 29, Folder 3, Smith Papers, MC 35a, MHS. The misuse of state funds by the prison warden seems to have been a recurring problem. For years to come, some residents of the state expressed concern over financial mishandling by Warden Frank Conley, who assumed control of the prison at the turn of the century. At one point, Conley purchased a $30,000 home on an annual salary of $5,000. On January 19, 1922, State Attorney General Wellington Rankin filed charges against the warden. After one of the most costly trials in the state's history, the court exonerated Conley of any wrongdoing. Richard Hines, "Wellington Duncan Rankin: The Man behind the Myth," (M.A. thesis, Washington State University, 1996), 55–61.
30. Governor Smith to Mrs. M.F. Sherman, April 30, 1898, Box 29, Folder 3, Smith Papers, MC 35a, MHS.
31. Miss Carrie Waefer to Governor Smith, May 12, 1898, Governor Smith to Miss Carrie Waefer, May 13, 1898, Box 27, Folder 4, Smith Papers, MC 35a, MHS.
32. Secretary of War Russell A. Alger to Governor Smith [telegram] April 15, 1898, Box 29, Folder 6, Smith Papers, MC 35a, MHS. When President McKinley sent telegrams to each of the states to announce their quotas, he suggested that these numbers be filled by the "regiments of the National Guard or State Militia." Although most of the governors adhered to the president's request, Governor John Leedy of Kansas totally bypassed the guard hierarchy and recruited volunteers from the general population. Other governors selected officers from outside of the guard structure. Cooper, *Rise of the National Guard.*
33. Governor Smith to R.A. Alger [telegram], April 26, 1898; Adjutant General [hereafter cited as AG] Henry C. Corbin to Governor Smith [telegram], April 27, 1898, Box 29, Folder 6, Smith Papers, MC 35a, MHS.
34. Senator Thomas Carter to Governor Smith [telegram], April 26, 1898, Governor Smith to Secretary of War Alger [telegram], April 28, 1898, AG Corbin telegram to Governor Smith, April 29, 1898, Box 29, Folder 6, Smith Papers, MC 35a, MHS.
35. Lt. Alexander Laist, "Official History of the Operations of the First Montana Infantry, U.S.V. in the Campaign in the Philippine Islands," in *Campaigning in the Philippines* by Karl Irving Faust (San Francisco: Hicks-Judd, 1899), 3; *Helena Independent*, April 28, 1898.
36. Laist, "Official History…of the First Montana," 4; AG Corbin to Governor Smith [telegram], May 5, 1898, Box 29, Folder 6, Smith Papers, MC35a, MHS.
37. Laist, "Official History…of the First Montana," 4.
38. AG Corbin to Governor Smith [telegram], April 27, 1898, Box 29, Folder 6, Smith Papers, MC 35a, MHS.

39. Forms for the Physical Examination of a Recruit, Drawer 2, Captain Charles F. Morrison Papers, MMHM, LA, Bldg. T-15, Fort Harrison; *Adjutant General Report, 1897–1898*, 29.
40. AG Corbin to Governor Smith [telegram], May 9, 1898, Box 29, Folder 6, Smith Papers, MC35a, MHS.
41. Governor Smith to AG Corbin [telegram], May 9, 1898, Box 29, Folder 6, Smith Papers, MC 35a, MHS.
42. *Adjutant General's Report, 1897–1898*, 14.
43. John E. Rickards to Governor Smith, July 26, 1898, Box 29, Folder 6, Smith Papers, MC 35a, MHS.
44. Russell A. Alger, *The Spanish-American War* (Freeport, New York: Books for Libraries Press, 1971), 7.
45. Nankeen cloth originated in China and is a brownish-yellow cotton fabric. Erna Risch, *Quartermaster Support of the Army: A History of the Corps, 1775–1939* (Washington, D.C.: Center of Military History, U.S. Army, 1989), 516, 524.
46. Unknown newspaper article, Drawer 2, Flag Presentation, 1st Montana Regiment Folder, MMHM, LA, Bldg. T-15, Fort Harrison; *Laws, Resolutions, and Memorials of the State of Montana Passed at the 9th Regular Session of the Legislative Assembly, Helena,* 1905.
47. Helena *Weekly Herald*, May, 19, 1898 (typed facsimile on 3x5 card), Drawer 2, Flag Presentation, 1st Montana Regiment Folder, MMHM, LA, Bldg. T-15, Fort Harrison.
48. Helena *Weekly Herald*, May 26, 1898 (typed facsimile on 3x5 card), Drawer 2, Mascot Dewey Folder, MMHM, LA, Bldg T-15, Fort Harrison.
49. Bozeman *Avant Courier*, May 28, 1898 (typed facsimile on 3x5 card), Drawer 2, Mascot Dewey Folder, MMHM, LA, Bldg. T-15, Fort Harrison.
50. *Helena Independent*, May 25, 1898 (typed facsimile on 3x5 card), Drawer 2, Mascot Dewey Folder, MMHM, LA, Bldg. T-15, Fort Harrison.
51. *Anaconda Standard*, May 25, 1898.
52. Ibid.
53. Governor Smith to Senator Carter, April 28, 1898 [telegram], Box 26, Folder 14, Smith Papers, MC 35a, MHS.
54. Senators Carter and Mantle to Governor Smith, May 4, 1898 [telegram], Box 27, Folder 2, Smith Papers, MC 35a, MHS.
55. Governor Smith to Secretary of War Alger, May 4, 1898 [telegram], Box 29, Folder 6, Smith Papers, MC 35a, MHS.
56. Senator Carter to Governor Smith, May 5, 1898 [telegram], Senator Mantle to Governor Smith, May 5, 1898 [telegram], Box 27, Folder 2, Smith Papers, MC 35a, MHS. Senator Mantle had been a long-time Butte resident. Senator "oily Tom" Carter had been an ally of Amalgamated Copper's Marcus Daly, and therefore had close ties to Butte.
57. *Adjutant General's Report, 1897–98*, 33–36.
58. Douglas R. Hartman, *Nebraska's Militia: The History of the Army and the Air National Guard, 1854–1991* (Virginia Beach, Virginia: Donning, 1994), 56; Cosmas, *An Army for Empire*, 107; *Correspondence Relating to the War with Spain, Including the Insurrection in the Philippine Islands and the China Relief Expedition, April 15, 1898, to July 30, 1902* (Washington, D.C.: Center of Military History, U.S. Army, 1993), 625.
59. Cosmas, *An Army for Empire*, 132, 137; *Correspondence Relating to the War with Spain*, 512.
60. Hartman, *Nebraska's Militia*, 56.
61. Quotation comes from Cosmas, *An Army for Empire*, 132.
62. Hartman, *Nebraska's Militia*, 56; *Quartermaster Support of the Army*, 541.

63. Senator Mantle to Secretary of War Alger, July 21, 1898 [telegram], *Correspondence Relating to the War with Spain*, 304; Senator Carter to Secretary of War Alger, July 29, 1898 [telegram], *Correspondence Relating to the War with Spain*, 330.
64. Senator Carter to Secretary of War Alger, August 6–7, 1898 [telegram], *Correspondence Relating to the War with Spain*, 362.
65. Ibid., 625; Circular: Montana Adjutant General's Office, 1903, 4.
66. *Butte Miner*, October 24, 1899; Helena *Daily Independent*, May 30, 1899; *Correspondence Relating to the War with Spain*, 624.
67. Helena *Daily Independent*, May 30, 1899.
68. Ibid.; *Butte Miner*, October 24, 1899.
69. *Correspondence Relating to the War with Spain*, 624; Helena *Daily Independent*, May 30, 1899.
70. Helena *Daily Independent*, July 5, 1898.
71. *Correspondence Relating to the War with Spain*, 561; Helena *Daily Independent*, March 10, 1899.
72. The islands of Negros, Panay, and Cebu are in the central part of the Philippines between the main islands of Luzon to the north and Mindanao at the south. Maj. Thompson to Signals, Washington, May 28, 1899 [telegram], *Correspondence Relating to the War with Spain*, 997.
73. General Otis to Agwar, Washington, D.C., May 30, 1899 [telegram], *Correspondence Relating to the War with Spain*, 998.
74. 2nd Lt. Alfred Clifton to Maj. R.E. Thompson, May 31, 1899, Drawer 2, Captain George Tilly, Signal Corps, U.S.V. Folder, MMHM, LA, Bldg. T-15, Fort Harrison.
75. General Otis to Agwar, Washington, D.C., June 1, 1899 [telegram], *Correspondence Relating to the War with Spain*, 999.
76. Maj. R.E. Thompson to Chief Signal Officer, U.S. Army, June 7, 1899, Drawer 2, Capt. George Tilly, Signal Corps, U.S.V. Folder, MMHM, LA, Bldg. T-15, Fort Harrison.
77. U.S. Army Center of Military History, Historical Resources Branch, "Spanish-American War: Volunteer Forces," www.army.mil/cmh-pg/documents/spanam/ws-stat.htm.
78. Sexton, *Soldiers in the Sun*, 22; Laist. "Official History…of the First Montana," 5; *Anaconda Standard*, Lt. Greenan Papers, MMHM, LA, Bldg. T-15, Fort Harrison.
79. Senators Carter and Mantle to President McKinley, June 2, 1898, Senator Mantle to President McKinley, June 16, 1898, Drawer 2, Col. Harry C. Kessler Folder, MMHM, LA, Bldg. T-15, Fort Harrison. Harry Clay Kessler served as a lieutenant with the 104th Pennsylvania Volunteers during the Civil War. After coming to Montana in 1875, Kessler established the *Butte Miner*. He joined the Montana National Guard in 1887, and held the rank of colonel in that organization until the beginning of the Spanish-American War. Laist, "Official History…of the First Montana," 39. General Harrison Gray Otis served with the 12th Ohio Infantry during the Civil War. Enlisting in June 1861 as a private, Otis rose through the ranks to become a lieutenant colonel by 1865. On May 27, 1898, Otis reenlisted as a brigadier general of volunteers and served in the Philippines until July 2, 1899. Francis B. Heitman, *Historical Register and Dictionary of the United States Army from Its Organization, September 29, 1789, to March 2, 1903*, (Washington, D.C.: Government Printing Office, 1903), 762.
80. *Correspondence Relating to the War with Spain*, 556.
81. "What the Boys Do," *Anaconda Standard*, Lt. Grennan Papers, MMHM, LA, Bldg. T-15, Fort Harrison.
82. *Correspondence Relating to the War with Spain, 556.*

83. "They Had a Hot Fight," *Anaconda Standard*, Lt. Grennan Papers, MMHM, LA, Bldg. T-15, Fort Harrison.
84. Ibid.
85. Ibid.
86. Circular: Montana Adjutant General's Office, 2, 4; "The First Montana," *Anaconda Standard*, Lt. Grennan Papers, MMHM, LA, Bldg. T-15, Fort Harrison.
87. "From Lieut. Knowlton," and "Thus Far It's Been Pretty Rocky," *Anaconda Standard*, August 17, 1898.
88. Ibid.
89. Laist, "Official History…of the First Montana," 8; "Thus Far It's Been Pretty Rocky," *Anaconda Standard*, August 17, 1898.
90. Ibid.
91. "He Likes Honolulu," *Anaconda Standard*, August 17, 1898.
92. "From Manila," Helena *Daily Independent*, Drawer 2, Private Asa L. Fisk Folder, MMHM, LA, Bldg. T-15, Fort Harrison.
93. Ibid.
94. Laist, "Official History…of the First Montana," 10; "From Manila," Helena *Daily Independent*, Drawer 2, Private Fisk Folder, MMHM, LA, Bldg. T-15, Fort Harrison; "Jensen Is Exonerated," *Anaconda Standard*, Drawer 2, Private Fisk Folder, MMHM, LA, Bldg. T-15, Fort Harrison.
95. CMH, *American Military History*, 326–27, 335–36.
96. Ibid., 336; Sexton, *Soldiers in the Sun*, 43–45.
97. Artificers were skilled mechanics. Although artificers were used during the War of 1812, the necessity of this designation became even more apparent during the Seminole War when southern militia refused to do routine repairs. Risch, *Quartermaster Support of the Army*, 230; Circular: Montana Adjutant General's Office, 1–3; Laist, "Official History… of the First Montana," 11–12. Paxson did not receive his formal discharge until December. William B. Knowlton was promoted to 1st Lt. to replace Paxson on December 15, 1898. Adjutant General Corbin to Governor Smith, December 15, 1898, Box 29, Folder 6, Smith Papers, MC 35a, MHS.
98. Hartman, *Nebraska's Militia*, 66; Sexton, *Soldiers in the Sun*, 70–75.
99. General Otis to AG Corbin, January 11, 1899 [telegram], *Correspondence Relating to the War with Spain*, 877.
100. Laist, "Official History…of the First Montana," 14.
101. Charles Sutton to Governor Smith, January 22, 1899, Box 31, Folder 1, Smith Papers, MC 35a, MHS. In reply, after hostilities broke out, Governor Smith indicated that any action on the petition at that time would be useless, but that he would take up the matter with the Secretary of War as soon as peace was restored. Governor Smith to Charles Sutton, March 1, 1899, Box 31, Folder 1, Smith Papers, MC 35a, MHS.
102. Otis quoted in Sexton, *Soldiers in the Sun*, 77–78.
103. Laist, "Official History…of the First Montana," 14–15; Sexton, *Soldiers in the Sun*, 90–91; Hartman, *Nebraska's Militia*, 66–67.
104. Sexton, *Soldiers in the Sun*, 93; Laist, "Official History…of the First Montana," 17–18.
105. Sexton, *Soldiers in the Sun*, 93; Laist, "Official History…of the First Montana," 18. In his report to Washington, D.C., General Otis indicated that total casualties amounted to 175. General Otis to Adjutant General Corbin, February 5, 1899 [telegram], *Correspondence Relating to the War with Spain*, 894. Four victims of the February 5 fight suffered only minor wounds, while the two wounded soldiers who eventually died included Private

John Serenson, shot in the head, and Private William Myersick, shot through the lungs. General Otis to AG Corbin, February 6, 1899 [telegram], *Correspondence Relating to the War with Spain*, 895.
106. Sexton, *Soldiers in the Sun*, 96–97.
107. "On the Battlefield," *Anaconda Standard*, March 21, 1899.
108. "Tells Of The Fighting," *Anaconda Standard*, March 22, 1899
109. Ibid.
110. Injury Report, 1st Montana, February 10, 1899, Drawer 2, Lt. Col. R B. Wallace Folder, MMHM, LA, Bldg. T-15, Fort Harrison. A woman, Muriel Bailey, who for some reason was near the Montana line during the Battle of Caloocan, spoke to Lt. Col. Wallace as he was brought back to the rear on a stretcher. After she asked how he felt, Wallace replied he was "all right," and there was "no reason for bringing him back at all. It was a Mauser." "Are only Mausers," Helena *Daily Independent*, April 17, 1899. Little is known about Muriel Bailey, but there is a possibility she was serving as a nurse. Recruitment for the Hospital Corps during the war remained a constant problem. Those that did enlist often lacked the necessary medical training. To alleviate this situation, the U.S. Army for the first time in its history employed professionally qualified nurses to staff military hospitals in the states and overseas. Cosmas, *An Army for Empire*, 248–49.
111. "Heard the Bullets," Helena *Daily Independent*, June 15, 1899.
112. "Are only Mausers," Helena *Daily Independent*, April 7, 1899.
113. *Butte Miner*, October 24, 1899.
114. "Heard the Bullets," *Independent Record*, June 15, 1899; "Tells of the Fighting," *Anaconda Standard*, March 22, 1899; *Correspondence Relating to the War with Spain*, 900–1.
115. "Letter from Manila," Bozeman *Avant Courier*, April 15, 1899. Dunn's father received a letter from a family friend, who had visited Tommy in San Francisco. The letter writer mentioned that Tommy was "accompanied by a guard," and assumed this was necessary because Tommy was on "sick parole." Other reports indicate that Dunn was in the guardhouse and, in fact, apparently had arrived in San Francisco under guard. There is, however, no indication of any infraction on Dunn's part, though it might be surmised he was experiencing behavioral problems due to his serious head wound. "Bullet through His Head," Helena *Daily Independent*, May 6, 1899; *Weekly Independent* (3x5 typed facsimile), May 26, 1899, Drawer 2, Private Thomas G. Dunn Folder, MMHM, LA, Bldg. T-15, Fort Harrison; "To Welcome Tommy Dunn," Helena *Daily Independent* (3x5 typed facsimile), July 17, 1899, Drawer 2, Private Thomas G. Dunn Folder, MMHM, LA, Bldg. T-15, Fort Harrison.
116. Laist, "Official History…of the First Montana," 22; "Lieut. French Dead," Helena *Daily Independent*, February 24, 1899.
117. Laist, "Official History…of the First Montana," 23–24, *Report of the Adjutant General, 1897–1898,* 22.
118. Laist. "Official History…of the First Montana," 24–25; Faust, *Campaigning in the Philippines*, 167–68.
119. "Letters from Manila," *Anaconda Standard*, June 6, 1899.
120. Ibid.
121. Faust, *Campaigning in the Philippines*, 168–69; Sexton, *Soldiers in the Sun*, 117–18; General Otis to AG Corbin, March 31, 1899 [telegram], *Correspondence Relating to the War with Spain*, 953.
122. Laist, "Official History…of the First Montana," 26–27; Sexton, *Soldiers in the Sun*, 110, Hartman, *Nebraska's Militia*, 61.

123. Laist, "Official History…of the First Montana," 28.
124. Edward White and W.B. Trembly of the 20th Kansas, the two soldiers who swam across the river, were awarded the Medal of Honor. Interestingly, these two men chased surprised insurgents from their trenches by throwing mud balls. Col. Funston, who led the raid, likewise received the Medal of Honor, and was promoted to brigadier general. Faust, *Campaigning in the Philippines*, 186–87; Sexton, *Soldiers in the Sun,* 143–45; Laist, "Official History…of the First Montana," 29.
125. 1899 Journal, June 16, 1899, Folder 1, Alexander Robertson Papers, Small Collection 1690, MHS.
126. Ibid.
127. Ibid.
128. Ibid.; Laist, "Official History…of the First Montana," 31.
129. Ibid., 32; "Comrade Tells Tale of Colonel Wallace," *Billings Gazette*, June 23, 1940; Fort Huachuca, Arizona, Medical Report, Drawer 2, Lt. Col. Wallace Folder, MMHM, LA, Bldg. T-15, Fort Harrison; General Otis to Agwar, Washington, D.C., August 26, 1899 [telegram], *Correspondence Relating to the War with Spain*, 1059.
130. "Didn't Like the Delay," *Anaconda Standard*, August 24, 1899. Bright's disease is an inflammation of the kidneys frequently resulting in renal failure.
131. General Otis to Agwar, Washington, D.C., August 8, 1899 [telegram], General Otis to Agwar, Washington, D.C., August 22, 1899 [telegram], General Otis to Agwar, Washington, D.C., August 26, 1899 [telegram], *Correspondence Relating to the War with Spain*, 1049, 1057, 1059.
132. Mabel B. Pace to Governor Smith, August 25, 1899, Box 31, Folder 1, Smith Papers, MC 35a, MHS.
133. Governor Smith to Mabel Pace, September 1, 1899, Box 31, Folder 1, Smith Papers, MC 35a, MHS; Laist, "Official History…of the First Montana," 33, 35.
134. *Anaconda Standard*, October 24, 1899; *Souvenir Edition: The Butte Miner*, October 24, 1899. The regiment presented a bronze Spanish cannon to the citizens of Montana. Engraved across the butt end were the words "Barcelona, June 24, 1776." Col. Kessler had thought the date significant, and after lengthy negotiations with the Spanish military had managed to buy the cannon for 300 Mexican dollars. The regiment requested that it be exhibited on the grounds of the state's capitol, then currently under construction. "Historic Old Gun," Helena *Daily Independent*, November 11, 1899.
135. "French's Body Here," Helena *Daily Independent*, April 15, 1899.
136. An abridged article based on the original manuscript of Chapter 4 in *Splendid Service* appeared as "'First to Respond to Their Country's Call': The First Montana Infantry and the Spanish-American War and Philippine Insurrection, 1898–1899," in *Montana: The Magazine of Western History* (Autumn 2002): 44–57.

Butte's Company G in 1898 before service in the Philippines. After the war, Company G's reconstitution in Butte proved short-lived, with the unit mustering out in June 1907. The same fate befell Butte's Company B (1901–1913). Miners and unions held adversarial perceptions that guardsmen were "strikebreakers," which led to a general malaise and understrength enlistment rates for these units. In 1954, the 143rd Ordnance Company, Direct Automotive Support, was the first guard unit organized in Butte since the 1914 riots. *MMHM*

5

Dick Act and National Reorganization, 1900–1910

Susan Paras

There is no reason why the Montana National Guard should not rank first... and lead the way to the founding of a National Military Reserve.—Montana Adjutant General Charles F. English, November 30, 1900.

The forest fires have proved the sterling worth and absolute necessity of the National Guard. Not only have its members rendered efficient service, but also they have proved capable, dependable men.—Gallatin Forest Supervisor D.T. Conkling, August 27, 1910.

Twelve companies of the Montana National Guard served as the 1st Montana Infantry, U.S.V., in the Philippines in 1898–1899.[1] Given the exigencies of the overseas conflict, the state and its regiment had responded quickly. The 1st Montana was rapidly mustered in, then shipped off to the Pacific to effectively campaign, and returned home to a hero's welcome. With a few strokes of the pen, federal activation had bypassed complicated administrative procedures—one day they were a state militia; the next, a federal force. The simplicity of this arrangement did not reoccur when activation procedures were later applied in 1910 to fight Montana forest fires.

Standing in the shadow of the U.S. Army continued to be problematic for the National Guard across the country. How could it fully meet proscribed regular army standards as a part-time military entity? How should it incorporate state duties that were outside of federal supervision or direction? Some critics argued that these tasks could not be adequately met or combined. The implications of these questions confronted the National Guard as the federal government and the states pondered arrangements for the units returning from the Philippines and Cuba.

It would gradually dawn on the authorities that activating guard units for an international crisis was a less complicated process than calling up individual units for emergency situations within a state or territory. In the case of the Philippines campaign, of course, National Guard units retained their state and local identities, but also became full-time federal components—armed, led, billeted, provisioned, and paid by the regular army. In contrast, during a domestic activation, a National Guard unit in most instances was armed, led, billeted, provisioned, and paid by the state. Instead of integration into a well-oiled regular army and its procedures, National Guard units were left to the whims of governors, fickle state legislatures clutching tight purse strings, and a citizenry frequently divided over political issues.

The authorities became aware that the Militia Act of 1792 needed revision to meet new 20th-century realities. The old legislation had worked adequately regarding frontier warfare, earlier civil disturbances, and even the Civil War, but the 20th century introduced new roles and responsibilities that challenged and strained the limits of the original legislation.

The indisputable fact that the federal government could successfully use state militias to help carry out its overseas policies was proven in the Philippines and Cuba. The skepticism of many in the regular army notwithstanding, it was clear to most in the federal government that the militia was a critical component in enforcing the nation's will. With America's growing political and economic interests overseas, the federal government understood more than ever the importance of timely access to National Guard troops.

The calling-up of militia to assist a relatively small regular army had broad appeal for other reasons, too. National Guard augmentation of the regular army helped skirt the thorny issue of maintaining a large and expensive professional army in peacetime. The citizen soldier concept, moreover, had an egalitarian link, based on the legend of the Roman leader, Cincinnatus, who abandoned his farm to take up arms and then laid them down again at the conclusion of hostilities to resume civilian responsibilities.

With the conclusion of the Cuba and the Philippines campaigns, the militia regiments returned home as America evaluated the guard's first involvement in an overseas international conflict. The war confirmed the need for a better-trained and equipped reserve when inadequacies were exposed in the activation. At the same time, the victory instigated a nationalistic fervor that swept the nation. All of these factors prompted a series of efforts to strengthen the nation's soldiery. Consequently, in the first decade of the 20th century, the United States adopted significant reforms regarding the organized militia and the regular army.

The terms of enlistment for the men in the 1st Montana Volunteer Infantry expired when they were mustered out of federal service. Afterward, only 114 infantry and cavalry soldiers remained on the rosters. Adjutant General Charles F. English informed the Montana legislature that this low number "left our State with the least number of organized Militia to her credit of any in the Union."[2] Without adequate funding for equipment, uniforms, and training, Montana guardsmen, English warned, were encountering obstacles jeopardizing the militia's existence. With sufficient state support, however, "there is no reason why the Montana National Guard should not rank first…and lead the way to the founding of a National Military Reserve."[3]

Efforts to reconstruct the guard were made difficult by the parsimonious Montana legislature. Unlike larger guard organizations enjoying strong state and legislative assistance, such as in New York, Pennsylvania, and Illinois, the smaller state units often received minimal support. Montana legislators allocated just $2,500 to retain the militia, hampering the guard's ability to reorganize itself.[4]

Meanwhile, the organized militia's national representative body—the Interstate National Guard—met in an Indianapolis convention in January 1900 to help draft a bill to increase annual federal appropriations from $400,000 to $2,000,000.[5] In April 1900, 38 states, including Montana, were represented by this organization in Washington, D.C.[6] After passing through the House of Representative's Militia Committee, the bill was introduced to Congress and within two months President Theodore Roosevelt signed it into law. The Militia Act of June 5, 1900, raised the annual National Guard appropriation to $1 million, and authorized the War Department to compensate the militia for the remaining amount ($1 million) through federal issuance of rifles, ammunition, uniforms, and other equipment.[7]

In return for the federal appropriations, the National Guard was expected to demonstrate its capability as a federal reserve force. Eventually, under Section 1661 of the Revised Statutes, state units were required to maintain at least 100 "regularly enlisted, and organized men" for each congressional delegate. At the time, Montana was deficient in this regard. Faced with the mission of tripling the guard's membership, Adjutant General English recommended that new units be first organized in counties large enough to adequately support companies of 45 men. Ideally, with added enlistment, Montana's annual federal allocation could increase from $2,587 to $6,500. Combined with the $2,500 set aside by the state legislature, the organized militia thus would be entitled to a $9,000 budget for the upcoming year.[8]

Reorganization of the Montana National Guard, now designated as the 2nd Montana Infantry Regiment, officially began in the spring of 1901 when the state legislature appropriated $5,000 for that purpose. Efforts were concentrated in western Montana due to that region's greater population.[9] Under the leadership of English's successor, Adjutant General R. Lee McCulloch of Hamilton, the first infantry unit, Bozeman's Company A, mustered into service on May 30, 1901, under the command of Capt. Alexander Wessitsh.[10] McCulloch held the new company in high regard. "The petitioners belong to the very best class of young men in Bozeman," he wrote to Governor Joseph Toole.[11]

Following Bozeman's lead, other Montana communities contacted the Adjutant General's Office with petitions for guard units, and the new enlistees in these proposed units were willing to accept outdated Springfield rifles and furnish their own uniforms. McCulloch was amazed at the growing fervor. During the summer of 1901, he visited Butte and Big Timber to muster in companies B and C. By the following September, McCulloch was optimistic and hoped to raise the guard's membership to the goal of 300 within the following month.[12]

By late 1901, units at Red Lodge and Livingston mustered in as companies D and E; and by November 30, 1902, state membership would surpass 400 officers and enlisted men. When McCulloch resigned in August 1902, Shirley Ashby assumed the adjutant general post. He oversaw the completion of the regiment's reorganization, officially finalized on December 1, 1903. The Montana National Guard had transformed itself into a military entity comprised of more than 400 soldiers organized in seven companies (formed into two battalions), and one battery.[13]

Company	**Location**	**Date**	**Roll**	**Commander**
Battery A	Helena	May 30, 1901	60	W.A. Moore
Company A	Bozeman	May 30, 1901	53	A. Wessitsh
Company B	Butte	August 23, 1901	49	S.G. Jeans
Company C	Big Timber	August 26, 1901	64	G.H. Preston
Company D	Red Lodge	October 12, 1901	51	J.Z. Verne
Company E	Livingston	October 14, 1901	63	M.J. Walsh
Company F	Dillon	April 2, 1902	58	J.T. Young
Company H	Kalispell	July 1, 1902	60	W.A. Swaney[14]

Meanwhile, the federal government began adjusting the outstanding accounts accrued by the states in supplying, equipping, and transporting soldiers for federal service during the recent war. In 1898, Congress had passed legislation requiring the treasury secretary to reimburse the state governments for these expenses.[15] The Montana guard had participated in the Philippines campaign with the understanding that it would be reimbursed upon its return. Also, during their service, men took personal equipment and supplies abroad. In 1900, the federal government requested the states to forward inventory reports to the treasury secretary accounting for expenses.

In October 1901, Montana's Adjutant General McCulloch created a Board of Survey to report on the monies owed to Montana and its veterans. Board members Capt. W.A. Moore, Capt. A. Wessitsh, and Capt. Steve G. Jeans met in Helena, October 14–16, compiling an inventory and report of equipment used during the activation.[16] Montana, as well as several other states, however, had not kept an adequate inventory for items taken into federal service. Lacking such a list, the board based its findings on requisition forms, veterans' testimony, officers' affidavits, and receipts signed by Montana Adjutant General James W. Drennan in 1897. On October 16, 1901, the board concluded that $5,201.47 in equipment and supplies had been worn out, and that $9,917.44 in property taken into active duty was either damaged, deficient, or now missing. Several years passed, however, before a final settlement was concluded with the federal government.[17]

The new companies mustering in during the reorganization still used outdated rifles and in many cases supplied their own uniforms. Of the 395 Springfield breech-loading .45 caliber, black-powder rifles retained by the Montana guard in 1901, only 30 percent were fit for use.[18] Within the year, the War Department issued new supplies, uniforms, and equipment worth more than $10,000. On January 5, 1902, 300 Krag-Jorgensen Model 1898 .30–.40 caliber magazine rifles, together with "slings, wiping rods, breech covers, knife bayonets...50,000 rounds of ball cartridges, [and] 10,000 rounds blank cartridges," arrived at the Helena armory. The guardsmen welcomed the modern Krag rifles, the "first smokeless powder, small caliber, repeating rifle to be adopted by the United States government."[19]

In August, the War Department sent a second shipment, including 400 each of blankets, campaign hats, blouses, trousers, and legging pairs, totaling $7,389.61. Although exceeding Adjutant General McCulloch's expectations, the shipment still fell short of entirely outfitting the new companies. Nevertheless, he remained hopeful that in 1903 there would be "a sufficient amount to the credit of the State to fully and thoroughly equip" the guard. He continued to lobby the state legislature for increased appropriations.[20]

In 1899, Montana's citizens had displayed their appreciation to the returning veterans when presenting them with ornate medals commemorating the Philippines campaign. The state government itself, however, did not honor the 1st Montana Volunteer Infantry until 1903.[21] On September 29, Adjutant General Shirley Ashby issued Circular No. 1, commissioning the design and creation of a bronze tablet inscribed with the names of volunteers who died during the conflict.[22] Upon its completion, the tablet was placed on display in the main corridor of the State Capitol Building in Helena.[23] A year and half later, on February 19, 1905, Montana effectively commemorated the guardsmen's duty in the Philippines when the 1st Montana's Kessler Banner was selected as the state flag with some modifications.[24]

Across the country, the National Guard continued to transform itself into a more integrated military reserve. Federal legislation signed on January 21, 1903, marked the state militias' greatest political victory since their establishment. Formally titled "An Act to Promote the Efficiency of the Militia, and for Other Purposes," it came to be known as the Dick Act for its most influential political supporter, Ohio Representative Charles W. Dick. A lieutenant colonel in the 8th Ohio Volunteers during the war, Dick was elected president of the National Guard Association in 1902, and he chaired the House Militia Affairs Committee when the militia bill was introduced. His political status and relationship with Secretary of War Elihu Root played a key role in gaining bipartisan support for the 1903 legislation.[25]

The Dick Act repealed several provisions of the Militia Act of 1792. Though retaining the requirement that state militias be comprised of able-bodied men between the ages of 18 and 45, it separated the militia into two categories—the organized militia or National Guard, and the Army Reserve. The act extended the three-month federal service maximum to nine months, and added a clause offering state militia companies an option to join the volunteer army as single units after the nine-month expiration. This clause protected state militia units that wanted to remain intact during extended federal service.[26]

The legislation also established an Office of the Adjutant General, under the direction of the Assistant Secretary of War, to oversee the operations and needs of the National Guard's many units.[27] The U.S. president was authorized to muster guardsmen into federal service "to repel invasion, suppress rebellion, or enforce federal law" with the consent of individual state governors. The Dick Act also required that the "organization, armament, and discipline of the organized militia" had to meet federal requirements by 1908. To facilitate this five-year transformation, Section 1661 of the Revised Statutes authorized a one-time federal appropriation of $2 million to cover training costs for the National Guard.

The Dick Act, moreover, required the War Department to assist the National Guard with its reorganization. It prepared a model military code for legislatures to reference when the states modified their own military codes to meet federal standards. Federal pay was granted for summer training camps, guard units were required to conduct joint maneuvers with the regular army, and drill and instruction were required 24 times a year.[28]

The new legislation generally was seen as a victory for the National Guard. However, a modern historian, Jim Dan Hill, has claimed that "the Dick Act was not a political victory for the guardsmen as much as it was a reluctant Federal recognition of the National Guards' demonstration of its inherent vitality" when reorganizing so swiftly after "complete demobilization" following the end of the Spanish-American War.[29] For the first time since 1808, however, state militias were required to conform to federal army standards. And, for the first time ever, states were required to maintain inventories of federally-issued equipment.

The Dick Act provided direct guidelines to enable the National Guard to meet regular army standards, but the task of reorganizing and restructuring nearly 40 independent state militias obviously would be difficult. Immediately following the 1903 enactment, Secretary Root contacted individual state militias to inquire whether they were aware of the benefits and responsibilities. Out of 1,943 militia units, 23 percent were either completely unaware of their new obligations or failed to respond to Root's inquiry.[30] Hoping that the National Guard could become a "functional reserve unit," Secretary Root urged state militias nationwide to prove themselves worthy of their status and assert their position as models for volunteer soldiery.[31]

Despite some concerns about domination by the regular army, most guard organizations readily accepted national control in return for federal appropriations and recognition.[32] On December 1, 1903, the 2nd Montana Infantry Regiment was federally recognized as the 2nd Regiment of Infantry, retaining its seven companies organized into two battalions, and one light battery. Three weeks later, General Order No. 65 issued by the War Department grouped individual state militias into eight geographical divisions, with each division consisting of several departments. Montana joined Minnesota, North Dakota, and portions of Idaho and Wyoming in the Northern Division, Department of Dakota, headquartered at Omaha, Nebraska.[33]

State legislatures worked quickly to seek approval from the War Department to secure federal appropriations and equipment. Montana enacted the 1904 Montana Military Code, which paralleled army requirements. It provided strict guidelines for mustering in new companies, and required each company to maintain at least 45 enlisted men. If a company fell below 45 men for two consecutive months, it would be immediately disbanded. Section 28 mandated that guardsmen serve for three years, conform to federal standards, and, of course, participate in drills organized by the state of Montana.[34]

Out of the $2 million allowance provided to National Guard units by the federal government, Montana was entitled to arms and equipment worth $6,372.53.[35] In November 1903, the War Department sent 152 Krag .30 caliber magazine rifles, gun slings, protective covers, and ammunition to the Helena armory—a total value of $3,469.20. Later, in August and September 1904, more than $4,000 of supplies including tents, knapsacks, field ovens, cooking utensils, and miscellaneous camp supplies arrived at the Helena armory. By December 1904, Adjutant General Ashby was pleased to report that all Montana guardsmen were completely outfitted. While the equipment issued to the Montana National Guard was not the most up-to-date, the organization considered itself fortunate. As late as 1905, only 53 percent of units nationwide were considered adequately prepared for field service.[36]

The 1903 Dick Act demonstrated the dedication of Congress and the War Department in raising the status of the National Guard. This strong federal backing gave Adjutant General Ashby the confidence to aggressively pursue state support. In his 1903–1904 biennial report, Ashby identified the guard's top priorities. He requested that Montana make an application to the War Department requesting a regular army officer instructor, and to muster in five additional infantry companies, establishing three full battalions. He also asked for $20,000 to fund the guardsmen's annual encampment.[37]

Both state and federal appropriations remained essential to the Montana guard's success. The state's 1904 Montana Military Code provided for the salary of the adjutant general and required the state treasury to absorb drill pay and transportation costs. Under Section 1661 of the Dick Act, the federal government paid for transportation, subsistence, and salaries for state soldiers attending summer training camps. However, it was unclear who would pay for the upkeep of the rifle ranges and camping grounds. While serving at National Guard encampments was the greatest attraction to current members and prospective applicants, the Montana guard had foregone summer camps since 1897. Under Section 18 of the 1897 Montana State Military Code, guardsmen were required to attend encampments at the State Military Reservation, or old Fort Ellis, for 10 days each year.[38]

Located near Bozeman, dilapidated Fort Ellis was barely adequate for training, with neither running water nor a sewer system. Vacated by the regular army in 1886, it intermittently was used by the National Guard for summer training. In return for free housing, Horace Smith, and later A.C. Harding, both Philippines veterans, guarded the structures from civilian looters and scavengers, maintained the grounds, and made minimal structural repairs.[39] In June 1904, Adjutant General Ashby petitioned the War Department for "additional" funding to hold the state encampment. The regular army's military secretary, however, responded that the War Department was not required to fulfill requests outside the initial provisions established by Section 1661.[40]

To help sustain and increase membership, Adjutant General Ashby reinstated the long-suspended state rifle competition between individual companies, raising unit esprit de corps.[41] In 1903, Bozeman's Company A won the silver trophy, while in the following year, Helena's Battery A marksmen surpassed their competitors.[42]

Meanwhile, the War Department sponsored a national rifle contest, with participation by teams from both the regular army and the militia. During the first year's competition, a National Guard team won the trophy. The Montana guard did not participate until 1907 when 15 officers and enlisted men, all winners from the state rifle competition, entered the contest at Camp Perry, located about 30 miles from Toledo, Ohio.[43] Under direction of the team captain, Adjutant General A.M. Alderson, the rifle team included range officers, scorers, and a target spotter. The National Rifle Match's popularity continued to spread rapidly, with 43 state militias participating in the competition by 1909.[44]

Shortly after passage of the Dick Act, the regular army sent an inspector-instructor to review the Montana guard and oversee completion of an annual report, as required by regulations. In April 1904, the U.S. Army's Maj. Zerah W. Torey arrived in Helena. Together with Adjutant General Ashby and Col. Bray, he recommended that the state militia forego annual encampments during 1904–1905 in order to equip, arm, and clothe the entire 2nd Infantry Regiment.

In May of the following year, Maj. Torey, along with Ashby's successor, A.M. Alderson, again reported on the status of the Montana National Guard. Torey assessed Helena's Battery A and each of the infantry companies, reporting his findings to the War Department. Companies A, D, and H at Bozeman, Red Lodge, and Kalispell received favorable reports. Company A received the highest compliment from Torey, who stated it was "a creditable organization and could be relied upon in any emergency."[45] The most recent units added to the state militia, Glendive's Company I and Billings' Company K, also received high praise.[46] The establishment of a National Guard unit in the Great Plains community of Glendive marked a significant shift in state guard demographics. For the first time, a guard company was active in the far eastern part of Montana.[47]

Companies B, C, E, and F at Butte, Big Timber, Livingston, and Dillon, and Battery A, Helena, received poor grades due to "improper instruction and lack of officers' instruction."[48] Companies E, F, and Battery A were harshly criticized. Torey observed that between 1904 and 1905, Livingston's Company E lost 61 men. When asked the reason for this drastic reduction from 68 to 7 soldiers, the company's captain blamed opposition from local workingmen and unions. Torey took little pity in the officer's explanation, commenting that organized labor was just as strong during the prior year when Company E received good marks. He blamed the commanding officer's negligence for the unit's demise.[49] Consequently, companies E, F, and Battery A were disbanded.

The federal government, in addition to providing annual inspections, offered guard officers the opportunity to participate in professional military courses at U.S. Army training schools. On January 14, 1904, Acting Adjutant General W.P. Hall in Washington, D.C., informed Montana's Governor Toole about these opportunities for federal instruction, specifically at the General Service and Staff College at Fort Leavenworth, Kansas, and the Artillery School at Fort Monroe, Virginia. Although Montana guardsmen had participated in regular army instruction at Fort Harrison, this was their first opportunity to pursue a truly professional military education.[50] Officers also would receive training when participating in joint maneuvers with the U.S. Army in 1906 and 1908 at American Lake (now part of Fort Lewis), near Tacoma, Washington.[51]

In 1906, Montana's militia organization remained one of the smallest in the National Guard system[52]—despite increasing its membership by more than 260 men in the past three years while mustering in a hospital unit at Helena, two light artillery batteries, and a short-lived second unit at Butte (Company G).[53] The guard also now included a regimental band. In 1904, 20 Finnish immigrants enlisted in Company D at Red Lodge and shortly received permission to form a regimental band, the first since 1899. By March 1907, the band's home base was relocated to Billings.

Later that same year, the state militia established a military tribunal, appointing Maj. Jesse Roote of Company B (Butte) as Judge Advocate General.[54] Any non-commissioned officer or other enlisted man accused of violating the military code of Montana or regular army guidelines appeared before Roote and three other appointed officers, who held authority to investigate, acquit, or court-martial an accused individual.[55]

While the Montana guard continued to request state financial support and expand its organization, National Guard lobbyists in Washington, D.C., pursued further federal appropriations. On June 22, 1906, these efforts were rewarded when Congress approved an increase of $2 million under Section 1661 of the Dick Act. Assistant Secretary Robert Shaw Oliver wrote to Montana Governor E.L. Norris and Adjutant General A.M. Alderson, strongly suggesting that Montana pass statutes parallel to the federal provisions so as not to jeopardize these set-aside funds.[56]

General Orders No. 222 issued by the War Department required that state militia companies now be comprised of 1 captain, 1 first lieutenant, and at least 58 enlisted men. The current revised Montana Military Code, however, maintained the outdated quota of a minimum of 45 soldiers. In response, Adjutant General Alderson proposed reforms, which were submitted to the 1907 state legislature. The proposals died in the military committee.[57] Montana Inspector General John J.W. McGuinness, rightly or wrongly, blamed this response on the growing strength of organized labor and its influence on the state legislature. The 1907 legislature appropriated a smaller sum of $5,000 to maintain the militia.[58]

The Montana guard, however, was not the only state militia confronting difficulties. By 1908, it became obvious that a five-year deadline for most state militias to conform to regular army standards was not feasible. Consequently, Congress amended the 1903 Dick Act on May 27, 1908.[59] The amendments passed in 1908 symbolized a clear victory for the guard.[60] It extended the conformity deadline to January 21, 1910, safeguarded the National Guard's position as the first reserve unit of the regular army, and expanded the militia's federal military role.[61] The President retained the power to call up the National Guard on threat of war or invasion, and the 1908 amendments allowed the guard to serve both within and outside the United States. More importantly, new provisions granted the President control over the militia's length of federal service, as long as it did not extend beyond an individual guardsman's enlistment expiration date.[62]

At the same time, the War Department established the Division of Militia Affairs (DMA) in Washington, D.C., to facilitate the development of the National Guard. With Lt. Col. Erasmus M. Weaver at the helm, the DMA assumed all responsibilities previously assigned to the National Guard Adjutant General's Office and worked with the regular army to bring the organized militia up to federal standards.[63] The regular army inspector-instructors assigned to state militias educated guardsmen in federal administrative procedures as well as training in tactical maneuvers.

Additionally, Congress created a separate annual disbursement of $2 million. Combined with the $2 million set aside by the 1906 amendments to Section 1661, this raised the national militia's federal appropriations to $4 million annually.[64] Despite Montana's inability to fully achieve U.S. Army standards, the War Department approved an equipment issuance to the state. The shipment, totaling $7,214.35, included bronze infantry cap ornaments, drab breeches, khaki coats, and leggings.[65] When charged against the total allotment set aside for the state militia, however, the equipment and uniform nearly expended Montana's total budget, thwarting the Montana guard's chances of participating in 1908 joint encampments.[66] The War Department redistributed Montana's money allotted for encampments to other states.

Montana's officers, however, eventually were granted an opportunity to attend a 1908 joint encampment with the regular army; the War Department, for reasons never fully explained, seized Nebraska's allotment of $14,000 and assigned it to Montana. Combined with allowances saved from suspending the 1908 rifle competition, the Montana guard had accumulated $22,000 and sent its 2nd Infantry officers to joint maneuvers at American Lake on August 16–25, 1908.[67] Company officers assigned to their posts prior to July 25 were invited to attend. They arrived at American Lake armed, uniformed, and equipped for field service. Instructed by regular army officers, the guard officers participated in simulated problems to defend the western coastline.[68]

In 1908, federal appropriations continued to be assigned to the guard budget. On July 29, the state's attorneys won an important settlement when federal courts ordered the treasury secretary to pay Montana $31,368 in compensation for the guard's participation in the Philippines conflict. With attorney costs totaling $4,205, Montana veterans were entitled to over $27,162. By February, $13,950 was paid to living veterans of the 1st Montana Volunteers, and $977.55 issued to the heirs of fallen soldiers.[69] On August 3, Governor Toole appointed three Philippines veterans—Julius Barney, Colin S. Hill, and Adolph Faessler—to distribute the money.[70] This settlement ended the final chapter of the Montana guard's involvement in the Philippines campaign.

On March 5, 1909, Phil Greenan replaced A.M. Alderson as Montana's adjutant general, and by year's end Greenan assured the War Department that the Montana guard had complied with the Dick Act.[71] This was not accomplished without sacrifice. In order to put the state in good standing with Washington, D.C., the Montana guard had to forego a 1909 summer encampment. Guardsmen, however, looked forward to the state rifle competition, held July 28–30 at the Fort William Henry Harrison[72] rifle range. The participating marksmen, organized into company teams comprised of a captain and 10 shooters, entered several categories, including all-ranges, rapid fire, and skirmish competitions. At the conclusion of the match, the guardsmen with the 15 highest aggregate scores were selected to represent Montana at the national rifle competition on August 9–13 at Camp Perry, Ohio. Though falling short of a medal at the national competition, the team received high praise from Greenan. In an August 11 letter to Governor Norris, Greenan applauded their performance. "Yesterday was a day here that tried the best of the shooters on the range, and our men stood up mighty well."[73]

Montana also mustered in four new companies. On February 12, 1909, Inspector-General John McGuinness accepted Company D at Lewistown. Within the following year, strong support in the northwestern town of Kalispell, coupled with a rapid increase in population, spurred the organization of Company F on February 7, 1910. Kalispell now maintained two company units.[74] On April 4, Company L also was organized in the northwest timber boomtown of Libby. On March 7, applicants in eastern Montana mustered in as Company E at Miles City. Statewide by November, the Montana guard totaled 52 officers and 761 enlisted men, a significant increase from the 34 officers and 437 enlisted men reported in the previous January.[75]

As America continued to grow as a world power, the reorganization of the National Guard focused on potential national and international involvements. Consequently, policy makers failed to foresee that the guard's first major test would be fighting massive forest fires in the western mountains. In May and June 1910, record-breaking heat caused severe drought conditions in western Montana, northern Idaho, and northeastern Washington, resulting in tinder-dry forests "ready to explode at the touch of a spark."[76] The fire season started in the Blackfeet National Forest of northwestern Montana toward the end of April. By late May, several small fires caused by lightning, careless campers, and sparks from railroad car wheels burned throughout the region.[77]

The U.S. Forest Service, established only five years earlier, earnestly sought to justify its recent creation by singly controlling the conflagrations. Only reluctantly did it solicit help from other agencies.[78] Initially, the Forest Service contracted hundreds of temporary fire fighters to combat the blazes, and by July 15 nearly 3,000 men were involved.[79] After draining the employment offices in Butte, Helena, and Spokane, the Forest Service's northern region supervisor, William B. Greeley, ordered the closure of logging camps and mines in order to persuade loggers and miners to join fire fighters at the lines.[80] As the situation grew more desperate, forest supervisors hired men off the street, often including vagabonds and men with criminal records. Some arrived at the fire lines intoxicated, disinterested, or incapable of doing hard labor.[81]

By mid July, more than 3,000 small fires burned in the national forests stretching along both sides of the Bitterroot Range in Montana and Idaho. With fires growing in the Kootenai, Cabinet, Flathead, Lolo, and Bitterroot national forests, concern spread throughout the region.[82] With the demand for fire fighters and the threat to local communities, it was questionable whether all of western Montana's guard companies would be participating in summer joint maneuvers with the regular army at American Lake, or if Governor Norris would permit 15 marksmen and 4 officers, including Adjutant General Phil Greenan, to attend the rifle match in Ohio.

As the flames spread largely unchecked in the forest surrounding Libby, local residents quickly joined fire crews. One week prior to the scheduled departure of the Montana guard to American Lake, Libby's Mayor E.W. Dow pleaded with Governor Norris to excuse Libby's Company L from the joint maneuvers. "We [have] shut down our entire works and sent all of our crew from the sawmill and woods to help fight," Mayor Dow reported. "You will be taking...sixty young able-bodied men which...might mean the saving or loosing [sic] of the town."[83]

In a telegram to Governor Norris dated July 28, Kootenai National Forest Supervisor Dorr Skeels reiterated the mayor's concerns, though conditions by then seemed to have turned for the better. "Situation so improved that thirty men...can be spared for encampment," he related, but he recommended that the "remainder of the company [be] held to control fires."[84] By July 31, most of the fires in western Montana appeared contained, and Governor Norris permitted guardsmen to attend the summer encampment and the national rifle competition.

Based on Forest Supervisor Skeels' recommendations, the governor indeed sent only half of Company L, along with the other Montana companies, to American Lake south of Tacoma on August 8.[85] At American Lake, 53 officers and 532 enlisted men, including the regimental band, participated in joint maneuvers. Meanwhile, the rifle team, under the leadership of Adjutant General Greenan, represented Montana at the national match in Ohio.[86]

Although most fires seemingly were controlled by early August, relief was only temporary and danger increased. Within days of the guardsmen's departure, the winds picked up, transforming small blazes into powerful infernos. Overwhelmed by fires raging out of control, Forest Supervisor Greeley turned to the national government for help.[87] In response, President William Howard Taft authorized ten U.S. Army companies to fight fires in the Coeur d'Alene, Lolo, and Flathead national forests. On August 11, a battalion of the 14th U.S. Infantry cut short maneuvers at American Lake and proceeded east to join the fire lines.[88] By the next day, two additional battalions of the 25th U.S. Infantry boarded trains heading toward critical areas in Montana.[89]

In response to the President's action, Governor Norris ordered the prompt return of Montana guardsmen from American Lake. On the morning of August 13, the First Battalion, comprised of companies from Kalispell, Glendive, and Big Timber under the command of Maj. Dan Donohue, departed on the Great Northern Railroad. Later that afternoon, the remaining companies likewise boarded coaches bound for Montana.[90] Before any of these troops arrived, however, high humidity slowed the fires, and by August 15 nearly 3,000 small and 90 large fires were largely restricted.[91] In a few days, Montana guardsmen were back at their home stations.

On August 20, gale force winds again swept across the region, combining hundreds of small fires into massive conflagrations up to 30 or 50 miles across in northern Idaho and western Montana.[92] The walls of flames gained speed across the Bitterroot Range in the Lolo National Forest, sweeping through the towns of Taft, Haugan Junction, and DeBorgia, and moving northward in the Kootenai National Forest.[93] Lolo National Forest Supervisor Elers Koch later recounted the horrific beginnings of the 48 hour holocaust. "Fire lines…melted away under the fierce blast," he remembered. "The sky turned a ghastly yellow, and at four o'clock it was black dark ahead of the advancing flames." Koch also repeated a description reported by another witness. "The air felt electric, as though the whole world was ready to go up in a spontaneous combustion."[94]

The Kootenai National Forest endured severe damage on August 21 as the flames destroyed mining camps near Sylvanite and threatened Troy and Libby.[95] As the firestorm closed in on Libby, Mayor Dow and Capt. Paul D. Pratt, commander of Libby's Company L, sent a frantic message to Governor Norris. "We must have help at Libby immediately," they wrote, "we cannot handle situation."[96] In the absence of Adjutant General Greenan at the Ohio rifle match, the governor assumed control over the Montana guard in his role as commander-in-chief.

After receiving the urgent telegram, Governor Norris left the capital for northwest Montana to assess critical needs and assign regular army troops already en route to the Kootenai, Cabinet, and Flathead national forests.[97] With most of the telegraph lines burned down, the governor initially could not communicate with Libby. Fortunately, it was determined that contact could be made with northwest Montana by sending telegrams to San Francisco, then linking through Seattle and Spokane to Libby.[98]

Though a rise in humidity around 1 a.m. on August 22 slowed the fires on the Idaho slopes of the Bitterroots, the conflagrations in Montana went unchecked. The firewall in the Kootenai National Forest swept across mountains and valleys. Libby still remained in grave danger. Several ranches located as close as eight miles south of town were destroyed.[99] Later that day, conditions at Kalispell also worsened as a firestorm burned the surrounding mountains. Making matters worse for fire fighters, most of the critical hot spots were remote from Forest Service trails. The advancing 30-mile long blaze forced men to retreat from the fire lines. Reporting on conditions in the Kootenai National Forest, one journalist noted that the "camps…burned out before the fire fighters were able to gather their equipment and the problem of getting new supplies is difficult to meet."[100]

The situation in the Gallatin National Forest near Bozeman likewise grew critical on August 22. New blazes quickly combined into a conflagration burning out of control. The governor was in Libby when his private secretary, Will Aiken, forwarded Gallatin National Forest Supervisor D.T. Conkling's urgent plea, requesting that Bozeman's Company A combat a fire already devastating a five mile section of forest.[101] The exhausted fire crews, numbering about 250 men, were having only minimal success against the flames.[102]

At the same time, blazes in the Snowy Mountains, only 16 miles from Lewistown, also were fanned by the extreme conditions, gaining speed while heading for the community. The Lewistown Commercial Club petitioned the governor to call up Lewistown's Company D to fight the blaze. A telegram to the governor exclaimed, "willing to go, but want authority before moving."[103] The guardsmen waited for orders from the War Department. As a reserve unit of the U.S. Army, the Montana National Guard could only be summoned by the War Department after all available regular troops were assigned. Thus, Governor Norris had to wait for the federal government's reaction to the crisis before intervening. With Libby, Troy, and Kalispell in serious danger and receiving a request for 250 U.S. Army soldiers, the War Department sent the last five available companies in Montana and the Dakotas to the fire lines. By August 22, 30 regular army companies had been called up.[104]

Later the same day, President Taft wired Governor Norris: "Will you telegraph me what the exact situation is?" Rather than ordering the state militia to the fire line, however, Taft instead asked Norris whether he intended "to place state troops in the threatened towns to do police work?"[105]

Taft's inquiry about having the National Guard do "police work" complicated state procedures and the governor's ability to authorize the call-up during the crisis. Nevertheless, Governor Norris mobilized units to join U.S. Forest Service employees and regular army troops at the fire lines. Shortly before his departure for Helena on August 23, he called up several companies and ordered others to remain on alert at their home stations. The governor instructed Capt. E.W. Williams of Bozeman's Company A to "assemble command and...proceed to co-operate with Forest Supervisor Conkling in fighting forest fires" in the Gallatin National Forest. He also ordered Lewistown's Company D, under Capt. James Croft, to join Forest Supervisor J.B. Seeley and his fire crews in the Snowy Mountains. And, in response to ever growing concerns in northwest Montana, Norris ordered Kalispell's Company F, commanded by Capt. L.A. Foote, to travel southward to Ronan. The governor also directed Lt. M.L. Doering to lead Kalispell's Company H to the lumber town of Eureka, located near the Canadian border.[106]

Most guardsmen responded to the governor's orders immediately. Due to the absence of Adjutant General Greenan and with other officers being gone, however, the guard's chain of command was disrupted. This situation, coupled with Taft's opinion about the guard doing "police work," caused confusion.

Kalispell's Capt. Foote and Lt. Doering realized that more than half of their men already were fighting fires in a citizen's role. Thus, less than half of their soldiers were available for activation as a unit. There was dissension, too. Some members of companies F and H, Kalispell, refused to fight fires: "They could not be called out in fact, for any such purpose and would rather take their discharges rather than do so." Upon hearing this, Capt. Foote argued that "the governor, under the state militia law…has authority to call out state troops for any purpose upon authority from the war department." This seemed to have no impact on the dissenters. According to the Kalispell *Daily Interlake*, this faction of guardsmen took their discharges from the state militia.[107]

The remaining members of Kalispell's Company F left August 24 for Ronan, while Company H departed two days later to Eureka. Company F had assembled at the local armory on the night prior to their departure. Despite their intended role as fire fighters, they left early the next morning in "heavy marching order, with each soldier carrying ninety rounds of ammunition." Upon their arrival at Ronan, Blackfeet National Forest Supervisor Haines welcomed the troops, and immediately escorted them to fire lines near Olney.[108]

On August 23, despite some snow dusting the higher elevations and rain falling in the valleys, Libby and Kalispell remained bone dry. Fears of another fire storm terrified local residents and Forest Service employees. Later that day, District Supervisor Greeley wired Norris from Kalispell, requesting that the governor call out all available militia units to stave off blazes at the danger points.[109] Simultaneously, Forest Supervisor Ralph N. Bushnell informed the governor of large fires burning out of control south of Bozeman.[110] In turn, Norris sent an urgent telegram to Adjutant General Greenan at Camp Perry in Ohio, requesting his timely return to the state. "Fire conditions serious," he wrote, "your services greatly needed here."[111] Within 24 hours, Greenan and the Montana rifle team forfeited the last part of the competition and boarded a train bound for Helena.[112]

Within hours of Greenan's departure, rainfall weakened the grip of the Kootenai fires, particularly near Libby and Kalispell, and gave fire fighters in the Cabinet and Gallatin national forests a reprieve. Even though heavy precipitation extinguished fires in the Snowy, Belt, and Bitterroot ranges, Norris ordered the troops to remain on alert. "Winds constitute an ever present source of danger," he warned.[113] Contrary to the governor's precautionary measures, Kootenai Forest Supervisor Skeels was now confident that his men could contain three remaining large fires. Skeels informed the governor that state assistance was no longer needed.[114]

Relief proved temporary. Within a few days strong winds and warm weather returned, again producing ideal conditions for flames to swell. On August 26, some small fires sprang up at Elk Park, 17 miles north of Butte. As winds fanned the flames into several large fires, 24 Butte citizens with mining equipment fought the blaze. Capt. Vickers, commander of Butte's Company B, stood ready for Governor Norris' order, which was not forthcoming. [115] (This inaction in fighting fires may have acerbated the strong anti-guard sentiment already existing among Butte's labor unions.) Meanwhile, Bozeman's Company K had barely reached home when several fires re-ignited in the Gallatin National Forest, developing into widespread flames. The soldiers remaining in the field tried to push back the fire. On August 30, Company C stationed at Big Timber was called out for the first time, combating a large blaze in the Boulder Reserve, located 12 miles away. With fires still burning in the Snowy and Belt mountains, members of Lewistown's Company D closely monitored the status of that area.[116]

The fire season finally concluded on September 1 when cooler temperatures and an early heavy snowfall extinguished the blazes.[117] The vast 1910 fires had a profound impact on the Northwest and, in some respects, the entire nation.[118] More than 3 million acres of forest were destroyed, enough timber "to build from 50,000 to 55,000 four- and five-room cottages."[119] The fires destroyed six boomtowns in northern Idaho and western Montana, burned down portions of Sylvanite, Montana, and Wallace, Idaho, and threatened several other communities. Amazingly, the guard and regular army suffered no fatalities. Others were not so lucky—at least 85 people died. Of these, 72 Forest Service employees and pickup laborers perished in the Coeur d'Alene fire, 2 in the Pend Oreille National Forest, and 4 in the Cabinet National Forest; 7 other people also were victims, including 2 at Wallace, 1 at Taft, 3 homesteaders near Newport, Washington, and 1 prospector at the head of the St. Joe River.[120]

"The forests staggered, rocked, exploded, and then shriveled under the holocaust" of August 20–21, according to historian Betty Goodwin Spencer in *The Big Blowup* (1956).[121] Another writer, Ruby El Hult, noted that for several days smoke darkened skies as far away as Watertown, New York.[122] Hult, in her book *Northwest Disasters* (1960), also provides this vivid account of the terrifying holocaust: "On those two terrible days, August 20–21, fires had surged like great red rivers through that double tier of National Forests on both slopes of the Bitter Root Mountains…not rivers in channels but rivers in flood, inundating the land in great irregular destructive blotches."[123]

On August 27, Adjutant General Greenan arrived in Montana to resume command. Immediately, Governor Norris turned leadership back to Greenan and to regimental commander Col. George W. Reif and Maj. Dan Donohue of the First Battalion.[124] Norris initially had activated five western Montana units, though a number of guardsmen already were out on the fire lines as citizen volunteers. The five companies served diligently, while the remaining six Montana companies reported nightly to their home stations. Eventually, three of the latter units also were called up during the last week of August.

For their efforts, guardsmen received praise from both state and federal authorities. Governor Norris already had publicly commended the guard on August 25, expressing his appreciation to Maj. Donohue and the entire regiment for their prompt response. Five days later, he declared that the emergency "gave the general public a better idea of the situation in the National Guard of this State."[125] Gallatin Forest Supervisor Conkling also praised the men of Bozeman's Company A for their courageous assistance.[126] "The forest fires have proved the sterling worth and absolute necessity of the National Guard. Not only have its members rendered efficient service, but also they have proved capable, dependable men."[127]

Letters sent by Washington officials, including from Acting Secretary of Agriculture James Wilson, also praised the guard for its willingness to join the Forest Service in the struggle. "Please accept thanks for the assistance rendered by the State troops in fighting forest fires," he wrote. "Your hearty cooperation is greatly appreciated."[128]

Fighting the great fires of 1910 proved a defining moment for the Montana National Guard, establishing an enduring legacy. No governor before had called upon the militia to counter the calamitous effects of nature. Guardsmen forged a new identity for themselves—that of assisting Montana communities and government agencies in dire need during natural disasters.

Just before the turn of the 20th century, the 1st Montana Infantry Regiment had returned from the Philippines to a joyous welcome from Montana's citizens. Patriotism and pride enabled the Montana guard to reorganize quickly despite shortages in federal and state appropriations. Men from local communities seeking membership in the militia were fully aware of the shortages, and often willingly supplied their own uniforms and equipment.

Within a decade, the Montana National Guard had expanded to 12 companies and aligned itself with regular army standards, while receiving national appropriations in return for stricter federal control. Significantly, the creation of new companies in eastern Montana at Billings, Miles City, and Glendive now gave the Montana guard a strong claim as a statewide organization. Perhaps most importantly during this period, the Montana guard had earned respect for its assistance in fighting the 1910 conflagrations, thereby protecting life, home, property, and one of the state's most prized resources—its forests.

Notes

1. *Biennial Report of the Adjutant General, 1897–1898*, 16, 21–27.
2. *Biennial Report, 1899–1900*, 3, 5.
3. Ibid., 4–5.
4. William H. Riker, *Soldiers of the States* (Washington, D.C.: Public Affairs Press, 1957), 60; *Biennial Report, 1899–1900*, 7.
5. The $400,000 federal appropriation was established by the Militia Act of 1808 and the amount had not been raised for more than 90 years. Martha Derthick, *The National Guard in Politics* (Cambridge: Harvard University Press, 1965), 21; Riker, *Soldiers of the States*, 60–61. For further information relating to the Interstate National Guard, see *Proceedings of the 1st Annual Interstate National Guard Association*, December 7–8, 1897.
6. *Biennial Report, 1899–1900*, 10.

7. Derthick, *National Guard in Politics* 22; Jerry Cooper, *The Rise of the National Guard: The Evolution of the American Militia, 1865–1920* (Lincoln: University of Nebraska Press, 1997), 109; Riker, *Soldiers of the States*, 68.
8. *Biennial Report 1899–1900*, 10; Circular [no number], War Department, January 15, 1901, Box 24 Folder E-2, Record Group 168, National Archives. Under section 16 of the 1897 Montana Military Code, each company was required to maintain at least 1 captain, 1 first lieutenant, and 40 soldiers; *State of Montana 1897 Military Code*.
9. According to the 1900 Montana county assessor's report, nearly 80 percent of the estimated 31,258 men available for military duty resided in the western and central regions of the state; *Biennial Report, 1899–1900*, 6–7. Agriculture dominated the economy of the eastern plains, resulting in a sparser population. Economics and population, however, were not the only factors that prompted western counties to organize company units. According to Montana historian K. Ross Toole, plains Montanans looked outward, not inward. "It was Congress, not the legislature" that "determined how the public domain was to be handled." It was the Eastern owned and managed railroads, not the local mining magnates that "had fingers in his pie"; K. Ross Toole, *Twentieth-Century Montana: A State of Extremes* (Norman: University of Oklahoma Press, 1972; reprint, 1979), 99–101. It also may be assumed that rivalry between the eastern and western regions may have caused dissension in Montana's legislature over the maintenance of the guard, which contributed to militia appropriations remaining at minimum levels for several years.
10. *Biennial Report, 1901–1902*, 5; Governor Joseph K. Toole to Adjutant General McCulloch, March 13, 1901, Box 7 Folder 7, Governor Joseph Toole Papers, Manuscript Collection 35a, Montana Historical Society, Helena, Montana [hereafter cited as Toole Papers, MC 35a, MHS].
11. Adjutant General R. Lee McCulloch to Governor J.K. Toole, April 26, 1901, Box 7 Folder 7, Toole Papers, MC 35a, MHS.
12. *Biennial Report, 1901–1902*, 5, 11. In 1901, Montana was entitled to receive arms and equipment valued up to $6,372.53, provided that the state maintained at least 300 men in the militia. Adjutant General R. Lee McCulloch to Governor Toole, September 8, 1901, Box 7 Folder 7, Toole Papers, MC 35a, MHS.
13. *Biennial Report, 1901–1902*, 5; On June 18, 1902, Governor Toole reported that the Montana National Guard comprised 412 men, "regularly organized, uniformed, and in actual service of the state...and that the average attendance at drills and parades...is 308." Governor J.K. Toole to Brig. Gen. M.I. Ludington, Quartermaster General U.S. Army, June 18, 1902, and Adjutant General R. Lee McCulloch to Governor Joseph K. Toole, August 4, 1902, Box 237 Folder 4, Montana Governors' Papers, Manuscript Collection, MC 35, MHS.
14. *Biennial Report, 1899–1900*, 10; *Biennial Report, 1901–1902*, 5–6; "Montana National Guard-Bibliography of Outline History," Vertical File M, Montana Historical Society Library, Helena, Montana. Discrepancies exist between the Montana *AG Reports* and Richard Lacey's *The Montana Militia*. On page 35, Lacey reports that Company B was organized in Big Timber and that Capt. G.H. Preston commanded Company C. The historian also claims Capt. J.J. Venire, not Capt. J.Z. Verne, commanded Red Lodge's Company D. Lacey does not provide footnotes and it is unclear where he obtained this information; therefore, it may be assumed that information reported in the 1900 and 1902 Montana state government documents is accurate. See Richard H. Lacey, *The Montana Militia: A History of Montana's Volunteer Forces, 1867–1976* (Dillon, Montana: Tribune-Examiner Press, 1976).

15. Lee Mantle to Governor Smith, October 18, 1898, Box 28 Folder 2, Montana Governors' Papers, MC 35, MHS; *1898 Mobilization Act, U.S. Statutes at Large* 30 (1898): 361–63.
16. *Biennial Report, 1901–1902*, 8.
17. Ibid., 7; Montana National Guard Board of Survey Report, October 14–16, 1901, Box 7 Folder 7, Toole Papers, MC 35a, MHS.
18. *Biennial Report, 1901–1902*, 8.
19. Ron Landsborough, "The Antique Firearm Network: Krag-Jorgensen Rifles," oldguns.com/uskrag.htm (accessed November 12, 1999). See also, *Proceedings of the 5th Annual Convention of the Interstate National Guard Association*, May 4–5, 1904, 38–44.
20. *Biennial Report, 1901–1902*, 8.
21. Montana citizens presented the veterans with a Silver medal "representing a goddess crowning the soldier with a laurel wreath." The words "'First to respond to their country's call' 1898. Campanas De Filipinos 1899" surrounded the image. The Montana state seal was imprinted on the back and donned with the caption, "First Montana U.S. Volunteers Second Div. 8th A.C." A ribbon attached the medal to a military bar. *Biennial Report, 1899–1900*, 10, 12–14.
22. The tablet inscription denotes the name, rank, company, regiment, date of enlistment, and date of death of each volunteer during the Philippines conflict. Circular 1, Montana Adjutant General's Office, September 29, 1903, in *Biennial Reports, 1872–1912*.
23. Governor Toole to American Bronze Foundry Company, February 11, 1904, Box 237 Folder 7, Montana Governors' Papers, MC 35, MHS.
24. *Laws, Resolutions, and Memorials of the State of Montana Passed at the 9th Regular Session of the Legislative Assembly, Helena*, 1905.
25. Cooper, *Rise of the National Guard*, 109, 111; R. Ernest Dupuy, *The National Guard: A Compact History* (New York: Hawthorn, 1971), 92; *Militia Act of 1903, U.S. Statutes at Large* 57 (1903): 775–79 [Dick Act]; Cooper, *Rise of the National Guard*, 109. Martha Derthick claims the Interstate National Guard was essentially an ineffective organization that could not agree on goals, leaving the future of the National Guard in the hands of Secretary of War Elihu Root; Derthick, *National Guard in Politics*, 22–24.
26. Jim Dan Hill, *The Minute Man in Peace and War: A History of the National Guard* (Harrisburg, Pennsylvania: Stackpole, 1964), 189; Dupuy, *A Compact History*, 92; Cooper, *Rise of the National Guard*, 109; Dick Act, 775–79.
27. The Office of the Adjutant General was renamed as the Division of Militia Affairs in 1908 and remained under the auspices of the War Department. Maurice Matloff, ed., *American Military History* (1969; reprinted and partially revised, 1973; reprint, Washington, D.C.: Center for Military History, 1988), 351.
28. Cooper, *Rise of the National Guard*, 110, 132; Dupuy, *A Compact History*, 92; Dick Act, 775; Matloff, *American Military History*, 351–52.
29. Ibid., 185.
30. Hill, *Minute Man in Peace and War*, 191.
31. Riker, 61, 68.
32. Ibid., 70.
33. Only the portions of Idaho and Wyoming that lay within Yellowstone National Park were included within the Department of Dakota. The state of South Dakota was assigned to the Department of the Missouri, headquartered at Chicago, Illinois. General Order No. 65, U.S. War Department, Washington, D.C., December 22, 1903, Box 237 Folder 7, Montana Governors' Papers, MC 35, MHS.
34. *1904 Military Code of the State of Montana* [*1904 Military Code*], 9.

35. *Biennial Report, 1903–1904*, 4–5.
36. Only 1,169 out of 2,151 units were completely outfitted. Hill, *Minute Man in Peace and War,* 199.
37. *Biennial Report, 1903–1904*, 9.
38. *1897 Montana State Military Code*, 5.
39. Section 18 of the *1897 Montana Militia Code* required guardsmen to attend training at Fort Ellis. *Biennial Report, 1899–1900,* 7; *Biennial Report, 1901–1902*, 5; *Biennial Report, 1903–1904*, 5.
40. *Biennial Report, 1903–1904* contains excerpts from the original correspondence, but does not identify the military secretary.
41. *Biennial Report, 1901–1902*, 10; *Biennial Report, 1903–1904*, 7.
42. Ibid.
43. General Orders No. 13, Montana Adjutant General's Office, August 13, 1907, Montana Military History Museum, Library Archives, Fort William H. Harrison, Helena, Montana [hereafter cited as MMHM, LA, Fort Harrison].
44. Dupuy, *A Compact History,* 93.
45. Adjutant General A.M. Alderson and Zerah Torey to Governor Toole, May 1, 1905, Box 237 Folder 8, Montana Governors' Papers, MC 35, MHS.
46. Forty-six men were mustered into Company K, located at Billings, on April 11, 1905. During the same year, 65 men residing in Glendive were mustered in as Company I. Adjutant General Alderson to Governor Toole, February 17, 1905, and Adjutant General A.M. Alderson and Zerah Torey to Governor Toole, May 1, 1905, Fred J. Marks, Glendive, to Governor Toole, January 15, 1905, Box 237 Folder 8, Montana Governors' Papers, MC 35, MHS.
47. Western and eastern Montana historically have been regions divided by sharp differences. Early population centers in western cities such as Helena, Butte, Missoula, and even Great Falls were dependent on the mining and timber industries, whereas ranching and farming predominated in eastern Montana. See K. Ross Toole, *Twentieth-Century Montana: A State of Extremes* (Norman: University of Oklahoma, 1972; reprint, 1979).
48. Adjutant General A.M. Alderson and Zerah Torey to Governor Toole, May 1, 1905, Box 237 Folder 8, Montana Governors' Papers, MC 35, MHS.
49. Ironically, Adjutant General Asbhy's successor, A.M. Alderson, was a member of Livingston's Company E. Alderson replaced Ashby as Adjutant General on January 6, 1905. Adjutant General A.M. Alderson to Governor Toole, January 6, 1905, Box 237 Folder 8, Montana Governors' Papers, MC 35, MHS.
50. Acting Adjutant General W.P. Hall, Washington, D.C., to Governor Toole, January 14, 1904, Box 237 Folder 7, Montana Governors' Papers, MC 35, MHS; Governor Toole to Secretary of War, October 8, 1906, Box 238 Folder 3, Montana Governors' Papers, MC 35, MHS.
51. John J.W. McGuinness, Montana, Col. and Inspector General, to Governor E.L. Norris, November 15, 1908, Box 242 Folder 9, Montana Governors' Papers, MC 35, MHS.
52. With less than 700 enlisted members, Montana was among the smallest regiments in the National Guard along with Delaware, Utah, and Wyoming. Cooper, *Rise of the National Guard,* 137, 139.
53. Company D, located at Red Lodge, and Butte's Company G were mustered out of service during June 1907. Both companies' membership had fallen below the 45 minimum requirement. On January 10, 1908, the Hospital Detachment, stationed at Helena, was transferred from the "medical department to the line," and was designated as Company G.

General Orders No. 7, Montana Adjutant General's Office, May 22, 1907, and General Orders No. 4, Montana Adjutant General's Office, January 10, 1908, MMHM, LA, Fort Harrison.

54. Maj. Roote practiced law in Butte. Even though Butte's Company B was disbanded in 1913, Roote retained his post as judge advocate general and briefly served as a summary court judge when martial law was declared in Silver Bow County in 1914.
55. Formal statement made by Jesse Bryan Roote, Maj., Judge Advocate General, Butte, Montana, March 26, 1906, Box 238 Folder 2, Montana Governors' Papers, MC 35, MHS.
56. Acting Secretary of War Robert Shaw Oliver to Governor J.K. Toole, June 11, 1907, Box 242 Folder 9, Montana Governors' Papers, MC 35, MHS.
57. Adjutant General Alderson to Governor Toole, June 21, 1907, Box 238 Folder 6, Montana Governors' Papers, MC 35, MHS.
58. John J.W. McGuinness, Montana, Col. and Inspector-General, to Governor E.L. Norris, November 15, 1908, Box 242 Folder 9, Montana Governors' Papers, MC 35, MHS.
59. Cooper, *Rise of the National Guard,* 110–12; John J.W. McGuinness, Montana, Col. and Inspector-General, to Governor E.L. Norris, November 15, 1908, Box 242 Folder 9, Montana Governors' Papers, MC 35, MHS. By January 8, 1908, only four states had conformed to Section 3 of the Dick Act: Idaho, Massachusetts, Wisconsin, and South Dakota. *Statement as to the Conformity of National Guard to Section Three of the Act of January 21, 1903,* Box 25 S3W2 R2 C25, Record Group 168, National Archives, Washington, D.C.
60. Cooper, *Rise of the National Guard,* 111.
61. Ibid., 110–12; John J.W. McGuinness, Montana, Col. and Inspector-General, to Governor E.L. Norris, November 15, 1908, Box 242 Folder 9, MC 35, MHS.
62. Dupuy, *A Compact History,* 93; Hill, *Minute Man in Peace and War,* 203–4.
63. Cooper, *Rise of the National Guard,* 112.
64. Ibid., 110.
65. Quartermaster General to Governor E.L. Norris, February 10, 1908, Box 238 Folder 6, Montana Governors' Papers, MC 35, MHS.
66. Acting Governor E.L. Norris to Assistant Secretary of War Robert Shaw Oliver, January 21, 1908, Box 238 Folder 6, Montana Governors' Papers, MC 35, MHS.
67. Erastmus Weaver, Chief Militia Division, to Adjutant General A.M. Alderson, July 15, 1908, Box 238 Folder 7, Montana Governors' Papers, MC 35, MHS; General Orders No. 12, Montana Adjutant General's Office, July 25, 1908, MMHM, LA, Fort Harrison.
68. "Companies act[ed] as coast artillery at the batteries and regiments of infantry to protect the fortifications from rear attack." Robert Shaw Oliver, Assistant Secretary of War, to Governor Toole, March 6, 1908, Box 238 Folder 6, Montana Governors' Papers, MC 35, MHS.
69. Governor Norris to Honorary C.M. Tinney, Department and Institution Auditor, Springfield, Illinois, February 1, 1910, and Julius Barney to Will Aiken, Helena, Montana, February 1, 1910, Box 239 Folder 2, Montana Governors' Papers, MC 35, MHS.
70. Governor Norris to Julius Barney, August 3, 1908, Box 241 Folder 7, Montana Governors' Papers, MC 35, MHS.
71. General Orders No. 1, Montana Adjutant General's Office, March 5, 1909, MMHM, LA, Fort Harrison, and duplicated in Box 238 Folder 8, Montana Governors' Papers, MC 35, MHS; Circular No. 2, Montana Adjutant General's Office, December 20, 1909, MMHM, LA, Fort Harrison.

72. Authorized by the U.S. Congress on May 12, 1892, and opened in 1895, Fort Harrison was named after the sitting president, Benjamin Harrison. When later realizing there was another fort of the same name in Indianapolis, Indiana, the Montana post was renamed Fort William Henry Harrison in 1906. Federal troops withdrew from the fort in 1913.
73. Adjutant General Phil Greenan to Governor E.L. Norris, June 17, 1909, Box 238 Folder 8, Montana Governors' Papers, MC 35, MHS; General Orders No. 5, Montana Adjutant General's Office, July 10, 1909, and General Orders No. 8, Montana Adjutant General's Office, July 31, 1909, MMHM, LA, Fort Harrison; General Orders No. 8, Montana Adjutant General's Office, July 31, 1909, General Orders No. 5, Montana Adjutant General's Office, July 10, 1909, Special Orders No. 15, Montana Adjutant General's Office, July 31, 1909, Adjutant General Phil Greenan to Governor Norris, July 26, 1909, and Adjutant General Phil Greenan, Camp Perry, Ohio, to Governor E.L. Norris, August 11, 1909, Box 239 Folder 1, Montana Governors' Papers, MC 35, MHS.
74. Kalispell's Company H was mustered into service in 1902.
75. Col. Inspector-General John J.W. McGuinness to Governor Norris, February 16, 1909, Box 238 Folder 8, Montana Governors' Papers, MC 35, MHS; *Biennial Report, 1909–1910,* 2.
76. Elers Koch, "History of the 1910 Forest Fires in Idaho and Western Montana," 2, Region 1, United States Forest Service, Missoula, Montana; Betty Goodwin Spencer, *The Big Blowup* (Caldwell, Idaho: Caxton, 1956), 34–37.
77. *Daily Missoulian,* May 1, 1910; Spencer, *The Big Blowup,* 36.
78. The national forest system at this time was divided into six regions across the United States, with each region directed by a "forester." Within each region, multiple "national forests" were designated and managed by "forest supervisors." Each national forest was further divided into smaller units, overseen by "forest rangers." Region 1, including 40,949,772 acres with headquarters at Missoula, encompassed forests in northeast Washington, the Idaho Panhandle, Montana, and northwest South Dakota. Forester William B. Greeley in Missoula oversaw approximately 22 national forests; and, in turn, forest supervisors directly managed the national forests. With each national forest ranging between 250,000 and 400,000 acres, the managers were overwhelmed in attempting to contain the 1910 fires with existing Forest Service employees. Spencer, *The Big Blowup,* 27–32; Ruby El Hult, *Northwest Disaster: Avalanche and Fire* (Portland, Oregon: Binfords and Mort, 1960), 100; see also Curtis W. Buchholtz, "The Last Summer at Lake McDonald," *Montana: The Magazine of Western History* 26 (4) (1976): 22–29, for a discussion of the early development of the U.S. Forest Service.
79. Spencer, *The Big Blowup,* 39.
80. Koch, "History of the 1910 Forest Fires," 2; Hult, *Northwest Disaster,* 100. Of the $742,976 granted to the Forest Service's district one for annual expenditures beginning July 1, only $30,000 was "placed at the disposal of the district forester for use as occasion may require in putting out fires"; *Daily Missoulian,* July 1, 1910. According to Libby's *Western News,* fire fighting costs in the Kootenai forests alone totaled more than $50,000 during the summer of 1910; Libby *Western News,* September 15, 1910.
81. Spencer, *The Big Blowup,* 39–40.
82. Ibid., 38.
83. Mayor E.W. Dow, Libby, to Adjutant General Greenan (copy to Governor E.L. Norris), July 25, 1910, Box 239 Folder 3, Montana Governors' Papers, MC 35, MHS.
84. Kootenai Forest Supervisor Dorr Skeels to Governor E.L. Norris, July 28, 1910, Box 239 Folder 3, Montana Governors' Papers, MC 35, MHS.

85. Governor E.L. Norris to Mayor E.W. Doe, July 30, 1910, Box 239 Folder 3, Montana Governors' Papers, MC 35, MHS. On August 4, 1910, Libby's *Western News*, however, reported that 38 men and 4 officers attended joint maneuvers at American Lake, Washington, located near Tacoma.
86. *Biennial Report, 1909–1910*, 6; General Orders No. 10, Montana Adjutant General's Office, August 12, 1910, MMHM, LA, Fort Harrison.
87. On August 3, 1910, the *Daily Missoulian* announced, "Men, men, men is the frenzied cry of the forestry officials...the available supply [of men] is now almost exhausted."
88. *Great Falls Tribune*, August 9, 1910; Elers Koch, Lolo Forest Supervisor during the Great Fire of 1910, reported that President Taft authorized the use of 10 regular army companies to fight fires on August 8. Koch, "History of the 1910 Forest Fires," 3; see also Hult, *Northwest Disaster*, 104. Betty Goodwin Spencer supports this claim, and reported that by August 10 more than 200 regular army soldiers were fighting fires in Yellowstone National Park; Spencer, *The Big Blowup*, 65–66. Since the blaze swept through federally owned national forests, the regular army was called upon by the War Department. Within the week, however, the situation worsened, prompting the timely return of Montana guardsmen from joint maneuvers; *Biennial Report, 1909–1910*, 8.
89. Spencer, *The Big Blowup*, 66–68; *Helena Independent*, August 16, 1910. Lolo National Forest Supervisor Elers Koch claimed that the regular army's role during the Great Fire of 1910 was rather insignificant; Koch, "History of the 1910 Forest Fires," 3.
90. *Helena Independent*, August 17, 1910.
91. Elers Koch, "When the Mountains Roared: Stories of the 1910 Fire," printed by the U.S. Department of Agriculture, Forest Service, Northern Region, Coeur d'Alene National Forest, no date, 3.
92. Ibid., 2.
93. Koch, "History of the 1910 Forest Fires," 3, and "When the Mountains Roared," 24; see also Hult, *Northwest Disaster*, 151, and Spencer, *The Big Blowup*, 238.
94. Koch, "When the Mountains Roared," 4. This 48-hour period was historically known as the "holocaust of 1910." For additional interesting and credible sources regarding the great fires of 1910, see Stephen J. Pyne, *Fire in America* (Princeton: Princeton University Press, 1982), and Richard C. Davis, ed., *Encyclopedia of American Forest and Conservation History*, 2 vols. (New York: Macmillan, 1983). The latter offer a broad historical overview of fires in the United States. Three additional sources include Hal K. Rothman, ed., *I'll Never Fight Fire with My Bare Hands Again* (Lawrence: University Press of Kansas, 1994), U.S. Department of Agriculture, Forest Service, Northern Region, *Early Days in the Forest Service*, 2 vols. (Missoula, Montana, 1944), and "Fighting Forest Fires—Then and Now," Theodore Shoemaker, October 1955 (reprinted in Elers Koch, "When the Mountains Roared"). Compilations of memoirs written by the first Pacific Northwest Forest Service employees are included in a file identified as Fire Management—1910 Fires, #5100, Region 1 Archives, Forest Service, U.S. Department of Agriculture, Missoula, Montana. A pictorial essay by Don Miller and Stan Cohen, *The Big Burn: The Northwest's Great Forest Fire of 1910* (Missoula, Montana: Pictorial Histories, 1978; revised 1993), examines the holocaust through reprinted correspondence, photographs, and newspaper headlines. While Miller and Cohen's book somewhat minimally addresses associated issues related to Montana, it does provide a vivid account of the summer of 1910, particularly in Idaho. Numerous journal articles also focus on the fire. For example, Tina Solberg, Bill Elmore, et al., "'All Hell Broke Loose:' The Forest Fires of 1910," *Montana Historian* 8 (2) (May 1978): 14–19, and George W. Reynolds, "Nature Sets the Stage," Garrett B. Holloway,

"Golden Anniversary of Fiery Horror," and Joe B. Halm, "An Eye-Witness Account," in "Death of a Forest—The Terrible Idaho-Montana Fire of 1910," *Montana: The Magazine of Western History* 10 (4) (October 1960): 46–58. Newspaper accounts include: "1910 Was Year of Holocaust in Forests," Kalispell *Daily Interlake*, July 3, 1961; "Rescue Mission in 1910 Fire," Libby *Western News*, October 19, 1967; and "More from the Quarries of Last Chance Gulch," *Helena Independent*, September 4, 1997.

95. In the Kootenai National Forest, fires burned at the head of Fisher Creek, while new blazes starting on the Yaak River traveled east toward Sylvanite. Winds also forced an offshoot of the blaze westward from the Kootenai National Forest, through the Kaniksu National Forest in Idaho and Washington. In comparison to other national forests located in western Montana, the Kaniksu National Forest escaped extensive destruction. *Western News*, August 25, 1910; Spencer, *The Big Blowup,* 178–79; Koch, "When the Mountains Roared," 23; Hult, *Northwest Disaster,* 198–200.
96. Paul D. Pratt and Mayor E.W. Dow, Libby, to Governor Norris, August 20, 1910, Box 239 Folder 3, Montana Governors' Papers, MC 35, MHS.
97. Kalispell *Daily Interlake*, August 23, 1910.
98. *Daily Missoulian*, August 23, 1910.
99. *Great Falls Tribune*, August 23, 1910.
100. Ibid., August 20, 1910; Spencer, *The Big Blowup,* 91.
101. Will Aiken, Helena, to Governor E.L. Norris, Libby, August 22, 1910, Box 239 Folder 3, Montana Governors' Papers, MC 35, MHS.
102. *Billings Gazette*, August 23, 1910.
103. Will Aiken, Helena, to Governor E.L. Norris, Libby, August 22, 1910, Box 239 Folder 3, Montana Governors' Papers, MC 35, MHS.
104. *Billings Gazette*, August 23, 1910.
105. President William H. Taft, Executive Office, Beverly, Massachusetts, to Governor E.L. Norris, August 22, 1910, Box 239 Folder 3, Montana Governors' Papers, MC 35, MHS. Portions of this telegram were reprinted in the *Helena Independent* on August 23, 1910.
106. Will Aiken to Spokane *Daily Chronicle*, August 23, 1910, Box 239 Folder 3, Montana Governors' Papers, MC 35, MHS; Governor E.L. Norris to E.W. Williams, August 23, 1910, 9:30 a.m., Box 239 Folder 3, Montana Governors' Papers, MC 35, MHS; Governor E.L. Norris, to James M. Croft, August 23, 1910, 9:30 a.m., Box 239 Folder 3, Montana Governors' Papers, MC 35, MHS. At the time of the call up, Capt. Snell, commander of Company H, was at the National Rifle Match at Camp Perry, Ohio. *Billings Gazette*, August 24, 1910.
107. The number of guardsmen resigning is unavailable. *Daily Interlake*, August 23, 1910.
108. Ibid. The *Biennial Report, 1909–1910* stated that Col. George W. Reif and Maj. Robert Eaton accompanied the Kalispell units into the field. According to the *Daily Missoulian*, Company F arrived at the fire line on August 29. *Biennial Report, 1909–1910,* 13; *Daily Missoulian*, August 30, 1910.
109. District 1 Supervisor William Greeley to Governor E.L. Norris, August 23, 1910, Box 239 Folder 3, Montana Governors' Papers, MC 35, MHS.
110. Spencer, *The Big Blowup,* 170.
111. Governor E.L. Norris to Adjutant General Greenan, Camp Perry, Ohio, August 23, 1910, Box 239 Folder 3, Montana Governors' Papers, MC 35, MHS.
112. Adjutant General Greenan, Camp Perry, to Governor E.L. Norris, August 24, 1910, Box 239 Folder 3, Montana Governors' Papers, MC 35, MHS; *Great Falls Tribune*, September 1, 1910.

113. *Billings Gazette*, August 26, 1910.
114. Forest Supervisor Dorr Skeels, Libby, to Governor E.L. Norris, August 25, 1910, Box 239 Folder 3, Montana Governors' Papers, MC 35, MHS.
115. *Billings Gazette*, August 27, 1910, and *Great Falls Tribune*, August 27, 1910.
116. 1st Lt. Tom L. Pittman, Lewistown, to Governor E.L. Norris, August 26, 1910, Box 239 Folder 3, Montana Governors' Papers, MC 35, MHS.
117. *Western News*, September 1, 1910.
118. The vast conflagration prompted the U.S. government to revolutionize forest fire management policies. For further information see John J. Little, "The 1910 Forest Fires in Montana and Idaho: Their Impact on Federal and State Legislation" (M.A. thesis, University of Montana, 1968).
119. Quote in Spencer, *The Big Blowup*, 238.
120. Koch, "When the Mountains Roared," 25.
121. Spencer, *The Big Blowup*, 80.
122. Hult, *Northwest Disaster*, 203.
123. Ibid., 197.
124. *Billings Gazette*, August 26, 1910.
125. Governor Norris to Dan J. Donohue, Maj., Second Regiment, Glendive, August 25, 1910, Box 239 Folder 3, Montana Governors' Papers, MC 35, MHS. Governor Norris to Lt. E.P. Neill, Company K, Kalispell, August 30, 1910, Box 239 Folder 3, Montana Governors' Papers, MC 35, MHS. This was a response to correspondence sent from E.P. Neill, 1st Lt. of Company K. Neill, reporting, "I have been in the National Guard for nine years...and have always found them ready to do their duty at personal inconvenience without thought or expectation of public acknowledgement. Usually they don't get either. In Montana, where until quite recently, the guard has been hindered rather than helped, your proclamation [*Billings Gazette*, August 28, 1910] appealed to me." E.P. Neill, Company K, to Governor Norris, August 28, 1910, Box 239 Folder 3, Montana Governors' Papers, MC 35, MHS.
126. Forest Supervisor D.T. Conkling to Governor Norris and Adjutant General Greenan, September 12, 1910, Box 239 Folder 3, Montana Governors' Papers, MC 35, MHS.
127. *Billings Gazette*, August 28, 1910.
128. Acting Secretary of Agriculture James Wilson to Governor Norris, August 31, 1910, Box 239 Folder 3, Montana Governors' Papers, MC 35, MHS.

6

Trials of Reorganization: Peacekeepers or Tin Soldiers, 1911–1914

Susan Paras

The militia must show patience and tact...cannot take the initiative; must keep their temper under a steady fire of vile names and derision. They must submit to being called cowards who do not dare to shoot.—Walter M. Pratt, 1912.

There were a few who yelled "scabs," "tin soldiers" and so on. I thought the "tin soldier" appelation [sic] fitted me.—Corporal Theodore Wiprud, 1914.

William Howard Taft, while serving as Secretary of War, made the far reaching decision of transferring jurisdiction of the Division of Militia Affairs from National Guard control to the regular army. (Taft would become the 27th U.S. president three months later.) He explained that the Division of Militia Affairs, established in 1908, had faltered in the process of integrating state units with regular army standards. Brigadier General Albert L. Mills, a former cavalry officer, took command of Militia Affairs as chief of staff. Mills, assisted by a group of hand-picked regular army officers, devised new plans to align state militias with federal military requirements.[1]

In 1910, the War Department detailed two regular army officers to oversee officer training at Fort Harrison. Between May 2 and 6, 48 guard officers attended the instruction conducted by Maj. Dana T. Merrill of the 28th U.S. Infantry. The high attendance rate, the guardsmen's willingness to learn, and their marked improvement prompted Merrill to offer a winter correspondence school.

Montana's Adjutant General, Phil Greenan, welcomed the proposal and ordered all regimental staff, field, and line officers to participate in the correspondence instruction.[2] Under the supervision of Montana's battalion commanders—Maj. Dan J. Donohue, Maj. John J. McGuinness, and Maj. Robert N. Eaton of the First, Second, and Third battalions—the officers were assigned ten lessons that emphasized four major areas: minor tactics, infantry drill regulations, map reading, and administrative procedures.[3] The guard officers' performance and dedication impressed Capt. Merrill.

In the fall of 1910, Adjutant General Greenan visited individual units throughout the state to evaluate progress. Upon completing the tour, Greenan reported that company officers scheduled unit drills, yet frequently did not attend these exercises. Geographical distances played a factor in some of these cases, but did not explain the negligence of a number of officers who resided near their company's station. Greenan criticized these officers for a lack of leadership and their units' shortcomings. "When officers are guilty of neglect of duty," he counseled, "it is showing an extremely bad example to the enlisted men, and the enlisted men can hardly be blamed for being guilty of the same character of offense." Accordingly, Greenan ordered regimental, battalion, and company commanders to complete quarterly reports, evaluating subordinate officers' attendance rates and leadership capabilities.[4]

On June 15, 1910, Acting Secretary of War Robert Shaw Oliver had inquired about arrangements for the Montana guard's annual encampment.[5] In response, Greenan reported that old Fort Ellis was unsuited as a military camp. The grounds were plowed up and fenced in, and the buildings run down and inadequate. Greenan also explained that five of the regiment's companies were located more than 350 miles from Bozeman, and Libby's Company L was nearly 500 miles away. He recommended moving future summer encampments to Fort Harrison.[6] Early in 1911, Oliver concurred.[7]

Though regular army troops would continue to train at Fort Harrison until 1913, the Montana National Guard took over portions of the post in 1911 and held its summer encampment there between July 17 and 22. A number of the companies needed further training regarding integration into a regimental formation.[8] Under the direction of the 14th U.S. Infantry stationed at Fort Harrison, the 2nd Montana worked extensively on drills and marching formations.[9] A non-commissioned officer from the 14th Infantry was assigned to each company, participating in all formations and "at all times acted as a friend, guide and mentor for the organization." On July 21, the entire regiment participated in a tactical exercise with the 14th Infantry's Second Battalion. While the regular army troops were positioned in the "hills west of the post," the Montana regiment successfully devised and implemented an offensive plan to take the hill. The guardsmen received high marks for their performance.[10]

At the conclusion of the encampment, Capt. Arthur W. Ferguson of the 14th Infantry was assigned to compile a Field Inspection Report regarding the Montana regiment. It was clearly evident that individual companies were yet lacking in organization and training. In fact, Ferguson noted that with the exception of a couple of the companies, the state militia was somewhat in disarray, despite an adequate supply of federally issued equipment, uniforms, and supplies. The guard's performance particularly was hindered by high absenteeism. "The majority of companies," Capt. Ferguson reported, "displayed a woeful lack of company training and most of them reached camp with a large percentage of absentees."[11]

Ferguson credited Kalispell's Company H, commanded by Capt. James J. Snell, for having the best unit in the regiment and acknowledged Snell's excellent leadership. Regardless of the fact that 24 of the company's 46 enlisted men were absent from the summer camp, Ferguson praised the Company H soldiers. Capt. Einar Rivenes, of Glendive's Company I, also received recognition. Although the company lacked experienced officers and adequate weapons training, Ferguson noted that Rivenes was "one of the best officers in the regiment." Ferguson concluded, "this company is well handled and in very good condition."[12]

Other companies showed reparable inadequacies, but companies B and G, stationed at Butte and Helena, were beyond restitution and immediately disbanded. With the resignation of Butte's Richard B. Vickers shortly before the encampment, Lt. Louis C. Lamont took over B Company, but faced insurmountable obstacles. Meanwhile, the Helena unit was poorly represented at the encampment and those who attended showed inadequate motivation, leaving Ferguson to conclude that the company was "not fit for any duty."

Company M, mustered into service at Fort Benton on March 13, 1911, suffered from dissension in its leadership. Ferguson reported that company commander Capt. Frank Chittum, a Philippines veteran, lacked the necessary confidence of his officers, Lt. John V. Carroll and Lt. William F. Wilford, to motivate and lead the Fort Benton unit. Ferguson warned Company M that unless its commanding officers put aside their differences, it would be disbanded.[13]

Whereas each of the Montana companies maintained annual rosters of between 42 to 65 men, company absentee rates at the encampment ranged from 8 to 29 each.[14] Many blamed low attendance on the long distances involved—e.g., Libby's Company L had to travel 465 miles to reach Helena, and Glendive's Company I had come 467 miles. Additionally, some guardsmen lived as far as 20 miles from their unit's armory. Ferguson acknowledged this factor in a state as large as Montana; it created difficulties in maintaining attendance at normal drills. Also, the widely separated units seldom had an opportunity to train in either battalion or regimental formations, other than at summer encampments and during biennial maneuvers with the army. However, he optimistically noted, "if this regiment could be placed in a camp of instruction…for one month…[then] it could be put in shape and fit for any duty…and could be made into a first rate fighting machine."[15]

Ferguson called "the aggregation of officers…absurd," and also directed the regiment to focus on membership retention and new applicants. He recommended the elimination of all officers in the staff departments, transferring these responsibilities fully to Adjutant General Greenan. Consequently, the quartermaster general, commissary general, chief of engineers, and chief signal officer positions were terminated. He also demanded the resignation of six unqualified officers across the state.[16] After Butte's Company B and Helena's Company G were mustered out, Ferguson clearly established what he expected of the remaining units at the next encampment, scheduled for the following July. He warned that unless serious action was undertaken, more companies would be disbanded.

During the winter of 1911, officers again participated in correspondence instruction, now headed by Merrill's replacement, Capt. Ira Fravel of the 19th U.S. Infantry.[17] Upon the completion of their winter assignments, 60 commissioned and non-commissioned officers attended six-days of training at Fort Harrison in May 1912.

In a 1912 report to the War Department, Capt. Fravel sympathetically noted how Montana's extensive geographical area and small population hampered the militia's progress. In the more populated states, such as New York or Pennsylvania, multiple companies or a battalion might be assigned to a single armory, thereby benefiting from tighter supervision and operation.[18] In Montana, on the other hand, great distances between units made it difficult for companies to fully muster together and train regularly.[19]

The Montana guard's performance improved slightly at the next biennial joint maneuver on July 14–23, 1912.[20] But again, attendance was a problem. Of 621 enlisted men, just 359 attended, while 9 of the 43 officers were absent.[21] The guard again drilled alongside the 14th U.S. Infantry, stationed at Fort Harrison and Fort Missoula. However, inexperience and insufficient training hampered the guard officers during the tactical exercises with the regulars. In reporting to the War Department, Capt. Fravel noted that the Montana guard benefited from the joint maneuvers, but regular army standards still remained to be achieved. According to Fravel, many officers assumed that rank automatically imbued them with additional knowledge; however, without a "thorough grounding in the ordinary subjects," he commented, "they will not be able to perform their duties satisfactorily in case they are called into active service."[22]

Additional difficulties soon arose. During Montana's 12th Legislative Session, convening in January 1912, a new militia law was enacted to amend the outdated 1897 state military code. Adjutant General Greenan proudly reported to officials in Washington, D.C., claiming the 1912 act would enable the 2nd Montana Infantry to meet federal regulations.[23] The brigadier general's prediction proved premature. When the law went before Montana voters in the November 21 general election, it was repealed. Frustrated, Greenan accused Montana citizens for giving "too-little credit" to guardsmen. He pleaded with Montana legislators to revise the "old militia" law to ensure the state followed federal standards. Otherwise, he warned, "the state cannot hereafter participate in the Federal appropriation."[24]

Guard supporters, from their point of view, blamed the legislation's failure on organized labor and particularly the Socialist Party, which publicly denounced the militia bill and used the controversial measure in their political platform during the 1912 election. Capt. Ferguson was taken aback by the strong opposition. "Socialist speakers," he wrote to the War Department, "would get on a box in the street and harangue on the militia bill for an hour at a time."[25]

Modern historians have suggested that the citizens' repeal of the 1912 militia bill, interpreted by many at the time as a means to increase the governor's authority to call out the militia in suppressing labor demonstrations, was a direct challenge to the powerful Anaconda Copper Mining Company. Furthermore, Progressives joined "organized labor" in opposition to the proposed law, "arguing that the [Anaconda] Company had pushed it through so that the militia could be used to crush strikes."[26] Union and worker opposition also affected a number of politicians initially favoring the measure. Aware of the growing influence of organized labor and its disdain for the state militia, and attempting to maintain their own political careers, a number of state representatives who voted for the bill remained silent after the referendum was defeated.[27]

In 1912, the Montana legislature, strongly influenced by the large working-class participation in recent voting, set aside a mere $10,000 to maintain the regiment and $5,000 to repair the state armory in Helena. Considering that $30,000 had been allotted in 1911, this was an astonishing blow to the 700-member National Guard.

By 1913, it became obvious that recruitment was adversely affected by the labor movement's opposition.[28] In certain localities this sentiment grew so strong "as to render it impracticable to successfully maintain an organization."[29] Particularly in Havre and Butte, labor organizers sought to dismantle the local units. Many in Havre, a key Great Northern Railway town, viewed guardsmen merely as strikebreakers. "Some members of the Union feel or pretend to feel that the Militia is hostile to their interests," observed 1st Lt. A.A. Hofmann, Montana's inspector-instructor in 1913. Unions forbade members from joining the guard and publicly ridiculed the organization.

Butte, western Montana's key mining and smeltering center, had always been a "veritable hub of unionism." Similar to Havre, its population was growing rapidly in 1913.[30] Of Butte's 40,000 residents, more than 14,000 men were affiliated with labor organizations. Montana's inspector-instructor reported that "the Guard [was] despised and hated...there [was] little love lost between the Militia and organized labor."[31] During the "holocaust of 1910," the governor's reluctance to call out the Butte company to quell blazes in nearby Elk Park also may have added to soured relations. Butte's Company B had become completely demoralized. It was anticipated that Company B would be mustered out of service, which indeed did occur.[32] Havre's Company C remained active for only two years, being mustered into service in August 1911 and disbanded on August 8, 1913.

As the recruitment challenge mounted, the regiment's inspector-instructor warned that the guard needed to attract dedicated applicants in order to maintain an adequate strength of 58 men per company. As early as 1911, Capt. Ferguson noted that "Guard applicants must exhibit a strong sense of patriotism, particularly in areas where local politics were dominated by labor organizations."[33] Adjutant General Greenan and the Montana inspector-instructor, Lt. A.A. Hofmann, scrambled to devise ways to attract new members to the floundering organization. They prioritized the guard's budget, placing new uniforms at the top of the list. In addition to the olive-drab wool service uniforms, Montana guardsmen were issued dress blue uniforms, for use at special functions and public appearances. Furthermore, the guard leadership continued to strive for a more professional-like organization; they admonished those members who might participate in activities resembling a fraternal order. Capt. Fravel also encouraged Montana guardsmen to remain active in community affairs.[34]

Interest and participation were encouraged by the annual marksmanship contest, particularly in regard to the selection of Montana's top rifle team. As in prior competitions, participants accumulated points based upon their "marksmanship, attendance at drill, soldiery appearance, intelligence, ability to teach, cheerfulness, and military courtesy." Soldiers with the 15 highest aggregate scores were selected to represent Montana at the national contest. Beginning with the match at Fort Harrison on July 28–31, 1913, however, new regulations required the Montana team to include at least seven new marksmen never before representing the state at Camp Perry, Ohio.[35]

While Montana guardsmen faced challenges at home, war clouds in Europe and revolutionary strife in Mexico made American military intervention on the international scene appear imminent. The Division of Militia Affairs tightened its grip on the reserve, issuing Circular 8 on August 1, 1913.[36] According to the order, individual state militias were expected to fulfill a quota of 12 companies, and were required to reorganize into battalions comprised of at least four companies each. Circular 8 also ordered the states to streamline their organizations by reducing the number of officers, based on regulation regimental membership rolls. Excess officers were to be retired or demoted. State militias unable to immediately meet the new standards (specifically the smaller regiments in the West), were granted six months to comply.[37]

Working within these constraints, the Montana guard quickly dismissed the regimental headquarters and abandoned one of the battalion headquarters. The affected officers were demoted or placed on the militia's reserve list.[38] To accommodate for the regiment's insufficient overall strength, Adjutant General Greenan reorganized eight companies into two battalions. Maj. Dan J. Donahue was given command of the First Battalion, consisting of Bozeman's Company A, Miles City's E, Billings' K, and Kalispell's M. Major John J. McGuinness was appointed commander of the Second Battalion, made up of Lewistown's Company D, Kalispell's companies F and H, and Libby's Company L.[39]

In the fall of 1914, the guard would be called upon due to tensions and disorder arising in Butte and Silver Bow County.[40] Lacking access to a sufficient number of federal troops in Montana, Governor Samuel V. Stewart activated the state militia to control the disruptions. Because their training had focused on military drill and tactical field exercises, the guardsmen were rather unprepared for enforcing martial law. The situation in Butte, however, returned to relative calm when the guardsmen arrived, allowing martial law to be administered for two months. The regiment's presence in Butte, nevertheless, would consummate the "state police" stereotype, negating some of the goodwill that guardsmen earned during the 1910 fires.

The origins of the Butte disruptions in 1914 came from within the ranks of labor itself. As the timber and particularly the mining industries flourished in Montana, labor union membership had soared, eventually influenced by European immigrant groups and other workers with radical agendas. The Butte Workingmen's Union, founded in 1878 and later renamed the Butte Miners' Union (BMU) in March 1885, had maintained a solid presence in Silver Bow County for decades. With the creation of the Western Federation of Miners (WFM) in May 1893, the BMU also become the Western Federation's first local unit. While the WFM pushed for better wages in the hazardous mines, it largely ignored other issues plaguing workers, such as health benefits, living and working conditions, and high prices in company-controlled towns. When the radical Industrial Workers of the World (IWW) arrived in Butte in the early 1900s, the BMU's determination to retain control in Silver Bow County resulted in a stand-off between the two groups. Organized in Chicago in 1905, the IWW not only sought to advance the cause of labor, but also had dedicated itself to eliminating the capitalist system, replacing it with a classless economy.

The IWW challenged the WFM, which prided itself in its traditional ideology and congenial relationship with Butte's largest employer, the Anaconda Copper Mining Company. Competition between the IWW and the WFM, and between traditional and radical elements within the Butte Miners' Union itself, reached a climax in 1914.[41]

Upset over the traditionalists' victories during a recent union election, the disaffected members of the WFM-BMU Local No. 1, referring to themselves as "progressives," sought to gain control of the union. The progressives charged the traditionalist officials, who were closely aligned with the WFM, with three counts—favoring the Anaconda Copper Mining Company over the needs of the union's constituents, devising a new policy to check union cards at the Anaconda Company gates, and embezzling membership dues.[42] Additionally, rumors abounded that WFM President Charles F. Moyer was negotiating with officials of the United Mine Workers Union to amalgamate the smaller union within the national organization. This infuriated progressive unionists wishing to remain independent.

Members from both sides in the Butte Miners' Union felt pushed over the edge. Violence first erupted on June 13, 1914, during Butte's annual Miners' Day Parade, an event celebrating unionism.[43] Angry progressives led by "Muckie"

McDonald broke up the parade and stole the Western Federation's safe. Unable to control the situation, Butte Sheriff Tim Driscoll frantically wired Governor S.V. Stewart on June 14 requesting that regular army troops be sent to Butte, arguing that the guard was incapable of controlling a situation of this magnitude.[44] The governor immediately apprised President Woodrow Wilson of the crisis in Butte. "Unless situation improves troops will be moved to Butte tomorrow," he reported. By that evening, members of the 2nd Montana Infantry assembled at their home stations and were issued 90 rounds of ball cartridges and two days' rations.[45]

On June 15, Governor Stewart arrived in Butte to personally assess the situation. He found the town curiously quiet. When local officials asked whether he had called up the National Guard, Stewart answered cautiously. Although unconvinced by Butte's peaceful facade, he denied having activated the state militia. Upon returning to the capital, Stewart ordered the guardsmen to return to their homes, but to remain alert. He also emphasized to the officers that orders issued from the governor's office were confidential, not to be leaked to the press.

Despite this precaution, the governor's actions became known to the public. On June 16, the *Butte Miner* and the *Anaconda Standard* reported that Stewart informed President Wilson that without the support of federal troops, the state's guardsmen, numbering several hundred, would be overcome by 12,000 angry Butte miners. Neither newspaper, however, published the president's response. Previously, Wilson promised the governor that "necessary steps" would be taken if the emergency required the service of the regular army, but he added, "it would be highly inconvenient and hardly necessary to make an intermediate transfer of troops to [forts] Harrison or Missoula."[46]

Governor Stewart's reluctance to believe that discord in Butte had abated proved correct. Tensions escalated within a few days of his departure. On June 17, a number of members of Butte Miners Union No. 1 met to decide whether to remain in the WFM or to organize separately. The outcome of the vote overwhelmingly favored creation of a new organization. On June 22 they formed the Butte Mine Workers' Union (BMWU), with Muckie McDonald as president. Immediately, the WFM countered that the new BMWU was controlled by the IWW.[47] WFM President Charles Moyer arrived in Butte on June 19 to try and settle the dispute between the traditionalists and progressives, but four days later a frustrated Moyer informed Governor Stewart that chaos reigned and demanded action regarding what he felt was an injustice imposed upon the WFM. He blamed the incendiary situation on IWW agitators and the negligence of Butte's Socialist mayor, Lewis J. Duncan.[48]

On June 23, the situation worsened, evolving into physical confrontation. Men of the WFM's Butte Miners' Union No. 1 held a regularly scheduled meeting at the Miners' Union Hall, while members of the BMWU crowded outside and blocked the front entry. Suddenly shots rang out, igniting violence between the two groups. The rioting stopped momentarily when the city was rocked by 25 separate dynamite blasts. The three-story Miners' Hall was leveled. As fear gripped Butte, the city police refused to intervene. By June 25, Butte quieted again, but the situation remained tense. Mayor Duncan reassured Stewart that peace was restored and persuaded the governor to refrain from calling up the National Guard. In return, he promised to use city police to protect Butte's residents.[49]

While Silver Bow County remained a hotbed of confrontation throughout the summer, the Montana guard continued with its regular training schedule. Between June 24 and 30, nearly 600 guardsmen attended joint maneuvers with the regular army at Fort George Wright near Spokane, including a simulated battle against the army troops stationed there. In late August, several Montana companies again trained with the Fort Wright regulars, but were recalled shortly because conditions in Butte required their presence.[50]

Contention had escalated again. Boasting a membership of 5,000, the newly established Butte Mine Workers' Union intended to displace the Western Federation of Miners by forcing the Anaconda Company to acknowledge the BMWU "as the miners' sole and legitimate bargaining agent."[51] Outside events now came into play. With the march to war in Europe, mineral markets had declined sharply, forcing American copper mines to reduce production by nearly 50 percent. The Anaconda Company laid off 2,000 workers on August 1.[52]

Ever determined to assert itself, the BMWU imposed its own closed shop. On August 26, its officials inspected the membership cards of workers arriving at the mines for their shifts, turning away 34 men without BMWU cards. The BMWU leaders "marched the men to a nearby vacant lot…[where they] were put on 'trial.'" Thirty-one were released after agreeing to join the new union, but the remaining three, loyal WFM members, were run out of town.[53]

Almost immediately, Anaconda Copper closed its mines. Fearing the actions of jobless and angry miners, distressed local businessmen petitioned the governor to send in the National Guard to prevent a possible "insurrection."[54] Stewart promptly wrote to Mayor Duncan, inquiring whether city authorities could "protect life and property." Duncan answered that Butte was under control and he criticized the businessmen's premature reaction, claiming they were unfamiliar with labor unions. Questioning the city's ability to control an outbreak, the governor again eyed federal assistance. On August 28, he telegrammed Montana Senators T.J. Walsh and H.L. Myers. "Butte situation remains critical," Stewart warned. "Citizens much alarmed and apprehensive…some already think martial interference must ultimately obtain."[55]

Senator Walsh replied the following day, forwarding President Wilson's response. Federal "troops could be landed within 24 or 48 hours," he relayed, but "incapacity of militia to deal with situation must first be demonstrated."[56]

Governor Stewart planned for the worst. On August 28, he had wired Secretary of War Lindley Garrison and requested four machine guns. Later that evening, the governor sent another urgent telegram to the senators. "Will probably be forced to take some action within twenty-four hours...we will probably not wait for co-operation of Government."[57]

On the following day, he directed Adjutant General Greenan to assemble the ten companies of the 2nd Montana Infantry and to arm each soldier with 100 cartridges. The governor's direct orders were clear: "Each member...must report for duty. No excuses will be taken...quick mobilization is requested."[58]

Within 24 hours, the situation in Butte worsened. During the early morning hours of August 30, dynamite blasts leveled Anaconda Copper's Parrot Mine employment office and street riots followed.[59] Unable to manage the situation, Sheriff Tim Driscoll sent an urgent message to the governor asking that regular troops be sent immediately.[60] Without first verifying Driscoll's request with Mayor Duncan, Governor Stewart promptly directed Adjutant General Greenan to mobilize the state militia at the armory in Helena.[61] "On request of Sheriff, District Judge, and citizens have ordered militia mobilized," the governor wrote to federal authorities.[62] Several companies arrived at Helena on August 31, immediately pitched tents, and began target practice while awaiting further orders.

Stewart's mobilization of the guard prompted positive and negative responses from citizens. Some Billings residents applauded the governor's actions, as did several Butte businessmen.[63] Other citizens criticized the governor for relying on the Montana National Guard and pleaded for the use of federal troops. "Threats are openly made that they will drive the militia out," one Butte citizen warned. "There are a great [number of] I.W.W.'s here and a great many foreigners from Bulgaria, Servia [*sic*], and Greece who will not hesitate to fight the militia," he concluded.[64]

Others told Governor Stewart that military intervention was unnecessary because local officials had the situation under control. Mayor Duncan and the BMWU lashed out at the governor's decision. The mayor vehemently denied that he had asked for the National Guard, and he claimed that the only way to achieve calm was to prevent the guardsmen from entering Butte. The BMWU echoed the mayor's claim, while also agreeing to keep the peace if the state militia did not intervene.[65] The governor justified his decision. "I have no time to bandy words with Mayor Duncan...who says that life and property has not been jeopardized," he argued. "Does this declaration square," he asked, "with a well known fact that within the past 48 hours an organization similar to the Vigilantes of early days has sprung up in Butte made up of responsible citizens for the avowed purpose of protecting their property and protecting their lives?"[66]

On the morning of August 31, Stewart wired President Wilson just hours prior to the guardsmen's departure from Helena to Butte. "Authentic reports estimate armed resistance from one to five thousand...I strongly request that you order some Federal troops to accompany us in. The presence of Federal troops will doubtless prevent armed resistance whereas the entrance of the Guard alone will precipitate test of strength and incident[al] loss of life. If you will wire me that Federal troops will accompany us we will wait for them."[67]

Entraining for Butte, August 31, 1914.
History Second Regiment Infantry National Guard Montana (1916)

Receiving no immediate response, the governor ordered the regiment's departure from Helena. At 1:30 p.m. on August 31, approximately 400 Montana guardsmen, armed with Model 1903 .30 caliber Springfield rifles, boarded 14 gondola railway cars.[68] Four Maxim machine guns and two Gatling guns recently sent by the War Department went with the regiment; the manned guns, surrounded by sandbags, stood mounted on a flat car directly behind the locomotive.[69] The guardsmen were alarmed by rumors that agitators intended to dynamite the tracks; consequently, protective measures were taken. A pilot locomotive preceded the guardsmen's train to warn of danger. Several miles before entering Silver Bow County, the guardsmen's train switched from the main line to the Anaconda Copper railway to confuse potential attackers.[70] Several guardsmen feared the worst. "It was doubtful if some of us would return home," recalled Corporal Theodore Wiprud, a member of Company D.[71]

They reached the outskirts of Butte that evening and, to avoid a potential nighttime confrontation with rioters, camped on a hill overlooking the city. The next day, the guardsmen approached Butte's city limits. They were led by Maj. "Dynamite" Dan Donohue, a Philippines veteran and former state legislator. They found the streets curiously quiet.[72] At 10 a.m. that same day, Governor Stewart issued a "Proclamation of Martial Law for Silver Bow County," turning complete jurisdiction of the city over to the Montana National Guard, which in turn, established arrangements under the "Martial Law Proclamation by the Commanding Officer." This required the closure of all Butte saloons, imposed press censorship, prohibited public meetings, and imposed a strict curfew. The proclamation also established a military court to try citizens violating these orders. Major Jesse B. Roote, a prominent Butte attorney and the guard's judge advocate general, would oversee civilian cases assigned to the summary court. Major John J. McGuinness would preside over the military commission for cases involving transgressions by officers or enlisted men.[73]

The governor's actions continued to attract the federal government's attention. In light of Stewart's feelings of "apprehension," Secretary of War Lindley Garrison ordered a battalion of the 14th U.S. Infantry from Spokane's Fort George Wright to proceed to Fort Harrison on September 1. Secretary Garrison reminded the governor, however, that "no federal troops c[ould] be sent to Butte or be used to quell disorder…I cannot…send any federal troops to accompany the National Guard."[74] This explanation notwithstanding, the governor was pleased with the secretary's response. He informed Garrison that even though the Montana guardsmen would quickly restore order in Butte, the presence of federal troops at Helena would undoubtedly "prevent resistance and minimize loss of life."[75]

Quickly taking control of Butte's streets and posting guards, the guardsmen restored calm. The men established quarters in the Silver Bow County Courthouse. During martial law, they were prohibited from fraternizing with local residents, particularly "girls who loiter," and from consuming alcohol.[76] Butte's residents, however, would be permitted to enter and conduct business at the courthouse during regular hours. In the days ahead as tensions decreased, a less regimented atmosphere would soon develop inside the courthouse. The *Butte Miner* reported that guardsmen "sang and danced…and staged…boxing contests" for entertainment.[77]

(After about a week, access to the building was restricted when it was discovered that prostitutes took advantage of the easy access and got in after hours. Wiprud explained that "those seeking 'girls' were not to be denied. A searchlight on the roof of the Courthouse spotted lovemakers at an entrance to a nearby church, in an open lot and other places to the amusement of onlookers. The searchlight had been installed to spot large gatherings of potential trouble makers."[78] Soon afterward, soldiers on guard duty were ordered to allow courthouse access only to individuals with legitimate business.)

By the second day in Butte, the governor informed Washington, D.C., that the "National Guard is in complete control."[79] Shortly, arrests were being made. On September 3, the military courts convened, with Maj. Roote hearing criminal cases in the summary court. Within a few days of Roote's hearings, however, the summary court became a target of criticism. On September 5, Montana Senator Thomas J. Walsh strongly advised Governor Stewart to repeal criminal trials conducted by the military tribunal and to return prosecution to the county's regular courts. The guard was called to Butte to merely aid the "ordinary officers of the law," he argued. Fearful of repercussions to the military court's sentences, Walsh also warned the governor that decisions handed down by the summary tribunal could be overturned by a federal court.[80]

Upon receiving the senator's correspondence, Governor Stewart immediately forwarded the recommendations to Maj. Donohue. Although the governor authored the martial law proclamation allowing a military tribunal, he redirected the blame elsewhere. In a September 10 letter to Senator Walsh, Stewart wrote, "I have placed everything in his [Donohue] hands." "While I do not feel disposed to interfere,…I shall impress upon him…the justice of the position."[81]

Based upon Senator Walsh's recommendations, Maj. Donohue took the first step in returning judicial power to Silver Bow County. On September 15, he restored the county's criminal court and permitted it to hear charges reported before September 1. All crimes committed prior to martial law were to be tried in the regular courts.[82]

Early in September, however, Judge Advocate General Roote already had exercised his judicial powers. He had ordered guard units to destroy liquor owned by saloon owners who violated the military code when remaining open for business.[83] On September 9, the *Anaconda Standard* reported that Kalispell's Company F, under orders of the judge advocate general, had confiscated $900 worth of liquor belonging to two saloons, pouring "every drop of wet goods from barrels, bottles, cases and demijohns" into the gutter.[84] The next day, the *Butte Miner* reported that a barber was given a 60-day jail sentence for refusing to cut the hair of guardsmen. On another occasion, a miner was arrested when he cursed soldiers as they crossed his path. The miner was subsequently acquitted of all charges after he saluted the American flag in Roote's presence.[85] It was clear to many that the judge, a prominent Butte attorney and the only permanent National Guard member in Silver Bow County, had abused his authority.

In the eyes of a number of Butte's residents, the guard's presence had brought security. But to other people, the regiment epitomized all of the negative stereotypes attributed to the militia. Letters poured into the governor's office and to the Montana senators, supporting or complaining about the National Guard's presence in Butte. Unaware that the regiment actually was undertrained for this kind of duty, some Butte residents praised the state militia for its professionalism. "There is a spirit of determination to do their duty no matter how distasteful it may be, and to do it as they have been taught it should be done," the *Anaconda Standard* had reported on September 1.[86] The Carpenter's Union and the Butte Chamber of Commerce also praised the governor for sending the state militia, and he also received supportive correspondence from some of Montana's farmers. W.M. Woodings, of Chinook in Blaine County, claimed that "had a single shot been fired on the troops entering Butte…rural Montana would have gone to Butte in overpowering strength in support of law and order."[87]

While most hostility directed at the guardsmen was verbal, reports indicate there were some physical threats. On September 16, a local plumber's apprentice was arrested and charged with planning to poison the guardsmen. He suggested to a plumber working at the courthouse that they place poison in the building's pipes.[88] On another occasion, an individual assaulted a physician who had treated three guard members.[89] Contaminated food sent to the courthouse, such as maggot infested meat, made it necessary to inspect all incoming provisions. These actions, however, had little effect on the performance of daily duties.[90]

With the exception of routine outside guard duty, rifle practice, and drilling, the men were ordered to remain on the courthouse grounds. The troops conducted rifle practice at the Rocky Mountain Rifle Club, where several officers also were trained to fire Colt .45 revolvers.[91] The regiment's most intimidating weaponry was in the hands of the machine gun platoon, outfitted with the four machine guns and two Gatling guns. Corporal Theodore Wiprud was assigned to the machine gun platoon shortly before the regiment's departure for Butte. Normally a member of the regimental band assigned to Company D, Wiprud had arrived at Helena on August 28. Along with the rest of the regiment, Wiprud was given hasty rifle practice. By the following day, Corporal Wiprud's poor vision and dismal performance on the firing range prompted officers to transfer him to the machine gun platoon. "If I had slight knowledge of a rifle," he reflected years later, "I had none whatsoever of the Gattling [*sic*] gun…here I was a corporal [bandsmen rank] of a machine gun unit."[92]

Wiprud was amazed at the power of the Gatling, which "had revolving barrels and…its fire was destructive because dum dum bullets were used." Under the direction of Capt. J.L. Tucker, the inexperienced machine gun platoon conducted target practice on September 27 in front of a large curious crowd of Butte residents. Despite their inexperience, they successfully operated the machine guns, firing 225 rounds a minute at targets a mile and a half away. Additionally, the two Gatling guns, each operated by two guardsmen, had the capacity of firing 300 rounds per minute, reaching targets up to a distance of 2,800 yards.[93]

By September 21, Butte had enjoyed three weeks of relative calm. As tensions eased, so too did the guard's responsibilities. The regimental band, stationed with Valier's Company D, for example, began performing evening concerts for Butte audiences. The soldiers' isolation, however, began to take a toll.[94] Restless guardsmen lobbied for permission to walk freely across the demarcation lines to visit cafes, attend church, and to see theatrical performances. Wiprud recalled that the guardsmen often attended "The Whip," a British-style melodrama. Rather than clapping, many of the guardsmen sitting in the balcony stomped their feet. "On more than one occasion," recounted Wiprud, "the manager…warned the boisterous audience that they might be the cause of a disaster."[95]

A number of men also began frequenting local saloons or visiting the red light districts. John Davis, the regimental band leader and a rather cocky individual, regularly entered drinking establishments. Davis's example sheds light on attitudes in Butte. "Upon entering one saloon he went up to the bar and slammed his pistol on the counter and called loudly for service. He received a look of disgust from the bartender," and was refused.[96]

Governor Stewart now noted that the guard occupation force, with each soldier being paid $3 a day, was becoming expensive for the state, especially as harmonious conditions persisted in Butte. The activation cost the state treasury $60,000 a month, prompting the governor to order Maj. Donohue to send about half of the regiment home.[97] On October 1, they departed Butte.[98] The remaining troops were consolidated into five provisional companies. The remaining men from companies B (Roundup) and C (Shelby) were combined into Company C under the command of Capt. Conway; companies A (Bozeman) and M (Choteau) were consolidated as Company M under Capt. Verge; Kalispell's company H remained independent under Capt. Snell; and the retained elements of companies K (Billings) and E (Miles City) made up Company K with Capt. Morris and Capt. Moore in charge. The machine gunners stayed to man the specialized Maxim and Gatling guns. The reorganized battalion was placed under the command of Capt. E.H. Williams of Bozeman.[99]

Meanwhile, the 14th U.S. Infantry from Spokane, temporarily stationed at Fort Harrison, complained about the outdated quarters and requested permission to return to Fort George Wright. Nevertheless, Governor Stewart remained convinced that the state militia's success depended upon retaining federal troops at Fort Harrison. The "disturbing elements," the governor warned Senator Myers, "are simply lying low with the hope that there will be an early withdrawal…and in that case there will be trouble."[100] Myers agreed and persuaded the Secretary of War to extend the federal troops' stay until spring, on the condition that they be transferred over to Fort Missoula.[101] The army troops arrived at their new quarters on October 12.[102]

As the streets of Butte remained quiet, the summary court's sentences drew critical attention from state and federal officials. On October 2, Maj. Roote sentenced the man assaulting the physician who had treated the guardsmen. The penalty—12 months in prison and a $1,000 fine. Later that day, another person was fined $200 for "insulting the uniform of the National Guard." The individual had walked into a tailor shop and, after throwing around military clothing, was apprehended.[103] Reacting to public pressure and heeding Senator Walsh's recommendation, Maj. Donohue temporarily suspended the military court beginning October 3, while he met with state officials in Helena to redefine Roote's judiciary power.[104]

As state officials criticized the military tribunal, a few local citizens defended Maj. Roote and argued that the civil courts of Silver Bow County were corrupt. "Without the military court the militia may as well be recalled for of what use will they be if…all offenders [are tried] before the civil courts of this county… [Roote] has done more to restore order than a thousand soldiers," claimed a Butte resident.[105]

The arrest of Muckie McDonald.
History Second Regiment Infantry National Guard Montana (1916)

Criticisms of the tribunal, however, outweighed support. On October 8, the Montana Supreme Court ruled that neither the militia nor the governor possessed authority to convict arrested individuals.[106] This decision was handed down after the supreme court examined petitions sent from prisoners held at the Silver Bow County jail, who claimed they were illegally arrested and imprisoned. Four labor union members tried in the military court had been convicted and sentenced to 11-month prison terms and $500 fines. They sought to overturn the military court's ruling.[107] With the supreme court's decision, it was clearly determined that beyond transactions involving military personnel, all other cases, particularly those covered under state and federal laws, were to be handled by the ordinary courts.[108]

In his defense, Maj. Roote suggested that the right to a writ of habeas corpus could be suspended because Silver Bow County was in a state of anarchy. Therefore, martial law superseded an accused person's legal rights, and the military courts replaced civil authority. "Under martial law," he summarized, "the constitution[al] guarantees of life, liberty, and property cease to exist, as does violators right to habeas corpus."[109] This failed to persuade the higher court. On October 9, the military tribunal was suspended indefinitely.

By mid October, it was clear that the governor wanted to return jurisdiction to local officials. "The regular authorities may begin the active assumption of their duties," reported the *Anaconda Standard* on October 13.[110] Two days later, the newspaper noted that although the governor had ordered the departure of 250 guardsmen, troopers were remaining in Butte "indefinitely" to enforce martial law.[111] Meanwhile, city and county peace officers returned to work under Provost Marshall Frank Conley's supervision.[112] The guardsmen continued to bivouac in the county courthouse. Though the demarcation lines surrounding the building were removed, soldiers still served on guard duty in Butte as a precautionary measure.[113]

On November 12, Governor Stewart ended martial law and returned all civil jurisdiction to the local authorities. After 73 days in Butte, the guard left for the armory in Helena. Two days later they were released from duty and returned to their homes.[114] Stewart praised the men for their quick response to state service. "The crisis was upon us—a crisis the gravity of which was realized by all who were conversant with conditions in the State's metropolis—and it became necessary to take the extreme step of calling upon the National Guard."[115]

Within 24 hours of mobilization in late August, over 400 guardsmen had reported for duty. By mid-September, nearly 600 had been sent to Butte. Despite early reports of potential miner violence and vigilante reaction, not a single hostile shot was fired during the occupation. Aside from a couple of demonstrations outside the jail, "no incidents marked the administration of martial law."[116]

During martial law, several hundred arrests were made, with 26 writs of habeas corpus issued, of which only one case was eventually sustained. On the other hand, no one was ever convicted for inciting the June 13 riot, of dynamiting the Miners' Union Hall on June 23, or of leveling the Parrot Mine employment office on August 30.[117] In sum, 44 officers and 685 enlisted men served in Butte during the fall of 1914. The total cost was $125,141.37, with $96,836 for pay and $14,417.20 for subsistence.[118]

While the 2nd Montana Infantry could point with pride to effectively easing the situation during martial law, the regiment's presence in Butte nonetheless provoked a spirited debate over the militia's policing power. This adversely affected the guard's reputation and prestige in the eyes of some citizens and officials. Judge Advocate General Roote's summary court, in particular, was criticized.

Corporal Theodore Wiprud, however, may have captured the essence of the situation during the festering union disputes. He felt that the appellation "tin soldiers" was, at least in his view, applicable. The guard, not trained for enforcing martial law, nevertheless successfully performed its task. "The reaction of the crowd generally I thought was an illustration of what a show of force by uniformed soldiers...can accomplish...no matter how poorly trained. [However] if something untoward had happened it would have been ev[e]ry man for himself."[119] For Butte and the Montana National Guard, the militia's effective show of force in the fall of 1914 was not followed by "something untoward."

Notes

1. Jim Dan Hill, *The Minute Man in Peace and War: A History of the National Guard* (Harrisburg, Pennsylvania: Stackpole, 1964), 210; Jerry Cooper, *The Rise of the National Guard: The Evolution of the American Militia, 1865–1920* (Lincoln: University of Nebraska Press,

1997), 112; Martha Derthick, *The National Guard in Politics* (Cambridge: Harvard University Press, 1965), 30.

2. *Biennial Report of the Adjutant General, 1909–1910,* 7.
3. General Orders, No. 11, Montana Adjutant General's Office, November 26, 1910, Montana Military History Museum, Library Archives, Fort William H. Harrison, Helena, Montana [hereafter cited as MMHM, LA, Fort Harrison].
4. General Orders, No. 13, Montana Adjutant General's Office, December 21, 1910, MMHM, LA, Fort Harrison.
5. Assistant Secretary of War Robert Shaw Oliver to Governor E.L. Norris, June 15, 1910, Box 239 Folder 2, Montana Governors' Papers, Manuscript Collection 35, Montana Historical Society, Helena, Montana [hereafter cited as Governors' Papers, MC 35, MHS].
6. Originally named Fort Benjamin Harrison, the post was commissioned by the U.S. Army in 1892. Adjutant General Greenan to Governor E.L. Norris, June 24, 1910, Box 239 Folder 2, and Governor Norris to Asst. Secretary of War Robert Shaw Oliver, June 30, 1910, Box 239 Folder 2, Governors' Papers, MC 35, MHS.
7. Lt. Col. Thomas H. Rees, Corps of Engineers, to Governor E.L. Norris, December 20, 1911, and Governor Norris to Capt. H.J. Brees, 1st Cavalry, aide-de-camp, San Francisco, California, Box 239 Folder 4, Governors' Papers, MC 35, MHS.
8. Field Inspection Report, 2nd Montana Infantry, July 17–22, 1911, MMHM, LA, Fort Harrison.
9. Walter M. Pratt, *Tin Soldiers: The Organized Militia and What It Really Is.* (Boston, 1912), 90.
10. Field Inspection Report, 2nd Montana Infantry, July 17–22, 1911, MMHM, LA, Fort Harrison.
11. Ibid.
12. Ibid.
13. On November 30, 1912, Company M remained stationed at Fort Benton, with Capt. William F. Wilford, 1st Lt. John V. Carroll, and 2nd Lt. Patrick Egan as commanding officers. *Biennial Report, 1911–1912.*
14. Field Inspection Report, 2nd Montana Infantry, July 17–22, 1911, MMHM, LA, Fort Harrison.
15. Ibid.
16. Ibid. See also "Report of the Camp of Instruction, Organized Militia of Montana, Fort Harrison, May 6–11, 1912," by Capt. A.W. Ferguson, Folder MNG-1912, Miscellaneous Original Military Documents, MMHM, LA, Fort Harrison.
17. Governor E.L. Norris to Mr. W.J. McCormick, Missoula, Montana, June 9, 1911, Box 239 Folder 4, Governors' Papers, MC 35, MHS.
18. *Biennial Report, 1911–1912.*
19. "Report of the Camp of Instruction, Organized Militia of Montana, Fort Harrison, May 6–11, 1912," by Capt. A.W. Ferguson, Folder MNG-1912, Miscellaneous Original Military Documents, MMHM, LA, Fort Harrison.
20. General Orders, No. 19, Montana Adjutant General's Office, July 5, 1912, Folder MNG, 1912: Field Inspection Report, 2nd Infantry Montana Regiment, July 15–22, 1912, MMHM, LA, Fort Harrison.
21. Company L (Libby) was absent, and companies D (Lewistown) and G (Helena) were mustered out of service prior to the encampment. "Field Inspection Report, July 16–22, 1912," by Ira Fravel, 1st Lt., 19th Infantry Folder MNG-1912: Field Inspection Report, 2nd Montana Infantry Regiment, July 15–22, 1912, MMHM, LA, Fort Harrison.

22. 1st Lt. Ira F. Fravel, 19th Infantry, to Chief, Division Militia Affairs, Washington, D.C., October 5, 1912, Folder MNG-1912: Miscellaneous Original Military Documents, MMHM, LA, Fort Harrison.
23. *Biennial Report, 1911–1912.*
24. Ibid.
25. Special Report: Changes in State Militia Law, Capt. A.W. Ferguson to Chief, Division of Militia Affairs, Washington, D.C., November 21, 1912, Folder MNG-1912, Miscellaneous Original Military Documents, MMHM, LA, Fort Harrison. According to historian Nick Salvatore, much of organized labor supported Socialist political platforms. See Nick Salvatore, *Eugene Debs: Citizen and Socialist* (Urbana: University of Illinois Press, 1982).
26. Michael P. Malone, Richard B. Roeder, and William L. Lang, *Montana: A History of Two Centuries* (Seattle: University of Washington Press, 1976: rev. ed., 1991), 259–60.
27. Special Report: Changes in State Militia Law, Capt. A.W. Ferguson to Chief, Division of Militia Affairs, Washington, D.C., November 21, 1912, Folder MNG-1912, Miscellaneous Original Military Documents, MMHM, LA, Fort Harrison.
28. *Biennial Report, 1911–1912*, 8, 16. Jim Dan Hill, *The Minute Man,* 217. Inspector-Instructor Quarterly Report, by 1st Lt. A.A. Hofmann, Organized Militia of Montana, to Chief of Division of Militia Affairs, April 7, 1913, Part III, Folder MNG-1913, Miscellaneous Original Military Documents, MMHM, LA, Fort Harrison.
29. Inspector-Instructor Quarterly Report, by 1st Lt. A.A. Hofmann, Organized Militia of Montana, to Chief of Division of Militia Affairs, April 7, 1913, Part III, Folder MNG-1913, Miscellaneous Original Military Documents, MMHM, LA, Fort Harrison.
30. K. Ross Toole, *Twentieth Century Montana: A State of Extremes* (Norman, Oklahoma: University of Oklahoma Press, 1972; reprint 1979), 123; see also Vernon H. Jensen, *Heritage of Conflict: Labor Relations in the Nonferrous Metals Industry up to 1930* (Ithaca: Cornell University Press, 1950), 289. Richard E. Lingenfelter, *The Hardrock Miners: A History of the Mining Labor Movement in the American West, 1863–1893* (Berkeley: University of California, 1974) recounts the development of mining in the American West, including a chapter devoted to Butte. For late 19th and early 20th century Butte history, see Michael P. Malone, *The Battle for Butte: Mining and Politics on the Northern Frontier, 1864–1906* (Helena, Montana: Montana Historical Society Press, 1981: reprint 1995); Jerry Calvert, *The Gibraltar: Socialism and Labor in Butte, Montana, 1895–1920* (Helena, Montana: Montana Historical Society Press, 1988); and Paul Andrew Frisch, "The 'Gibraltar of Unionism': The Working Class at Butte, Montana, 1878–1906" (Ph.D. diss., University of California, Los Angeles, 1992). Several engaging historical accounts of Butte have been written, including Work Projects Administration, *Copper Camp: Stories of the World's Greatest Mining Town, Butte, Montana* (New York: Hastings House, 1943); David M. Emmons, *The Butte Irish: Class and Ethnicity in an American Mining Town, 1875–1925* (Urbana: University of Illinois, 1989); and Mary Murphy, *Mining Cultures: Men, Women, and Leisure in Butte, 1914–41* (Urbana: University of Illinois Press, 1997). Additionally, Murphy has collaborated with Bill Walker on a bibliography specific to Butte; see Mary Murphy and Bill Walker, *Butte, Montana: A Selected Bibliography* (1980).
31. Inspector-Instructor Report, April 7, 1913, Folder Fort Harrison, MNG (1913), Miscellaneous Original Historical Documents, MMHM, LA, Fort Harrison.
32. Ibid. *Havre Plaindealer*, August 16, 1911, and *Havre Daily Promoter*, June 24, 1916.
33. Report of the Camp of Instruction, Organized Militia of Montana, Fort Harrison, May 6–11, 1912, by Capt. A.W. Ferguson, and "Status of the Montana National Guard," May 20, 1912, Brig. Gen. Commander Marion P. Maus, Folder MNG-1912, Miscellaneous Original Military Documents, MMHM, LA, Fort Harrison.

34. Inspector-Instructor Report, April 7, 1912, Folder Fort Harrison, MNG (1913), Miscellaneous Original Historical Documents, MMHM, LA, Fort Harrison.
35. General Orders, No. 8, Montana Adjutant General's Office, June 11, 1913, Folder Fort Harrison, MNG (1913), Miscellaneous Original Historical Documents, MMHM, LA, Fort Harrison. The Montana rifle team placed third in Class C at the national match during August 1913. Adjutant General Phil Greenan to Governor S.V. Stewart, August 29, 1913, Box 239 Folder 7, Governors' Papers, MC 35, MHS.
36. Cooper, *Rise of the National Guard,* 114–15, 139.
37. Circular No. 8, War Department, Office of the Chief of Staff, Division of Militia Affairs, Washington, D.C., August 1, 1913, and General Orders, No. 10, Montana Adjutant General's Office, October 1, 1913, Box 239 Folder 7, Governors' Papers, MC 35, MHS.
38. Lt. Col. Michael J. Walsh, Maj. Robert N. Eaton, Capt. Charles N. Sargent, Capt. Gerald W. Lansing, 1st Lt. Charles M. Bennett, 1st Lt. Charles Floyd Jump, and 2nd Lt. Charles C. Owings were placed on the militia's reserve list. Ironically, Lt. Col. Walsh and Maj. Eaton had been categorized "incompetent" by regular army inspector-instructors assigned to the regiment between 1911 and 1913, but were never demoted nor dismissed for their inept performance. General Orders, No. 10, Montana Adjutant General's Office, October 1, 1913, Box 239 Folder 8, Governors' Papers, MC 35, MHS; Circular No. 8, War Department, Washington, D.C., August 1, 1913, Box 239 Folder 7, Governors' Papers, MC 35, MHS.
39. Colonel Dan J. Donohue, formally the regimental commander, was demoted to major upon reorganization. General Orders, No. 10, Montana Adjutant General's Office, October 1, 1913, and Circular No. 8, War Department, Washington, D.C, August 1, 1913, Box 239 Folder 7, Governors' Papers, MC 35, MHS.
40. Guardsmen stationed across the nation had participated in relatively few labor-related conflicts in the early part of the 20th century. Cooper, *Rise of the National Guard,* 148.
41. Jerry W. Calvert, *The Gibraltar,* 89; Jensen, *Heritage of Conflict,* 289. For more on the IWW, see Melvyn Dubofsky, *We Shall Be All: A History of the Industrial Workers of the World* (Urbana: University of Illinois Press, 1988) and Philip S. Foner, *The Industrial Workers of the World: 1905–1917* (New York: International Publishers, 1965).
42. The progressives argued that assessments levied by the national officers to support strikes in Michigan, combined with local dues, amounted to a full day's pay for union members each month. Later, the progressives stressed that they were in favor of the additional dues, but questioned whether the money reached Michigan. Jensen, *Heritage of Conflict,* 325–27, 330, and Calvert, *The Gibraltar,* 80–82.
43. Jensen, *Heritage of Conflict,* 138; Toole, *Twentieth Century Montana,* 132.
44. Sheriff Tim Driscoll, Butte, to Governor S.V. Stewart, June 14, 1914, Box 180 Folder 7, Governors' Papers, MC 35, MHS.
45. Governor S.V. Stewart to President Woodrow Wilson, June 14, 1914, Box 180 Folder 7, Governors' Papers, MC 35, MHS; Adjutant General Phil Greenan to 2nd Montana Infantry company commanders, June 14, 1914, Kermit Edmonds Collection, File MNG 1914, Miscellaneous Original Documents, MMHM, LA, Fort Harrison.
46. Jensen, *Heritage of Conflict,* 329, and Butte *Anaconda Standard,* June 15, 1914; Governor Stewart to 2nd Montana Infantry, June 16, 1914 (memorandum), Kermit Edmonds Collection, File MNG 1914, Miscellaneous Original Documents, MMHM, LA, Fort Harrison; Governor Stewart to President Wilson, June 15, 1914, Box 180 Folder 7, Governors' Papers, MC 35, MHS; *Butte Miner,* June 16, 1914, and *Anaconda Standard,* June 16, 1914; President Woodrow Wilson to Governor S.V. Stewart, June 17, 1914, Box 180 Folder 7, Governors' Papers, MC 35, MHS.

47. Historians disagree over the causes of the dissension between the liberal and conservative factions of WFM-BMU Local No. 1. K. Ross Toole and Vernon H. Jensen both suggest the IWW not only influenced liberal WFM members to renounce their membership, but also persuaded them to organize the Butte Miner Workers' Union. Other historical accounts suggest that the IWW had nothing to do with the split between the progressive and conservative unionists in 1914. Jensen, *Heritage of Conflict,* 330, 332, 344; Calvert, *The Gibraltar,* 83–84; Toole, *Twentieth Century Montana,* 134; Governor Stewart to Senator H.L. Myers, June 17, 1914, Box 180 Folder 7, Governors' Papers, MC 35, MHS.
48. Jensen, *Heritage of Conflict,* 330, 332; Calvert, *The Gibraltar,* 83–84; Toole, *Twentieth Century Montana,* 137–38; Charles Moyer to Governor Stewart, June 23, 1914, Box 180 Folder 7, MC 35, MHS.
49. Jensen, *Heritage of Conflict,* 335, and Toole, *Twentieth Century Montana,* 135; Governor Stewart to President Woodrow Wilson, June 23, 1914, and Governor Stewart to Senator H.L. Myers, June 23, 1914, Box 180 Folder 7, Governors' Papers, MC 35, MHS.
50. Butte *Anaconda Standard,* June 22, 1914; "A Crisis in the Making," 13, Theodore Wiprud Collection, SC 111, K. Ross Toole Archives, Mansfield Library, University of Montana, Missoula, Montana [hereafter cited as Wiprud Collection, SC 111, UM]. Portions of Wiprud's memoirs have been published; see Theodore Wiprud, "Butte: A Trouble Labor Paradise," *Montana, Magazine of Western History* 21 (4) (1971): 31–38. Corporal Wiprud embarked on a medical career serving in several prestigious positions: as Executive Director of the Medical Society of the District of Columbia (1938–1962); Professor, Georgetown University School of Medicine, Washington, D.C. (1944–1949); and Associate Medical Advisor to the Director of Selective Service, District of Columbia (1948–1962).
51. Calvert, *The Gibraltar,* 85.
52. Jensen, *Heritage of Conflict,* 345; Calvert, *The Gibraltar,* 85; see also *Engineering and Mining Journal,* September 5, 1914, 449.
53. Calvert, *The Gibraltar,* 86.
54. Ibid., 86, 87; Jensen, *Heritage of Conflict,* 344, 345; Governor Stewart to Senators H.L. Myers and T.J. Walsh, August 29, 1914, Box 180 Folder 7, Governors' Papers, MC 35, MHS.
55. S.V. Stewart to T.J. Walsh and H.L. Myers, Washington, D.C., August 27, 1914, Box 180 Folder 7, Governors' Papers, MC 35, MHS.
56. T.J. Walsh to S.V. Stewart [telegram], August 28, 1914, Box 180 Folder 7, Governors' Papers, MC 35, MHS.
57. S.V. Stewart to T.J. Walsh and H.L. Myers, Washington, D.C., August 28, 1914, Box 180 Folder 7, Governors' Papers, MC 35, MHS.
58. Telegrams were sent to the following commanding officers: E.H. Williams (Bozeman), James J. Snell (Kalispell), Ralph L. Morris (Billings), William P. Morse (Miles City), James Stanford (Valier), Oliver S. Perry (Kalispell), Charles M. Bennett (Libby), Walter L. Verge (Choteau), Frank P. Baird (Roundup), and John J. Conway (Shelby). It should be noted that by August 1914, the 2nd Montana Infantry had undergone several organizational changes. Company B (Butte) was reassigned to Roundup, and placed under the command of Capt. Frank P. Baird. Company C (Big Timber) was reassigned to Shelby, with Capt. John J. Conway as commanding officer. After the disbanding of Lewistown's Company D, it was mustered in at Valier, under Capt. James Stanford. Company M, having been stationed at Miles City, was disbanded and reorganized at Choteau, under the command of Capt. Walter L. Verge. Adjutant General Phil Greenan to 2nd Montana Infantry Company Commanders, August 29, 1914 (memorandum), Box 180 Folder 7, Governors' Papers, MC 35, MHS.

59. Toole, *Twentieth Century Montana,* 138; see also Calvert, *The Gibraltar,* 87, and Jensen, *Heritage of Conflict,* 344–45.
60. Sheriff Tim Driscoll to Governor S.V. Stewart, August 30, 1914, Box 180 Folder 7, Governors' Papers, MC 35, MHS.
61. Governor S.V. Stewart to Adjutant General Greenan, August 30, 1914, Box 180 Folder 7, Governors' Papers, MC 35, MHS.
62. Governor S.V. Stewart to H.J. Myers and T.J. Walsh, Washington, D.C., August 30, 1914, Box 180 Folder 7, Governors' Papers, MC 35, MHS.
63. Thomas Arthur, Billings, to Governor Stewart, August 30, 1914, and Governor Stewart to President Woodrow Wilson, August 31, 1914, Box 180 Folder 7, Governors' Papers, MC 35, MHS.
64. Charles E. Sheme, Butte, to Governor Stewart, August 31, 1914, Box 180 Folder 7, Governors' Papers, MC 35, MHS.
65. Jensen, *Heritage of Conflict,* 345; *Anaconda Standard,* September 1, 1914.
66. Jensen, *Heritage of Conflict,* 346.
67. Secretary of War Garrison responded to the governor on September 1. S.V. Stewart to President Woodrow Wilson, Washington, D.C., August 31, 1914, Box 180 Folder 7, Governors' Papers, MHS.
68. *Anaconda Standard,* September 2, 1914; Governor S.V. Stewart to Lindley M. Garrison, Secretary of War, September 1, 1914, Box 239 Folder 8, Governors' Papers, MC 35, MHS.
69. On September 7, 200 additional guardsmen arrived in Butte to help enforce martial law. In total, Company A (Bozeman), Company C (Shelby), Company D (Valier), Company E (Miles City), companies F and H (Kalispell), Company G (Glasgow), Company K (Billings), Company L (Libby), and Company M (Choteau) arrived in Butte during September. Telegram sent by Adjutant General Greenan, August 29, 1914, Box 180, Folder 7, Governors' Papers, MC 35, MHS; *Anaconda Standard,* September 8, 1914; "Crisis in the Making," 12–13, Wiprud Collection, SC 111, UM.
70. Ibid., Wiprud Collection, SC 111, UM.
71. "As a Corporal Saw It," 5, Wiprud Collection, SC 111, UM.
72. Wiprud recounts the rumors that dominated the soldiers' conversations. One individual, he recalled, reported that "the flag flying over the courthouse in Butte had been torn down by the rioters." "Crisis in the Making," 12, and "As a Corporal Saw It," 4, Wiprud Collection, SC 111, UM.
73. It should also be noted that Judge Advocate General Roote had remained in his appointed office even though Company B, stationed at Butte, was disbanded and reassigned to Choteau in 1914. Silver Bow County Martial Law Proclamation, 1914, Folder 1, Silver Bow County Martial Law Proclamation (1914), Small Collections 1852, MHS. Byron L. Bargar, *Law and Customs of Riot Duty: A Guide for National Guard Officers and Civil Authorities* (Columbus, Ohio, 1907), presents one guardsmen's interpretation of laws regulating riot duty during the early 20th century. Montana was not the only western state that called out the state militia for such duties; see George G. Suggs Jr., *Colorado's War on Militant Unionism* (Detroit: Wayne State University Press, 1972).
74. Secretary of War Lindley M. Garrison to Governor S.V. Stewart [telegram], September 1, 1914, Box 239 Folder 8, Governors' Papers, MC 35, MHS.
75. Governor Stewart to Senator T.J. Walsh, September 1, 1914, Box 180 Folder 7, Governors' Papers, MC 35, MHS; Governor S.V. Stewart to Secretary of War Lindley M. Garrison, September 1, 1914, Box 239 Folder 8, Governors' Papers, MC 35, MHS.

76. *Butte Miner*, September 15, 1914; "Crisis in the Making," 12, Wiprud Collection, SC 111, UM. Appendix A lists the arrangements of the soldiers' quarters at the courthouse.
77. *Butte Miner*, September 5, 1914; see also *Anaconda Standard*, September 2, 1914.
78. "As a Corporal Saw It," 9, Wiprud Collection, SC 111, UM. For information on prostitution in Butte, see Mary Murphy, "Women on the Line: Prostitution in Butte, Montana, 1878–1917" (M.A. thesis, University of North Carolina, Chapel Hill, 1983).
79. S.V. Stewart to T.J. Walsh and H.L. Myers, Washington, D.C., September 2, 1914, Box 180 Folder 7, Governors' Papers, MC 35, MHS.
80. Senator T.J. Walsh to Governor Stewart, September 3, 1914, and Senator T.J. Walsh to Governor Stewart, September 5, 1914, Box 180 Folder 7, Governors' Papers, MC 35, MHS.
81. S.V. Stewart to T.J. Walsh, Washington, D.C., September 10, 1914, Box 180 Folder 7, Governors' Papers, MC 35, MHS.
82. Jensen, *Heritage of Conflict*, 349.
83. *Anaconda Standard*, September 9, 1914.
84. The two saloons were owned by James Meade and Frank Sfurm of 811 North Montana Street and 1302 East Second Street, respectively. Major Donohue permitted Butte's saloons to reopen on September 10, 1914. *Anaconda Standard*, September 9, 1914, and October 9, 1914.
85. Calvert, *The Gibraltar*, 89; *Anaconda Standard*, September 10, 1914.
86. Ibid., September 1, 1914.
87. H.A. Feertz, Great Falls, to Governor S.V. Stewart, September 16, 1914; W.M. Woodlings, Chinook, to Governor Stewart, September 28, 1914; Governor Stewart to Mrs. Ada Dawson, Butte, September 15, 1914; and Charles Austin, Butte, to Governor Stewart, September 12, 1914, Box 180 Folder 9, Governors' Papers, MC 35, MHS.
88. *Butte Miner*, September 16, 1914.
89. Ibid., October 2, 1914.
90. "As a Corporal Saw It," 12, Wiprud Collection, SC 111, UM.
91. *Butte Miner*, September 20, and 23, 1914.
92. "As a Corporal Saw It," 5, Wiprud Collection, SC 111, UM.
93. *Anaconda Standard*, September 2, 1914; "Crisis in the Making," 12, Wiprud Collection, SC 111, UM.
94. *Butte Miner*, October 1, 1914.
95. "As a Corporal Saw It," 10, Wiprud Collection, SC 111, UM.
96. Ibid., 12, Wiprud Collection, SC 111, UM.
97. Governor S.V. Stewart to Maj. Dan Donohue, September 21, 1914; and Governor S.V. Stewart to D.M. Kelly, Montana Attorney General, September 21, 1914, Box 180 Folder 9, Governors' Papers, MC 35, MHS; *Butte Miner*, October 1, 1914.
98. Major Donohue to Governor S.V. Stewart, September 23, 1914, Box 180 Folder 9, Governors' Papers, MC 35, MHS; *Butte Miner*, November 12, 1914; "Crisis in the Making," 12, Wiprud Collection, SC 111, UM.
99. *Butte Miner*, October 4, 1914.
100. S.V. Stewart to Henry L. Myers, September 24, 1914, Box 180 Folder 9, Governors' Papers, MC 35, MHS.
101. S.V. Stewart to Henry L. Myers, September 24, 1914, Box 180 Folder 9; and Governor Stewart to President Woodrow Wilson, October 4, 1914, Box 180 Folder 10, Governors' Papers, MC 35, MHS; *Anaconda Standard*, October 9, 1914.

102. Henry L. Myers, Washington, D.C., to S.V. Stewart, October 12, 1914, Box 180 Folder 10, Governors' Papers, MC 35, MHS; *Anaconda Standard*, October 9, 1914.
103. *Butte Miner*, October 2, 1914.
104. Ibid., October 4 and 6, 1914; Governor Stewart to Maj. Dan Donohue, October 3, 1914, Box 180 Folder 10, Governors' Papers, MC 35, MHS.
105. Anonymous letter sent to Governor Stewart, October 3, 1914, Box 180 Folder 10, Governors' Papers, MC 35, MHS.
106. It should be noted that Governor Stewart telegrammed Maj. Donohue on October 7, 1914, informing him that the conviction of Edward Ross, Owen Smith, and C.W. Malone by the military tribunal for carrying concealed weapons was revoked by the "Governor...and Commander-in-Chief of the National Guard." S.V. Stewart to Dan Donohue, Butte, October 7, 1914, Box 180 Folder 10, Governors' Papers, MC 35, MHS.
107. *Butte Miner*, October 9, 1914.
108. Silver Bow County Martial Law Proclamation (1914), Small Collections 1852, MHS; Jensen, *Heritage of Conflict*, 349.
109. Major Jesse B. Roote to Adjutant General Phil Greenan, December 26, 1914, Folder 1/3, National Guard, Record Series 158, MHS.
110. *Anaconda Standard*, October 13, 1914.
111. Ibid., October 16, 1914.
112. Frank Conley, the warden of the Montana State Prison located at Deer Lodge, was appointed Silver Bow County Provost Marshal. Calvert, *The Gibraltar*, 345.
113. *Anaconda Standard*, October 16, 1914.
114. National Guard historian Jerry Cooper in *Rise of the National Guard*, p. 149, reports that the Montana National Guard occupied Butte until December 28. Whereas Cooper's information is based upon information provided by the Army War College (AWC 9744-C), other primary evidence disproves this assertion. Acting Governor to Brig. Gen. Phil Greenan, November 12, 1914, and November 14, 1914, Box 180 Folder 10, Governors' Papers, MC 35, MHS.
115. "To the Officers and Enlisted Men of the Second Regiment of Infantry, National Guard of Montana," from the Governor, November 21, 1914, Box 180 Folder 10, Governors' Papers, MHS. The governor also expressed his appreciation to Adjutant General Greenan. Minimal correspondence exists between the governor and Greenan during the crisis, and Greenan remained in Helena throughout the duration of martial law.
116. *Butte Miner*, November 12, 1914.
117. Jesse B. Roote to Adjutant General Phil Greenan, December 26, 1914, Folder 1/3, National Guard, Record Series 168, MHS; Calvert, *The Gibraltar*, 90.
118. Adjutant General Phil Greenan to Governor Stewart, December 12, 1914, Folder MNG-1914, Miscellaneous Original Historical Documents, MMHM, LA, Fort Harrison.
119. "As a Corporal Saw It," 8, Wiprud Collection, SC 111, UM.

7

"Splendid Service": The Mexican Border, Labor Conflict, and World War I, 1915–1919

Matthew Godfrey

You are the living exemplification of the preparedness of which we have been talking for months.—L.L. Totten, during the Montana guard's departure for the Mexican border.

It is with pride in our success that I extend to you my sincere thanks for your splendid service to the army and to the nation.—Major General John J. Pershing, addressing the American Expeditionary Force at the conclusion of World War I.

In the summer of 1914, America's foreign policy faced challenging times as the European powers and their colonial empires became engulfed in World War I. For nearly three years, the United States remained neutral, maintaining a long-standing tradition of avoiding involvement in Europe's wars. President Woodrow Wilson reminded the country that "every man who really loves America will act and speak in the true spirit of neutrality."[1]

However, atrocities attributed to the Central Powers eventually pushed America closer to participation on the Allied side. The German submarine campaign especially vexed Americans. In 1915, Germany declared that the sea lanes around the British Isles were a war zone, and warned citizens of neutral nations that they were at risk when entering the area. On May 7, a German submarine carried out this threat by sinking the British liner *Lusitania*; of the 1,198 fatalities, 128 were Americans. This, and other incidents, hardened growing negative attitudes toward the Central Powers.[2]

At the same time, events in Mexico threatened American economic interests in Latin America, as well as the security of the U.S. border. In 1910, the Mexican Revolution began when Francisco I. Madero assumed the presidency after long-time dictator Porfirio Díaz was deposed. Madero's takeover unleashed further disruptions. Reactionary forces, led by General Victoriano Huerta, were displeased with Madero's reforms and mounted a successful military coup by 1913. This infuriated many revolutionaries, including Venustiano Carranza, who took up armed resistance. Carranza soon defeated Huerta and took control of the nation's government, but the extensive fighting had thrust the country into increased instability, further threatening the U.S. border and American business interests in Mexico.[3]

In the fall of 1915, the situation became more provocative when another revolutionary leader, Francisco "Pancho" Villa, pointedly created tension between the two countries. Villa was resentful of American support for Carranza and sought an opportunity to advance his personal ambitions by creating a new crisis. In March 1916, Villa's troops raided the small town of Columbus, New Mexico, directly across the international border, and killed 17 Americans.[4]

With the southern border troubles, along with possibility of entering the European war, the strengthening of America's armed forces became a pressing issue in Washington, D.C. It also highlighted disagreements between the National Guard and the War Department as to the federal government's responsibilities toward the guard and the practicality of using the militia as a national reserve force. The Militia Act of 1903 and subsequent amendments had designated the National Guard as the organized reserve for the regular army. Since the Spanish-American War, however, a number of regular army officials had expressed dissatisfaction with the National Guard's overall performance. Brigadier General Emory Upton had especially voiced opposition, claiming the guard lacked sufficient training and military education.[5]

Because of its reserve force designation under the 1903 Militia Act, the guard requested increased federal funding, but the national government, responding to regular army concerns, refused additional aid unless more federal control could be exerted over the militia. President Wilson, looking for a way to ease tensions in the dispute, provided a compromise by pushing Congress to pass new legislation. Subsequently, the National Defense Act was approved on June 3, 1916.[6] It "was one of the most important pieces of military legislation in U.S. history," in part because it expanded the role of the National Guard in the American military.[7]

The president and Congress had the authority to call out the militia, "for any purpose requiring the use of troops in excess of those of the Regular Army." The government considered the guard to be part of the U.S. Army, subject to inspection and regulation by the War Department. In return, the guard received an annual federal appropriation providing for "arms, ordnance stores, quartermaster stores,...camp equipage, and all other military supplies...as are now or may hereafter be authorized by law."

In order to ensure the militia's readiness in times of national emergency, the act required the guard to submit to the same discipline as the regular army, and to double the number of annual drills. Summer camps were lengthened, and to make such training more attractive, the federal government reimbursed the states for the added costs incurred. Before passage of this act, guard units annually conducted

Ready for duty—Montana National Guard companies boarding at a Helena train station.
MMHM

MMHM

24 drills and engaged in 5 days of summer training. The new law required 48 drills a year, with 1½ hours of training constituting 1 drill, and assembling for a 15 day summer encampment.[8]

Most states appreciated the increased funding, but the additional regulation and oversight irritated some capitols, including Montana's. Before the legislation passed, Brig. Gen. A.L. Mills of the War Department testified before the House Committee on Military Affairs claiming that some states, including Montana, objected to increased federal control of state militias. After hearing this charge, however, Montana's Adjutant General Phil Greenan and Governor Samuel V. Stewart took exception and "absolutely" denied Mills' statement. Probably at that stage they did not want to offend those in the federal government who now held significant authority over the National Guard.[9] Publicly, at least, they offered no objections to the legislation.

Philip Greenan's appointment as Montana Adjutant General dated from March 5, 1909. Earlier, he served during the Philippines campaign, where he was wounded. *History Second Regiment Infantry National Guard Montana (1916)*

For President Wilson, the National Defense Act came at an opportune time. The hostility between the United States and Pancho Villa's forces had sharply escalated, and American soldiers were being assigned to the border. A few days after the raid on Columbus, Carranza reluctantly approved President Wilson's request to allow U.S. troops to cross the international boundary in pursuit of Villa. On March 15, 1916, General John J. Pershing ordered 6,000 U.S. soldiers to begin entering Mexico.[10]

In the weeks following, Villa's forces eluded the Americans while wreaking vengeance along the U.S. border. On May 5, Villa's soldiers attacked Glenn Springs and Boquillas, Texas. These incidents forced Maj. Gen. Hugh L. Scott and Brig. Gen. Frederick Funston to ask Wilson for 150,000 additional troops and to call-up the National Guard in Texas, New Mexico, and Arizona. The army did not have these extra troops available, but Wilson did grant the generals' second request on May 9, sending 5,000 Southwest guardsmen to the border. Tensions further increased when President Carranza, leery of the increasing American intervention in Mexico's northern regions, informed Pershing not to advance further or he would be met by Mexican forces. Concerned about Carranza's warning, and aware of the insufficient number of troops on the long rugged border, Wilson ordered the country's National Guard into federal service on June 18.[11]

That night, Secretary of War Newton D. Baker transmitted a telegram to Governor Stewart in Montana: "Having in view the possibility of further aggression upon the territory of the United States from Mexico, and the necessity for the proper protection of that frontier, the president has thought proper to…call out the organized militia and the national guard necessary for that purpose."

The telegram instructed Montana to assemble one regiment of infantry at Fort Harrison for federal service.[12] At the time, the governor was in Ranchester, Wyoming, and thus Lieutenant Governor W.W. McDowell ordered Adjutant General Greenan to call up the 2nd Montana Infantry. McDowell also sent word to Governor Stewart, who promptly returned on June 20.[13]

Because the president had signed the National Defense Act less than three weeks earlier, many units exhibited uncertainty and confusion about their new role as federal troops. Most militias reported for service insufficiently manned, equipped, and trained. Indeed, several states fell considerably short of army expectations.[14] The regular army had no reason to think that Montana's militia would be any different. In fact, on May 31, 1916, Adjutant General Greenan had received an annual inspection report from the chief of the Division of Military Affairs, stating that many First Battalion members had not attended the required number of drills. The inspector also complained that the battalion was not fully equipped for field service, had engaged in insufficient rifle practice, and needed to give more attention to "extended order, fire control, bayonet work, and signaling of musicians."[15]

Hoping that the guard would indeed redeem itself, Adjutant General Greenan issued general orders to the state's companies outlining the mobilization. Units needed to recruit to full strength, assemble in uniform at their home stations on June 19, and then depart for Fort Harrison. Greenan also instructed the officers to inventory all equipment. Then, in coordination with federal mustering officials, it would be decided what equipment would be needed in federal service. The federal government would provide for any deficiencies.[16]

As news of the mobilization spread, Montanans expressed support as well as some reservations. Secretary of War Baker alleviated these concerns by declaring that, according to President Wilson's policy of "watchful waiting," the soldiers would guard the border and not enter Mexico. The guard's main function, announced Baker, was to ensure no further Mexican incursions into the United States.[17]

With the June 19 mobilization, new recruitment began in earnest under the direction of the regimental commander, Col. "Dynamite Dan" Donohue, a Butte physician with 25 years of guard experience. Initially, the guard targeted an expansion of its 875 members to 1,836 men, the authorized full wartime strength.

(In actuality, the regiment sent 1,070 soldiers to the border.)[18] Donohue opened recruiting stations in Helena, Butte, Great Falls, Lewistown, and Missoula. Armories across the state increased their efforts, too. New recruits needed to be from 5 feet 4 inches to 6 feet 3 inches in height, weigh between 120 and 190 pounds, be able to speak, read, and write English, have generally good health, and be an American citizen.[19]

Colonel "Dynamite Dan" Donohue. *History Second Regiment Infantry National Guard Montana (1916)*

In addition, recruitment parades were organized in Helena to further stimulate interest in enlistment. Meanwhile, an overtly critical newspaper editor presented his own view of the type of person the guard wanted: "A man past thirty whose sisters support him"; "a smart alec whose father owns a big automobile and permits him to run it"; and "a young rascal...who has already deserted a wife and baby because he was too ornery to support them."[20]

While establishing the recruitment effort, Donohue also focused on bringing all of the guard units to Fort Harrison. Recent heavy summer rains left water pooled over the railroad tracks in places, disrupting normal traffic to Helena. Additionally, Fort Harrison was soaked to the point that officers feared an outbreak of sickness if the troops were encamped there. The adjutant general postponed mobilization by one day.[21]

As the rainstorms ceased, the units began their trek to Fort Harrison. Montana's communities responded with banquets and parades, and send-offs at the train stations. At a banquet in Kalispell, former state congressman W.J. Brennan proclaimed that the guardsmen represented "the flower of the young manhood of Flathead county." The Reverend L.L. Totten, the event's organizer, declared: "You are the living exemplification of the preparedness of which we have been talking for months. This requires patriotism of the highest order." Similar support abounded across Montana.[22]

Reverend Totten, however, also expressed the ingrained prejudice many Americans felt toward Mexicans in those times. He declared: "Some one remarked today, 'It is a shame to sacrifice American boys for dirty Greasers,' but history has shown that it is always the citizen of the highest type who must sacrifice himself for those lower in the scale."[23]

The men arrived at Fort Harrison, June 23-26, and were examined by War Department physicians to determine their fitness for duty. According to a newspaper account, this consisted of "an exceedingly thorough examination from the soles of [a recruit's] feet to the top of his head." If a man stammered when speaking, had stiff finger joints, stiff ankles, corns, or bunions, or if he could not hear a whisper 20 feet away, he was rejected.[24] One newspaper reported that some recruits "were released for broken arches, poor eyes, broken ribs, and many little physical defects that in no way hindered their usefulness as soldiers."[25] According to one report, approximately 2 officers and 216 enlisted men were disqualified. Many of the rejected men were upset and charged that the physical standards were unrealistically high.

As outlined in the National Defense Act, soldiers mustering into federal service had to swear allegiance not only to their state, but also to the United States. The great majority of guardsmen across the nation willingly did so; however, some refused to take the federal oath, thereby expressing their displeasure with increased federal control of their units.[26] Montana had only slight difficulties in this regard, unlike in some other states. Only two Montana guardsmen refused to take the federal oath. They were promptly arrested. After court martial proceedings had begun, the War Department informed the guard that the oath was "a matter of individual volition," and not a court-martial offense.[27] Most Montana communities approved the oath. For example, when a company in Billings swore to obey the orders of the president, "a rousing cheer was given, as [the men] stood with bared heads offering their lives to their country."[28]

After the physical examinations, a rigorous training schedule began at Fort Harrison. The soldiers attended classes and conducted drills, including 1½ hours of calisthenics each day. By holding to "strict military discipline," Col. Donohue hoped to adequately prepare the troops for deployment to the border.[29]

As the troops trained, the recruiting effort continued. On one occasion, a fife and drum corps of guard veterans marched through Helena's streets carrying American flags and a banner proclaiming: "One hundred recruits wanted tomorrow morning."[30] Enlistees had to be at least 18 years old, but some zealous under-aged boys lied to get in. One 17-year-old, Frank Peoples, apparently lost his enthusiasm soon after enlisting and asked his uncle to write to Governor Stewart explaining the situation. Stewart recommended, however, that the young man remain in the service, since admitting that he lied about his age would lead to a court martial.[31] For the most part, recruitment efforts succeeded and some company rosters increased significantly. Glasgow's Company G, for example, expanded its numbers from 65 to 93 in just a few days.[32]

After a short time at Fort Harrison, orders arrived from the War Department assigning the 2nd Regiment to the Mexican border. Their initial destination was Nogales, Arizona, but this was soon changed to Douglas, Arizona, located approximately 75 miles east of Nogales.[33] According to some accounts, Senator

Thomas J. Walsh persuaded Secretary Baker to assign the Montana units to guard the Calumet and Phelps Dodge smelters located in Douglas, owned by William A. Clark, one of Montana's copper kings. (Clark apparently was pleased with the change in destination, as he later supplied the Montanans' camp with running water, "at his own expense.")[34] With the destination known, the troops excitedly prepared for the trip to Douglas.

On June 25, the U.S. mustering officer, A.A. Hoffman, accepted Montana's companies into federal service, a procedure completed on July 1. On July 2, the troops boarded trains and began the long trip to the border.[35] After traveling to Billings, the regiment proceeded south toward Denver. They arrived on July 4 and "marched around the streets for exercise" in a summer snowstorm.[36] Next, they went to El Paso, Texas. A local newspaper declared that the regiment consisted of "some of the bravest and strongest men in the state of Montana," who were "happy to have the chance to get away from home."[37] From El Paso, the regiment journeyed west to Douglas by way of Columbus, New Mexico, where buildings still were undergoing repairs from damage sustained during Villa's raid. Finally, around 8:30 p.m. on July 6, the trains pulled into Douglas, in the extreme southeast corner of Arizona. The regiment slept until 3 a.m., before marching to a site near the New Jersey National Guard encampment.[38]

The soldiers had their work cut out for them, as cactus, brush, and sand hills covered the camp site. The troops spent a day removing the vegetation and leveling ground,[39] and then set up eight-man tents. By the end of the second day, "every company street was in excellent order, a strange contrast to the uneven brush covered prairie on all sides."[40] Because Arizona's summertime "rainy season" would begin in a few days, they also dug open drains for water run-off. Their diligence paid off when a heavy shower turned the New Jersey camp into a "sea of mud," whereas the Montanans remained "snug and dry," while giving "their fellow-sufferers the laugh."[41]

However, construction materials for mess halls, latrines, bathhouses, and other buildings had yet to arrive. The lack of sanitary structures soon led to a dysentery outbreak.[42] In addition, at least 200 men did not have blankets, bed sacks, or mess kits.[43] In time, however, as the adjutant general reported, "many conveniences tending toward the comfort and safety of the men were added."[44] These eventual improvements, combined with the efforts of physicians in administering typhoid and smallpox vaccinations, mitigated the effects of disease.[45]

Three days after arriving in camp, the regiment began a regular schedule. Reveille sounded at 5 a.m., followed by 20 minutes of exercise, usually a two-mile march. Breakfast commenced at 6 a.m., and a two-hour drill began at 7 a.m. The troops ate dinner at noon, drilled in the afternoon from 3 to 5 pm., had supper at 6 p.m., and then spent the evening engaged in guard, fatigue, or kitchen duty, relaxing in camp, or visiting Douglas. Colonel Donohue required all soldiers to return to quarters by 11 p.m. Drills were suspended on weekends and passes were issued to those not on guard duty or a detail. Each Sunday, regimental chaplain John L. McMullen of Butte conducted Catholic services, while the Reverend William C. Pippey of Company C and Sgt. Armstrong of Company M led worship for other denominations.[46]

The Montana guard was given the task of patrolling eight miles of the border, with each company scheduled to take its turn in arranged order. Mexican army units, meanwhile, jealously watched their side of the border. Confrontational tension prevailed between the two forces.

On one occasion, Sidney's Company L captured a Mexican woman and six men who had crossed the border. They quickly were confined to a tent. With the aid of a lieutenant who spoke Spanish, they learned that the men were soldiers recently discharged from Frontoras, the Mexican base south of Douglas. The patrol fed them, provided blankets, and sent them to Agua Prieta, the large Mexican town directly across the border.[47]

At times, encounters with Mexican soldiers took on dangerous aspects, as "about three thousand Mexican [troops were] watching their side of the line,"[48] sometimes firing across the border at Americans. On one occasion, Mexican soldiers two miles west of Agua Prieta fired a number of shots at a patrol. Because the American sentinels could not see the attackers in the dark, they did not respond.[49] The Montanans frequently were under sniper attack during the first month, "but luckily for the Mexican soldiers, no [one] was injured," as one American newspaper trumpeted.[50]

Despite the sniper danger, the Montanans only suffered two fatalities during their border duty, both health related. On August 30, Private Kenneth W.

Captain John V. King, the regimental adjutant.
History Second Regiment Infantry National Guard Montana (1916)

Lt. Orville L. Anderson of Company D (Valier) and Lt. Harry Johnson of the Machine Gun Company. During World War I, Anderson died in action on the Western Front, August 1, 1918. *History Second Regiment Infantry National Guard Montana (1916)*

Pickett of Helena had died from the early dysentery outbreak, and, on October 9, Corporal Donald A. Smith from Conrad succumbed to complications from an appendectomy.[51] Their deaths bolstered patriotic feeling in the militia and back in Montana. Pickett's funeral was held in Helena on September 8 under the direction of Adjutant General Greenan. Speakers not only eulogized Private Pickett, but also called for more recruits. "I appeal to you, young men," the Reverend Eugene Milne Cosgrove stated, "to make the supreme gift to your country by preparing yourself for her service through an adequate military training." Kenneth Pickett, said Cosgrove, was a strong and manly youth "like the mountains from which he came," who offered "his life in heroic sacrifice to his country."[52]

Meanwhile at the Douglas camp, recreational facilities were provided to break up the monotony of bivouac life and the continual patrols in the desert heat and torrential afternoon thunderstorms. Chaplain McMullen obtained a large recreational tent for the troops, making available books and other publications, games, stationery, a piano, an organ, a phonograph, and a moving picture machine. This "Enlisted Men's Club" tent soon became the center for off-duty activities. [53]

Sports also played an important role in camp life. Boxing and wrestling matches between men from different regiments became popular. Supposedly, Montana's men won every contest, never "yielding the palm."[54] Different companies also competed in baseball. By September, for example, Baker's Company I had won two games and lost one, but expected to win the remainder of its contests as it "now [had] some line up."[55]

Two soldiers also began publishing a four-page weekly newspaper, the *Montana Bugle*. The machine gun company's Sergeant A.R. Dorris and Corporal Karl R. Peterson of Glasgow's Company G released the first edition during the last week of July. It presented news about the various companies and the border area, and included national stories, orders from Col. Donohue, and camp gossip and jokes. A success not only within the guard, it was avidly read by citizens in Montana.[56]

One of the popular features in the *Montana Bugle* was the frequent writing of F.B. Camp from Kalispel's Company F. Camp presented a humorous and often sarcastic view of military service, new recruits or "rookies," and camp life in general. Although not fine poetry, his efforts provided entertaining ruminations about border duty, both for the troops and the families back home, as in this example:

> Did you ever have to dig a ditch to hold the surplus rain,
> Make the water run up the hill and then run down again,
> Dig until your aching back was yelling loud with pain,
> And the typhoid in your punctured arm was swelling up a vein?
> No? Well we have to do this thing right here in Douglas.[57]

Titles of Camp's poems included "What a Rookie Thought of Border Duty," "A Rooky's Letter Home," "Memories of Montana or Visions of a Soldier," "Impressions of a Few Days in Douglas, Arizona," "The Sunny Side of Soldier Life," and "Incipient Diarrhoea." He also penned a moving tribute to Private Kenneth Pickett.[58]

Meanwhile, some soldiers, mainly from Miles City, grumbled without humor about living conditions on the border. R.P. Heren of Miles City notified Governor Stewart that some parents had received "pathetic" letters from several of their sons, claiming a food shortage in camp.[59] The governor responded that he had heard nothing about such a deficiency, but he would investigate. A few days later, the *Miles City Daily Star* printed an anonymous letter from a soldier noting a lack of soap, towels, home newspapers, and tobacco.[60]

The governor found nothing amiss; the troops had plenty of food and other necessities.[61] Chaplain McMullen told the governor that provisions were adequate and that the only explanation he could give for the negative letters was the attempt of some soldiers to seem more heroic and self-sacrificing in their communities back home. McMullen thought that such reports should be read with "the proverbial grain of salt."[62]

Colonel Donohue expressed his opinion in more humorous terms: "The horrible suffering caused amongst the men of this command from the shortage of ice cream can never be told." To prove that no food shortages existed, he provided a list of camp meals to the *Helena Daily Independent*. Menus included bacon, oatmeal, and hotcakes for breakfast; veal, chicken, and potatoes for dinner; and corned beef, macaroni and cheese, and roast beef hash for supper. "This regiment needs recruits, not dainties," Donohue concluded.[63] This explanation and the outpouring of letters from the border refuting the negative charges brought the matter to a close.

As the summer wore on and tensions with the Mexicans lessened somewhat, a quieter routine prevailed. As a result, an increasing number of soldiers requested release to either attend school in Montana, help out with harvest at home, to provide for wives and children, or for other reasons. Although Governor Stewart actually had no control over such matters, letters poured into his office requesting his attention. An early example of this occurred even before the regiment had reached the border. Glasgow's county attorney, George Ruffcorn, had his family ask the governor to discharge him for two principle reasons—he had a wife and family to support, and there was "a lot of criminal work" to perform in the county.[64] But because Ruffcorn was now serving in uniform for the federal government and not the state, Governor Stewart had no jurisdiction over the situation. Regardless, Ruffcorn asked the governor to enlist the aid of Senator Thomas Walsh.

In early August, Ruffcorn received a discharge. "Were it not for the fact that my wife and mother needed my support I would gladly remain until the expiration of my service," Ruffcorn wrote.[65] Colonel Donohue expressed a different opinion: "Ruffcorn got his discharge the other day and he lied to get it and is a yellow cur," the colonel proclaimed in a letter to the governor. In the same missive, Donohue expressed his disappointment with the guard's discharge rate, which exceeded the number of incoming recruits. "It is a most discouraging situation," he wrote.[66]

The regular army agreed with Donohue. In the first months of the border campaign, the army had willingly released guardsmen showing "a bona fide intention of entering or returning to colleges or schools at the beginning of the Fall Term in 1916."[67] But after numerous soldiers left, the army reconsidered. On September 5, 1916, Secretary of War Baker informed Governor Stewart that the military would no longer grant discharges for those wanting to attend school. The general inability to replace discharged soldiers with new recruits probably influenced this decision.[68]

Even with the discharges, the Montana regiment apparently gained widespread respect from regular army officers during the border deployment. Although federal officers frequently enough criticized guard units,[69] Montana's soldiers received compliments in newspaper reports. Early on, when the 2nd Regiment traveled through Columbus on the way to Douglas, army officers remarked that the Montana soldiers "were the best looking outfit that had passed through there."[70] Major General George Bell, the commander of the border patrol, claimed that the Montana regiment comprised "one of the best

A detachment of Montana soldiers on the border.
History Second Regiment Infantry National Guard Montana (1916)

equipped and drilled state militia forces on the Mexican border."[71] The citizens of Douglas also characterized Montana's troops as "loyal, brave and obedient," a "hell-roaring regiment," and a merry and brave "lot of true blues...which was ready for any eventuality and patriotic to the core." Several years later, the Montana guard's official history of the border campaign reported that the U.S. Army's inspector general declared the 2nd Regiment as "the best National Guard organization on the border" because of its military competence and morale.[72]

As the Montana men continued their patrols and further training, the weeks wore on. By autumn 1916, Pancho Villa was hiding in the mountains of Mexico and his diminished forces—now more like a bandit band—only occasionally descended to liberate prisoners and secure ammunition and supplies in Mexican towns. He seemingly had lost interest in raiding U.S. border towns, thus the threat of aggression virtually disappeared.[73]

The War Department gradually began removing guard units in October. Montana men were among the first to leave.[74] Most guard units, however, would not return home until later, in January or February 1917. In fact, when the United States entered World War I in April 1917, thousands of guardsmen remained on the border.

On October 2, 1916, Adjutant General Greenan received orders from the War Department to demobilize the 2nd Regiment at Fort Harrison. The *Helena Daily Independent* estimated that more than 1,000 men would return, although the cavalry, which had arrived at Douglas in August, would remain on the border. In addition, some of the men had obtained jobs at the nearby Douglas smelters, thereby choosing to stay in Arizona. The returning troops packed their gear and wished those staying behind good luck. On October 11, the regiment departed by train for Helena. "The boys are mighty glad to be moving," one soldier declared, "and everyone is happy."[75]

After the long journey north and upon their arrival in Helena, they paraded through the city streets "like a group of college boys, gloating over a gridiron victory."[76] The soldiers demobilized at Fort Harrison, completing four months of federal service.[77] Guardsmen had happy reunions with "mothers, wives, sweethearts, and friends" who had journeyed to Helena, and some quickly married their girlfriends. It was a joyous few days.[78]

For Col. Donohue, who had been in the National Guard system for nearly 25 years, it was a time to express his criticisms. He claimed that two main problems existed within the militia—first, its reliance on married men to staff its regiments, and second, politicians secured the release of members who wanted to return home. "While a few of each state gladly give of their time and money in an effort to make the national guard a success, the great mass of people shirk their duty and will never answer their country's call until war has actually started." Donohue was specifically criticizing the guard's inability to gain sufficient recruits and keep them in the service, not their soldierly merits. The only solution he could see was "compulsory military training."[79] Shortly, with the U.S. entry into World War I, Donohue's wishes would largely become reality when the federal government established the draft.

For the moment, however, Donohue and the 2nd Regiment concentrated on demobilization. On November 3, the troops departed from Helena to their home stations, taking with them gold coins received as federal pay. The regular army officers who directed the mustering out departed as well. For Montana's troops, the Mexican border campaign had ended. Because of the training and equipment received, however, the guard was now "better prepared than ever before to meet any exigency of war."[80]

For the next few months, the Montana guard enjoyed a well-deserved rest, but this proved brief as the United States drew closer to entry in World War I. President Wilson, vexed over Germany's resumption of unrestricted submarine warfare, severed diplomatic relations in February 1917. A few weeks later, tension worsened. On March 1, American newspapers published an intercepted telegram from German Foreign Secretary Arthur Zimmerman to the German ambassador in Mexico, proposing that if Mexico allied itself with Germany, it would receive the territories lost in the Mexican-American War of 1846–1848. Such German intrigue infuriated the American public, which increasingly clamored for war. Wilson called for a special session of Congress on April 2, at which time he asked for a declaration of war against Germany. Four days later on April 6, the United States officially entered the conflict.[81]

At the time, the U.S. Army consisted of only 200,000 men.[82] A few days before his address to Congress, President Wilson had summoned the National Guard into federal service. On March 25, the Montana governor's office received a telegram from Secretary of War Newton D. Baker calling up the 2nd Regiment. As during the Mexican border mobilization, Governor Stewart happened to be on vacation; consequently, Lieutenant Governor McDowell transmitted the orders to Adjutant General Greenan. The federal order declared that the government needed troops to provide "a more perfect protection against possible interference with postal, commercial and military channels and instrumentalities of the United States." The 2nd Regiment was placed under the command of the Western War Department, headquartered in San Francisco. Secretary of War Baker also informed Montana that the Western department would issue additional instructions later.[83]

The 2nd Regiment commenced mobilizing at Fort Harrison, where 1,539 men reported for duty between March 26 and April 5. Colonel John J. McGuinness, a border campaign veteran and secretary to Montana's attorney general, replaced Col. Donohue as commander of the guard.[84] At the fort, officers swore the soldiers into federal service. Further instructions from the Western War Department came in April. The First Battalion, consisting of companies A, E, F, and K, was ordered to guard utilities and other facilities in Butte, Missoula, Helena, and Bozeman. The Second Battalion, including companies D, G, H, and I, was assigned the same responsibilities in Great Falls, Whitefish, Shelby, and Miles City. The Third Battalion with companies B, C, L, and M remained at Fort Harrison as a reserve force, along with the Machine Gun Company, Headquarters Company, Supply Company, and Medical Detachment.[85]

The War Department also clearly delineated the guard's responsibilities in dealing with labor strikes. The troops should "prevent any interruption [of] transcontinental [railway] traffic or any action threatening such interruption." If strikers committed any such acts, the guard must consider them to be disloyal to the country. The units were instructed to "impress upon the minds" of strikers and agitators that the militia had federal authority to "protect persons and property threatened with damage and to prevent acts of violence."[86]

Throughout 1917, more strikes would occur in the United States than at any other time in the country's history.[87] In March, the state already had expected labor unrest from the Industrial Workers of the World. The radical IWW protested not only about working and social conditions, but also stood against U.S. involvement in the World War, claiming the conflict was due to the machinations of the elite and business classes in Europe and America. On March 16, Governor Stewart had learned from P.L. Howe of the Imperial Elevator Company that Lincoln County might need state troops "to protect lives and property in that district." Apparently, IWW advocates, or "Wobblies," from Idaho and Washington had flooded into northwest Montana hoping to foment public protests and strikes. Though nothing had occurred yet, Howe expected trouble.[88]

After the declaration of war and as word of the guard's responsibility to protect industrial and commercial enterprises spread, requests for troops poured into Governor Stewart's office. Drummond, for example, asked for soldiers to guard its railroad bridge, while the Valier-Montana Land and Water Company in the Great Falls vicinity desired protection for its dams. The Royal Milling Company, also in Great Falls, declared that "socialists and anarchists" had subjected its men to "all kinds of abuse" and threatened to destroy company property. Colonel McGuinness, however, made it clear that the guard could only interfere "in case of actual violence or threatened violence." If strikers remained orderly, it had no authority.[89]

Compounding the situation, many Montanans believed that the more radical labor leaders would stop at nothing to hinder the war effort. Governor Stewart himself felt that labor troubles could be traced to "German influence" and "German money." The Royal Milling Company appealed for troops on the grounds that the mill supplied flour to the Allied governments and if strikers damaged any property, "it would cause a serious loss to the country."[90]

Despite the tensions of the times, many strikers still felt they had legitimate grievances regarding working conditions in Montana's timber and mining industries, and many wanted to act on those concerns. The tense situation finally exploded in mid-April 1917 when a strike shut down the Eureka Lumber Company in Lincoln County.[91] The northwest Montana laborers agitated for higher pay and improved working and living conditions in the lumber camps, and better treatment by company supervisors. Since the War Department had not assigned troops to Eureka, Governor Stewart requested that soldiers be sent in to put down the strike. The War Department complied. Company I was the only Montana unit included with the out-of-state troops sent to the Eureka area. The soldiers' presence quickly stopped the agitation, and by the end of the month logging operations resumed.[92]

Some citizens, including editor Leo H. Faust of the *Libby Times*, thought it was a "damnable outrage" that units had been ordered to Eureka. "There has been no development in the labor situation here which justifies state authority in publishing to the world that Lincoln county is unable to police its own territory." Others in Eureka, however, expressed unqualified support for the troops, declaring that the *Libby Times* editorial was "uncalled for" and disappointing.[93] Labor agitation, however, continued to plague Eureka into the summer. Throughout May and June, an Oregon company apparently remained there to control the situation.[94]

Disputes in Butte also flared up in the summer of 1917. June 5 was registration day for the newly instituted nationwide draft, causing a heated demonstration in Butte, mainly among the city's Irish and Finnish populations. In Ireland at the time, Irish revolutionaries were fighting for independence from Great Britain. Butte's Irish did not want America siding with the English in the World War, and they had persuaded the Finns that draft registration meant immediate induction.[95] More than 400 men and women paraded in the streets with a red banner proclaiming "Damn With War." Meanwhile, a large crowd of counter-protestors prevented their passage. Soldiers from Roundup's Company B and Kalispell's Company F disbursed the demonstration at bayonet point and, together with the local police, arrested 65 individuals.[96]

A more serious situation arose on June 8 after an electrical fire broke out in the Speculator Mine, owned by the North Butte Mining Company. It was one of America's worst mine tragedies. Carbon monoxide suffocated 162 men, a number of whom were trapped by cement bulkheads in the tunnels. Workers blamed management for negligence in the placement of these bulkheads. The disaster exacerbated tensions between labor and management, and a strike shortly began at the Elm Orlu Mine on June 11.[97] In response, Governor Stewart sent 123 men from Company B, which had been training at Helena, thereby increasing the number of guardsmen in Butte to more than 200. According to one officer, the troops were sent mainly to provide "assistance that might be needed in this city in any emergency."[98] No clashes occurred, but the strike continued and relations between workers and management remained deeply strained.

In August, the situation in Butte worsened after Frank Little, an outspoken radical leader (he famously proclaimed he was "half Indian, but all IWW"), was taken from a boardinghouse room by five men, tied to an automobile bumper, dragged behind the car, then severely beaten and hanged. A note left on his body warned other labor agitators that similar actions would follow if they did not stop their protests.[99]

To prevent further violence, the government sent in additional troops, including men from the Washington Coast Artillery. In a special order dated July 25, 1st Lt. Harry C. Brumbaugh of the Western War Department also assigned Montana's companies F and K to guard the mines and utilities in Butte. After a few days, as tension lessened, most of the Montana men ceased guard duty by August 1. Some guardsmen, however, remained behind to keep the peace during Little's funeral procession, attended by 3,000 people on August 5.[100]

In mid July, the Western War Department had informed the Montana guard to prepare for overseas service. On July 18, the Western department combined units from Idaho, Oregon, Washington, Wyoming, and Montana into the 41st Division, and assigned it for training at Camp Fremont in Palo Alto, California. Subsequently, Col. McGuinness informed Governor Stewart that he would recall Montana troops from state duties on August 1.

Management and business leaders became concerned about the guard's approaching departure. As early as July 6, Governor Stewart had asked the U.S. Adjutant General to notify him about any plans for replacing the 2nd Regiment with other troops in Montana. The adjutant general evidently replied that the governor should rely on local police forces for law enforcement. Later, Stewart replied to concerned management and business leaders, saying there was "no reason in the world why they should not be given a full measure of protection" by local law enforcement authorities.

Labor problems would continue to trouble Montana, especially Butte, throughout the World War I period. With Montana's guardsmen serving in Europe, federal forces were called in to put down strikes and quell labor disturbances. Many of Butte's residents resented the federal intrusion and called into question the conduct of the soldiers. U.S. District Attorney Burton K. Wheeler in Butte also accused the troops of holding prisoners without warrants, bayoneting strikers, and committing "extralegal, violent activities." The army defended its actions, but damage to its reputation had been done.[101]

In the first weeks of August 1917, 2,050 officers and enlisted men of the 2nd Regiment gathered at Fort Harrison, ready for federal action. Meanwhile, the U.S. Army's high command had spent the summer organizing for America's upcoming massive overseas operations. Major General John J. Pershing had sailed to France in May to supervise the war effort. Each division of the American Expeditionary Force (A.E.F.) was authorized to include 1,000 officers and 27,000 enlisted men, divided into four regiments of infantry, three regiments of artillery, one regiment of engineers, three machine gun battalions, a field signal battalion, and ammunition, supply, and sanitary units. Each regiment was to include 100 officers and 3,000 men, organized into three battalions, with each battalion consisting of four companies of 250 men each. The 41st Division included not only National Guard units from Washington, Oregon, Montana, Wyoming, and Idaho, but guardsmen from Colorado, North and South Dakota, New Mexico, and the District of Columbia were added later.

In the War Department's incorporation of the country's National Guard for federal service, Montana's 2nd Infantry Regiment was redesignated as the 163rd Infantry Regiment of the 41st Division.[102] The department also informed the 41st Division that its training site had been changed to Camp Greene near Charlotte, North Carolina.[103] As the Montana guardsmen prepared to leave, citizens across the state showed their support. Local businesses compiled a scrapbook for the 163rd Infantry, complete with letters of support. The Great Northern Railway extended its "best wishes for a speedy termination of the war" and a safe return of the troops. Likewise, the Great Falls Meat Company declared: "You, young men, representing the best manhood of our state...are going forth, knowing that your country, your state, your county and your town stand behind you."

Other businesses expressed their willingness to do their part at home while the soldiers were away. "Like you, your home folks are willing and ready to sacrifice as long as is necessary," the Glendive State Bank proclaimed, "until final victory is assured." The Commercial National Bank of Great Falls declared, "this is our war as well as the war of you men in uniform."[104]

In September, a battalion of Montana's 163rd arrived at North Carolina's Camp Greene and began drilling with regular army troops. The War Department designated Montana's soldiers as part of the 82nd Infantry Brigade of the 41st Division, under the command of Maj. Gen. Hunter Liggett. According to Corporal James J. Morris, a Company D guardsman from Great Falls, 200 regular army officers taught the troops combat bayonet techniques, trench digging, the use of hand grenades, and how to construct barbed wire entanglements.

Because of the defensive nature of the war in Europe, some of the soldiers were surprised when they received extensive training for offensive operations. On the Western Front, stretching from Switzerland to the North Sea, the opposing armies had constructed elaborate trench networks, and resorted to massive machine gun fire and artillery barrages to effectively halt enemy advances. Indeed, General Pershing remarked that the French and British troops had become so accustomed to defensive trench warfare that they rarely went on the offensive. Pershing became convinced, however, that the introduction of large numbers of American troops and an aggressive strategy would turn the tide for the Allies. Consequently, he had proposed that American training centers continue to teach the troops offensive operations.[105]

Recreational and entertainment opportunities at Camp Greene included sports, especially football. Company D's Corporal Jim Morris noted that the Montana men, with "the flower of the [state's] high school teams," supplied many players to the regimental squad.[106] When off duty, guardsmen visited Charlotte and often were invited to dine in family homes.

Corporal Morris also noted the intense sense of competition between guardsmen and regular soldiers that pervaded Camp Greene. He boasted that a "company of Nat. Guard can clean about 6 regiments of these regulars," and that the militia troops were "a duce of a lot better than the regulars in drilling, men and every thing." Contention was acerbated by a regulation insignia worn by guardsmen on their uniforms. As stipulated in the 1916 National Defense Act, guardsmen wore a red star on their sleeves to distinguish them from regular army soldiers. A National Guard adjutant general remarked, "I can't think of anything that is more disgusting than that red letter."[107]

During the first week in November, the battalion was ordered to Camp Mills near Long Island, New York, thereby clearing the way for additional regular army troops to train at Camp Greene. Accordingly, on November 12 the Montana men arrived at Camp Mills by way of Washington, D.C., and Philadelphia. At the camp, the battalion rejoined the two other Montana battalions of the 163rd, which had departed the state on October 26. The reunited regiment also received a number of new conscripts requiring training. New equipment was issued and sailing lists prepared for embarkation to Europe. During leave time, some soldiers took in New York City's Chinatown and Great Bowery, while others visited Boston.[108]

Drawing near to the embarkation date, on December 1 the regiment was transferred to Camp Merritt, New Jersey, where the men enjoyed "light duty, warm barracks, [and] fair grub."[109] There, Secretary of War Baker reviewed the troops.[110] On December 14, after two feet of snow blanketed the area, the men went by train from Camp Merritt to the Hoboken, New Jersey, docks. They boarded the U.S.S. *Leviathan* and the next morning set sail on the nine-day journey to England.[111]

The voyage was relatively uneventful, other than the men dealing with seasickness and conducting abandon ship drills. As the *Leviathan* neared England, a number of British and U.S. vessels joined in a convoy. On December 24, 1917, they docked at Liverpool and the troops boarded trains for a rest camp at Winchester, near London. As the 163rd traveled to their destination, "friendly people met [them] at stations and wished [them] luck." One soldier reported that the British welcomed the sight of "big Westerners from over the sea com[ing] to fight their fight."[112]

Indeed, the British, French, and Belgians would express much appreciation for the influx of Americans, believing they could provide the manpower and resources to turn the tide in the vast conflict. Engaged in war since 1914, most of the Allied countries were weary of fighting; their armies were afflicted with low morale, and experiencing manpower and materiel shortages. Furthermore, in 1917 the Germans mounted a great offensive on the Western Front to try and win the war before American men and equipment tipped the balance. Also, Russia was knocked out of the conflict after Tsar Nicholas II was deposed. The revolutionary Bolshevik party eventually took over, suing for peace with the Central Powers. Germany and the Austro-Hungarian Empire could now send more troops against the western Allies. Considering these circumstances, General Pershing had recommended committing 1 million American troops to the conflict by May 1918.[113] As part of this buildup, the 163rd had arrived in England.

The American high command, however, would relegate the 41st Division to replacement and depot status, and to training other troops. Consequently, when other divisions at the front required replacements in their ranks, soldiers from the 41st would be provided to them. Thus, Montana men from the 163rd were variously parceled out, to such units as the 42nd and 91st divisions. In all, 3,000 163rd men would be transferred to other outfits.

After arriving in France, the three Montana battalions were assigned to Bordeaux, Langres, and St. Aignan, where they underwent additional training.[114] Corporal Morris noted: "We may never all be together again because we are pretty well split up now in different outfits."[115] True enough, they were widely dispersed across the Western Front. Their individual stories are many—too many for the space allowed here. Especially intriguing and no doubt representative, however, are the examples of Captain Orville L. Anderson and Corporal James J. Morris.

Captain Orville Anderson had enlisted in the Montana National Guard as a private in February 1910. Soon after reenlisting in 1913, he was commissioned as a 2nd Lieutenant. Anderson resigned two months before the Mexican border campaign, but rejoined when the guard called for more recruits. At the border, he served as a 1st Lt. in Valier's Company D. With the federal call-up in 1917, Anderson became a captain and was assigned to Billings' Company K. Soon after, on June 25, he married Lucy Dingman and on October 26 departed with his battalion for Camp Mills, New York.

After arriving in France, Anderson and Company K were sent to Le Courveau as replacements for the U.S. Marine Corps.[116] As company commander, Anderson had to complete the usual paperwork and be prepared for surprise inspections by the AEF's inspector general office.[117] A chore he found particularly trying was sending Company K men to replenish other units at the front. "It is mighty hard to see the company broken up," he wrote. "I intend not to become so attached to the next outfit."[118] Perhaps equally as difficult was disciplining disorderly men. After one barroom fight, for example, he had to demote one of his best sergeants. "Damn the booze!" he exclaimed afterwards. "It is at the bottom of all our troubles in the army."[119]

Anderson soon entered extensive combat. In April 1918, he was transferred to the First Army Corps training school at Gondrecourt, where he received additional instruction in infantry combat tactics.[120] Anderson then led a squad into "No man's land" between the opposing trenches. They planted an explosive device to blast a hole in the barbed-wire, thereby clearing a path for a combat patrol in attacking the enemy. "Patroling [sic] is very interesting," he remarked, "especially when a Very light [a pyrotechnic signal flare] strikes about a foot from where you are hugging the ground."[121]

Soon after completing the training school, Anderson transferred to Verdun. Two years earlier, the Germans launched one of the great offensives of the war against the French at Verdun, but eventually abandoned the effort when British and French armies attacked farther north along the Somme. On March 18, 1918, Pershing had assigned the 2nd Division to this area.[122]

One night, Anderson again visited "No man's land" with 34 French soldiers. They encountered an enemy patrol, "but neither side seemed anxious to fight."[123] On another occasion, a Very light fired by the Germans illuminated his patrol, but by keeping "perfectly still" until the flare dimmed, they escaped detection. "It is all most interesting," Anderson commented.[124]

Not long afterward, Anderson returned to his regular company at Montrichard, where he resumed the usual activities of conducting drills and training. The respite from battle was short-lived. On May 28, he again went to the front, this time with the 128th Division in the Alsace-Lorraine region, an area that

France had lost to Germany at the conclusion of the Franco-Prussian War in 1871. Here, Anderson experienced constant German artillery barrages, as well as sleeping in "cots full of 'Cooties.'"[125] He also dug trenches, fired at a German sniper, and protected a company on a mission between the lines.[126]

When noting his first wedding anniversary, Anderson wrote: "I wonder if we shall see another anniversary around, and whether we may spend it together," he mused that night. "If I live, I believe I will be at home with my wife a year from now."[127] The prospect seemed rather dim, however, because within the next few days Anderson endured a 45-minute artillery barrage, knocking him to the ground twice, and was shot at by a German sharpshooter. On July 12, he was granted a 10-day pass, a reprieve from the front.[128]

On July 25, Anderson returned to the lines, this time on the Aisne River, 20 miles from Soissons. Here, Allied forces would begin a counteroffensive to repel the Germans at the Second Battle of the Marne. The Allies hoped to break the German hold on the region between the Aisne and Marne rivers. The offensive eventually accomplished this purpose. Captain Anderson's personal story regretfully ended here. He was killed on August 1, only 36 days after his first wedding anniversary.[129]

In contrast, Corporal James J. Morris, also of Company D, served a relatively short time at the front and spent much of his time studying French, exploring the countryside, and participating in sports activities. Morris had enlisted in Great Falls at the start of the war, much to the chagrin of his pacifist Quaker parents. Indeed, no one in the family had been in military service since the 1600s.[130] He went with the 163rd's First Battalion to France, assigned to Bordeaux. His letters to his parents reveal that the battalion had relatively little to do in the first few weeks.

In February 1918, he informed his mother not to worry about him facing combat, because for much of the time he merely sat "on a soft chair with…feet cocked up on a table reading a novel."[131] He also studied French,[132] watched Charlie Chaplain movies, and took hikes in the countryside,[133] while receiving training in gas warfare and practicing the tossing of hand grenades. In April 1918, the battalion began training new recruits and passed the time by "showing them they don't know anything." (By the summer of 1918, 290,000 men were trained in 41st Division camps.)[134]

By June, the regiment had moved to Montrichard, where the transfer of soldiers to other units accelerated. Morris, however, remained assigned to camp, where he expressed frustration that other guardsmen were at the front while he merely practiced his French. Yet shortly, he saw action in the Second Battle of the Marne (the same campaign in which Captain Anderson was killed).[135]

Ever aware of the increasing number of American troops arriving in France, the German high command formed plans to drive the Americans and French from Chateau-Thierry, a town near the Marne River, thereby forcing the Allied commanders to the peace table. The Germans laid out a surprise attack, but the Allied forces were prepared. In July, the Germans launched the massive assault. The French, along with the 42nd Division (National Guard) and other American troops, clung to their positions through barrage after barrage of high explosives and poison gas. Eventually, the Germans conceded defeat, later claiming that the "savage roughness" of the Americans had held the Marne.[136] Morris's letters do not detail his participation in the campaign, but certainly he experienced the dangers of war.

In August and September, Morris instructed new recruits at Montrichard, swam in the Cher River, competed in track and basketball, listened to an army band, and traveled about as he could. "We are working and playing hard lately," he wrote at one point.[137] In September, the army designated Company D as a "Model Company." Morris admitted that he did not know exactly what that entailed; perhaps it meant that the army would "charge admittance of a franc to watch [them] work."[138]

Whatever the meaning, the army decided to train Company D personnel as officers, Morris included. In October, he was sent to an Officer's Training School at La Valbonne. Then came the news they hoped for. Allied offensives in the Meuse-Argonne region had devastated enemy defenses and pushed the German army to the brink of collapse. On November 11, the Germans signed an armistice, bringing the war to an end. Morris remained in officer's training, receiving a commission as a 2nd Lt. in January 1919.

After the armistice, U.S. troops, including the 163rd, served in occupation posts in German territory. Pershing, however, advocated sending American soldiers home as soon as possible. In March 1919, the 41st Division, including the 163rd and 2nd Lt. Morris, returned to the United States. The division demobilized at Camp Dix, New Jersey, but not all Montanans returned home at the same time. Some still served in other divisions. By August 1919, however, all American soldiers had left Europe.[139]

The Montanans fought with distinction. For example, Capt. Charles L. Sheridan, who served alongside his friend, Capt. Orville Anderson, was wounded three times in three different engagements. He received the Distinguished Service Cross, Belgian War Cross, and the Croix de Guerre, and later became adjutant general of the Montana National Guard.

Seventeen other guardsmen also received the Distinguished Service Cross, including William Belzer, who had been at the Mexican border as a member of Glasgow's Company G. 2nd Lt. Belzer entered France with the 163rd machine gun company, but transferred early in 1918 to the 135th U.S. Aero Observation Squadron. This unit took part in the St. Mihiel offensive in September and the Meuse-Argonne attacks from September to November.

During the World War I period, 3 officers and 123 enlisted men of the Montana National Guard died in battle, 28 succumbed to disease, and 19 officers and

289 men were wounded. For Montana as a whole, 39,276 served in the armed forces, including guardsmen, draftees, and regular enlistees, out of a state population of 496,131. Of these, 934 died and 2,469 were wounded.[140]

All certainly deserved General John J. Pershing's commendation to the American service man:

> To the glory of the citizen-soldier, our troops have faithfully fulfilled their trust...Whether keeping lonely vigil in the trenches, or gallantly storming the enemy's stronghold; whether enduring monotonous drudgery at the rear, or sustaining the fighting line at the front, each has bravely and efficiently played his part. By willing sacrifice of personal rights; by cheerful endurance of hardship and privation; by vigor, strength and indomitable will, made effective by thorough organization and cordial co-operation, you inspired the war-worn Allies with new life and turned the tide of threatened defeat into overwhelming victory...It is with pride in our success that I extend to you my sincere thanks for your splendid service to the army and to the nation.[141]

Notes

1. As cited in Leon H. Canfield, *The Presidency of Woodrow Wilson: Prelude to a World in Crisis* (Rutherford, New Jersey: Fairleigh Dickinson University Press, 1966), 60, 65–66.
2. Ibid., 65–66.
3. Ibid., 43–48.
4. Ibid., 48–49.
5. Maj. Gen. Bruce Jacobs, *Tensions between the National Guard and the Regular Army* (Washington, D.C.: Historical Society of the Militia and National Guard, n.d.), 1–3.
6. Jerry Cooper, *The Militia and the National Guard in America since Colonial Times: A Research Guide* (Westport, Connecticut: Greenwood Press, 1993), 99; Jerry Cooper, *The Rise of the National Guard: The Evolution of the American Militia, 1865–1920* (Lincoln: University of Nebraska Press, 1997), 153–54; Canfield, *Presidency of Woodrow Wilson*, 71.
7. Renee Hylton and Robert K. Wright Jr., *A Brief History of the Militia and National Guard* (Washington, D.C.: Departments of the Army and the Air Force, 1993), 21.
8. "National Defense Act," *United States Statutes at Large*, 39, sec. 2, 166, sec. 67, 199, sec. 78, 202, sec. 92, 206, sec. 111, 211; *Military Laws of the State of Montana*, comp. Phil Greenan (Helena, Montana: Independent Publishing, 1919), 28–29. Exactly how the Montana guard units intended to conduct 48 drills each year is unclear, as the troops served on active duty for most of 1916, 1917, and 1918. However, if a unit assembled 1 weekend per month, it could fulfill 4 drills monthly, thus meeting the required 48 drills annually.
9. Phil Greenan to A.L. Mills, March 6, 1916, Drawer 2, Montana National Guard, 1916: Miscellaneous Original Historical Documents, Vertical File, Montana Military History Museum, Library Archives, Building T-15, Fort William H. Harrison, Helena, Montana [hereafter cited as National Guard, 1916: MOHD, MMHM, LA Building T-15, Fort Harrison].
10. Canfield, *Presidency of Woodrow Wilson*, 48–49; Paul J. Vanderwood and Frank N. Samponaro, *Border Fury: A Picture Postcard Record of Mexico's Revolution and U.S. War Preparedness, 1910–1917* (Albuquerque: University of New Mexico Press, 1988), 11.

11. Ibid., 11–12; Canfield, *Presidency of Woodrow Wilson*, 49; Cooper, *Rise of the National Guard*, 156; Clarence C. Clendenen, *Blood on the Border: The United States Army and the Mexican Irregulars* (London: Collier-Macmillan, 1969), 276, 289.
12. Newton D. Baker to Samuel V. Stewart, June 18, 1916 [telegram], Box 235 Folder 4, Governor Samuel V. Stewart Papers, Manuscript Collection 35, Montana Historical Society, Helena, Montana [hereafter cited as Box 235 Folder 4, Stewart Papers, MC 35, MHS].
13. Acting Governor to Brig. Gen. Phil Greenan, June 18, 1916, Will Aiken to S.V. Stewart, June 19, 1916, S.V. Stewart to Will Aiken, June 19, 1916, Box 235 Folder 4, Stewart Papers, MC 35, MHS.
14. Cooper, *Rise of the National Guard*, 156.
15. The Chief, Division of Militia Affairs to the Adjutant General of Montana, May 31, 1916, Box 1 Folder 1, Montana Adjutant General Records, Record Series 223, Montana Historical Society, Helena, Montana [hereafter cited as Box 1 Folder 1, General Records, RS 223, MHS].
16. "General Orders No. 9, June 19, 1916," Box 235 Folder 4, Stewart Papers, MC 35, MHS.
17. "Call Entire National Guard," *Helena Daily Independent*, June 19, 1916; "Companies H and F Receive Orders," Kalispell *Daily Interlake*, June 19, 1916.
18. "National Guard and Organized Reserve Units Mobilized in 1916 for Mexican Border Duties," History, Army National Guard File, Drawer 1, National Guard Association of the United States Library, One Massachusetts Avenue, Washington, D.C. [hereafter cited as NGAUS].
19. "Wanted—100 Men from Helena for Montana National Guard," *Helena Daily Independent*, June 26, 1916.
20. "Second Regiment, National Guard of Montana Mobilized at Fort Harrison, Awaits Orders," *Helena Daily Independent*, June 25, 1916.
21. "Hurry Call for State Troops Sent Governors, Montana May March Away Sunday," *Helena Daily Independent*, June 23, 1916.
22. See, for example, "Company K Boys Had to Hustle Grub," *Billings Gazette*, June 29, 1916; "Company G," *Glasgow Courier*, June 30, 1916; "Form Company A Auxiliary," *Bozeman Daily Chronicle*, July 18, 1916.
23. "Banquet Given to National Guard," Kalispell *Daily Interlake*, June 21, 1916.
24. "Rigid Tests for Recruits," *Bozeman Daily Chronicle*, June 22, 1916.
25. "Many Good Men of Co. K Sent Home through Severe Tests of War Department Examiners," *Billings Gazette*, July 2, 1916. A.A. Hoffman to the Chief of the Militia Bureau, War Department, August 16, 1916, Drawer 2, National Guard, 1916: MOHD, MMHM, LA Building T-15, Fort Harrison; "Percent Unfit in Guard High," *Helena Daily Independent*, June 29, 1916.
26. Cooper, *Rise of the National Guard*, 157.
27. The Chief of the Militia Bureau to the Adjutants General of all States and the District of Columbia, September 13, 1916, Box 235 Folder 6, Stewart Papers, MC 35, MHS; "Two Guardsmen Refuse the Oath," *Helena Daily Independent*, June 28, 1916.
28. "Billings Boys Mustered In," *Billings Gazette*, June 29, 1916.
29. "Regiment All Here," *Helena Daily Independent*, June 26, 1916.
30. Ibid.
31. Mrs. Lovenstein to S.V. Stewart, July 1, 1916, S.V. Stewart to Mrs. Lovenstein, July 3, 1916, Box 235 Folder 5, Stewart Papers, MC 35, MHS. For another example, see Mrs. J.E. Walker to S.V. Stewart, August 20, 1916, Ibid.

32. "Glasgow Boys to Leave for Mexico," *Glasgow Courier*, June 23, 1916.
33. J.D. Barrette to A.A. Hoffman, June 28, 1916, Eben Swift, "Special Orders No. 142," Drawer 2, National Guard, 1916: MOHD, MMHM, LA Building T-15, Fort Harrison.
34. Col. Fred Lang Oral History Transcript, Box 1 Folder 1, Fred Lang Collection, Montana Historical Society, Helena, Montana [hereafter cited as Lang Oral History, MHS]. Richard H. Lacey repeats Lang's account in *The Montana Militia: A History of Montana's Volunteer Forces, 1867–1976* (Dillon, Montana: Dillon Tribune-Examiner Press, 1976),
40. "Montana Boys Are Heartiest," *Billings Gazette*, August 19, 1916.
35. Col. Erastus H. Williams, "Second Montana Volunteers Served on Mexican Border, '16," Drawer 2, Montana National Guard, 1900–1916: *History Second Regiment Infantry National Guard Montana*, Vertical File, MMHM, LA Building T-15, Fort Harrison; A.A. Hoffman to the Chief of the Militia Bureau, August 16, 1916, Drawer 2, National Guard, 1916: MOHD, MMHM, LA Building T-15, Fort Harrison.
36. Lang Oral History, MHS; Lacey, *Montana Militia*, 40–41.
37. "Company E Is Now Encamped at Douglas, N.M.," *Miles City Daily Star*, July 15, 1916.
38. "Company G at Mexican Border," *Glasgow Courier*, July 14, 1916; Lang Oral History, MHS; Lacey, *Montana Militia*, 40–41.
39. "Company G at Mexican Border," *Glasgow Courier*, July 14, 1916.
40. "Morris Tells of Army Life," *Billings Gazette*, July 11, 1916.
41. *History Second Regiment Infantry National Guard Montana*, comp. W.M. Swarthout (n.p., 1917), 7.
42. Ibid., 9.
43. "National Guard Service on the Mexican Border—Alpha by State" File, Drawer 1, NGAUS.
44. Williams, "Second Montana Volunteers Served on Mexican Border," Drawer 2, Montana National Guard, 1900–1916: *History Second Regiment Infantry National Guard Montana*, MMHM, LA, Building T-15, Fort Harrison.
45. Ibid., 9.
46. Ibid., 9, 13; "Boys Drilling When Mex Pass," *Billings Gazette*, July 28, 1916; "Company G at Mexican Border," *Glasgow Courier*, July 14, 1916.
47. Ibid.; "Boys Drilling When Mex Pass," *Billings Gazette*, July 28, 1916; "Captain B.O. Reynolds Writes Interesting Letter Regarding Welfare of Company I," *Sidney Herald*, July 28, 1916.
48. *History Second Regiment Infantry National Guard Montana*, 13.
49. "Second Mont. Fired At by Mexican Snipers," *Miles City Daily Star*, August 4, 1916.
50. "Montana Troops Are under Fire from Snipers," newspaper clipping, Box 1 Folder 1, Gerald Wesley Lansing Papers, Small Collection 203, Montana Historical Society, Helena, Montana [hereafter cited as Lansing Papers, SC 203, MHS].
51. *History Second Regiment Infantry National Guard Montana*, 9; "Kenneth Pickett Dead on Border," *Helena Daily Independent*, August 31, 1916; "Conrad Man Dies at Border Camp," Drawer 2, Montana National Guard, 1916: "2nd Montana Infantry Regiment—Newspaper Articles from Home Stations of Each Company," Vertical File, MMHM, LA Building T-15, Fort Harrison.
52. "In Memory—Kenneth Pickett," Box 1 Folder 2, Kenneth W. Pickett Papers, SC 1260, MHS. See also "Fitting Service for Pickett by Montana Troops," *Helena Daily Independent*, September 5, 1916.
53. *History Second Regiment Infantry National Guard Montana*, 11.
54. Ibid., 11–13.

55. "With Boys on Border," *Baker Sentinel*, September (n.d.) 1916.
56. Karl Peterson previously served as a reporter for the *Glasgow Courier* while A.R. Dorris had worked as editor and manager of the *Saco Independent* before border service. "2d Montana Have Paper," *Baker Sentinel*, July 28, 1916; "Montana Boys Drill and Hike," *Billings Gazette*, August 27, 1916; Corporal Karl R. Peterson, "With the Boys of Company 'G,'" *Glasgow Courier*, n.d.; "Soldier Boys Newspaper Mont. Bugle," *Miles City Daily Star*, July 28, 1916; "Montana Troops Enjoy Army Life," *Helena Daily Independent*, July 24, 1916; *History Second Regiment Infantry National Guard Montana*, 13. The *Montana Bugle* can be found in a Miscellaneous File, MMHM, LA Building T-15, Fort Harrison.
57. "With the Boys of Company 'G,'" *Glasgow Courier*, n.d.
58. For copies of F.B. Camps' poems, see Drawer 2, National Guard, 1916: MOHD, MMHM, LA Building T-15, Fort Harrison. See "National Guard Service on the Mexican Border—Alpha by State" File, Drawer 1, NGAUS.
59. R.P. Heren to S.V. Stewart, July 16, 1916, Box 235 Folder 5, Stewart Papers, MC 35, MHS.
60. "Boys on the Border Feel Neglected and Forgotten," *Miles City Daily Star*, July 22, 1916; S.V. Stewart to R.P. Heren, July 17, 1916, Box 235 Folder 5, Stewart Papers, MC 35, MHS.
61. The army, however, banned the consumption of watermelon because the rinds were "the only kind of garbage that cannot be properly disposed of." Rinds could not be buried or burned and attracted flies and other insects, leading to unsanitary conditions. "Watermelon Taboo in Army Camps and Guardsmen Gloomy," *Billings Gazette*, August 6, 1916.
62. John L. McMullen to S.V. Stewart, July 26, 1916, Box 235 Folder 5, Stewart Papers, MC 35, MHS.
63. "Need Recruits Not Dainties on the Border," *Helena Daily Independent*, August 23, 1916.
64. W.M. Ruffcorn to S.V. Stewart, July 1, 1916, Box 235 Folder 5, Stewart Papers, MC 35, MHS.
65. George W. Ruffcorn to S.V. Stewart, August 2, 1916, Box 235 Folder 5, Stewart Papers, MC 35, MHS.
66. Col. Dan J. Donohue to Governor Sam V. Stewart, August 10, 1916, see also S.V. Stewart to T.J. Walsh, July 3, 1916, George W. Ruffcorn to S.V. Stewart, July 10, 1916, S.V. Stewart to George W. Ruffcorn, July 17, 1916, Box 235 Folder 5, Stewart Papers, MC 35, MHS.
67. Captain, Cavalry, Aide-de-camp, to S.V. Stewart, n.d., Box 235 Folder 6, Stewart Papers, MC 35, MHS.
68. Maj. Gen. Frederick Funston to S.V. Stewart, September 5, 1916, Box 235 Folder 6, Stewart Papers, MC 35, MHS; Cooper, *Rise of the National Guard*, 159–60.
69. For example, a Montana newspaper reported that the War Department believed the militia was "no good" and it should be replaced by a compulsory military service system. "Percent of 'Slackers' in Militia Is Very High," *Helena Daily Independent*, October 25, 1916. One army officer claimed that the border campaign only strengthened his view that the militia system was inadequate, while another exclaimed, "the Lord help such troops if they ever have to go against trained regulars." As cited in Cooper, *Rise of the National Guard*, 163.
70. "Company G at Mexican Border," *Glasgow Courier*, July 14, 1916.
71. "Montanans Draw Very High Praise of Commander Bell," *Helena Daily Independent*, August 19, 1916.

72. *History Second Regiment Infantry National Guard Montana*, 2. See also Williams, "Second Montana Volunteers Served on Mexican Border," Drawer 2, Montana National Guard, 1900–1916, MMHM, LA Building T-15, Fort Harrison; "Montana Boys Are Pride of Troops Encamped in Great Base at Douglas," *Helena Daily Independent*, August 14, 1916; "Montana Gets Praise," *Baker Sentinel*, July 21, 1916; "Montana Boys Have Best Camp," *Billings Gazette*, September 22, 1916.
73. Clendenen, *Blood on the Border*, 337.
74. Cooper, *Rise of the National Guard*, 167.
75. "Soldiers Home within Ten Days," *Helena Daily Independent*, October 3, 1916; "Regiment Routed over Many Roads," *Helena Daily Independent*, October 9, 1916; "Some of Boys to Stay in Douglas," *Billings Gazette*, October 16, 1916.
76. "Second Montana Is Here," *Helena Daily Independent*, October 16, 1916.
77. A few displayed grisly souvenirs; i.e., the bones of Mexican soldiers picked up from one of Villa's battlefields. Although the officers informed the men that anyone caught stealing bones would be arrested, it became a mark of distinction for some to pilfer human remains. "Claim to Have Bones of Some Villa Bandit," *Helena Daily Independent*, October 20, 1916.
78. "Second Montana Is Here," *Helena Daily Independent*, October 16, 1916.
79. "Brands Militia Total Failure," *Helena Daily Independent*, October 19, 1916.
80. "Men of Militia Fold Tents and Leave the City," *Helena Daily Independent*, November 4, 1916; "Affairs of Militia Are Being Wound Up," *Helena Daily Independent,* November 11, 1916; "Montana Will Be Better Prepared," *Helena Daily Independent*, November 8, 1916.
81. David M. Kennedy, *Over Here: The First World War and American Society* (Oxford: Oxford University Press, 1980), 10–11; Edward M. Coffman, *The War to End All Wars: The American Military Experience in World War I* (New York: Oxford University Press, 1968), 7–8.
82. Chester K. Shore, *Montana in the Wars* (Miles City, Montana: Star Printing, 1977), 66.
83. Secretary of War Baker to Gov. S.V. Stewart, March 25, 1917, see also Secretary to the Governor to P.L. Howe, March 19, 1917, Acting Governor to Brig. Gen. Phil Greenan, March 26, 1917, Box 239 Folder 12, Stewart Papers, MC 35, MHS.
84. The records do not clearly state why McGuinness replaced Donohue, but it is probably due to the latter going into retirement.
85. "Initial return of the 2nd Regiment of Montana Infantry from Mch 25/17 date of call of President to Apr 30/17, date last troops mustered in," Box 6 Folder 11, Montana Adjutant General Records, RS 223, MHS; Charles L. Sheridan, "Colonel Charles Sheridan Traces Military History of Montana; Troops Served Bravely Against Germans during World War," *Three Forks Herald* newspaper clipping, "World War, 1914–1918," Vertical Newspaper File, MHS; Lacey, *Montana Militia*, 45.
86. Hayden to Commanding Officer, Second Montana Infantry, April 21, 1917, Box 240 Folder 1, Stewart Papers, MC 35, MHS.
87. Kennedy, *Over Here*, 262.
88. P.L. Howe to Governor S.D. [sic] Stewart, March 16, 1917, see also Secretary to the Governor to P.L. Howe, March 19, 1917, Box 239 Folder 12, Stewart Papers, MC 35, MHS.
89. S.M.C. Hughes to S.V. Stewart, May 1, 1917, Box 240 Folder 1, Stewart Papers, MC 35, MHS; Col. James T. Stanford to Maj. Jesse B. Roote, April 28, 1917, J.W. Sherwood to S.V. Stewart, April 27, 1917, Box 239 Folder 12, Stewart Papers, MC 35, MHS; Col. John J. McGuinness to Honorable S.V. Stewart, May 5, 1917, Box 240 Folder 1, Stewart Papers, MC 35, MHS.

90. J.W. Sherwood to S.V. Stewart, April 27, 1917, Box 239 Folder 12, Stewart Papers, MC 35, MHS; S.V. Stewart to Hon. Henry L. Myers, June 30, 1917, Box 240 Folder 3, Stewart Papers, MC 35, MHS.
91. Michael P. Malone, Richard B. Roeder, and William L. Lang, *Montana: A History of Two Centuries* (Seattle: University of Washington Press, 1991), 270–71.
92. Ibid., 271; Arnon Gutfeld, *Montana's Agony: Years of War and Hysteria, 1917–1921* (Gainesville: University Presses of Florida, 1979), 34–35; C.A. Weil to Governor S.V. Stewart, April 25, 1917, Box 239 Folder 12, Stewart Papers, MC 35, MHS.
93. Leo H. Faust, "A Damnable Outrage," *Libby Times* newspaper clipping, F.D. Becker to S.V. Stewart, May 14, 1917, Box 240 Folder 1, Stewart Papers, MC 35, MHS.
94. Graham Fletcher to Hon. S.V. Stewart, June 21, 1917, Box 240 Folder 2, Stewart Papers, MC 35, MHS.
95. Gutfeld, *Montana's Agony*, 14.
96. "Anti-Draft Riot in Butte Nipped," *Roundup Record*, June 8, 1917; "Anti-Draft Mob in Butte Dispursed with Bayonets," Kalispell *Daily Interlake*, June 6, 1917; U.S. Department of Justice, "Use of Federal Military to Quell Domestic Disturbances in Butte, MT," 39, Glasser File, Silver Bow County Archives [hereafter cited as SBCA], Butte, Montana; Gutfeld, *Montana's Agony*, 14.
97. Gutfeld, *Montana's Agony*, 14–16; Jeanette Prodgers, *Anaconda Almanac* (Butte, Montana: The Author, 1997), 42; see also Malone, Roeder, and Lang, *Montana*, 274.
98. "Company B on Guard Keeps Peace at Butte," *Roundup Record*, June 15, 1917; Prodgers, *Anaconda Almanac*, 42; Malone, Roeder, and Lang, *Montana*, 274. The *Billings Gazette* reported on June 15 that three companies from Montana's 2nd Regiment were in Butte. Presumably, this included Company B (Roundup), Company F (Kalispell), and Company K (Billings). "New Butte Union Calls On Miners to Be Strikers," *Billings Gazette*, June 15, 1917
99. Gutfeld, *Montana's Agony*, 23–29.
100. "Butte Lynchers Not Yet Known," Kalispell *Daily Interlake*, August 2, 1917; "3,000 Parade at Little Funeral," *Daily Interlake*, August 6, 1917; Malone, Roeder, and Lang, *Montana*, 275; "Use of Federal Military to Quell Domestic Disturbances," 52–61, Glasser File, SBCA; Harry C. Brumbaugh, "Special Order No. 64," Box 240 Folder 3, Stewart Papers, MC 35, MHS. Company B from Roundup had returned to Helena by August 2, as "their services were no longer needed" in Butte. "Despite the Draft Recruiting Continues," *Roundup Record*, August 3, 1917. Similarly, on August 3, Maj. Gen. Hunter Liggett, the commanding officer of the Western War Department, sent a telegram to the adjutant general in Washington, D.C., stating that the situation in Butte was quiet and he recommended that no additional troops be sent to the area. Liggett to Adjutant General [telegram], August 3, 1917, Butte (1917), Internal Disturbance (Geographical File), Abraham Glasser File, Record Group 60, Department of Justice, National Archives, Washington, D.C.
101. *Historical and Pictorial Review, National Guard of the State of Montana 1940* (Baton Rouge, Louisiana: Army and Navy Publishing, 1940), xxiii; John J. McGuinness to S.V. Stewart, July 24, 1917, S.V. Stewart to the Adjutant General, July 6, 1917, Governor Stewart to C.D. French, July 27, 1917, see also Governor Stewart to A.L. Jordan, July 11, 1917, Box 240 Folder 3, Stewart Papers, MC 35, MHS; Gutfeld, *Montana's Agony*, 70–79.
102. *Order of Battle of the United States Land Forces in the World War. Volume 2—American Expeditionary Forces: Divisions* (Washington, D.C.: Government Printing Office, 1931–

1949; reprint, Washington, D.C.: U.S. Army Center of Military History, 1988), 265 (page reference to reprint edition); Shipley Thomas, *The History of the A.E.F.* (New York: George H. Doran, 1920), 47, 449, 485–86; Brief Histories of Divisions, U.S. Army, 1917–1918, Drawer 2, "Montana Military History: 1917–1918: 'Brief Histories of Divisions, U.S. Army,'" Vertical File, MMHM, LA Building T-15, Fort Harrison.

103. "First and Second Montana Regiments; Their Fighting Records in Two Wars," *Reed Point Review* newspaper clipping, "World War, 1914–1918," Vertical Newspaper File, MHS. Cooper, *Rise of the National Guard*, 168; *Historical and Pictorial Review*, xiii; Lacey, *Montana Militia*, 45; Shore, *Montana in the Wars*, 66; "Montana's National Guard Celebrates 130 Years of Service," *Ft. Harrison Post Dispatch* 2 (Fall 1997): 3. Some states were disturbed by the incorporation of National Guard units into federal organizations and the renaming of regiments. Whether or not Montana reacted similarily is unclear from the sources available. Cooper, *Rise of the National Guard*, 169.

104. *History and Commemoration of the Second Regiment Montana Infantry: A Photographic Record of Enlistment* (n.p., 1917), 1, 31, 34, 35.

105. Brief Histories of Divisions, U.S. Army, 1917–1918, Drawer 2, MMHM, LA Building T-15, Fort Harrison; Jim Morris to Martin and Mary Morris, September 29, October 11, 1917. The James Joseph Morris Papers consist of letters sent to his parents, June 10, 1917, to January 20, 1919, providing a glimpse into Morris's World War I experiences, and also includes photographs and his service record. The papers are in the possession of Morris's daughter, Laela Jo Lindner, of Houston, Texas [hereafter cited as Morris Papers, LJL]. Coffman, *The War to End All Wars*, 5–6; "Final Report of General John J. Pershing," *United States Army in the World War, 1917–1918, Volume 12: Report of Commander-in-Chief, A.E.F., Staff Sections and Services* (Washington, D.C.: Historical Division of the Department of the Army, 1948), 21–22.

106. Jim Morris to Martin and Mary Morris, October 30, 1917, Morris Papers, LJL.

107. Ibid., October 30, November 9, 1917; Bruce Jacobs, "No Red Stars, Please," Executive Council File, SDF/1981, Drawer 11, NGAUS.

108. Jim Morris to Martin and Mary Morris, November 9, 12, 22, 24, December 2, 1917, Morris Papers, LJL; Charles L. Sheridan, "Colonel Charles Sheridan Traces Military History of Montana," *Three Forks Herald* newspaper clipping, "World War, 1914–1918," Vertical Newspaper File, MHS. Corporal Morris clearly was delighted at receiving the new equipment, including bayonets, rifles, canteens, belts, raincoats, and overcoats. "Everything [is] more efficient than it used to be," he stated, "except the Reserve officers." Jim Morris to Martin and Mary Morris, December 7, 1917, Morris Papers, LJL.

109. Ibid.

110. "First and Second Montana Regiments; Their Fighting Record in Two Wars," *Reed Point Review* newspaper clipping, "World War, 1914–1918," Vertical Newspaper File, MHS.

111. Charles L. Sheridan, "Colonel Charles Sheridan Traces Military History of Montana," *Three Forks Herald* newspaper clipping, "World War, 1914–1918," Vertical Newspaper File, MHS; December 14, 15, 1917, Diary of Orville L. Anderson Diary [typescript], Box 1 Folder 1, Orville L. Anderson Papers, Small Collection 289, Montana Historical Society, Helena, Montana [hereafter cited as Anderson Diary, Anderson Papers, SC 289, MHS].

112. Ibid., December 17, 20, 22, 24, 1917; Lacey, *Montana Militia*, 46.

113. "Final Report of General John J. Pershing," *United States Army in the World War, 1917–1919*, 17.

114. Ibid., 54–55; Thomas, *The History of the A.E.F.*, 47–48, 485–86; Lacey, *Montana Militia*, 46–47; Charles L. Sheridan, "Colonel Charles Sheridan Traces Military History of Montana," *Three Forks Herald* newspaper clipping, "World War, 1914–1918," Vertical Newspaper File, MHS. The 42nd was known as the "Rainbow Division," a name proposed by Maj. Douglas MacArthur. The 42nd included soldiers from 26 states and sailed to Europe in November 1917. The 91st Division consisted mainly of draftees from eight western states including Montana, and arrived in France on July 20, 1918. Hylton and Wright, *History of the Militia and National Guard*, 23; Brief Histories of Divisions, U.S. Army, 1917–1918, Drawer 2, MMHM, LA Building T-15, Fort Harrison.
115. Jim Morris to Martin and Mary Morris, March 28, 1918, Morris Papers, LJL.
116. *History Second Regiment Infantry National Guard Montana*, 30; Special Orders No. 82, April 19, 1917, Box 239 Folder 12, Stewart Papers, MC 35, MHS; War Diary Memoranda, Box 1 Folder 1, Anderson Papers, January 4, 1918, Anderson Diary, Anderson Papers, SC 289, MHS.
117. January 10, 1918, Anderson Diary, Anderson Papers, SC 289, MHS.
118. Ibid., March 15, 1918.
119. Ibid., February 28, 1918.
120. Ibid, March 26, April 2, 12, 13, 1918.
121. Ibid., April 11, 1918.
122. "Final Report of General John J. Pershing," *United States Army in the World War, 1917–1918*, 16–17, 25.
123. May 1, 1918, Anderson Diary, Anderson Papers, SC 289, MHS.
124. Ibid., April 30, 1918.
125. Ibid., June 3, 1918.
126. Ibid., May 1, 28, 30, June 6, 15, 23, 24, 1918.
127. Ibid., June 25, 1918.
128. Ibid., July 2, 6, 11, 1918.
129. Ibid., July 25, 1918; Coffman, *The War to End All Wars*, 251–61; "Final Report of General John J. Pershing," *United States Army in the World War, 1917–1919*, 35–36; "First and Second Montana Regiments; Their Fighting Record in Two Wars," *Reed Point Review* newspaper clipping, "World War, 1914–1918," Vertical Newspaper File, MHS.
130. Laela Jo Lindner, "James Joseph Morris," Morris Papers, LJL.
131. James J. Morris to Mary Morris, February 25, 1918, Morris Papers, LJL.
132. Ibid., March 10, 1918.
133. Ibid., March 3, 10, 28, 1918.
134. Ibid., April 14, 1918; Charles L. Sheridan, "Colonel Charles Sheridan Traces Military History of Montana," *Three Forks Herald* newspaper clipping, "World War, 1914–1918," Vertical Newspaper File, MHS.
135. James J. Morris to Martin and Mary Morris, June 21, July 17, 30, August 2, 1918, Morris Papers, LJL;
136. Coffman, *The War to End All Wars*, 222–27; "Final Report of General John J. Pershing," *United States Army in the World War, 1917–1919*, 34–36.
137. James J. Morris to Martin and Mary Morris, August 16, 1918, Morris Papers, LJL.
138. Ibid., September 5, 7, 1918.
139. "Transcript from Record of Service," Morris Papers, LJL; Coffman, *The War to End All Wars*, 355; Lacey, *Montana Militia*, 51; *Historical and Pictorial Review National Guard of the State of Montana*, xxiv. Morris went on to attend a year of college at the University of Montana, and then with his father established the Morris Construction Company. He

continued personal study throughout the rest of his life, especially philosophy, agriculture, geology, finance, and languages. Lindner, "James Joseph Morris," Website.

140. Lewis and Clark County American Legion Souvenir Booklet, "Montana Military History: 1917–1918—American Legion Souvenir Booklet," Vertical File, Drawer 2, MMHM, LA Building T-15, Fort Harrison; Lacey, *Montana Militia*, 52; Dennis Gordon, "Montana's Birdmen of World War I," *Montana: The Magazine of Western History* 29 (July 1979): 38–40; Charles L. Sheridan, "Colonel Charles Sheridan Traces Military History of Montana," *Three Forks Herald* newspaper clipping, "World War, 1914–1918," Vertical Newspaper File, MHS.

141. General Orders No. 38-A, February 28, 1919, Personal Papers of Thomas C. Cooper, Cage Accession #371, MMHM, LA Building T-15, Fort Harrison.

8

Rebuilding to Stability: The 1920s

Suzanne Julin

The work has been slow and at sometimes discouraging but it has brought some results.—Adjutant General Charles L. Sheridan, 1922.

Late in 1922, Adjutant General Charles L. Sheridan, a Bozeman native and World War I veteran cited for heroism in action, submitted his first biennial report to Governor Joseph Dixon. He reminded the governor that a number of other states had effectively reconstituted their National Guard units during or immediately after the war. Reorganizing Montana's guard, however, "has been slow and at some times discouraging, but it has brought some results."[1]

Sheridan's discouragement was understandable, though eventually he succeeded in an admirable manner. Federal policies during World War I had extinguished the pre-war National Guard. This now necessitated a complete rebuilding. In Montana, the effort began with the reorganization of Company A at Sidney on February 3, 1921, and would officially end on January 20, 1924, with federal recognition of all the Montana units authorized by Congress at the time.[2]

This rebuilding would dominate guard activities during the first half of the 1920s, setting the stage for stabilization and peacetime service lasting into the late 1930s.

For the country as a whole, the decade following World War I was a period of changed attitudes and readjustment. The great cost of the European conflict in money, materiel, and casualties affected the way many Americans felt about the military and armed ventures in general. They were disillusioned with self-sacrifice. Anti-war and anti-military sentiment, as well as isolationism from international affairs, became common attitudes—deeply rooted among much of the populace.

At the same time, the country experienced broad social and economic changes. An exponentially growing consumer orientation led to a greater demand for goods and services, which promoted more sophisticated advertising, business, and production methods. The nation's spectacular financial growth expanded speculative investments. As many of these ventures bore fruit, people began investing in Wall Street as an alternative to saving.

Automobiles became much more common, with a corresponding expansion in improved highway systems—fostering further domestic, commercial, and urban reorientations. Radio and motion pictures immediately disseminated information and trends, and promoted new nationally recognized personalities and heroes. On top of it all, an extended period of national prosperity throughout most of the 1920s led many to believe that the good times were here to stay.[3]

World War I had affected Montana very directly. Men from the state served in large numbers— about 28,000 were drafted, a quota based on a probable overestimate of the state's population. Thousands of others enlisted in the armed services, or were inducted as members of guard units. Altogether, over 39,000 men from a population of less than a half-million, nearly 10 percent, went into military service. This was a ratio one-quarter higher than for other states. As a result, Montana suffered greater per capita casualties than other parts of the country.[4] Montana citizens had a special reason to reflect on the sacrifice of war.

Attitudes toward the war also impacted labor issues in Montana. Numerous workers and labor sympathizers retained anti-military sentiments, as well as resentment regarding the guard's strike-breaking role. Among the most radical in this regard was the Industrial Workers of the World, which blamed the European and American elite upper-classes for causing, and then profiting, from the war. The IWW advocated a classless society in America and the world, with the control of production in the hands of workers. Divisiveness grew as pro-labor and anti-war factions became increasingly juxtaposed to business and pro-military groups. After strike-related shootings at Butte in 1920, the use of federal troops to quell the demonstrations further increased labor's enmity toward the military. Aggressive countermeasures by politicians, government, and business, however, subsequently began weakening the labor movement.[5]

The nation's post-war economic growth did not benefit Montana to the full extent as in other regions. Montana's economy depended on producing agricultural, mining, and lumber commodities, which indeed were in great demand during the war. After the armistice, however, markets weakened, particularly regarding agricultural products as the European nations brought their farmlands back into full production. In addition, federal price supports were cancelled, and the state suffered from a drought lasting well into the 1920s, particularly affecting northeast Montana. Many farmers in marginally productive agricultural areas lost their property; banks failed, and thousands of rural residents left the state. The situation would ease somewhat when the drought ended in the mid-1920s, but the hard times left many with feelings of cynicism and bitterness over the lack of government intervention to ease the crisis.[6]

These circumstances impacted the Montana National Guard as it rebuilt during the 1920s. Anti-military sentiment hampered enlistment, and economic difficulties affected state funding. Nevertheless, a sense of duty and better guard salaries would attract recruits.

National Guard units had experienced extensive transformation when activated for World War I, with the U.S. Army reconfiguring units or incorporating them among revised organizations. The 2nd Montana Infantry was re-designated as the 163rd Infantry. Under section 111 of the National Defense Act of 1916, the guardsmen were discharged from the state militia upon their 1917 induction into the U.S. Army. Therefore, when leaving federal duty after the World War, these men had no further military obligation.

Though Congress amended the National Defense Act in 1920, allowing guard personnel called into federal service to return to guard membership after discharge,[7] Montana's Adjutant General Sheridan still confronted difficulties. In the *Instructors Annual Report*, April 1922 to April 1923, Major H.B. Keen, a regular army officer conducting inspections of the Montana guard, summarized the situation as follows: "General scattered condition of units, Labor opposition, lack of interest in most localities among ex-servicemen, poor armories, small state appropriation. The appropriation, as passed by the Legislature, was $50,000 for two years. All appropriations were cut by the Governor in order to hold within the income of the State. The National Guard appropriation was cut $10,000 in the general cut. This leaves only $20,000 per year, an amount too small to work with."[8]

As Keen observed, the "scattered condition of units" and "poor armories" hampered reorganization.[9] Sidney's Company A, for example, did not have an armory and rented a hall for drills. "The building that they had at first blew down last year," the inspector noted, "and they have to take the hall when they can get it."[10] Company H in Kalispell drilled in a former church, which Major Keen considered too small. He described other armories as cramped or inadequate for close order drill and bayonet practice. The inspector classified the units themselves as ranging from very good to poor. The deficiencies he attributed to inadequate training, poor attendance, and restricted activity in those communities harboring anti-military sentiment.[11] The distribution of supplies was somewhat haphazard, and some organizations allowed men to take equipment home against regulations, particularly pistols. High turnover rates, a relatively large number of extremely young recruits, and inexperienced or unenthusiastic officers compounded the situation.[12]

Labor opposition in communities with a strong union tradition tended to discourage the formation of guard units.[13] In his 1923 report, Keen noted: "The state as a whole does not seem behind the Guard. In some localities the support is all that could be asked for. Montana is a strong [labor] Union state, and consequently we receive a great deal of opposition. That part of the State on the Great

Northern R.R. in the North East is the best section for Guard units. All the large towns are opposed to the Guard."[14]

Colonel Fred Lang, who rejoined the guard after serving in World War I, recalled that "recruiting was terrible after the war."[15] Adjutant General Sheridan also believed it was more difficult to convince Montanans to enlist because "there were so few of our young men who had not seen service during the war."[16] (In fact, by 1927 only about 250 war veterans were enlisted in the Montana guard.[17]) In Sheridan's view, "the whole country was war weary." Most states, indeed, experienced difficulty recruiting veterans into the National Guard.[18]

In 1924, the War Department planned to test its improved organizational strategies—as outlined in the 1920 National Defense Act—when calling out the U.S. Army, National Guard, and the Army Reserve in a rapid mobilization on National Defense Day, scheduled for September 12.[19] Maj. Gen. C.G. Morton, Commander of the IX Corps Area (one of nine corps established across the country by the 1920 act), had advised Montana Governor Joseph Dixon in May of the organizational plans for the event. Each corps area contained one Army, two National Guard, and three Reserve divisions. In July, Morton's chief of staff, A.V.P. Anderson, followed up in a note to Governor Dixon, complimenting him on his "aggressive action in plans for the Defense Test in Montana." The governor's preparations, however, quickly encountered opposition and he seemed to vacillate, being aware of broad anti-military sentiment.

During the next few weeks, the governor received a number of letters and telegrams urging him to take a stand against the planned mobilization. The communications were from both local individuals and national organizations opposed to the event. [20] Dixon replied to one correspondent, "I am sure there must be some mistake in the matter as I have ordered no mobilization of the state guard on that day and do not intend doing so."[21] To a Synod of Wyoming representative, the governor explained he was descended from Quakers and believed "that the response to the mobilization gesture…would not be a very enthusiastic one."[22]

Nevertheless, the National Defense Day event occurred on September 12, 1924, when 1,500,000 men across the nation volunteered to attend. Citizens of local communities also participated. In Billings, for example, 600 civilians attended the day's program at the Babcock Theater.[23]

The next year, the War Department again planned a mobilization test. While proclaiming July 4 as National Defense Day, President Calvin Coolidge noted that each state's participation should be voluntary. Montana's newly elected governor, John E. Erickson, received letters and telegrams from peace and religious groups (both local and national) opposed to the event.[24] For example, the Silver Bow League of Women Voters wrote "to express its disapproval of any plan for an annual 'Muster Day' or 'Mobilization Day,' or 'Defense Test Day,' or any day of Militaristic gesture whatsoever."[25]

In a reply to another correspondent, Governor Erickson said he designated July 4 as Defense Day in Montana "after considerable mental reservation,"[26] but he also responded warmly to another rare letter supporting his action in making the proclamation. State leaders in these times walked a fine line, given the deeply polarized public mood. During the 1925 event, some state governors withheld their guard units from active inclusion. Participation in general declined from the previous year. All of Montana's National Guard companies, however, took part.[27]

During this period of drought and agricultural depression, Governor Joseph Dixon, a progressive Republican, had earlier tried to introduce tax reform. In particular, he hoped to impose reasonable taxes on mine production. He was opposed, however, by Anaconda mining and its company-supported press, and by many conservative Republicans controlling both houses of the legislature. In 1924, Democrat John E. Erickson, supported by the Anaconda Company, and whose campaign stressed thrift and economy, defeated Dixon's reelection bid.

Erickson's thrift probably affected the state appropriation for the National Guard. State funds paid for facilities and storage rental, clothing allowances, new recruit examinations, incidental office costs, and the salaries of the adjutant general, military storekeeper, and stenographer—i.e., expenses not covered by federal funding. Between March 1, 1921, and November 1, 1922, during Governor Dixon's administration, the organization had $22,045.02 in state appropriated funds. After Governor Erickson's election in 1924, the state appropriated $20,000.

The guard continued to request increased state appropriations, noting that for every $1,000 the Montana legislature granted, the federal government contributed about $10,000. Though the drought finally abated and the state's financial problems eased,[28] in 1927 new Adjutant General Erastus Williams commented to the chief of the Militia Bureau: "We are having our usual battle with our State Legislature for funds sufficient to run the guard for the next two years."[29]

In addition to the affects of anti-military sentiment in Montana, the guard became embroiled in another factional issue of the times. In 1925, two mothers of guardsmen wrote to Governor Erickson, complaining about several guard officers disregarding the 18th Amendment—the Prohibition of alcohol. The mothers accused guard officers of drinking, for allowing the consumption of liquor at the summer encampment, and of not supporting Prohibition. They specifically described the officers' behavior. The governor responded, assuring them he took their complaints seriously.[30]

The following year, a guard captain sold some of his company's equipment to a local Army and Navy store. Because the army was changing uniforms and equipment, he believed he was justified in selling the soon-to-be outmoded items. He later pled guilty to petty larceny and the guard subsequently dismissed him.[31] A lawyer representing the business owner making the purchases wrote to

Adjutant General Williams, saying he talked to local citizens about the captain and they indicated he was unreliable. The attorney added, "newspaper publicity given these matters has been a little stronger than we anticipated....I do not want [the businessman] to go to another lawyer and have the matter opened up and get more publicity."[32] The attorney clearly was concerned about negative publicity over the incident, which could not have reflected well on the state militia.

Such incidents reinforced the negative views that some segments of the public felt toward the military. A sergeant contacted Governor Dixon to air his grievances regarding treatment in his community: "There are three of us here...and every time we dress to go to drill a bunch in town make all manner of fun of us and say things that sure hurt. So we [want] to [know] just what the National Guards are used for and in black and white so we can show them where they are wrong for if we can't stop it we would like very much to be excused from drills here after."[33]

Though obstacles remained in rebuilding the organization, there also was a new incentive for recruitment. The 1916 National Defense Act had guaranteed substantial federal funding. Before World War I, the largest annual support for the country's National Guard was $6 million, but in the 1920s (and the 1930s), federal expenditures would average $32 million annually. Regular pay for guard members, and the added economic benefit to local communities, was more substantial than before—an inducement for enlistment and gaining support from local commercial interests. Under the act, the U.S. government provided funds for drill and summer camp pay, for armaments and equipment, and for physical structures serving training and storage needs. Previously, the states bore responsibility for most of these expenses.[34]

Across the nation, young men began turning to the guard as a source of income. By the mid 1920s, 381 college and high school students were enrolled in the Montana guard. In fact, many could afford to remain in school only because of drill pay. For the Montana guard as a whole, 38% were students; 15%, farmers; 32%, laborers, railroad workers, and business and government employees; 8%, professionals, businessmen, or elected officials; and 7%, classified as "miscellanous."[35]

Retaining a local guard unit was economically important for a number of communities. When Poplar's Company B was scheduled for inspection in 1926, a local newspaper urged all guardsmen to attend, warning that a lackluster turnout could result in the loss of the unit. The company's payroll, "amounts to about $9,600 a year, all of which is spent right here in Poplar. This is a big item, and it means considerable to the city."[36] When rumors circulated about removing units from Baker and Wilsall in 1919, Governor Erickson received letters from citizens protesting such action.[37]

By the mid 1920s, some of the urban opposition to military affairs seemed to be waning. For example, a Billings Commercial Club representative wrote to

Adjutant General Williams in 1926, urging him to consider Billings for assigning a unit. The request cited the availability of young men as recruits, good training facilities, and stressed the community's support for the National Guard. Billings, indeed, was assigned a unit. In 1929, the Headquarters Company of the Third Battalion also came to Billings after the Wilsall unit was disbanded. Adjutant General Williams had delayed this move until after the 1929 legislative session to avoid conflict with legislators wanting companies in their communities.[38]

Initially, of course, the task of rebuilding the Montana guard had fallen chiefly under the guidance of Adjutant General Charles Sheridan. Despite many obstacles, Sheridan prevailed. As a part of this three year effort, he instituted a newspaper publicity campaign and sought the support of veteran and civic associations. Sheridan completed the official reorganization in 1924, his last year as adjutant general.[39] The organization increased more than in any other state in the IX Corps area. It ranked 20th among all states and territories in terms of strength of organization in proportion to population, even though Montana's appropriations ranked 44th.

On January 1, 1925, Erastus H. Williams, another World War I veteran, had taken over as adjutant general, a position he held until his death in 1937. During Williams' tenure, membership nearly tripled and federal funding more than quadrupled. He also would add a medical unit to the state guard.[40] Adjutant generals Sheridan and Williams, of course, not only built up units, they also oversaw training. Under the 1916 act, state units were required to drill 48 times annually, with each drill period lasting at least 1½ hours. In addition, each unit needed to participate in encampments for at least 15 days each year.[41]

The guard also conducted schools for officers and non-commissioned officers. Meanwhile, regular army personnel continued to be assigned as instructors-inspectors in Montana. Some guard officers and selected enlisted men attended War Department service schools in other locations. In 1923, for example, an officer attended the Infantry School at Camp Benning, Georgia; another went to the Field Medical School in Carlisle, Pennsylvania; and eight enlisted men participated in a Cooks and Bakers School in San Francisco. In addition, officers participated in correspondence courses, receiving lessons on a weekly basis.[42]

The annual 15-day summer encampment provided the most essential training for the Montana guard as a whole. In 1922, the first encampment of the reorganized Montana National Guard convened at Fort Missoula, with 14 officers and 256 men participating. Typically, a summer camp was named for the governor; in that year, Governor Joseph Dixon visited "Camp Dixon" and reviewed the troops. In 1923, the Montana guard conducted training at Camp Lewis, Washington. In the following year, 765 enlisted men and 56 officers encamped at Fort Harrison, where officers and enlisted men of the First Battalion, 4th U.S. Infantry, assisted in instruction.

In 1925, the War Department issued a license to Montana to utilize 600 acres on the Fort Harrison Military Reservation. The state paid nothing for the license, but assumed responsibility for maintaining the property and agreed not to interfere with the Veterans' Bureau Hospital, which utilized the remainder of the fort grounds. Summer encampments were held here throughout the rest of the decade.[43]

At Fort Harrison, the enlisted men bivouacked in canvas wall tents with dirt floors, until federal authorities funded the addition of wooden floors. The platforms were stored in a nearby warehouse between encampments. From 1925 to 1930, the federal government expended approximately $110,000 on construction and improvements, including the tent floors, kitchens, mess halls, latrines, showers, a water system, and an electrical system. With electrical lights, the men no longer relied on candles or lanterns in the evenings. Summer camp participation during the 1920s grew from a total of 270 officers and men in 1922, to about 900 in 1929.[44]

The 1924 Fort Harrison encampment involved a variety of activities. In preparation for the summer camp, an officers' school convened from June 8 to 11, with attendees receiving instruction from 7 a.m. until 9:30 or 10 p.m. each of the four days. Bozeman's service company, which included the regimental band, arrived two days before the full encampment to make preparations. Meanwhile, 18 companies and the medical detachment traveled toward Helena on special trains to begin training on June 14. A reunion of the "old" 163rd Infantry also was organized, with about 100 war veterans attending.[45]

Poplar's Company B played a prominent role in this encampment. Two-thirds were from the Yankton and Assiniboine tribes, many of them war veterans. Before they left for camp, a capacity crowd feted them at an Indian dance hall near Poplar with speeches, ceremonies, and dancing. After arriving at Fort Harrison, the company entertained the other soldiers and local citizens one evening with traditional Native American dances. Company B also played in the camp's baseball championship finals.

On June 21, Company B formally adopted General E. DuMont into their tribe. A member of the French embassy, DuMont received the title "High Eagle" while being presented a porcupine quill necklace. In reciprocation, a few weeks later General DuMont sent Company B a French flag, which Sheridan presented to Company B at the Fort Peck Indian Fair in September. In addition to the Poplar unit, Sidney's Company A also was predominantly Native American. And again, a number of them were war veterans.[46]

In the 1920s, rifle competitions remained a popular venue for training. In 1922, 14 guardsmen attended the National Rifle Match at Camp Perry, Ohio. Since only three of them had previously participated in competitive marksmanship contests, Sheridan's expectation of not performing well proved true. In 1923, a rifle instruction camp was held at Fort Harrison, attended by teams of between five and eight men from different companies. The 15 best marksmen attended the national competition, placing 91st in a field of 98 teams; Sheridan considered this a good showing in view of their sparse training. Another rifle instruction camp was held in the following year and the intervening training had borne fruit. The 16 men attending the Camp Perry national matches placed 42nd out of 97 teams. Montana teams continued attending the national match throughout the 1920s. In 1923 and 1924, 27 rifle and pistol clubs also were formed in Montana, with Harlowton hosting competitions.[47]

Montana guardsmen also served at ceremonial and public functions. For instance, guardsmen from Culbertson, Froid, and Bainville in northeast Montana participated in a celebration at old Fort Union in July 1925.[48] In the following year, Queen Marie of Romania visited Montana during a cross-country tour. Eleven guard officers and enlisted men were assigned to escort her when traveling through Montana. A descendent of Queen Victoria of England as well as Czar Alexander II of Russia, Queen Marie received much public attention; 119 stories about her appeared in the *New York Times* between October 1 and the end of the year. While traveling toward Washington, where she would attend the dedication of the Maryhill Mansion and art museum on the Columbia River, her journey was punctuated by side trips. She visited the University of Montana, where students greeted her with college chants, and Glacier National Park, where she and her children were adopted into the Blackfoot tribe.[49]

In July 1926, a Montana honor guard also attended Prince Gustavus Adolphus and Princess Louise of Sweden when they visited Livingston on their way to Yellowstone National Park. Governor John E. Erickson and his wife, as well as 78-year-old Livingston resident Hannah Shogren, once a cook for the Swedish royal family, attended the community's ceremonies, which included a performance by rodeo riders. In the spring of 1927, Livingston's howitzer company honored President Calvin Coolidge, firing a 21-gun salute when Mr. and Mrs. Coolidge and their son briefly stopped in Livingston, also en route to Yellowstone. Governor Erickson presented Coolidge with a fly rod before a crowd of about 3,000 people.[50]

On September 6, 1927, the Montana State Fair hosted the greatest public hero of the decade, Charles A. Lindbergh. In the previous spring, Lindbergh was the first to fly solo across the Atlantic. His instant celebrity pushed other personalities in the news into the background.[51] More than 25,000 people and 3,800 automobiles converged on Helena for Lindbergh's arrival by plane and appearance at the state fair. Montana guardsmen and local law enforcement officers cordoned off the landing area at the city golf course and kept nearby streets free of traffic. Helena's Headquarters Company and the Helena city police provided Lindbergh's escort to the fair, where the 163rd Regimental Band, Campfire Girls, and Boy Scouts preceded Lindbergh, Governor Erickson, Mayor Perry Witmer, and other dignitaries. Meanwhile, a Headquarters Company detachment remained at the landing site, guarding Lindbergh's plane, the Spirit of St. Louis, which was protected by a barbed wire barrier immediately after Lindbergh's landing.

Lindbergh's speech—to the largest gathering in Montana up to that time—focused on the need to further develop commercial aviation. His visit was part of a country-wide tour featuring at least one stop in every state. Lindbergh also spent several days in Butte, leaving his plane there while vacationing.[52]

Lindbergh heightened the interest in aviation. In July 1928, the small town of Froid in far northeast Montana sponsored a national air meet, part of a tour originating from Detroit, Michigan. A detachment from Culbertson's Company E and Bainville's Second Battalion Headquarters Company assisted when 20,000 people converged at Froid on Sunday, July 26. About 40 planes landed at the small town, including one flown by Mrs. Phoebe Omlie, the only woman pilot on the tour. Froid's newspaper complimented the National Guard for its crowd management.[53]

In another well established role for the guard, some members again served as fire fighters. In late summer 1929, a timber blaze in northwest Montana and Glacier National Park destroyed several logging camps, homesteads, and summer homes. On August 24, Governor Erickson issued General Order Number 12, ordering Adjutant General Williams to mobilize as many guard elements as he considered necessary to protect people and property. Williams made arrangements for transporting 400 troops by train from Bainville, Froid, Culbertson, Poplar, Glasgow, Harlem, and Chinook, if their participation became necessary.[54]

Williams also ordered 3 officers and 12 enlisted men from Kalispell's Company F to report for duty. Captain Carl Anderson would lead this detachment to Columbia Falls, setting up a command post and assisting in fire fighting directly north of the community. The detachment embarked with equipment and supplies by 2 p.m., arriving in Columbia Falls an hour later. They established the quarters in a vacant house offered by the city's mayor. A local power company provided electricity and telephone service without charge, and a Columbia Falls restaurant agreed to provide each man with a 40¢ meal three times a day. For $2, a farmer sold the detachment a load of straw for filling their bed sacks.

The men burned the tall grass between the railroad grade and the town, creating a vegetation-free barrier against the fire. For three days, about 100 acres of grass were intentionally set afire around the town's border, and for the next two days the detachment continued patrolling. No buildings were destroyed, nor any injuries suffered. On August 28, the danger having passed, Adjutant General Williams ordered the detachment home, dismissing them later that day.[55]

By 1930, the total strength of the Montana National Guard stood at 1,173 officers and enlisted men, the maximum allowed by the War Department.[56] Under the leadership of adjutant generals Charles Sheridan and Erastus Williams, the

Montana guard had fully reorganized, despite political, monetary, and social obstacles and the "war weariness" affecting much of the population.

The Montana National Guard was a stable organization, prepared to meet the challenges ahead.

Notes

1. *Biennial Report of the Adjutant General of Montana, 1921-1922,* 1. Sheridan received the French Croix de Guerre, Belgian War Cross, and the American Distinguished Service Cross. He was cited for heroism in action near Cieges, France, in 1918. Richard H. Lacey, *The Montana Militia: A History of Montana's Volunteer Forces, 1867–1976* (Dillon, Montana: Dillon Tribune-Examiner Press, 1976), 52; Liberty County *Farmer* (Montana), June 18, 1924.
2. "Bibliography of Outline History, 163rd Infantry," Montana National Guard, Vertical Files, Montana Historical Society, Helena, Montana [hereafter cited as MHS].
3. Robert S. McElvaine, *The Great Depression: America, 1919–1941* (New York: Times Books, 1984), 10–17, 37–46; Neil A. Wynn, *From Progressivism to Prosperity: World War I and American Society* (New York: Holmes and Meier, 1986), xvi, 200–1; Ellis W. Hawley, *The Great War and the Search for Modern Order: A History of the American People and Their Institutions, 1917–1933* (New York: St. Martin's Press, 1979), 85–87, 144–46, 165–69; Emily S. Rosenberg, *Spreading the American Dream: American Economic and Cultural Expansion, 1890–1945* (New York: Hill and Wang, 1982), 99–103.
4. Michael P. Malone and Richard B. Roeder, *Montana: A History of Two Centuries* (Seattle: University of Washington Press, 1976), 207–8, 219; Lacey, *Montana Militia,* 52. The 163rd Infantry returned to the United States on February 12, 1919, and was mustered out at Camp Dix, New Jersey, February 21. "Bibliography of Outline History, 163rd Infantry," Montana National Guard, Vertical Files, MHS.
5. Malone and Roeder, *Montana,* 208–15; Jim Shoemaker to Erastus Williams, March 20, 1926, Box 36 Folder 3, Governor John Erickson Papers, Manuscript Collection 35, Montana Historical Society, Helena, Montana [hereafter cited as Erickson Papers, MC 35, MHS]; Butte *Miner,* April 22, 23, 1920; Joseph W. Upshaw, Ret., interview by Staff Sgt. Milo McLeod, June 1, 1985, transcribed tape recording, Oral History 1268, Montana Historical Society, Helena, Montana [hereafter cited as Upshaw interview, OH 1268, MHS]; Joseph W. Upshaw, Ret., interview by Sgt. Orlan J. Svingen, May 5, 1985, transcribed tape recording, Drawer 3, Montana Military History Museum, Library Archives, Fort William H. Harrison, Helena, Montana [hereafter cited as Upshaw interview, MMHM, LA, Fort Harrison]; Robert K. Murray, *Red Scare: A Study in National Hysteria, 1919–1920* (Minneapolis: University of Minnesota, 1955), 29–31.
6. Malone and Roeder, *Montana,* 216–19, 222, 282–83.
7. Jerry Cooper, *The Militia and the National Guard in America since Colonial Times: A Research Guide* (Westport, Connecticut: Greenwood Press, 1993), 106–7; Jerry Cooper, *The Rise of the National Guard: The Evolution of the American Militia, 1865–1920* (Lincoln: University of Nebraska Press, 1997), 168–74; *United States Statutes at Large,* XXXIX, sec. 111, 211; *United States Statutes at Large,* XLI, sec. 111, 785.
8. *Instructors Annual Report, National Guard, 1923,* Box 1 Folder 12, Montana Adjutant General Records, Record Collection 223, MHS.
9. *United States Statutes at Large,* XXXIX, sec. 93. 206.

10. *Report of an Inspection of Company 'A' 163rd Infantry N.G. of Montana, February 16, 1923,* Box 1 Folder 12, Montana Adjutant General Records, RC 223, MHS.
11. *Report of an Inspection of Company 'A' 163rd Infantry N.G. of Montana, February 16, 1923; Report of an Inspection of Company 'B' 163rd Infantry, N.G. of Montana, February 14, 1923; Report of an Inspection of Company 'E' 163rd Infantry N.G. of Montana, February 15, 1923; Report of an Inspection of Company 'H' 163rd Infantry N.G. of Montana,* n.d.; *Report of an Inspection of Headquarters Co., 1st Bn. 163rd Inf., N.G. of Montana, February 15, 1923,* Box 1 Folder 12, Montana Adjutant General Records, RC 223, MHS; H.B. Keen, Major Infantry, to Adjutant General of Montana, May 1, 1924, Box 1 Folder 13, Montana Adjutant General Records, RC 223, MHS.
12. H.B. Keen, Major Infantry, to Adjutant General of Montana, May 1, 1924, Box 1 Folder 13, Montana Adjutant General Records, RC 223, MHS; Wm. V. McCreight to the Adjutant General, April 28, 1924, Box 1 Folder 13, Montana Adjutant General Records, RC 223, MHS.
13. Malone and Roeder, *Montana,* 208–9, 211–15; Jim Shoemaker to Col. Erastus Williams, March 20, 1926, Box 36 Folder 3, Erickson Papers, MC 35, MHS; Upshaw interview, June 1, 1985, OH 1268, MHS; Upshaw interview, May 5, 1985, MMHM, LA, Fort Harrison.
14. *Instructors Annual Report, National Guard, 1923,* Box 1 Folder 12, Montana Adjutant General Records, Record Collection 223, MHS. This opposition continued at least into the next decade. In 1939, Montana's attorney general objected to plans for the organization of a unit in Butte, saying "rank and file of Butte are against establishment of National Guard in Butte and consider this as move on part of Anaconda Copper to provide Guard for use during strike." Harrison J. Freebourn, Attorney General to Maj. Gen. M. [sic] H. Blanding [telegram], Entry 344 Box 587, State Dec file 1922–45, 325.4 Montana, Army-National Guard Bureau, Record Group 168, National Archives, Washington, D.C. [hereafter cited as RG 168, NA].
15. Col. Fred Lang, interviewed by 2nd Lt. Greg Murray and Sgt. Charles Hull, transcribed tape recording, Fall 1972, Box 1 Folder 1, Montana National Guard Collection, Small Collection 1226, MHS.
16. *Biennial Report, 1921–1922,* 1; Cooper, *Rise of the National Guard,* 173.
17. Billings *Gazette,* July 10, 1917; "History of National Guard in Montana," *The Montana Legionnaire,* May 1927.
18. *Biennial Report, 1921–1922,* 1.
19. "The Defense Test," September 12, 1924, Box 27 Folder 2, Governor Joseph M. Dixon Papers, Manuscript Collection 35, Montana Historical Society, Helena, Montana; Maj. Gen. C.G. Morton to Joseph M. Dixon, May 13, 1924, Box 27 Folder 2, Dixon Papers, MC 35, MHS.
20. *United States Statutes at Large,* XLI, sec. 3, 759; Cooper, *Rise of the National Guard,* 174; A.V.P. Anderson to Joseph Dixon, July 21, 1924; Daniel S. McCorkle, Moderator of the Synod of Wyoming, to Governor Joseph M. Dixon, August 4, 1924; Frederick J. Libby, National Council for Prevention of War, to "Friend," July 28, 1924; Frederick J. Libby to Joseph M. Dixon, August 1924; Hanna Clothier Hull, Women's International League for Peace and Freedom, to Joseph M. Dixon, August 9, 1924; Charlotte Jones to Governor Dixon, August 15, 1924, Box 27 Folder 2, Dixon Papers, MC 35, MHS.
21. Joseph Dixon to Mrs. Charlotte Jones, August 18, 1924, Box 27 Folder 2, Dixon Papers, MC 35, MHS.

22. Joseph Dixon to Daniel S. McCorkle, August 5, 1924, Box 27 Folder 2, Dixon Papers, MC 35, MHS.
23. Billings *Gazette,* September 12 and 13, 1924; Helena *Independent,* July 4, 1925. The latter news article reviewed the previous year's activities.
24. Maj. Gen. Charles T. Mencher to Governor John Erickson, June 4, 1925; Paul Jones to Hon. J.E. Erickson, May 28, 1925; Anna E. Bowersox, Silver Bow League of Women Voters, to Hon. J.E. Erickson, May 27, 1925; Henry Van Englen, J.N. MacLean, Jesse Lacklen, W.L. Young, Frank E. Henry, John R. Hahn, Edwin Johnson, Woolsey Couch, Members of the Missoula Ministerial Association, to Honorable J.E. Erickson, n.d.; S.R. Logan to J.E. Erickson, June 17, 1925; Students of the 34th Annual Southern Students' Conference, June 25, 1925; Box 36 Folder 3, Erickson Papers, MC 35, MHS; Malone and Roeder, *Montana,* 221–22.
25. Anna E. Bowersox, Silver Bow League of Women Voters, to Hon. J.E. Erickson, May 27, 1925, Box 36, Folder 3, Erickson Papers, Box 36 Folder 3, MC 35, MHS.
26. J.E. Erickson to S.R. Logan, June 27, 1925, Box 36 Folder 3, Erickson Papers, MC 35, MHS.
27. Governor to Dr. Charles L. Bovard, July 17, 1925, Box 36 Folder 3, Governor Erickson Papers, MC 35, MHS; Helena *Independent,* July 4, 1925; Billings *Gazette,* July 5, 1925; Erastus H. Williams to J.E. Erickson, July 13, 1925, Box 36, Folder 3, Erickson Papers, MC 35, MHS.
28. Malone and Roeder, *Montana,* 220–22; Cooper, *Rise of the National Guard,* 175; *Biennial Report, 1921–1922,* 8; "National Guard Information," Box 51 Folder 10, Erickson Papers, MC 35, MHS.
29. Erastus H. Williams to Gen. Creed C. Hammond, January 18, 1927, Entry 344 Box 587, State Dec file 1922–45, 325.4, RG 168, NA.
30. Mrs. Clyde McLemore to John E. Erickson, June 24, 1925; Governor to Mrs. Clyde McLemore, July 2, 1925; Mrs. F.J. Wheeler to Governor Erickson, June 9, 1925; Governor to Mrs. F.H. [sic] Wheeler, June 17, 1925, Box 36 Folder 3, Erickson Papers, MC 35, MHS.
31. Bozeman *Daily Chronicle,* n.d.; Office of the Adjutant General, General Order No. 11, September 21, 1926, Box 1 Folder 1, Montana National Guard Collection, SC 1226, MHS.
32. Hubert D. Bath to Col. Erastus H. Williams, January 22, 1926, Original Historical Documents file, MMHM, LA.
33. Sgt. A. Borden to Governor, November 12, 1923, Box 17 Folder 1, Dixon Papers, MC 35, MHS.
34. Cooper, *Militia and the National Guard in America,* 118–19; "Bozeman Recognized as 'National Guard City,'" *The 163rd Infantry Journal,* 1(2) (February 25, 1930): 3; *United States Statutes at Large,* XXXIX, sec. 67, 199; sec. 94, 206; sec. 110, 209–10.
35. Cooper, *Rise of the National Guard,* 175–76; "National Guard Information," n.d., Box 51 Folder 10, Erickson Papers, MC 35, MHS.
36. Poplar *Standard,* November 19, 1926.
37. Governor to R.B. Lowry, September 16, 1925, Box 36 Folder 1, Erickson Papers, MC 35, MHS; Governor to W.O. Hutchinson, March 30, 1929, Box 36, Folder 4, Erickson Papers, MC 35, MHS.
38. Jim Shoemaker to Col. Erastus Williams, March 20, 1926, Box 36 Folder 3, Erickson Papers, MC 35, MHS; Erastus H. Williams to Capt. H.C. Dempewolf, February 29,

1929, Box 1 Folder 7, Montana Adjutant General Office Records, RC 223, MHS; *Biennial Report, 1929–1930*, 1.

39. "Bibliography of Outline History, 163rd Infantry," n.d., Montana National Guard, Vertical Files, MSH; Charles L. Sheridan to Chief, Militia Bureau, May 24, 1924, Entry 344 Box 587, State Dec file 1922–45, 325.4, RG 168, NA.
40. Edgar A. Sirmeyer to John E. Erickson, January 16, 1925, Box 5 Folder 10, Erickson Papers, MC 35, MHS; Lacey, *Montana Militia*, 57; "History of the National Guard," *The Montana Legionnaire*, May 1927; *Historical and Pictorial Review of the National Guard State of Montana* (Baton Rouge, Louisiana: Army and Navy Publishing, 1940), 68. By the end of 1938, the Montana National Guard would include 60 officers and 1,174 enlisted men, with units in 24 locations, and federal funds received totaled $395,431.82 during 1937 and 1938. *Biennial Report, 1937–38*, 1–2.
41. *United States Statutes at Large*, XXXIX, sec. 92, 206.
42. *Biennial Report, 1923–1924*, 3–5; *Biennial Report, 1929–1930*, 6; *Instructor's Annual Report, National Guard, 1923*, 7, Box 1 Folder 12, Montana Adjutant General Records, RC 112, MHS; *Biennial Report, 1925–1926*, 2–3.
43. *Biennial Report, 1921–1922*, 3; Governor Joseph Dixon to Adjutant General Charles S. Sheridan, August 25, 1922, Box 27 Folder 1, Dixon Papers, MC 35, MHS; *Biennial Report, 1923–1924*, 3; Revocable License, March 17, 1925 (copy), Box 36 Folder 3, Erickson Papers, MC 35, MSH; *Biennial Report, 1925–1926*, 3; *Biennial Report, 1925–1926*; *Biennial Report, 1927–1928*, 3–4; *Biennial Report, 1929–1930*, 6. The property covered by the license was described as "[t]he area known as the pasture of said reservation, comprising approximately six hundred (600) acres, bounded on the outside by a 'pipe rail' reservation fence; exclusive of the areas occupied by the 'parade' buildings, the 'aviation field' and the 'golf field.'" Revocable License, March 17, 1925 (copy), Box 36 Folder 3, Erickson Papers, MC 35, MSH.
44. *Biennial Report, 1925–1926*, 3; SFC Kermit Edmonds to Col. Ray Read and Montana Military Museum files, November 30, 1997, Miscellaneous Museum Files, MMHM, LA, Fort Harrison; *Biennial Report, 1921–1922, 3; Biennial Report, 1929–1930, 6.* The memorandum to Col. Read summarizes an interview by Edmonds with John Barrows Sr. and John Barrows Jr. on November 29, 1997.
45. *Biennial Report, 1923–1924*, 3–4.
46. Ibid.; Kermit Edmunds to Historical Files, n.d., Drawer 2, The Indian Companies, Museum Files, Drawer 2, MMHM, LA; Helena *Daily Independent*, June 12, 18, 22, 1924; Poplar *Standard*, June 6, 13, 27, September 19, 1924. Adjutant General Sheridan also was ceremonially adopted into the tribe.
47. *Biennial Report, 1921–1922*, 4; *Biennial Report, 1923–24*, 3; *Biennial Report, 1925–1926*, 4; *Biennial Report, 1927–1928*, 4; *Biennial Report, 1929–1930*, 6.
48. *Biennial Report, 1925–1926*, 4.
49. Jules Abels, *In the Time of Silent Cal* (New York: G.P. Putnam's Sons, 1969), 139–42; *New York Times Index*, Vol. XIV, No. 4, October–December, 1926 (New York: New York Times, 1926), 424–26; *New York Times*, November 3, 9, 1926; *Biennial Report, 1925–1926*, 4.
50. Helena *Daily Independent*, July 2, 1926; Livingston *Enterprise*, August 23, 1927.
51. Frederick Lewis Allen, *Only Yesterday: An Informal History of the 1920s* (New York: Harper and Row, 1931; Perennial Library Edition, 1964), 180–84.
52. Helena *Independent*, September 6, 7, 1927; *Biennial Report, 1927–1928*, 2; SFC Kermit Edmonds to Col. Ray Read and Montana Military Museum Files, November 30, 1997,

summarizing interview with John Barrows Sr. and John Barrows Jr. on November 29, 1997, Miscellaneous files, MMHM, LA.

53. *Biennial Report, 1927–1928*, 2; *Froid Tribune*, June 6, July 13, 27, 1928.
54. *Biennial Report, 1929–1930*, 5; General Order No. 12, Box 36 Folder 4, Erickson Papers, MC 35, MHS; Erastus H. Williams to J.E. Erickson, Box 36 Folder 4, Erickson Papers, MC 35, MHS.
55. Capt. Carl E. Anderson to Adjutant General, August 29, 1929, Box 36, Folder 4, Erickson Papers, MC 35, MHS; Kalispell *Daily Inter-Lake*, August 19, 21, 23, 26, 29, 1929; Cooper, *Rise of the National Guard*, 175.
56. *Biennial Report, 1929–1930*, 1–2.

Governor's Day, June 20, 1933. Camp Cooney. *MMHM*

9

From Peace to War: The 1930s

Suzanne Julin

During these last three years of depression the pay rolls of this company have been a very material aid in keeping many families off the county and other charitable agencies [relief rolls], and have meant much also to our local business men.— Hugh H. Waldrow of Froid, Montana, to Governor Frank H. Cooney, May 20, 1933.

In the early 1920s, rural Montana and its small communities had suffered economic depression due to drought and falling agricultural prices. Many who joined the Montana National Guard during this period were working men or youngsters needing extra income.[1] In the 1930s, drought and hard times struck again, but this time the entire nation shared in the suffering caused by the Great Depression. Again, men enlisted in the guard for much needed income in addition to a sense of duty to Montana.

As farm values fell during the 1930s, many rural Montanans left for other regions in hopes of finding a better life. The state's timber industry likewise declined, along with the construction industry. Even the mighty Anaconda Copper Mining Company fell on difficult times. In desperation, fiscally conservative leaders tightened the state's budget strings even further.

President Franklin D. Roosevelt and his New Deal policies brought some relief to Montana, instituting agricultural and work programs, such as the construction of Fort Peck Dam on the Missouri River. These efforts provided much needed income for many of the state's beleaguered citizens and their communities. As the decade neared its end, the state and national economies finally began to improve, as drought ended and the country prepared for war.[2]

This decade took the Montana National Guard from being a peacetime operation to making preparations for participation in World War II. Erastus H. Williams, a dedicated soldier and World War I veteran, guided the organization from 1925 until 1937, serving as regimental commander as well as adjutant general.[3] His long tenure coincided with an era of stability for the Montana guard. After the rebuilding efforts of the early 1920s, guard units became important social and economic components in their local communities, and continued their role of aiding citizens during emergencies. A new adjutant general, John W. Mahan, would lead the Montana guard at the end of the 1930s, recruiting new members, training them, and making preparations for World War II mobilization.

In 1930, the Montana guard published *The 163rd Infantry Journal*, edited by H.S. Bruce and available for a year's subscription at $1. The 16-page *Journal* contained reports from Montana units as well as National Guard news from around the country. Also included were inspirational essays, letters, humor and jokes, advertisements from supporters including local businesses, and accounts describing guardsmen's social and recreational activities in their communities. *The 163rd Infantry Journal* provides a comprehensive glimpse of guard activities for a typical year at the start of the decade.[4]

A main purpose of the *Journal* was to describe training at the company level in local armories. For example, the Third Battalion Headquarters Company in Billings began its February 10, 1930, meeting with physical training, and then turned to telephone and central switchboard instruction. Also in February, Livingston's Howitzer Company made preparations for firing-range practice when warm weather returned, including the use of .45 caliber pistols, 37-mm artillery, and 3-inch trench mortars.[5] Company D of Harlowton, with 15 new recruits, met on Wednesday nights, reporting good attendance and effective drilling despite the bad winter weather. First Sergeant Harlin Lucas claimed the drills became so engrossing that "'Boy Friend' has no time for sweethearts on drill nights."[6]

In the spring, the Froid unit, part of Company L split between Froid and Scobey, trained in military hygiene and first aid, becoming familiarized with artificial resuscitation and using tourniquets. During inspection near the end of the drill, the men were closely questioned regarding guard duty orders and weapons terminology. Lewistown's Company K reported leasing land for a 300-yard target range, located about 5½ miles from town. The Miles City Medical Detachment, having acquired a new commander and several new recruits, was now holding double drills. Earlier, the unit faced disbandment when a number of men left to attend college or take jobs elsewhere and the commanding officer resigned, moving out of state.[7]

The Regimental Headquarters Company in Helena prepared for the annual inspection, putting its men through "rigid drills" at a regular meeting. The headquarters elements included the Intelligence Section for "scouting, mapping and patrolling," the Pioneer Section charged with planning "fortifications, roads and bridges" as well as using explosives to destroy transportation networks if an attack threatened, the Wire Section operating a field telephone system, the Message Center and Courier Section handling communications, and the Radio Section equipped with several radio sets.[8]

The *Journal* reported on the rewards and efficiency ratings that units received. Harlowton's Company D, for example, earned the highest possible rating in the annual federal inspection; Captain Langston was forced to make good on a promise for this achievement, treating his men to "a big feed at the Sweete Shoppe."[9] Private George Darby of Lewistown's Company K received a billfold and cigarette case, awarded to the most skilled participant in bayonet training. Captain Charles H. Perkins, a regular Army instructor posted to Montana, provided a trophy for the annual rifle competition. Each drill night, Company D gave prizes contributed by the officers and community businesses to a soldier judged the best-dressed in uniform. Helena's Regimental Headquarters Company did the same, providing a $1 prize; in addition, soldiers were given $2 if they brought in a recruit. The manager of Lewistown's Fox-Judith Theater invited Company K as guests at a showing of *Men without Women*, in recognition of the high rating they earned during the spring inspection. The company marched from the drill area to the movie house. Company L of Froid and Scobey won the rifle marksmanship trophy for the second time.[10]

Typical unit entertainment activities included the Livingston Howitzer Company's April 15th sponsoring of an exhibition basketball game, three boxing matches (each ended in a draw), wrestling, indoor baseball, and refreshments. Captain Carl Anderson treated Company F at Kalispell to a night at the local movie theater.[11] Billings' Company H had a "keen feed" after its April 8 drill, where hot dogs, hamburgers, coffee, and Eskimo pies were served.[12]

Hosting or participating in community dances, balls, fund raisers, and other events also were popular activities, reinforcing the guard's positive interactions with local citizens. Uniformed guardsmen from Glasgow's Company G attended a wedding dance immediately after a February 27 drill, "even down to the[ir] ten-pound shoes. With the aid of these large boots and an intense love of dancing the boys succeeded in making their appearance very apparent."[13] Sidney's Company A held a successful military ball, despite bad weather and the orchestra's failure to arrive; "The Dream Band" from Culbertson was thwarted by a snowdrift between Fairview and Sidney and turned back to Fairview. Attendees at Company A's dance nevertheless were undeterred. They put together a make-shift four-piece band, and dancing commenced after a close-order drill demonstration. All was recorded on film for a special weekend showing at the local theater.[14]

Company F of Kalispell hosted its military ball at the Island Park Pavilion, featuring Pete Miller and the Orientale Ballroom Orchestra. Three hundred and fifty couples attended, with the proceeds going to the camp mess fund, "so we can have better eats while we are encamped at Helena, Mt." the unit reported to the *Journal*.[15] Wolf Point's Company E planned a military ball as a fund-raiser and invited attendees to "make whoopee with the Guards."[16]

Miles City's Medical Detachment fielded a basketball team in a local league, posting a 7–1 record. In Sidney, the Montana Dakota Power Company installed a radio in Company A's armory on February 27 so the men could listen to a nationally broadcast boxing match. The Glasgow Chamber of Commerce bought a trophy for the highest scorer in local tryouts for the state marksmanship team. If the same soldier won the cup three years in a row, it became his possession. In the meantime, the Chamber of Commerce displayed the trophy with the winners' names engraved on it.[17]

Harlowton's Company D invited the local community to a program where citizens were served hot dogs "a la army grub line style." This was followed by the soldiers demonstrating their drilling skills. Boxing contests were held, including a match between two 5-year-old boys, with musicians entertaining between the bouts. The evening ended with more hot dogs, sandwiches, and coffee.[18] The 163rd Regimental Band, part of Bozeman's Service Company, presented a concert at the Farm and Home Week held at Montana State College.[19] The Third Battalion Headquarters Company in Billings planned to raise money for new caps, garrison belts, and trousers: "The boys figure this will give them a well-balanced uniform…and something mighty attractive in connection with their parades when called upon in their home town and social functions."[20]

Although these social and recreational activities created camaraderie and positive interaction with local communities, the guard's major emphasis, of course, was training. In the early and mid 1930s, summer camps were held at Fort Harrison. (After 1937, the organization would begin participating in annual maneuvers in the state of Washington.[21])

The 1930 summer encampment followed tradition by naming the bivouac "Camp Erickson" after the current governor. On Saturday, June 14, the units arrived in Helena by railway and settled into quarters partially prepared by the Service Company. Men were posted on guard duty. Next morning, the 163rd Regimental Band presented a concert. Afterward, everyone had the day off except those men on camp duty. On Monday, field training began in battalion and regimental operations.

On Tuesday, June 17, the First Battalion conducted a parade and formal guard mount under review of the battalion commander, Maj. Lyman E. Moore.[22] The *Journal's* editor remarked, "this and succeeding parades never failed to wipe away every indication of a blasé attitude…it is possible that the human heart is stirred because in a body of troops is symbolized service; the potential offering without any reservation of the greatest sacrifice for home and country."[23] The Second and Third battalions paraded on Wednesday and Thursday, under the review of the battalion commanders, respectively Maj. George V. Finley and Maj. E.K. Cheadle.

Regular army officers were in attendance for inspections and evaluations. Colonel C.S. Lincoln, Chief of the National Guard Division of the IX Corps Area, inspected the camp; Col. R.J. Burt, Chief of the Militia Bureau Training Section, observed training exercises; and Col. W.S. Little, Instructor of Medical Units, IX Corps Area, likewise arrived, spending two days at Camp Erickson.[24]

Recreational activities included baseball, boxing, and track and field events. Silver cups went to Bozeman's Company C for accumulating the most points in track and field, Livingston's Howitzer Company for the baseball championship, and Poplar's Company B for the boxing title. Lt. Herman G. Klemme, the regiment's chaplain as well as the Morale, Recreation, and Athletic Officer, arranged the events and proved to be a good competitor himself. He pitched for the regimental team in a baseball game against a Helena civilian team, striking out 14 opponents in 17 times at bat.[25] In referring to Klemme, the *Journal* editor noted, "if anybody thinks this 'sky pilot' is a 'softy' he'd better keep that opinion to himself."[26] On the second weekend in camp, Helena citizens attended the Sunday service, which featured a sermon by Klemme, band music, and a male chorus. Guardsmen not on guard duty had the day off.

On Tuesday, June 24, designated as "Governor's Day," the camp honored Montana Governor John E. Erickson. Colonel Erastus H. Williams, serving as both the regimental commander and state adjutant general, called on the governor at his office at 3 p.m. They motored to the camp with an escort of American Legion officials in accompanying cars. A 17-gun salute from Livingston's Howitzer Company greeted the governor. Next, three young Helena women, selected by the Women's Club at the request of the American Legion, received commissions as honorary officers in a special ceremony. Then, at 5 p.m., the governor, Col. Williams, and other officials reviewed the troops. Following this, the three Helena women presented silver cups to Sidney's Company A for rifle marksmanship and to Company M of Harlem and Chinook for machine gun proficiency. That evening, the American Legion and the regiment hosted the governor and other officials at a dinner and show. The next day, the regiment paraded through Helena, and Governor Erickson presented the trophies to the winners of the camp's sporting events.[27]

The 1936 summer encampment, also at Fort Harrison, featured a similar routine. The men arrived in Helena on Saturday, June 13, and spent Sunday on their own after religious services. The weekday schedule began at 7:15 a.m. with calisthenics, followed by typical training activities, such as drilling and range firing. One exercise required the soldiers to practice defending against tank attacks. On Saturday, June 20, a regimental parade and rifle competitions were held. The training schedule culminated on a final day when commanders maneuvered their battalions in attack formations west of camp.[28]

During their training, guardsmen were "double-timed" to and from calisthenics and drilling, marching at 128 steps per minute. During inspection, the men were required to wear service hats "well forward and straight on head," while the officers donned Sam Browne belts with well polished buckles and proscribed leggings, "top well up to knee, edges smooth. Bleached tie straps

PROHIBITED."[29] Men were cautioned to remember to salute during the playing of the national anthem, and, if driving vehicles, not to pass automobiles carrying regimental or visiting officers.[30]

Looking forward to the following year's regularly scheduled armory drills, Col. Williams outlined unit objectives, including training in close and extended order drill, ceremonial duties, pitching tents, crowd control, proper equipment utilization, weapons firing, communications, patrolling, and combat principles. He directed headquarters companies to give special attention to instructing rifle, machine gun, howitzer, and medical units, and also to provide training in protection against chemical warfare agents.[31]

During the difficult years of the Great Depression, drill pay provided an important source of income for local men and their communities.[32] In 1930, for example, the Bozeman Service Company's fall quarter payroll was $2,400. The *Journal* reported that "practically all of this enormous amount of money is spent in the city."[33] The Montana guard and local communities also benefited from President Roosevelt's New Deal when the Works Progress Administration built new armories, helping to remedy a long-standing need for better facilities. The federal construction funds boosted local economies, too. During a typical period in 1937–1938, the federal government allocated $395,431.82, including $171,500 in drill pay and $68,000 for construction projects, as well as other cash disbursements.[34]

The state occasionally determined it was necessary to disband or relocate some units, which could be a matter of contention in local communities. People in Froid, for example, learned in May 1933 that their "split unit," Company L of Froid and Scobey, would be mustered out. A number of Froid's townspeople and businessmen immediately asked the governor to reconsider.

One letter summarized the unit's importance to the local economy: "An armory has been provided for this Company at considerable expense...The sentiment of the entire community is against the removal of this company from this point, inasmuch as the company owes its inception and growth to its present status to the backing of this community; and further feels indignant that an order has already been made directing the discontinuance of Co. L... During these last three years of depression the pay rolls of this company have been a very material aid in keeping many families off the county and other charitable agencies [relief rolls], and have meant much also to our local business men."[35]

The manager of the Farmers' Union Oil Company also reminded the governor that for 10 years the community had provided men and officers to the unit, and noted that townspeople were unhappy about the potential removal. Froid's Commercial Club urged that the Scobey platoon be moved to Froid, thus strengthening the unit by joining it together in one place.[36] In the pleas coming from Froid, economic considerations were not the only factor. Local radical politics in northeast Montana, called a "red scare" by many, also made the presence of a National Guard unit important to many citizens.

The nation as a whole was deeply divided by the "red scare" of the 1930s. As most Americans experienced widespread suffering caused by the worsening economic situation, a number of people came to view capitalism as a failure and the cause of the Great Depression. Some desperately turned to socialist beliefs, and some joined the Communist Party or supported Communist political candidates. Other Americans had juxtaposed views and believed these attitudes were dangerous. Some worked to eradicate them. In 1938, for example, the U.S. House of Representatives established a Special Committee on Un-American Activities to investigate suspected Communists.[37]

Montana's "red scare" dated back to World War I and the agricultural depression of the early 1920s. A number of people in northeast Montana, in particular, had become active in radical politics. This part of Montana, of course, was deeply affected by the vagaries of crop failures and an unforgiving climate. Even during World War I when wheat prices were high and most producers prospered, farmers in northeast Montana struggled. Many residents were Scandinavians with a tradition of social and political activism and joining cooperative ventures. Near the end of the war, a significant number embraced proposals advocated by the Non-Partisan League, a radical farm organization originating in North Dakota. The league called for state ownership of banks and grain elevators, reform of railroad operations, direct political action, and the equitable taxation of large corporations, which in Montana meant the Anaconda Company in particular.[38]

At Plentywood in 1918, socialists along with Non-Partisan League activists had formed the People's Publishing Company. Charles Taylor, a Midwestern native working at the League's Northwestern Service Bureau, came to Montana to serve as editor for the group's newspaper. A colorful, committed man, "Red Flag" Taylor had a larger-than-life reputation among his supporters, and no doubt contributed to the strength of the radical movement in northeast Montana. When the Non-Partisan League began to fade, Taylor and others reorganized under the auspices of an earlier area organization, the Progressive Farmers' Club. They successfully placed their candidates in many Sheridan County offices during most of the 1920s.[39]

Taylor used the *Producers News*, which had wide local circulation, to promote a radical agenda and harass adversaries, even minor ones. When a Plentywood restaurant stopped advertising in the *News*, for example, Taylor ran front page coverage claiming cockroaches and even a cooked mouse were found in the cafe's food. Resentment against Taylor and his tactics grew. Some attributed a 1926 absconding of more than $100,000 in county funds to Taylor and an accomplice. Opposition also developed from an active new editor at the *Plentywood Herald*. The political fortunes of the reformers began to decline, even with the onset of the Great Depression.[40]

By the 1930s, the Communist Party had become the major supporter of the *Producers News* and Taylor eventually was replaced when more radical leaders took over local activities, including the establishment of a Young Communist training center. In 1932, the funeral for a teenage daughter of a radical leader was devoid of religious rites and laden with Communist symbols and rhetoric, which alienated many local people even further. The same year, the *News* backed a slate of candidates openly running as Communists, but all went down to defeat. The county's activists eventually succeeded in reinstating Taylor to the paper, but the extreme actions of the Communists exerted a permanent effect on most public opinion.[41]

In early 1933, several attendees of the Young Communist training program broke into the local Red Cross office and stole winter clothing. This may have been the final turning point for many local residents. Although the *News* continued to operate for a few more years, support in the community dropped to the point that Communist candidates in 1934 received only half the votes of 1932. Taylor published the last edition in March 1937, after the worst days of the Great Depression had passed and Roosevelt's New Deal programs had taken affect.[42]

Thus, when news of the impending disbandment of Froid and Scobey's Company L reached Sheridan County, shortly after the Red Cross incident in 1933, a number of citizens urged Governor Frank H. Cooney to reconsider. One correspondent referred to "a considerable 'Red element' which raided our Red Cross depot at the County Seat."[43] A Sheridan County senator wired, "the unit

Company L marching in formation. The Froid/Scobey unit of far northeast Montana was disbanded on June 8, 1933, and reorganized in Billings. *MMHM*

is considered a necessity owing to conditions in this section of which I am sure you are aware."[44]

The Commercial Club in Medicine Lake also expressed concern in a telegram: "We believe this unit of the National Guard is a dire necessity in this community to assure safety and peace. Please recognize the rebellious activities of the communistic organization in this section and realize the need of the retention here of Co. L."[45] Two businesses also sent a telegram referring to the overall situation: "If there ever was a time when [a unit] is needed in this community [it is] now with the red movements that have been the last year in Sheridan County and Roosevelt Co."[46] Another writer more subtly stated, "personally I think due to various attitudes in this section it would not be a very wise move at the present time."[47]

Governor Cooney, however, refused to yield to the pressure. He informed the county sheriff that Adjutant General Williams had advised him that the federal government did not approve of split companies. Rather, Washington, D.C., encouraged National Guard companies to be located in larger towns with more potential recruits. To another citizen, the governor responded, "this is really in compliance with Federal orders and I have no authority to stop these orders. You realize," he continued, "that most of this expense is paid for by the Federal Government and they simply tell us what to do." (In actuality, the 1916 National Defense Act gave states the right to assign locations for their units.) Consequently, Froid and Scobey's Company L was disbanded on June 8, 1933, and reorganized in Billings.[48]

Long after the guard's post-World War I reorganization, a number of Montana units continued to make do with inadequate armories or buildings designed for other purposes. Under the National Defense Act, the federal government provided funds for most National Guard expenses, but not for administrative costs or the construction of local unit facilities. The erection of new armories had to be paid for by state appropriations or local dollars,[49] but the economic hard times severely limited any available funds. In the late 1930s, however, the federal government's Works Progress Administration (WPA) began providing assistance for armory construction in Montana, which helped alleviate this long-standing problem.

The WPA was created under the auspices of the Emergency Relief Appropriations Act of 1935 to combat massive unemployment due to the Great Depression. The WPA program focused on creating jobs for laborers, construction and agricultural workers, carpenters and other skilled men, and for more specialized occupations, including artists, writers, historians, and various other professionals.[50]

Late in 1936, Col. Williams reported to the governor that 12 months of organizational work by his adjutant general's office resulted in the start of plans for facilities at Livingston, Lewistown, Glasgow, Chinook, Harlem, Culbertson, Bainville, and Poplar. Also, new armories were slated for Kalispell, Wolf Point, and Harlowton. Plans for Helena, Billings, and Sidney showed promise for coming later. Williams also informed the governor that these projects totaled $600,000 in federal funds. The adjutant general's office sponsored the initial projects, but the towns in which they were located would serve as fiscal agents and become the legal owners of the buildings.[51]

The importance of this effort resulted in the state legislature creating the Montana Armory Board in 1939. The board, which the WPA accepted as the sponsor for the buildings, investigated potential locations, worked with local communities in developing plans, and issued bonds for construction. On August 21, 1939, for example, the board voted to issue $125,000 in bonds on a trust indenture for the construction of an armory, drill hall, and arsenal in Helena. Also, $50,000 in bonds was provided for a new armory and drill hall in Bozeman. The revenue from the bonds was to be used in conjunction with funds from the adjutant general's office.[52]

Plans were delayed, however, when a suit was filed against each member of the Montana Armory Board, the adjutant general, Lewis and Clark County and its commissioners, the City of Helena and the members of its council, and the City of Bozeman and its commission members. Concerned about state budgeting, plaintiff M.M. Geboski claimed that the legislation allowing the creation of the armory board was unconstitutional because, among other considerations, it conferred powers that should be limited to the legislature, made armories state facilities that required state funding, and established an administrative body that could create a debt against the state. The case went before the Montana Supreme Court, which decided in favor of the defendants and thus confirmed the Montana Armory Board's constitutionality.[53]

After nearly a year's delay caused by the suit, the board continued its plans to build the Helena and Bozeman armories, as well as proposed armories in Billings, Kalispell, Poplar, and Harlowton, and to complete an armory in Glasgow. The funds provided by the revenue bonds would equal 40 percent of the proposed construction costs. The board also voted to request WPA assistance in financing the remaining 60 percent, citing national defense as a justification for the expenditure of federal funds. On August 21, 1940, the board voted to authorize 225,000 Montana Armory Board bonds, in $1,000 denominations.[54]

Despite determined efforts, the Montana Armory Board failed to see all projects to completion. In December 1941, the governor issued Executive Reorganization Order No. 26, which instructed the armory board to cease activities relative to proposed construction at Kalispell, Harlowton, and Billings. This canceled at least $118,000 of bonded indebtedness, and required future projects

Vehicles in front of the tile and brick ordnance shop and the QM warehouse at the guard's training grounds at Fort Harrison, 1930s. *MMHM*

to proceed "on a contract basis with direct grants of money from some federal agency or supported by valid agreements with local governmental units." The board was cautioned to take "great care" in future bond issues by arranging "maturities that…will fit in with maturities on present obligations."[55] Declining national WPA funding, financial issues due to the Armory Board's decisions, and federal activation of the National Guard in 1940 probably contributed to the governor's call for fiscal reorganization and restraint, as well as the cancellation of the pending projects.

During the 1930s, federal funds also were expended on improvements at the guard's Fort Harrison installations. From 1931 to 1934, federal money paid for the construction of an infirmary, storage facility, camp incinerator, kitchen ranges, and road improvements. Federal dollars also were used to purchase 24 passenger/cargo trucks and 2 station wagons. In 1936, WPA funds covered repairs on buildings at the fort, much of it necessitated by earthquake damage in the previous fall; $4,308.28 was expended for 11,000 man-hours of labor and $1,541.72 for supplies. The workers, all of whom were on the government's relief rolls, repaired doors, tables, and benches, replaced broken tile, painted the woodwork, and made other improvements. During the 1939 fiscal year, $600 in guard funds and contributions from officers and enlisted men provided sponsoring moneys for additional WPA projects at the fort, including construction of a new kitchen, recreation hall, and women's restroom.[56]

During the 1930s, the Montana guard continued a traditional role of participating in public ceremonies and events. On August 23, 1930, for example, a detachment from Kalispell's Company F provided crowd control for a ceremony at Summit, Montana, marking the opening of the Roosevelt Highway and the dedication of the Theodore Roosevelt monument at Marias Pass. About 2,000 people attended the event, in which Miss Corinne Roosevelt Alsop, one of Roosevelt's nieces, laid the cornerstone of the Roosevelt Memorial Arch. Records pertaining to the development of the highway were deposited under the arch.

Colonel Williams made arrangements for the National Guard's presence at the ceremony, but it was accomplished with some frustration. He asked the Great Northern to transport the troops free of charge, or at least to arrange a convenient travel schedule for the detachment. When the railroad refused, the adjutant general authorized Kalispell's Capt. Anderson to transport the men by truck and car. A.L. Jordan of Columbia Falls, who made the initial request for the guard's assistance, passed on a compliment from one of the people attending; the detachment was "courteous and mannerly, we thought they would be officious and impertinent, but it was certainly most wonderful to have them here.'"[57]

In the same year, a detachment from Wolf Point's Company E provided assistance at a Wolf Point Bridge celebration, and Kalispell's Company F and Glasgow's Company G helped with an Army air tour. The air tour's appearance in Kalispell proved anticlimactic, as the four planes arrived several days late.

In August 1934, nearly 240 officers and enlisted men served as guards during President Franklin D. Roosevelt's trip to the Belt, Glasgow, and Fort Peck areas. During this visit, the Sioux and Assiniboine conferred chiefdom on the president. Roosevelt, who had visited the state in 1932, would return again in 1937.[58]

The guard was also called upon during natural and civil emergencies. In the fall of 1935, numerous geological fault zones at and around Helena erupted in scores of frequently spaced tremors. Just before 10 p.m. on October 18, a particularly powerful shock occurred, followed by more minor jolts, causing major ruin. In Helena, the tremors killed four people, knocked out power, and damaged many buildings, including the Helena armory, or "old arsenal," which had officially opened in 1890. The structure suffered severe harm. After the worst jolts, rescuers pulled an extensively injured officer from the debris.

Headquarters Company went into action. Soon, men were patrolling Helena's streets, guarding the armory to prevent the looting of supplies and equipment, and assisting in knocking down dangerously weakened structures. A tent camp at the guard's summer encampment site temporarily housed earthquake victims. Another jolt on November 1 proved the death knell for the armory.

In the aftermath of the 1935 Helena tremors, a 163rd guardsman with a Browning Automatic Rifle, along with another rifleman, are assigned to direct fire at a weakened chimney on a public building and complete its collapse. *MMHM*

A large portion of the front brickwork collapsed and the rear of the building sustained further damage. The structure subsequently was razed, with some of the salvaged material used in constructing a recreation building at Fort Harrison under the auspices of the WPA.[59] Hundreds of tremors continued to strike the Helena area for the rest of the year and into early 1936.

Three years later in 1939, Governor Roy E. Ayers received urgent requests on March 23 and 24 for assistance in the mountainous Red Lodge vicinity, where a murderer named Earl Durand was running loose near the Wyoming-Montana border. J.M. McFate, the sheriff of Montana's Carbon County, said Durand and possibly other perpetrators were "armed with high powered rifles and are barricaded in the mountains in such a way that we are desperately in need of artillery or heavy guns which are in the possession of the national guard of Montana only."[60]

The 26-year-old Durand had been sentenced to a 75-day jail term for poaching. In escaping from jail in Cody, Wyoming, he killed two law officers, then took refuge in a canyon north of Cody. On March 22, he shot and killed two deputized men from a 100-member posse attempting to force him out of hiding. Governor Ayers responded by ordering the Montana National Guard to assist in the fugitive's capture, in part because lawmen believed Durand's only escape route led north, where the lives of Montana citizens could be endangered.

The adjutant general contacted the Livingston Howitzer Company, ordering an eight-man detachment with a howitzer and trench mortar to the area. These men would serve as deputies under the Carbon County sheriff. Gas bombs from the Casper National Guard Armory also were sent. Before the Livingston detachment was in place, however, posse members rushed Durand's hideout only to find he had escaped by climbing a canyon ridge. The next day, a high school student shot and killed Durand as he was trying to hold up a bank in Powell, Wyoming.[61]

In the mid 1930s, as Germany, Italy, and Japan expanded their armed forces and pursued expansionist policies, the United States remained committed to avoiding involvement in another global conflict. However, the 1935 Italian attack on Ethiopia, Japan's assault on China beginning in 1937, and the 1939 German invasion of Poland finally resulted in full-scale warfare in Europe and much of Asia, heightening America's sense of impending international danger. The nation's long-held desire to remain neutral became increasingly tempered by the specter of a French and British defeat, and ensuing threats to America's own security. In June 1940, shortly before France surrendered to Adolf Hitler, President Roosevelt publicly announced that America was sending arms and materiel to the Allies and making preparations for its own defense.

In actuality, the National Guard had become involved in the country's military build-up several years earlier. In 1935, Congress called for all guard units to increase enlistment and fill their rosters.[62] The Montana National Guard expanded its ranks, eventually including the establishment of the 116th Quartermaster unit, operational by 1939 and headquartered at Malta. Also, beginning in 1937, the Montana guard began holding summer encampments in the state of

Washington, training alongside regular army units. Most of Montana's war preparedness work was guided by John W. Mahan, appointed adjutant general after Erasmus H. Williams died on February 13, 1937. A Helena attorney, Mahan served as judge advocate prior to taking the post. Mahan had enlisted in the Montana guard in 1912, and served in the Mexican border campaign and World War I.[63] Under Mahan, the state organization achieved its required enlistment levels, completed additional training, and would later enter active duty with the U.S. Army.

Early in 1939, the IX Corps Area directed each state adjutant general to formulate plans for induction of guard units into federal service. In September, Mahan also received word from the Secretary of War that 225 enlisted slots were added to Montana's quota and that every effort should be made to quickly fill the quota. Training schedules expanded by adding 7 days of full-time duty, and increasing annual armory drills from 48 to 60.[64] Under the governor's direction, Adjutant General Mahan issued General Orders No. 5, instructing unit commanders to begin the new recruiting campaign. He advised discretion: "Only sufficient recruiting publicity should be given to the extent required to obtain this necessary increase with the least practicable delay."[65]

Mahan's caution reflected Washington, D.C.'s concern that a widely publicized recruiting campaign would unduly alarm citizens, since anti-war and isolationist sentiment still remained prevalent among much of the population. A few days later, Mahan wrote to his guard officers, stating that General Blanding of the National Guard Bureau believed the War Department's enlistment instructions were simply meant to test the National Guard's efficiency. In case anyone missed the point, however, Mahan added: "It is not desired to give any more publicity to the recruiting campaign than is necessary in each community…you should be careful not to permit an energetic reporter to print a story indicating that this expansion has anything whatever to do with mobilization or anticipated mobilization because it does not."[66]

By November 3, 1939, the successful recruiting campaign allowed the Montana guard to reach an authorized strength of 1,413 enlisted men and officers. In December and January, the guard conducted seven days of wintertime field training. The 1940 summer encampment was held at Camp Murray, Washington, with Montana guardsmen training with regular army units. Finally in August 1940, Congress authorized the president's request to call up the National Guard for 12 months of active duty, beginning September 16, 1940. The mobilization was intended to strengthen and broaden the regular army's capabilities and to prepare guard members for training draftees.[67]

Montana guardsmen assembled at their local armories and departed for Camp Murray and Fort Lewis, Washington, on September 21–22, for a year of training under the regimental commander, Col. E.M. Birely. Meanwhile, the state staff detachment was assigned to Montana's Selective Service Headquarters.[68]

Adjutant General Mahan now turned his attention to the continued expansion of the Montana guard. Although Montana apparently had been allotted the 190th Field Artillery, this unit's organizing was not authorized by the calls for increased enlistments. Mahan, and Williams before him, believed this authorization was imminent, and successfully gained state legislative funding to form artillery units. The National Guard Bureau, however, now informed Mahan that authorization would not be forthcoming, nor was it likely that other units would be assigned to the Montana guard. In April 1940, the 190th Field Artillery allotment was withdrawn.[69]

Nevertheless, Mahan continued attempts to increase the size and role of the Montana organization. In the fall of 1940, he requested the formation of home defense units, citing as justification a large "Communistic element" in Butte, and the need to protect the state's hydroelectric plants, copper and zinc mines, and three transcontinental railroads. In his zealousness to obtain these new units for national defense, he met with the National Guard Bureau's major general; later, he wrote to apologize for his demeanor during that meeting. Despite Mahan's determined efforts, the federal agency did not authorize additional units. Shortly, Mahan resigned from the post of adjutant general, and Governor Roy Ayers appointed Maj. Frederick A. Lange of Helena as his replacement.[70]

Notes

1. Michael P. Malone and Richard B. Roeder, *Montana: A History of Two Centuries* (Seattle: University of Washington Press, 1976), 216–19, 222; Jerry Cooper, *The Rise of the National Guard: The Evolution of the American Militia, 1865–1920* (Lincoln: University of Nebraska Press, 1997), 175–76; "National Guard Information," n.d., Box 51 Folder 10, Governor John E. Erickson Papers, Manuscript Collection 35, Montana Historical Society, Helena, Montana [hereafter cited as Erickson Papers, MC 35, MHS].
2. Malone and Roeder, *Montana*, 226–32.
3. Richard H. Lacey, *The Montana Militia: A History of Montana's Volunteer Forces, 1867–1976* (Dillon, Montana: Dillon Tribune-Examiner Press, 1976), 57–58; "History of the National Guard," *The Montana Legionnaire*, May 1927.
4. *Biennial Report of the Adjutant General of Montana, 1929–1930*, 7; *The 163rd Infantry Journal*, February 25 to July 1, 1930. The Montana Historical Society Archives and the Montana National Guard Museum retain a total of 10 copies of *The 163rd Infantry Journal*, all published in the first half of 1930, including a July 1 "Souvenir of Camp" issue covering activities at the June 14–28 summer encampment. Apparently the publication was short-lived.
5. *The 163rd Infantry Journal*, February 25, 1930, 9, 13.
6. Ibid., 11.
7. Ibid., February 25, 1930, 8; March 10, 1930, 8; March 25, 1930, 11.
8. Ibid., March 10, 1930, 12.
9. Ibid., April 10, 1930, 11.
10. Ibid., February 25, 1930, 8, 11; March 10, 1930, 8; April 10, 1930, 10; April 25, 1930, 3, 10.

11. Ibid., 9; February 25, 1930, 14.
12. Ibid., April 25, 1930, 11.
13. Ibid., March 10, 1930, 13.
14. Ibid., March 25, 1930, 13.
15. Ibid., April 25, 1930, 12.
16. Ibid.
17. Ibid., February 25, 1930, 8; March 10, 1930, 9; March 25, 1930, 7.
18. Ibid., 11.
19. Ibid., February 10, 1930, 6; April 10, 1930, 13.
20. Ibid., February 25, 1930, 9.
21. *Biennial Report, 1937–1938*, 2.
22. *The 163rd Infantry Journal*, July 1, 1930, 1–2.
23. Ibid., 2.
24. Ibid., 1–4.
25. Ibid., 2–3.
26. Ibid., 3. "Sky pilot" is a slang term for a clergyman.
27. Ibid., 4–7.
28. Office of the Adjutant General, Training Memorandum Number 1, Master Schedule, Montana National Guard, Fort William H. Harrison, Montana, June 13–17, 1936, 7–10, Box 81 Folder 15, Governor Elmer Holt Papers, Manuscript Collection 35, Montana Historical Society, Helena, Montana [hereafter cited as Holt Papers, MC 35, MHS].
29. Ibid., 2–3.
30. Ibid., 5.
31. Office of the Adjutant General, Training Memorandum Number 2, Annual Armory Training Program for the Training Year July 1, 1936, to June 30, 1937, 3–5, Box 81 Folder 15, Holt Papers, MC 35, MHS.
32. Cooper, *Rise of the National Guard*, 175–76.
33. *The 163rd Infantry Journal*, February 25, 1930, 14.
34. *Biennial Report, 1937–1938*, 2.
35. Hugh H. Waldrow to Governor Cooney, May 20, 1933, Box 60 Folder 3, Governor Frank H. Cooney Papers, Manuscript Collection 35, Montana Historical Society, Helena, Montana [hereafter cited as Cooney Papers, MC 35, MHS].
36. R.[S.] Harbs to Governor F.H. Cooney, May 29, 1933, Box 60 Folder 3, Cooney Papers, MC 35, MHS; H.C. Skarie to Governor F.H. Cooney, May 29, 1933, Box 60 Folder 3, Cooney Papers, MC 35, MHS.
37. Robert S. McElvaine, *The Great Depression: America, 1929–1941* (New York: Times Books, 1984), 202–6.
38. Malone and Roeder, *Montana*, 207, 225.
39. Charles Vindex, "Radical Rule in Montana: The Agonizing Years," *Montana: The Magazine of Western History* 18(1) (January 1968): 3–12.
40. Ibid., 10–12.
41. Ibid., 12–14.
42. Ibid., 14–16.
43. Edw. S. Powers to Governor Cooney, May 20, 1933, Box 60 Folder 3, Cooney Papers, MC 35, MHS.
44. Lars Angvick to Governor Cooney [telegram], May 22, 1933, Box 60 Folder 3, Cooney Papers, MC 35, MHS.

45. Medicine Lake Commercial Club, Jos. F. Dolin, Pres. to Governor Cooney [telegram], May 21, 1933, Box 60 Folder 3, Cooney Papers, MC 35, MHS.
46. Farmers Elevator Company, Quality Cash Store to Governor Cooney [telegram], May 20, 1933, Box 60 Folder 3, Cooney Papers, MC 35, MHS.
47. John Brudie to Governor Cooney, May 20, 1933, Box 60 Folder 3, Cooney Papers, MC 35, MHS.
48. Governor to Hans C. Madsen, Sheriff, May 26, 1933; Governor to Edw. S. Powers, June 5, 1933, Box 60 Folder 3, Cooney Papers, MC 35, MHS; *United States Statutes at Large* XXXIX, sec. 68, 200; Erastus H. Williams to Chief, National Guard Bureau, August 8, 1933, Box 1 Folder 7, Montana Adjutant General's Office Records, Records Collection 223, Montana Historical Society, Helena, Montana [hereafter cited as RC 223, MHS]; *Biennial Report, 1933–1934,* 1.
49. "Report of An Inspection of Company 'A' 163rd Infantry N.G. of Montana," February 18, 1923; "Report of an Inspection of Company 'H' 163rd Infantry N.G. of Montana," n.d.; "The Organization," n.d., Box 1 Folder 12, RC 223, MHS; Cooper, *Rise of the National Guard*, 175; *United States Statutes at Large,* XXXIX, Sec, 67, 199–200; *Biennial Report, 1925–1926*, 3; "National Guard Information," n.d., Box 51 Folder 10, Erickson Papers, MC 35, MHS; Jerry Cooper, *The Militia and the National Guard in America since Colonial Times: A Research Guide* (Westport, Connecticut: Greenwood Press, 1993), 119.
50. WPA work continued until 1943, by which time the agency's original objectives were made moot by the massive buildup of a wartime economy and full employment of the nation's work force. McElvaine, *The Great Depression*, 152–53, 254–55, 265–75, 297, 322.
51. *Biennial Report, 1935–1936,* 3–4; Col. Williams to Governor, November 20, 1936, Box 81 Folder 15, Holt Papers, MC 35, MHS; *Biennial Report, 1937–1938, 3.*
52. Minutes, Special Meeting, Montana Armory Board, August 21, 1939, *Minutes, Montana Armory Board, 1939–40,* Office of Col. Ray Read, Command Historian, Montana National Guard, Helena, Montana [hereafter cited as Command Historian, MNG].
53. M.M. Geboski, Plaintiff, No. 9004, State of Montana in the Supreme Court, June Term, 1940 v. Montana Armory Board of the State of Montana, et al., 2–6, Box 1 Folder 16, RC 223, MHS; Minutes, Special Meeting, Montana Armory Board, July 8, 1940, *Minutes, Montana Armory Board, 1939–40*, Command Historian, MNG.
54. Minutes, Special Meeting, Montana Armory Board, July 8, 1940; Minutes, Special Meeting, Montana Armory Board, August 21, 1940, *Minutes, Montana Armory Board, 1939–40,* Command Historian, MNG.
55. Executive Reorganization Order No. 26, December 10, 1941, Box 1 Folder 16, RC 223, MHS; *Historical and Pictorial Review of the National Guard State of Montana* (Baton Rouge, Louisiana: Army and Navy Publishing, 1940), contains photographs of armories in Great Falls, Livingston, Harlem, Malta, Harlowton, Glasgow, Bainville, Culbertson, Whitehall, Lewistown, and Chinook, and a sketch of the Helena Armory. Dates and circumstances of construction are not indicated.
56. *Biennial Report, 1931–1932,* 5; *Biennial Report, 1933–1934*, 2; *Biennial Report, 1935–1936,* 2; *Final Narrative Report on O.P. 13-135*, September 8, 1936, Box 1 Folder 3, RC 223, MHS; *Biennial Report, 1937–1938,* 3; John W. Mahan to Chief, National Guard Bureau, April 25, 1939, Box 1 Folder 4, RC 223, MHS.
57. Erastus H. Williams to Governor, August 30, 1930; A.L. Jordan to Carl Anderson, August 25, 1930, Box 36 Folder 4, Erickson Papers, MC 35, MHS; Kalispell *Daily Interlake,* August 25, 1930; A.L. Jordan to Carl Anderson, August 25, 1930, Box 36 Folder 4, Erickson Papers, MC 35, MHS.

58. Cooper, *Rise of the National Guard,* 175; *Biennial Report, 1929–1930,* 5; *The 163rd Infantry Journal,* February 10, 1930, 7; *Biennial Report, 1933–1934,* 3; Malone and Roeder, *Montana,* 233.
59. Kermit Edmonds, "From Brick to Concrete," *Montana Militiaman,* 27(3) (Fall 1989): 10–11; "Earthquake Kills Man in Helena; Buildings Wrecked, City in Panic," and other unidentified clippings, Helena, Montana, Earthquake, 1935 (2), Vertical Files, MHS; *Biennial Report, 1935–1936,* 3; Anthony I. Qamar and Michael C. Stickney, "Montana Earthquakes, 1869–1979," Memoir 51, Montana Bureau of Mines and Geology, 1983, 12; *Biennial Report, 1939–1940,* 3; Resolution of the State Board of Examiners, March 13, 1939, Box 1 Folder 4, RC 223, MHS.
60. R.L. Esmay to Governor [telegram], March 23, 1939; Ed O'Donnell to Governor [telegram], March 23, 1939; J.F. McFate to Governor, March 23, 1939; W.H. Moore to Governor [telegram], March 23, 1939, Box 85 Folder 14, Governor Roy E. Ayers Papers, Manuscript Collection 35, Montana Historical Society, Helena, Montana [hereafter cited as Ayers Papers, MC 35, MHS].
61. Governor to John W. Mahan, March 23, 1939, Box 85 Folder 14, Ayers Papers, MC 35, MHS; Billings *Gazette,* March 24, 1939; March 25, 1939; March 26, 1939.
62. A. Russell Buchanan, *The United States and World War II,* Volume I (New York: Harper and Row, Harper Torchbook edition, 1964), 2–16, 22, 30–34; Cooper, *Rise of the National Guard,* 177; *Historical and Pictorial Review,* 68.
63. John W. Mahan to the Chief, National Guard Bureau, March 12, 1937; Albert H. Blanding to Adjutant General of Montana, March 25, 1937 Box 1 Folder 7, RC 223, MHS; *Biennial Report, 1931–1932,* 2; John W. Mahan to Maj. Gen. John F. Williams, September 14, 1940, Entry 344 Box 587, State Dec file 1922–45, 325.4 Montana, Army-National Guard Bureau, Record Group 168, National Archives, Washington, D.C. [hereafter cited as RG 168, NA]; *Historical and Pictorial Review,* v.
64. Horace F. Sykes to All State Adjutants General and All Instructors, January 12, 1939; Blanding to Adjutant General [telegram], September 21, 1939, Box I Folder 7, RC 223, MHS; C.H. Miller to the Adjutant General of Montana, September 21, 1939, Box 1 Folder 7, RC 223, MHS.
65. General Orders No. 5, Extract, September 25, 1939, Box 1 Folder 7, RC 223, MHS.
66. John W. Mahan to Commanding Officers of the Units Affected by General Order No. 5, September 26, 1939, Box 1 Folder 7, RC 223, MHS.
67. John F. Williams to Adjutant General of Montana, November 3, 1939, Box 1 Folder 7, RC 223, MHS; Executive Order 8530, August 31, 1940, Box 1 Folder 5, RC 223, MHS; *Biennial Report, 1939–1940,* 3; Cooper, *Rise of the National Guard,* 177; Cooper, *Militia and the National Guard,* 124;
68. Summary of interview with Joseph Upshaw by SFC Howard Anderson, SSG Milo McLeod, Sgt. Orlan Svingen, June 1, 1985, State Armories, Havre 1911, Drawer 3, MMHM, LA; A.V. Vinton to Adjutant General, September 28, 1940, Entry 344 Box 587, State Dec file, 1922–45, 325.4, RG 168, NA; *Biennial Report, 1939–1940,* 4; Helena *Independent Record,* June 24, 1951; State of Montana, Office of the Adjutant General, *Directory of the Organizations and Units Montana National Guard* (Helena, Montana: Haegele, [1943]), 5. The year of training was extended by 18 months in August 1941. State of Montana, Office of the Adjutant General, *Directory of the Organizations,* 5. The *Directory of Organizations* states that a total of 1,579 officers and enlisted men were inducted.

69. John W. Mahan to Chief, National Guard Bureau, March 12, 1937; Albert H. Blanding to Adjutant General of Montana, March 25, 1937, Box 1 Folder 7, RC 223, MHS; John W. Mahan to Albert Blanding, April 10, 1937, Albert H. Blanding to John W. Mahan, April 21, 1937, John F. Williams to Adjutant General of Montana, April 29, 1940, Entry 344 Box 587, State Dec file 1922–45, 325.4, RG 168, NA.
70. John W. Mahan to John F. Williams, November 16, 1940; A.V. Vinton to John F. Williams, November 22, 1940; John F. Williams to John W. Mahan, November 26, 1940, Entry 344 Box 587, State Dec file 1922–45, 325.4, RG 168, NA; John W. Mahan to Roy E. Ayers, December 3, 1940; Governor to Sam W. Mitchell, December 3, 1940, Ayers Papers, Box 85 Folder 14, MC 35, MHS.

10

Answering FDR's Call to Arms: The 163rd Infantry Regiment, 1940–1942

Michelle Tabit

The majority of us didn't mind it too much, for we were thoroughly enjoying our hitch in the armed forces... Of course there was some beefing, but a soldier who doesn't beef, is not a true soldier.—Sergeant James J. Eder (Company B, Poplar, Montana), September 1941, at Fort Lewis, Washington.

We put a crew of cooks to work in the ships galley on the night shift, and as a result we had fresh baked bread, sausages and tomatoes etc. for our Christmas dinner.—Sergeant Earle Clark (Company A), on board the *Van Heutz* in the Coral Sea, December 1942.

In the 1930s, America watched with growing concern as European and Asian nations fell under the control of fascist dictatorships. In 1933, Adolf Hitler began transforming Germany into a military state to regain national prestige lost in the 1919 Versailles Treaty following World War I. In Italy, Benito Mussolini increased dictatorial control since coming to power in 1922. By the late 1930s, Japan intensified its imperial ambitions in the Far East under the guidance of Hideki Tojo, the nation's vice minister of war, and later prime minister.

Japan's military clique planned to vigorously pursue a "Greater East Asia Co-Prosperity Sphere" policy, eventually establishing economic and political control in the western Pacific extending from Manchuria and China to Thailand and New Guinea.[1] The expulsion of British, Dutch, French, and American control and influence in Asia was part of this agenda. Cooperation and shared opportunity with other Asian countries, however, really did not fit into the plan. The Japanese Empire mostly wanted a free hand to exploit Asian resources without Western interference.

Japan's military aggressions in Manchuria (1931–32) and China (beginning in 1937) foretold of future conflict with the United States and Great Britain. After signing the Tripartite Pact with Germany and Italy in the spring of 1940, Japan, as an "Axis" power, pursued ever more aggressive actions in Asia.

With tensions growing in Europe and Asia, President Franklin D. Roosevelt's administration shifted to an ever more supportive posture in regard to the European democracies and China. As an added deterrent to the Axis nations, Roosevelt also believed that the United States should begin rearming. It became clear to astute observers that America was moving military preparedness forward.

The Montana adjutant general had received word from the IX Corps commanding general that Congress had authorized an increase in the country's National Guard ranks, effective for the 1937 fiscal year. Pursuant to this directive, Montana created the 2nd Battalion (less Company C), and the 116th Quartermaster unit becoming operational on April 1, 1939.[2]

In 1937, Montana's 163rd Infantry Regiment joined with other 41st Division men from Oregon, Washington, and Idaho (including the 161st, 162nd, 186th regiments and their attached artillery, quartermaster, medical, and other units) to begin summer training with the U.S. Army's 3rd Infantry Division at Fort Lewis, south of Tacoma, Washington.[3] From 1937 on, the 41st and 3rd divisions became friendly but earnest rivals until the 41st finally left for the South Pacific in 1942. (The regular army's 3rd Division eventually went to the European Theater, where it fought ably in 1944–1945, while suffering high casualties.)

Over the next two summers, 163rd Infantry soldiers, as an element of the 41st Division, continued attending training sessions at Fort Lewis and adjacent Camp Murray,[4] in addition to increased annual drilling in Montana. In 1940, the intense three-week training period at Fort Lewis alerted the 163rd guardsmen to an impending federal call-up to active duty.

During this period, relations continued to deteriorate between the United States and the Japanese Empire. The American government instituted an embargo on trade with Japan, and soon would freeze all Japanese assets in the United States. Across the Atlantic, France had fallen to Hitler, and the Battle of Britain raged on, while in Asia, Japan continued its aggression in China and French Indo-China. As awareness of the worldwide fascist threat became ever more apparent, Roosevelt accelerated America's military preparedness. In the summer of 1940, the president finally federalized the National Guard in accordance with Section 111 of the National Defense Act, thereby ordering the reserve into full-time military duty.

Within months, over 300,000 guardsmen would be entering active service. Robert Patterson, the under secretary of war, later declared that this action boosted America's confidence during these foreboding times—"their presence in the field gave the country a sense that it had passed the lowest ebb."[5] Pursuant to the Selective Service Training Act of 1940, National Guard troops reported for one year of training. (In late summer 1941, however, as America's involvement in World War II became ever more imminent, Congress extended this term of service to 18 months.)

At full mobilization, the activation totaled 302,000 guardsmen, including 21,000 commissioned officers and 281,000 enlisted men.[6] This nearly doubled the size of the U.S. Army, adding a total of 18 divisions and 29 Army Air Corps squadrons to the nation's active duty force. Eighty regiments were organized in the call up. As a result, the entire National Guard would be on active duty when the United States entered World War II in December 1941.

The Montana guard's activation began on August 27, 1940, when Major General George A. White, the commander of the 41st Division, issued an "Immediate Action Order," alerting all command staffs to prepare their units for federal induction.[7] In Montana, Adjutant General John Mahan and Governor Roy E. Ayers issued orders calling up the 163rd Infantry Regiment to duty as part of the 41st Division.[8]

Men from all walks of life—farmers and ranchers, laborers and high school boys, businessmen and professionals, lumberjacks and Native Americans—readily responded to their nation's call.[9] The families at home knew there would be many changes in the months ahead, but they supported their men as they left to report for duty. Though the guardsmen were being called up for just one year, they sensed they might be serving longer. Units from Whitefish, Kalispell, Helena, Whitehall, Bozeman, Livingston, Great Falls, Chinook, Lewistown, Harlowton, Billings, Glasgow, Wolf Point, Poplar, Culbertson, Bainville, and Sidney answered the call.

At the time of mobilization, the regiment consisted of three rifle battalions, a regimental headquarters company, a service company, and a medical company. Under the leadership of Colonel Everett M. Birley, the Montana men assembled at their home stations throughout the state.[10] Colonel Birley requested that each unit recruit up to full strength by September 16, 1940, the date of full activation. In August 1940, the *Wolf Point Gazette* had reported that Adjutant General Mahan believed the 163rd would achieve its fully authorized strength of 1,508 men when the one-year training began.[11] Mahan was largely correct. Units eventually increased their enlistment rolls with new enlistees.

At the time, the Montana National Guard consisted of 119 officers, a warrant officer, and 1,631 enlisted men. As guardsmen assembled at their home stations for the induction process, they were given physical examinations and began basic conditioning. Men under 18 years of age and those with physical disabilities or special dependents were eliminated. In all, 17 officers and 154 enlisted men received honorable discharges or were released from active federal service because of physical disqualification or personal hardship. After the pre-induction evaluation, the regiment consisted of 102 officers and 1,477 enlisted men. However, the 21 units of the Montana National Guard would fill their sections, squads, and platoons with additional recruits.

Initially, the 163rd men had hastily erected tents at their home stations or established makeshift training centers at armories, bivouac sites, and fairgrounds

Men in chow line at Bozeman Fairgrounds during induction into active duty status, September 16, 1940. *MMHM*

throughout Montana. Commissioned and noncommissioned officers alike found themselves assigned to new duties as on-the-job training became a way of life. The manual of arms, close order marching, and combat drills were practiced at the home stations. Veteran guardsmen, whose experience consisted of a few hundred days and nights of camp life and training, directed the newer members in the basic aspects of army life, including military courtesy, stripping and assembling weapons, guard duty, and kitchen police (KP). Classroom training focused on the Articles of War and Interior Guard Duty. New recruits also memorized General Orders and learned how to properly wear their uniforms and organize their packs.

After completing the initial mustering-in activities, the 163rd received orders to relocate to Camp Murray, just outside of Tacoma, Washington. Troop trains began rolling across Montana on September 21, collecting up the various 163rd units. They arrived at Camp Murray on September 23 and bivouacked. Within a few weeks—following hours of marching and drilling in frequent Pacific Northwest drizzle—men began referring to the post as "Swamp Murray." The challenging circumstances at Camp Murray simulated a combat-like setting, however, that ultimately served the regiment well in the Pacific. Although they despised the mud, moisture, remoteness, and cold, the men accepted their circumstances and were determined to become competent soldiers.

During this initial period, the regiment saw numerous changes, with the most dramatic in regard to leadership. Shortly after arriving at Camp Murray, Colonel Everett Birley, the 163rd commander, failed to pass a physical examination and was replaced by Lt. Colonel George C. Bloomquist. It was under

Bloomquist's leadership that the regiment would transform itself into a cohesive combat force. According to 2nd Lt. Howard A. McKinney, "Bloomquist was a splendid tactician and disciplinarian...and the regiment owes much to him for its sterling record."[12]

In later recollections, soldiers said they most remembered the rainy conditions at Camp Murray. From day to day it seemed to never stop drizzling. This made their first task of organizing a livable and comfortable wintertime training camp difficult. Work details were commonplace, and the men quickly learned that picks and shovels would play an important role in their lives. The regiment transformed a relatively well drained, grassy spot into livable quarters. Initially, the encampment consisted of rows of khaki-colored pyramid tents, but without floors, electric lights, or sidewalks. With the exception of outhouses, showers, and mess halls built by private contractors, few permanent buildings existed in the regimental area.

After two months at Camp Murray, the army began making improvements. Soon, each tent was equipped with a wooden floor, Sibley stove, and light socket. The government also was constructing a new divisional cantonment on the Fort Lewis Reservation, due for completion in the spring of 1941. But for now, the men remained in tents. Winter rains set in almost daily. Trampled grassy areas turned to mud, but this was an important training experience, as ditch digging for water runoff became an art form.[13]

Intensive field training began in October 1940. Chief among the skills the 163rd units needed to acquire was learning how to work together as an overall combat team. Adjutant General Mahan exclaimed: "The [Montana] National Guard...needs training in the field as a Regiment, but, in my judgment, within two or three months it will be as good as any outfit in the United States."[14] Officers who served during World War I, as well as younger men from college ROTC programs, usually filled the 163rd's command slots. Often, officers read training manuals only an hour or so before giving instruction to the troops in training sessions. According to Lt. McKinney's recollections, "any good private with ambition to read the field manual knew more or as much as the instructor."[15]

There were some openings in rank and grade, and members of the regiment anxiously competed for coveted "stripes." Some earned rank quickly, while others, though equally qualified, did not.[16] The men of the 163rd soon increased their proficiency in close order drill, marksmanship, and other skills required of good soldiers. The long hours of arduous training was paying off—the enlisted men and officers in the regiment soon learned to effectively work together in squads, platoons, companies, and battalions, and then as part of a regiment and a division.

Meanwhile in Montana, Adjutant General Mahan in October 1940 heatedly requested the formation of additional National Guard units to remain in the state as a home guard. The Chief of the National Guard Bureau denied the request. Facilities, equipment, and supplies were not available for such units. Shortly, Mahan resigned from his post, and Governor Ayers replaced him with Maj. Frederick A. Lange of Helena.

The regiment originally had minimal equipment and many recruits even lacked sufficient uniforms prior to their arrival at Fort Lewis. Some had received World War I leftovers, such as all-wool tunics and knickers with wrap-around leggings. The regiment also was short of vital equipment ranging from sidearms and rifles, to machine guns and radios. Many guardsmen trained with sticks for machine guns, stovepipes for artillery pieces, and trucks for tanks. With improvisation and hard work, however, the 163rd men soon performed like a long established regular army unit.

Originally, the training included at least one field problem a week. By December 1940, the regiment's weekly schedule increased to two or more field problems, with infantry and artillery deployed in tactical defensive and offensive operations. The training focused on the regiment's ability to operate and fight independently for days at a time. Multi-day drills also provided the 163rd with communications skills and field bivouac experience.[17]

After 13 weeks of diligent training, the regiment received an 11-day furlough during the winter holiday season. General George A. White, the 41st Division commander, encouraged the men to take full advantage of it. A few of the soldiers remained at Camp Murray for guard duty, and some were quarantined with measles, but most left for Montana. Unbeknownst to them, this would be the last Christmas at home with their families and friends for a long time.

Returning to training with a renewed sense of vigor, they noted that only nine months remained in their one-year call-up. The next few months at Camp Murray saw other changes for the 163rd. Hundreds of Selective Service recruits (draftees) began arriving, which would bring the 41st Division up to battle strength. The new men, however, needed basic training. How could the regiment conduct primary training for the new inductees, while at the same time conduct advanced training for the guardsmen? General White's staff resolved the problem by choosing the most capable and well trained officers and noncommissioned officers from the 41st Division's ranks, forming a cadre to train the new men quickly and efficiently. After 13 weeks of basic training, the recruits would be ready for assignment to their permanent companies.

As the new recruits arrived in early 1941, they were sent for their training to newly constructed barracks at Fort Lewis. By April 1941, the entire 163rd was readied for relocation to the new divisional cantonment—amongst two square miles of gleaming white barracks, warehouses, theaters, mess halls, offices, and service clubs. The regiment conducted an orderly move from Camp Murray to the new quarters. On April 18, the entire 41st Division completed the relocation. The many recent enlistees and draftees now were fully combined with the guards-

Fort Lewis main gate, south of Tacoma, Washington. *MMHM*

men in the new Fort Lewis cantonment. Meanwhile, General White and his staff remained in tents at Camp Murray, directing divisional training from there.

A number of privates and NCOs continued their personal education by attending night classes at the nearby Clover Park school in Tacoma. When the call-up came, some of the youngest men were still attending high school; they had yet to graduate.[18] Consequently, educational offerings at Fort Lewis and the Clover Park school allowed them to earn diplomas. Not only did some enlisted men spend extra time in the classroom, but Colonel Bloomquist required the 163rd's officers to attend his training lectures.

In addition to regular training, the men participated in numerous work details, including the construction of basketball courts, football fields, and baseball diamonds. When completed, these facilities provided much appreciated recreational opportunities. Army life was not all work, of course. On many a rainy evening at the Camp Murray tents, men had relaxed in conversation around the warmth of their Sibley stove.[19] Bus service from the base into town provided the opportunity to attend movies, sight-see, run errands, and visit a bar during off-duty hours. The bonds that the men established in their free time carried over into their training, adding cohesion as a military unit.

A nearby post canteen provided beer and other necessities, and men of the 163rd took it over "lock, stock and beer case." According to Lt. McKinney, "it was our boys, which drank the beer, caused the riots and claimed the canteen."[20] Native Americans from Poplar and the Fort Peck Indian Reservation made up a large part of Company B. Known as the "Indian Company," these men would earn a very positive reputation throughout their years of service. Company B soldiers, however, spent more time at the canteen than men from other companies, since Native Americans were denied the right to purchase liquor in some nearby civilian areas. It was rumored, too, that Company B's "war whoops" and yells discouraged men from other units, such as the 162nd and 186th regiments, from visiting the canteen. Montana's Company C also was known for throwing a beer bash at least once a month.

Company E men purchased a "big Chrysler" and toured the Pacific Coast while on three-day passes. Later when on maneuvers in California, they lent the Chrysler to a group of nurses, who promised to buy new tires in return for borrowing the car. Unfortunately, the men received a letter, explaining the nurses had totally demolished the automobile in an accident.[21]

After seven months, the 163rd began participating in larger maneuvers with other 41st Division regiments. The first set of these war games was with Washington's 161st Infantry. Lacking sufficient weapons and equipment, the troops used sticks depicting mortars, while trucks with flags represented tanks. Sticks labeled "machine-guns" or "anti-tank-guns" substituted for the real thing, and empty sidearm holsters were common.[22] Company B was assigned a truck with white flags affixed to it, signifying that it was a tank. Frequently the "tank" became stuck and the infantry had to push it out of the mud. Ill-equipped as they were, the 163rd trained long and hard. They frequently participated in rapid, long marches under simulated combat conditions. The artillery, quartermaster, engineer, and medical units participated in simulated combat situations, too.

Lt. Colonel Mark W. Clark, a training monitor representing the Army Chief of Staff, noted the excellent progress of the 41st Division in reports to Washington, D.C.[23] On March 29, 1941, he remarked: "Training has been progressing splendidly...Divisions are well up-to-date in carrying out schedules prescribed by GHQ [General Headquarters]...Commanders and key noncommissioned officers are becoming experienced in their duties and general improvement is most noticeable."[24] The GHQ chief of staff, Lt. General Lesley McNair, declared the 41st Division to be the top ranked National Guard division in the country and one of the top three divisions in the whole army.

In the spring of 1941, the 41st was ordered to participate in war games in California. GHQ was anxious to determine how well trained the division was after months of drilling and maneuvers. As Lt. Colonel Clark explained, "General McNair is very interested in this phase of training and feels that it is particularly important...that the corps commander see how the divisions are progressing... and determine their eligibility...for advancement to the next phase of training."[25]

As part of the 41st Division, the 163rd prepared for departure in May 1941. Lack of a sufficient number of serviceable vehicles plagued the division at that time. It was "very short in useable transportation," Lt. Colonel Clark observed. "The obsolete stuff simply cannot make the trip, and every truck we're short makes that many more men go by rail, and reduces combat efficiency."[26] In addition, the guardsmen lacked adequate radio and telephone equipment, making it necessary to use runners and command cars for communications. It was clear to all that the training in California would require an equipment upgrade, and Washington, D.C., did its best to provide.

The training maneuvers would pit the 41st Division against troops stationed at Fort Ord, near Monterey. The simulated battles were scheduled to take place on the Hunter Ligget Military Reservation, 18 miles outside of King City. On May 19, the regiment began the week-long, 1,100-mile journey to central California. In all, about 2,500 men traveled by truck in a long motor convoy. The trip proceeded smoothly, with stops twice a day to serve meals, and in the evening to make camp.[27] En route, however, one driver rolled a vehicle on a soft shoulder and a man was killed.[28]

Troops from other outfits participating in the maneuvers made the journey by train. By the time the 163rd arrived in Jolon, California, on May 25, other units already had arrived and were encamped. Training in Jolon would last for 2½ months, involving 65,000 men in the most realistic war games conducted on the Pacific Coast up to that time.

When the regiment arrived, it made camp at Ruby Gulch, a dry-wash at the foot of a steep sided mountain range. The nearby San Antonio River at least allowed for bathing facilities. According to a Company A report, the site "embodied all of the hardships they would encounter during the war, terrific desert heat, exceptionally cold nights, sand, dense undergrowth and all the usual insects and poisonous reptiles, an excellent training ground...every different difficult terrain feature was represented in this God Forsaken country."[29] The climate was hot, the grassy slopes were slick as glass, the meals irregular, and the water supply wanting.

During the first few weeks, training focused on basic conditioning to accustom the men to the climate. Each day, the troops participated in marches up and down the hillsides in the blazing sun, with the drilling became longer and harder. Evening entertainment, however, softened the rigors of training. Radio and screen celebrities, including Marlene Dietrich, Claudette Colbert, Jack Benny, and Ray Bolger, performed in open-air theaters, and projectors were set up for movies. The small town of Jolon, about five miles from the base, had a small combination store-post office, which included a beer hall frequented by the men. Intermittently, passes were granted, allowing men to visit San Francisco, Monterey, and Los Angeles. Some toured the Hearst Ranch and the San Antonio Mission in their off time. Those men with relatives in California had an opportunity to visit.

During the war games, the divisions were divided into two opposing forces. The 41st was combined with the regular army's 3rd Infantry Division as the "Blue Army." They faced the "Red Army," comprised of the 7th and 40th divisions, the latter a California and Utah National Guard outfit. During the last ten days of the training, the two armies squared off. The red forces were assigned as defenders; the blue divisions were the attackers. The Blue Army pushed through the Red Army, sending it about 15 miles backward. For some, the maneuvers became real hostilities, as men put aside their simulated weapons and took to fist fighting. When the blue team out-scored the red, recognition went to the 163rd regimental commander, Colonel Bloomquist, for his "Bloomkrieg-Tactics."

According to McKinney, Bloomquist's theory was to grab high ground and dig in; the men utilized these tactics over and over again in the hot California sun.

When the California war games ended in early July 1941, the entire 41st Division was assembled for a pep talk from General White, who praised them for their achievement. He concluded his remarks by announcing a ten-day furlough. A number of the new men who joined the 163rd in the spring were from California, so they began their leave from Jolon. Personnel from other states boarded troop trains for the return to Fort Lewis, with many passing their time drinking beer and gambling. On arriving in Washington, men in the division began taking furloughs. According to command policy, however, only half of the garrison could be away at one time. Consequently, schedules were arranged so that enough men would be present to continue the training.

On August 1, a full-scale schedule resumed as the 163rd prepared for maneuvers with the Fourth Army in the rain-drenched forests of Washington's Olympic Peninsula. Operations began on August 10 with an imaginary "Asian" force invading the West Coast under the cover of fog banks. The 41st was deployed south and west, spreading over the Olympic Peninsula. Summer rains and mud complicated the maneuvers, presenting a constant challenge of freeing mired vehicles and keeping men in dry socks. The 163rd continued to learn valuable skills, including how to move troops at night through wet, boggy woods, managing truck convoys in hauling up supplies and weapons, and in setting up effective defensive perimeters.

The operations failed to clearly produce an announced winner. McKinney noted: "The maneuvers high spot according to the [news]papers was the 163rd Infantry's cornering the enemy in a berry patch." He also observed, "were it not for the newspaper the majority of the 163rd would never have known the outcome of the maneuver at all."[30] The overall purpose of the maneuvers, of course, was to ensure that the units were prepared to defend the West Coast.[31]

The 163rd returned to Fort Lewis with a sense of excitement. Their one-year of service soon would be over and many eagerly looked forward to returning to their homes, families, and jobs. However, talk of impending American involvement in the war now was more pronounced than ever. In late August 1941, Congress debated a bill to extend the National Guard's period of active service to 18 months. The measure passed in mid-September. General White, in an attempt to boost the 41st Division's morale, issued an unprecedented 15-day furlough and promised to work to obtain additional leaves during the holidays. The furloughs came in stages, allowing normal training to continue.

On September 2, a 41st Division parade had commemorated one year of active service. Wives, parents, additional family members, public officials, and dignitaries received invitations. A hearty crowd of Montanans arrived to show their support for the 163rd. The guests toured the barracks, recreational areas, and training grounds, enjoying their time with the troops.

Garrison life again settled into a routine. Each company had a fully furnished recreation room for entertainment. While off-duty, the men continued to find new interests in the surrounding civilian communities, and they wrote letters home regularly. The 163rd also organized a regimental football team—the Montana Ramblers. Company B, known for men with good athletic ability, had several participate. The Ramblers played a number of games and boasted a winning record. They earned the right to play in the championship game at the end of the season, losing a close contest decided in the last moments.

As garrison life continued, the men received training in gas warfare and decontamination, participated in tank operations, and spent time on the target range. They barracks were kept spotless, and their shoes received a daily coat of polish. The routine helped the time pass. According to Sgt. James J. Eder of Company B, "the majority of us didn't mind it too much, for we were thoroughly enjoying our hitch in the armed forces…Of course there was some beefing, but a soldier who doesn't beef, is not a true soldier."[32] Meanwhile, rumors of an early discharge circulated around camp.

The second year of training seemed to be off to a good start, but then events in November left the troops unsettled. Whereas guardsmen had their time extended, U.S. Army recruits who were obligated for just one year of service started receiving discharges. Others with dependents, personal hardships, or who were over the age of 28 also were being released.

An alarming incident occurred on November 23 when Maj. General George A. White, the 41st Division commander, passed away at his home in Clackamas, Oregon. White became ill during the California maneuvers, but retained command, though against the advice of his physician. With his death, men throughout the division felt a sense of loss. His compassion as a leader along with his respect for all soldiers, no matter what their rank, had endeared him to the men. According to an authoritative account, "his formula was sternness tempered with a sympathetic understanding of the soldier's makeup…men in his ranks swore by him."[33] In Portland during the funeral, guardsmen carried his casket to a final resting-place in Riverview Cemetery.

During the following weeks, other changes occurred within the 41st Division. Word began circulating that the 161st Regiment (mainly Washington men) was being brought up to full combat strength. Consequently, volunteers from such 163rd units as companies A, B, and K joined the 161st Infantry in order to help it achieve regimental combat capacity. Reportedly, a number of Company K men might have joined the 161st for quite personal reasons. According to Private First Class Don E. Rohrig, author of Company K's unit history, "K Company gave up many trained men, most of whom at the time were in some military doghouse or were considered to be malcontents."[34] Company B's commander, Lt. Walter Rencheler, transferred 32 of his men. Also when it was reported that the 161st would be sent to the Philippines, Fiji, or Turkestan, 15 men from Company A volunteered.

The 163rd, meanwhile, remained unsure of its future. By mid-November, as Washington's 161st prepared to move overseas (eventually assigned to the 25th "Tropic Lightning" Division during the South Pacific campaigns), the rest of the 41st Division—the 186th, 162nd, and 163rd regiments—began the process of triangularization.[35] The old "square" division used since World War I consisted of two brigades, with each brigade comprised of two regiments. Under the new system, each infantry division would have three regiments, thereby eliminating the "brigade." In addition, artillery, engineer, and tank battalions would be incorporated into these combat groups.[36] The new triangularized division was smaller, more maneuverable, and actually had more firepower.

On December 2, Brigadier General Horace H. Fuller, from the Command and General Staff School at Fort Leavenworth, Kansas, took over the 41st Division's leadership. Fuller had formerly commanded artillery at Fort Lewis; consequently he already knew the 41st Division's strengths and weaknesses. "I have watched the progress of this Division since its induction into federal service," the general explained. "Its record is one of achievement and it is recognized as one of the topflight divisions in the army…I feel highly honored in assuming the command of this organization."[37]

General Douglas MacArthur and General Horace H. Fuller confer at Humboldt Bay, New Guinea, on April 22, 1944. General Fuller took command of the 41st Division at Fort Lewis on December 2, 1941, and guided the division through the New Guinea campaigns until being relieved during the Biak invasion on June 14, 1944. *U.S. Army*

In the week before December 7, 1941, a number of guardsmen over 28 years old were looking forward to returning to civilian life. All that was keeping them from going home were x-ray exams; however, a shortage of film had prevented this. While waiting, they had returned uniforms and equipment to supply sergeants, and relaxed around the barracks or went off-duty into surrounding communities. The weekend promised to be an enjoyable one. With pay in hand, men scattered to Pacific Northwest towns. Meanwhile, the Montana Ramblers were slated to play a charity game against a Red Cross team.

On Sunday, December 7, the devastating Japanese air assault on the U.S. Pacific fleet in Hawaii changed everything.[38] The news hit like a bombshell. McKinney recalled, "Japan's attack on Pearl Harbor found the regiment in one of its usual payday throes. Putting it bluntly many were still battling with liquor and having a good time in general."[39] The charity football contest between the Montana Ramblers and the Red Cross eleven was called in the fourth quarter due to the announcement.[40]

Radio broadcasts throughout the region informed off-duty military personnel to report immediately to their garrisons. Men from Company K and other units stood "stunned in the streets of Tacoma and Seattle by commands from loud-speakers to return to camp."[41] They quickly boarded buses to return to their barracks.

Fort Lewis went on full alert as the post began teeming with soldiers reporting for duty. All furloughs and discharges were canceled. Blackout conditions went into effect in case of an enemy air attack, and preparations began for assigning units to defensive positions. Supply sergeants issued equipment and distributed weapons, but arms and munitions still were in short supply and some men were deployed without rifles.

Before dawn on December 8, the division began preparing for deployment along the Washington coast. Within a week, pockets of troops were assigned to positions extending from the Canadian border, south along Puget Sound from Bellingham to Everett, and on the Olympic Peninsula from Port Angeles to Aberdeen, where some companies drew cold, grueling patrol duty along the outer coast.

The troops spent wet, windy days and nights policing roads and beaches. Company A, for example, received orders to guard a local Port Angeles airport and 20 miles of coastline. According to a Company A soldier, "we were on the alert for any invasion or apparent sabotage."[42] Meanwhile, they bivouacked in a local park. The reality of war hit home when Private Collier accidentally shot himself in the leg.[43] The Company K men were ordered to Bellingham, where they moved into a National Guard armory. In the following days, they too patrolled beaches and dug foxholes, while monitoring the U.S.-Canadian border area.

For the next month, guard duty, beach patrols, and other wartime preparations filled the lives of every soldier in the division, causing anxiety and eventually monotony as the weeks passed. Replacements from Camp Roberts in California began arriving in mid-December, bolstering such units as companies A, B, and K by filling positions left vacant after men left to join the 161st Infantry. As replacements filtered in, Christmas arrived. Some companies returned to Fort Lewis before the holiday season, but others did not. For example, Company K celebrated Christmas in Bellingham, and later moved to a Civilian Conservation Corps camp at Quilcene on the northeast Olympic Peninsula. Homesickness blunted their enthusiasm as the holiday season passed.

During the weeks that followed, it became apparent that Japan's massive, multi-pronged sea, land, and air assaults were focused on the Southwest Pacific and the Asian mainland, and not Hawaii or the West Coast. The 41st Division received orders to return to Fort Lewis, while the 3rd Division took over the defensive positions. After weeks of experiencing cold, mud, rain, and snow while deployed along the coast, the Fort Lewis cantonment was a welcome sight to the men.[44]

The 41st Division was being prepared to move overseas,[45] and considerable change would occur between December 1941 and February 1942. The ranks were increased with new Army recruits, while other men transferred in from the 186th Infantry, bringing the 163rd up to full combat strength. Some from the 163rd applied for flight training; when receiving approval, they transferred out as aviation cadets. Staff personnel sections and first sergeants were kept busy day and night during this period.[46] By now, the 163rd retained about 1,600 Montana men, or nearly half of the regiment's total number.

The "rumor mill" went into full swing as the troops wondered about where they might be sent. New equipment and supplies continued to arrive, giving rise to speculation. Sun helmets, dust respirators, and other hot weather clothing and equipment persuaded many to think Australia was their destination, but no one knew for certain.[47]

The regiment received orders to depart for San Francisco on March 7, 1942. The final days at Fort Lewis were a whirlwind of activity as the men prepared for the deployment. They purchased personal items—toiletries, shoe-polish, beer, etc.—and spent long hours in line to make phone calls and tell their wives, parents, and sweethearts good-bye. Sometimes the heavily used pay phones overflowed with returned change, quickly grabbed up by the soldiers waiting in line.[48] Each weekend, relatives and friends arrived by automobile for a final visit and farewell.

At midnight on March 7, the regiment boarded railway cars to set out for California. At this late hour, there were no crowds and no last minute good-byes, but only a military band playing briefly as the troops entrained. The men were loaded down with weapons, duffle bags, and other equipment. Arriving in San Francisco two days later, they were assigned to temporary barracks in the Fontana Building, an abandoned macaroni factory. Companies A and B received orders to guard Pier 35, where the largest ship afloat, the luxury liner *Queen Elizabeth,* was docked. For the next two weeks, guard duty came in four-hour shifts, with eight hours off between. Anticipation ran high through the regiment. As one soldier later noted, "all of us figured that we would leave on this empress of the seas, but mum was the word, for our own protection."[49]

For the next two weeks, the regiment stood guard while the *Queen Elizabeth* was reconditioned as a troop carrier. Adam Preteovich of Company A recalled that for three days workers removed nothing but mirrors from the luxury craft.[50] Lavish furnishings in the staterooms were replaced with bunks stacked four high to accommodate large numbers of men.[51] With renovations completed, rumor became reality when the 163rd boarded the *Queen Elizabeth* for a destination yet undisclosed. At 1:10 p.m. on March 19, under a clear afternoon sky, the ship weighed anchor. Men watched with heavy hearts as they sailed under the Golden Gate Bridge into the Pacific Ocean, watching Nob Hill and Sausalito recede into the haze.

When the "*Lizzie*" set sail,[52] several large African American engineering and service units also were aboard (these men later earned high praise for performing essential roles during the Pacific campaigns). Some aboard the *Lizzie* feared prejudice problems might develop, but congeniality prevailed. Two additional transports, the *Coolidge* and *Mariposa,* each carrying 4,500 men, also were part of the convoy. Two cruisers, one American and the other British, escorted the transports. Unbeknownst to most in the convoy, American submarines escorted the ships during the first leg of the journey. The convoy cruised in a zigzag to thwart any attempts by enemy submarines to get into position to launch torpedoes.

The *Queen Elizabeth*'s only stop during the voyage occurred when the convoy pulled into Nuka-hiva, the largest port in the Marquesa Islands, where an American tanker waited. Tension ran high during refueling. Naval vessels and observation planes hovered around, on guard for lurking Japanese submarines or attacking aircraft, though the presence of the latter was unlikely in this remote region of the Pacific. Men of the 163rd manned weapons on the *Lizzie*'s deck. McKinney recalled, "large ack-ack guns, 20mm affairs, [and] every .50 caliber gun, and anti-tank gun…[was] set up for use against submarines and torpedo planes."[53] Despite the stress, the men noted the lush, green beauty of the island's coconut, palm, and banana trees. After a day in port, the *Queen Elizabeth* pulled anchor, resuming a westerly course for Australia.

Due to severely cramped conditions during the 22-day voyage, duties were largely limited to morning and afternoon lifeboat drills, and to cabin inspections, lectures, and calisthenics.[54] Strict blackout conditions prevailed at night to prevent enemy submarines or planes from detecting the convoy's passing. During the first days, men spent time at the railing, staring out across the expansive ocean and watching for flying fish, sharks, and porpoises. The novelty soon wore off, however, and the men resorted to more typical off-time activities—playing cards, gambling, and visiting the canteen. McKinney noted that the African American soldiers "played craps morning until night…the 163rd played some, but devoted much more time to poker and blackjack."[55] The stakes often were low, since many had spent most of their pay during the last weeks in the states.

"Land!" someone finally shouted. "The cry brought everyone on deck or to the port-holes." On April 6, Easter Sunday, the *Lizzie* entered Sydney Harbor, Australia's foremost seaport.[56] The men were filled with relief and excitement.

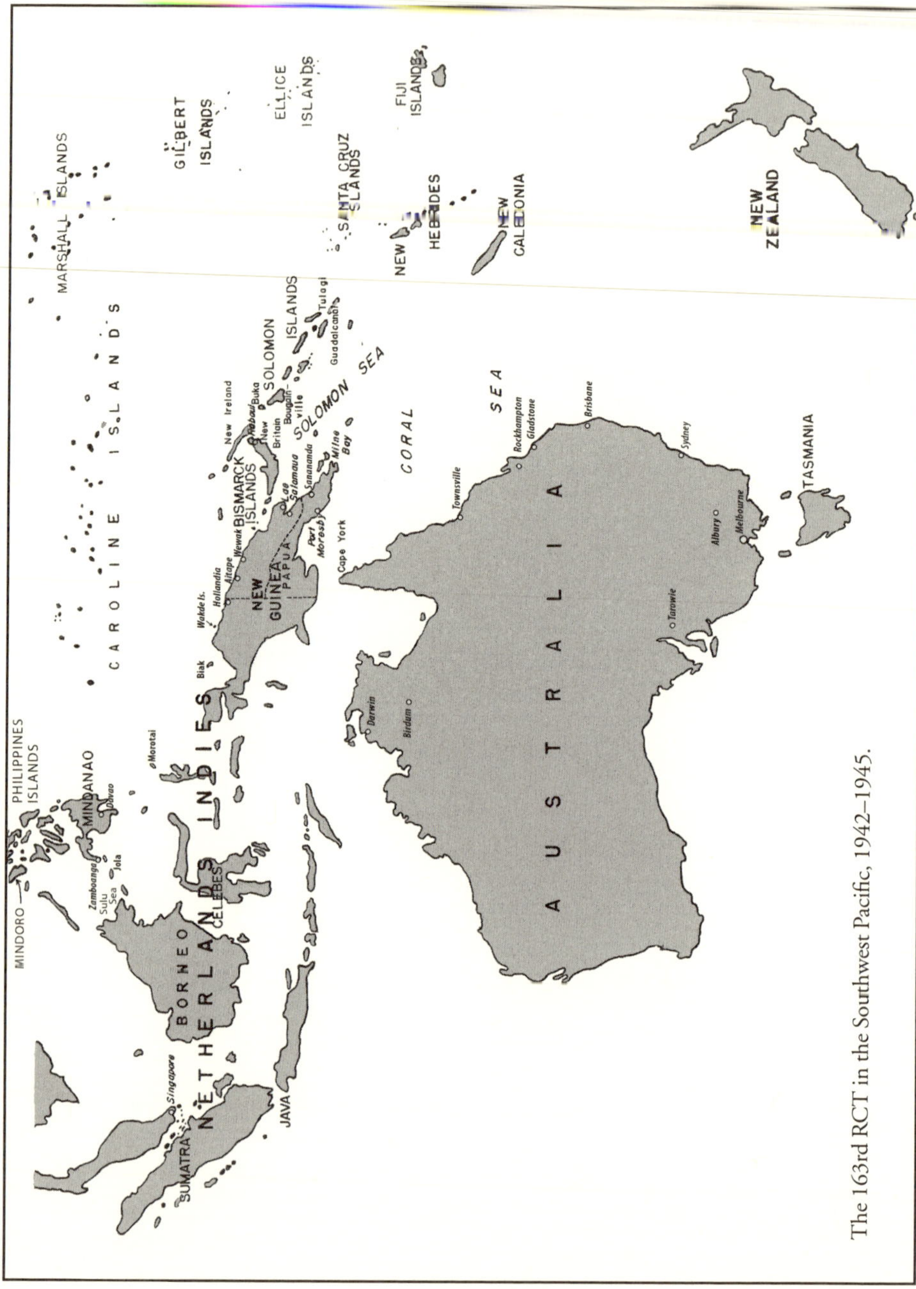

The 163rd RCT in the Southwest Pacific, 1942–1945.

The Sydney Bridge, the city's red rooftops reflecting in the sun, and the *Queen Mary* (the *Queen Elizabeth's* sister ship) sailing out of Sydney harbor were enduring sights. Many hoped this would be the end of their travel by water, but this was not so.[57]

Four Dutch vessels waited in the harbor for transporting the troops to Melbourne, further down the southeast coast of Australia. The regiment's 2nd Battalion was ferried over to the *Van Heutz*, while the 3rd Battalion transferred to the *Cremer* (these and 27 other Dutch vessels of the K.P.M. Line had escaped the Japanese advance in the Dutch East Indies and now served essential roles as transports for Allied forces in the Southwest Pacific Area). Due to a shortage of ships and a dock strike, other units remained aboard the *Lizzie* for several hours, awaiting arrangements for railway transportation to Melbourne.[58] Those continuing by boat envied the men going by rail. Normally, the Sydney to Melbourne voyage took two days, but the small Dutch vessels required four days to ply the Tasman Sea's rough waters. The men spent their time below decks. One Company A soldier recalled: "The longer this trip lasted the rougher the sea became." However, "after four days of this nightmare, the sea became quiet and we docked at Melbourne."[59]

As they disembarked, the Americans received a warm welcome from the local population. Newspapermen snapped pictures and jotted down notes. According to Sgt. James Eder, "the Aussies all turned out to see what the Yanks looked like."[60] Many of them wept at the sight of U.S. troops. Australia was practically defenseless at this point in the war and lay vulnerable to the quickly advancing Japanese. In February, Japanese carrier- and land-based planes in the conquered Dutch East Indies had devastated Darwin harbor in northern Australia.

Two years earlier, the majority of Australia's combat forces went to North Africa and the Mediterranean to fight the European fascist powers. Many of these troops now were returning to defend their homeland, but most would not be in operational positions for some months.[61] Thus, the arrival of American troops gave the Australians new hope at a time when the Japanese set their sights on New Guinea, just to the north.

Within hours of docking, the 163rd boarded diminutive rail coaches taking them to Seymour, about 60 miles inland. To the Americans, the quaint little passenger cars looked very old fashioned, like something from the 1890s.[62] Traveling by train gave the men a chance to view the countryside and its small towns. "The tracks never circled a hill," Sgt. Eder later noted, "they went right up, and right down on the other side, just like a roller coaster in one of our amusement parks… it was fun while it lasted."[63]

Upon arriving at Seymour, the men transferred to Australian military trucks for the final leg to their new quarters, located about seven miles outside of the community. The 163rd was assigned to Camp 25 and Camp 25A, previously used by Australia's militia during training. The men immediately set up their bivouac. Over the next several days, the camp essentially was dismantled and rebuilt in a scattered pattern as a precaution against air attack.

After their long inactive journey across the Pacific, the men began working themselves back into shape. The regiment adopted a 13-week training schedule. They focused on such small unit tactics as maneuvering at night, arm and hand signals, and map and compass reading. The training also included "wigwagging," using white and orange colored flags to send messages in code. Long marches were conducted in the nearby hills for conditioning.[64] McKinney observed: "We carried five-gallon bottles of water in our packs, and marched up and down mountains," which "most of the Montana men believed were only foothills."[65]

As the Southern Hemisphere's hot, sultry summer faded into winter, rain turned the camp into a quagmire, similar to "Swamp Murray." However, "the down pour here, made the hardest rain storm in Washington seem like a shower."[66] The rolling, treeless hillsides turned to mud, the bivouac area flooded, and some equipment floated away; but training continued.

In mid-May, the remaining elements of the 41st Division arrived at Melbourne and received orders to proceed to Seymour. The 41st had been the first American division sent to Australia. Shortly afterward came the 32nd Division, another National Guard outfit from the upper Midwest, whose ranks likewise were bolstered with new enlistees and draftees. For a time, the 41st and 32nd were the only U.S. divisions assigned to Australia, although significant air corps, engineer, and other smaller units likewise were sent to the southern continent. Training intensified in the months that followed. Thirty-mile marches with full field packs were common. Everything learned in the Fort Lewis, California, and Olympic Peninsula war games was put to the test.

Weekend passes in Melbourne offered a respite from the demanding training schedule. At first, only a few curious soldiers ventured into the city. When these men returned with stories of a "soldier's paradise," where liquor, warm hospitality, and friendly females were plentiful, visits to Melbourne increased.[67] The Australians were extremely accommodating. As one soldier later recalled, "people invited us to spend our leaves at their homes, with everything furnished, free of charge."[68] Although the Americans initially found some difficulty in adjusting to the use of Australian money, driving on the "wrong" side of the road, and the speech differences, they adapted quickly. In fact, the Americans soon incorporated Australian slang into their daily talk. In summary, "to the men of the 41st, in those first two months, Australia was Melbourne, Melbourne was heaven, and heaven was theirs, for the taking."[69]

Celebrating Independence Day, July 4, 1942, was a festive occasion for the U.S. troops when Melbourne threw a huge party for the Americans. Company commanders permitted most of the men to attend. For many, it would be their last visit to Melbourne before heading north to face the harsh realities of war.

The following days were spent in making preparations for another move. With men, equipment, and vehicles loaded on rail cars, the regiment set out on a seven-day journey to Rockhampton, halfway up Australia's east coast in Queensland. Stops were made on the way—at the borders of New South Wales, Brisbane, and Queensland—where the troops changed trains.[70] "Each state we passed through had a railroad system of its own, and [seemed to have] a different gauge of track; we had to change trains every time we entered a different state," explained Adam Preteovich. Upon arrival at Rockhampton, ground was cleared and the camp set up. Australian workers pitched in, building latrines, mess halls, and other facilities. The troops then resumed with jungle warfare training.

Rockhampton's warmer, even hot, climate provided a welcome change from the rain and cold at Seymour. Being closer to the equator, the men now were acclimatizing to the conditions they would face when entering combat. Another significant change occurred around this time. Colonel Bloomquist, the 163rd's commander since the autumn of 1940, had become ill and was ordered to return to the United States.

The regiment now was assigned a new leader, Colonel Jens A. Doe, a career army officer. Under Colonel Doe, the regiment received its final tactical training before meeting the Japanese in battle. Doe was a West Point graduate who had commanded the 17th Infantry Regiment in the Jolon, California, war games, where the 17th took punishment from the 163rd. Colonel Doe quickly endeared himself to his new regiment and would receive a promotion to brigadier general after its first combat action.[71]

Brig. Gen. Jens A. Doe confers with an aide, 1st Lt. Rob D. Trimble. In late 1942, Doe took over command of the 163rd RCT during training in Australia's Berserk Mountains and guided the regiment in the Sananda, Aitape, Wakde, and Biak operations in New Guinea. In June 1944, he replaced General Horace H. Fuller as 41st Division commander. *U.S. Army*

The troops conducted training in the thick jungles of the Berserk Mountains, participating in nighttime tactics, patrol and ambush methods, compass use in thick undergrowth, jungle hygiene, tree climbing and sniping, reconnaissance techniques, and hand-to-hand combat. They also were instructed in boat operations and beach landings. Each company rotated out for a 10-day amphibious training course in the choppy waters of Pumicestone Channel at Toorbul Point, not far from Brisbane. During this phase of their training, the 163rd worked closely with Australian commandos. Conditioning took on a realistic form; the commandos delighted in seeing how difficult they could make life for the Americans. Some training problems took place under simulated battle conditions, with explosives detonated along the beach. "They resorted to every trick they knew," a Company B man recalled, "and were quite surprised that we countered every time with something one of us would think up on the spur of the moment."[72] Following the amphibious training, the 163rd could now perform in an amphibious assault should the need arise.

The men next received a week of leave at the beaches near Yeppoon. Some companies even elected to have noncommissioned officers perform kitchen duties, thereby giving privates time off. The men participated in some sports, but swimming and relaxing on the sand proved most popular. After returning to duty, the 41st Division men were summoned before Lt. General Robert Eichelberger, the I Corps commander in Australia, for a short but important talk. He said they would soon see action.

From Rockhampton, the regiment prepared for departure from the nearby port of Gladstone. Everything was made combat ready, Lt. McKinney observed. "This was a hectic week...everyone took off for town...they wanted one last fling."[73]

Boarding the same Dutch ships that brought them to Melbourne, the regiment set sail on December 19. Morale was high as they left the port and strains of "Anchors Aweigh" drifted through the air. The men now learned their destination—they were going north to Port Moresby in southeast New Guinea. Passing time in the usual way, they played poker, blackjack, pinochle, and craps. Also, as on the *Queen Elizabeth*, the stakes remained low; many of the men spent most of their pay back in Rockhampton.

Christmas 1942 found them sailing on the Coral Sea in a war zone. The 3rd Battalion, traveling on the *Cremer*, celebrated with a dinner of C-rations, hard tack, and stew. The 2nd Battalion aboard the *Van Heutz* was more fortunate. Earle Clarke of Company A recalled: "We put a crew of cooks to work in the ships galley on the night shift, and as a result we had fresh baked bread, sausages and tomatoes etc. for our Christmas dinner."[74]

On December 27, the 163rd landed in New Guinea. The regiment moved quickly to a bivouac at Bootless Inlet, just outside of Port Moresby. En route, the 163rd saw the first signs of war—destroyed buildings, bomb craters on the hillsides, and damaged vessels bobbing helplessly in the sea, all due to Japanese air raids. The most alarming sight was the "airplane graveyard," where twisted wreckage lay along the road leading to the camp. Mixed among the wrecked American and Australian planes, however, they saw metal airframe scraps bearing the "Rising Sun" emblem.[75]

The regiment hastily dug slit trenches and foxholes for protection against nighttime bombing. The effort paid off; that very night the 163rd earned its "baptism by fire." Sgt. Eder explained: "As soon as we closed our eyes there'd be an air raid alert, and we'd have to jump into our slit trenches, where the mosquitoes practiced dive bombing us...while enemy planes were overhead."[76] Several times that first night, Japanese two-engine bombers flew over, dropping bombs on airstrips near the camp.

Just twelve months earlier, the 163rd Infantry Regiment had been guarding the Washington coast in the aftermath of the Pearl Harbor attack. Now the regiment had crossed the Pacific, landed on the New Guinea coast, and stood poised to meet the Japanese in combat—just on the other side of the Owen Stanley Mountains.

Notes

1. Robert A. Divine, *The Reluctant Belligerent: American Entry into World War II*, 2nd ed. (New York: John Wiley and Sons, 1979), 97.
2. Major General Albert M. Blanding to the Adjutant General of Montana, memorandum, "Increase in Strength of the National Guard, Fiscal Year 1937," 325.4 Montana, Box 587, Entry 344, Records of the National Guard Bureau (decimal file 1922–45), Record Group 168, National Archives II.
3. "An Overview History of the 163rd Infantry Regiment: From the Late 1930s through the Sananada Campaign," slide presentation, SFC Kermit M. Edmonds, 19 pages, Drawer 3, Montana National Guard, History of the 163rd during World War II, Montana Military History Museum, Library Archives, Fort William Henry Harrison, Helena, Montana [hereafter cited as MMHM].
4. Camp Murray, a state-owned facility, stood immediately northwest of the main part of the U.S. Army's Fort Lewis. The two military posts still exist today. Alan Archambult, Historian, Fort Lewis Museum, telephone conversation, September 16, 1999.
5. Untitled typed manuscript, 1, Drawer 3, Montana National Guard, History of the 163rd in World War II, MMHM.
6. Although mobilization records from the National Guard Bureau total 301,000, an additional 1,000 Selective Service replacements were assigned to guard units. National Guard Association of the United States, *The Nation's National Guard* (Washington, D.C., 1954), 39.
7. "Mobilization Phase 163rd Infantry, 1940," 11-page manuscript, n.d., Drawer 3, Montana National Guard, History of the 163rd during World War II, MMHM.
8. William C. Benson, *The History of the 163rd Regiment Montana National Guard* (Helena: Montana State Historical Society), 13.
9. "History of the 163rd Infantry," shelf #53, random articles clippings and photos, 1–2, MMHM.
10. "Mobilization Phase 163rd Infantry, 1940," 2, MMHM.
11. "Montana Guard Will Send Full Quota, 1500 to Camp," *Wolf Point Gazette*, August 1940, Drawer 3, Montana National Guard 1940–1945, World War II History of the Montana National Guard Units, MMHM.
12. Colonel Howard A. McKinney, "History of the 163rd Montana National Guard," Box 67, MMHM, 12. For citation purposes in *Splendid Service*, page numbers have been

assigned to this manuscript. McKinney's personal account of the 163rd Infantry was written as a supplement to William F. McCartney's official history, ordered by the War Department and dating from 1948 (*The Jungleers: A History of the 41st Infantry Division* [Washington, D.C.: Infantry Journal Press]). While engaged in military operations at Sananda, New Guinea, in 1943, McKinney was awarded the Silver Star for gallantry in action. In the 1950s, McKinney wrote his addendum to the official 1948 history, offering what he described as "the human side" of the regiment's training and combat experiences. It is based on diary entries, memoirs, letters, telegrams, and orders. In addition, McKinney incorporated accounts offered by other 163rd men, including a copy of Company K's unit history.

13. McKinney, "History of the 163rd," 5, MMHM.
14. Adjutant General John Mahan, Montana, to Major-General John F. Williams, Chief of the National Guard Bureau, memorandum, "RE: New Units," 325.4 Montana, Box 587, Entry 344, Record Group 168, National Archives II.
15. McKinney, "History of the 163rd," 3, MMHM.
16. Ibid., 4.
17. "Mobilization Phase 163rd Infantry, 1940," 7, MMHM.
18. Howard McKinney remembered signing up for $1 per drill; guardsmen participated in one drill per week, and received a check every three months. Howard A. McKinney, tape-recorded interview by Jodie Foley, September 9, 1995, Oral History 1261, Montana Historical Society, Helena [hereafter cited as MHS].
19. "Headquarters, Company 'A' 163rd Infantry, Office of the Company Commander," Entry 427, Folder 341-INF (163) -0 to 341-INF (163) -0.1, World War II Operations Reports 1940–45, Box 10633, World War II Operations, Record Group 407, National Archives II.
20. McKinney, "History of the 163rd," 10, MMHM.
21. McKinney, tape-recorded interview by Jodie Foley, September 9, 1995, Oral History 1261, MHS.
22. "Mobilization Phase 163rd Infantry, 1940," 8, MMHM.
23. Ibid.
24. Lt. Colonel Mark W. Clark, U.S. Army General Headquarters, the Army War College, Washington, D.C. to Wayne, Headquarters IX Army Corps, Office of the Commanding General, Fort Lewis, Washington, letter, dated March 29, 1941, Folder 322, IX Army Corps GHQ, HQ Army Ground Forces General HQ, U.S. Army (GHQ) Box 357, decimal file 1940–March 9, 1941, Records of Headquarter's Ground Forces, Record Group 337, National Archives II.
25. Lt. Colonel Mark W. Clark, to Lt. Colonel D.D. Eisenhower, GSC, Chief of Staff, IX Army Corps, Fort Lewis, Washington, April 5, 1941, Folder 322, IX Army Corps (GHQ), HQ Army Ground Forces General HQ, U.S. Army (GHQ) Ground Section AG Box 357, Project Decimal File 1940–March 9, 1941, Record Group 337, National Archives II.
26. Lt. Colonel Mark W. Clark, Army War College, Fort Lewis Washington, April 23, 1941, Folder 322, IX Army Corps (GHQ), HQ Army Ground Forces General HQ, U.S. Army (GHQ) Ground Section AG Box 357, Project Decimal File 1940–March 9, 1941, Record Group 337, National Archives II.
27. The convoy stopped at Vancouver Barracks, Bend, Klamath Falls, Red Bluff, Marysville, and Modesto before arriving at the Hunter Ligget Military Reservation. William

F. McCartney, *The Jungleers: A History of the 41st Infantry Division* (Washington, D.C.: Infantry Journal Press, 1948), 7.

28. Letter from Ike to Wayne, RE: Hunter Liggett Military Reservation, May 29, 1941, 322, IX Army Corps (GHQ), HQ Army Ground Forces General HQ, U.S. Army (GHQ) Ground Section AG Box 357, Project Decimal File 1940–March 9, 1941, Record Group 337, National Archives II.
29. "Headquarters, Company 'A' 163rd Infantry, Office of the Company Commander," Entry 427, Folder 341-INF (163) -0 to 341-INF (163) -0.1, World War II Operations Reports 1940–45, Box 10633, World War II Operations, Record Group 407, National Archives II.
30. McKinney, "History of the 163rd," 28, MMHM.
31. McCartney, *The Jungleers,* 11.
32. Ibid.
33. Ibid., 12.
34. McKinney, "History of the 163rd," 138, MMHM.
35. Renee Hylton and Robert K. Wright Jr., *A Brief History of the Militia and National Guard* (Washington, D.C.: Department of the Army and Air Force Historical Service Division, Office of Public Affairs, National Guard Bureau, 1993), 29.
36. Elbridge Colby, "The National Guard of the United States: A Half Century of Progress," Ph.D. dissertation, Kansas State University, 1977, 14–15.
37. McCartney, *The Jungleers,* 16.
38. William L. O'Neil, *A Democracy at War: America's Fight Abroad in World War II* (Cambridge, Mass.: Harvard University, 1993), 1.
39. McKinney, "History of the 163rd," 34, MMHM.
40. "History of the 41st - 163rd Infantry (Company B) 9-16-40 thru 1945, Wakde 5-18-44, Ibdi Ridge," Entry 427, Folder 341-INF (163) -0 to 341-INF (163) -0.1, Box 10633, World War II Operations Reports 1940–48, Record Group 407, National Archives II.
41. McKinney, "History of the 163rd," 138, MMHM.
42. "Headquarters, Company 'A' 163rd Infantry, Office of the Company Commander," 6, Entry 427, Folder 341-INF (163) -0 to 341-INF (163) -0.1, World War II Operations Reports 1940–45, Box 10633, World War II Operations, Record Group 407, National Archives II.
43. Ibid.
44. Ibid., 7.
45. Random articles clippings and photos, History of the 163rd Infantry, shelf #53, MMHM.
46. According to members of the 163rd, the men applying to flight school were fortunate. They were assigned to more casual barracks postings, often with a long wait, before being sent to an aviation school. In many instances these men received furloughs of from 30 to 90 days. McKinney, "History of the 163rd," 40, MMHM.
47. Ibid.
48. Ibid., 41.
49. "History of the 41st - 163rd Infantry (Company B) 9-16-40 thru 1945, Wakde 5-18-44, Ibdi Ridge," 8, Entry 427, Folder 341-INF (163) -0 to 341-INF (163) -0.1, Box 10633, World War II Operations Reports 1940–48, Record Group 407, National Archives II.
50. Adam Preteovich, tape-recorded interview by Jodie Foley, September 9, 1995, Oral History 1647, MHS.
51. Throughout the war, the *Queen Elizabeth* transported not only thousands of National Guard and regular U.S. Army troops, but also numerous females in the Women's Army

Corps (WACS) and Women Accepted for Volunteer Emergency Service (WAVES). More than 350,000 women served in uniform during World War II, with a peak strength of 271,000, first in administrative or clerical fields, then gradually in nontraditional, more hazardous roles. Although women were excluded from combat assignments, a number came in harm's way and were killed, wounded, or taken prisoner. WACS and WAVES from Montana participated in World War II, although these women were not directly involved with the 163rd Infantry Regiment. Regarding women in World War II, see the following: Rosalind Rosenberg, *Divided Lives: American Women in the Twentieth Century* (1992); Rose Rosenthal, *Not All Soldiers Wore Pants: A Witty World War II WAC Tells All* (1993); Sherna Berger Gluck, *Rosie the Riveter Revisited: Women, the War, and Social Change* (1987); Paula Nassen Poulos, ed., *A Women's War Too: U.S. Women in the Military in World War II* (1996).

52. In Company K's unit history, the men began to refer to the *Queen Elizabeth* as the *Lizzie*, and it spread throughout the regiment. McKinney, "History of the 163rd," 142, MMHM.
53. Ibid., 43.
54. Ibid., 140.
55. Ibid., 42.
56. "History of the 41st - 163rd Infantry (Company B) 9-16-40 thru 1945, Wakde 5-18-44, Ibdi Ridge," 7, Entry 427, Folder 341-INF (163) -0 to 341-INF (163) -0.1, Box 10633, World War II Operations Reports 1940–48, Record Group 407, National Archives II.
57. "Headquarters, Company 'A' 163rd Infantry, Office of the Company Commander," 8, Entry 427, Folder 341-INF (163) -0 to 341-INF (163) -0.1, World War II Operations Reports 1940–45, Box 10633, World War II Operations, Record Group 407, National Archives II.
58. Samuel Milner, *United States Army in World War II: The War in the Pacific, Victory in Papua*, vol. 7 (Washington, D.C.: Center of Military History, United States Army, 2003), 26; "Corrections and Comments on History Manuscript," 1, random articles clippings and photos, History of the 163rd Infantry, Box 67, MMHM.
59. "History of the 41st - 163rd Infantry (Company B) 9-16-40 thru 1945, Wakde 5-18-44, Ibdi Ridge," 7, Entry 427, Folder 341-INF (163) -0 to 341-INF (163) -0.1, Box 10633, World War II Operations Reports 1940–48, Record Group 407, National Archives II.
60. Ibid., 8.
61. When off-duty Australian soldiers and 163rd men mingled in Melbourne, some minor flare-ups arose over local women. McKinney, tape-recorded interview by Jodie Foley, September 9, 1995, Oral History 1261, MHS.
62. McKinney, "History of the 163rd," 46, MMHM.
63. "History of the 41st - 163rd Infantry (Company B) 9-16-40 thru 1945, Wakde 5-18-44, Ibdi Ridge," 8, Entry 427, Folder 341-INF (163) -0 to 341-INF (163) -0.1, Box 10633, World War II Operations Reports 1940–48, Record Group 407, National Archives II.
64. McKinney, "History of the 163rd," 142, MMHM.
65. McKinney, tape-recorded interview by Jodie Foley, September 9, 1995, Oral History 1261, MHS.
66. "History of the 41st - 163rd Infantry (Company B) 9-16-40 thru 1945, Wakde 5-18-44, Ibdi Ridge," 8, Entry 427, Folder 341-INF (163) -0 to 341-INF (163) -0.1, Box 10633, World War II Operations Reports 1940–48, Record Group 407, National Archives II.
67. "Headquarters, Company 'A' 163rd Infantry, Office of the Company Commander," 9, Entry 427, Folder 341-INF (163) -0 to 341-INF (163) -0.1, World War II Operations

Reports 1940–45, Box 10633, World War II Operations, Record Group 407, National Archives II.

68. "History of the 41st - 163rd Infantry (Company B) 9-16-40 thru 1945, Wakde 5-18-44, Ibdi Ridge," 8, Entry 427, Folder 341-INF (163) -0 to 341-INF (163) -0.1, Box 10633, World War II Operations Reports 1940–48, Record Group 407, National Archives II.
69. McCartney, *The Jungleers,* 27.
70. Adam Preteovich, tape-recorded interview by Jodie Foley, September 9, 1995, Oral History 1647, MHS.
71. McKinney, "History of the 163rd," 57, MMHM.
72. "History of the 41st - 163rd Infantry (Company B) 9-16-40 thru 1945, Wakde 5-18-44, Ibdi Ridge," 10, Entry 427, Folder 341-INF (163) -0 to 341-INF (163) -0.1, Box 10633, World War II Operations Reports 1940–48, Record Group 407, National Archives II.
73. McKinney, "History of the 163rd," 68, MMHM.
74. Ibid.
75. "History of the 41st - 163rd Infantry (Company B) 9-16-40 thru 1945, Wakde 5-18-44, Ibdi Ridge," 7, Entry 427, Folder 341-INF (163) -0 to 341-INF (163) -0.1, Box 10633, World War II Operations Reports 1940–48, Record Group 407, National Archives II.
76. Ibid., 12.

A Papuan native in ceremonial regalia. *MMHM*

11

Twenty-two Days of Combat in Papua: The Sananda Front, 1943

Michelle Tabit

They presented an impressive sight, four men to a roughly constructed stretcher... Sometimes the wounds of the men they carried were repulsive and sickening to the eye... no man felt too good over this reception... any illusions we had of the glories of war were quickly dispelled.—Company A's Lt. Howard A. McKinney of Sidney, Montana, at Soputa, New Guinea, early January 1943.

We would surely have made an interesting picture, sitting there staring at one another... there was no wild cheering, as Hollywood would have it... just a group of tired, bewildered men, each in his own way giving thanks to his maker for victory.—Company B's Sergeant James J. Eder of Poplar, Montana, at Sananda, New Guinea, late January 1943.[1]

In March and April 1942, only a few months after the Pearl Harbor attack, Japanese forces swept across the South Pacific and advanced to New Guinea's north shore, landing in parts of Dutch New Guinea in the western half of the island, and in the Australian mandate of North East New Guinea in the east central part. In the following months, the invaders solidified their positions along much of the vast island's 1,400-mile northern coast.

Meanwhile, with Australia largely undefended and under threat of Japanese invasion, regular Australian Army brigades were returning from the Mediterranean and North Africa, where they had battled German and Italian armies. In the interim, Australia relied largely on often hastily formed and outnumbered militia forces, which nevertheless determinedly faced the Japanese in eastern New Guinea.

In early May 1942, the Japanese planned to take Port Moresby and the southeast coast of New Guinea with a seaborne attack. U.S. aircraft carrier action, however, turned back the invasion force in the Battle of the Coral Sea. In late July 1942, the Japanese again stepped up operations in New Guinea—this time by land. Maj. Gen. Tomitaro Horii and the elite South Seas Detachment of Japanese jungle fighters, along with other combat and engineering units, landed in the Territory of Papua, another Australian possession. In this far-eastern New

Guinea operation, 11,000 Japanese soldiers soon established a base and improved the transportation network among several small settlements along 11 miles of the northern coast—from Gona at the west, to Buna on the east, with Sananada Point in the middle as the focus of this effort. In following months, thousands of additional troops came by the sea lanes.[2]

During the next two months, the invaders pushed southwest on the barely passable Kokoda track, crossing the mountainous Papua Peninsula toward Australian-held Port Moresby. In peacetime, Port Moresby had a population of only 2,000 citizens, but now it teemed with Australian and American servicemen and native workers, improving the nearby airfields, harbor facilities, and land defenses. For the enemy, the seizure of Port Moresby would not only eliminate a growing Allied base, but also provide a "spring-board" for further Japanese expansion across the Coral Sea. From here, the enemy intended to advance into the archipelagos east of Australia, thereby cutting off America's all-important sea and air routes to Australia. This would effectively knock Australia, with its 7 million people, out of the war. Port Moresby also would be an important base for invading Australia itself, should the Japanese decide to do so in future planning.

By late August, the Japanese penetrated deep into the jungle and forests of the incredibly steep-cut Owen Stanley Mountains, pushing undermanned Australian militia forces back in a brutal equatorial campaign. Men sweltered in high humidity during the daytime, and shivered at night in the frigid mountain air and torrential rains. Combat casualties were heavy and thousands on both sides were afflicted with tropical disease and exhaustion. By early September, the Japanese approached within 32 miles of their objective, seeing the Coral Sea in the distance. However, they did not advance any farther. Australian soldiers from the 7th Division (newly arrived from the Middle East), the 39th militia brigade, and other combat units faced the enemy in the Imita Range, south of Ioribaiwa. In addition, American and Australian planes strafed and bombed Japanese supply routes as the enemy's supply effort broke down in the extremely difficult terrain.

On cautionary orders from Tokyo, General Horii was directed to halt, and then pull back. The high command was concerned about recent Japanese sea and land battles elsewhere in the Pacific, particularly in the struggle with the U.S. Navy and Marines at Guadalcanal in the Solomon Islands, 800 miles east of New Guinea. Tokyo now gave Guadalcanal top priority for men, ships, planes, and supplies, though some support continued to come to New Guinea by sea. General Horii would consolidate his forces in fortified positions on the north New Guinea coast, with the possibility of renewing the Port Moresby assault later. As the Japanese retreated, Australian forces took the opportunity to go on the offense.

The Japanese survivors, still fighting the Australians along the Kokoda trail, withdrew north to Gona, Sanananda, and Buna, where approximately 5,500 men (soon strengthened with fresh troops to over 6,500) had time to prepare formidable defenses in the swamps, mangrove trees, tall Kunai grass, and coconut plantations along the coast. Meanwhile at Aussie-held Milne Bay far out on the easternmost tip of New Guinea, the Australians and Americans were preparing important new airstrips, which the Japanese intended to knock out. Here, Australian troops and some U.S. Army engineers thwarted a Japanese sea-borne assault. This was the first Allied victory in land fighting against the Japanese in the Southwest Pacific. The tide began turning in the Allies favor, but only barely so.

In challenging the Japanese in the Owen Stanley Mountains, the Australians suffered extensive casualties from combat, exhaustion, and especially malaria and other diseases. With American assistance required for besieging the Japanese on the north coast, General Douglas MacArthur, Commander-in-Chief of the Southwest Pacific Area, now committed the first U.S. ground troops to combat. The two American infantry outfits in Australia—the National Guard's 32nd and 41st divisions—awaited MacArthur's orders.[3] After Lt. Gen. Robert Eichelberger, the I Corps commander, consulted with the division commanders, it was determined that the 126th Regiment of the 32nd Division would go into action first, largely because the division was housed in inadequate training facilities and needed to relocate anyway. MacArthur began moving the 126th, and also shortly the 32nd Division's other two regiments (the 127th and 128th), to New Guinea.

The 41st Division remained at Rockhampton. Having better training arrangements than what the 32nd Division had, they continued their jungle training under a knowledgeable staff. This served the 41st Division men well because they later entered combat better prepared than the 32nd Division regiments.[4] Among other combat skills, the training included nighttime perimeter security, patrolling and navigating in thick jungle, counter measures for sniping, familiarity with Japanese small unit tactics, equipment maintenance in an equatorial climate, and physical conditioning and toughening.

Meanwhile, the 32nd Division under Australian field command set out to assist in taking Buna and Sanananda on the Papua Peninsula's north shore. The Japanese—entrenched in a vast array of bunkers on several narrow, heavily garrisoned fronts with the Solomon Sea shoreline at their back, and taking full advantage of lethal firing positions in the swamps, Kunai grass, and thick jungle—fought tenaciously against the Australian and U.S. forces. The 32nd Division lacked the artillery, tanks, and especially flame-throwers that American troops and marines would have in subsequent island campaigns. In late 1942 and early 1943, National Guard and Australian soldiers in New Guinea normally assaulted the enemy's fiercely defended bunkers with only light infantry weapons, grenades, and satchel explosives. The small handful of tanks available proved effective at times, but normally could not maneuver in much of the area's swampy terrain.

Conducting infantry operations was difficult in the dense foliage and bogs where opposing positions often stood less than 50 yards apart. Enemy snipers kept everyone vigilant. Men slogged through deep mud and standing water, struggled across streams swollen by heavy rains, drank unsafe water, and contracted tropical diseases. The stench of decomposing bodies— Japanese, Australian, and American—permeated the humid jungle.[5] The Allied operation soon bogged down.

By late November 1942, MacArthur realized the Buna front had reached a point of stagnation. At Port Moresby, he summoned the I Corps commander, General Robert Eichelberger, and issued a harsh direct order: "Go out there, Bob, and take Buna or don't come back alive."[6] The same words also were meant for Eichelberger's chief of staff. Eichelberger took over at the front.

After several weeks of some of the severest fighting of the Pacific war, Australian forces finally took Gona (on the west) in mid December. Then, the Americans and Australians conquered Buna (to the east) in early January. Conditions were unbelievably harsh and difficult. For example, during one attack by a 32nd Division company, the men were wading in neck deep water when they were stopped by enemy fire during daylight. There they remained standing throughout the long insect-infested night, with only their helmeted heads sticking out of the cold swampy muck permeating their clothes, weapons, and equipment.

The high losses due to combat and disease were alarming. Furthermore, the Australian forces and the 32nd Division still needed to take Sanananda and clean up dangerous enemy pockets, while other roaming Japanese soldiers continued to infiltrate through the jungle. The 126th Regiment was decimated by casualties and the tropical illnesses that most contracted. From a total of 3,171 men when entering the combat zone in mid-November, the 126th would be reduced to 611 when finally evacuated to Port Morseby on January 22.

The taking of Gona and Buna were important stages on the road victory. The final main objective of the campaign, however, had yet to be achieved. In the middle—at points no more than a few miles inland from Sanananda Point—1,000 or more Japanese troops occupied especially strong defensive lines on the coast and in the swamps and jungle. These were centered in perimeters around the junction of the important Killerton and Sanananda tracks. Branches of the former track extended northwest toward nearby Cape Killerton, while the Soputa-Sanananda trail (called the Motor Transport, or M.T., supply road by the Allies) led northeast to Sanananda Point, also close by. Near this trail junction, inland from the coast just a couple of miles, the Japanese held strong positions,[7] generally in areas around the Allies' fortified "Huggins Roadblock." The roadblock was named for Capt. Meredith M. Huggins of the 126th Infantry, a staff officer who desperately held the position despite determined Japanese assaults in December 1942.[8] Importantly, the Huggins position blocked Japanese use of the Sanananda track in this vicinity, but the enemy controlled other sections of the road, both north and south. The few roads through this soggy terrain were essential to both sides in moving equipment, supplies, and combat units.

At this time, the 163rd Regimental Combat Team was called upon to assist or relieve exhausted, depleted Australian and American troops. The 163rd would be the only 41st Division regiment entering this phase of the fighting.

As related in the previous chapter, the 163rd arrived at Port Moresby on December 27, 1942, bivouacking at nearby Bootless Inlet. During the next three days, the men received jungle flashlights, rubberized food bags, mosquito gloves, hunting knives, and machetes. On December 30, the 163rd's commander, Colonel Jens A. Doe, announced that the regiment was going to the front. The 163rd would be conducting offensive operations, holding vital positions, and protecting the Dobodura and Popondetta airstrips, two landing field complexes located more than 6 miles inland from the north coast. Both the enemy and the Allies were receiving support from the sea lanes. Air transport and supply, however, were becoming key to the Allies' success.[9]

In final preparation, the 163rd received ammunition and rations, and last minute instructions from commanding officers. According to Stanley C. "Black Bart" Davison: "Captain Van Duyn, commanding officer of Company C, gave us a pep-talk reminding us this would probably be the last time we were all together and what a fine company we had—made us all feel good."[10]

That same day, Colonel Doe and his regimental staff left Port Moresby by plane for Popondetta airfield on the other side of the Owen Stanley Mountains. The 1st Battalion and part of the 2nd Battalion followed to the airstrips, which took two days. The 3rd Battalion and remaining elements of the 2nd likewise were flown over the mountains within several days, completing the regiment's deployment along with attached engineer, medical, signal, and other units, but without artillery. The regimental roster, including the 550 attached troops, numbered 3,820 men at this time.

A 1st Battalion soldier recalled the trip over the rugged Owen Stanley range as "an unforgettable forty-minute flight: the climb from sea level to 6,500 feet, the risky trip through the misty pass with jungle-covered mountains extending upward from each wing tip, the tree-top hedge hopping descent to Dobodura airstrip hacked out of a Kunai grass-covered plain."[11] Tension ran high throughout the flight.[12] The unarmed two-engine transports, carrying about 20 passengers, flew in skies infested by Japanese fighter planes coming from air strips to the northwest and north.[13] As the men quickly debarked, native stretcher bearers ran from the jungle with wounded and debilitated soldiers, loading them onto the transports for the return to Port Moresby.

The 163rd men set out with full field packs in the nearly unbearable jungle heat. They were directed along a 12-mile trail, reaching forward positions in two days. Along the route, they passed through the settlement of Dobodura not far

Infantrymen in typical lowland Papua terrain. Supplies and ammunition for front line positions were laboriously hand carried by soldiers and native porters. The soldier in the middle of the photo is hauling a bucket filled with ammunition or rations. Also, note two strands of communication wire staked along the swampy track. *MMHM*

from the airfields. "It wasn't what we expected," one member of Company B recalled. "We sort of figured that there would be some sort of village, with at least one store; but it turned out to be only a few native huts, occupied by sick and wounded Yanks and Aussies waiting to be transported to one of our base hospitals; or waiting to get back into action."[14]

During the arduous, single-file trek, the men crossed swampy areas in ankle to waist deep water. The heavy tropical canopy blocked the sun's rays from the jungle floor, and thick leafed softwood trees offered hiding places for Japanese snipers. Visibility in the jungle was often just 5 to 30 yards when a man stood, and reduced to a couple of yards when he was prone.[15] During one of the rest periods, the regiment consumed coffee, cheese, and hardtack.[16] With the coming of night, many could not find dry places for sleeping; most tried to slumber while lying on muddy ground or wet tree roots. At midnight on December 31—as 1942 came to a close—the Australians at the front celebrated the New Year by firing a barrage from their limited number of 25-pound howitzers and other artillery pieces.

Beginning at 3 a.m., the 163rd men set out again on the muddy track, often through high, thick-bladed Kunai grass. They passed more natives carrying wounded men back to Dobodura. As Company A's Lt. Howard A. McKinney later recalled, "they presented an impressive sight, four men to a roughly constructed stretcher...Sometimes the wounds of the men they carried were repulsive and sickening to the eye." McKinney added: "No man felt too good over this reception...any illusions we had of the glories of war were quickly dispelled."[17]

The 163rd was attached to the 7th Australian Division, commanded by Maj. Gen. George A. Vasey. On December 31, Australian guides had led advanced American command personnel to forward positions at Huggins Perimeter, where the 163rd would be relieving exhausted Aussie soldiers (see Sananada Front map). According to Capt. "Black Bart" Davison, "we started off at a fast clip... God knows how far...We came to a place called Moore's Outpost [where] we were given Aussie helmets so the Jap snipers wouldn't know we were Americans, or fresh troops."[18] For several hours, the men observed the area while their Australian guides pointed out enemy positions.

Once Colonel Doe's 163rd regimental headquarters was established at Huggins Roadblock, the leading 1st Battalion units moved into the forward positions, taking over complete responsibility by January 3. Company C, with one platoon from Company D, took over Perimeter Kano to the northeast, while the 1st Battalion's B, D (minus the one platoon at Kano), and Headquarters companies occupied Huggins Perimeter. Company A (minus one platoon at Moore's Outpost, 400 yards east of Huggins) defended the jungle supply trail bulging around Japanese positions, just east of the main Soputa-Sanananda Point track (or the Motor Transport, or M.T., road, as it was called by the Allies).

Colonel Doe assigned the code name Musket to his regimental headquarters at the Huggins Roadblock. The Japanese and the Allied positions were a mosaic of interspersed perimeters, basically around the junction of the Cape Killerton and the Sanananda Point roads. Two strong enemy perimeters were located between Kano and Huggins, while others were situated to the south of Huggins and north of Kano. To the south of the enemy's large southern perimeter, the Australian 18th Brigade would arrive in a few days to take over from other Aussie troops and the U.S. 126th Regiment, which had fought to an exhausted stalemate.

Initially, the 1st Battalion's task was to attempt to clear the enemy's middle two perimeters straddling the Sanananda road—one on the east side of the trail, and the other, about twice as large, on the west. These were concentrated in an area several hundred yards across, between Kano and Musket. As with many enemy positions, the Japanese bunkers stood on higher, better drained ground, forcing attacking Allied units to advance through low, swampy areas.

The 163rd's expansive Musket Perimeter consisted of two borders. An interior ring contained Colonel Doe's regimental headquarters and the switchboard as well as an aid station, the main ammunition dump, field kitchens, and 81-mm

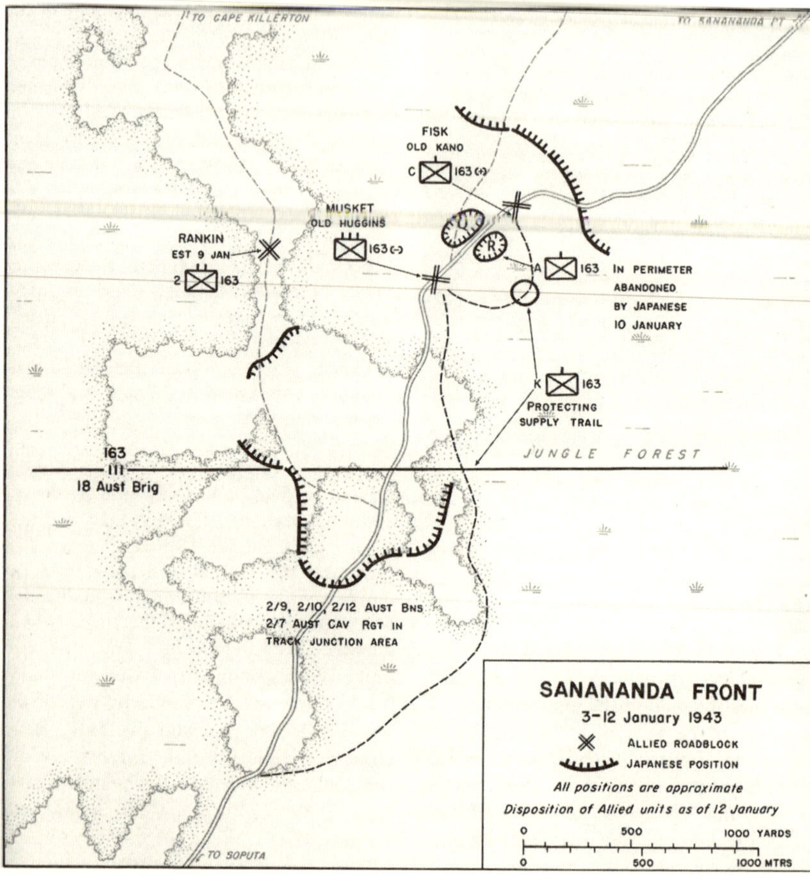

Adapted from Samuel Milner, *United States Army in World War II... Victory in Papua* (1957).

mortars. The exterior ring was manned by squads from three companies, arranged in either square or circular formations, to defend from all sides. Each squad had its own straddle trench (latrine) and water seep (hand dug wells) spaced about 15 yards apart. Situated between the two rings were the various company headquarters and forward munition dumps. The entire Musket area was crisscrossed with trenches, making it a well defended position.

Japanese snipers immediately proved challenging on the day the 1st Battalion moved into position. The American troops quickly responded, thanks to their jungle warfare training. They established two-man sniper observer posts in the trenches along the forward edges of the perimeter, and in trees on the flanks and at the rear. Small counter-sniping patrols on the ground, covered from above by riflemen climbing up wire and wood-rung ladders into the trees, began picking off Japanese marksmen.

In the 163rd's jungle training, Australian veterans had warned that nighttime muzzle flashes from a weapon revealed a man's position to enemy infiltrators. The Aussies recommended throwing hand grenades instead. To stop Japanese infiltrators at night, the troops also rigged booby traps—mainly hand grenades tied to trees with the pins connected to trip wires.

The men took turns in groups of three manning each individual perimeter position at night. In addition to an M1 Garand rifle (firing an 8-cartridge en-bloc clip), a sniper rifle, or a Browning Automatic Rifle (BAR) with a 20-cartridge magazine, each man had three or four hand grenades. Captain Davison warned his men, "if you hear a branch break on the outside of the perimeter, just pull the pin and toss the grenade."[19] The men received strict instructions not to leave their positions at night, no matter how urgent the need, lest they risk being mistaken for Japanese and fired upon. After a man was accidentally shot, the men obeyed this rule as if their lives depended on it, which it did, of course. (These procedures became common doctrine for Allied forces throughout the Pacific war.)

As early as January 2, elements of the 163rd set out to begin breaking the seven-week stalemate at Sananda. The Musket position was in a comparatively open area with vines and a few low trees, except around the outer edges of the large perimeter where the jungle resumed. Mostly, the dense vegetation and swampy terrain prevented mass troop movements. Instead, small units and combat patrols inched forward through the swamps and tropical growth, locating enemy bunkers and conducting infiltration missions.[20]

The Japanese bunkers mostly were built with coconut-tree logs, typically 6 to 8 feet long, with the larger ones up to 30 feet in length. The bunkers were partially underground, and covered over with earth and camouflaged by palm branches and quick-growing tropical vegetation. The log walls frequently were reinforced with sheet metal, iron rails, and sand-filled oil drums. The bunkers were arranged short distances apart in circular or oval patterns, providing excellent concealment and fields-of-view for interlocking support during firefights.

In small unit action during this time, Staff Sgt. Joseph Reddoor, a full-blood Sioux from Poplar's Company B, distinguished himself by leading reconnaissance and combat patrols into enemy areas. His actions helped knock out several Japanese pillboxes. On one fateful mission, Sgt. Reddoor was wounded, and Sgt. Arthur Belgrade, without regard for his own safety, rushed to Reddoor's aid. For their bravery, Reddoor later would be granted the Silver Star, while Belgrade earned the Distinguished Service Cross. Both men also received Purple Hearts for being wounded.[21]

Patrols conducted between January 4 and 7 provided a good introduction for the regiment in utilizing their equatorial combat training. They also became accepting of the discomfort associated with jungle fighting. "If it wasn't raining, it was dripping from the previous shower…each square foot of earth was home for bugs and insects," McKinney explained. "The soldier with his C ration, shelter half and rifle was fair game for everything capable of stinging or biting."[22]

A disabled soldier carried on a stretcher by local natives. The Australians and Americans relied on Papuan porters to carry supplies and litters, whereas the Japanese brought in 1,200 forced natives from Rabaul and New Britain Island. *MMHM*

Both sides endured the stench of death, hanging heavy over the area. Dense rains frequently turned the roads to mud, limiting the amount of supplies coming to the front lines. McKinney explained, "a bath and a change of clothes was not for the front line troops…neither friend nor foe was prepared to survive this unforgiving tropical environment for long."[23]

Each day in combat, the new troops learned something new about warfare. As one general pointed out, "it's the kind of war where little things are important, where men tape their identification 'dog tags' so the tags won't jingle; where they prefer to be bearded rather than clean shaven because the whiskers are camouflage; where of two men on patrol, one may spot a Jap position and the other be completely unable to see it."[24]

In this close-in combat environment with obscured visibility, the enemy tended not to utilize artillery or planes. The Japanese also had learned that the trajectories of their own mortar shells frequently did not penetrate the thick tree canopy above their own positions; when a mortar projectile exploded in the jungle over them, metal fragments rained down on their own men. This concern sometimes limited their use of mortars.[25] For the Allies, a shortage of artillery and the obscurities of spotting targets in a jungle environment also proved restrictive. They eventually often called off close air support because their own planes could mistakenly fire into or bomb friendly positions. Combat for both sides was mostly limited to the use of small arms and grenades.

Combat patrols soon identified the outlines of the two Japanese strongholds—which they called perimeters Q (on the west) and R (east)—straddling the Sananda track between Musket and Kano. At this time, Sgt. Harold Poynter of Company B, known for his "lone wolf" style and deadly sniping, gathered valuable information about the position and strength of the enemy.[26] Malaria soon disabled Poynter, sending him to a Port Moresby hospital. For gallantry in action, Poynter later received the Silver Star.

By day's end on January 7, the 2nd Battalion, under Major Walter R. Rankin, had joined the advanced elements of the 163rd, guarding the Motor Transport trail south of Musket. At this time, Colonel Doe ordered the 1st Battalion to prepare to attack, thereby hoping to shrink the two enemy perimeters between Musket and Kano. If the attack succeeded, the rest of the 1st Battalion would move into the Kano area and Major Rankin's 2nd Battalion would take over around Musket.

On January 8, Company B from Musket attacked the larger enemy perimeter (Q) at dawn, while Company C from Kano and Moore assaulted the eastern Japanese perimeter (R). Although the two companies were covered by all the mortars and machine guns that the battalion could muster, neither attack succeeded. The Australian field artillery, firing obliquely from the southeast, only briefly supported the assault due to a shortage of ammunition and the difficult angle of range. Company B made a frontal approach on Perimeter Q along a creek. While B Company crossed the little stream, the enemy opened fire with six or seven machine guns. One man recalled, "it was like swimming in a swarm of bees."[27] Company B retreated, occupying positions in waste-deep water about 30 yards from the objective. Company B remained there until night, when Company E relieved them. In the early dawn hours, after some sleep and a hot meal,

Company B returned to the forward positions and Company E resumed its deployment with the 2nd Battalion along the supply trail.

Meanwhile, in the attack from Kano, Company C probed the enemy's east perimeter (R) while wading waist-deep in swamp water, swollen by the previous day's rain. The troops tried to advance under heavy fire, but the swamp was too deep and the enemy fire too intense. After losing several men, including 1st Lt. Harold R. Fisk, Company C pulled back to its original position at Kano.

At a later date when 163rd men occupied Perimeter R, they found the body of Lt. Fisk, killed while leading a platoon in the January 8 action. When recovering his body, they saw that the left arm and calves of the legs were severed. After a closer examination around the former Japanese position, they found the bones of a recently cooked left forearm; a chief surgeon of Australia's 7th Division subsequently described the remains as those of a young man less than 25 years of age. Near the bones, they also found a helmet filled with wild figs.[28]

While it was known that the Japanese were physically depleted from months of combat, and extremely short of food, medicines, and supplies, this was the first time that 163rd men saw evidence of cannibalism. Some starving Japanese had resorted to eating the flesh of Americans and Australians killed in combat. After December, the Japanese high command had been unable to adequately resupply its troops in eastern Papua by submarine or barges. During subsequent patrols, American soldiers found other bodies in a similar state, many without identification tags.[29] Later, dog tags of men who had been cannibalized were found in the pockets of dead Japanese soldiers. In Harold Fisk's honor, the 163rd renamed Kano, as Perimeter Fisk. Eventually, Lt. Fisk was posthumously granted the Silver Star for gallantry in action during the January 8, 1943, attack.[30]

On January 9, Major Rankin's 2nd Battalion pushed out from its position along the M.T. road, through Musket, and then advanced southwesterly one-half mile to the Killerton trail, with the intention of blocking it as an escape route for any Japanese moving north. As they advanced, communication wire was laid down to maintain telephone contact with headquarters. Approaching a clearing along the Killerton Trail, Rankin sent a Company G platoon to protect his left flank when moving out of the jungle. Because of this maneuver, enemy mortar and small arms fire erupted from just yards away, to the south. A portion of the battalion managed to cross the trail, but enemy machine gun fire and mortar shells prevented further advance. In the hours that followed, Capt. William C. Benson and the other Company G men occupied trench positions west of the trail.

In the meantime, the rest of the 2nd Battalion, under Capt. Paul G. Hollister, had faced northward, moving forward a couple of hundred yards under light opposition. The battalion established a perimeter on the Killerton trail almost due west of Musket. The new position was named Rankin after the battalion commander. This mission achieved its goal of effectively cutting off this

Japanese escape route north, but the battalion's advance this day cost 4 killed and 7 wounded, and other casualties occurred in following days.[31] In the meantime, the 1st Battalion continued attacking the Japanese perimeters between Musket and Kano.

The 3rd Battalion, led by Major Leonard A. Wing, reached the front lines on January 10.[32] On their arrival, the 3rd Battalion's Company K assisted the 1st Battalion's Company A in guarding the supply route on the east. Also, companies I, L, and M of the 3rd Battalion relieved Company B of the 1st Battalion at Musket.

That same day, Corporal Paul H. Knight from the Antitank Company, after reconnoitering on his volition, noted an absence of enemy activity in enemy Perimeter R just east of the Sananda track. Quickly responding, Colonel Doe ordered Lt. McKinney of Company A at Moore's Outpost to lead his 2nd platoon forward and investigate. Without firing a shot, McKinney and the platoon entered the abandoned enemy lines in the waning daylight hours. Heavy rain from the previous day had flooded the Japanese trenches and gun positions, which may have contributed to the enemy's hasty departure and redeployment. They left behind considerable equipment, including a water-cooled .50-caliber machine gun, two mortars, some hand grenades, ammunition, and a cache of rifles.[33] The enemy had either moved to other positions, or, as would become evident, were attempting to infiltrate individually or in groups through Allied lines, trying to escape to Japanese-held Salamaua and Lae, many miles northwest up the coast.

McKinney opted to keep his platoon in the abandoned Japanese positions rather than return to the company. Mindful of twilight counterattacks and nighttime harassment, the platoon formed a defensive perimeter amidst the Japanese dead. The men sat mostly submerged in the flooded positions, with only their heads, shoulders, and weapons above water, an all too common occurrence in the Papua campaign. "The Sanananda Trail was all that separated us" from the manned enemy perimeter to the west, recalled McKinney, and "the stench of abandoned dead was terrible."[34]

As morning dawned, the men buried the enemy dead and reorganized the position to accommodate the rest of Company A's arrival, less the 3rd platoon, which remained at Moore's Outpost. With their arrival, the company set up an observation post, using a lone tree stump five-feet-high and three-feet-wide, enabling them to monitor the enemy perimeter just west across the road. Several machine guns helped fortify the new position. The men stocked up on ammunition, rations, and other equipment in preparation for engaging the enemy. It was here that Lt. Fisk's defiled remains were found.

On the morning of January 12, on the far south, the newly arrived 18th Australian Brigade veterans,[35] led by Brigadier George Wooten, set out with orders to eliminate the remaining Japanese positions south of Musket and Rankin. The

163rd would execute a series of feints in the action, while the regiment's heavy weapons would provide support.

At 7:45 a.m., artillery and mortar concentrations set the stage for the assault. The Australian 2/9 moved off to the northeast, while the 163rd's Company K covered its right flank. Preceded by three light tanks, the Australian 2/12 attacked in column straight up the narrow Sananada road. The tank attack proved ill-fated. An enemy 3-inch anti-tank shell pierced the lead tank, disabling its radio. The tank commander managed to get the vehicle off the road, but could not communicate a warning to the following vehicles, which were hit when moving forward. The second tank veered uncontrollably along the road until eventually destroyed by the enemy. The third tank, though knocked out by mines and anti-tank shells, was later retrieved. Without the tanks, the Australians still managed to kill many Japanese soldiers in the fierce struggle, but gained little ground and failed to penetrate most of the enemy positions.

This day alone, the Australians lost 34 killed, 66 wounded, and 51 missing (some of whom later were recovered).[36] Japanese losses were never entirely determined, but certainly were heavy. The day's fighting appeared to be inconclusive, but in two days it became apparent that the Japanese will to resist at Sananada was faltering, largely because of the events of January 12. At this point, General Vasey ordered patrols dispatched from Musket to ascertain how far north the Japanese positions extended.

On January 13, Lt. McKinney received orders to deploy his Company A platoon in scouting the Japanese perimeter (Q) just to the west of the Sananada trail. At daybreak, the 2nd platoon moved in single-file about 50 yards until reaching a small trail. They crawled in an attempt to cross the Sananada track without being detected. Continuous rain helped muffle their movements as they moved toward the Japanese perimeter.

Crawling past an abandoned Ford sedan, which the Japanese acquired in the Philippines invasion and later brought to Papua, McKinney deployed a squad of close-interval skirmishers in two directions, while the third remained near the sedan.[37] The first squad crawled noiselessly through water 2 to 6 inches deep. "An enemy soldier came within fifteen feet of our lead squad," McKinney recalled, "brushed his teeth and disappeared back" in the Japanese positions.[38] After this close encounter, the squad crept forward another 30 feet, at which time Lt. McKinney lobbed a hand grenade at one of the Japanese bunkers, signaling the squads to attack.

Almost instantly, the enemy responded with machine gun fire, but the men continued the assault, throwing grenades and firing. Meeting furious Japanese resistance, McKinney's progress halted. The firefight continued as McKinney withdrew his men to the Ford sedan, by now riddled with bullets. From there, they returned to give their report. They provided information that soon enabled the entire company to attack and take these Japanese positions. Gathering this intelligence came with a price—four men were wounded, one fatally.

Early in the morning of the next day, January 14, a 163rd patrol discovered a sick Japanese soldier hiding in the bushes south of Musket. The prisoner was delivered to the Australians for interrogation. The enemy soldier revealed that Lt. Col. Hatsuo Tsukamoto had ordered "all able bodied Japanese to withdraw from two nights before, while the sick and wounded were to remain." The captured man further noted "that he had left with some other sick, but due to malaria and dysentery had not been able to keep up."[39] This information revealed that Japanese resistance was crumbling and they were mounting a mass withdrawal. The overall Japanese plan soon became apparent; as many troops as possible would be evacuated by in-coming motor launches sent to the Kumusi and Mambare rivers, 20 to 50 miles to the northwest. They were then to be taken to Salamaua and Lae, farther up the New Guinea coast.

This information altered General Vasey's hold-and-strangle tactics, and instead a full assault was quickly ordered. Vassey sent the 18th Brigade and 7th Cavalry Regiment against the Japanese positions at the south, while all available units of the 163rd were ordered to block the enemy's escape to the north. The Australians set out on the attack.

Meanwhile, the 163rd's Company A, led by Lt. John Boid, minus the 3rd platoon, attacked the enemy position (Perimeter Q) just west of the Sananda road. The 2nd platoon, commanded by Lt. Frank T. Nugent, who had McKinney's scouting intelligence, led the assault, followed by the 1st platoon under Lt. Houston.[40] Striking due west, Houston's platoon broke through the first line of bunkers while taking heavy fire from deep inside the perimeter. After occupying these enemy positions, they held their ground until companies B and C reinforced them. Company B had orders to take positions on the west, which completed a stranglehold around the enemy.

Sgt. Paul Ziegle of Company A and another rifleman assaulted a Japanese bunker containing a .50 caliber machine gun. Ziegle reached the bunker, fired into the machine gun nest, and killed three men. (Sgt. Ziegle earned the Distinguished Service Cross for this action.)[41]

Using hand grenades, rifles, and automatic weapons, the 163rd continued to attack enemy bunkers, taking them one by one. In two days, they cleared and secured Perimeter Q. Because the fighting was contained in close proximity, Sgt. Gonzales and Lt. McKinney of Company A carefully monitored the perimeter to prevent companies A and B from miscommunicating and firing at one another. Shortly, they received word that the 3rd Battalion's companies I, K and L would relieve them late in the afternoon.

The combined attacks were successful. All of the objectives were being taken south of Musket, as men from Australian and American units linked up and shook hands.

On January 15, General Vasey arrived at Musket where he met with Colonel Doe and laid out the second stage of the assault, which became known as the "Victory Phase."[42] Vasey ordered his 18th Brigade to move up on the west along the Killerton trail and through the 163rd's 2nd Battalion at Perimeter Rankin and on toward the coast, and then sweep east (see Sananada Front, Last Phase map). Meanwhile, the 127th Infantry Regiment of the 32nd Division, situated to the northeast, would move west along the shoreline. Vasey also was sending the 163rd's 2nd Battalion from the Perimeter Fisk area to wipe out Japanese perimeters along the road bend north on the Sananada road.[43] These movements were expected to complete the envelopment of the Japanese. Allied reserve troops would mop up any disorganized enemy elements to the south.

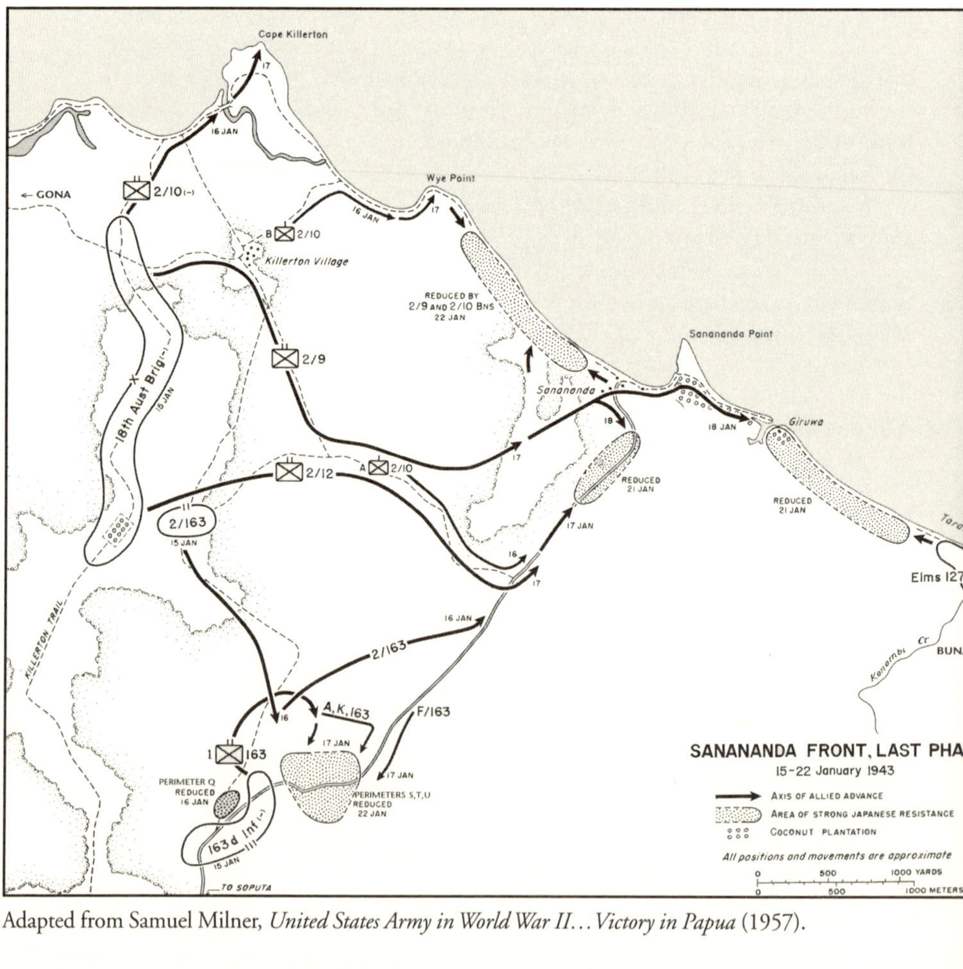

Adapted from Samuel Milner, *United States Army in World War II... Victory in Papua* (1957).

Based on intelligence from several Japanese prisoners, the 163rd knew the approximate strength and armaments of the remaining enemy forces they confronted to the north. According to Sgt. James Eder of Company B, the positions were "heavily defended...yet despite the strength of their perimeters, the Jap garrison was starving."[44] On the Killerton trail, companies E and G moved out of Rankin. Aided by 18th Brigade and 2nd Battalion mortars, the units led by Major Rankin reduced three enemy perimeters on the southern flank. At least 100 Japanese died in the assault, many of them having been escapees from the track junction.

The fluid, altering combat situation was keeping the headquarters' intelligence officers busy in designating the combatants' intricate array of blue and red positional marks being recorded on regimental maps. The officers discussed plans for attacking the Japanese perimeters northeast of Fisk, identified as S, T, U, and V, which formed a 375-yard semi-circle on the Sanananda road.[45] During the meeting, the 1st Battalion's Lt. Col. Harold Lindstrom ordered platoon leader Lt. McKinney to take over command of Company A. Companies A, B, and C were directed to jointly encircle Perimeter S north of Fisk, requiring a frontal attack by Company A across 200 yards of open terrain. The 1st Battalion's mortars and machine guns would provide covering fire. Company A would move on the right and Company C on the left, with Company B in reserve.

Meanwhile, the 2nd Battalion would advance from a coconut plantation on a branch of the Killerton trail and then swing east, severing the Sanananda trail between Perimeter S and the Sanananda Point beaches, cutting off the Japanese escape routes to the north. The 3rd Battalion would follow, mopping up Perimeter Q, and serve as the regimental reserve.[46]

As dawn broke on January 16, the 1st Battalion men prepared for the assault. Reconnaissance from the night before indicated that tall Kunai grasses would provide the best cover for the attack. Unsure of the enemy's numbers or precise location, McKinney decided to advance Company A on a wide front, hoping to find a weak spot that would allow the entire company to gain jungle cover. Companies A and C moved forward under the protection of light machine gunners, who, until they ran out of ammunition, raked the treetops for snipers and kept the enemy pinned down in their positions.

"The Japs being crafty and not asleep, had set up a light and heavy machine gun that laid down a very effective crossfire," a member of Company A recalled. "They let us get practically into their perimeter past these two machine gun nests, and then their experience in jungle fighting came to the fore," he continued. "Instead of just raking the field with machine gun and sniper fire, they concentrated on shooting at the base of the grass that was moving."[47]

During the advance, a mortar round landed behind McKinney, wounding his runner and severing the communications wire, impairing McKinney's ability to communicate with Company C for over an hour.[48] Company A had advanced to within 50 yards of the enemy emplacements before the supporting fire stopped, forcing the men to lie silently, waiting for Company C to advance on the left. To avoid drawing machine gun fire, the Company A men laid low in the grass. "It was miserable hot," McKinney explained. "This was one of the few Guinea days without cloudy skies and rain…[The] sun nearly scorched our hands on our rifles…men passed out from the heat."[49] The soldiers dug shallow depressions, seeking cooling water.

Meanwhile, Colonel Lindstrom learned that McKinney's Company A was pinned down, too close in for mortar support, and too spent to continue the attack. Lindstrom then maneuvered Company C into a position in advance of Company A, and ordered Company C and most of reserve Company B to engage the enemy's flank. The encirclement of the enemy was complete, but the line of Japanese bunkers was too strong to be taken that day.

Colonel Lindstrom had the men dig in and establish Perimeter AD, strategically centered approximately 400 yards west of the Sananada road. From its new positions, the 1st Battalion could destroy any enemy troops that tried to flee north toward the coastline. Augmented by Major Rankin's 2nd Battalion from the Killerton trail, the 163rd would now be able to effectively fight against perimeters S, T, and U.[50]

When communications were restored, McKinney learned that companies C and B had bypassed his position. Meanwhile, Lindstrom sent a Company B platoon to reinforce McKinney's Company A, but it too was immediately pinned down. In response, Lindstrom ordered the withdrawal of A Company and the B Company platoon. The troops crawled back into the protection of the jungle, where a guide sent by Colonel Lindstrom was waiting to lead them over to the new perimeter.

Also during this period, the Australian 18th Brigade had advanced north along the Killerton Trail, while the 163rd's 2nd Battalion was heading east through the "Coconut Garden." In the meantime, the 3rd Battalion continued its role in reducing Japanese pockets remaining between Musket and Fisk, and supported the rest of the 163rd's attack with its heavy weapons.

As the 2nd Battalion proceeded down the Killerton road, "our Company and that of G were to cut our way through the jungle traveling parallel to one another," explained Company F's Robert F. Marlow. "At a prescribed time we were to reach the Japanese perimeter and deliver the joint attack with the First Battalion."[51]

After a meal and short rest, the troops moved easterly and cut the Sananada trail about 1,000 yards from enemy lines. The rapid execution of their orders earned the 2nd Battalion the title of "Rankin's Racers." They had cut two tracks through 1,400 yards of terrain to reach the Sananada trail.[52] In that day the "racers" sped northerly along the road, cleared its west side of enemy forces, made contact with the Australians in forward positions nearer the coast, then turned and cleared a large area to the east. Their rapid pace would enable them to join with Australian infantry units in the capture of the vital Sananda Point locality.

As they had made their way through the dense jungle and swamps, however, several men became separated from their platoons. Major Rankin, in an attempt to regroup, ordered his troops to establish a temporary perimeter, allowing them to gather up those who had become separated.

In continuing the advance, an ambush of Company F's scouting party forced Company G to take the lead. While patrolling a side trail, they discovered a clearing with native huts and soon realized they were approaching a Japanese hospital area, but also quickly learned that armed and able enemy soldiers were hiding among the patients and corpses. When the Americans approached, they met enemy fire from the huts, including machine gun bursts coming from the rafters. Enemy mortars were firing from the cemetery, and rifle fire came from trenches.

"Tokyo Rose" was a name given by U.S. troops to several female propagandists employed by the Japanese government on their Zero Hour radio program. The soldiers enjoyed the American music played in the broadcasts from Tokyo. During the Sanananda campaign, the men of the 163rd were called "Bloody Butchers," the only American regiment in the Pacific to be singled out for this personal invective in the Tokyo Rose broadcasts. Throughout the remainder of the war, Radio Tokyo referred to the regiment as "The Butchers." Three times Tokyo Rose announced that the 41st Division had been wiped out—the last on the eve of the attack at Biak in 1944.

Company F's Sgt. Marlow offered this account: "We started down the trail and after going approximately 200 yards we came up on a group of native huts, the stench of dead bodies was terrific and we came to the conclusion we were entering a Japanese hospital...they lay side by side as many as 12 in a row having died of wounds and sickness."[53]

It was then that the Japanese opened fire. The men had no choice but to deal methodically with this situation. They shot each body, dead or alive, in the huts. It was at the "hospital lot" that the 163rd earned the nickname, "the Bloody Butchers of Sanananda," on Tokyo radio after word of this event reached Japan. Tokyo Rose warned in a broadcast, "Butchers of Sanananda, you will never leave New Guinea."[54]

During its movements of January 15–16, elements of the 2nd Battalion had rendezvoused with the 1st Battalion. The 2nd Battalion's Company H had remained back at the Coconut Garden to guard the trails junction, while

Companies F and G, led by Rankin, renewed the attack. Major Rankin distinguished himself by reconnoitering an area ahead of his troops, where he personally directed mortar and artillery fire from an exposed position within a few yards of the enemy.[55] (Walter Rankin, of Bozeman, later received the Distinguished Service Cross.) These combined efforts completely broke the enemy's resistance. For a mile north of its junction with the Soputa-Sananada road, the Allies were holding the Killerton trail.

The 3rd Battalion had accomplished its mopping up missions as well and by mid-afternoon on January 16, companies K and L succeeded in completely cleaning out Perimeter Q, thereby eliminating all enemy resistance along the Sanananda Trail from Soputa to Fisk. They also worked on improving the route, enabling vehicles to bring up supplies and evacuate the wounded.

The exact strength and location of the enemy's defenses still remained unclear. Accordingly, on the evening of January 16, Company B's Sgt. Eder was ordered to conduct a reconnaissance southward from Perimeter AD. Eder's three-man patrol located the enemy's Perimeter S, which had turned back Company A on the previous day. Not learning any more useful information from the reconnaissance, Company B quietly dug in 100 yards from the Japanese bunkers.

On January 17, Capt. Robert Hamilton of Company B, in conjunction with Company C, gave the order to attack the enemy positions S, T, and U. Moving forward cautiously, Lt. Mackenzie scouted the bushes and discovered a half-dozen enemy bunkers on the far bank of a chest deep, five-yard-wide, stream. When Company B's 2nd platoon pushed forward, the Japanese opened fire. Two point men crossed the stream, throwing hand grenades and firing Thompson submachine guns to clear the way for the rest of the 2nd platoon. The 1st platoon closed up behind in the center of the line, while drawing machine gun fire. However, the forward scouts reported back that they could find no way to flank the enemy positions. "Two lines of Jap bunkers stretched as far as they could see," recalled a member of Company B. Consequently, Captain "Hamilton thought it was time to dig in for the night."[56]

Company B established a diamond-shaped defense perimeter near the first line of Japanese pillboxes. "We spent the night in rain filled trenches and foxholes, amid the gagging stench of decaying Japanese bodies," one soldier remembered. And, "to top it off, it started raining, and maggots from the dead, floated into our trenches…there was no escape from them."[57]

In the same attack on January 17, company C also had received orders to reduce Perimeter S. The plan of attack had called for Company B, as described above, to drive ahead and clear the enemy bunkers, while Company C would attack straight ahead on the left. Capt. Jack Van Duyn of Company C and Capt. Hamilton of Company B had linked four rifle platoons and the 60 mm mortar squads into a telephone party line to their dual command post. This allowed them to receive reports about breaks in the Japanese perimeter, as well as to coordinate their advances. The system also permitted one commander to monitor the phone lines, while the other fought at the front line with his unit.[58]

Staff Sgt. John L. Mohl and Corporal Wilbur H. Rummel led Company C's assault.[59] They crossed the creek, knocked out six bunkers in quick succession, and created a hole in Perimeter S for Company C to pass through. (For these outstanding acts of bravery, both Sgt. Mohl and Corporal Rummel received the Distinguished Service Cross.)

At this time, the Company B men were moving out as well (as described above), crossing the creek and knocking out one of the bunkers only to find themselves up against other bunkers. Throughout the day, B and C companies worked in concert trying to breech the enemy lines. "Just as our attack seemed to pierce the perimeter, the Japs left their broken first and second lines," Sgt. Eder explained, and "they formed a new line, some 30 yards back and held us as dusk began to fall."[60] The two weary companies went into a defensive position, waiting for another try at the enemy position in the morning.

Meanwhile, companies A and K also had moved out the morning of January 17, planning to envelop the enemy position on the M.T. road. While trying to reach the road, they ran into a Japanese strong point in a bend about 250 yards behind Perimeter S, which halted their advance.

Company F, operating east of the trail, also met heavy opposition during the morning confrontation. They encountered a double line of log and dirt bunkers dispersed over a large area. It became necessary to use 81 mm mortars, and with the help of Australian artillery, a barrage was laid down lasting over 30 minutes. According to Company F's Robert Marlow, "smoke and dust filled the air and to me it seemed the half hour would never end. It seemed impossible that any human could ever survive what I would call 'an inferno of hell' but that's what we were to find out later."[61]

Log bunkers were destroyed and many Japanese killed, but Company F, after advancing 150 yards past the bunker line, found itself wedged between two shoulder-deep streams with Japanese machine gunners to the front and right flank. The men succeeded in taking out one of the machine gun nests in the encounter, but not the second. As the daylight hours faded and ammunition dwindled, Major Rankin dispatched Company E to relieve Company F. It would take two days of continuous shelling and repeated assaults to force the Japanese to abandon this perimeter. This local engagement drew to a close. Marlow later noted that what "ended now was just another victory over the enemy…[and] a dark future in this war lay ahead…what price we had to pay."[62]

On January 19, Companies B and C resumed their attack on Perimeter S. They assaulted the position straight on, while Company I moved against the southern end of Perimeter U. Preceding the assault, Australian 25 pounders fired 250 shells, while 750 rounds were launched from 81 mm mortars at Musket. Company M lent machine gun support from Perimeter Fisk, sweeping the

Porters carrying equipment alongside a motor track. The bridge probably was intentionally constructed just below the river surface to prevent detection by attacking aircraft. The levels of Papuan streams, however, fluctuated wildly depending on rainfall in the mountains and lowlands. *MMHM*

trees and ground for snipers. As Company I began its assault against the enemy bunkers, an errant mortar shell from Fisk landed amidst the company and killed Capt. Dupree and Sgt. James W. Boland. This loss of leadership due to friendly fire caused the platoons to falter, giving the enemy just enough time to exit the bunkers and get into firing positions, thereby repulsing the attack.

The next day, January 20, while companies B and C continued their assault on Perimeter S, companies A and K advanced along a trail near the northwest side of Perimeter T while supported by heavy machine guns on their right flank and by light machine guns out front. The attack proceeded smoothly with the men breaking into the Japanese defenses and fanning out inside. Their deadly fire killed a number of Japanese soldiers and confined others to their bunkers, until men could get close enough to throw hand grenades inside. The Japanese were shot whenever they emerged. Other Japanese retreated and attempted to regroup. As the daylight hours waned, a wounded Japanese soldier crawled out from the brush and surrendered—interrogators learned that the companies were approaching the Japanese headquarters.

In an assault directed against Perimeter T on the morning of January 21, companies A and K struck hard, with a perfectly timed concentration of artillery, mortar, and machine-gun fire. They breached the perimeter defenses and fanned out. This softened the enemy resistance to companies B and C as well. Together, the four companies advanced south along the M.T. road, taking perimeters S and T. Australian field artillery laid down a 15-minute barrage, followed by a series of 81 mm mortar barrages from an American unit. Unfortunately, some of the projectiles rained down on Company B, instead of the Japanese. "Some of us were buried by earth," recalled Sgt. Eder, but "we dug out our B men with no casualties."[63]

Company C withdrew, while 1st Battalion headquarters ordered Company B to remain in place. Another barrage of field artillery was requested, this time finding its intended target—the Japanese perimeter. Several enemy soldiers died instantly, while others were confined to their bunkers. Infantrymen from all the companies stormed into the area, lobbing grenades into the trenches, killing scores of enemy soldiers. After the attack, 525 Japanese dead were counted.[64] The 1st Battalion had overran perimeters S and T, while Company B cut off all escape routes. Perimeter U, however, remained intact across the Sanananda road.

Meanwhile, Company B's ranks had dwindled to 30 men, not nearly enough to storm Perimeter U. "Our phone had gone dead," Eder recalled. Without communications, "B grimly sat in our defensive position from 21 Jan. through 25 Jan."[65]

During the night of January 21, Company K came under attack as Japanese machine-gun fire rained down from the trees, followed by a fixed-bayonet assault by 70 enemy soldiers. Company K succeeded in fending off the attack with mortars, followed by a counter-attack. The return assault cut down Japanese soldiers as they fled from their shelters followed by machine gun fire. Meanwhile, Lt. McKinney with 13 men from Company A had set out to determine the strength of the remaining enemy forces. They found little resistance—the mortars launched the night before had been extremely accurate. Perimeter S had been liquidated.

On January 22, the 3rd Battalion's companies I and L attacked Perimeter U, east of the Sanananda trail, from the south. The infantry movement with supporting fire was well coordinated, as the troops moved in with a last mortar salvo. Resistance was weak and by noon the position was overrun. The mop-up was done with the aid of Company E, which had occupied the northeast end of the perimeter, supporting the attack with machine gun fire. The enemy fought desperately, but it was apparent the end was near. All organized resistance on the M.T. road had been broken, and, by evening, mopping up on both sides of the trail was complete.

Meanwhile, on the north end of the Sanananda trail, the Australian 18th Brigade and the U.S. 127th Infantry had encountered little resistance. With enemy perimeters along the coast also cleared, the battle of Sanananda was essentially over.

The 2nd and 3rd battalions spent January 23 mopping up between the 1st Battalion and Fisk. They encountered small arms fire, mostly from snipers. The 163rd men responded with heavy machine guns. Patrols entered pillboxes that had tunnels leading to dugouts some distance away. Some enemy soldiers were hiding underground and fought tenaciously, sometimes finally killing themselves with pistols or grenades rather than surrendering.

With the primary combat objectives achieved, the regiment now turned to other tasks. Some units buried the enemy dead, while others improved the M.T. road to facilitate the trucking of supplies from the Popondetta and Dobodura airstrips.

Meanwhile, Capt. William Benson's Company G received orders to patrol east of the 1st Battalion's bivouac. During this patrol, they captured two Japanese soldiers, whom they delivered for questioning at an Australian holding area. During the interrogation, the prisoners revealed that 200 Japanese soldiers had been hiding in the Kunai grass 700 yards south of where they had been captured. The others had scattered with the appearance of the patrol.[66]

Company G, along with other troops, also was ordered to patrol the mouth of the Kumusi River, located some 20 miles off to the west, to prevent the enemy's escape by sea. The combined force moved up the beach by land or barges in hot pursuit of the remaining enemy soldiers fleeing the Sanananda area. Company G soon engaged them, fighting a tenacious running battle to the Kumusi River. Few prisoners were taken, primarily because the Japanese refused to be seized. Some demanded to be shot rather than face the dishonor of capture.

Meanwhile, for three days Sgt. James Eder's Company B had sat without food or communication, waiting for orders. Finally, as Eder explained, "tired of sitting around doing nothing, a runner was sent back to our company command post." When he returned, "and informed us that we were all finished fighting, that the enemy had been exterminated...we would have surely made an interesting picture, sitting there staring at one another...there was no wild cheering, as

Hollywood would have it, just a group of tired, bewildered men, each in his own way giving thanks to his maker for victory"[67]

In the days that followed, Company B passed the time hunting for souvenirs, mainly Japanese firearms, money, and officers' swords. Sgt. Eder, as the senior NCO in Company B, received orders to march the men back in a "victory parade" to Soputa. Company B had suffered exceptionally high casualties—of its original 71 men, 25 were killed and 28 wounded or debilitated, leaving only 18 to march to Soputa. When passing the Musket graveyard, where Australian and American soldiers were buried, Eder said "most of us feared to look aside."[68]

While they were marching in formation, a jeep pulled up, mounted with a two-star general's flag. Company B came to attention, saluting General Horace H. Fuller, the 41st Division commander. As the men continued past the jeep, one of the general's staff remarked, "General, there goes what remains of one company—the raggedest, stinkingest, and fightingest outfit in the 163rd—Company B."[69]

Colonel Doe had remained at the front lines during the last days of the Sananda fight, directing the 163rd's final assaults on January 21 and 22. For outstanding leadership, he would be promoted to Brigadier General and appointed as assistant division commander. (Doe also earned the Distinguished Service Cross.)

On Sunday, January 23, Major Leonard Wing and the 3rd Battalion proceeded on the Jumbora road, with orders to relieve the Australian 14th Brigade and establish a defensive perimeter near the beach. They headed west for Gona Mission and the nearby Gona track a few miles from the beach. Arriving in the evening, they were greeted by the Australians and crowds of Papuan villagers.

Two platoons from Company K took up defensive positions at Gona. Another had stayed back at Jumbora, where supplies were transported by motor vehicles from Soputa. Pvt. Don Rohig described the devastation they observed:

> Gona Mission is merely a large white cross and a few fire-charred uprights today. Bomb craters of immense proportions abound. Some remnants of thatched huts are left, a few complete except that they have collapsed inwardly upon themselves from concussion. The hull of a big Japanese freighter, the seaward side torn and gutted, leans crazily askew far out in Honicote Bay. The coconut palms along the beach are scorched, blackened, and denuded of foliage, standing like skeletons of sentries watching the sea towards Rabaul for the Invader.
>
> Airplane wreckage is strewn chaotically, the metal and fuselage twisted and fused and broken. Japanese equipment and bones litter the black, volcanic sand of the waterfront...The corpses had been buried on the edge of the sand, and the tropical combers which worry the Gona sands daily encroach upon the fresh graves.[70]

In the days that followed, the 3rd Battalion dispatched daily reconnaissance patrols, seeking trails and jungle hiding-places where the enemy might be lurking.

Meanwhile, Company A was assigned guard duty at the vital Amboga River crossing just west of Gona, in relief of Australian 18th Brigade soldiers. Under Lt. Frank T. Nugent's command, Company A was transported to the site in three captured Japanese trucks. Upon arriving, they sought concealment for their perimeter.

"Finally a spot was decided upon and we started to unload men and equipment," a Company A man reported. "Then all Hell broke loose and was over quicker than we can tell it; five Japs, apparently lost from their main body, were in hiding at the base of an immense stump."[71] One of them threw a grenade at the Company A men, but it ricocheted off a tree limb, bounced back, and exploded among the Japanese, killing them. Company A suffered no losses in the exchange and buried the five enemy soldiers where they lay.

Patrols were conducted twice a week, including 25-mile-long operations to Sangara Mission, and 12-mile patrols to the Jumbora. These each took two days. They confronted enemy snipers and a few remaining stragglers. Company A remained at Amboga until mid March, and then boarded small riverboats taking them to a base at Oro Bay, located southeast down the coast.

The 163rd had performed with determination during the Sananandaoperation. In recognition, Colonel Doe commended "the officers and men of the 163rd Infantry Combat Team for the fine planning, organization and individual excellence in execution of the successful operations of January 16, 1943, against the strongest point of the Japanese main defenses between Soputa and Sananda Point, New Guinea."[72]

A similar message came from I Corps commander Lt. Gen. Eichelberger. "As Commanding General of the Advance New Guinea Forces may I extend my heartiest congratulations and deep gratitude for the part each of you has played in inflicting upon the Japanese the…defeat they have suffered." Eichelberger gave further praise: "Realizing the difficulties and almost insurmountable obstacles which faced you in the accomplishment of your mission it was with a great deal of pride that I reported to the Commander in Chief the important contribution of your Regiment to our momentous victory."[73]

The 41st Division's commanding officer, General Fuller, likewise extended his compliments. "I wish to congratulate the Division for its soldierly manner and excellent conduct of operations."[74]

The Montana State Legislature wired its compliments to the regiment. "With vibrant admiration for your magnificent victory over the Japanese on the Papuan Peninsula of New Guinea and elsewhere[,] with prayers for the wounded and with undying resolve to carry on the high purpose of our noble dead[,] the hearts of the people of Montana are with you beating as one every hour of every day."[75]

The 163rd's nearly month-long fight was costly, with 85 men killed in action (KIA), 12 dying of wounds (DOW), 4 missing, and 238 wounded in action (WIA).[76]

American Combat Casualties, Less the Missing[77]

41st Division—			
163rd RCT	85 KIA	12 DOW	238 WIA
32nd Division—			
126th RCT	266 KIA	34 DOW	728 WIA
127th RCT	182 KIA	29 DOW	506 WIA
128th RCT	138 KIA	25 DOW	434 WIA
Div. Attach.	16 KIA	0 DOW	14 WIA*

* Not included in these statistics for the 15,000 Americans participating in the campaign were the thousands hospitalized due to combat fatigue, heat prostration, operational non-combat injuries, and especially tropical diseases and infections.

In the six-month campaign, the more numerous Australian units suffered about twice as many casualties as the four American regiments. Combat, disease, and suicides, of course, took a vast toll of Japanese lives. Relatively few enemy soldiers were captured, while a limited number escaped to the northwest.

The Sananda effort showed that the 163rd's extensive training at Camp Murray and Fort Lewis, in the Hunter-Ligget war games, and at the Australian camps, paid off. Of course, the men could not have been completely prepared for the reality of jungle warfare. Only actual combat could do that. "At its best a slit-trench is a unromantic and despicable place," McKinney noted, "but at times not even a white cottage with green shutters and a rolling lawn would feel as comfortable as those holes, when enemy lead came pouring your way."[78]

McKinney also noted: "Even with death all around the men still retained a sense of humor, which kept them going when their bodies told them to stop."[79] The men of the 163rd now were experienced, hardened, and savvy. The Montana regiment had carved out its own piece of history, playing an important role in one of the earliest land combat victories against the Japanese in World War II.

Notes

1. "History of the 41st - 63rd Infantry (Company B) 9-16-40 thru 1945, Wadke 5-18-44, Ibdi Ridge," 17, Entry 427, Folder 341-INF (163), Box 10633, Office of the Adjutant

General, Records of the Adjutant General's Office 1917-, Record Group 407, National Archives II.

2. Lida Mayo, *Bloody Buna* (New York: Doubleday, 1974), 26.
3. William H. Riker, *Soldiers of the States: The Role of the National Guard in American Democracy,* (Washington, D.C.: Public Affairs Press, 1957), 84–85.
4. At the time, the Allies were engaged in something of a "poor man's war" in the Pacific, with most resources being funneled into the European theater. Samuel Milner, *United States Army in World War II: The War in the Pacific: Victory in Papua*, vol. 7 (Washington, D.C.: Center of Military History, United States Army, 2003), 92.
5. Howard Apter, "MacArthur's Jungleers, Without the Glory They Deserved, the Men of the Sunset Division Destroyed the Japs in the Caves and Jungles of New Guinea," *Saga: The Magazine for Men* (September 1962), 27–29.
6. Mayo, *Bloody Buna*, 113.
7. In the Sananananda area, Japanese outer perimeters often had a depth of 15 yards or less. "Notes on Jungle Warfare No. 1," author unknown, "41st Division, 163rd Infantry, History of the Unit, 14 December 42–20 July 43," Entry 427, Folder 341-Inf (163) -0.3, Box 10634, World War II Operations Reports 1940–48, Record Group 407, National Archives II.
8. Mayo, *Bloody Buna*, 124.
9. "Outline for Defense," notes taken by Colonel Doe, "41st Division, 163rd Infantry, History of the Unit, 14 December 42–20 July 43," Entry 427, Folder 341-Inf (163) -0.3 Operations Reports, Box 10634 World War II Operations Reports 1940–49, Record Group 407, National Archives II.
10. "Diary of Stanley C. 'Black Bart' Davison, December 27, 1942 to June 28, 1943," 1, random articles, History of the 163rd Infantry, Box 67, RBC, Montana Military History Museum, Library Archives, Fort William Henry Harrison, Helena, Montana [hereafter cited as MMHM].
11. Untitled manuscript, 3, Montana National Guard, History of the 163rd during World War II, Drawer 3, MMHM.
12. Howard A. McKinney, "History of the 163rd," 75, MMHM.
13. Ibid., 74.
14. "History of the 41st - 163rd Infantry (Company B) 9-16-40 thru 1945, Wadke 5-18-44, Ibdi Ridge," 13, Entry 427, Folder 341-INF (163), Box 10633, World War II Operations Reports 1940–48, Record Group 407, National Archives II.
15. "41st Division, 163rd Infantry, History of the Unit, 14 December 42–20 July 43," 2, Entry 427, Folder 341-Inf (163) -0.3 Operations Reports, Box 10634, World War II Operations Reports 1940–48, Record Group 407, National Archives II.
16. "Headquarters, Company 'A' 163rd Infantry, Office of the Company Commander," 11, Entry 427, Folder 341-INF (163), World War II Operations Reports 1940–45, Box 10633, World War II Operations, Record Group 407, National Archives II.
17. McKinney, "History of the 163rd," 75, MMHM.
18. "Diary of Stanley C. 'Black Bart' Davison," 3, MMHM.
19. Ibid., 3.
20. Ronald H. Spector, *Eagle Against the Sun: The American War with Japan,* (New York: Vintage, 1985), 228–29.
21. "History of the 41st - 163rd Infantry (Company B) 9-16-40 thru 1945, Wadke 5-18-44, Ibdi Ridge," 14, Entry 427, Folder 341-INF (163), Box 10633, World War II Operations Reports 1940–48, Record Group 407, National Archives II.

22. Howard A. McKinney, "With 'A' Company, 163rd Infantry at Sananada, New Guinea," 4, MMHM. This 22-page typed manuscript details combat activity at Sananada.
23. Ibid., 4–5.
24. William F. Boni, "Falls Youth and other Montanans within 50 Yards of Japanese Outpost in New Guinea," 1, newspaper clipping, January 10, 1943, random clippings and articles, shelf #52, MMHM.
25. I.C.B. Dear, *The Oxford Companion to World War II,* ed. by M.R.D. Foot (Oxford: Oxford University Press, 1995), 760.
26. "History of the 41st - 163rd Infantry (Company B) 9-16-40 thru 1945, Wadke 5-18-44, Ibdi Ridge," 15, Entry 427, Folder 341-INF (163), Box 10633, World War II Operations Reports 1940–48, Record Group 407, National Archives II.
27. Ibid., 16.
28. "41st Division, 163rd Infantry, History of the Unit, 14 December 42–20 July 43," 6, Entry 427, Folder 341-Inf (163) -0.3 Operations Reports, Box 10634, World War II Operations Reports 1940–48, Record Group 407, National Archives II.
29. Ibid.
30. General Orders No. 5, "Citations, Posthumous, for Gallantry in Action," February 7, 1943, signed by Capt. James P. Cassidy, Assistant Adjutant General; LTC Ray Read office, uncategorized boxes of Hargis Westerfield materials, Box 1 of 4, MMHM.
31. Milner, *United States Army in World War II... Victory in Papua*, 342.
32. "41st Division, 163rd Infantry, History of the Unit, 14 December 42–20 July 43," 7, Entry 427, Folder 341-Inf (163) -0.3 Operations Reports, Box 10634, World War II Operations Reports 1940–48, Record Group 407, National Archives II.
33. Milner, *United States Army in World War II... Victory in Papua,* 343.
34. McKinney, "With 'A' Company, 163rd Infantry at Sananada New Guinea," 6–7, MMHM.
35. An Australian brigade was roughly the size of an American regiment. Untitled manuscript, 8–9, Montana National Guard History of the 163rd during World War II, Drawer 3, MMHM.
36. Milner, *United States Army in World War II... Victory in Papua,* 345.
37. McKinney, "With 'A' Company, 163rd Infantry at Sananada New Guinea," 7, MMHM.
38. Ibid.
39. "41st Division, 163rd Infantry History of the Unit, 14 December 42–20 July 43," 8, Entry 427, Folder 341-Inf (163) -0.3 Operations Reports, Box 10634, World War II Operations Reports 1940–48, Record Group 407, National Archives II.
40. McKinney, "With 'A' Company, 163rd Infantry at Sananada New Guinea," 7, MMHM.
41. Ibid., 8.
42. Dr. Hargis Westerfield, Col. Robert M. Hamilton, and Sgt. James J. Eder, "B Co. Infantry: Sananada: The Victory Phase," *Jungleer* (June 1974) 10–11
43. Ibid., (December 1973) 10–11.
44. Ibid., (June 1974) 10–11.
45. Dr. Hargis Westerfield, *Montana in the Wars,* ed. by Chester K. Shore (Miles City, Montana: Star Print, 1977), 120.
46. McKinney, "With 'A' Company, 163 Infantry at Sananada New Guinea," 9, MMHM.
47. "Headquarters, Company 'A' 163rd Infantry, Office of the Company Commander," Entry 427, Folder 341-INF (163), World War II Operations Reports 1940–45, 10633, World War II Operations, Record Group 407, National Archives II.

48. An interesting note in Captain Davison's diary explains that, while on reconnaissance in the jungle, Davison and another man from Company C discovered a trail with U.S. communications wires along it. They thought the Japanese might be using the wire in some way to monitor the 163rd's communications. Davison decided to cut the wires and see who came to repair it. Corporal Seeger returned with information that they were 2nd Battalion wires. Davison quickly had the wires repaired and left the area. In his diary, McKinney questions how the outcome that day may have differed were it not for the communications breakdown. "Diary of Stanley C. 'Black Bart' Davison," 9–10, MMHM.
49. Col. Howard McKinney and Dr. Hargis Westerfield, "A Co. 163rd INF in fighting Japanese Perimeters at Sanananda," 5, MMHM.
50. Westerfield, Hamilton, and Eder, "B Co. Infantry: Sanananda: The Victory Phase," *Jungleer* (June 1974) 10–11.
51. Sgt. Robert F. Marlow of Company F wrote an operations summary for the company: "WWII, The Battle for Sanananda Point: A History of Co. F, 41st Infantry Division," 2–3, History of the 163rd during World War II, random articles, RBC box #67, MMHM.
52. Richard H. Lacey, *The Montana Militia: A History of Montana's Volunteer Forces, 1867–1976* (Dillon, Montana: Dillon Tribune-Examiner Press, 1976), 71.
53. Robert F. Marlow, "WWII, The Battle for Sanananda Point: A History of Co. F, 41st Infantry Division," 4, History of the 163rd during World War II, random articles, RBC box #67, MMHM.
54. "History 41st Division, 341-0, Jan 43…1945," Entry 427, Folder 341-0.1," Box 10526, World War II Operations Reports 1940–48, Record Group 407, National Archives II. See also, Dear, *The Oxford Companion to World War II*, 1119.
55. Untitled manuscript, 11, Montana National Guard, History of the 163rd during World War II, Drawer 3, MMHM.
56. Westerfield, Hamilton, and Eder, "B Co. Infantry: Sanananda: The Victory Phase," *Jungleer* (June 1974) 10–11.
57. "41st Division, 163rd Infantry History of the Unit, 14 December 42–20 July 43," 16, Entry 427, Folder 341-Inf (163) –0.3 Operations Reports, Box 10634, World War II Operations Reports 1940–48, Record Group 407, National Archives II.
58. Untitled manuscript, 16, Montana National Guard, History of the 163rd during World War II, Drawer 3, MMHM.
59. Westerfield, Hamilton, and Eder, "B Co. Infantry: Sanananda: The Victory Phase," *Jungleer* (June 1974) 10–11.
60. Ibid.
61. Marlow, "WWII, The Battle for Sanananda Point: A History of Co. F, 41st Infantry Division," 8, MMHM.
62. Ibid.
63. Westerfield, Hamilton, and Eder, "B Co. Infantry: Sanananda: The Victory Phase," *Jungleer* (June 1974) 10–11.
64. "41st Division, 163rd Infantry History of the Unit, 14 December 42–20 July 43," Entry 427, Folder 341-Inf (163) -0.3 Operations Reports, Box 10634, World War II Operations Reports 1940–48, Record Group 407, National Archives II.
65. Westerfield, Hamilton, and Eder, "B Co. Infantry: Sanananda: The Victory Phase," *Jungleer* (June 1974) 10–11.
66. McKinney, "History of the 163rd," 94, MMHM.
67. "History of the 41st - 63rd Infantry (Company B) 9-16-40 thru 1945, Wadke 5-18-44, Ibdi Ridge," 17, Entry 427, Folder 341-INF (163), Box 10633, Office of the Adjutant

General, Records of the Adjutant General's Office 1917-, Record Group 407, National Archives II.

68. Westerfield, Hamilton, and Eder, "B Co. Infantry: Sananda: The Victory Phase," *Jungleer* (June 1974) 11.
69. Ibid.
70. McKinney, "History of the 163rd," 158, MMHM.
71. "Headquarters, Company 'A' 163rd Infantry, Office of the Company Commander," 17, MMHM.
72. General Order No 7, Headquarters One Sixty Third Infantry Office of the Regimental Commander, 17 June 1943, Jens A. Doe, Colonel, Infantry Commanding Musket CT. "41st Division, 163rd Infantry History of the Unit, 14 December 42–20 July 43," Entry 427, Folder 341-Inf (163) -0.3 Operations Reports, Box 10634, World War II Operations Reports 1940–48, Record Group 407, National Archives II.
73. Advanced Echelon New Guinea Force, To the Officers and Men of the 163rd Infantry Regiment, January 24, 1943, R.L. Eichelberger, LT. Gen., U.S. Army, Commanding, "41st Division, 163rd Infantry History of the Unit, 14 December 42–20 July 1943, Entry 427, Folder 341-Inf (163) -0.3 Operations Reports, Box 10634, World War II Operations Reports 1940–48, Record Group 407, National Archives II.
74. General Order No 7, Headquarters 41st Infantry Division APO #41, F/g 26 April 1943, H.H. Fuller, MMHM.
75. Telegram from Lt. Col. Charles R. Dawley, AMABKO, W 55 Via Beam, Helena, Montana, "41st Division, 163rd Infantry History of the Unit, 14 December 42–20 July 43," Entry 427, Folder 341-Inf (163) -0.3 Operations Reports, Box 10634, World War II Operations Reports 1940–48, Record Group 407, National Archives II.
76. "An Overview History of the 163rd Infantry Regiment: From the late 1930s through the Sanananda Campaign," 19, slide presentation, SFC Kermit M. Edmonds, 19 pages, Drawer 3, Montana National Guard, History of the 163rd during World War II, MMHM.
77. The chart and statistics are derived from Milner, *United States Army in World War II… Victory in Papua*, 370–1.
78. McKinney, "History of the 163rd," 102, MMHM.
79. Ibid., 101.

Troops unloading supplies during the Aitape invasion. *U.S. Army*

12

Island Hopping in the Pacific: New Guinea and The Philippines, 1943–1945

Michelle Tabit

The thoughts of going back to civilization, good food, wine, women, and song was noticeable as ever with the boys singing and laughing merrily... telling each other what they intended to do when they reached Australia.—Company B's Sergeant William C. Davidson in July 1943, following the Papua Campaign.[1]

Little tho, did he realize that some day he would see men dying, hear the crack of the rifle, the swish of a mortar, men crying for medics, and bombs whistling and exploding all around him.—Sgt. Davidson.[2]

Following the Sananada-Gona fighting, the 163rd eventually began making its way southeast 20 miles to the large Allied base at Oro Bay. To the combat-weary veterans, the breezes from the Solomon Sea and bivouacking atop a mosquito-free knoll, 1,200 feet above the harbor, provided some welcomed relief in New Guinea's sultry tropical environment. The regiment received orders to establish their encampment on the side of a steep hill, with the incline serving as shielding from enemy air observation. Initially, the troops saw this task as practically impossible. Sgt. James Eder observed, "we've learned that there[']s no such thing as an impossibility in the army."[3]

Here, they hacked away the vegetation, eventually establishing a bivouac much improved over what they recently were accustomed to. Each 16-square-foot canvas pyramid tent had a bamboo floor and six beds. Frequent interruptions occurred when men were pulled away to serve as stevedores, unloading supplies and equipment from ships in the harbor. After several weeks of working on the docks and establishing their camp, the regiment resumed its training regimen. Marksmanship was maintained at a high level on the firing ranges.

Patrolling continued, as did improvement work on roads. With rest, relaxation, and medical care, the regiment revived. As men from Company A noted, however, "just as we would finish erecting one floor and tent to sit back with a sigh of relief, additional men would return from the hospital necessitating another construction job."[4]

For the first time in months the regiment had time for recreation. Entertainers and stage shows were flown in to perform for the men, including the Irish tenor John Fogarty, and comedian Joe E. Brown. The Activities and Recreation Office supplied volleyballs and nets, prompting contests between the enlisted men and their officers. Some carved tropical wood, into everything from picture frames to furniture. Others collected scrap metal and other parts from downed Japanese planes, fashioning the materials into bracelets, ashtrays, utensils, miniature planes, and wristwatch bands.[5]

New uniforms and stacks of mail finally caught up to them. Only first-class letters had been delivered in the combat areas, and now some of the men received up to a half-year stack of newspapers and magazines. The regiment also opened a makeshift library, while radio and a "Victorola" record player provided other entertainment. Each night, men gathered to listen to the enemy's Zero Hour program. Radio Tokyo broadcasted anti-American propaganda, but also played American "swing tunes," actually lifting the men's spirits. "We often thought of sending in requests," a Company B soldier joked, "but figured Japan might stop the broadcasts, if they thought we were enjoying them."[6]

The balance of the regiment's time was relatively uneventful. March 28, 1943, however, proved memorable when a large enemy air raid struck Oro Bay. According to Company A men, "the exciting event was when the Japanese bombers broke formation directly over our area and peeled off to dive bomb Oro Bay."[7] The men had a bird's-eye view of the planes as they swooped in to attack shipping and harbor installations. American aircraft engaged the enemy, destroying several bombers. "One plane [of ours] was hit, but the losses by the Japs, made up for the loss," Sgt. Eder noted. The 163rd witnessed additional air attacks from the relative safety of their hilltop bivouac. "There were other raids, but the enemy always got the worse of it."[8]

On May 30, the men held an outdoor memorial, honoring fallen comrades and the wounded. The chaplain reminded all present that "the acts of heroism, shown by these men, shall not have been in vain: We have pledged ourselves to avenge their sufferings."[9] The following week, Maj. Gen. Horace H. Fuller, the 41st Division commander, visited the regiment and decorated several soldiers with awards, including the Purple Heart and the Distinguished Service Cross.[10]

On June 11, the regiment received orders to return to the Cape Killerton area, the scene of their combat operations in the previous January. The last hours at Oro Bay proved hectic as the men packed up gear and equipment in total darkness during a night-time air raid. The next morning, trucks transported the 163rd back to Cape Killerton, where they moved into a bivouac previously occupied by their sister regiment, the 186th Infantry. The camp stood only a few hundred yards from the shoreline—the ocean breezes and sandy beach provided a relaxing environment. As the men patrolled in this locality, they recalled that just five months earlier, about 1½ miles from their current bivouac, they had fought in one of the bloodiest battles in the Southwest Pacific Area. But now, the scene was quiet and peaceful. The hulk of the 16,000-ton transport, the *Francisco Maru*, stood offshore, lodged in a coral reef. A former luxury liner retrofitted for service by the Imperial Japanese fleet, it now bobbed helplessly in the bay.

Life for the regiment had calmed considerably. After serving as stevedores at Oro Bay, the tranquility of easy duty at a tropical beach was welcomed. "We got our first good food here," a Company A soldier recalled, "fresh eggs and steak."[11] Vegetables, bread, meat, and butter arrived once a week.

While at Cape Killerton, word came that the regiment had earned a Presidential Unit Citation for its success at Sananada. All took pride in the recognition. General MacArthur also visited on July 2, inspecting the troops and briefing the command staff about future plans. The regiment now learned it would return to Australia.

On July 6, the 163rd received the official order to move to Dobadura, beginning the trip back to Rockhampton. Meanwhile, the 186th Regiment returned to relieve the 163rd at Cape Killerton. The troops boarded trucks on July 11, and after spending the night at Dobadura, C-47 transports flew them over the Owen Stanley Mountains. At Port Moresby, the 163rd occupied a temporary bivouac. Awaking at 3 a.m. on July 15, they piled into trucks transporting them to the docks. They then embarked on a "Victory" ship,[12] the *Newenhall,* for Australia.[13]

The men felt exhilaration. After six months in New Guinea, they longed to return to Australia. According to Sgt. William C. Davidson of Company B, "the thoughts of going back to civilization, good food, wine, women, and song was noticeable as ever with the boys singing and laughing merrily."[14]

Two days later, on July 17, the *Newenhall* docked at Townsville, at the eastern base of Australia's Cape York Peninsula. The regiment transferred gear and equipment to railroad cars bound for Rockhampton. The two-day train trip further lightened their spirits, as they played poker and shared liquor.

On the evening of July 20, the 163rd arrived at Rockhampton. Trucks meeting the men at the station transported them 13 miles to their new bivouac—home for the next eight months. Much to the men's dismay, the company commanders required that improvements be completed before any passes were issued. Previously serving the 186th, this camp featured new conveniences, including refrigerators, lights, radios, bathhouses with showers, modern latrines, and good food.[15] With the satisfactory completion of facility improvements, the men began receiving furloughs.

On July 23, the I Corps commander, Lt. Gen. Robert L. Eichelberger, visited the regiment, congratulating the men for their achievements. He promised to let people back home know about the 163rd's efforts. Seven-day passes were issued. With the inclusion of time for travelling, this gave the men 15 days off. Most went south to Melbourne and Sydney; others remained in Rockhampton.[16]

Various recreational activities were available in the Rockhampton locality. Some men visited the mining town of Mount Morgan, a couple hours drive away. Others relaxed on the Yeppoon beaches, 18 miles out on the coast. It was "a little summer resort on the Pacific," recalled Captain McKinney. "Here we swam, danced and dated the few girls," but added, we "attempted to eat and drink, but, failed miserably as the few pubs and hotels were crowded to capacity with troops at all times."[17] Men also visited Emu Park, a smaller, more crowded beach, yet it had one special attraction—nurses. Here, the 1st Field Hospital leased summer cottages to house its medical staff. According to one soldier, "nurses were only for the officers at Rockhampton and they received quite a play from the brass of the division."[18]

As part of their daily routine, the troops at the camp had opportunities to visit Rockhampton almost nightly, attending movies and dances. Some romanced new sweethearts, sometimes referring to them by the Aussie term "Sheilas." Regimental command also authorized company dances in the mess halls. Both the American and Australian Red Cross organizations arranged for young ladies to attend these affairs. On one such occasion, "our 163rd band arrived at seven o-clock," Sgt. Davidson recalled, "and by eight, two large buses containing sixty five beautiful Australian girls with their hostesses arrived. There were red heads, blondes, brunettes and everything a 'Yank' could have wished for."[19] The dancing continued for hours. As the evening ended, the men escorted their companions to the buses and bade them farewell. "As they drove away, the lights faded out into the night like a dream," a soldier remembered, and "this brought to a close an evening of music, dancing and merriment that was by far, the biggest treat we had ever had up to that time."[20]

September 10, 1943, likewise was an especially eventful day. While on a tour of the Southwest Pacific Area, Eleanor Roosevelt visited Rockhampton and the 163rd. Arriving at 9 a.m., she toured the camp, observing the daily training routine. PFC Icenhower of Company A ran the obstacle course for her, while Sgt. Clifton B. Thomas and his squad from the 1st platoon gave a demonstration on how to knock out enemy pill boxes. Later that day, Mrs. Roosevelt along with General Fuller and Lt. Gen. Walter Krueger, the U.S. Sixth Army commander, viewed a regimental parade. [21] The event culminated with an address from the First Lady, offering her thanks and congratulations for a job well done.[22]

Nevertheless, after a couple of months of rest and good food, the reality of being sent on future combat operations set in. The regiment resumed a strict training routine. The 163rd men had learned valuable lessons during their time in battle, which served the regiment well when instructing replacements coming from the United States. Most of the recruits had been in the U.S. Army less than four months; 163rd NCOs gave the newcomers nighttime lectures on combat tactics. The replacements came in sizeable numbers. On August 8, for example, about 89 recruits arrived at Rockhampton, causing Company B's 1st Lt. Frank E.

Maxam to note, "it now seemed that we were over strength after being down to less than a hundred."[23] The new men quickly adapted to the regimental routine, and, according to members of Company A, friendships grew fast between the veterans and raw recruits.[24] Also, considerable shuffling had taken place among the ranks because of casualties, promotions, and the arrival of the new men.

During the next several months, the training remained strenuous, with long marches, overnight problems, and additional jungle training, climaxing in December with amphibious operations near Brisbane. On December 17, the 163rd boarded troop trains bound for the Toorbul Point training area. The regiment worked intensely, practicing amphibious tactics and beach landings. According to Company B men, "it was tough training and long hours but plenty of good food and sleep put us into shape."[25] While at Toorbul Point, the regiment celebrated its third Christmas season away from friends and family. The Montana men missed the Rocky Mountain snow and evergreen-fir Christmas trees. "By sheer coincidence, numerous Xmas pkgs. were received on Christmas day, making the holiday a little more home-like in that dismal area."[26] The remainder of the regiment's training at Toorbul Point progressed smoothly, with the men returning to Rockhampton on January 14, 1944.

After a week, training again intensified. The men started with one-day marches, but these were soon extended to three-day and eventually five-day maneuvers. Typically, the regiment marched all day with full field packs and made camp at sunset. A final march, considered an endurance test, lasted seven days. Besides the forced marches, jungle combat tactics received a good deal of the usual emphasis, as did night problems. Much needed replacement equipment also was arriving.

In early February 1944, the War Department announced a rotation program, allowing for the return of men who had lengthy service in combat zones. Among various requirements, eighteen months of overseas duty and six months of combat in a forward area earned a soldier the highest priority for being returned to the United States. Thus began a "sweating it out" process for each man, regarding whether he might survive in combat long enough to eventually fulfill these requirements. Men of the 41st Division who received orders to return to the United States rotated back to Fort Lewis, where they were reassigned to stateside duties.[27]

During these months, the Joint Chiefs of Staff in Washington, D.C., had developed long-range plans for advancing to the Philippines-Formosa region in a vast two-pronged approach—(1) The bulk of the U.S. Navy's ever-expanding fleet, with Marine and Army units, would proceed westward through the Central Pacific via campaigns in the Marshall, Mariana, Palau, and other archipelagos nearer Japan; (2) MacArthur's Allied assault in the Southwest Pacific Area would continue northwest through New Guinea and to the Philippines.

Consequently in the Southwest Pacific Area, orders were issued for Allied forces to jump several hundred miles by sea from eastern New Guinea to Hollandia and Aitape, about half-way along the northern New Guinea coast. This movement would bypass strong, well-garrisoned Japanese positions at Wewak and Hansa Bay, located at about the mid-point between Lae and Hollandia.

Meanwhile, Allied naval and air forces were achieving superiority at sea and in the skies, which was essential in the operations. Taking Hollandia's broad Humboldt Bay would provide large cargo ships, troop transports, and combat vessels with an excellent base for subsequent operations. Also, smaller naval units operating from Aitape and Hollandia, such as PT boats,[28] could disrupt the enemy barge and small-craft traffic attempting to resupply and move troops for the increasingly isolated Japanese garrisons along the New Guinea coast. Allied aircraft at Hollandia and Aitape's airfields also could dominate local skies and provide key support for future advances.[29]

After the bloody frontal assaults conducted at Buna, Gona, and Sananada, General MacArthur and his staff had improved strategy and tactics, trying to reduce the rate of Allied combat casualties. Taking full advantage of ever increasing sea and air dominance, Allied forces relied on amphibious landings along the New Guinea coast, usually hitting the Japanese where they least expected it, while bypassing and strangling enemy garrisons left in isolation with little or no hope of supply or reinforcement. Currently, the Australians were mopping up retreating enemy forces beyond Lae and Salamaua, a couple hundred miles west of Gona.

Similar tactics were being applied in the Solomon, Bismarck, and Admiralty archipelagos to the north. After securing Guadalcanal in February 1943, Allied forces had steadily advanced to the northwest, paralleling the New Guinea operations to the south across the Solomon and Bismarck seas.

On February 25, the 41st Division received orders to relocate for a new combat operation in New Guinea.[30] The division departed Rockhampton on March 12 for the port of Gladstone, about 85 miles away. Part of the division went by troop train, while the other traveled by truck convoy. After arriving at Gladstone, the division began the long process of loading ships for the voyage to recently ceased Finschhafen, across the Huon Gulf from Lae and Salamaua in northern New Guinea.

Meanwhile, General Fuller reported ahead to the I Corps commanding staff at a key base on Goodenough Island, near the far-eastern tip of New Guinea. Fuller and his advance staff consulted with Chief of Staff, G-3, Quartermaster, and G-1 officers and together worked out details for assaulting Hollandia and the Aitape airfields, which were located 125 miles east of Hollandia. The 163rd was tapped for the Aitape assault as part of the "Persecution Task Force." The 167th Field Artillery and other engineering and supporting units, and the 127th

Infantry from the 32nd Division, also would participated in this attack. Brig. Gen. Jens A. Doe would lead the Persecution Task Force.

The larger "Reckless Task Force," under the command of Lt. Gen. Eichelberger, would invade Hollandia. The plan called for the 41st Division's 186th and 162nd infantry regiments and the 146th, 205th, and 218th field artillery battalions—identified as the Letterpress Landing Force—to be incorporated with other elements, including 24th Division regiments, in the assault.[31] After the Goodenough Island meeting, General Fuller and his staff moved their 41st Division headquarters to Cape Cretin near Finschhafen.

On March 18, the *Cape Cleare* arrived in Gladstone harbor and the men soon were busy loading equipment, supplies, and ammunition. The 163rd then boarded and set sail for Finschhafen. "Rolling out into the great ocean was mysterious, yet adventurous," Sgt. Davidson recalled. "The deck was crowded with men looking out across the hazy waters to get their last glimpse of Australia."[32]

For nine days, the men played cards, watched movies, and attended live entertainment programs as the convoy proceeded around eastern New Guinea. On March 27, the *Cape Cleare* entered Finschhafen harbor, where wheeled, amphibious landing craft—DUKWs[33] —ferried the men to shore. Sgt. Davidson described Finschhafen as "a beautiful place, palm trees bending their long slender bodies toward the sea and a picture an artist would attempt to paint. We had seen pictures such as these in movies, art galleries, and storybooks, but it didn't seem real."[34] The division's men were pleasantly surprised to encounter American nurses and Red Cross volunteers.

Over the next few days, the division remained in a temporary bivouac and received additional equipment, while the men attended lectures focusing on the upcoming operation. During one such talk, Captain Maxam[35] of Company B began by saying: "Fellas, we're going to make a beach landing!" A sense of unease passed among the soldiers, until Maxam explained they would be rehearsing a landing under tactical conditions, "just like the real thing."[36] The regiment, however, was not informed about their ultimate objective—the Japanese airstrips near Aitape. For security reasons, the command staff kept this a secret until later.

The 163rd's practice landing was scheduled to take place 12 miles from Lae on a beach resembling the actual objective. Captain Maxam also explained that the assault would be fully supported with 105-mm howitzers, anti-aircraft weapons, jeeps, trucks, bulldozers, and tanks, the most appreciated of all.[37] This had not been the case at Sananada, of course. The 163rd also now had additional personal weapons, including a new type M1 grenade launcher and the bazooka, effective against both tanks and bunkers.[38]

At 6:45 a.m. on April 7, the amphibious "dress rehearsal" began in the harbor. When the landing ramps dropped in the practice assault, the men disembarked and spread out along the beach to assigned positions. Tanks, trucks, jeeps, and artillery followed the troops ashore. A man from Company B remarked, "it was more or less an [exercise] to familiarize ourselves with the tanks and to learn how to follow a tank under fire."[39] Some confusion ensued during the regiment's practice landing. Afterward, the command staff worked out improvements for the actual operation.[40]

General MacArthur and his staff opted to attack Hollandia and Aitape, rather than closer Wewak or Hansa Bay, after intelligence revealed that the Japanese 18th Army under Lt. Gen. Hatazo Adachi was regrouping in the Wewak area, where the Japanese expected the next Allied assault. In attacking Hollandia, the Allies were jumping 500 miles forward, bypassing some 40,000 Japanese troops centered around Wewak.

The plan called for the larger Reckless Task Force to land on both sides of Hollandia—at Humboldt and Tanahmerah bays—with a simultaneous assault by the smaller Persecution Task Force near Aitape, located east about midway between Hollandia and Wewak. The 163rd Infantry alone would conduct the morning assault near Aitape. The Aitape and Hollandia landings were scheduled for the same day.[41]

The last of the replacement troops arrived on April 11, bringing the division to full strength. Over the next few days, the men loaded the assault ships. Ready for battle, the force set sail under sealed orders. Sgt. Davidson recalled: "Two days out, we were told that 'D-day' was April 22nd, and Aitape our objective."[42]

Aboard ship, the 163rd regiment ate k-rations, as the good food provided in Australia faded in memory. Limited sleeping quarters meant that some men had bunks, while others slept on deck. Tension ran high the night before the landing. "At this point," according to a Company A report, "the old combat men" thought "it was just another job of hell, but many of the new men, still to have their first taste of combat were thinking in terms of the future as heroic deeds, fear and thoughts of hatred."[43]

The Hollandia Assaults

By April 17, all of the LCIs (Landing Craft, Infantry) had left Finschhafen. The following day, the last of the LSTs (Landing Ship, Tank), destroyers, and other vessels left the ports, proceeding to a rendezvous point in the Bismarck Sea north of the Admiralty Islands.[44] On the morning of April 20, the combined Hollandia-Aitape troop convoy assembled, forming an armada of more than 100 ships.[45] Supporting aircraft carrier and naval bombardment groups also sailed in nearby waters. In the evening hours of April 20–21, the Aitape task force separated and disappeared into the night, while the Hollandia convoy proceeded on toward its objective.

General Robert Eichelberger's Hollandia landing forces consisted of regiments from the 24th and 41st divisions as well as attached units. In landings at Hollandia and Humboldt Bay (to the east), and Tanahmerah Bay (to the west), the ultimate objective was to seize several airdromes. The two bays were separated by 25 miles of the Cyclops Mountains peninsula, with the airfields located inland on a plain at the southern base of the Cyclops peaks, equidistant between the two bays. The beach assaults, set for 7 a.m. on the morning of April 22, unfolded smoothly. American and Australian cruisers and destroyers—firing eight-, five-, and 4.7-inch guns—along with other vessels, began shelling the beaches at 6 a.m., or "H hour minus 60 minutes."[46]

At Humboldt Bay, targets ranged from Hollandia and Cape Soeadja at the northwest end of the harbor to Cape Dijar, six miles southeast. The naval barrage pounded the beaches with special attention given to the shore west of an inner body of water, called Jautefa Bay, and to "Pancake Hill" just northwest of the landing beaches.[47] In addition to the naval fire, two rocket-equipped LCIs, firing 288 rockets per barrage, zeroed in on the beaches.[48] At 6:30 a.m., U.S. carrier aircraft from Task Force 58 began strafing and bombing the beaches and adjoining areas up to two miles inland. According to an official account,[49] the "air strike was completed at H-4 [H hour minus 4 minutes] when the first assault waves were 500 yards from the landing beaches."[50] The 41st Division's 162nd and 186th regiments landed on the "White" beaches with virtually no Japanese resistance, though some fighting occurred in subsequent advances.

Meanwhile, at H-hour in Tanahmerah Bay, following a similar bombardment, the first wave of 24th Division soldiers arrived approximately eight minutes late, but nevertheless landed on the "Red" beaches with nothing amiss against light enemy action.[51] Overall, the landing progressed as expected, taking the Japanese completely off guard.[52] Four days later on April 26, having overcome some Japanese resistance, the 29th and 41st divisions linked up at the enemy airfields.[53] All objectives in the Hollandia operation had met with success.

The Aitape Area Landing

The Persecution Task Force assault led by Brig. Gen. Doe also went well. The landing was supported by planes from 8 escort aircraft carriers, along with naval gunfire and rockets from 5 destroyers and 12 other vessels, which were backed up by A-20 and B-25 bombers of the Allied air forces. The 163rd led the initial assault, followed up a day later by the 127th.

At 6:45 a.m., April 22, the landing craft carrying the 2nd and 3rd battalions came in abreast toward "Blue" beach (with the 2nd Battalion on the west and the 3rd to the east). Under overcast skies and in smoke from the shelling and the burning enemy installations, the task force stormed ashore a half mile too far east at Wapil, a small native village about 12 miles southeast of Aitape. Nevertheless, this miscue turned out to be advantageous; Wapil had this locality's best operational beach for LSTs and other landing vessels.

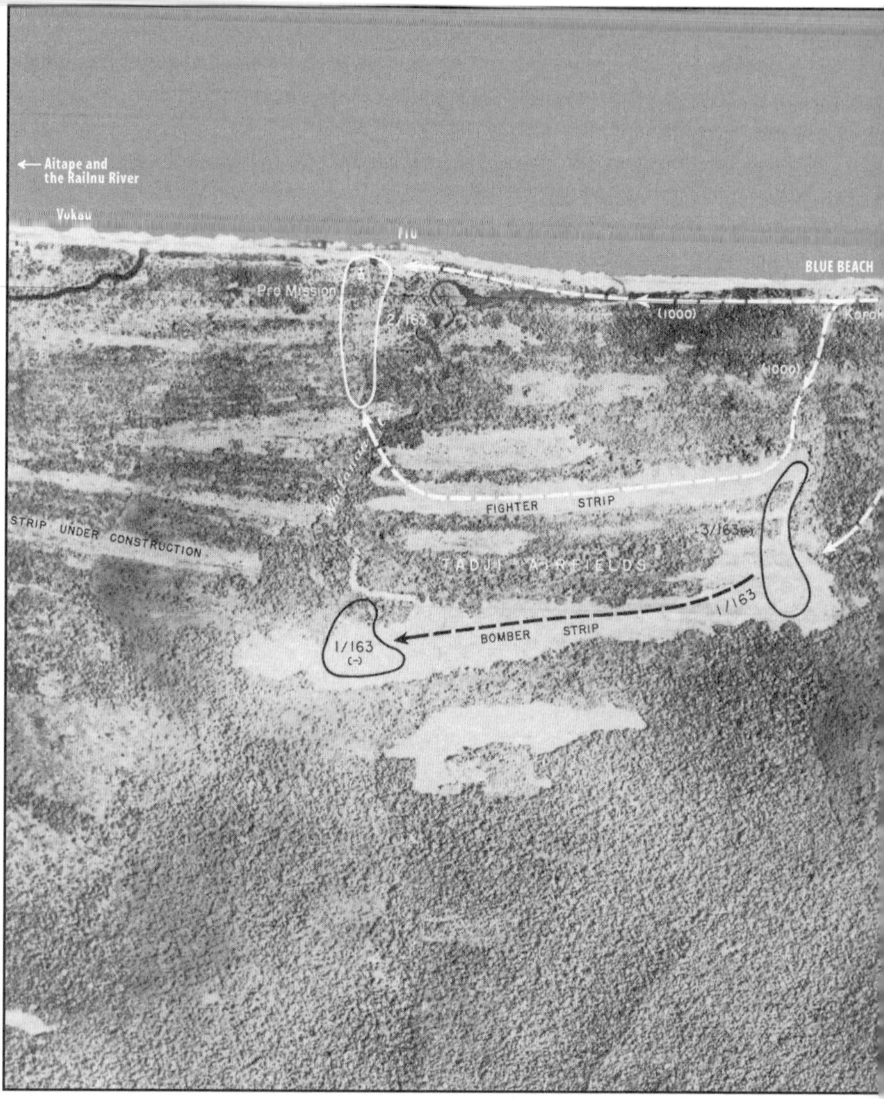

Aitape landings and the Japanese airfields at Tadji, April 22, 1944. Modified from Robert Ross Smith,

The enemy was taken by surprise, firing scattered shots and running into the jungle, leaving breakfasts uneaten. The Japanese force, probably totaling about 1,000 men, consisted mostly of service units and antiaircraft artillerymen, with about 240 combat troops. The 2nd Battalion quickly turned west along the coast to secure a trail extending to the main objective—the airstrips. Meanwhile, detachments of the 3rd Battalion secured the beachhead, and eventually

...ited States Army in World War II... The Approach to the Philippines (1953).

advanced through several small settlements east along the shore, establishing an outpost on the west side of the Nigia River, three miles away.

The 1st Battalion soon came ashore to join the 2nd Battalion in securing the Tadji airstrips, 1,000 yards inland. American engineers also had landed, immediately improving the beach area and local roads. The assault plan called for Australian engineers to follow the same day, to quickly begin preparing the airstrips for

Allied fighter planes. "The landing was successful," recalled one member of the 1st Battalion, "in that we suffered no casualties"[54] while encountering only one Japanese soldier and several Korean laborers.[55]

The 163rd's mortar companies D, H, and M also landed with orders "to fire at the earliest practical time in the support of the operation," and "to be prepared to execute fire in support of either the 1st or 2nd Battalions in their attack on the airdromes." The 1st Battalion's troops were quickly organized by 11 a.m., and passed through the 3rd Battalion's beachhead positions, pushing inland with elements of the 2nd Battalion on their right toward the Tadji airfields. The 1st Battalion's plan called for companies A and B, with Company C in reserve, and less mortar Company D, to secure the Tadji's fighter strip and the bomber field parallel to it, several hundred yards further south.

By early afternoon, the objectives were reached by the 1st Battalion and the 641st Tank Destroyer Battalion, while meeting no enemy resistance. Squads fanned out along the sides of the runways, cautiously moving from crater to crater left by the Allied air and sea bombardment. The soldiers remained low to the ground in case of enemy sniper fire. Tanks led the way in front of each company. "These were the modern weapons of the war that we had prayed for during the Sananda Campaign," recalled Sgt. Arthur Belgrade of Company B.[56]

Company B crossed the east end of the bomber runway and continued along the south side, while Company A moved down the north side. "A few wrecked planes were strewn about the airstrip," Sgt. Belgrade recalled, "as our bombers and fighters gave this place a real going over."[57]

More than halfway up the runway, Company B sighted a camouflaged shack. Quickly, tank cannon blasts along with machine gun bursts destroyed it. "Every man was lying on the ground, waiting and listening for returned fire." Much to Sgt. Belgrade's surprise, "there wasn't any."[58]

The tanks rolled on, spraying machine gun bullets at other shacks or anything of a suspicious nature. Meanwhile, half-way along the runway, Company A suffered its first casualty when a stray 81-mm mortar fragment killed Private First Class Snyder.[59] The company resumed its course down the runway expecting an encounter, but the enemy was gone. According to a Company B member, "good running trucks were left on the trails by Nips who had to leave them behind. This was an indication that they were caught off guard and we captured quite an amount of supplies and equipment."[60]

Meanwhile, at mid-afternoon on the same day, the Australian engineers began work on the fighter strip. The Australians operated their equipment through the nighttime under floodlights, completing the task in less than 48 hours. Shortly, 25 Royal Australian Air Force P-40 fighters flew in. These and additional planes soon provided support for Eichelberger's "Reckless Task Force" at Hollandia to the west, and for attacks on by-passed Japanese positions toward Wewak, southeast down the coast.

Before sunset of the first day, the 1st Battalion established defensive perimeters at the bomber airstrip, with a supporting tank platoon for added protection. Meanwhile the bulk of the 3rd Battalion guarded the eastern end of the two airstrips. The 2nd Battalion dug in to the north, perpendicular to the coast line and facing west. As a Company A soldier explained, "although we hadn't seen the enemy, the men were extremely tense & jittery."[61] Throughout that sleepless first night, outposts guarding the 1st Battalion's perimeter reported no activity by Japanese soldiers. Nevertheless, some men in their foxholes tossed hand grenades at an imagined enemy.[62]

The second day's operations proved similar, except heavy rains turned the roads into quagmires. Armored vehicles of the 603rd Tank Company led the way toward an unfinished enemy airstrip to the east, and then on to the Raihu River at a point about two miles from its mouth. Meanwhile, the 3rd Battalion's positions at the beachhead and on the east had been taken over by elements of the 127th Infantry, now coming ashore. This freed up the 3rd Battalion to join the 2nd Battalion in making a six mile westward probe along the coast, parallel to the sweep by the 1st Battalion.

The operation met minimal resistance, but had a mishap. "One of the tanks attached to us had fallen through" a Japanese bridge, a member of Company B recalled, and was "almost fully covered with mud and water."[63] At the end of the day, the 1st Battalion established a perimeter on the east side of the Raihu River, but without tank protection. At the same time, the 2nd and 3rd battalions also dug in, further down the east bank of the stream and at its mouth.

After the incident with Company B's accompanying tank, the remaining armored vehicles returned to regimental headquarters. The 1st Battalion's second night in New Guinea was quieter than the first, with few, if any, panicked men needlessly lobbing hand grenades in the darkness.[64]

On the morning of the third day, April 24, the 1st and 2nd battalions were ordered to continue the advance across the Raihu River and on to Tadji village, located on the coast just west of the stream's mouth. Information gathered by intelligence officers[65] from the natives supposedly indicated that 3,000 Japanese were waiting across the Raihu River—somewhere between that stream and Tadji.[66] At 7 a.m., the 1st Battalion crossed the Raihu. "We started to wade across the river in a single column and it was hip high deep," Sgt. Belgrade recalled, "so we held our rifles above our heads until we got to the other side."[67]

The 1st Battalion troops followed a trail north through dense trees and thick vines, climbing their way over a rugged high point, while constantly on the lookout for the enemy. "At the top of the hill, sitting on the porch of the native hospital, we found two Nips taking breakfast," said Private Hargis Westerfield. "They reached for their rifles," but a sergeant "tommy-gunned one man's brains out," while "the other fled over the ridge."[68]

After the 163rd Infantry seized the Tadji fighter strip, Australian engineers quickly made improvements for the arrival of 25 Royal Australian Air Force P-40 fighters. *U.S. Army*

The 1st and 2nd battalions met about two hours after starting the advance and secured Tadji unopposed. Next, the 1st Battalion was ordered to patrol trails to the south and west, while the 2nd Battalion continued on two miles to occupy Aitape at Rohm Point on the coast. The 1st Battalion and the supporting 3rd Battalion then were ordered to bivouac back on the river's east side. Few changes in these dispositions would occur in the next few days.

"So this campaign ended, as all campaigns should end," reminisced Private Westerfield regarding his company, "with a bath while floating on one's back in the deep Aitape River, [refreshingly] chilled from the rains in the mountains, and with no one dead, and only one wounded."[69]

Over the course of the next week, patrols moved west along the beaches and inland to investigate native settlements while searching for retreating enemy soldiers. At Kamti village, five miles in the interior, Company L's 2nd platoon finally encountered determined Japanese resistance. On April 28-29, these 39 men of the 3rd Battalion repelled attacks by an estimated 200 enemy soldiers. Company M's heavy machine guns ultimately helped thwart the assaults. The platoon withdrew, while Battery A of the 126th Field Artillery fired 240 rounds of 105-mm shells into the enemy positions. Company L then went back into Kamti with no opposition. The battalion had lost three killed and two wounded, while the Japanese dead totaled about 90.[70]

On another patrol, Company K captured a runner for a Japanese general, carrying a map showing the scattered locations of enemy troops in the area. It also identified their headquarters in Atterap, about ten miles away.[71] A special assault force, under the command of Lt. Houston and comprised of Company A, the 2nd platoon of Company B, and a .30-caliber machine gun squad from Company D, received orders to take Atterap. On the morning of April 30, the detachment set out through the dense jungle, slogging carefully down a muddy trail toward the objective. During the first day's march, they encountered only two Japanese soldiers; one fled into the jungle while the other was killed. A mile outside of Atterap, the troops dug in, establishing a temporary bivouac. The 2nd platoon sent out reconnaissance patrols in an attempt to locate the enemy, but only discovered a few starving natives. The Japanese were gone.

During this period, Company A also set up ambushes along the principle jungle trails used by the Japanese, and 42 enemy soldiers were killed.[72] Other 163rd units also did patrol and outpost work. As of May 4, an estimated 525 Japanese had died in the Aitape operation, while 14 Americans were killed and 23 wounded.[73]

The 163rd's participation in the overall operation lasted two weeks. Beginning on May 6, all of the 163rd's outposts around the Tadji area were relieved by the 127th Infantry of the 32nd Division. Eventually, the 32nd's other two regiments arrived, too. All three regiments were veterans of Buna. The 32nd Division—originally a Wisconsin-Michigan National Guard outfit—eventually was reinforced by the Texas National Guard's 112th Cavalry, the 31st Division's 124th Infantry, and the National Guard 43rd Division. Later that summer in this locality, these troops became engaged in massive, bloody battles, holding out against major elements of the Japanese 18th Army, coming 100 miles west through the jungle from Wewak to attack the American held airstrips.

The Hollandia-Aitape assaults were an unqualified success.[74] MacArthur and his staff later considered them one of the crowning achievements of all Southwest Pacific Area operations. It neutralized enemy air and land forces throughout north central New Guinea, while increasing the overall effectiveness of the Allied air forces. Hollandia, in particular, provided excellent anchorage for future amphibious operations.

Attacks on Japanese positions accelerated throughout New Guinea. Intelligence sources indicated that off to the west—about 140 miles beyond Hollandia—the enemy was entrenching for a stand at Wakde Island and the nearby coastal town of Sarmi, recently flattened by Allied bombing. The latter was a former Dutch administrative center for western New Guinea. Again, the 163rd was called upon.[75]

Invasion of the Arare Beaches and Wakde Island

The focus of the operation was a stretch of shoreline near Wakde Island, located 20 miles east of Sarmi. Along the coastal plain, the Japanese maintained defensive positions, bivouacs, depots, and storage areas for 11,000 troops, half of them

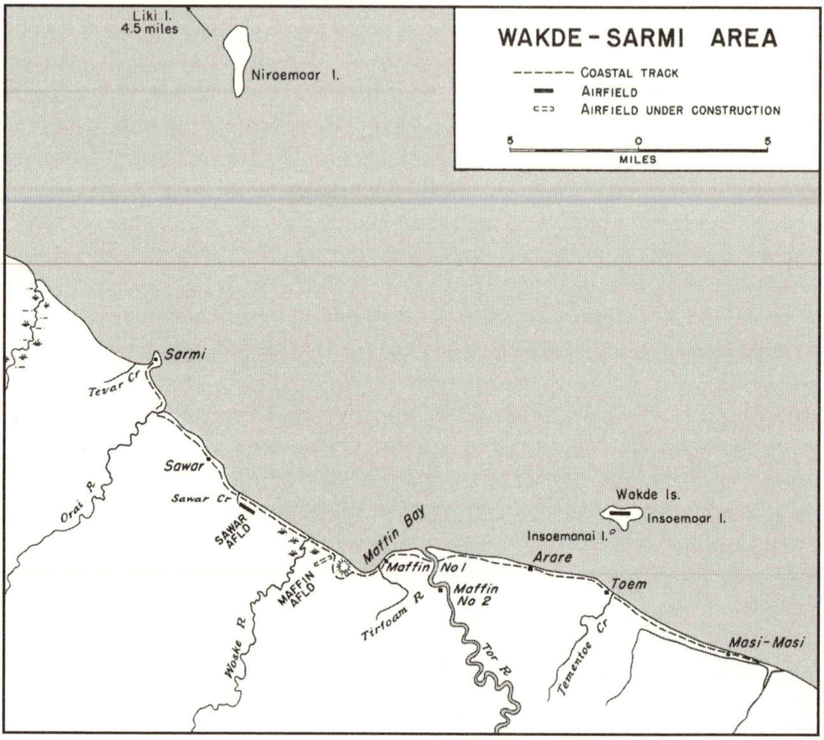

From Robert Ross Smith, *United States Army in World War II... The Approach to the Philippines* (1953).

battle hardened veterans. This number proved to be nearly twice what American intelligence officers had anticipated.

At about the mid-point between Wakde Island and Sarmi, the Japanese had established airstrips at Maffin Bay and near Sawar, recently hit hard by Allied air attacks. A more important airstrip, however, covered about half of Wakde Island. Less than 1 x 2 miles in size, the island stood several miles offshore from two small mainland settlements—Toem (on the east) and Arare (to the west). Seizure of Wakde Island as a fighter base was key to further Allied advances.

Wakde Island itself had too little suitable shoreline for an initial landing and was too small for establishing sufficient supply dumps during an assault. Also, an attacking force might be subjected to enemy artillery fire from the nearby mainland. Consequently, the Arare beaches on the mainland, just to the southwest of Wakde Island, were chosen for the initial attack. By establishing a beachhead on the mainland, and eliminating enemy positions and artillery, it then would be possible for troops to cross the bay and take the Wakde Island airfield. A small islet—Insoemanai Island—just south of Wakde also would be occupied to provide mortar and machine gun support for the assault.

The 163rd had become one of the highly regarded outfits in the entire Southwest Pacific Area and MacArthur's staff again tapped the regiment for important action.[76] The 163rd only recently had gone into bivouac near the captured Tadji airstrips. By working throughout the night of May 13–14, the assault ships assigned for the small invasion were loaded with the 163rd and attached units, plus their equipment. On May 15, their course was westward 300 miles, joining other vessels from Humboldt Bay, with the destination yet unknown for most of the men. In the meantime, cruisers and destroyers rendezvoused with the convoy off the Admiralty Islands on the night of May 16, keeping in contact by radar. As the convoy neared Wakde Island and the Arare-Toem beaches, word was finally let out.

On the evening of May 16, when briefing his men about the objective, Captain Maxam explained: "The Navy was shelling it [Toem] and our bombers were blasting it nite and day," and the entire regiment "would land on Toem, and the next day [the 1st Battalion would] hit the island of Wakde." The mainland attack would start the very next morning, May 17. As a Company B trooper later noted, this left "most of us speechless."[77]

In a cold drizzly dawn, but soon followed by sunshine, the Navy began shelling enemy positions. As one man later recalled, "we saw a destroyer go within a few hundred yards of Wakde Island and throw hundreds of shells into its installations, then return to its original position to shell the mainland."[78] There was no return fire from the enemy.

As the smoke began clearing, and with a calm sea, waves of 3rd Battalion troops boarded landing craft and assaulted the Arare beaches, with Company I spearheading the attack in eight LCVPs at 7:15 a.m. They met minimal Japanese resistance. With succeeding waves coming in, the 3rd Battalion secured the beachhead, and fanned out in search of pockets of enemy resistance.[79] Engineering units came next, making improvements in the landing area, while being protected and assisted in the unloading by most of Company I. The 2nd and 1st battalions and the artillery soon followed.

The 3rd Battalion, meeting occasional enemy rifle fire, sent men west a couple miles toward the Tor River to protect the right flank. Meanwhile, the 2nd Battalion deployed eastward along a coastal road toward Tementoe Creek, quickly occupying Toem by 9:30 a.m. Occasional Japanese stragglers were encountered during these movements. The enemy obviously was surprised, and probably regrouping beyond the reach of the Americans. The 1st Battalion, not scheduled for assaults on this day, followed along to Toem, 2½ miles east, to prepare for the next day's attack on Wakde Island. The 191st Field Artillery Group, the 163rd Infantry's Cannon Company, and the 167th Field Artillery Battalion supported the 2nd Battalion's eastward move, while shelling Wakde Island as well.[80]

The 2nd and 1st battalions, due to the light enemy activity, almost casually dug in at Toem in clear view of Wakde Island just three miles away.[81] Meanwhile, tiny Insoemanai Island, 3,500 yards offshore and only 600 yards from Wakde Island, also was seized by a small amphibious landing force supported by two destroyers and two LCI rocket ships. Company E, the three heavy-weapons companies, and a 4.2-inch mortar company landed against no resistance—the island was unoccupied. This regimental Provisional Groupment would provide the 1st Battalion with additional mortar and machine gun support during the following day's Wakde Island landing. When the regimental artillery on the mainland began shelling Wakde Island, however, the Provisional Groupment on Insoemanai Island began receiving machine gun and mortar fire from Wakde's defenders, killing one man and wounding four others in the most determined enemy action of the day. Also, an American artillery round meant for Wakde fell short on Insoemanai Island, killing another soldier and injuring six.

In the morning hours of May 18, 1,500 men began the assault on the southwest side of Wakde Island, with the 1st Battalion's Company B in the leading wave at 9:10 a.m. Immediately following came companies A and C, as well as the 2nd Battalion's Company F, plus two Sherman tanks, by 9:25 a.m.[82] Two other tanks scheduled for the initial assault were delayed. For the previous 24 hours, naval, air, and artillery bombardments poured thousands of cannon rounds and bombs onto Wakde's shores, thought to be defended by perhaps as many as 1,000 enemy. Also, the regimental Provisional Groupment on Insoemanai Island swept the beaches with machine gun and mortar fire as the landing craft went in.

"No one could still be alive after that terrific pounding," noted a Company A soldier, nevertheless "500 yards from the beach, we received the surprise of our lives," when "bullets began slapping the water around the assault boats."[83]

"The men crawled on their stomachs like snakes"—163rd men during the Wakde Island landing, facing stiff Japanese resistance. *U.S. Army*

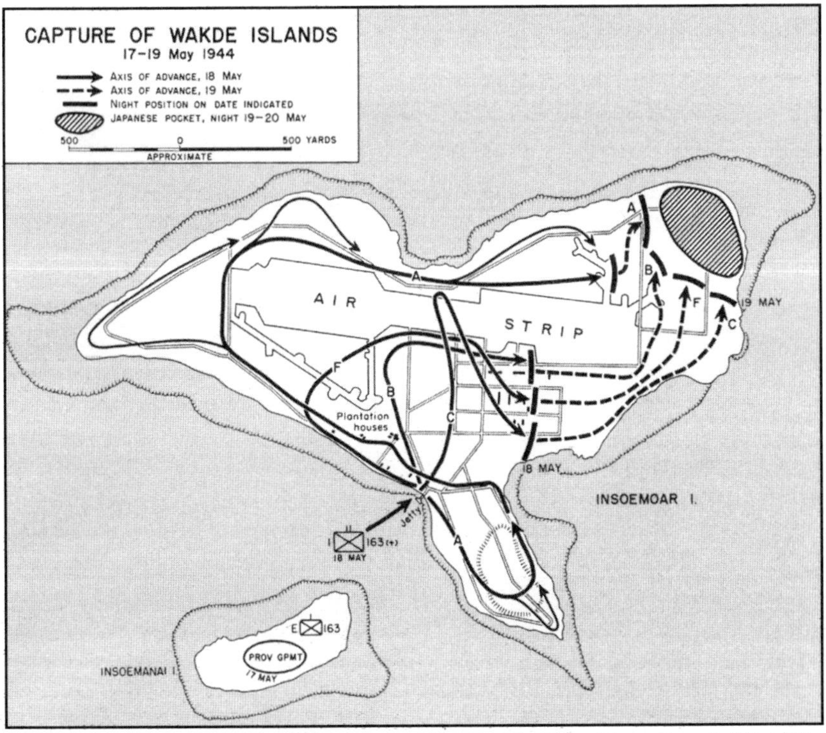

The 163rd RCT at Wakde Island. From Robert Ross Smith, *United States Army in World War II... The Approach to the Philippines* (1953).

The companies met fierce enemy resistance when storming ashore. Eight landing craft were damaged that day, and the exposed operators of the LCVPs suffered 5 dead and 30 wounded. Among the infantry casualties were three company commanders—one killed, and two wounded. Executive officers took over leadership. After securing part of the beach, the two Sherman tanks came up, breaking the stalemate against strongly entrenched enemy machine gunners and snipers in bunkers and pillboxes. "The men crawled on their stomachs like snakes moving forward to keep in contact with the men in front of them," Sgt. Bilbao recalled.[84]

Combat frequently was close, often with enemy positions cleared by hand grenades, small arms fire, and flamethrowers. Soon the enemy fell back, leaving behind deadly suicide squads to hold up the battalion's advance. The island defenses included about 100 bunkers, numerous foxholes and slit trenches, and at least two concrete air raid shelters, plus the enemy occupied coral caves on the eastern shore. Downed trees of Wakde's neglected and overgrown coconut plantation, as well as destroyed plantation buildings, numerous bomb and artillery craters, and thick brush, also provided the enemy with cover.

As the landing force fanned out, Company A cleared stiff resistance on the small peninsula jutting from the island's south shore, and then was ordered to sweep through the other companies to the north side of the island and take the air strip. Eventually, A, B, F, and C companies were deployed across the small island from north to south. As Company A men advanced to the west end of the airfield, they discovered "the strip itself was ¾ of a mile long with revetments at each end," and "all of these contained wrecked Jap planes—perfect hiding places for numbers of Jap snipers and MG nests."[85]

Cautiously combing masonry revetments and moving east in the narrow corridor between the airstrip and the northern shore, Company A deployed the 1st platoon and two 3rd platoon squads to determine the enemy's strength. The 1st platoon soon became engaged in a firefight while other enemy shooting pinned down the 3rd platoon squads. Recently arrived from Insoemanai Island, a Company D heavy weapons platoon moved in from the rear. Under support from Company D, the 1st and 3rd platoon squads withdrew to Company A's main lines.

Not long after, a Company B platoon arrived with tank reinforcement and flushed out the Japanese soldiers. By sunset, Company A swept across the island to the east end of the airfield, establishing a defensive perimeter opposite to a main Japanese pocket on the northeast tip of Wakde. Tanks evacuated the wounded to the beachhead and returned with water and ammunition. Company A, though exposed, experienced a relatively quiet night.[86]

Meanwhile, Company B reached the south central side of the airstrip with only minimal resistance, when the reorganized enemy began attacking again. "The Nips were…screaming and even hollered out to us to get the hell out of here and leave them alone," a Company B man recalled. "They charged in groups of fifteen and were mowed down in groups of fifteen."[87] After several unsuccessful attempts to storm the perimeter, the enemy withdrew to regroup.

Tanks reinforced by a Company F platoon came to Company B's aid. The next Japanese attack was fierce. "It seemed like ages before the tanks came up and they cut…down [the enemy] from the trees like sun melting butter on a hot, sultry day," a Company B soldier noted.[88] After the tanks entered the battle, the Japanese withdrew and company B dug in. "During the night, the Japs opened up every five minutes more or less,"[89] and several attacked the perimeter. "They were easily cut down by our rifle and machine gun fire. We didn't receive any casualties that night."[90]

Also on this day, Company C briefly swept north past companies B and F against stiff opposition to the center part of the airfield, meeting with Company A men. Several men were killed and wounded when sprinting across the exposed runway. During the day's movements, the "heavily shelled areas provided the enemy excellent cover and concealment," reported 1st Lt. Floyd R. Stanfield. "It was difficult to locate the exact position of the enemy, except by his movement." Japanese "ground snipers therefore caused considerable trouble."[91]

Company C drew intense fire, but tank support insured that the company reached the airstrip. The company, when moving through the brush following behind tanks in skirmish order, fired into likely enemy hideouts. On one occasion, "the first and third tanks were charged by lone Japs, bent on putting a few rounds down the tube," but "riflemen got both of these," reported Lt. Stanfield.[92] (By this time in the Pacific, it was recognized that infantrymen needed to protect tanks from infiltrating enemy soldiers. Acting individually or in small groups, the Japanese came in suicide attacks, throwing themselves with explosive charges directly under armored vehicles or climbing up to shoot through tank portals.) Later in the day, Company C was sent to the opposite or south end of the battalion's line, based on the south shore.

At the end of the first day, Company A's nighttime perimeter was the most advanced and isolated. The nearest other company position was 500 yards southwest, where B, F, and C companies were deployed north to south. In the rear positions during the night, a small group of Japanese attacked the battalion command post, but were repelled with the help of Company D's heavy weapons—12 Japanese lay dead, while 3 Americans were wounded.

On the second day, May 19, Company A moved a short distance forward to assault the difficult northeast revetment area, forming a skirmish line to flush out enemy soldiers. Japanese also were found in a beach cave against which rifle fire proved ineffective. Company A's Private Gallagher moved forward, "with a flame thrower and neutralized the cave."[93]

A typical coconut log bunker occupied by the enemy on Wakde Island. *U.S. Army*

An infantry squad supports a Sherman tank on Wakde Island, clearing enemy machine gun and sniper nests. Armor provided mobile cannon and machine gun fire while infantrymen guarded against Japanese soldiers throwing satchel charges under the tanks or placing grenades in the track wheels. *U.S. Army*

To the south, companies B, F, and C, with the aid of tanks, conducted a joint northeastward advance, clearing out determined resistance in caves, thick brush, demolished structures, and aircraft wreckage. Back at the beachhead, construction equipment was coming ashore, and engineers already were repairing the western end of the airstrip under occasional sniper fire. The first planes would land two days later.

By the end of the second day, the remaining organized Japanese troops were forced into a triangular area about 500 yards wide on the northeast tip of the island. The diminished enemy force was tightly compressed by companies A, B, F, and C, lined up northwest to southeast.

On the morning of the third day, May 20, action began when 37 enemy soldiers, apparently infiltrating past Company C's lines in the night, attacked engineer units at the beachhead. After the fire fight, 36 enemy lay dead, with 1 wounded soldier taken prisoner. At the island's northeast tip, companies A, B, F, and C cleaned out the last concentrated enemy pocket by the afternoon. According to Company C's Lt. Stanfield, "we noticed some evidence of suicide by grenades and rifles…no prisoners were taken."[94]

That same day, the companies returned to the mainland. Two days later, however, Company L was sent to Wakde to seek out a few remaining Japanese

A concrete air raid shelter used as a defensive position by the Japanese. *U.S. Army*

who were shooting at the engineers. After eliminating eight snipers, Company L returned to the mainland after four days.

According to an official U.S. Army account, the final number of Japanese casualties on Wakde Island numbered 759 dead and 4 captured; meanwhile more than 50 were killed on the mainland by May 20. Included among the enemy dead were members of the elite Marine Tigers. On Wakde Island, the Americans lost 40 dead and 107 wounded. During the first day's landing and operations, Company B alone suffered 42 casualties. Meanwhile, for the companies on the mainland during this time, action continued but casualties were light.[95]

Control of Wakde Island provided the Allies with a strong foothold in western New Guinea. As at the Tadji airfields, however, the 163rd's replacements in the Wakde area—the Arizona National Guard's 158th Infantry, the 6th Division, and other units—later fought fierce battles against regrouped enemy forces coming east through the jungle. Though suffering high casualties and some withdrawals, the Americans nevertheless prevailed in protecting the Wakde and Sarmi airfields.

The 163rd at Biak

As the 163rd concluded its brief but intense fight with the enemy at Wakde Island, the 41st Division's other two regiments (the 162nd and 186th), as the main combat component of "Hurricane Task Force," were engaging the Japanese

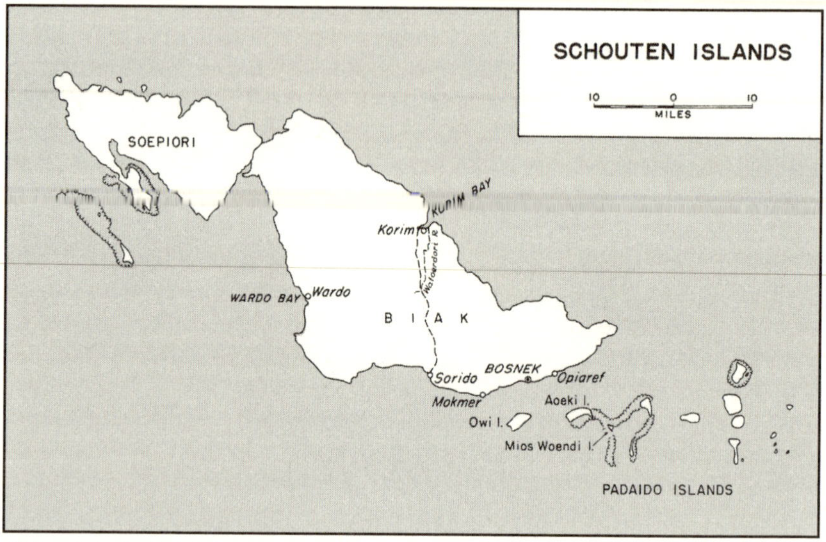

Biak and the Padaido Islands. From Robert Ross Smith, *United States Army in World War II… The Approach to the Philippines* (1953).

on Biak Island, 180 miles northwest of Wakde.[96] Taking possession of three airdromes—from east to west, at Mokmer, Borokoe, and Sorido—on Biak's southeast coast would give Allied air forces full control of Dutch New Guinea and would serve as a key base for reclaiming the Philippines.[97]

Biak is a coral island, irregularly shaped and about 25 miles across at its larger southern bulge. The topography is characterized by a series of rugged ridges between extensive flats. Above the sandy beaches and narrow coastal plain stand jungle-clad coral cliffs and terraces, as high as 300 feet and often honeycombed with passages and caves. The numerous Japanese in the area used these places to great advantage.[98]

On May 27, the landing assaults around the small Bosnek settlement met with slight resistance and gave little indication of the bitter struggle ahead. General Eichelberger later felt that the enemy intentionally lulled U.S. forces into a false sense of security, and then, from the dominating cliffs and caves overlooking the beaches, launched "a savage counterattack" the next day. On May 28, aided by tanks, the Japanese succeeded in throwing back American troops as they attempted to advance west toward the Mokmer airdrome. The 41st's commander, Gen. Horace Fuller, soon reported that the situation was grave.

The 163rd's 1st and 3rd battalions, the Antitank Company, and the regimental headquarters were aware of the situation when leaving the Wakde Island area.[99] Private Westerfield noted: "On May 30 the 163rd RCT boarded LCIs to fight the Nips who were rumored to be defeating the Division on Biak."[100] The

2nd Battalion and the Cannon Company were temporarily left behind in defensive positions at Toem, to follow in about two weeks.

During the two-day voyage to Biak, the men relaxed, played cards, and prepared equipment. As Biak came in sight, one observer noted, "torpedo boats and several destroyers were patrolling the waters...hundreds of troops had dug in all along the beach." Sand was piled "around their ack-ack guns and we could see trucks running up and down the newly made road, like automobiles on Hollywood Blvd in 1940."[101] The two battalions landed at Bosnek, taking over protection of the beach head, docking area, and supply dumps, while serving as the 41st Division reserve.

On June 1, the battle's main action again shifted westward from Bosnek toward the airfields, with the 162nd and 186th regiments fighting on the ridges and caves and the inland plateau. Every foot of ground was taken slowly after painful climbing and digging in: "It took one regiment five days to reduce one monstrous cave... [It was] railroad-terminal large with almost countless offshoots, crannies, entrances and hidden exits. It is estimated that 1,100 Japs died in it. It contained two complete portable hospitals, giant radio station, as well as living quarters, power plant and food dumps."[102]

As the battle continued, the 1st Battalion, less Company A, received orders to take over a 186th Infantry position on "Ghost Ridge Pass," near the Ibdi pocket, about two miles west of Bosnek. The 186th would move westward, as the 1st Battalion patrolled north, east, and west behind Bosnek. Meanwhile, the 163rd's 3rd Battalion also patrolled to the west on the ridges and plateau, protecting the beaches and supply area.[103]

"The ridge was about five hundred yards from the shore and one had to climb almost straight up," recalled a 1st Battalion soldier.[104] After several hours of ascending, with intermittent stops, the battalion reached the crest and continued to Ghost Ridge Pass. Lt. Arthur Merrick[105] and Company B troops established defensive positions behind a series of coral rocks. Beginning at 8:30 p.m., the men observed a nighttime air raid. Enemy planes dropped flares along the ridge, giving Japanese bombers a clear view of the beach positions. However, "the last Jap bomber that attempted to unload his explosives burst into a thousand burning pieces. The explosion could be seen for miles," and "our shore batteries knocked down four more bombers during the night." Otherwise the 1st Battalion's first night on "Ghost Ridge" remained quiet, with no shots fired or grenades thrown by the men.

Meanwhile, in the first days of June, Company A had been ordered to investigate the small Padaido Islands off Biak. Their first stop was at Owi, four miles away. They landed unopposed and the 1st platoon scouted the area, while the remainder of the men moved on to Mios Woendi. "We found this island to be a true conception of a Hollywood South Sea Island, minus women of course," a Company A man recalled.[106] Again, there was no trace of the enemy.

The invasion force dock area, Biak. *U.S. Army*

On the second day, Company A resumed the sweep through the small islands. That morning, as a soldier later explained, "our LCI in support was attacked by Jap Zeros & bombers, but missed their mark." Another noted, "P-38s and P-47s quickly came to the scene engaging the Jap planes and we had the pleasure of seeing the Zeros falling in flames, after a furious dogfight."[107] By late afternoon, Company A, after retrieving the 1st platoon from Owi, returned to Biak where it assisted in establishing the battalion's bivouac and guarded the battalion hospital. More air raids occurred during the next few days.

After patrolling and protecting Ghost Ridge, the 1st Battalion was relieved on June 4 by other troops. "We gave them all the details there were and left them our hand grenades and best wishes," a Company B soldier recalled.[108]

At the beach during the next week, the 163rd patrolled along the supply lines. "We never saw or killed any Japs in that particular area," reported a soldier, "but the patrols did find a Jap perimeter about three miles up the beach from our positions on the roadblock."[109] Shortly, the regiment relocated. Trucks met the troops and transported them up to around Ibdi pocket, where the 3rd Battalion held another roadblock. There the 163rd established a new base of operations.

Meanwhile to the west, the other 41st Division regiments were progressing slowly in securing Biak's all-important Mokmer airdromes. Lt. Gen. Krueger, commander of Allied ground forces in the Southwest Pacific Area, was becoming dissatisfied with the operation. He expected Gen. Horace Fuller's 41st Division to accelerate the seizure with the 163rd reinforcement. Five days after the 163rd's two battalions arrived, however, Fuller was no closer to wrapping up this essential part of the Biak campaign. On June 5, General MacArthur indicated he too was concerned about the delay.

According to Southwest Pacific Area inspectors sent to assess progress, there appeared to be some lack of determination in executing the task force plans.[110] Reports also indicated that reconnaissance of the enemy positions was ineffective, and Fuller was not making full use of his assistant division commander, Brig. Gen. Jens A. Doe. Enemy resistance continued to mainly check the attempted advances.

Actually, the delays were largely caused by a lack of sufficient troops and the continuous fighting, along with the extremely difficult terrain, intense heat, and scarcity of water, which left the troops exhausted.[111] On June 13, General Fuller reported the fatigue and extensive reduction of his troops. He requested reinforcements from General Krueger, who reluctantly sent the 34th Infantry of the 24th Division, arriving on June 18.

Krueger, although frustrated by the slow progress, had delayed taking any action against Fuller, hoping that the airdromes would soon be secured. By June 14, it became apparent this was not happening. Under pressure from MacArthur, who believed that the future of the Biak operation was at stake, Krueger relieved Fuller as the Hurricane Task Force commander. Lt. Gen. Robert Eichelberger, the I Corps commander, took over on June 15. Eichelberger was in an unenviable situation, for he had been a classmate of Fuller's at West Point and the two were life-long friends. Not long after Eichelberger's arrival, the stressed General Fuller, on his own initiative, also resigned as commander of the 41st Division. (He later would be assigned to another position elsewhere[112]). At Eichelberger's suggestion, the 163rd's Jens A. Doe took over leadership of the 41st Division.

By this time, the 3rd Battalion was assigned with other regimental formations in the far western sector around the Mokmer airfields. One of Doe's first orders as division commander was to increase the tempo of patrolling in order to precisely locate and then effectively engage the well-concealed enemy. From the ridges and "West Caves" above the beaches near Mokmer field, the Japanese continued their heavy attacks. Located less than a mile from shore, the West Caves consisted of three large sumps, or openings, in the coral ridges, connected by a network of tunnels and caverns—altogether an area only a couple of hundred yards wide. Pillboxes, bunkers, and foxholes ringed the cave entrances, while extensive log and coral defensive emplacements stood along a spur ridge in front.[113]

Wresting control of the West Caves was critical. Accordingly, 3rd Battalion soldiers received orders on June 19 to hold their current position at the "Sump Hole" near the West Caves, while the 162nd Infantry continued a frontal assault, and the 186th Infantry attacked from the north and east. Both 186th and 163rd men engaged in hard fighting in the ridges and hills approximately a mile north of the West Caves. These deployments, plus those of the 34th Infantry just to the west, eventually guaranteed the security of the three closely-placed airfields, located below on the coastal plain.

For several days, the attempts at capturing the West Caves were unsuccessful. Finally, on June 23, a demolition detail from the 116th Engineers lowered two 500-pound TNT charges into the entrances. A few Japanese somehow survived the massive explosions and fled the caves but were quickly shot down. In the following days, enemy resistance dwindled and eventually ceased.

By now, with reinforced troops and more effective tactics, Eichelberger's forces were finally winning the battle. Nevertheless, stiff enemy resistance continued 1 to 3 miles east of the Mokmer airfields in the 163rd's 2nd Battalion sector. Other 1st and 3rd battalion companies also were ordered here onto the main ridge between the coastline's Parai Defile (on the west) and the coastal village of Ibdi (to the east), about a mile apart. Between these points, they engaged the enemy in the "Ibdi pocket," no more than a half-mile from the sea. The terrain consisted of a series of knife-like east-west ridges, separated by depressions and crevices up to 50 feet deep, and connected in places by cross-ridges. Thick jungle covered the coral landscape. Approximately 600 of the enemy manned massive pillboxes, smaller coral caves and crevices, and foxholes at the bases of large trees.[114]

A portion of the Parai Defile—a coral landscape honeycombed with caves and depressions, all covered by a thick jungle canopy. Beginning in mid June 1944, the 163rd cleared stubborn Japanese defenses on the Parai Defile and in the Ibdi pocket just to the east. *U.S. Army photograph*

Lt. Merrick informed the men of Company B that they would lead an attack, with Company A to follow and Company C in reserve.[115] Meanwhile, "105s [howitzers] were zeroed in on the ridge and pumped thousands of rounds day and night to soften it up for the troops."

The next day, B Company's early morning advance killed 26 Japanese in one cave, with 9 slain in another. But as Sgt. Davidson later noted, the company's successful "pre-dawn infiltration assault" soon ended. Now, "our combat patrols found defeat and death ahead in this brushy plateau of the Ibdi pocket with its low, hidden ridges and masked pillboxes."[116]

After moving over a fourth ridge, the battalion's advance was halted by Japanese troops in coral bunkers. Companies B and C formed a defensive perimeter as a fierce firefight continued throughout the afternoon. Company A's 3rd platoon was assigned in front, while the 2nd platoon deployed on a half-moon shaped ridge covering the line's left flank. Company C dug in on the right. As the fighting continued, artillery pounded the Japanese positions. By nightfall, the battle of attrition finally quieted down. Elsewhere that night, an enemy air raid at 10 p.m. attempted to put the airdromes out of use.[117]

On June 25, with only four ridges taken and having suffered significant casualties, Doe withdrew the 163rd in lieu of an air strike. At 5:30 a.m., B-24 heavy bombers dropped a devastating 75 tons of bombs into the Ibdi pocket. Companies F and G then moved in, eliminating the remaining enemy positions.

The "East Caves," located about 1½ miles from the "West Caves," were similar in character. At one time perhaps 1,000 enemy personnel with medium to light ordnance occupied this position, attacking the Americans' important coastal supply road between Bosnek on the east and the airdromes to the west. Company I scouted the position, which subsequently was shelled by regimental artillery. By now, most of the Japanese here were either killed or withdrew to the island's interior. The East Caves remained an irritant, however, resulting in the Allied forces continuing to attack the position with mortars, tanks, artillery, aircraft, and naval fire; the 163rd launched numerous 81-mm mortar rounds. Subsequently, taking the position proved a relatively easier task. About July 3, an engineer explosives detail and Company E entered the caves and in a few days cleared them, encountering only 10 Japanese.[118]

Having accomplished the campaign's primary goals, Eichelberger turned control of the Hurricane Task Force over to Doe on June 27. By July 4, all enemy positions in the area were neutralized. For the remainder of the month, the tedious job of mopping up continued.

By the end of August, the 41st Division controlled Biak—a key point in MacArthur's 1,100-mile campaign along the New Guinea coast. After a few more assaults in New Guinea's far-western Vogelkop Peninsula, as well as at Morotai Island and in the Palau Islands to the northwest and north, the stage was finally set for invading the Philippines.

More than 8,000 Japanese died defending Biak; the cave fighting tactics developed by U.S. forces on the island set the standard for subsequent actions. Meanwhile, the 41st Division earned distinction as a "premiere bushmaster outfit of the world."[119] At Biak, too, the first tank-to-tank battles of the Pacific war occurred. "The score was decidedly one sided," recalled a soldier, "all eleven Nip tanks being destroyed and none of ours."[120]

At the close of the New Guinea operations, the 163rd remained in Biak for the next five months. "After that protracted campaign…up the Guinea Shore," reminisced Private Westerfield, "the rest camp on Biak was a blessing."[121] As Westerfield also noted, however, "during those four or five months of rest and training, another battle had to be fought…against nostalgia and monotony and melancholy." The men recuperated physically, but the heat and isolation tried their patience.

Training continued, but the men had little heart for it. Generally, "old stuff over again… weapons were fired; gas-masks were re-checked and tested in the gas chamber…short hikes were taken, along the new highway called the Oregon Trail…and they were slow sweaty plodding walks."[122] Training generally lasted half a day, leaving the remaining time for writing letters, reading, or playing basketball.

For most of the soldiers, the months passed slowly. "Great numbers of them went to extremes in gambling," reported Westerfield, "and there was drinking in abundance."[123] Another Christmas abroad came and went.

Since January 1944, men with 18 months overseas duty supposedly were eligible for rotation back to the United States, where they received a 21-day furlough and at least six months stateside duty. According to Westerfield, "with the great need for replacements, the program was all but a failure."[124] The Army also proposed a 30-day furlough in the states if a man agreed to return to the Southwest Pacific Area. Rotations and furloughs understandably resulted in bitter feelings due to its unequal application—most had served the same number of months overseas, yet not all were sent home.

The selective process was arbitrary, as "some CO's made the reasons for selection secret." In the determination of who should return to the United States, "wounds, illness, decorations, time in a combat area, general physical and morale condition, and good conduct might all enter the picture; and there was no official way of making the final selections."[125] Consequently, only the fortunate ones received early rotation.

By about this stage in the war, Montana men comprised an estimated 20 to 12 percent of the 163rd regimental roster. Change in the makeup of the ranks, of course, was due to casualties, sickness, rotation, and the numerous new replacements.

On to the Philippines

On October 20, 1944, the liberation of the Philippines began with a massive assault on Leyte Island, located about halfway up the east side of the Philippines archipelago. The invasion included the 1st Cavalry, 7th, 24th, 32nd, 77th, and 96th divisions.[126] Eight weeks later on December 15, another major landing occurred at Mindoro Island, just south of the large northern island of Luzon. Next, on January 9, Sixth Army troops stormed ashore at Lingayen Gulf on Luzon, north of the capital, Manila. On January 21, another powerful force hit the beaches at Subic Bay, even closer to Manila. With this landing came the announcement that the 41st Division, as part of the newly formed Eighth Army, would once again join the fight.

In early February 1945, the 163rd's long wait at Biak ended with the troops boarding trucks jammed with their equipment and rumbling away from the deserted campsite. They passed by "the great bomber base at Mokmer, [and] came to the sea and the fleet of transports."[127] The regiment set sail on the USS *Warren*, never to return to New Guinea.[128] Tokyo Rose had been wrong—the regiment did leave New Guinea to fight another day.

On February 9, the 163rd arrived at Mindoro Island, just south of Luzon Island, where the regiment prepared for the invasion of Mindanao. This operation would be a back track to the far south—Mindanao sat at the southern end of the Philippines. After Luzon, Mindanao was the biggest island in the Philippines.

At the bivouac on Mindoro, Sgt. Harold Ingle of Company H watched two P-38 fighters crash in mid-air. "One sheared off the tail of the other—then exploded." An accident occurred again on February 14 when a bomber pilot misjudged a landing. "With wheels already down, he struck the earth where trenches had been hastily dug when Jap ships blasted the area. All J Co. rushed over to help, but exploding ammo from the gun belts repelled us." The crew, however, managed to escape unhurt.[129]

By February 19, the regiment's camp on Mindoro was completed—a neat tent city. For a short while, one soldier recalled, "nothing could be more pleasant—men engaged in baseball games and rested."[130] On March 5, however, the regiment packed and prepared to leave. The following day, they hiked to the beach where LCIs waited to transport them to Mindanao.

By this time, the 41st Division was split up. On February 28, the 186th landed on Palawan, in the far-western Philippines, to eliminate the Japanese on that vast, long, narrow island—a task that continued through June for most of the regiment. Meanwhile, on March 10, 1945, the 162nd and 163rd assaulted the tip of Mindanao's Zamboanga Peninsula, jutting far out westward in the Sulu Sea.

Before H-hour, cruisers and destroyers bombarded the beachhead and inland up to 2,500 yards, including the extreme flanks at Caldera Point and Zamboanga City, the capital of Mindanao. Also, the 13th Air Force saturated the area with bombs in preparation for the landing. The enemy, however, had largely abandoned a vast network of defenses in the lowlands because of the fierce pre-invasion bombardments. The Japanese mainly withdrew to other fortifications in the hills. At 9:15 a.m., the 162nd landed at San Mateo and immediately fanned out, moving against light resistance to take the western side of the peninsula. The 163rd followed, landing on a beach two miles from Zamboanga City, which was located near the tip of the peninsula. The 163rd had orders to continue the attack east.

The 162nd spearheaded the operation under the command of Lt. Col. Harold M. Lindstrom of Tacoma, formerly a battalion leader in the 163rd. The immediate objectives were the Wolfe airdrome, 1,000 yards inland, in addition to the San Roque airstrip on the outskirts of the city. Within thirty minutes, the troops overran Wolfe field. The airdrome was not in serviceable condition, but construction of a "cub strip" commenced immediately and by 4 p.m. small planes began landing.[131] At noon, with the airfield secured, General Doe established his division command post here, officially assuming control of the ground forces.

The 162nd began probing the approaches to Malaguatay, Masilay, and San Roque, while Company F of the 162nd moved west along a coastal road to established a blocking position. Meanwhile, the 658th Amphibious Tractor Battalion provided beach security on both flanks until the 163rd launched an attack in the east on the Baliwasan River. The 163rd met two small enemy contingents in the advance. These delayed the regiment at Gavilan Point and then again just near the Zamboanga Road. When reaching the west flank of the Baliwasan River, the 163rd encountered several concrete pillboxes, two machine guns, and numerous booby traps. Several of the mines and booby traps hampered progress. Mine detector teams from the 116th Combat Engineers Battalion accompanied the infantry and cleared the beach roads of enemy mines. With that flank secured, the regiment bivouacked for the night, approximately 300 yards east of the 162nd's Company F roadblock.[132]

The next day, March 11, the Americans captured Zamboanga City—much damaged except for the docks and jetties, which remained in fair condition. In their hasty flight, however, the enemy left the city power and water systems in usable condition. In the days ahead, with continuing tank and air support, and due to the critical work done by combat engineers in building support roads and bridges, the 163rd continued moving forward. As the Japanese retreated, they intermittently fired artillery and mortars, and left booby traps and mines.

This normally constituted the enemy's resistance, along with scattered rifle or machine gun fire—a common pattern during the widespread operations in the Philippines. Before the end of the war, 16 U.S. divisions participated in more than 40 landings in the Philippines. Some operations, nevertheless, were the typical savage slugfests that Americans expected against the Japanese, but many other actions were fast paced and wide ranging.

The 163rd experienced a brutal occurrence on the morning of March 13 as the regiment continued its advance inland against cleverly concealed enemy positions around Pasananca. The 1st and 2nd battalions initially encountered mortar and small arms fire. Suddenly, the Japanese electrically detonated a store of torpedoes buried in a hillside, 100 yards west of the Pasananca Road. The explosion obliterated a hillside, clearing an area 300 yards square in the process. At the time, the 1st and 2nd battalions were advancing abreast—they suffered 65 dead and wounded.[133] Undaunted, General Doe's men picked up the assault on March 14, with precision bombing support from three squadrons of B-24s.

Action on the morning of March 16 was typical as Company G rifleman followed several tanks into battle. "On that day, a Japanese mountain gun, 20mm cannon, and machine guns pinned down the entire company," recalled Westerfield. "The lead tank carried a bulldozer [blade]; it dropped the blade and charged the pillbox and rolled up the entrance and sat upon the roof." And then, "it sank down a few feet...the crew of the pillbox moaned for awhile and then quit moaning." With the pillbox neutralized, the tanks blasted away at four smaller emplacements and silenced the 20-mm gun. Afterward, the tanks trained their guns on a lone Japanese strong point. This forced about 75 enemy soldiers to charge out of the stronghold, but "the tanks' machine-guns spun and toppled them."[134]

Securing the Zamboanga coastal plain, the two regiments next faced the problem of driving out the Japanese entrenched in the nearby high ground, particularly around Mount Capisan. On March 20, the 1st Battalion of the 186th, which had been fighting on Palawan, was sent in as reinforcement. For a week, a pitched uphill battle continued from ridge to ridge against determined resistance. By about March 21, the advance had won a commanding position near Mount Pulungbata, and on March 30, Japanese soldiers withdrew further into the mountains, driven along by relentless aerial bombing and artillery fire. On March 30–31, relatively fresh 186th troops relieved the 163rd, which returned to a bivouac area. Two days later, Mount Capisan was seized.

Since the Zamboanga landing, some 3,000 of the estimated 6,000 to 7,000 enemy soldiers in the area were fatalities in combat. Overwhelmed by the hard hitting invasion, they were "demoralized, disorganized, and suffering severely from lack of food."[135]

The Sulu Archipelago

Following action on the Zamboanga Peninsula, the 163rd received orders to eliminate Japanese positions in the Sulu archipelago, a chain of islands stretching southwest from Zamboanga to within a few miles of the huge island of Borneo. This would be an island hopping operation. According to intelligence reports, supposedly the bulk of Japanese forces had evacuated to Borneo.

On April 2, the 163rd's 2nd Battalion landed on Bongoa and Sanga Sanga, the northernmost prominent islands of the archipelago. Preceded by air and naval bombardment, the regiment encountered light and ineffective mortar and 20-mm fire during the operation. Poor beach conditions hampered the unloading of supplies, but by 1:40 p.m. the battalion was firmly established ashore. On April 3, the 2nd Battalion occupied Bongoa Town without a struggle, enabling the command to declare the area secure by April 6. Company A of the 873rd Aviation Engineer Battalion began construction of the Sanga Sanga airfield.

The 2nd Battalion then mopped up in Bongoa's Kabogan Peak area and sent patrols elsewhere across the island, meeting only scattered enemy resistance. The battalion, less Company F, then departed and rejoined the rest of the 163rd on Jolo on April 10, the day after the initial assault there. The remaining Company F provided security at the Sanga Sanga airstrip and coordinated the guerilla elements on Bongoa, which continued seeking out enemy stragglers.

Meanwhile, the 1st and 3rd battalions had attacked Jolo Island, the largest of the Sulu group, which General MacArthur previously had chosen to bypass. It was estimated that 2,300 Japanese soldiers were garrisoned on Jolo, which was centrally located in the Sulu chain. On April 9, elements of the 163rd with supporting troops stormed ashore, expecting heavy resistance, but there was none. Communication with native guerilla forces on the island had resulted in information identifying the best beachhead. By 8:45 a.m., the shore was secured, and by late afternoon, the Mount Patikul area, about four miles from Jolo City, was occupied by elements of the 3rd Battalion. Meanwhile, the 1st Battalion came in on LCMs to the Jolo Town dock, on the island's north side. In Jolo, enemy "box mines" and 75-mm shells buried nose up represented the only obstacles encountered. Jolo was in ruins, however, being burned by the Japanese during their withdrawal.

The Sultan of Sulu, Muhammed Janail Abririr II, leader of 300,000 "Mahammedans" in the archipelago, personally welcomed the 163rd. His irregular forces would assist in taking Jolo.[136] The 1st Battalion next attacked and captured Zettle airfield and Mount Bangkal, while Company I of the 116th Engineers completed the occupation of Jolo Town, repairing the dock facilities and clearing the remaining land mines. In cooperation with local guerillas, elements of the 163rd assaulted the enemy and captured Mount Daho. Meanwhile, Company L, supported by tanks, encountered only light resistance, and by early morning on April 11, took Mount Mausing. Company A also secured Mount Datu, 1,000 yards from Mount Agao, while meeting only weak opposition. Motorized patrols reconnoitered the area and met no resistance. During the night of April 11, the enemy attempted to infiltrate the 1st and 3rd battalion perimeters on Mount Mausing and Mount Agao, but both attacks were repulsed.

The 2nd Battalion continued dealing with hostile remnants outside of Jolo Town, while simultaneously the 1st and 3rd battalions continued moving against increasing enemy resistance, capturing their objectives by April 15. The Japanese conducted nightly attacks, which were repeatedly repelled. Between the start of the invasion on April 9 and up to April 15, 324 enemy soldiers were killed, and 3 taken prisoner.

Guerillas acting in concert with the 163rd attacked toward Mount Daho, meeting with minimal resistance, until coming under heavy 20-mm fire from the heights of Mount Daho itself. After determined efforts by the guerillas failed to dislodge the enemy, the 1st Battalion went in, supported by artillery and air strikes. Beginning on April 17, daily air, artillery, and infantry attacks eventually broke through the stubborn Japanese defenses. By April 24, Mount Daho was secured. For the rest of the month and into May, the 163rd, augmented with native forces, continued to sweep across the island.

Eventually in the Eighth Army's Sulu campaign, Tawi Tawi would be taken near the southern end of the archipelago. From there, and from other captured or newly established installations in the Sulu Sea, Australian and Dutch troops launched an invasion of northern Borneo near the end of the war. By that time, however, the 163rd had been called elsewhere.

Back to Mindanao

In mid May, the 3rd Battalion, followed by the 1st Battalion, was sent back to participate in the Eighth Army's Davao Gulf operations on the southeast side of Mindanao. Here, after skirmishes, the combined forces of the 163rd and 186th took the large important city of Davao.[137] The Americans frustrated Japanese attempts to move or organize their troops, and exerted steady pressure as enemy casualties mounted. Between May 23 and June 20, 1,345 Japanese soldiers died and 103 Japanese and 274 Formosans were captured on the Zamboanga Peninsula. The 41st Division's casualties at this time were relatively light.

The Mindanao campaign ended for the 41st Division on June 20, when relieved by the 93rd Infantry Division. The 41st Division returned to Zamboanga, where it would remain in training and rehabilitation. As on so many occasions before, the first task was to establish a bivouac. "The regiment framed their tents in bamboo and leveled the old Jap entrenchment along the bluff and began training," Westerfield explained.[137] Soon, instructions came for the planned invasion of Japan.

On August 1, staff officers attended a conference at the Sixth Army command post, receiving information about the upcoming Olympic Operation—the initial assault on the Japanese home islands. Soon, the division's staff informed the 163rd that it would be participating in the attack on Kyushu, Japan's southernmost large isle. Training became intense in the following days for what appeared to be the regiment's most daunting task yet—landing in Japan itself.

Meanwhile on the international scene, the Allies' Potsdam Declaration of July 26 demanded that Japan surrender unconditionally or face "prompt and utter destruction." The declaration called for an end to Japan's military regime, punishment of its war criminals, withdrawal from all occupied territories except the home islands, and disarmament. With the Allies' occupation of Japan, the western powers intended to establish a democratic political system, while promising to allow the economy to rebuild. Military occupation would end when Japan installed a "peacefully inclined and responsible government."

On July 28, Japan's militarist dominated government rejected the Potsdam demands, though there were some stirrings behind the scenes to accept surrender, mainly in civilian circles. Japan's resolve faltered between August 6 and 9, 1945, however, when two atomic bombs were dropped on the home islands and the USSR declared war on Japan. The following day, August 10, the Japanese government announced its willingness to accept the surrender terms, with the proviso that it did "not compromise any demand which prejudices the prerogatives of His Majesty as Sovereign Ruler."

Meanwhile, rumors swept through the regiment at Zamboanga, and "bulletin boards graphically depicted the B-29s destruction of the great industrial cities in Japan."[138] Then, on August 15, to the great relief of the 163rd soldiers, Japan surrendered. The men celebrated as training ceased for three days and the regiment was issued passes. Fireworks lit the beach at night, and a parade in Zamboanga commemorated the Allied victory.

Now, word circulated that the regiment would serve with occupation forces in Japan. Training resumed and continued through the end of August. On September 1, Col. William J. Moroney called a meeting of the entire regiment, announcing that the time and place for serving in the occupation would soon be released. Meanwhile, training programs proceeded, and the regiment's men received elementary instruction in the Japanese language.

Occupation of Japan

Early on the morning of September 18, the men boarded the transports *Saint Mary*, *Highland*, *Yancy*, and *Rutland* and set sail. The convoy stopped at Buckner Bay, Okinawa, on September 25, where the regiment practiced "fire and abandon ship drills." On September 28, the convoy's ships left harbor to avoid a typhoon and struggled in rough seas until returning to Okinawa on October 1.

On October 5, the ships entered Japan's Bungo Strait between Kyushu and Shikoku, where mines littered the waters. Escorting destroyers fired .50-caliber machine guns to detonate mines. "All men stuck close to their abandon ship stations," recalled a soldier. A Japanese coastal pilot guided the convoy through the minefields. One observer noted: "Japan looked pretty good from aboard ship—very beautiful scenery on all side." Another added: "The men were anxious to land and see the country of the enemy."

On October 5, at 3:30 p.m., the 2nd Battalion disembarked at Kure in southern Honshu, not far from Hiroshima. The remainder of the regiment came ashore the next morning around 7 a.m. The troops proceeded inland to a prearranged camp at Hiro. Over the next few weeks, the men improved the camp, conducted reconnaissance, inspected Japanese military installations, and directed the enemy's disarmament at Yano, Yoashiura, Kure, and Hashinommatzu.

On November 22, Thanksgiving Day, all enlisted men were released from duty. "Details were pulled by highest NCOs," recalled one soldier. The weather now cooled considerably, resembling the winter climate in the northern United States. On December 25, the Montana men remaining in the regiment celebrated their last Christmas away from home. According to William McCartney, "much time was spent in decorating the barracks, mess halls and recreation rooms and for a change the men had real Christmas trees." Nevertheless, "many longed to go home, but morale remained high."[139]

On January 1, 1946, the 41st Division officially was deactivated. During the next several weeks, the men made their way to Nagoya, and from there, embarked for the United States. After five long years, the regiment returned home.[140]

Notes

1. "History of the 41st - 163rd Infantry (Company B) 9-16-40 thru 1945, Wakde 5-18-44, Ibdi Ridge," 21, Entry 427, Folder 341-INF (163) –0 to 341-INF (163) –0.1, Box 10633, Office of the Adjutant General, Records of the Adjutant General's Office 1917–, Record Group 407, National Archives II.
2. Ibid., 18.
3. Ibid., 21.
4. "Headquarters, Company 'A' 163rd Infantry, Office of the Company Commander," 18, Entry 427, Folder 341-INF (163) -0 to 341-INF (163) -0.1, 1940–45, Box 10633, World War II Operations Reports 1940–48, Record Group 407, National Archives II.
5. Ibid.
6. "History of the 41st - 163rd Infantry (Company B) 9-16-40 thru 1945, Wakde 5-18-44, Ibdi Ridge," 19, Entry 427, Folder 341-INF (163) –0 to 341-INF (163) –0.1, Box 10633, Office of the Adjutant General, Records of the Adjutant General's Office 1917–, Record Group 407, National Archives II.
7. "Headquarters, Company 'A' 163rd Infantry, Office of the Company Commander," 19, Entry 427, Folder 341-INF (163) -0 to 341-INF (163) -0.1, 1940–45, Box 10633, World War II Operations Reports 1940–48, Record Group 407, National Archives II.
8. "History of the 41st - 163rd Infantry (Company B) 9-16-40 thru 1945, Wakde 5-18-44, Ibdi Ridge," 18, Entry 427, Folder 341-INF (163) –0 to 341-INF (163) –0.1, Box 10633, Office of the Adjutant General, Records of the Adjutant General's Office 1917–, Record Group 407, National Archives II.
9. "Headquarters, Company 'A' 163rd Infantry, Office of the Company Commander," 19, Entry 427, Folder 341-INF (163) -0 to 341-INF (163) -0.1, 1940–45, Box 10633, World War II Operations Reports 1940–48, Record Group 407, National Archives II.
10. "History of the 41st - 163rd Infantry (Company B) 9-16-40 thru 1945, Wakde 5-18-44, Ibdi Ridge," 20, Entry 427, Folder 341-INF (163) –0 to 341-INF (163) –0.1, Box

10633, Office of the Adjutant General, Records of the Adjutant General's Office 1917–, Record Group 407, National Archives II.

11. "Headquarters, Company 'A' 163rd Infantry, Office of the Company Commander," 20, Entry 427, Folder 341-INF (163) -0 to 341-INF (163) -0.1, 1940–45, Box 10633, World War II Operations Reports 1940–48, Record Group 407, National Archives II.
12. A "Liberty" ship's maximum speed was 11 knots, making it easy prey for enemy submarines, consequently in 1942 a new "Victory" ship design capable of more speed was adopted. The vessels were 455 feet long and 62 feet wide, and the cross-compound steam turbine engines with double reduction gears developed 6,000 or 6,500 horsepower. The design was sleek compared to Liberty ships, and the hulls strengthened to avoid the fracturing that plagued the Liberty vessels. Victory ships were armed with a 5-inch stern gun, a 3-inch bow gun, and eight 20-mm machine guns. Frederic C. Lane, *Ships for Victory; a History of Ship Building under the U.S. Maritime Commission in World War II* (Baltimore: Johns Hopkins Press, 1951), 50.
13. "Headquarters, Company 'A' 163rd Infantry, Office of the Company Commander," 20, Entry 427, Folder 341-INF (163) -0 to 341-INF (163) -0.1, 1940–45, Box 10633, World War II Operations Reports 1940–48, Record Group 407, National Archives II.
14. "History of the 41st - 163rd Infantry (Company B) 9-16-40 thru 1945, Wakde 5-18-44, Ibdi Ridge," 21, Entry 427, Folder 341-INF (163) –0 to 341-INF (163) –0.1, Box 10633, Office of the Adjutant General, Records of the Adjutant General's Office 1917–, Record Group 407, National Archives II.
15. "Headquarters, Company 'A' 163rd Infantry, Office of the Company Commander," 20, Entry 427, Folder 341-INF (163) -0 to 341-INF (163) -0.1, 1940–45, Box 10633, World War II Operations Reports 1940–48, Record Group 407, National Archives II.
16. Ibid.
17. Col. Howard McKinney, "History of the 163rd Montana National Guard," 62, Box 67, Montana Military History Museum, Library Archives, Fort William Henry Harrison, Helena Montana [hereafter cited as MMHM].
18. Ibid.
19. "History of the 41st - 163rd Infantry (Company B) 9-16-40 thru 1945, Wakde 5-18-44, Ibdi Ridge," 2, Entry 427, Folder 341-INF (163) –0 to 341-INF (163) –0.1, Box 10633, Office of the Adjutant General, Records of the Adjutant General's Office 1917–, Record Group 407, National Archives II.
20. Ibid., 3.
21. Robert Ross Smith, *United States Army in World War II: War in the Pacific: The Approach to the Philippines,* vol. 3 (Washington, D.C.: Center of Military History, United States Army, 1996), 14.
22. "Headquarters, Company 'A' 163rd Infantry, Office of the Company Commander," 21, Entry 427, Folder 341-INF (163) -0 to 341-INF (163) -0.1, 1940–45, Box 10633, World War II Operations Reports 1940–48, Record Group 407, National Archives II.
23. "History of the 41st - 163rd Infantry (Company B) 9-16-40 thru 1945, Wakde 5-18-44, Ibdi Ridge," 2, Entry 427, Folder 341-INF (163) –0 to 341-INF (163) –0.1, Box 10633, Office of the Adjutant General, Records of the Adjutant General's Office 1917–, Record Group 407, National Archives II.
24. "Headquarters, Company 'A' 163rd Infantry, Office of the Company Commander," 21, Entry 427, Folder 341-INF (163) -0 to 341-INF (163) -0.1, 1940–45, Box 10633, World War II Operations Reports 1940–48, Record Group 407, National Archives II.
25. "History of the 41st - 163rd Infantry (Company B) 9-16-40 thru 1945, Wakde 5-18-44, Ibdi Ridge," 2, Entry 427, Folder 341-INF (163) –0 to 341-INF (163) –0.1, Box 10633,

Office of the Adjutant General, Records of the Adjutant General's Office 1917–, Record Group 407, National Archives II.

26. "Headquarters, Company 'A' 163rd Infantry, Office of the Company Commander," 21, Entry 427, Folder 341-INF (163) -0 to 341-INF (163) -0.1, 1940–45, Box 10633, World War II Operations Reports 1940–48, Record Group 407, National Archives II.
27. William F. McCartney, *The Jungleers: A History of the 41st Infantry Division* (Washington D.C.: Infantry Journal Press, 1948), 71.
28. Officially designated as "Patrol Craft Torpedo," fast-moving PT boats were armed with two torpedo tubes and .50-caliber machine guns, and were the equivalent to British MTBs and German E-Boats. I.C.B. Dear, *The Oxford Companion to World War II*, ed. by M.R.D. Foot (Oxford: Oxford University Press, 1995), 916.
29. Smith, *United States Army in World War II... The Approach to the Philippines,* 12–13.
30. "History of the 41st - 163rd Infantry (Company B) 9-16-40 thru 1945, Wakde 5-18-44, Ibdi Ridge," 4, Entry 427, Folder 341-INF (163) –0 to 341-INF (163) –0.1, Box 10633, Office of the Adjutant General, Records of the Adjutant General's Office 1917–, Record Group 407, National Archives II.
31. "G-3 Historical Report-Letterpress (Humboldt) Landing Force Hollandia Campaign, 41st Infantry Division, 22 April- 5 May 1944," 1, Entry 427, Folder 41st Inf Div, 341.3, 1-14 to 8-1944, Box 10554, World War II Operations Reports 1940–48, Record Group 407, National Archives II.
32. "History of the 41st - 163rd Infantry (Company B) 9-16-40 thru 1945, Wakde 5-18-44, Ibdi Ridge," 4, Entry 427, Folder 341-INF (163) –0 to 341-INF (163) –0.1, Box 10633, Office of the Adjutant General, Records of the Adjutant General's Office 1917–, Record Group 407, National Archives II.
33. DUKWs, officially designated a "Truck, 2-1/2 ton, 6 x 6, Amphibious," had power in all six wheels, a top speed of 50 mph on land and about 6 mph in water, and could haul over 5,000 pounds of cargo or personnel. It also could be mounted with .30- or .50-caliber machine guns, though generally they were unarmed and used behind the lines to move men, ammunition, and supplies across rivers and other wet terrain. C.B. Colby, *Fighting Gear of World War II: Equipment and Weapons of the American G.I.,* (New York: Coward-McCann, 1961), 39.
34. "History of the 41st - 163rd Infantry (Company B) 9-16-40 thru 1945, Wakde 5-18-44, Ibdi Ridge," 4, Entry 427, Folder 341-INF (163) –0 to 341-INF (163) –0.1, Box 10633, Office of the Adjutant General, Records of the Adjutant General's Office 1917–, Record Group 407, National Archives II.
35. On August 20, Captain Moss, a transfer from the 32nd Division, took command of Company A. At the same, time 1st Lt. Frank E. Maxam was promoted to captain and became Company B's commander. "Headquarters, Company 'A' 163rd Infantry, Office of the Company Commander," 21, Entry 427, Folder 341-INF (163) -0 to 341-INF (163) -0.1, 1940–45, Box 10633, World War II Operations Reports 1940–48, Record Group 407, National Archives II.
36. "History of the 41st - 163rd Infantry (Company B) 9-16-40 thru 1945, Wakde 5-18-44, Ibdi Ridge," 5, Entry 427, Folder 341-INF (163) –0 to 341-INF (163) –0.1, Box 10633, Office of the Adjutant General, Records of the Adjutant General's Office 1917–, Record Group 407, National Archives II.
37. Ibid.
38. Hargis Westerfield, the official 41st Division historian, compiled a 111-page typed manuscript containing unit recollections. The manuscript begins with induction in September

1940 and concludes with the surrender of Japan in August 1945; Hargis Westerfield, unpublished manuscript, 45, Box 4, LTC Ray Read office, State Area Command, Fort Harrison.

39. "History of the 41st - 163rd Infantry (Company B) 9-16-40 thru 1945, Wakde 5-18-44, Ibdi Ridge," 5, Entry 427, Folder 341-INF (163) –0 to 341-INF (163) –0.1, Box 10633, Office of the Adjutant General, Records of the Adjutant General's Office 1917–, Record Group 407, National Archives II.
40. Headquarters and Headquarters Battery, 41st Division Artillery (Designated for this operation, Letterpress Artillery), "History of the 41st Division, 163rd Inf., September 16, 1940–December 31, 1945 and beyond," 1, Folder 341-INF (163) -0.1, Box 10633, World War II Operations Reports 1940–48, Record Group 407, National Archives II.
41. Douglas MacArthur, *Reports of General MacArthur/Prepared by His General Staff: The Campaigns of MacArthur in the Pacific, Volume I* (Washington, D.C.: Center for Military History, 1994) 142–43.
42. "History of the 41st - 163rd Infantry (Company B) 9-16-40 thru 1945, Wakde 5-18-44, Ibdi Ridge," 5, Entry 427, Folder 341-INF (163) –0 to 341-INF (163) –0.1, Box 10633, Office of the Adjutant General, Records of the Adjutant General's Office 1917–, Record Group 407, National Archives II.
43. "Headquarters, Company 'A' 163rd Infantry, Office of the Company Commander," 22, Entry 427, Folder 341-INF (163) -0 to 341-INF (163) -0.1, 1940–45, Box 10633, World War II Operations Reports 1940–48, Record Group 407, National Archives II.
44. An LCI (Landing Craft, Infantry) was designed to deliver troops directly onto a beachhead. With a crew of 24 to 60 sailors, LCIs carried 200 soldiers, who descended from ramps on each side of the bow. The vessels measured 158 feet long and 23 feet wide, with a hull of ¼-inch steel plate. Propulsion was provided by two sets of quad General Motors 6-cylinder diesel engines, generating 3,600 HP per quad set. The flat-bottom hulls were designed for beach landings. LCIs were not designed for cross-ocean travel, yet given wartime urgency, they did sail from the United States to the European and Pacific theaters. A considerably larger vessel, the LST (Landing Ship, Tank) delivered troops, vehicles, and supplies directly onto beaches, without the need of docks, cranes, or other shore facilities. LSTs measured 328 feet long and 50 feet wide, and carried up to 2,100 tons. The lower part was a tank deck, where up to 20 Sherman tanks could be loaded. Lighter vehicles were stored on the upper deck; an elevator loaded and off-loaded vehicles, artillery, and other equipment from the upper deck. In later models, a ramp replaced the elevator. An LST had a maximum speed of 11.5 knots and a cruising speed of 8.75 knots. LSTs were lightly armed, typically with seven 40-mm and twelve 20-mm antiaircraft guns. James L. Mooney, ed. *Dictionary of American Naval Fighting Ships* (Washington, D.C.: Department of the Navy, Office of the Chief of Naval Operations, Naval History Division, 1977).
45. Headquarters and Headquarters Battery, 41st Division Artillery (Designated for this operation LETTERPRESS ARTILLERY), "History of the 41st Infantry Regiment, July 1917–June 1945," 2, Entry 425, Folder 341-INF (163) to 341-INF (163) 0.1, World War II Operations Reports 1940–48, Box 10526, Office of the Adjutant General, Record Group 407, National Archives II.
46. "H" meant "hour" and the number following it with a minus sign in front designated the minutes remaining until the actual landing began. Smith, *United States Army in World War II... The Approach to the Philippines,* 45.
47. The landing beaches were broken down into four primary locations referred to as White Beach 1, 2, 3, and 4.

48. "G-3 Historical Report-Letterpress (Humboldt) Landing Force Hollandia Campaign 41st Infantry Division 22 April- 5 May 1944," 2, Entry 427, Folder 41st Infantry Division 341.3, 1-14-43 to 8-1944, Box 10554, World War II Operations Reports 1940–48, Record Group 407, National Archives II.
49. Smith, *United States Army in World War II... The Approach to the Philippines,* 597.
50. "G-3 Historical Report-Letterpress (Humboldt) Landing Force Hollandia Campaign 41st Infantry Division 22 April- 5 May 1944," 2, Entry 427, Folder 41st Infantry Division 341.3, 1-14-43 to 8-1944, Box 10554, World War II Operations Reports 1940–48, Record Group 407, National Archives II.
51. Ibid.
52. Smith, *United States Army in World War II... The Approach to the Philippines,* 55.
53. Ibid., Map III.
54. "Headquarters, Company 'A' 163rd Infantry, Office of the Company Commander," 22, Entry 427, Folder 341-INF (163) -0 to 341-INF (163) -0.1, 1940–45, Box 10633, World War II Operations Reports 1940–48, Record Group 407, National Archives II.
55. The fate of the Japanese soldier and the Korean laborers is unclear.
56. "Master 163rd Infantry Regiment - Aitape (Persecution) Opn.-Operations Rpt., 22 April–17 May 1944," 2, Entry 427, Folder 41st Infantry Division 341-INF (163) –0.3 Operations Reports, 12-14-42 to 6-30-44, Box 10634, and "History of the 41st - 163rd Infantry (Company B) 9-16-40 thru 1945, Wakde 5-18-44, Ibdi Ridge," 7, Entry 427, Folder 341-INF (163) -0 to 341-INF (163) -0.1, Box 10633, World War II Operations Reports 1940–48, Record Group 407, National Archives II.
57. Ibid.
58. Ibid.
59. "Headquarters, Company 'A' 163rd Infantry, Office of the Company Commander," 22, Entry 427, Folder 341-INF (163) -0 to 341-INF (163) -0.1, 1940–45, Box 10633, World War II Operations Reports 1940–48, Record Group 407, National Archives II.
60. "History of the 41st - 163rd Infantry (Company B) 9-16-40 thru 1945, Wakde 5-18-44, Ibdi Ridge," 7, Entry 427, Folder 341-INF (163) –0 to 341-INF (163) –0.1, Box 10633, Office of the Adjutant General, Records of the Adjutant General's Office 1917–, Record Group 407, National Archives II.
61. "Headquarters, Company 'A' 163rd Infantry, Office of the Company Commander," 22, Entry 427, Folder 341-INF (163) -0 to 341-INF (163) -0.1, 1940–45, Box 10633, World War II Operations Reports 1940–48, Record Group 407, National Archives II.
62. Ibid.
63. "History of the 41st - 163rd Infantry (Company B) 9-16-40 thru 1945, Wakde 5-18-44, Ibdi Ridge," 7–8, Entry 427, Folder 341-INF (163) –0 to 341-INF (163) –0.1, Box 10633, Office of the Adjutant General, Records of the Adjutant General's Office 1917–, Record Group 407, National Archives II.
64. Ibid., 8. "Headquarters, Company 'A' 163rd Infantry, Office of the Company Commander," 22–23, Entry 427, Folder 341-INF (163) -0 to 341-INF (163) -0.1, 1940–45, Box 10633, World War II Operations Reports 1940–48, Record Group 407, National Archives II.
65. S-2 is the Intelligence Section. Smith, *United States Army in World War II... The Approach to the Philippines,* 598.
66. "Headquarters, Company 'A' 163rd Infantry, Office of the Company Commander," 22, Entry 427, Folder 341-INF (163) -0 to 341-INF (163) -0.1, 1940–45, Box 10633, World War II Operations Reports 1940–48, Record Group 407, National Archives II.

67. "History of the 41st - 163rd Infantry (Company B) 9-16-40 thru 1945, Wakde 5-18-44, Ibdi Ridge," 8, Entry 427, Folder 341-INF (163) –0 to 341-INF (163) –0.1, Box 10633, Office of the Adjutant General, Records of the Adjutant General's Office 1917–, Record Group 407, National Archives II.
68. Hargis Westerfield, unpublished manuscript, 51, Box 4, LTC Ray Read office, State Area Command, Fort Harrison.
69. Ibid.
70. "Headquarters, Company 'A' 163rd Infantry, Office of the Company Commander," 23, Entry 427, Folder 341-INF (163) -0 to 341-INF (163) -0.1, 1940–45, Box 10633, World War II Operations Reports 1940–48, Record Group 407, National Archives II; Richard H. Lacey, *The Montana Militia: A History of Montana's Volunteer Forces, 1867–1976* (Dillon, Montana: Dillon Tribune-Examiner Press, 1976), 74; Smith, *United States Army in World War II... The Approach to the Philippines,* 111.
71. "Headquarters, Company 'A' 163rd Infantry, Office of the Company Commander," 23, Entry 427, Folder 341-INF (163) -0 to 341-INF (163) -0.1, 1940–45, Box 10633, World War II Operations Reports 1940–48, Record Group 407, National Archives II.
72. Ibid.
73. Lacey, *Montana Militia,* 74.
74. "History of the 41st - 163rd Infantry Regiment, July 1917–June 1945," Entry 427, Folder 341-INF 2 (163) –0 to 341-INF (163) –0.1, World War II Operations Reports 1940–48, Box 10526, World War II Operations, Record Group 407, National Archives II.
75. MacArthur, *Reports of General MacArthur,* 150.
76. Ibid., 57.
77. "History of the 41st - 163rd Infantry (Company B) 9-16-40 thru 1945, Wakde 5-18-44, Ibdi Ridge," 10, Entry 427, Folder 341-INF (163) –0 to 341-INF (163) –0.1, Box 10633, Office of the Adjutant General, Records of the Adjutant General's Office 1917–, Record Group 407, National Archives II.
78. Ibid.
79. Ibid.
80. "Headquarters, Company 'A' 163rd Infantry, Office of the Company Commander," 24, Entry 427, Folder 341-INF (163) -0 to 341-INF (163) -0.1, 1940–45, Box 10633, World War II Operations Reports 1940–48, Record Group 407, National Archives II; McCartney, *The Jungleers,* 94.
81. Ibid.
82. The M4 Sherman, with a crew of five men, was the most numerous American tank used in World War II. The most common version, the M4A3, weighed over 31 tons, with a 75-mm cannon in a turret, which also often mounted a machine gun. A ball-mounted machine gun was located in the front hull. The M4A3 was powered by a Ford 450hp V8 engine, providing a top speed of 42 mph. Colby, *Fighting Gear of World War II,* 45.
83. "Headquarters, Company 'A' 163rd Infantry, Office of the Company Commander," 24, Entry 427, Folder 341-INF (163) -0 to 341-INF (163) -0.1, 1940–45, Box 10633, World War II Operations Reports 1940–48, Record Group 407, National Archives II.
84. "History of the 41st - 163rd Infantry (Company B) 9-16-40 thru 1945, Wakde 5-18-44, Ibdi Ridge," 12, Entry 427, Folder 341-INF (163) –0 to 341-INF (163) –0.1, Box 10633, Office of the Adjutant General, Records of the Adjutant General's Office 1917–, Record Group 407, National Archives II.
85. "Headquarters, Company 'A' 163rd Infantry, Office of the Company Commander," 25, Entry 427, Folder 341-INF (163) -0 to 341-INF (163) -0.1, 1940–45, Box 10633, World War II Operations Reports 1940–48, Record Group 407, National Archives II.

86. "Headquarters Company 'A' 163rd Infantry Office of the Commanding Officer," 25–26, Subject: Infantry and Tank Coordination in the Attack, To: C.O. 163rd Inf., APO #41, 12 Aug 44, "Wakde Toem Aitape Biak 41st Inf Div 163rd Regiment 1st Bn Co A May June 44," Entry 427, Folder 341-INF (163) –0.3 Box 10634, World War II Operations, Record Group 407, National Archives II.
87. "History of the 41st - 163rd Infantry (Company B) 9-16-40 thru 1945, Wakde 5-18-44, Ibdi Ridge," 13, Entry 427, Folder 341-INF (163) –0 to 341-INF (163) –0.1, Box 10633, Office of the Adjutant General, Records of the Adjutant General's Office 1917–, Record Group 407, National Archives II.
88. Ibid.
89. Ibid.
90. Ibid.
91. "Company C One Hundred Sixty Third Infantry, Office of the Commanding Officer," Subject: Infantry-Tank Assault Teams, To: The Commanding Officer First BN, One Hundred Sixty Third Infantry, A.P.O. Fourty-One, 31, July 1944, "Wakde Toem Aitape Biak 41st Inf Div 163rd Regiment 1st Bn Co A May-June 44", Entry 427, Folder 341-INF (163) –0.3, World War II Operations Reports 1940–48, Box 10634, Record Group 407, National Archives II.
92. Ibid.
93. "Headquarters, Company 'A' 163rd Infantry, Office of the Company Commander," 25, Entry 427, Folder 341-INF (163) -0 to 341-INF (163) -0.1, 1940–45, Box 10633, World War II Operations Reports 1940–48, Record Group 407, National Archives II.
94. "Company C One Hundred Sixty Third Infantry, Office of the Commanding Officer," Subject: Infantry-Tank Assault Teams, To: The Commanding Officer First BN, One Hundred Sixty Third Infantry, A.P.O. Fourty-One, 31, July 1944, "Wakde Toem Aitape Biak 41st Inf Div 163rd Regiment 1st Bn Co A May-June 44", Entry 427, Folder 341-INF (163) –0.3, Box 10634, World War II Operations, Record Group 407, National Archives II.
95. MacArthur's staff listed American losses for the operation at 16 killed, 83 wounded, and 2 missing. "Wakde Island Now Firmly in Yank Grip," newspaper clipping, circa 1944, Howard McKinney Scrapbook, shelf #49, MMHM; Smith, *United States Army in World War II... The Approach to the Philippines*, 231.
96. MacArthur, *Reports of General MacArthur*, 152.
97. Ibid.
98. Lacey, *Montana Militia*, 75.
99. MacArthur, *Reports of General MacArthur*, 152–53.
100. Dr. Hargis Westerfield, "A Co., Infantry: Combat Tour of Wakde," *Jungleer* (December 1972) 8–9.
101. "History of the 41st - 163rd Infantry (Company B) 9-16-40 thru 1945, Wakde 5-18-44, Ibdi Ridge," 2, Entry 427, Folder 341-INF (163) –0 to 341-INF (163) –0.1, Box 10633, Office of the Adjutant General, Records of the Adjutant General's Office 1917–, Record Group 407, National Archives II.
102. The regiment referred to here was not the 163rd; however, the quote illustrates the nature of the enemy's often-intricate defensive systems on Biak. "History of the 41st - 163rd Infantry Regiment July 1917–June 1945," Entry 427, Folder 341-INF (163) -0 to 341-INF (163) -0.1, World War II Operations Reports 1940–48, Box 10526, World War II Operations, Record Group 407, National Archives II.
103. "History of the 41st - 163rd Infantry (Company B) 9-16-40 thru 1945, Wakde 5-18-44, Ibdi Ridge," 2, Entry 427, Folder 341-INF (163) –0 to 341-INF (163) –0.1, Box

10633, Office of the Adjutant General, Records of the Adjutant General's Office 1917–, Record Group 407, National Archives II; Smith, *United States Army in World War II... The Approach to the Philippines,* 312–13.

104. Ibid.
105. Lt. Arthur Merrick assumed command of Company B after the battle at Wakde Island when Capt. Frank Maxam was wounded. Ibid.
106. "Headquarters, Company 'A' 163rd Infantry, Office of the Company Commander," 27, Entry 427, Folder 341-INF (163) -0 to 341 INF (163) -0.1, 1940–45, Box 10633, World War II Operations Reports 1940–48, Record Group 407, National Archives II.
107. Ibid.
108. "History of the 41st - 163rd Infantry (Company B) 9-16-40 thru 1945, Wakde 5-18-44, Ibdi Ridge," 5, Entry 427, Folder 341-INF (163) –0 to 341-INF (163) –0.1, Box 10633, Office of the Adjutant General, Records of the Adjutant General's Office 1917–, Record Group 407, National Archives II.
109. Ibid., 6.
110. Smith, *United States Army in World War II... The Approach to the Philippines*, 342.
111. McCartney, *The Jungleers*, 118.
112. General Fuller left Biak on June 18. After departing from the SWPA, he became Deputy Chief of Staff at Admiral Lord Louis Mountbatten's Southeast Asia Command headquarters. Smith, *United States Army in World War II... The Approach to the Philippines,* 341–44.
113. Ibid., 301.
114. Ibid.
115. "History of the 41st - 163rd Infantry (Company B) 9-16-40 thru 1945, Wakde 5-18-44, Ibdi Ridge," 7, Entry 427, Folder 341-INF (163) –0 to 341-INF (163) –0.1, Box 10633, Office of the Adjutant General, Records of the Adjutant General's Office 1917–, Record Group 407, National Archives II.
116. Sgt. William C. Davidson, Corporal Ray Wilcopolski, with Dr. Hargis Westerfield, "The Division History, No. 28: B Co., 163rd Inf.: Battle on Ghost Mountain," *Jungleer* (June 1965) 12–13.
117. Ibid.; "History of the 41st - 163rd Infantry (Company B) 9-16-40 thru 1945, Wakde 5-18-44, Ibdi Ridge," 9–10, and "Headquarters, 163rd Infantry, Office of the Company Commander," 27–28. Entry 427, Folder 341-INF (163) -0 to 341-INF (163) -0.1, 1940–45, Box 10633, World War II Operations Reports 1940–48, Record Group 407, National Archives II.
118. Smith, *United States Army in World War II... The Approach to the Philippines*, 388–89.
119. "History of the 41st Infantry Regiment, July 1917–June 1945," 2, Entry 425, Folder 341-INF (163) to 341-INF (163) 0.1, World War II Operations Reports 1940–48, Box 10526, Office of the Adjutant General, Record Group 407, National Archives II.
120. Ibid.
121. Hargis Westerfield, unpublished manuscript, 79, Box 4, LTC Ray Read office, State Area Command, Fort Harrison.
122. Ibid.
123. Ibid., 81.
124. Ibid., 83.
125. Ibid.
126. MacArthur, *Reports of General MacArthur*, 14852.

127. Hargis Westerfield, unpublished manuscript, 8, Box 4, LTC Ray Read office, State Area Command, Fort Harrison.
128. "Prologue (Biak to Mindoro, P.I.," 2, G-3 Historical Report-Occupation of Japan-Campaign 41st Infantry Division 8-15-45 through 11-3-45, Entry 427, Folder 41st Infantry Division 341.3 INF (163) —0.3 Operations Reports, Box 10557, World War II Operations Reports 1940–48, Record Group 407, National Archives II.
129. Uncategorized Hargis Westerfield materials, including Dr. Hargis Westerfield, "Japanese Shellfire at Zamboanga," *Jungleer* (unidentified issue), 1, in Box 3 of 4, LTC Ray Read office, State Area Command, Fort Harrison.
130. Ibid.
131. "Prologue (Biak to Mindoro, P.I.," 3, G-3 Historical Report-Occupation of Japan-Campaign 41st Infantry Division 8-15-45 through 11-3-45, Entry 427, Folder 41st Infantry Division 341.3 INF (163) —0.3 Operations Reports, Box 10557, World War II Operations Reports 1940–48, Record Group 407, National Archives II.
132. "History of the 41st – 163rd Infantry July 1917–June 1945," 4, Entry 425, Folder 341-INF (163) –0 to 341-INF (163), Box 10526, World War II Operations Reports 1940–48, Record Group 407, National Archives II; G-3 Historical Report-Occupation of Japan-Campaign 41st Infantry Division 8-15-45 through 11-3-45, 4, Entry 427, Folder 41st Infantry Division 341.3 INF (163) —0.3 Operations Reports, Box 10557, World War II Operations Reports 1940–48, Record Group 407, National Archives II.
133. Ibid., 6.
134. Hargis Westerfield, unpublished manuscript, 95, Box 4, LTC Ray Read office, State Area Command, Fort Harrison.
135. "Prologue (Biak to Mindoro, P.I.)," 11, G-3 Historical Report-Occupation of Japan-Campaign 41st Infantry Division 8-15-45 through 11-3-45, Entry 427, Folder 41st Infantry Division 341.3 INF (163) —0.3 Operations Reports, Box 10557, World War II Operations Reports 1940–48, Record Group 407, National Archives II.
136. McCartney, *The Jungleers*, 153.
137. "History of the 41st Division 163rd 8-2-44 through 11-30-45," 5, Report of Operations 6 April—20 June 45 Master V-4 Sulu Historical Report Jolo Operations, Entry 427, Folder 41st Infantry Division 341.3 INF (163) —0.3 Operations Reports, Box 10557, World War II Operations Reports 1940–48, Record Group 407, National Archives II.
137. Hargis Westerfield, unpublished manuscript, 105, Box 4, LTC Ray Read office, State Area Command, Fort Harrison.
138. Ibid., 109.
139. "Occupation of Japan, Report of Operations Aug 15–Nov 45," 1–3, 6–7, 13, 41st Div 163rd INF, Entry 427, Folder 41st Infantry Division 341.3 INF (163) —0.3 Operations Reports, Box 10557, World War II Operations Reports 1940–48, Record Group 407, National Archives II.
140. For additional sources regarding the 163rd Regiment and the 41st Division during World War II, see Martin Kidston, *From Poplar to Papua: Montana's 163rd Infantry Regiment in the Pacific in World War II* (Farcountry Press, 2004); Francis Bernard Catanzaro, *With the 41st Division in the Southwest Pacific: A Foot Soldier's Story* (Indiana University Press, 2002). In regard to the 162nd Regiment of the 41st Division, see Paul C. Wilson, *The Sunset War: The 41st Infantry Division in the South Pacific* (Authorhouse, rev. ed., 2003).

210th Engineer Combat Company, June 1949. *MMHM*

13

Post World War II Period: Reorganization, 1945–1955

Jennifer Ross-Nazzal

Although the war is over, we are still living in an unsettled and troubled world. Therefore, it is imperative that we have not only a strong regular army, but a strong national guard. The new national guard, trained and ready for any emergency, can play a vital role in keeping America secure.—Montana Adjutant General S.H. Mitchell, 1946.

In 1945, the United States emerged from World War II as the world's greatest superpower, armed with nuclear might. The Soviet Union, however, swiftly transformed into a global competitor with the detonation of its own nuclear device in 1949. The same year, Chinese Communists drove the Nationalist Chinese off the Asian mainland to the island of Taiwan.

In 1950, the Cold War heated up when with the Communist bloc's ally, North Korea, overran most of South Korea before United Nations forces turned the invaders back. Against this dangerous backdrop, having a reorganized, well trained, and quickly deployable National Guard took on urgency in America. In this period, veterans of the 163rd Infantry Regiment formed the foundation and mentored new recruits for a reconstituted Montana guard.

Unlike in World War II, however, the Montana Army National Guard was not called up during the Korean conflict, 1950–1953. The Montana Air Guard, on the other hand, activated for stateside duty from April 1, 1951, to January 1, 1953 (see Chapter 20), and some airmen transferring to U.S. Air Force units did see action on the Korean Peninsula.

The post World War II era brought change to the Montana National Guard. Compared to some other states, Montana was slower to reorganize its units due to recruiting difficulties in a region with a relatively small population and because of artificially high enlistment expectations placed on the state. Nevertheless, successful reorganization occurred. Technological advances brought new equipment, more vehicles, and innovative training, and a second reorganization in 1953 resulted in the Montana guard shifting from being an infantry regiment to a new, rapid deployment, armored cavalry force.

Postwar planning for reorganizing the country's National Guard began in the late stages of World War II. Based on estimations, the National Guard Bureau (NGB) and the War Department eventually approved a tentative figure of 654,426 men for the postwar National Guard—more than double the prewar number.[1] This high estimate reflected the challenges in an ominous international environment. Called the M-Day (Mobilization Day) Force, the federal government expected the National Guard "to be mobilized at an hour's notice."[2] Led by Maj. Gen. E.A. Walsh, President of the National Guard Association, most decision-makers saw the guard playing an integral role in the defense structure of the United States.

In a 1944 letter to the House Select Committee on Postwar Military Organization, General Walsh argued that the guard had earned a place "in the Military scheme of things of this Nation. To destroy the National Guard or relegate it to an inferior position in the Postwar Military Establishment…is utterly inconceivable."[3] Congress eventually approved an expanded role for the guard as Walsh and others envisioned.

Walsh was successful in receiving funding because the War Department realized America's need to prepare for a possible confrontation with the Soviet Union. "They assumed that war might come again by 1952," historian Elbridge Colby observed, "and that the contemplated National Guard force should be raised by 1948 so as to have three years of training at useful strengths before another call to service might come."[4]

In 1946, Montana Governor Sam C. Ford accepted the War Department's authorization of 3,975 men in 31 units for the reorganized Montana guard, which was about equal to the 163rd's fully recruited strength during World War II. In addition, the National Guard Bureau designated Helena as the state headquarters. The 163rd Regimental Combat Team initially was allocated 200 officers and 3,362 enlisted men, and the new 186th Fighter Squadron and supporting air units were slated for 39 officers and 172 enlisted men. There were further plans to expand the organization with a medium-maintenance ordnance company of 7 officers and 124 enlisted men, and a guard band comprised of 1 warrant officer and 28 enlisted men.

Furthermore, the NGB separated the 163rd RCT from the 41st Division. It no longer would be affiliated with its pre-World War II peer units in Idaho, Oregon, and Washington. Instead, the 163rd was under the direct command of the Sixth Army in San Francisco. Also, the bureau selected Col. S.H. Mitchell as the state's commanding officer and adjutant general.[5] Mitchell retained the rank of Col. in the regular army while serving as a brigadier general in the guard.

The federally mandated troop level would fluctuate over time. In a October 1946 report to Governor Ford, Adjutant General Mitchell noted that the Montana guard's ground troop allotment now was 3,788 men.[6] In 1947, the allotment for the air unit was 353.[7] Two obstacles would linger in the postwar reorganization—enlistment difficulties, and the shortage of serviceable armories.

Enlistment

> *The re-emergence of the National Guard after WWII was a painful and stormy business. The period from September 1945 almost to the time when it became evident that members of the Guard were once again going to war [in Korea] was marked by confusion and controversy, extensions of inter-service rivalry, and the reappearance of ancient doubts and distrust and, perhaps more serious, the leadership of the Guard was frequently in disarray.*—Major General Bruce Jacobs (Ret.), Montana National Guard.[8]

As late as May 1946, the War Department dragged its feet on which specific Montana cities would be allocated guard units. On May 13, for example, Adjutant General Mitchell announced that the 186th Fighter Squadron was still without a home. The War Department was concerned about the state's ability to recruit the minimum number of personnel needed to sustain a fighter squadron. In Washington, D.C., national decision-makers suggested that the 186th be transferred from its then-current base in Denver to McChord Air Base in Tacoma, Washington. Nevertheless, Montana eventually received the unit. Mitchell reassured the people of Montana that the assignment of units would ultimately be determined by Governor Ford and himself.[9]

In the summer of 1946, U.S. Representative Mike Mansfield reported receiving news "from the chief of army engineers [that] the postwar Montana national guard had been granted use of nearby Fort Harrison."[10] The Montana guard was returning to familiar quarters in the Helena area.

The continuing reorganization, however, gained speed slowly, even with the direct support of General Joseph Stillwell, commander of the Sixth Army Corps. Stillwell, who commanded American forces in the China-Burma-India theater in the critical days of World War II, arrived in Montana in early June for an inspection tour. Stillwell promised Governor Ford and Adjutant General Mitchell, "all the assistance and power of the Sixth army" in the reorganization effort.[11]

Other obstacles hindered quick reorganization. First, the War Department refrained from finalizing plans for any specific state until all states, along with Hawaii, Puerto Rico, and the District of Columbia, had accepted their unit allotments, which was not achieved until August 24, 1946.[12] Next, recruitment expectations rose substantially for Montana. At the time of federal induction in 1941, Montana had 1,703 enlisted men, compared with the new postwar expectations now running as high as 4,141 men. This was nearly 2½ times larger than Montana's prewar strength. Finally, the guard was slow to reorganize due to the inaction of lawmakers. In 1946, Congress indeed had allocated funds to the states, but the Montana assembly failed to enact legislation necessary for dispersing the federal support.

Mitchell hoped the state legislature would correct this in the next year, conceding that "definite plans will not be made until after the 1947 legislature has convened."[13] Earlier in 1946, Governor Ford had sent a letter to Maj. Gen. Butler B. Miltonberger, Chief of the National Guard Bureau, explaining the situation regarding the state legislature. "Activation of the organization cannot commence until the Legislature has made the necessary appropriations." Ford assured General Miltonberger that once the legislature met in early 1947, "adequate funds will be provided to organize and maintain the National Guard."[14]

The guard still lacked sufficient new personnel, thus enlistment remained a top priority. Ford and Mitchell actively strove to meet the federal government's expectations. Speaking to the Veterans of Foreign Wars, Governor Ford asked for support. "We want a strong Guard in Montana, well trained and well equipped," he explained. "We cannot succeed without the assistance of your organization and the people of Montana."[15]

At a ceremony in Helena, Mitchell also pointed out the task ahead. "The new organization being formed at present is stepping into a large pair of shoes but is confidently putting one foot forward at a time, with a view to climbing the stairs of fame and honor with a sure foot." He added, "with the material we have to work with, that is, our sons and brothers, there is little question as to the success of our new Montana national guard."[16]

Civic groups became involved. Prior to World War II, guard companies were closely knitted to their local communities. They represented "a center of activity...everybody in town knew everybody that belonged in the guard...It was part of the community," Col. Joe Upshaw later recalled.[17]

The prewar guard units were located in Kalispell, Whitefish, Helena, Whitehall, Bozeman, Livingston, Great Falls, Billings, Sidney, Chinook, Harlowton, Glasgow, Culbertson, Harlem, Malta, Wolf Point, Bainville, and Poplar. State-owned armories stood in Helena, Bozeman, and Poplar, with county-owned armories in Livingston, Great Falls, Lewistown, Chinook, Culbertson, Glasgow, and Bainville.

Reorganization required community support. In order to reestablish units in towns and cities, communities themselves sent veterans, including Upshaw and Warrant Officer Carl King in the case of Chinook, to visit the adjutant general's office in Helena to express the desire to retain guard units.[18] According to Upshaw, "the communities sold themselves to the headquarters in Helena rather than the headquarters having to go out and say we'd like to put a unit in your town."[19] Other guard veterans, such as Col. James Barfknecht, also later recalled that people wanted units back in their towns. Barfknecht believed it was important for local economies, especially for towns in rural areas.[20] 1st Sgt. Buzz Sadorf from Glendive echoed Barfknecht's sentiments.[21]

After the reorganized guard's second annual summer training at Fort Harrison in 1949, the Chinook company was the only unit to immediately receive its pay. The money appeared to go directly into the town's economy. "We are the only unit that paid their men after they had returned from camp," recalled a Chinook soldier. "Our money is spent at home. Maybe this is one of the reasons the town is behind us so strongly."[22] Warrant Officer Carl King, also of Chinook, likewise noted that the men received their pay upon returning from a summer camp, "so that the payroll will be spent locally."[23]

Community backing obviously proved important in reorganizing local guard companies, but federal recognition was essential. The latter depended on a couple of factors.[24] First, units needed access to training and drilling facilities with adequate security, and each unit was required to maintain rosters of enlisted men and officers at proscribed levels. The federal government devised a phased plan designed to bring units up to full strength within two years. In order to receive "initial" federal recognition, a new unit needed to have recruited 25 percent of its allotted officers and 10 percent of enlisted men. Each phase transpired over three month periods, "to allow units to meet organizational strengths gradually."[25] The two year plan, with eight phases, was outlined as follows:

	Officers	Enlisted Men
Initial strength for federal recognition	25%	10%
Phase I	25%	10%
II	30%	20%
III	40%	30%
IV	50%	40%
V	60%	50%
VI	70%	60%
VII	80%	65%
VIII	90%	70%
Required at the end of Phase VIII	100%	80%

Despite the efforts of the governor, adjutant general, and other guard and community leaders, figures for 1948 illustrate the guard's recruitment difficulties. In April, the NGB authorized 3,576 ground troops, but the state only had a roster of 633 men, and therefore was at 17.7 percent strength.[26] Such high expectations for Montana, along with a lack of enthusiasm among veterans to re-enter the military in the postwar period (not uncommon following America's wars) resulted in a low enlistment rate.

Col. Barfknecht recalled that recruitment for his Bozeman unit relied mostly on word of mouth. Barfknecht also noted that guard members spoke at "knife and fork clubs," such as Kiwanis and Lions luncheons, to encourage enlistment.[27] His unit did not reach full strength until the outbreak of the Korean War in 1950, when young men began joining in larger numbers to fulfill their military obligation in wartime. 1st Sgt. Sadorf remembered that his Glendive unit gained new enlistees primarily because the company recruiter taught at the local high school. But Sadorf also noted that the expanding Selective Service call-up eventually increased recruitment, as draft age men sought an alternative to serving in the regular armed forces.[28]

Glendive's Lt. Col. Darrel Hoover likewise noted recruitment occurred primarily through word of mouth, and that a truly organized recruiting program was not adopted "until much later." Hoover attributed the lack of recruitment and retention in the immediate postwar period to the "inconvenience" of attending weekly meetings and the two week annual summer encampment. Besides, he believed men simply were "not interested in the military" in the late 1940s.[29]

Dick Williams of Helena recalled: "A friend of mine [joined] and I was working with him and he talked me into" enlisting.[30] Sgt. Sadorf gave the same reason for joining. "Someone just talked me into it. It was something to do."[31] Hoover likewise signed up at the insistence of a friend. "We had a lot of friends who joined, so he said 'Let's join.'" Hoover planned on serving 3 years, but stayed for 27. "Kind of like an old horse," he recalled, "you just get ploddin' down the trail and keep going."[32]

Though some progress was achieved, Adjutant General Mitchell now directed a more organized solution for increasing recruitment. In the guard's *Biennial Report, 1948–1950*, Governor Ford noted that units were not achieving allotted strengths and he demanded an increased effort.[33] Mitchell directly ordered unit commanders to increase recruiting efforts to fulfill basic federal expectations: "We are short approximately 100 enlisted men in the ground units and approximately 170 men in the Air unit." To meet federal demands, he recommended recruiters target younger men, particularly "17 and to 18½ year olds."[34] Mitchell earlier noted that the guard received over $1 million worth of equipment "ranging from tanks to mess kits," but did not have sufficient men to use all the equipment.[35]

The Montana guard had already begun placing recruitment advertisements in newspapers, often in full page presentations. In the *Helena Independent Record* on July 6, 1947, for example, an enlistment ad noted Helena's "State Headquarters detachment, the famous 163rd Infantry Company, and the 3669th Ordnance Company!" The advertisement proclaimed that "Helena's own National Guard needs you!" and went on to list openings, imploring men as young as 17 to "Live at home! Learn and earn in the National Guard!"[36] Another full-page ad appeared in the same newspaper on September 14, 1947. Under Harry S. Truman's picture and the president's message on the importance of the National Guard, it reminded war-weary readers that the guard was needed for keeping the peace.[37]

Chinook's tank company likewise sought to increase enlistment through its hometown paper, the *Chinook Opinion*. On July 24, 1947, a full-page ad called for men at least 17 years of age to join "Chinook's own National Guard." Included were sketches of Uncle Sam saluting the U.S. flag and men taking the enlistment oath.[38] In September, the Chinook unit tried again: "Serve your country in your free time." Ten reasons were listed as to why men should join, including "the training you want," extra pay, recreational activities, and the chance to earn the "respect of your friends and neighbors."[39] Two days later, another appeal specifically focused on the extra money a soldier could earn; with a fist full of cash, a uniformed guardsman was depicted walking with open arms toward his running wife and daughter. The advertisement informed prospective recruits that a private earned $157.50 per year, while the highest-paid enlisted rank, a first sergeant, earned $346.50 a year. "Your spare time is money in the new National Guard."[40]

These advertisements and other efforts prompted enlistment, but the need for more men remained. Capt. Robert Smith, leading a new Helena company, noted that his unit required mechanics, truck drivers, clerks, carpenters, and supply personnel.[41] Age restrictions had eased in order to fill needed positions. Under a new policy taking effect in April 1947, "any veteran holder of the silver star or higher decoration may enlist until reaching his 55th birthday."[42] A month later, seven World War II veterans joined up in Helena.[43]

National Guard Day, September 16, 1947, also was an opportunity for units to promote recruitment. An NGB directive required the Chinook company commander to bring in 56 new recruits to reach the proscribed unit strength,[44] while also informing Adjutant General Mitchell to enlist 545 men throughout the state.[45] Governor Ford urged "the people of the state of Montana [to] further in any way they can the cause and strength of the national guard."[46] Gains were made, but Mitchell's intensified enlistment campaign ended in November without yet reaching adequate strength. "Vacancies still exist in all three Helena guard units," Mitchell noted in late December.[47]

Shortly, General Mark Clark, the new Sixth Army commander, announced that another recruitment drive would occur during the annual Army Week, April 6–10, 1948. "We cannot build alone," announced Clark. "We must have civilian support and for that reason I have declared Recruiting week to coincide with Army day as a means to focus the attention of all people upon the critical necessity of increasing enlistments."[48] But once again, the Montana guard was unable to achieve its allotted strength.

Adjutant General Mitchell continued to believe that the country's National Guard could only reach mandated levels with federal intervention. Since the end of World War II, many in the nation's military establishment advocated the reinstitution of the draft or some other universal military service requirement, in order to fill the ranks of the regular armed forces and also encourage enlistment in the National Guard and Reserve. As the Cold War intensified, these views gained ground. In the spring of 1948, the House of Representatives passed H.R. 6274, a Selective Service bill for men aged 19 and 26 (discharged veterans in this age group, of course, were exempted).[49] The bill passed through Congress, and President Truman signed it into law on June 28, 1948.

In preparation for new enlistments, Mitchell announced the opening of a recruiting office in downtown Helena. The adjutant general urged men "to join the Montana national guard and take advantage of exemption from conscription in the regular armed forces."[50] In addition, during the reorganized guard's first annual training camp at Fort Harrison that year, Mitchell had men from each unit open recruiting booths in Montana towns.[51]

By now it was evident that Montana could not reach the overly optimistic enlistment goal envisioned during the mid 1940s reorganization. By 1948, more realistic unit strength levels finally were advocated by the National Guard Bureau. Public indication for this came at the end of July, with Mitchell announcing enlistment "almost" at ceiling strength.[52] Other evidence had come in May 1948,[53] when Maj. Gen. Kenneth F. Cramer,[54] the National Guard Bureau chief, announced that Montana was one of 28 states being "100 per cent" organized.[55] Again, on November 16, 1949, Maj. Gen. Cramer would reaffirm, "Montana has completed organization of its National Guard."[56]

Mitchell informed his unit commanders that, as of August 5, 1948, he received new reduced allotment rosters.[57] The new ceiling strengths were 900 for the ground troops and 319 for the air unit,[58] much less than the previously advocated numbers.[59]

Mitchell assured General Cramer that the Montana guard was doing everything possible in reaching the new ceiling troop strength. "For example, we recently authorized both air and ground units to offer a prize to the member bringing in the most recruits"—the award, a free trip to San Antonio, Texas. Mitchell noted that some unit commanders offered $2 to a guardsman bringing in a recruit. "To our knowledge, no stone has been left unturned which would benefit the recruiting program."[60]

A few months earlier, Mitchell had reported that 14 of Montana's allotted 27 units had received federal recognition,[61] and progress was continuing. In a February letter to General Cramer, Mitchell asserted that all units were striving to achieve the federally-mandated recruitment plan of at least a 3.3 percent increase per month.[62] In March, just two months before Cramer's first announcement that the Montana guard was 100 percent reorganized, the NGB general stated to Mitchell, "to date no unit of Montana has been placed on probation, and I sincerely hope you will maintain such a fine record."[63]

In April, the NGB noted that the Montana guard had 633 men in the 163rd, the lowest percentage for states reorganizing regimental combat teams.[64] Yet in that same month, Cramer announced to the nation that the guard was 100 percent reorganized.[65] Clearly, as late as May 1948, the Montana guard yet had difficulties in recruiting the necessary men to officially complete its reorganization.[66]

At one point, Mitchell told bureau chief Cramer that, indeed, the Montana guard had fallen short of its recruitment goal during the fall of 1947. "Unfortunately, we lost an [Air Guard] airplane [near Helena in September]...and for 30 or 45 days immediately following that, all of our personnel in the State were vitally concerned with locating these people and a good percentage of the personnel did, at that time, participate in air and ground search for the missing aircraft." Thus, Mitchell partially blamed what became known as the Sperry incident for the guard's inability to achieve its recruitment goals during the last quarter of 1947.[67]

One explanation for Montana's fluctuating allotment figures might be found in the NGB's reaction to an upcoming decision by the Gray Board.[68] As General Bruce Jacobs later noted: "A significant and powerful assault on the National Guard came forth in the recommendations of a blue-ribbon panel headed by Gorden Gray, then assistant secretary of the Army and Chairman of the 'Committee on Civilian Components' appointed by the Secretary of Defense." Gray eventually recommended that the National Guard be merged with the Army Reserve, thus becoming federalized and leaving the governors and states "out of the picture."[69]

To counter the Gray Board's assault, the National Guard Bureau may have lowered Montana's strength allotment (along with such other states as New Hampshire and Nevada) to make it more feasible for the guard to "complete" its reorganization before the Gray Board's recommendation was made public. If this indeed was done as a self protective measure by the National Guard Bureau, it may have contributed to the eventual rejection of the Gray Board's findings in Washington, D.C.

By the end of 1949, the postwar reorganization of the Montana National Guard was complete, at least on paper, and the federal government's eight-phase, two-year plan had ended. With 31 units and a total of 1,811 men, the state's roster had expanded beyond its prewar figure by 108 men.

Armories

> *A responsibility of the State in the operation of the Montana National Guard is the furnishing of armory facilities for training purposes and for the storage of supplies and equipment. This has been, and remains a major problem in Montana. Some of the State-owned and most of the rental space is entirely inadequate for effective assembly and instruction of troops and does not provide adequate or secure storage facilities.*—Montana Adjutant General S.H. Mitchell, 1950.[70]

There were other hurdles in the reorganization. Montana and other states initially felt concern over whether the NGB could secure promised federal funds on an annual basis. According to a report in the July 1947 *National Guardsman*: "States which were all set to begin organizing numerous ground units, held back, for fear that their plans could not be supported financially by the Federal government."[71] Indeed, a House Appropriations Committee decrease left the bureau with a $110 million budget, nowhere near the anticipated $200 million for an expanded national militia force. Nevertheless, progress continued.

Modern tactical operations required more vehicles and equipment than prior to World War II. Being aware of Montana's lack of a proper infrastructure, Adjutant General Mitchell in the summer of 1945 wrote to the National Guard Bureau, addressing the need for federal funds to construct barracks, facilities, and armories.[72] "I do not believe that the strength of the National Guard should be predicated on the ability of the states to provide adequate housing for troops and necessary training and storage facilities. The National Guard is essentially a federal force as well as state, and it seems reasonable to expect that the federal government should assume at least part of the burden of providing armories and storehouses."[73]

Meanwhile, Governor Sam C. Ford turned to a civilian group, the Armory Board, to assess the situation. After the board completed its investigation, Chairman L.H. Richardson wrote a detailed letter to Ford on December 31, 1946, outlining the group's findings. Richardson recommended that some plan or policy needed to be outlined by the governor. Richardson suggested a bond measure—raising taxes between 2 and 2½ percent—to secure cash for building new armories, but doubted this could "be floated." He also noted reluctance among some community leaders to accept even a partial financial obligation in constructing new armories for their hometown units. More fundamentally, he doubted the willingness of the state and federal legislatures to appropriate sufficient funds for armory construction.

The Armory Board itself, having the duty of managing and constructing armories, was in debt. During the war it sold bonds for facilities and now needed to pay them back. "How to pay for and how to maintain them is a major problem," Richardson acknowledged. As an advocate, however, Richardson noted that a tax imposed on Montana citizens to build new armories would be cheaper than paying for yet another war, "with its immense waste, economic displacement, and terrific cost." He urged the governor to draw up a plan of action and impress upon the state legislature the need for funding.[74] The governor agreed that "providing adequate facilities for the national Guard is a matter of tremendous importance to the State." Ford, however, felt uncertain about how far the state legislature was willing to go in providing support.[75]

In a 1948 letter to Governor Ford, Adjutant General Mitchell basically reiterated Richardson's report while including an assessment of new facilities and armory construction priorities. Mitchell also sent his recommendations to the

National Guard Bureau. He believed Montana needed eight new armories. In descending order of importance, this included Kalispell, Sidney, Billings, Harlowton, Havre, Butte, Miles City, and Glendive. Another three armories would be required when units in Dillon, Cut Bank, and Wolf Point received federal recognition. Mitchell did not provide a cost estimate for constructing the 11 armories.[76]

A few months later, Sam C. Ford failed in a re-election bid, and John W. Bonner became the new governor. When taking office, Bonner asked Armory Board chairman Richardson to devise a plan that could alleviate the armory problem. In early 1950, Richardson again outlined his ideas. "It would be very unjust and unwise to string this matter along any further," Richardson noted. Although federal money was still unavailable, the Armory Board had managed to amass over $1 million worth of assets by 1950, prompting Richardson to suggest it be used to initiate construction of new armories. He felt that construction could not begin until the governor, as the guard's commander-in-chief, instituted the process: "No one of the Montana Armory Board feels that they have the authority to proceed with construction without an expression in writing from you." He believed that if Governor Bonner initiated construction, it could force either the state or federal legislatures, or both, to provide necessary funding.[77]

Fort Harrison had shortcomings, too. Assistant Adjutant General Robert A. Keyes of the NGB noted security deficiencies due to inadequate fencing and patrolling. Keyes estimated that nearly $20,000 was needed just to fix the broken fences where the Montana guard stored vehicles and supplies.[78]

The armory issue provoked some competition between communities. In 1949, for example, when rumors arose that Helena would receive federal authorization for a new armory, Lewistown's Lloyd V. Eastman, Secretary-Manager of the Central Montana Chamber of Commerce, wrote to the Armory Board. Eastman asked when his hometown would get its armory.[79] In reply, Richardson dismissed the Helena report as "newspaper talk." He assured Eastman that no funds were yet appropriated to any city for an armory.[80]

Facility insufficiencies for a number of units persisted into the 1950s. Not only were old armories often inadequate, but during the war some were taken over by local governments and civic groups for other uses. Consequently, some of the reorganized guard units had no access to their former training quarters, and often rented any available structure for conducting drills.[81] Even armories that guardsmen themselves helped pay for were confiscated by local and state governments in the early 1940s. In 1936–1937, each man in the Chinook unit had contributed one drill's pay a month to fund an armory, erected in coordination with the federal WPA. During the World War II period, however, the county took ownership of the armory, converting it into a bowling alley.[82]

When the Chinook unit reorganized in 1947, Captain Oliver Hallingstad diligently began acquiring appropriations for a new facility. By 1948, he announced that the federal government had set aside approximately $25,000 for a storage room for "mobile equipment and a repair shop to serve all National Guard units in this part of the state." By September, Adjutant General Mitchell and others selected a site "at the east side of town directly north of the city disposal plant" for the new construction. Furthermore, "a deal was made with the city council for a 99-year government lease on the lots."[83] Mitchell attributed the success of garnishing federal money to Captain Hallingstad, and believed the facility would increase the effectiveness of the Chinook unit and be a valuable asset to the town.[84] Building began in early June 1949 after Captain Hallingstad announced the contract was awarded to the Schellin Construction Company, a Chinook firm.[85]

In March 1949, Mitchell announced $150,000 was available from the NGB to help alleviate storage problems. The money was tentatively slated for new buildings—not armories—for the units at Chinook, Malta, and Kalispell, "as well as repairs and alterations to warehouse buildings at Fort Harrison and Helena." Mitchell also announced that a Department of the Army civil engineer would work with local contractors in drawing up plans and specifications for the new facilities. In addition, he noted that any local community that was willing to donate property would have the opportunity to receive new guard buildings. "The fine spirit of cooperation and civic interest in the National Guard in these communities is evidenced by their gifts of the necessary land which made construction possible," Mitchell announced.[86]

In regard to Fort Harrison, the state adjutant general's office as early as 1946 had informed Governor Ford about its inadequacies. At the time, the War Assets Administration and the Federal Housing Administration were using nearly all of Fort Harrison's garage and storage space. Consequently, the guard sought new space for motor pools and repair shops on the post cemetery grounds. In 1949, Mitchell received authorization from W.J. Russ, Chief of Facilities and Construction for the NGB, to proceed: "The post cemetery at Fort William Henry Harrison, Montana, is placed in an inactive status and authority is granted to amend the existing license to the State of Montana, which authorizes the Montana National Guard to use and occupy certain lands at the subject installation, to include the area of the said cemetery."[87]

In the postwar period, the new types of training, the added vehicles and field equipment, and increasing unit sizes were significant factors in rendering aging armories and rented facilities inadequate.[88] Culbertson shared its training facility with a school, while Harlowton rented a store basement. The Havre unit occupied a basement in a grocery store, and later rented the third floor of Cowan Hall at Northern Montana University.[89] The Bozeman unit did not have a functional armory.[90]

Glendive made due in an old dairy barn. The rented loft, earlier converted into a roller skating rink, served as an assembly area, with a supply room at the west end and other space for offices.[91] Lt. Col. Hoover described the barn as an insecure make-shift facility. "It could easily be broken into. We were lucky nobody did. When we received our first tank," Hoover recalled, "we had to store it outside."[92] The Billings unit rented space at the Midland Empire Fair Grounds because "it was the only building available in the city of Billings adequate for National Guard purposes."[93]

Hoover also noted: "It was pretty well known at state headquarters where the armories were needed 'cause we simply didn't have any...what we had was next to nothing."[94] As late as 1950, the adjutant general reported, "many armory and storage facilities for units of the Montana National Guard are inadequate"[95]

Complicating matters, both national and local support sometimes faltered. In late 1949, the Armory Board's Richardson wrote to Kalman & Company Inc., the Minnesota-based firm granted the contract to build the Harlowton armory. Richardson informed the firm that the beginning of construction had yet to be authorized due to a failure in federal funding. "I do not see at this moment a chance of Federal Funds," Richardson lamented. "Our waiting has been in vain." He dismissed the idea of raising more bonds to pay for construction since taxpayers were too "touchy" on the matter of increased taxation.[96]

Five months later, E.A. Swanz, owner of the Graves Hotel in Harlowton and signatory of a deed transferring land to the guard, wrote to Richardson regarding obligations under the deed. "As you remember, this deed was given with the understanding that if the armory was not built, the deed was to be returned to me. Since the proposed armory never materialized beyond the planning stage, I would like the property deeded back from the Armory Board to me."[97]

A month later, Charles Walton, clerk for the Wheatland County Board of Commissioners, followed up with a letter to the Armory Board requesting a quit claim to the deeded land. Walton reminded the board that the deed was transferred on December 4, 1940, and according to the operative paragraph, "if the said Armory is not partially erected one year from this date, the said Grantee covenants to Quit Claim the land hereinabove described to the grantor herein." Walton requested that the land be returned to the original owner.[98]

Other ownership questions unfolded in Kalispell where the city deeded land to the state in 1949. In January 1954, Kalispell's city attorney, Forrest C. Rockwood, wrote to Attorney General Arnold Olsen asking for guidance on laws pertaining to raising money for a town armory. Rockwood noted that there were no city laws authorizing the city to raise money for a building in which the title holder would be another entity, in this case the State of Montana.[99] Olsen answered in February, agreeing with Rockwood that if the city raised the necessary funds to build an armory, then the city—and not the state—should hold title to the structure. Olsen suggested that Rockwood contact Col. Harry Thode, the U.S. property and disbursing officer in Helena, for further information.[100]

Events took a negative course. On August 9, 1954, Kalispell's Rockwood again contacted Olsen, notifying him that the city council passed a resolution declaring the armory land "forfeited and the title reverted" to the city. According to the wording of the 1949 agreement, the land was to revert back to the city if "the state did not use said property for armory purposes."[101] In response, Montana's Attorney General Olsen said it was his understanding that only the state legislature could disclaim a gift of land, thus "there can be no revision of these lots to the City of Kalispell…in the absence of legislative action."[102] The affair had come to an impasse.

Meanwhile, the Armory Board diligently continued its work. Success finally was on the horizon, but yet delayed. Under the National Defense Facilities Act of 1950, Congress indeed had granted federal assistance for the construction of National Guard armories. The legislation authorized states to receive $3 in federal money for every $1 raised in state funding. Not until five years later, however, were all hurdles overcome and armory construction underway in Montana.

In 1955, the Montana legislature adopted House Bill 139, finally granting the Armory Board authority to construct armories.[103] Five units, with the Kalispell company ranking first, needed armories immediately. Another four ranked as "first priority" included Sidney, Glendive, Billings, and Miles City.[104] Attorney General Mitchell estimated that the Kalispell and Billings armories would cost $120,000 each, while the Sidney, Glendive and Miles City[105] armories would require $80,000 each.[106]

The "second priority" list included Fairview, Plentywood, Dillon, Choteau, Harlowton, Anaconda, Big Timber, Butte, Deer Lodge, Hamilton, Thompson Falls, Whitefish, and Polson. In total, Mitchell predicted that overall armory construction costs at the primary and secondary locations would be $1,480,000. When adding six vehicle storage facilities and six hangars, Mitchell estimated that the entire construction plan entailed $1,640,000, with Montana's share being $410,000.[107] Armory construction began in earnest in 1956, with Sidney being the first location to enter into a construction agreement, followed quickly by Billings.[108]

1953 Reorganization

It was great. Everybody rides! After five years of walking it was a relief.
—Lieutenant Colonel Darrel Hoover (Ret.), Glendive.[109]

In 1953, the Montana National Guard underwent one of the most significant changes in its history[110] when redesignated as an armored cavalry regiment.[111] On February 20, the Secretary of the Army ordered the conversion, effective March 1, 1953.[112] Col. Joe Upshaw recalled that with increased mechanization and maneuverability in modern warfare, there was a need "for a rapid strike

A gun tractor and towed field artillery piece on parade, 1950s. *MMHM*

force." Consequently, "light armor with its inherent capabilities could answer the need."[113]

With the 1953 redesignation, the Montana guard reformed as the 163rd Armored Cavalry Regiment (Light), along with the 443rd Armored Field Artillery Battalion with 105-mm self-propelled howitzers, and the 210th Engineer Battalion. The old regimental combat team designation, of course, was eliminated.[114] In December, Montana also was assigned the 639th Field Artillery Battalion, with 155-mm towed howitzers.[115]

In January 1954, Choteau's Company F, 163rd Armored Cavalry, and Anaconda's Company A, 210th Engineers, received federal recognition.[116] In March, the guard received additional units, including the Headquarters and Headquarters Detachment, 495th Ordnance Battalion, and the143rd Ordnance Company, Direct Automotive Support.[117] The 143rd Ordnance Company was the first National Guard unit in many years to be assigned to Butte, where distrust still ran deep due to the National Guard's riot breaking duties in earlier decades. It is noteworthy that Butte accepted an ordnance company in 1954, rather than a combat unit that might be perceived as being available for crowd control. Later that summer, the guard also gained the Headquarters and Headquarters Battery, 154th Field Artillery Group.[118]

In regard to the reorganization, Col. Upshaw thought that "the people who were already in the Guard were ready for it, they wanted something...especially those infantry men, something that they could fight with and also ride in. They were tired of walking."[119] According to Culbertson's Stanley C. Oelkers, changing from infantry to armored cavalry was a most interesting experience. He noted that most townspeople in Culbertson had never seen a tank. When the guard unloaded a tank there, half the town turned out to watch.[120] Col. Barfknecht believed that reorganization was a "morale booster." More opportunities for promotion to NCO ranks existed in the armored cavalry than in the infantry.[121]

1st Sgt. Sadorf likewise noted that men welcomed reorganization because "everybody had a vehicle to ride in."[122] "It was great," agreed Lt. Col. Hoover of the Glendive unit: "Everybody rides! After five years of walking it was a relief." Though Hoover enjoyed his years in the guard, being an infantryman was not his favorite experience: "It was so hot when we were infantry. I didn't think much of walking. I always figure you needed a horse under you to make some good ground." Armored cavalry did not provide "a horse, but it was mounted."[123] The 1953 reorganization brought more units into the guard, boosted morale, and generally had a smoother transition than the 1947 reorganization.

Training

> *Training in battle "know-how" takes first place over everything else.*—Col. W.R. Rankin, 1948.[124]

Postwar training was significantly improved. The 163rd's commander, Col. W.R. Rankin, offered this assessment at the 1948 summer encampment: "Our training program is giving the men basic knowledge in the technique of firing new weapons and battle tactics for the platoon, company and regiment. If the men who went into World War II had had the training that we can now give, I feel that we would have lost fewer men."[125]

As Col. Upshaw and others noted, equipment and financial shortages hindered prewar training; instead, much time was spent in close order drill and inspecting personal uniforms. "There had been no monetary support for the Guard during the period between the two wars, especially after the depression hit. There was just no money for it. So all the stuff we had was World War I equipment."[126] The 163rd had routinely trained with outdated rifles and pistols, and during the prewar annual training at Fort Lewis, "we went around and had people carrying fence posts instead of" 81-mm mortars.[127] Upshaw "didn't see a mortar for several months. They hadn't been put in production yet."[128] Lt. Col. Hoover also recalled that before World War II, some guard units used stove pipes to represent mortars and broom handles for rifles.[129]

After World War II, up-dated equipment became more readily available and the training more individually specific and technical in artillery, tank, infantry, and support units. Attendance at U.S. Army instruction schools gradually became proscribed. From the tank units, for example, some men were sent to Fort Knox, Kentucky, and Fort Irwin, California, for armor training.

The postwar training program fell into four categories—home station drills, field training, special instruction, and service schools, a formula with origins in the prewar period. Armory or home station drills were scheduled weekly, 48 times a year, with each drill period about two hours long. The men assembled in full formation, followed by the officers and NCOs conducting instruction, usually lectures, films, and hands-on experience regarding equipment and technical topics.[130]

Some units held 24 four-hour drills a year, instead of the 48 two-hour drills.[131] In Chinook, for example, drills occurred on Thursday nights for four hour periods. Col. Upshaw noted that the Chinook guardsmen increased their efficiency regarding tank operations, including weapons loading, communications, maintenance, and combat tactics, plus watching instructional films. Regular army instructors and observers with experience in tank warfare were assigned to help train the company.[132]

The Chinook unit became a tank outfit in 1947, but the men had little or no prior armor training. Col. Upshaw explained: "First of all, we did not realize the requirements of armor. Also, there was a great need for a training area. You cannot just go out and run tanks around the countryside because local people don't like it. You cannot get across bridges, or run down the roads. Also, the maintenance was horrendous, and that made it quite tough on us because we did not have the maintenance support that we needed. We didn't know what we needed at that particular time."[133]

By 1949, the Chinook unit received its fifth tank, another M4 Sherman. Lacking a secure armory, the unit did not stockpile ammunition. Sufficient amounts of ammunition, however, were delivered for firing exercises at the training ranges.[134] Some firing practice was conducted north of Helena, but most gunnery activity eventually occurred on the vast acreage of the Deer Lodge Prison Ranch.

The Chinook unit also lacked an indoor small-arms firing range,[135] which was needed since outdoor live-fire training exercises were hampered or prevented by inclement weather.[136] Plans were prepared to develop an indoor range in the old armory that the local community earlier turned into a bowling alley.[137] By 1951, the Chinook unit had its indoor range.

In the autumn of 1948, the NGB modified the drill training program. The first hour of a standard two-hour drill was to "be devoted to general training as a unit," a bureau spokesman stated. "During this period, the men will get practical instruction in team work which is essential to the modern military unit." In the second hour, guardsmen would meet in groups according to their specialties. Since the usual enlistments were for three years, groups were broken down into first, second, and third year levels, so that training became progressively more specialized. "All training will be concentrated on the minimal essential subjects needed to prepare the Guard for its M-Day mission." Maj. Gen. Cramer believed that the "new three year training plan means that the National Guard will be trained more quickly and more efficiently to take its vital part in keeping the peace."[138]

Annual summer camps were the second type of training. Most guardsmen travelled by train to Montana's first postwar encampment in 1948. Chinook, the only tank company in the state, had its single armored vehicle hauled on a rented Great Northern flatcar.[139] Col. Upshaw recalled: "When we got there, the other units really thought we were great people because we had something to ride in. Of course we only had one tank."[140] At the camp, trained personnel provided instruction in tank maintenance and tactics.

"Camp Ford," named for the current governor, was directed by Adjutant General S.H. Mitchell. After the men established their bivouac and unpacked equipment, training began in weapons instruction—"rifles, carbines, machine guns, pistols, 4.2 chemical mortars, 60-mm mortars, bazookas, flame throwers, and the 57-mm and 75-mm recoilless rifles."[141] The second week focused on tactics and specialized training. As daytime training ended, noncommissioned officers attended advanced classes in the evening.[142]

Nineteen units—from Kalispell, Missoula, Deer Lodge, Helena, Bozeman, Livingston, Billings, Chinook, Lewistown, Malta, Culbertson, Sidney, and Glasgow—participated in the first annual encampment held since 1939. "Montanans have the privilege of honoring the state guard whose members have an exceptionally fine record extending back 60 years," the *Helena Independent Record* announced. "It is with a great deal of pride and pleasure that Helena again welcomes the guardsmen to the home camp."[143]

On the encampment's second day, Spanish-American War veterans were guests of honor at a luncheon and afterward toured Camp Ford.[144] On June 19, Governor Ford paid a visit, viewing a demonstration of the 163rd's "new, postwar weapons." The guard air unit also conducted a bombing attack "to add realism to the display."[145] On June 21, outdoor maneuvers and weapons firing were halted due to inclement weather, forcing the men indoors for classroom training.[146] With the rain ending, outdoor training resumed the following day, including the 443rd Field Artillery Battalion returning to the firing range.[147]

The 163rd's commander, Col. W.R. Rankin, believed that the two week annual training was essential. "The new, modern national guard training will give our personnel the security of knowledge. Knowledge of the job to be done is the best safeguard that one can have in combat."[148] Rankin added: "With the training we now get, we will be ready if the turn of events is too unfortunate to bring another war to our nation."[149]

At the following year's encampment, a Chinook guardsman reiterated the necessity of summer training: "This will be a real experience for most of the men who have never seen artillery fired, much less firing it themselves."[150] Annual summer camps, of course, provided an opportunity for units to work together. In 1951, infantrymen from Havre's Company E were scheduled to train alongside Chinook's tank unit. Warrant Officer King noted: "This combination has been proven good in Korea, thus they will train together here and both companies should benefit greatly from the joint training."[151]

After the 1948 encampment, the National Guard Bureau revised the summer training program. The *Chinook Opinion* reported that the new summer camp "plan will be designed to test the year's armory instruction under practical field conditions." Measures also were being taken to "remove most of the present administrative load from the company commander giving him more time for training his outfit for its combat function."[152] Uniform training programs would be designed so that units in any one state would receive the same training as units in other states.

The annual summer encampment, of course, included recreational activities. Warrant Officer Carl King noted in 1952 that the Chinook unit "defended their volley ball title by winning the trophy for the second straight year." The Chinook softball team made it to the semi-finals before elimination by Dillon's Company G. In 1948, a movie theater at camp featured *The Greatest Show on Earth,* and a boxing tournament was sponsored.[153]

The third facet of instruction, officially referred to as special training, included particular schooling for guardsmen, usually consisting of live-fire practice preparatory to summer camp. In 1949, the NGB authorized two days of such training to improve proficiency with rifles and small arms.[154] In 1951, the bureau authorized 12 special training days with weapons, and in 1952, 6 days. Before the 1952 field training, it was estimated that approximately 50 percent of Montana's guardsmen fired their weapons for record.[155]

Attendance at regular Army service schools comprised the final type of training. Initially in the postwar period, the guard did not require officers and enlisted men to train with their active duty counterparts. It soon became acknowledged, however, that attendance at regular Army schools was important, not only for the proficiency of individuals but their units as well. In 1950, for example, two members of the Chinook unit attended the tank mechanics service school at Fort Knox. Another guardsman went to a radio school at Fort Benning. A Chinook guardsman recalled: "These courses are put out by the Army in regular army centers and the enlisted man gets regular Army pay and allowances while attending. Quite a chance for a young man."[156]

Commissioned officers, of course, attended U.S. Army service schools. For example, Chinook's new company commander, Lt. Robert H. Schellin, participated in a three-month program at Fort Knox in 1951.[157] Between 1950 and 1952, Adjutant General Mitchell reported that 81 officers and 204 enlisted men were sent to regular Army service schools. Most received artillery

163rd ACR tankers in front of a M4A3 Sherman with a 76mm gun, summer 1953. These men are training as drivers and gunners. *MMHM*

or infantry instruction, but some attended engineer, ordnance, and food service courses.[158]

Gradually, another essential form of training would be required for new recruits—Basic Training and Advanced Individual Training (AIT) at U.S. Army bases. In the 1940s, many enlisting in the guard were World War II veterans, often combat veterans, who, of course, previously received basic and other training during the war years. By the 1950s, however, significant numbers of new enlistees had no previous military involvement. These new recruits initially were trained by the Montana guard itself, but in 1957, some new recruits began attending Basic Training and AIT at U.S. Army training centers. By 1961, all new recruits were required to do so.[159]

Responses to Local Emergencies

> *The Governor of the State, as Commander-in-Chief of the Montana National Guard, is empowered to order any or all units or individuals into State service for the protection of life and property and the preservation of peace, order, and public safety.*—Adjutant General S.H. Mitchell, 1950.[160]

On September 17, 1947, a Montana Air National Guard twin-engine bomber disappeared from radar when flying through a snowstorm over mountains near Helena. Aboard the aircraft were Lt. Col. Willard Sperry, commander of the 186th Fighter Squadron, and Sgt. Charles Glover. Two weeks later, Major Clifford Owen, now acting squadron commander, asked local hunters for assistance in locating the missing aircraft. Although the 186th conducted air searches after the aircraft disappeared, they failed to locate the downed plane. Owen hoped that a hunter might have heard the crash or seen smoke.[161] By then, most realized the two airmen would not be found alive.

In late October, an aerial reconnaissance team spotted a "shiny" object on the ground near Craig, Montana. A search-and-rescue team investigated, but without result.[162] Another lead came a few days later. A sheepherder in the Rogers Pass area claimed he heard a "low-flying plane followed by an explosion" on the day Col. Sperry and Sergeant Glover disappeared while flying en route from Great Falls to Helena.[163] However, this lead, too, failed to locate the plane. Nearly two months after Sperry's bomber disappeared, the search was called off.[164] The wreckage eventually was found in the following year—on June 7, 1948.[165]

Three years later, another rescue effort had a better ending. In 1950, the Chinook unit launched "Operation Rescue," when three high school students became lost "somewhere south of town in sub-zero weather." Guardsmen John Shockley and Charles Peterson located the youths and returned them home safely.[166]

Also in 1950, the guard assisted civilian authorities during particularly severe winter weather. In "Operation Snowbound," Helena guardsmen operated bulldozers and plows throughout Blaine County. The governor also requested that the Montana Air National Guard conduct an aerial survey. Eventually the state was able to secure $50,000 in federal assistance to aid 12 counties.[167] The Blackfeet Indian Reservation became isolated in the same winter of 1949–1950 when "roads became impassable and food supplies ran low in many settlements." The Montana Air Guard dropped more than 12,000 pounds of food and clothing "furnished by local charities."[168]

Guardsmen were not called out in large numbers, however, until two years later when devastating floods overwhelmed parts of north-central Montana. The Milk River forced 1,000 Havre and Chinook residents to flee their homes. The governor declared a state of emergency and called out the guard. Havre's Company E patrolled Havre to ensure the safety of residents and protect homes from looting. The *Great Falls Tribune* reported that the "soldiers…joined police in guarding 300 homes and 12 flooded businesses."[169] In addition to guardsmen patrolling in Havre and Chinook, units at Malta and Glasgow were placed on alert.[170] Because of the critical need, the adjutant general kept Havre's Company E on duty until the floodwaters receded.[171] Both Company E and Chinook's Company M also directed traffic and provided drivers for trucks. A reporter with the guardsmen in Chinook noted they rescued domestic animals in addition to protecting property. Guardsman Armin Williams typically delivered groceries to people in areas with washed-out roads, and transported other people to safety. The guard also retrieved two expectant mothers, one stranded in a flooded home with six children.[172]

Chinook's Company M operated an emergency field kitchen for displaced persons. Col. Upshaw recalled: "We were set up to feed any people evacuated from their homes and who had to have a place to go; that was just a part of our duty...we had them sleep in the armory."[173] The guard provided cots and blankets, but encouraged people to bring mattresses if they could. Men called up for the emergency typically served from 4 to 10 days.[174] During this time, Col. Barfknecht guided federal, state, and local authorities in a flyover of the flooded area to determine the extent of the disaster.[175] The 1952 floods caused over $1,147,000 in damages to parts of Chinook, Havre, and Glasgow.

Individual guardsmen also participated in forest fire suppression. 1st Sgt. Buzz Sadorf helped out during a large conflagration in the Sandspring area, northwest of Jordan. Although his unit was not officially called up by the governor, Sadorf and other guardsmen from Glendive volunteered their assistance. They drove firefighters between a base camp and the fire lines in rotating shifts, 24 hours a day.[176] During another blaze, CW4 Dick Williams' unit, the 3669th from Helena, provided field kitchen service for firefighters.

In November 1950, Williams and the 3669th also provided assistance when a Northwest Airlines commercial flight "plowed into the side of a hill" near Butte. The governor activated Helena men to locate the aircraft and search for survivors. Members of the 3669th reached the wreckage by 11 a.m. the next day. There were no survivors in the tragedy. Williams and his fellow guardsmen dug the bodies from the wreckage in sub-zero weather. "That was probably one of the worst jobs I ever had," recalled Williams. Being election day, "I voted, then was sent to find the aircraft."[177] Guard officials also dispatched members of the 163rd Headquarters unit to assist in recovering bodies.

Notes

1. *Annual Report of the Chief National Guard Bureau* (Washington, D.C.: Government Printing Office, 1940), 14; *Annual Report of the Chief National Guard Bureau* (Washington, D.C.: Government Printing Office, 1946), 71.
2. According to the Department of the Army, "The M-Day Force is defined as the total strength in units and in individuals required by the Department of Army and available and capable constantly of performing their wartime missions promptly." *Department of the Army Policies Pertaining to the National Guard and Organized Reserve Corps* (Washington, D.C.: Government Printing Office, 1950); Lt. Col. Leonid Kondratiuk, e-mail to author, April 15, 1998; *Annual Report*, 1946, 106.
3. National Guard Association of the United States [hereafter cited as NGAUS], Statement of Policy Submitted to the House Select Committee on Postwar Military Organization,

by Maj. Gen. E.A. Walsh Box TF-2, Folder War Department Policies, NGAUS, National Guard Memorial Library [hereafter cites as NGML], Washington, D.C.

4. Elbridge Colby, *The National Guard of the United States: A Half Century of Progress* (Manhattan, Kansas: MA/AH Publishing, 1977), 9.
5. "Governor Sam C. Ford Will Accept Enlarged National Guard of 31 Units near War Size of 4,000 Troops," *Helena Independent Record,* March 10, 1946.
6. Col. S.H. Mitchell to Governor Sam C. Ford, October 18, 1946, Box 86 Folder 4, Governor Sam C. Ford Papers, Manuscript Collection [hereafter cited as MC] 35, Montana Historical Society [hereafter cited as MHS], Helena, Montana.
7. National Guard Bureau, "National Guard Troop Basis and Troop Allotments," (Washington, D.C.: National Guard Bureau, April 16, 1947), 27.
8. Maj. Gen. Bruce Jacobs, "Rebuilding the Guard 1945–1950: Tough and Turbulent," 1, undated manuscript, NGAUS, NGML.
9. "Location of Army Units in States Still Undecided," *Helena Independent Record*, May 13, 1946.
10. "Montana Army Unit Is Granted Use of Fort Harrison," *Helena Independent Record,* July 31, 1946.
11. "General Stillwell Sees Need for New Status of Guard," *Helena Independent Record*, June 5, 1946.
12. "Postwar National Guard Is Becoming Reality," *Helena Independent Record*, August 25, 1946.
13. "Montana Headquarters Detachment of Guard Is Organized," *Helena Independent Record*, October 24, 1946.
14. Governor Sam C. Ford to General Butler B. Miltonberger, March 9, 1946, Box 935 Folder 325.4, Records of the National Guard Bureau [hereafter cites NGB], Record Group 168, National Archives, Washington, D.C.
15. "Gov. Ford Seeks VFW Support for State Guard," *Helena Independent Record*, June 27, 1946.
16. "Montana Guard Colors Returned to State in Ceremonies Today," *Helena Independent Record*, November 11, 1946.
17. Col. Joe Upshaw joined the Chinook company in 1936, served in World War II, and held various positions in the Chinook unit and at state headquarters. After retirement, Upshaw continued to speak at local community gatherings on behalf of the National Guard. Joe Upshaw, tape-recorded telephone interview by author, April 18, 1998.
18. "Governor Sam C. Ford Will Accept Enlarged National Guard of 31 Units near War Size of 4,000 Troops," *Helena Independent Record*, March 10, 1946.
19. A 1985 interview with Dave Brere and Ed Azune, however, suggests that the Chinook community had not always fully supported the unit. "The townspeople didn't want a Guard unit in Chinook. They said, they don't spend their money here. They take their money to Havre, go to Great Falls, they spend their money there." One month, though, the paymaster and banks in Chinook paid guardsmen in $2 bills to track where the money was spent. All but $300 was exchanged in Chinook. "Then they said...we'll keep the Guard unit." Dave Brere and Ed Azune, tape-recorded interview by Milo McLeod, Chinook, Montana, August 24, 1985; Joe Upshaw, tape-recorded telephone interview by author, May 16, 1998.
20. Col. James Barfknecht enlisted in the guard in 1947, served in the Headquarters Company at Bozeman, Montana, and retired in 1977. James Barfknecht, tape-recorded telephone interview with author, May 7, 1998.

21. Sgt. Buzz Sadorf joined the Glendive unit in 1948. Buzz Sadorf, tape-recorded telephone interview with author, May 12, 1998.
22. "Tank Talk," *Chinook Opinion,* June 30, 1949.
23. Ibid., March 15, 1951.
24. "The National Guard, An Information Digest," October 1946, Filing Cabinet 2, The National Guard—An Informational Digest...1946 with supplement folder, NGAUS, NGML.
25. Ibid.
26. National Guard Bureau Status of Organization of RCT's as of April 30, 1948, Box 1 Folder 8, Adjutant General Mitchell Papers, RS 223, MHS.
27. Barfknecht interview.
28. Sadorf interview.
29. Lt. Col. Darrel Hoover joined the Glendive unit in 1948, a founding member of the company, and retired in 1975. Darrel Hoover, tape-recorded telephone interview by author, May 6, 1998.
30. CW4 Dick Williams originally enlisted in the 3669th Ordnance Company in Helena. Dick Williams, tape-recorded telephone interview by author, June 6, 1998.
31. Sadorf interview.
32. Hoover interview.
33. *Biennial Report, 1948–1950*, 36.
34. S.H. Mitchell to All Unit Commanders, All Battalion Commanders, Battalion and Regimental Staff Officers, August 5, 1948, Box 86 Folder 4, Governor Ford Papers, MC 35, MHS.
35. "Over $1,000,000 Worth of Army Material Is Here," *Helena Independent Record,* December 11, 1946.
36. "Helena's Own National Guard Needs You!" *Helena Independent Record,* July 6, 1947.
37. "Join Your Friends in the New National Guard," *Helena Independent Record*, September 14, 1947.
38. "Chinook's Own National Guard," *Chinook Opinion*, July 24, 1947.
39. "Serve Your Country in Your Free Time," *Chinook Opinion*, September 18, 1947.
40. "Your Spare Time Is Money in the New National Guard," *Chinook Opinion*, September 25, 1947.
41. "National Guard Will Accept Petitions for New Enlistments," *Helena Independent Record,* April 4, 1947. Applications for joining Captain Robert Smith's unit were accepted after April 4, 1947.
42. "Age Requirements Much Eased to Permit Enlistment in Guard," *Helena Independent Record,* April 16, 1947.
43. "Veterans Now Attached to Guard Units," *Helena Independent Record,* May 21, 1947.
44. "Tank Co. Begins Recruiting Campaign," *Chinook Opinion,* September 4, 1947.
45. "Montana N.G. Unit Will Compete in Recruiting Contest," *Chinook Opinion,* September 18, 1947.
46. "Guard Recruiting Program Gets Ford Backing," *Helena Independent Record,* September 9, 1947.
47. "Members of Guard Will Be Paid at Monday Meeting," *Helena Independent Record,* December 20, 1947.
48. "Gen. Mark W. Clark Announces Army Recruiting Week," *Helena Independent Record,* April 1, 1948.

49. "Guard Expects Full Strength to Be Easily Attained," *Helena Independent Record*, May 8, 1948.
50. "National Guard Sets Up Recruiting Station Uptown," *Helena Independent Record*, June 22, 1948; "Mitchell Urges State Men to Join Guard, Earn Draft Exemption," *Helena Independent Record*, June 22, 1948.
51. "Full Quota Asked for Nat'l Guard," *Chinook Opinion*, June 24, 1948.
52. "National Guard Ceiling Strength almost Reached," *Chinook Opinion*, July 22, 1948.
53. National Guard Bureau Press Release, May 6, 1948, NGAUS Library, NGML.
54. See also, General Kenneth F. Cramer to Adjutant General S.H. Mitchell, March 23, 1948, Box 935 Folder: 325.4 MT 1946–1948, RG 168, NA. Cramer reminded Mitchell of the necessity to fill the ranks. "I am sure that you and your staff are exerting real effort to accomplish the results desired. The very critical world situation is a constant reminder that an all-out effort must be made to insure an adequate national defense."
55. According to Adjutant General Mitchell, the Montana guard did not actually complete its reorganization until the last unit, Company L at Roundup, received federal recognition on October 20, 1949. *Biennial Report, 1948–1950*, 10.
56. National Guard Bureau Press Release, November 16, 1949, NGAUS, NGML.
57. S.H. Mitchell to all Unit commanders, August 5, 1948, Box 86 File 4, Ford Papers, MC 35, MHS.
58. In 1950, Mitchell would report that the guard's strength was 1,811 men. *Biennial Report, 1948–1950,* 10.
59. In 1952, Mitchell announced that the guard had lost nearly 300 men. *Biennial Report, 1950–1952,* 10.
60. S.H. Mitchell to Maj. Gen. Kenneth Cramer, February 13, 1948, Box 935 Folder: 325.4 MT 1946–1948, RG 168, NA.
61. Status of Federal Recognition of Regimental Combat Teams, January 31, 1948, Box 935 Folder 325.4, MT 1946–48, RG 168, NA.
62. S.H. Mitchell to Maj. Gen. Kenneth Cramer, February 13, 1948, Box 935 Folder: 325.4 MT 1946–1948, RG 168, NA.
63. Maj. Gen. Kenneth Cramer to S.H. Mitchell, March 23, 1948, Box 935 Folder: 325.4 MT 1946–1948, RG 168, NA.
64. Status of Organization of RCT's (Strength) as of 30 April 1948, Box 1 File 8, Mitchell Papers, RS 223, MHS.
65. Status of Organization of RCT's (Units) as of 31 May 1948, Box 1 File 8, Mitchell Papers, RS 223, MHS.
66. This difficulty also occurred in some other states, such Utah and Kansas. For example, see Richard Campbell Roberts, "History of the Utah National Guard, 1894–1954" (Ph.D. thesis, University of Utah, 1973), 432, 437; Brian Dexter Fowles, "A History of the Kansas National Guard, 1854–1975" (Ph.D. thesis, Kansas State University 1982), 305–7.
67. Lt. Col. Willard Sperry and Sgt. Charles Glover's aircraft, coming from Great Falls, was scheduled to pick up Adjutant General Mitchell in Helena and proceed to a National Guard conference in Ohio. Sperry and Glover were killed in the crash of their A-26 "Intruder." S.H. Mitchell to Maj. Gen. Kenneth Cramer, February 13, 1948, Box 935 Folder: 325.4 MT 1946–1948, RG 168, NA.
68. The Gray Board was charged with evaluating the role of the National Guard in the post World War II era.
69. Maj. Gen. Bruce Jacobs, "Rebuilding The Guard 1945–1950: Tough and Turbulent Times," 7, undated manuscript, NGML.

70. *Biennial Report, 1948–1950*, 29.
71. "Congress Economy Retards Guard's Reorganization," *The National Guardsman* 1 (July 1947): 18, in Box 1 Folder 15, William Cliff Benson Papers, Small Collection 1848, MHS.
72. The National Guard Bureau was aware of these difficulties and Montana was not the only state to experience armory shortages. Nebraska's adjutant general would not reorganize units until the guard received funding for buildings. Douglas R. Hartman, *Nebraska's Militia: the History of the Army and Air National Guard, 1854–1991* (Virginia Beach, Virginia: Donning Publishers, 1994), 173; Fowles, 306.
73. S.H. Mitchell to National Guard Bureau Chief, August 20, 1945, Box 935 Folder 325.4, MT 1946–1948, RG 168, NA.
74. L.H. Richardson to Governor Sam C. Ford, December 31, 1946, Box 87 File 2, Ford Papers, MC 35, MHS.
75. Governor Sam C. Ford to L.H. Richardson, January 9, 1947, Box 87 File 2, Ford Papers, MC 35, MHS.
76. S.H. Mitchell to Governor Sam C. Ford, July 12 1948, Box 87 File 2, Ford Papers, MC 35, MHS.
77. L.H. Richardson to Governor John W. Bonner, April 29, 1950, Box 125 File 10, Bonner Papers, MC 35, MHS.
78. Keyes, NGB, November 15, 1950, Box 1 Folder 1, Mitchell Papers, RS 223, MHS.
79. Lloyd V. Eastman to L.H. Richardson, April 7, 1949, Box 1 File 16, Mitchell Papers, RS 223, MHS.
80. L.H. Richardson to Lloyd V. Eastman, April 8, 1949, Box 1 File 16, Mitchell Papers, RS 223, MHS.
81. Joe Upshaw, interview by SSG Milo McLeod, tape recording, June 1985, MMHM.
82. Upshaw interview by author, April 18, 1998.
83. "Money Appropriated for National Guard Building," *Chinook Opinion*, September 9, 1948.
84. "National Guard Bldg. Assured for Chinook," *Chinook Opinion*, September 23, 1948.
85. "Chinook Firm Will Construct New Armory Storage Building Here," *Chinook Opinion*, May 12, 1949..
86. "National Guard Storage Building Assured Here," *Chinook Opinion*, March 17, 1949.
87. W.J. Russ to S.H. Mitchell, May 13, 1949, Box 1 File 2, Mitchell papers, RS 223, MHS.
88. S.H. Mitchell to Governor Sam C. Ford, Box 86 File 4, Ford Papers, MC 35, MHS.
89. Units in other states likewise had to make do with makeshift armories during this period. Wally Geutsen, interview by SSG Milo McLeod, tape recording, August 24, 1985, MMHM. James J. Pasma, notes from an interview by SSG Milo McLeod and SGT Orlan J. Svingen, Drawer 3, MMHM.
90. Barfknecht interview.
91. Sadorf interview.
92. Hoover interview.
93. S.H. Mitchell to R.V. Bottomley, June 2, 1947, Box 29 Folder 29, Attorney General Bottomley Papers, RS 76, MHS.
94. Ibid.
95. *Biennial Report, 1948–1950*, 22.
96. L.H. Richardson to L.C. Kalberg, November 15, 1949, Box 1 File 8, Mitchell Papers, RS 223, MHS.

97. At the bottom of the letter, a note was appended: "Larry - Please file - I handled this by phone. Rich." E.A. Swanz to L.H. Richardson, April 22, 1950, Box 1 File 16, Mitchell Papers, RS 223, MHS.
98. Charles Walton to Montana Armory Board, May 17, 1950, Box 1 File 16, Mitchell Papers, RS 223, MHS.
99. Forrest C. Rockwood to Arnold Olson (sic), January 22, 1954, Box 46 Folder 21, Attorney General Olsen Papers, RS 76, MHS.
100. Arnold Olsen to Forrest C. Rockwood, February 9, 1954, Box 46 Folder 21, Olsen Papers, RS 76, MHS.
101. Forrest C. Rockwood to Arnold Olson (sic), August 10, 1954, Box 46 Folder 21, Olsen Papers, RS 76, MHS.
102. Arnold Olsen to Forrest C. Rockwood, October 1, 1954, Box 46 Folder 21, Olsen Papers, RS 76, MHS.
103. House Bill No. 66, 1955, Box 1 File 28, Montana Legislative Assembly Records 34, MHS.
104. S.H. Mitchell to Arnold Olsen, April 22, 1955, Box 52 Folder 17, Olsen Papers, RS 76, MHS.
105. Representative Ray Grant to Arnold Olsen, August 1, 1955, Box 52 Folder 17, Olsen Papers, RS 76, MHS.
106. Minutes of Military Affairs Committee, January 21, 1955, Box 1 Folder 15, 3 Montana Legislative Assembly Records 34, MHS.
107. Recapitulation, Armory Construction Requirements, Montana National Guard, 1955, Box 1 Folder 15, LR 34, MHS.
108. Agreement for Construction of Armory at Richland County Fairgrounds Area, Sidney, Montana and Agreement for Construction of Armory at Airport Road, State Highway No. 6, Billings, Montana, Box 52 File 17, Olsen Papers, RS 76, MHS.
109. Hoover interview.
110. Lt. Col. Leonid Kondratiuk, personal conversation with author, February 1998.
111. Conversion, Reorganization, and Redesignation of National Guard Units, February 20, 1953, PRC Binder, Montana Army National Guard Environmental Office, Building 230, Fort William H. Harrison, Helena, Montana.
112. Conversion, Reorganization, and Redesignation of National Guard Units, February 20, 1953, PRC Binder, Env Bldg, National Archive Section, 1–4.
113. Upshaw interview by author, April 18, 1998.
114. NGB to S.H. Mitchell, January 26, 1953, Box Library Miscellaneous Rosters, 1, 1953–1955, NGAUS, NGML.
115. NGB to S.H. Mitchell, December 3, 1953, Box Library Miscellaneous Rosters, 1, 1953–1959, NGAUS, NGML.
116. NGB to S.H. Mitchell, January 26, 1954, PRC Binder, MT-ARNG EO, Bldg. 230, Fort Harrison.
117. NGB to S.H. Mitchell, March 17, 1954, PRC Binder, MT-ARNG EO, Bldg. 230, Fort Harrison.
118. NGB to S.H. Mitchell, July 19, 1954, PRC Binder, MT-ARNG EO, Bldg. 230, Fort Harrison.
119. Upshaw interview by author, April 18, 1998.
120. Stanley C. Oelkers, interviewer unrecorded, January 4, 1985, MMHM.
121. Barfknecht interview.
122. Sadorf interview.

123. Hoover interview.
124. "Col. W.R. (Barney) Rankin Cuts Details to Stress Important Work," *Helena Independent Record,* June 20, 1948.
125. "Training in Battle 'Know How' Features Guard Program," *Helena Independent Record,* June 20, 1948, in Box 1 Folder 6, William Cliff Benson Papers, SC 1848, MHS.
126. Upshaw interview by author, April 18, 1998.
127. Ibid.
128. Ibid.
129. Hoover interview.
130. *Biennial Report, 1948–1950,* 17–19.
131. Across the nation, drills normally were conducted once a week, until 1957–1960 when the states gradually converted to one weekend a month. Lt. Col. Leonid Kondratiuk, e-mail to author, April 29, 1998.
132. Upshaw interview by author, April 18, 1998.
133. Ibid. Upshaw also noted, "To fire a tank you have to clear a long ways ahead...that means that if you fire tanks, you have to establish safety zones to your left and to your right and also across that fan in front."
134. In 1949, for example, a guardsman in the Chinook unit noted that live-fire training would commence "as soon as ammunition arrives." "Tank Talk," *Chinook Opinion,* April 7, 1949.
135. Ibid.
136. "Tank Talk," *Chinook Opinion,* April 28, 1949.
137. In preparation for the second annual summer encampment at Fort Harrison, the Chinook unit scheduled a live-fire training exercise, but, as frequently occurred in 1949, range practice was canceled due to heavy rain. "Tank Talk," *Chinook Opinion,* May 26, 1949.
138. "National Guard Training Will Be Streamlined," *Chinook Opinion,* September 16, 1948.
139. "National Guard Unit Left Sunday for Training Period," *Chinook Opinion,* June 17, 1948.
140. Upshaw interview by author, April 18, 1998.
141. "163rd Regimental Combat Unit Will Train Here for Two-Week Period," *Helena Independent Record,* June 13, 1948.
142. Ibid. See also, "State Guardsmen Settle Down to Training Here," *Helena Independent Record,* June 14, 1948.
143. "Montana National Guard at Home Camp," *Helena Independent Record,* June 20, 1948.
144. "Guardsmen Begin Work on Firing Line as Plans Start for State Administration of Pending Draft," *Helena Independent Record,* June 15, 1948.
145. "Governor Ford Pays Official Visit to Guard Camp," *Helena Independent Record,* June 19, 1948.
146. "Rain Causes Halt in Field Activities at Camp," *Helena Independent Record,* June 21, 1948.
147. "National Guardsmen Back in Heavy Training Schedule," *Helena Independent Record,* June 22, 1948.
148. "Rankin Cuts Details," *Helena Independent Record,* June 20, 1948.
149. Ibid.
150. "Tank Talk," *Chinook Opinion,* June 23, 1949.
151. Ibid., March 22, 1951.
152. "National Guard Training Will Be Streamlined," *Chinook Opinion,* September 16, 1948.
153. "Tank Talk," *Chinook Opinion,* July 3, 1952. "National Guardsmen Back in Heavy Training Schedule," *Helena Independent Record,* June 22, 1948.

154. *Biennial Report, 1948–1950*, 18
155. *Biennial Report, 1950–1952*, 17
156. "Tank Talk," *Chinook Opinion*, January 5, 1950.
157. Ibid., November 15, 1951.
158. *Biennial Report, 1950–1952*, 17.
159. Lt. Col. Leonid Kondratiuk, e-mail to author, April 29, 1998.
160. *Biennial Report, 1948–1950*, 29.
161. "Guard Officials Ask Hunters to Help in Search for Plane," *Helena Independent Record*, October 15, 1947.
162. "Searchers Investigate New Clue in Hunt for Col. Sperry," *Helena Independent Record*, October 25, 1947.
163. "National Guard Planes Checking Herder's Story of Explosion," *Helena Independent Record*, October 31, 1947.
164. "Army Plans to Halt Its Search for Lost Guard Bomber," *Helena Independent Record*, November 15, 1947.
165. *Montana Air National Guard: The First 50 Years*, 4.
166. "Chinook Guards Make Quick Rescue Monday," *Chinook Opinion*, February 2, 1950.
167. "Operation Snowbound Fades before Busy Attack of Blaine County and Emergency Equipment," *Chinook Opinion*, February 9, 1950.
168. *Biennial Report, 1948–1950*, 34.
169. "Martial Law Clamped on Havre," *Great Falls Tribune*, April 3, 1952, in Box 2 File 33, Montana State Water Conservation Board Records, RS 37, MHS.
170. "Montana Flood Damage Estimated at $1,147,000," *Great Falls Tribune* April 5, 1952, in Box 2 File 33, Montana State Water Conservation Board Records, RS 37, MHS.
171. "Agreement Made to Keep Guardsmen on Duty This Week," *Havre News*, April 8, 1952.
172. "Flood Waters May Be Receding," *Havre News*, April 4, 1952.
173. Upshaw interview.
174. *Biennial Report, 1950–1952*, 39–40.
175. Barfknecht interview.
176. Sadorf interview.
177. Williams interview.

A "Priest" self-propelled 105-mm howitzer on the firing range west of Fort Harrison. In the mid 1950s, artillery units made up a large proportion of the Montana Army Guard, including the 443rd Armored Field Artillery Battalion (self-propelled 105-mm howitzers), the 154th Field Artillery Group, and the 639th Field Artillery Battalion (towed 155-mm howitzers). *MMHM*

14

Building a Cold War Army and National Guard Partner, 1955–1965

Mari Hillestad Knirck

We see no lines of entrenchment as we have known them in previous wars, no masses of men waiting in reserve. No roads jammed with trucks moving to the front. In fact we see no front, only a battle area.—General Willard G. Wyman, Commander of Continental Army Command.

Guard zealously your right to serve in the Armed Forces, for without them, there would be no other rights to guard.—John F. Kennedy.

National Security Policy

The sudden outbreak of the Korean War shocked America. Few, if any, had expected the United States to fight a war on the Korean Peninsula. Furthermore, Americans were alarmed when U.S. Army divisions—proven victors in World War II just five years earlier—were nearly driven out of South Korea in the summer of 1950. Adding to the anxiety, one year earlier the Soviet Union had ended America's four-year monopoly of nuclear military might.[1] Nuclear weapons in the hands of the Soviets erased any sense of full security that Americans may have felt after World War II. These events helped send war hero General Dwight D. Eisenhower to the presidency in 1952.[2]

Unsure of the future, America's leaders grasped what they believed to be two general sureties: (1) the major actions in the next war would not be land operations, but nuclear exchanges, and (2) the Army's role would no longer be to lead the fight overseas, but to protect the home front or serve as occupation forces.

From 1953 until 1961, the Eisenhower administration's National Security Policy—NSC 162/2—shaped national defense. Underlying this plan was the belief that a strong national economy would help generate security. Adversaries, particularly the Soviet Union, would see America's wealth as a reflection of power. Along with this principle came the concept of deterrence—labeled as nuclear "massive retaliation" by Secretary of State John Foster Dulles, and defined as an overwhelming "capacity to retaliate, instantly, by means and at places of our choosing."[3] Thus, the Eisenhower administration saw nuclear weapons as the means to both enhance national power and to serve as a deterrent to future war. When settling on nuclear weapons as the least expensive and most effective deterrent, NSC 162/2 proponents also pushed for budget cuts in conventional weapons programs, thus trimming military spending.

The Eisenhower administration developed a "New Look" for the country's defense. In the New Look concept, the U.S. Air Force—having separated from the U.S. Army and given independent status in 1947—would serve in the lead for defense. The Army, on the other hand, would be utilized for Civil Defense and controlling already bombed-out areas. A large standing army would not be necessary—hence a reduction in the Army's budget, but with an increase in Strategic Air Command funding and support.

The Army, nevertheless, was unwilling to accept a role as only an occupation or mopping up force, and criticized the New Look deterrence policy—arguing for either prohibiting nuclear weapons or using them sparingly, or for selecting tactical targets that would not involve a massive loss of human life. The Eisenhower administration considered these suggestions, but continued to see the Army's main "role and mission"[4] as maintaining post-attack order.

Nuclear deterrence, however, was but a theory and many questioned its effectiveness for preventing all major conflict. For example, General Matthew B. Ridgeway, Army Chief of Staff from 1953 to 1955, believed that this posturing overlooked the many possibilities for limited warfare in a complex, unsettled world. He remained committed to advocating preparations for ground wars. Nonetheless, the Army itself became allured by atomic technology and pushed for its own military applications, focusing on programs sure to gain Congressional support. These projects included the development of tactical nuclear weapons, Intermediate Range Ballistic Missiles (IRBMs), high altitude air defense, and research in space exploration. Meanwhile, the Pentagon largely put Ridgeway's wish list for conventional weaponry and equipment on the back burner.

Arguing for the likelihood of limited warfare in the future, the Army sought to secure its niche in the New Look doctrine. In a 1957 reorganization known as the Pentomic Concept, the Army adopted a tactical capability in using small atomic warheads. Ridgeway advocated a force that was "properly balanced and of adequate readiness" as the most "effective deterrent to general war."[5] Small nuclear weapons used tactically on a battlefield could allow breakthroughs in enemy lines, enabling a sizeable ground force of armor and infantry to eliminate the enemy at key points.

No one, of course, could fully predict the likely locations of future conflicts. Confrontations might develop in a wide range of geographic localities—tropical jungle, icy tundra, deserts, temperate zones, steppes and plains, and mountainous regions. Also, tactical responses would vary according to the nature of a conflict (i.e., whether conventional, guerilla, or limited or major nuclear warfare). The funding of major units fully manned, trained, and equipped for all these contingencies was impractical; the Army would not receive a budget large enough to do so. The Army's response was to develop a dual capability—train for the most critical scenario (i.e., a major nuclear exchange), but in doing so, also prepare to respond and adapt to other conflicts. This was attempted in the Pentomic restructuring.

The name "Pentomic" derived from the recurrence of the number "five" (*pentad*; grouping of 5) in the new line, battery, and other structures of reorganized divisions; and "tomic" referred to the mission or involvement in "atomic" warfare.[6] Under the Pentomic structure, the Army organized divisions divided into five "battle groups"—separately equipped, capable of operating independently, and each allotted a heavy battery. Each battle group consisted of five line companies (each comprised of five platoons), plus combat support and headquarters companies. With this reorganization, and the addition of field deployable delivery systems armed with small atomic warheads, the Army entered the nuclear age.

The reorganization accommodated what became the first expected rule-of-thumb when fighting a tactical nuclear land war—dispersal. Nuclear devices were expensive and not easily deployed. With this in mind, the Army realized that individual units in deployment should not become large enough to warrant the enemy's use of an atomic weapon against them. In fact, the Army wagered that the days of massive forces facing each other on a single front were in the past. Instead, smaller battle formations would be intentionally spread out. "We see no lines of entrenchment as we have known them in previous wars," envisioned General Willard G. Wyman, Commander of Continental Army Command, "no masses of men waiting in reserve. No roads jammed with trucks moving to the front. In fact we see no front, only a battle area."[7]

Each separated by many miles, battle groups were expected to disperse in various directions, supported individually by their permanently assigned headquarters and service companies for reconnaissance, maintenance, and medical needs. Each battle group sought to gain "key terrain," that is, to interdict the enemy's supply lines and communications.

To align itself with the Army's Pentomic Concept, the National Guard reorganized under the Combat Regimental System (CARS). This system assigned each regiment an allotted number of actively organized member units based on requirements to create a full field Army status. CARS affected armor, artillery, and infantry units, and sought to devise a long term and flexible organizational structure that could handle the complex land-combat missions envisioned under the Pentomic plan. Modern equipment required soldiers highly trained in its use and maintenance.[8] To meet this need, the Department of Defense Appropriation Act of 1959 authorized a manpower allotment of 400,000; CARS assigned the Reserve Structure with a total of 37 combat divisions (10 U.S. Army Reserve, and 27 Army National Guard).[9]

The Reserve Forces Act of 1955 had helped create a reservist force that could be quickly mobilized. The National Guard and the Army Reserve were now seen as fighting forces with sufficient numbers to meet full-strength manpower levels. In 1959, a year after the implementation of the Pentomic Reorganization, a paper entitled the "Image of the Modern Reserve Components of the Army" described the modern National Guard. No longer a heterogeneous group with undertrained units and personnel "without specific purpose or goal," the Reserve Components now were "a modern day Army, tailored to meet the requirements of the Army, trained with the same standards, and geared to the same tactical and technical concepts."[10]

In the 1958 reorganization, however, the Montana National Guard generally retained its basic structure—i.e., the 163rd Armored Cavalry Regiment and its field artillery.[11] Nonetheless, wrangling over force reductions continued on the national scene. William H. Harrison Jr. of the National Guard Association warned all adjutants general that "there are indications [there] will be reductions in both strength and units in 1961."[12] For 1956–1959, the president approved a budget for 360,000 reservists, but the Department of Defense had pushed Congress to fund for 400,000. To counter the threat of unit reduction and budget cuts, the National Guard across the country recruited heavily to show it could consistently reach the 400,000 allotment and therefore justify the full budget.[13]

By 1960, the doctrine of massive retaliation was increasingly challenged, not just by the Army, but in civilian circles as well. Some also questioned the feasibility of the Army's Pentomic answer to nuclear war, while others believed the next conflict would be conventional. Many asked: Just how flexible were the new battle groups? Army tests showed them to be "awkward and unwieldy," particularly for the division commander who led up to 16 subordinate units. Moreover, the Army admitted that the structure was ill-designed and unwieldy for conventional operations. It never really achieved its goal of dual capability for nuclear and conventional situations. One general later reflected, "every time I think of the… Pentomic division, I shudder. Thank God we never had to go to war with it."[14]

These concerns crystallized after President John F. Kennedy took office in 1961. The ground forces build-up in the tense face-off with the Communist bloc during the Berlin Crisis forced Washington, D.C., to reconsider massive retaliation concepts. It was clear that U.S. forces now were conventionally outgunned and outnumbered by the Soviet bloc. In response, the Kennedy administration introduced a revised strategic vision known as "Flexible Response," a balanced and incremental scale of military reaction, depending on the evolving nature of a conflict. This required a range of weapons, both conventional and nuclear, in equally effective operational proportions.

The new Flexible Response plan was conceptualized under General Herbert B. Powell, the Commander of Continental Army Command. Known as ROAD—Reorganization Objective Army Divisions (1961–1965)[15]—this system allowed greater flexibility in modern joint war plans than the Pentomic structure could provide.[16] Vice Chief of Staff General Clyde Eddleman hoped this new structure would provide what Pentomic could never really deliver—an organization sufficiently versatile and flexible for all nuclear and conventional battlefield situations.

Under ROAD, all infantry, mechanized infantry, and armored divisions held a common "base" structure, which included headquarters, three brigade headquarters, a military police company, aviation, engineer, and signal battalions, a reconnaissance squadron, divisional artillery, and support command. Individual units trained in specific types of tactics and conditions, which could be added to this base structure to create a fighting force capable of handling any particular battle style or environment.[17] Nine infantry battalions would replace the Pentomic battle groups as the "building block" of ROAD. The Pentagon believed that the new battalion configuration gave commanders better control, provided for simpler training, allowed wider dispersion in the field, and gave more career opportunities for officers. Also, each infantry battalion was being assigned the most modern weaponry, such as the Davy Crocket and the ENgin-Teleguide Anti-Char (ENTAC) missiles.[18] The Davy Crockett, developed in 1961, was a 150-pound rocket with nuclear warhead capability and a range of 1.4 miles.

Meanwhile, the Berlin Crisis delayed the Army's reorganization to ROAD. During the tense confrontation with the Soviets, the existing Pentomic divisions were on full alert, and some reserves were activated. While Montana was not included in the call-up, two National Guard divisions—Wisconsin's 32nd Infantry Division and the 49th Armored Division from Texas—plus other personnel, were ordered to active duty but not sent overseas.[19] In 1962, Secretary of Defense Robert McNamara replaced these active guard units with the first two ROAD divisions.[20]

In adopting new equipment such as helicopters, ROAD ultimately cost more to implement than the Pentomic organization. Another obstacle was finding enough soldiers to man the divisions at full strength; the Department of Defense refused to increase overall manpower authorizations.

The Department of Defense ordered reserve divisions to reorganize at the same time as the regular Army divisions, but a question arose over how many reserve divisions were required for the new system. Previous CARS studies suggested that 29 of the necessary 43 should come from the reserves. However, the Army staff, with the permission of the defense department, disagreed with these numbers. Instead, it cut each of the six army areas' Army Reserve divisions by three and retained only one division from each to achieve mobilization.[21]

The Army National Guard and U.S. Army Reserve began restructuring in 1962, but were given more time than the Army to complete the change.[22]

The army secretary and the defense secretary defined the role of the guard under ROAD, and in January 1962 the Senate Committee on Armed Services announced the new mission:

> The Army National Guard and Army Reserve should be designed primarily to augment our General Purpose Forces, that is, those forces other than our nuclear strike forces. Specifically, they should satisfy two requirements:
>
> (1) The ability on short notice to augment significantly the Active Army during periods of grave international tension or during limited wars. For this purpose we require a relatively small reserve force maintained at a very high state of readiness.
>
> (2) The ability to provide a base for a large-scale mobilization in the event of general war. For this purpose we need a large but not necessarily highly ready reserve establishment.[23]

In overview, not only had the Army regained its combat stature during the Kennedy years, but the National Guard was reaffirmed in its responsibility of augmenting Army troops. Retired Col. Gerald Miller later assessed these changes from a Montana perspective. "Reorganizations caused changes at the local level, but their effects were only marginal compared to the 'upper-level' changes. Pentomic and ROAD reorganization involved the principles under which the larger units were employed. Lower elements were kept aware of those concepts...but other than that it had little effect at our level."[24]

A National Guard Bureau memo brought "upper level change" home to Montana with a request to reorganize the field artillery under new Tables of Organization and Equipment (TOE). Following required inspections, the medical detachment consolidated and reorganized with headquarters and headquarters battery.[25]

By December 1961, Secretary of the Army Cyrus R. Vance requested that the states accept the new National Guard troop allotment of 23 divisions (6 armored and 17 infantry). In the original plans, the Army staff intended to redesignate 2 of the 17 infantry divisions as mechanized. Equipment shortages changed these plans, however, and kept all 17 divisions as standard infantry organizations.[26]

Secretary Vance informed Governor Tim M. Babcock of Montana that the ultimate goal of the 1962 reorganization was the "improvement in the operational readiness of the reserve components." Troop realignment directives (ultimately with a number of "reductions") that were sent to each of the adjutants general for their approval came with the added plea that the "military need for the types of units to be created by the reorganization is urgent."[27] This urgency, the government claimed, was caused by fiscal requirements.

S.H. Mitchell, in his last year as Montana's adjutant general, challenged the reduction of any reserve forces at a time of heightened Cold War tensions. He reasoned: "If fiscal economy is indeed the primary criteria, then the activation of new regular army units, which cost the Federal government many times the cost of maintaining ready reserve units is completely without justification."[28] A guard unit purportedly cost eight times less than one active, regular Army unit.[29] This prompted Mitchell to suggest with ire that what the Pentagon really desired was not a realignment to adjust to modern warfare or new weapons, but rather the "eventual eradication of the Militia system."[30]

A field communications operator. *MMHM*

For Montana, Mitchell warned, reorganization could mean the elimination of 10 full-time employees, the loss of 2 new armories at a cost of $250,000, and 350 trained officers and enlisted men[31] belonging to the field artillery.[32] Capt. Joseph W. Upshaw, President of the Montana National Guard Association, noted in a message to U.S. Representative James Battin, that "345 men and 16 full time technicians would be of great economic loss to the State." As a compromise, Upshaw suggested a reduction in strength per unit rather than the loss of artillery.[33]

Montana's Senator Mike Mansfield sent the MNG's concerns directly on to the secretary of defense, who promptly forwarded the complaint to the secretary of the army. The army secretary replied that Montana's fears were unfounded, and that, in fact, there would be no reorganizational changes affecting its current unit allotment. The only change would be the percentage of how many soldiers were needed to be retained within each unit, which swelled for some units and shrank for others, culminating in a shortfall of 91 enlisted men from the state's current manning level.[34] The Army also assured Senator Mansfield and the defense secretary that none of the recently built armories would be abandoned. Still, 91 Montanans found themselves let go by the time the guard completed its reorganization in May 1963.

While America remained focused on the threat of nuclear attack—and rapid changes in technology worldwide underscored this sentiment—ROAD strengthened battlefield mobility in the event of a ground war,[35] and attempted to consolidate systems in order to achieve the best use of resources.[36] It dropped the Pentomic Concept's criteria of having a "fixed standard divisional organization, completely equipped with multi-purpose and multi-capable equipment, suitable for all types of war under a variety of geographical conditions."[37] Instead it took on the concept of specialized divisions with transferable, interchangeable units. With the creation of these divisions suitable for particular missions (even down to the type of terrain), the Army also could readily incorporate new weapons and equipment into its organization.[38]

Civil Defense

Responsibility for implementing the Eisenhower administration's Civil Defense policy rested in three agencies—the Department of Defense (DOD), the Federal Civil Defense Administration (FCDA), and the Office of Civil Defense Mobilization (OCDM). Each organization reported to the President's Office. DOD handled military defense, both nationally and worldwide. The FCDA directed public Civil Defense, the relief and rehabilitation of local communities, and protecting the utilities necessary for commerce and industry to function. The OCDM provided logistical support for mobilizing and allocating resources to meet essential Army and community needs, and also was charged with securing economic stability.[39]

The National Guard Bureau, like the Army, believed the reserve should not be saddled with a primary role in Civil Defense. "There should be no action taken which would even imply that the ANG has a specific Civil Defense mission," the NGB argued. The bureau believed that assigning extensive control of Civil Defense to the National Guard might lead to a lack of public involvement, and also distract the guard from its combat mission.[40]

Nevertheless, ever since the Civil Defense Act of 1950 and Executive Order 10346, which was signed on April 18, 1952, both guard and reserve components[41] were directed to assist civil authorities in civil defense emergencies when requested or directed by FCDA officials. Beyond this, efforts were made to put the public in charge of as much of Civil Defense as possible.[42] Civil Defense groups nationwide worked closely with the National Guard to educate and disseminate information about air warning drills, fallout shelter locations, and general preparedness within communities.

When New York's Governor Nelson Rockefeller addressed Civil Defense directors in Grossinger, New York, on September 28, 1959, his comments about nuclear fallout in atomic warfare reflected fears felt across the United States. "No area of our country," stressed Rockefeller, "however remote, is immune from it. Protection against it cannot be improvised under attack. Such protection does not now exist. Recent evidence indicates that it is attainable under moderate cost." However, Rockefeller did not mention exactly what this moderately priced protection might entail. He added a somber reminder: "The last two operation alert exercises indicate that if the worst should come to pass and war should be forced upon us, three quarters of the estimated casualties will come from fallout."[43]

Meanwhile, the Office of Civil and Defense Mobilization published manuals describing how to build structures for protection from radioactive fallout. "The Family Fallout Shelter" booklet presented different OCDM recommended designs, with the more popular models constructed of wood readily approved by the National Lumber Manufacturers Association. Designs met OCDM recommendations in terms of "space, arrangement and degree of protection from radiation." The single-family sized units not only "protect from radiation, but" had "good blast resistance."

Fallout shelters also could have mundane utilizations. An "above-ground shelter is easily accessible and can serve additional uses such as storage of garden equipment and fruits and vegetables." Designs options were for both above and below ground shelters, with radiation protection contingent upon the amount of earth overburden. The OCDM suggested a minimum of two to three feet of covering soil. Bagged sand or dirt could protect entryways.[44]

Montana had no substantial urban centers that might warrant direct targeting by the Soviets, but an intercontinental Minuteman missile silo complex was located on Malmstrom Air Force Base, just outside of Great Falls. This facility included a control center with 10 powerful nuclear missiles located within 15 miles of the city. The Soviet's targeting of this complex might have caused Montana's citizens some concern; however, most did not seem to know quite what to make of fallout structures. Many citizens felt that fallout shelters probably would be rather ineffective.

An example of this ambiguity, perhaps, was expressed in a 1959 letter from Montana's Governor J. Hugo Aronson to Leo A. Hoegh, the OCDM director: "Thank you for your letter of September 11, regarding the demonstration of fallout shelters in Montana. The Host State Committee for the 1960 National Governors' Conference is considering your offer to put up a larger type shelter at Many Glacier [in Glacier National Park] to show the Governors of the 54 States and Territories and also to use it as added office space during the Conference."[45]

Indeed, three OCDM prototype shelters were exhibited in Helena, Great Falls, and Billings. Whether the shelters might have provided "office space," as the governor rather whimsically recommended, remains unknown.[46]

Meanwhile, guard unit leaders across Montana worked with local authorities to identify suitable existing structures for use as fallout shelters and for stocking water and emergency rations. MNG unit plans also included protecting public works, such as power and water utilities, and providing security. County and city government operations centers also were selected and stocked with supplies, but no effort was made to procure communication lines or set up instructional map boards at these sites. Instead, Civil Defense exercises were centered at law enforcement offices that already had maps and phones.[47]

Civil Defense matters were not an overriding concern for MNG operations, but the education regimen did include training in monitoring radiation levels and other after-effects of a nuclear attack. A Sixth Army headquarters memo from the Presidio in San Francisco instructed the guard to "survey radiologically contaminated areas following atomic and thermonuclear detonations in order to determine the extent of radiation hazard, radiation dose rates therein and the time which personnel may remain in such areas for the conduct of operations."[48]

Guardsmen in annual training sessions focused on some key Civil Defense categories requiring specialized training, including Radiological Monitoring, Civil Defense Adult Education, Shelter Management, Medical Self-Help, and Civil Defense Management.[49] Specific Chemical, Biological, and Radiological Teams handled testing for CBR agents. This included a control party and two or more survey parties comprised of two individuals each. A control party consisted of a team leader—an officer or NCO who oversaw CBR survey control points—plus an enlisted soldier serving as radio technician and driver. Ground survey teams included a monitor—an enlisted man trained in taking instrument readings, recording dose rates, and listing the time and location of each test—and an assistant operating as a driver and radioman.[50]

Though the MNG's primary unit training did not focus on Civil Defense, there was instruction in normal training that did pertain, including first aid, martial law, crowd control, and sanitation. Army National Guard personnel also could attend the Civil Defense School at Olney, Maryland. The MNG's past experiences in natural disaster relief also were pertinent in this regard.[51]

Nevertheless, on March 20, 1963, the governor reorganized Montana's Civil Defense program, passing the responsibility for operations to Adjutant General R.C. Kendall. The program concentrated on training and education at the county level. In July 1963, the Civil Defense agency hired three field coordinators to ensure this upgrade.[52] Kendall in a November 15, 1966, letter to Governor Babcock commented on responsibility, noting that the "primary objective" of the guard in Civil Defense should be to "develop an operation capability through State to local level of Government."

By 1966, all 56 counties had contributed to the program, as evidenced by the numerous assigned fallout shelters and trained volunteers and organizations put in place across Montana. "I believe that our objective for the next biennium," Kendall insisted, "must be in the areas of individual training and community shelter planning. It is significant that our plans call for the completion of the state community shelter program by the end of 1968. This plan will provide a shelter for each individual family in Montana. It will place in their hand directions for actually occupying the best shelter available to them in event of nuclear attack."[53] As testimony to the effectiveness of this organization, Adjutant General Kendall pointed out that most other western states emulated the MNG's integration of state military, disaster control, and emergency preparedness.

With Civil Defense being a federally supported program, 50 percent federal funding was provided to Montana's Emergency Operation Center facilities, which included radio, office, and warning systems equipment. However, the Office of Emergency Planning's contract with the government expired and was not renewed in January 1966. This meant the office became wholly dependent on Montana's already tight budget for Civil Defense. The AG reported that increased budgeting would be necessary in Montana.[54]

Modern Weaponry

The possibility of an adversary deploying small nuclear weapons in a tactical situation required the Army to integrate weapons systems capable of quickly changing between non-nuclear and nuclear arming.[55] Technological change greatly affected the Army by the late 1950s. A letter from Army planner Lt. Col. William R. Kintner to Henry M. Kissinger, then a Council on Foreign Relations member, indicated the importance of being able to institute design plan changes quickly. "New weapons require constant restructuring of forces and new strategy and tactical concepts. The upheaval this is causing in military circles," Kintner insisted, "is reflected in the fact that weapons...are tending to become obsolescent before they even become operational."[56]

As historian John S. Tompkins explained,[57] "the Army in the 1950s was like an aging corporation challenged to modernize or face extinction." Supporting the new missile programs in the 1950s, however, meant that other programs suffered. For example, the Army's 1957 budget assigned 43 percent of its funding to missiles and nuclear weapons, 4.5 percent to new vehicles, 4.3 percent to artillery, and 4 percent to aircraft. Buried among the discontinued conventional weapons programs were blueprints for a new generation of tanks.[58] To compete for federal research funds, the Army came up with innovative, futuristic, and even strange equipment designs. Disposable uniforms and maintenance-free trucks were some of the more creative, unlikely projects. None, however, surpassed the outlandish designs for a "flying jeep" hybrid aircraft.[59]

The Army, of course, proposed other sufficiently plausible projects and some of the most significant developments in modern weaponry of the 1950s involved warhead delivery systems. In 1953, initial plans called for a 280-mm cannon for nuclear artillery. While impressive in stature, the 280-mm giant was much too heavy for field use, thus existing artillery, such as 155-mm howitzers, were converted to accommodate a nuclear capability.[60] Also, a maneuverable, flexible rocket system was developed in 1954—the Honest John, fueled by a solid propellant rather than liquid fuel. Launched from a truck carrier, it could deliver an atomic warhead at a 22 mile range. It had some accuracy limitations, however, and weighed over three tons, too heavy to airlift. To correct this latter tactical deficiency, in 1956 the Army also developed the Little John, a solid propellant rocket with a lesser range of 10 miles. It was light enough for transport via helicopter.

In 1953, the Army acquired its first major missile, the Corporal, with a 75-mile range. At 46 feet in length, it proved unwieldy for Pentomic mobility and later was replaced by the Sergeant.[61] The Sergeant used a compact solid propellant, lessening the need for ground support vehicles as compared to liquid fuel rockets. The missile delivered either nuclear or non-nuclear warheads, with the added feature of an inertial guidance system that could withstand electronic jamming.[62]

To compete with the Air Force, the Army built up its air defense and surface-to-air missile (SAM) programs. The first SAM was the Nike Ajax. While it outperformed the Air Force version, the Bomarc, in 1954 testing, the Nike Ajax had a range of only 25 miles and a small warhead. It was replaced in 1956 by the Nike Hercules (a longer-range missile), the medium altitude Hawk, and the antiballistic missile Nike Zeus (in 1963).[63] Tested in the Pacific, the Nike Zeus could differentiate between a decoy and a live incoming target. By 1960, 15 Nike battalions were fully operational, with 5 more sites added the following year. Many guardsmen across the nation manned Nike missile installations, both the Ajax and Hercules, ready to blunt any potential Soviet air attack.[64]

The new Flexible Response concept of the early 1960s required an overhaul of conventional weapons as well. After the Berlin Crisis, weapons development turned to helicopters and to firepower designed more specifically for guerilla warfare. In 1961, nearly half of the $1.8 billion budget went toward non-nuclear weaponry.[65] Also, the M14 rifle had replaced the venerable M1 of World War II, and the new M60 machine gun replaced both the air-cooled and water-cooled .30-caliber machine guns. The lightweight M16 rifle and the small, hand-held M79 grenade launcher also were in use by the mid 1960s.[66]

In the late 1950s, a new series of 7.62-mm weapons were developed to fit NATO specifications. The M60 machine gun and the M14 rifle belonged to this new family, replacing .30-caliber arms in the American arsenal. Similar in dimensions to the M1, the M14 supported an M6 bayonet, used a 20-round box magazine, and served the M76 grenade launcher.[67] In agreements with governments in Western Europe, the 7.62-mm weapons developed by the United States fit the same uniform ammunition standards of the NATO allies.

Amid the new developments in conventional weapons, Secretary of Defense McNamara promoted and expanded the use of mobile helicopter forces, which in the 1950s had remained rather underdeveloped.[68] Beginning in 1962, large powerful Chinook helicopters were capable of transporting artillery and vehicles, as well as supplies and soldiers, under tactical conditions. The Chinook was the Army's first rear-ramp loading helicopter, and was capable of carrying three tons in the hold, or lifting eight tons by cable. After 1959, the troop-carrying UH-1 Iroquois helicopter, better known as the "Huey," also significantly increased tactical mobility.[69]

The 1960s also saw a significant upgrade in armor capabilities. With a diesel engine and 105-mm main gun, the M60 main battle tank provided increased firing range, armament, and power, replacing the M48 Patton series tank equipped with a 90-mm main gun.[70] The M48 was increasingly assigned to reserve units, though it was extensively used in Vietnam, while the M60 served as the main tank among Europe-based U.S. forces.

In 1960, the Army started replacing the bulky M59 and M75 Armored Personnel Carriers (APCs) with the sleeker M113. Lightly armored and fully tracked, it weighed only 11 tons (22,615 pounds when loaded; 18,200 pounds when air dropped). The M113 had an operational range of 200 miles, compared to the M59's 100-mile range, and its added benefits included increased durability,

A tank transporter and M4 "Sherman" tank. By the mid 1950s, the venerable M4 was outclassed by the M48 Patton medium tank. *MMHM*

less maintenance, and air-transport capability.[71] It could traverse through lakes, streams, and marshy terrain, and cruise at 40 mph on improved roads. Normally manned by two men and carrying 11 infantrymen, the M113 also often featured a cupola-style mounted .50 caliber machine gun.[72]

Modern advances also included new chemical weapons. The M91 Chemical Rocket Launcher, adopted by 1962, had the capability of spreading toxins over large targeted areas. The lightweight M91 launcher could be transported by air. With a range of up to 12,000 meters, rockets could be launched singly, in bursts, or in salvos of 45 rockets within 15 seconds.

Changes had not been made to gas masks since 1947. New design modifications eliminated the older version's bulky canister, employing instead lightweight filter material affixed inside a rubber face-piece. Developed in 1962, the M17 mask protected soldiers from chemical, nuclear, and biological agents.[73]

The Army Corps of Engineers meanwhile created modern night vision equipment, allowing "soldiers to shoot, build roads and bridges, drive any type of vehicle, including tanks; read maps and other documents; fuel a missile, and operate other missile support equipment, all in complete blackout."[74]

Since the Korean War, soldiers had available an improved type of flexible body armor that replaced earlier bulky vests containing heavy steel plates. The new vests consisted of multiple layers of a spot-laminated basket-weave style nylon, and were issued to all frontline combat troops.

For the Montana National Guard during this period, the technological changes, equipment modifications, structural reorganizations, and the regular Army's preferential position in procurement contributed to some chronic equipment shortages. For example, in 1956 the MNG was authorized 17 armored personnel carriers (M75s), but had to train with the 13 on hand.[75]

By 1962, the MNG retained inventory and equipment valued at $25 million, including 124 track vehicles, 691 wheeled vehicles, and 10 aircraft.[76] Yet in May, a National Guard representative reported insufficient funding to purchase repair parts and supplies for the equipment maintained at Fort Harrison. Adjutant General S.H. Mitchell added: "Shortages of major items of equipment, particularly radio and teletypewriter sets which are National Guard Bureau controlled items, continues to hamper the training of Montana Army National Guard units."[77]

In 1963–1964, reorganization of the Army National Guard caused much of Montana's equipment to be relocated to units in other states. In exchange, Montana received replacement materiel, including twelve 105-mm self-propelled howitzers, an M108 self-propelled howitzer, a number of M60 machine guns, telephone sets (TA 312/PT), three H-23B helicopters, two O-1A observation fixed-wing aircraft, and green berets, rucksacks, sleeping bags, and parachutes for Company C of the 19th Special Forces Group.

Despite these assets, shortages persisted in such basic items as tool and shop sets, wreckers, gas trucks, radios, and self-propelled artillery.[78] Yet, change and improvement had come in these years.

Notes

1. William W. Epley, *America's First Cold War Army, 1945–1950*. The Land Warfare Papers, No. 32, August 1999, Arlington: Institute of Land Warfare, Association of the United States Army, 1.
2. Unless otherwise noted, much of the following discussion on the defense policies of presidents Eisenhower and Kennedy is based on A.J. Bacevich, *The Pentomic Era: The U.S. Army between Korea and Vietnam* (Washington, D.C.: National Defense University Press, 1986), and John S. Tompkins, *The Weapons of World War III: The Long Road Back from the Bomb* (Garden City, New York: Doubleday, 1966).
3. "The Evolution of Foreign Policy," U.S. Department of State Bulletin, XXX, issued January 25, 1954.
4. Tompkins describes "roles and missions" as "the formal, legalistic definitions of purpose that spell out the function of each military service. To a civilian they are as dry as tax laws, but roles and missions [lay] at the bottom of nearly every squabble" between the Army and the Air Force after 1947. Tompkins, *The Weapons of World War III*, 56.
5. Bacevich, *The Pentomic Era*, 39.
6. Ibid., 5.
7. Ibid., 67.
8. "337 World-wide Army Info. Officer's Conf," 1962, Box 4244, Records of the National Guard Bureau, Record Group 168, National Archives II, College Park, Maryland.
9. "McGowan Report," Decimal File 326 Gen 1957, RG 168, NA II.
10. "Image of the Modern Reserve Components of the Army," Folder 334 General 1959, Box 3808, RG 168, NA II.
11. Press Release, "Helena Conference on Reorganization, March 23, 1959," Drawer 3, Vertical Files, Building T-15, Montana Military History Museum, Fort Harrison, Helena, Montana [hereafter cited as MMHM].
12. Major General William H Harrison Jr. served as adjutant general for the Army National Guard, as well as President of the National Guard Association. Memo from William H. Harrison Jr. to Adjutants General, May 15, 1959, Folder J-1, Box TF, National Guard Association of the United States Library, Washington, D.C. [hereafter cited as NGAUS Library].
13. "Army National Guard Strength and Training Reorganization," National Guard Association Memo, December 9, 1959, Folder J-1, Box TF, NGAUS Library. As of 1957, the National Guard consisted of 27 divisions (21 infantry, 6 armored), organized into 20 regiments and 285 battalions. There also were 148 headquarters and 426 separate companies and detachments. At the time, this was a larger organization of combat forces than the active Army. While there were no increased personnel or cost or requirements in the reorganization, it did mean a proposed reduction of 40,000 men for the ANG and a readjustment that would eliminate (or consolidate) a number of units. Western Governors' Conference Resolution, February 24, 1958, Folder "Reorganization," Box TF V-4, NGAUS Library.

14. Bacevich, *The Pentomic Era*, 135.
15. John B. Wilson, "Chapter 11: A New Direction—Flexible Response," in *Maneuver and Firepower: The Evolution of Divisions and Separate Brigades* (www.army.mil/cmh/books/Lineage/M-F/chapter11.htm), 2.
16. "337 World-wide Army Info. Officer's Conf.," Box 4244, RG 168, NA II.
17. ROAD concerned only the infantry, mechanized infantry, and armored divisions. Wilson, "A New Direction," 3.
18. Ibid., 4. See also Bacevich, *The Pentomic Era*, 94.
19. Wilson, "A New Direction," 8.
20. Ibid., 9.
21. Ibid, 11. ROAD included the elimination of more positions, but in the reserves, not the regular Army. In fact, the TOE strength of the reserve component structure dropped by one-third, roughly from 1,700,000 to 1,100,000. Pay drill status also decreased by 45 percent, with the number of paid soldiers reduced from 1,257,000 to 800,000. "Image of the Modern Reserve Components of the Army," Folder 334 General 1959, Entry 3444, Box 3808, RG 168, NA II.
22. Announcement made by President John F. Kennedy, NGB Memo, "Reorganization of Aviation Section Augmentation," May 25, 1961, Folder 325.4 Gen, Box 4058, RG 168, NA II.
23. Reorganization overview presented to the General Staff Committee on National Guard and Army Reserve Policy (Section 5 Committee), "Role of Reserve Components in National Defense," Folder 350.001 Gen Jan Thru May, Box 4244, RG 168, NA II, 11–12.
24. Colonel Gerald Miller (Ret.), interview by author, February 20, 2000.
25. National Guard Bureau Memo, "Reorganization Objectives Army Divisions," April 7, 1961, Folder 325.4 Gen, Box 4058, RG 168, NA II.
26. Infantry divisions included 2 tank and 6 infantry battalions, while armored divisions had 5 tank and 4 mechanized infantry battalions. Wilson, "A New Direction," 12.
27. Decimal File 1962 #325.1 NGR 75-4 Gen to 325.4 Air Fla, Folder 325.4 Governor's Letters on Reorganization 62, Box 4226, RG 168, NA II.
28. Adjutant General Spencer H. Mitchell to Senator Mansfield of Montana, 1962, Decimal File 325.4 Miss to 325.4 Air ND, Folder Mont 325.4, RG 168, NA II.
29. *Biennial Report, 1962–1964*, Montana State Library, Helena, Montana, 7.
30. Adjutant General S.H. Mitchell to Senator Mansfield, 1962, Decimal File 325.4 Miss to 325.4 Air ND, Folder Mont 325.4, RG 168, NA II.
31. Ibid.
32. The battalion was assigned self-propelled M7A "Priest" 105-mm howitzers. House Representative James Battin letter to Major General and Chief of the National Guard Bureau, D.W. McGowan, 1962, Decimal File 325.4 Miss to 325.4 Air ND, Folder Mont 325.4, RG 168, NA II.
33. Captain Joseph W. Upshaw to James Battin Telegram, May 2, 1962, Decimal File 325.4 Miss to 325.4 Air ND, Folder Mont 325.4, RG 168, NA II.
34. Secretary of Defense to Secretary of the Army, Decimal File 325.4 Miss to 325.4 Air ND, Folder Mont 325.4, RG 168, NA II.
35. "Fact Sheet Reorganization of Army Divisions," n.d., Folder 325.4 Gen, Box 4058, RG 168, NA II.
36. "1962 Current Policy Notes for Commanders," Folder 350.001 Gen Jan Thru May, Box 4244, RG 168, NA II.

37. "1961 Reorganization Objectives" Memo, Decimal File 1961 325.1 to 325.4, Folder 325.4 Gen, Box 4058, RG 168, NA II.
38. "Annual Worldwide Army Information Officer's Conference, 28–29 November, 1962," Folder "337 World-wide Army Info. Officer's Conf.," Box 4244, RG 168, NA II.
39. In 1959, New York City experienced "Operation Alert," a Civil Defense devised scenario involving a simulated nuclear attack. An estimated 1,200,000 people would have died from the atomic blast and heat, another 3,800,000 from exposure to fallout, while another 4,000,000 would suffer serious injuries. On a national basis, the figures projected close to 100 million deaths from fallout alone. "Basic Responsibilities after Attack," Memorandum by Department of Defense for FCDA and Office of Defense Mobilization regarding "Regional Roles," 23 January 1957, Decimal File #381 (AAA) Gen to 400.1912 Gen, Folder 384.51 General, Box 3179, RG 16, NA II.
40. National Guard Bureau's response to Westmoreland Memorandum regarding Civil Defense, "Role of Army Forces in Civil Defense," Decimal File 1957 #381 (AAA) Gen to 400.1912 Gen, Folder 384.51 General, Box 3179, RG 168, NA II.
41. General W.C. Westmoreland wrote: "I should like appropriate agencies of the staff to consider ways and means of emphasizing the emergency role of Army Forces in Civil Defense. Reserve and National Guard Forces should be considered in this action." November 1, 1957, Memorandum to Secretary of the General Staff from the Chief of Staff, "Role of Army Forces in Civil Defense," Decimal File 1957 # 381 (AAA) Gen to 400.1912 Gen, Folder 384.51 General, Box 3179, RG 168, NA II.
42. "Responsibilities for Civil Defense and other Domestic Emergencies," Department of Defense Directive #3025.1, 1957, Decimal File 1957 #381 (AAA) Gen to 400.1912 Gen, Folder 384.51 General, Box 3179, RG 168, NA II.
43. In 1957, Montana guardsmen became involved in "Operation Alert," which included three phases simulating an attack by the Soviets. The first phase, "Mobilization Emergency," took place June 5–July 11. This mock exercise included a situation in which a June 12 attack on a friendly nation in Southeast Asia prompted U.S. overseas forces to initiate a counterattack by June 20. The next phase, "Civil Defense," occurred July 12–14. This operation required moving to relocation sites, because certain military installations and headquarters had suffered virtual destruction. In this exercise, the locations of targets, ground zero, and the yield or type of burst for each atomic bomb had remained unknown until the time of the mock attack. The third and final stage, "Expansion of Mobilization Base," occurred July 15–19. The purpose of Operation Alert was explained in a Federal Civil Defense Administration memo sent to all Civil Defense directors. It was "to improve the readiness of the Nation to meet promptly and effectively in emergency situations resulting from enemy action, to test communications facilities, to provide additional training in the emergency functions at all echelons of government, to continue public education, and to test the performance of Federal Agencies in their immediate essential wartime functions." "Prototype Fallout Shelter, 1959," Press Release by Richard Amper, Press Secretary to New York's Governor Rockefeller, Folder 8, Governor John Hugo Aronson Papers, General Office Papers, Box 137, Manuscript Collection [MC] 35, Montana Historical Society, Helena, Montana [hereafter cited as MHS].
44. "The Family Fallout Shelter," Office of Civil Defense and Mobilization Pamphlet, AR-NGB Decimal File 1960, Box 3932, RG 168, NA II.
45. Governor J. Hugo Aronson to Leo A. Hoegh, September 15, 1959, Governor John Hugo Aronson Papers, General Office Papers, Folder 8, Box 137, MC 35, MHS. The Minuteman information is from an unpublished transcript, Colonel Gerald Miller (Ret.), provided to author, February 20, 2000.

46. Robert Keyes, Montana Director of Civil Defense, to Phillip Batson, Regional Director, Office of Civil Defense and Mobilization, October 9, 1959, Governor John Hugo Aronson Papers, General Office Papers, Folder 8, Box 137, MC 35, MHS.
47. Unpublished transcript, Colonel Gerald Miller (Ret.), provided to author, February 20, 2000.
48. "1957 6th Army Atomic Domestic Emergency Plan" Memorandum, NGB Decimal File 1957 #381, Folder 381 6th Army, Box 3179, RG 168, NA II, 2.
49. *Biennial Report, 1962–1964.*
50. Sometimes CBR teams utilized aircraft to conduct aerial surveys. An aerial survey party consisted of a pilot (officer or NCO) and a monitor (an enlisted man). While this was a potentially hazardous activity, it appears the teams were equipped with rather paltry equipment: radiac sets, radiacmeter, film badge, portable 2-way radio, binoculars, compass, flashlight, mask, chemical agent detector kit, liquid agent detector crayon and paper, protective ointment kit, weapon, first aid packet, and a wrist watch. "1957 6th Army Atomic Domestic Emergency Plan" Memorandum, NGB Decimal File 1957 #381, Folder 381 6th Army, Box 3179, RG 168, NA II, 2.
51. As early as 1955, the MNG ran Public Alert Signals—steady siren alarms lasting from three to five minutes at a time—that would warn of possible nuclear attack. Another Civil Defense precaution instituted in 1964 was the National Warning System (NAWAS). This system had direct telephone connections to 10 key warning points in Montana. These points then had the responsibility of relaying alerts to all of Montana's other counties. In 1964, 10 cities were chosen for this responsibility: Missoula, Kalispell, Butte, Billings, Helena, Great Falls, Lewistown, Miles City, Glendive, and Glasgow. Also in 1964, a radiological instrument repair station was installed at the state prison in Deer Lodge; Montana State College handled all work on the calibration systems. "Role of Army Forces in Civil Defense," Memorandum, 1957 Response to Westmoreland Memorandum by NGB Chief, Major General Edgar C. Erickson, Decimal File 1957 #381 (AAA) Gen to 400.1912 Gen, Folder 384.51 General, Box 3179, RG 168, NA II.
52. In terms of Civil Defense, the adjutant general office's duties included locating and stocking fallout shelters, organizing and training Civil Defense staff, keeping local assistance aware of operations, radiological monitoring, assisting at the state and county level with warning plans, manning Emergency Operations Centers, and inventorying and planning for achieving optimal fallout shelter effectiveness. The Civil Defense headquarters occupied four rooms on the third floor of the State Arsenal in Helena. The sub-basement held the Emergency Operation Center (EOC), which by 1966 included new ventilation, heat, emergency power, soundproofing, and office partitions. *Biennial Report, 1962–1964*, 42.
53. *Biennial Report, 1964–1966.*
54. Ibid.
55. 1962 Decimal File #337, Folder "337 World-wide Army Info. Officer's Conference," Box 4244, RG 168, NA II.
56. Bacevich, *The Pentomic Era*, 53–54.
57. Tompkins, *The Weapons of World War III*. See also, 1962 Decimal File #337, Folder "337 World-wide Army Info. Officer's Conference," Box 4244, RG 168, NA II.
58. Bacevich, *The Pentomic Era*, 99–100.
59. Ibid., 73, 99.
60. Ibid., 84. See also, C.B. Colby, *Fighting Gear of World War II: Equipment and Weapons of the American G.I.* (New York: Coward and McCann, 1961).
61. Bacevich, *The Pentomic Era*, 86.

62. "Current Policy Notes for Commanders," Folder 350.001 Gen Jan Thru May, Box 4244, RG 168, NA II, 2.
63. Bacevich, *The Pentomic Era*, 77.
64. "Image of the Modern Reserve Components of the Army," 2.
65. Tompkins, *The Weapons of World War III*, 86.
66. Ibid., 102.
67. Ibid.
68. Ibid., 57.
69. Ibid., 52.
70. 1962 Decimal File #337, Folder "337 World-wide Army Info. Officer's Conference," Box 4244, RG 168, NA II.
71. Ibid.
72. Army Training Manual TM 9-500, 1962.
73. 1962 Decimal File #337, Folder "337 World-wide Army Info. Officer's Conference," Box 4244, RG 168, NA II.
74. Ibid.
75. Folder "ORDNANCE-Montana-1957," Box 3190, RG 168, NA II.
76. *Biennial Report, 1960–1962.*
77. "Signal Supply Report No. 17," May 4, 1962, Folder 353.02 Mont, Box 4250, RG 168, NA II.
78. *Biennial Report, 1962–1964.*

A 163rd Armored Cavalry Regiment parade in Helena during the 1960s. *MMHM*

15

Reserve Forces Act (1955): 6-Months Active Duty, Monthly Training, and 2-Week Summer Camp, 1955–1965

Mari Hillestad Knirck

Technology undermined old assumptions, rendered traditional practices obsolete, and seemed to require a radical overhaul in the way that the Army equipped and organized itself.—John S. Tompkins, *The Weapons of World War III.*

The prison was a tension-ridden, overcrowded, disorganized mess, a powder keg set to explode at the slightest provocation.—Warden Floyd E. Powell, Deer Lodge Prison.

Education

The National Guard needed to adopt the latest technologies and fill its ranks with highly skilled soldiers to operate new systems and equipment. Mobility, inherent in the Pentomic and ROAD reorganizations, also demanded flexible and quick thinking leadership. In order to recruit men who would become skilled leaders and technicians, both the Army and the National Guard raised standards and reinvigorated education programs.[1]

In 1957, Army National Guard and U.S. Army Reserve officer instructional programs added new tests and requirements in order to quickly and effectively place higher qualified leaders into units.[2] The MNG's enlisted personnel also increasingly took part in a variety of educational opportunities at NCO and service schools, in and out of state, including training in maintenance, communications, administration, ordnance, etc.[3] An increasing number of courses reflected Cold War preparation in the event of a nuclear attack.[4] Scores of Montana soldiers received instruction at Fort Knox, Kentucky, Fort Olney, Maryland, Fort Sill, Oklahoma,[5] and other posts.[6]

Retired Col. Gerald Miller later explained the commitment that officer education entailed. "All Reserve officers have to meet the same time and education qualification standards as for those on active duty, so we had a never ending requirement for qualification training. Those requirements—added to maintaining our families, full-time civilian jobs, and National Guard positions that required an ever increasing amount of drill and training time—presented some real problems for unit members."

A number of soldiers could not handle the burden of these responsibilities and dropped out of officer training. According to Miller, however, "school teachers, government employees who were guaranteed their jobs and were allowed military training, and other seasonal employees...could often [have time to attend] military assignments or schools, and those people often became the best trained and most qualified unit members."[7]

At Army operated schools, most courses lasted two weeks and attendance could substitute for the annual two week field training.[8] In 1960–1962, Montana sent 98 officers, 8 warrant officers, and 62 enlisted personnel to U.S. Army schools.[9] Courses in 1964 reveal the MNG's focus during the Cold War—Chemical, Radiological, and Biological Warfare; Material Readiness; Equipment Records Systems; and Nuclear Weapons Employment Refresher Course.[10]

By 1957, 35 states had developed officer candidate schools (OCS).[11] Montana's newly formed academy opened in the spring of that year. Previously, Montana guardsmen usually earned commissions (if they were not prior U.S. Army officers) by taking correspondence courses under the "Ten Series" program. "I don't remember the exact numbers," Col. Miller recalled, "but it required about 300 study hours for about 100 credit hours, with no pay. It took me over a year to complete the study course."

The Montana Military Academy was launched just before Miller completed his coursework. Miller and another unit member, however, were close to completing their Ten Series work and were "grandfathered" in, commissioned as second lieutenants without attending the new academy. He believed they were perhaps the last officers in Montana to be commissioned under the Ten Series program.

The Montana OCS academy mandated that candidates attend two consecutive summer camps and ten weekend drills in Helena. "OCS," Miller recalled, "was a very concentrated instructional program; 'hands-on' with discipline and leadership highly emphasized."[12] The 432 instructional hours were divided into phases—the two summer sessions consisted of 262 hours of training and instruction, while the intervening winter-weekend drill phase entailed 170 hours. In keeping with principles established by the Reserve Forces Act of 1955, at least 296 hours of the lessons matched official stipulations provided by the U.S. Army Infantry School, Non-Resident Instruction Department.[13] Course work was the focus of the training.[14]

By the time an officer candidate approached graduation, he had undergone intense "harassment" training, described in an academy yearbook as "the well tested methods used to place an officer candidate under constant pressure, so he can be evaluated on his ability to perform under adverse conditions." The demanding course work included such topics as map and aerial-photography reading, weapons familiarization, administration, logistics, military law, and communications. Physical endurance was part of the regimen, including push-ups, double-timing, and other conditioning activities. Graduation from the Montana Military Academy required a 70 percent grade average and final approval by the commandant and tactical officers. Graduates were commissioned as second lieutenants.

Above all, an OCS candidate needed to have a profound desire for professional military achievement. "It is this intense desire that knots in your throat as you repeat the long awaited words of the oath of office at graduation ceremonies," a yearbook entry explained. Matching Miller's experience, all OCS graduates appeared before a federal recognition board. A number of graduates went on to serve in the active Army.[15] Newly minted commissioned officers were required to instruct at their home units.[16] Second lieutenants also needed to enroll and qualify in their assigned branch—e.g., Infantry, Armor, Artillery—through correspondence courses or active duty training lasting four to five months.

Miller remembered how this requirement added another heavy strain on his personal life. "My civilian job as a printer in a weekly newspaper made it difficult to be gone for that length of time," thus he took the correspondence course "20 Series" in Artillery. "That course again was several hundred study hours at no pay. Correspondence courses allowed us to remain at home and qualify," he noted, "but studying by yourself with no field work involved, and without an instructor present, made it a difficult choice and the education could not be as highly regarded as someone who attended active duty courses." Nevertheless, Miller made up for this deficiency by paying special attention to how the active duty graduates performed when serving in the field.[17]

During this period, enlistment standards for all guardsmen were elevated in regard to mental, moral, professional, and physical fitness. Previously, reservists did not have to meet a mental standard of any sort. The Air Force Quotient Test (AFQT), similar to one used by the active Army, now was instituted. The minimum score required for a guardsman was 10, but in two years rose to 21 (equivalent to the Army Standard Score of 80).[18] Those already serving who received less than minimal scores were transferred to "low mental category" groups. The inability to meet standards meant that a soldier might be transferred to the Standby Reserves, to the Retired Reserves, or be discharged.[19]

Training

In prior years, the MNG provided its own combat basic training for new recruits, but this began changing with the Reserve Forces Act of 1955 (RFA 55). This directive allowed National Guard recruits not having prior military experience to complete Six-Month Active Duty Training at U.S. Army training centers, such as at Fort Ord, California. Guardsmen and Reservists trained alongside regular Army inductees. A guardsman's six-month active duty typically included three phases—Combat Basic Training lasting 8 weeks, Advanced Individual Training, normally 8 to 12 weeks, and Basic Unit Training, 4 to 8 weeks.

Combat Basic Training served as the introduction to Army discipline, procedures, and military courtesy. Along with extensive physical training, the primary instruction included combat skills, close order drill, firearms training, map reading, guard duty, etc. After successfully completing basic training, a recruit moved on to Advanced Individualized Training (AIT) for instruction in a Military Occupational Specialty (MOS), such as a light weapons infantryman, truck driver, artilleryman, etc.

Once trainees returned from six-month active duty, they participated in their unit's normal drilling, which included the annual 15-day Active Duty Field Training program (summer camp) and 48 armory drills per year. If these attendance obligations were not met, a National Guard soldier could be inducted into the regular Army.

In 1957, Congress authorized increased funding for National Guard pay, allowances, equipment, and travel costs for attending training programs, including the six-month active duty.[20] The Army increased drill pay to ensure that RFA 55 would succeed in retaining more personnel meeting higher achievement standards. By 1958, 80 percent of National Guard units nationwide included personnel completing the six month training.[21]

Prior to RFA 55, the National Guard Bureau directed local units to drill once during each week, 48 times per year, under standards established by the 1948 reorganization. Under this schedule, an average weeknight session lasted about 2 or 2½ hours, barely sufficient time to service weapons, train with equipment, conduct classes, and pack up for the night. In the 1960s, the weekly drill schedule was dropped and, instead, training sessions were held one weekend each month. Weekend drilling proved more practical, allowing for more efficient hands-on exercises and training, frequently in the field.[22]

Retired guardsman Gerald Miller remembered what this meant for training standards. "Changing to a weekend reduced wasted time, and increased training from 10 to 16 hours as well. In general, the troops accepted the change very well because they lost only one weekend per month, rather than being tied to a once-a-week schedule under the old system. This improved training and morale because the men could demonstrate their competency. Maintenance problems did increase some because of more usage, but this was offset by the increased skills and training. Leadership greatly improved because leaders were actually 'leading' and not just acting as classroom instructors."[23]

The MNG's *Biennial Report* confirmed that the new weekend drilling—consisting of four combined four-hour assemblies—improved guard capabilities. "This system of conducting sixteen hours of instruction in the concentrated period of two consecutive days results in more effective training and training supervision." The report also attributed improved attendance to the weekend format.[24]

The MNG's 15-day summer field training usually was held at Fort William H. Harrison.[25] Federal directives assigned active Army personnel to each state to assist and advise in unit training, serving as liaisons between the guard and the regular Army. A number of these advisors, however, had preconceived views tagging National Guard performance as "inferior," despite the guardsmen's adherence to Army training standards. This bias, Miller believed, contributed to the guard often not receiving up-to-date equipment. "Although some reserve units might be assigned priority missions, they were at the bottom of the list to get required equipment. It was a 'given' that all new equipment would go to regular Army units, and their 'hand-me-downs' or obsolete items would eventually filter down to the reservists—some day!"[26]

In the *Biennial Report, 1960–1962,* Montana's adjutant general praised the new training emphasis and requirements established under RFA 1955. "The overall training and efficiency status," wrote Richard C. Kendall, "is such that the Guard is capable of performing its assigned missions and could be mobilized for any type of state emergency at a moment's notice."[27]

Summer Camps

Programs and regulations stipulated by the Commander of Continental Army Command provided the framework under which the MNG held its two-week summer training. Tactical exercises in security, blackout marches, field maintenance, supply, first aid, sanitation, etc. trained guardsmen to be self-sufficient in the field. Proficiency in battle tactics and weapons use was achieved through numerous live-fire exercises for infantry, armor, and artillery. The 15-day camps usually were scheduled for June, when college students could attend and after high school seniors completed graduation.

Although summer camp put guardsmen in situations as near to actual combat conditions as possible, it also allowed for time to relax and unwind. A number of officers and enlisted men brought wives and families to Helena for a "Helena holiday." The first days of camp, Saturday and Sunday, saw units converging on Fort Harrison, drawing equipment and organizing, before normally heading out to field sites by Wednesday. From Wednesday through Friday night, units underwent field training. Troops returned to base on Saturday for the "middle weekend." The men were free to join their families and friends in town until returning Sunday night. Training resumed in the field on Monday, lasting until Wednesday night when units returned to the garrison. On Thursday and Friday, they restored equipment and the garrison area to pre-summer camp condition, and traveled home on Saturday and Sunday.

On reflection, Col. Gerald Miller concluded that the middle weekend break was not in the best interest of training. "The 'middle weekend holiday' seemed to be a God given requirement, which lasted for several years, but hurt training

Lunch break during field training at Fort Harrison. *MMHM*

because units would get a rhythm going in their training, and then lose their 'edge' when they shut down for the weekend. Returning to the field after a 'holiday' made it difficult to operate as sharply and well as they should have. Finally someone dictated that the 'middle weekend' was a dead horse, and units did not return to garrison until field training was completed—and training greatly benefited from the change. Morale on the 'home front' took a beating because a lot of wives and families resented losing their 'Helena holiday,' but it was a big advancement for the training program."[28]

Annual training included considerable live-fire exercises. In 1958, more than 270 tons of ammunition was expended. Ammunition costs varied from 6½¢ per round for a .45 caliber pistol cartridge to $85 for a 155-mm howitzer shell. Approximately 2,000 guardsmen fired small arms at the Camp Aronson range, while the armor units practiced near Deer Lodge, and the artillery range was utilized in the Limestone Hills near Townsend.[29]

The Deer Lodge State Prison property was essential for field training by armor and other units. Col. William C. Benson of Bozeman, the regimental commander, had served for a time as the prison warden and saw the value of using the large penitentiary farm acreage. A long, rather rugged route could be utilized by vehicles in convoy between Fort Harrison and the prison property. Winding along U.S. Forest Service and county roads, units traveled to and from these locations in combat march column. Sometimes travel was conducted at night under blackout conditions. Units practiced night-time refueling, rested at halts, and proceeded on at early light. Springtime rains often harried the columns, creating potentially hazardous but essential training conditions. Miller remembered injuries resulting from vehicles slipping over embankments.

Miller also recalled an anecdote concerning the Deer Lodge farm road. "The prison farm site had its drawback—for the inmates. In one instance, a mistake in sighting artillery pieces resulted in a 1,000 yard error, with a cannon round bursting in the air above a prison ranch pickup driving down a cattle trail—the pickup was abandoned on the spot with a broken windshield and the three inmates traveling on foot, rapidly in three different directions. Someone else recovered the pickup for them."[30]

In April 1959, a battalion of the 163rd Regiment was sent to Camp Irwin, California, for armor training.[31] Most of the personnel traveled by special train, returning via the same means. Arrangements were made for the troops to visit Hollywood on a weekend and enjoy other tourist attractions.[32]

That summer, the 2nd Battalion and the Regimental Service Company conducted training near Deer Lodge on the tank proficiency course. Approximately 100 M47 tanks and more than 300 men honed their skills. Battalion S-2, Intelligence, commanded by Capt. Ward H. Bealy, assumed the role of aggressors and employed harassment tactics as the tanks traveled to the Deer Lodge site from Camp Aronson. The march adhered as closely as possible to actual battle conditions.[33]

Over the years, the MNG made improvements in live-fire evaluation tests. At first, tank units practiced on "static" ranges, with the targets obvious and fixed. "A couple of test shots established a range, and shooting after that was an easy task—but not very realistic," explained Miller. Training was improved by adding moving targets of different types, and incorporating other hidden targets, in an effort to catch tank crews unaware. More realistic situations gave crews much improved results.[34]

In 1958, the 163rd provided a nighttime demonstration of armor tactics.[35] The live-fire exercise—staged for battle training and as a public exhibition—simulated a full-scale tank attack at the Deer Lodge practice grounds. M41 light tanks participated in the maneuvers, which also incorporated artillery and infantrymen.[36] The weapons demonstration included tank and artillery fire, rocket launchers, 81-mm mortars, .50 caliber machine guns, and light weapons.[37]

The crowd witnessed an impressive illuminated demonstration as four magnesium flares soared simultaneously into the night sky, lighting up nearly a quarter-square-mile area.[38] The 639th Field Artillery Battalion, situated 8,000 yards from the target area, fired 155-mm howitzers, and the 443rd Armored Field Artillery Battalion, 5,000 yards distant, fired high explosive rounds. Spectators watched at a distance of 1,500 yards from the target area.[39]

Due to training acreage limitations, however, armor and artillery units normally did not train together.[40] During summer camp, tank units traveled to direct-fire ranges, while the artillery went elsewhere. According to Miller, separating units in this manner produced negative side effects. "Our commander attended headquarters briefings, and we socialized when together in garrison, but that was about it. Because of the separation, artillery officer advancement was limited—and the same thing applied to chemical, medical, communications, and other specialties."[41]

Also in 1958, the 210th Engineer Battalion and the 1049th Engineer Company from Shelby bivouacked for three days at Canyon Ferry Lake, constructing pontoon bridges.[42] At the same time, the 154th Field Artillery Group of Missoula, the 639th Field Artillery Battalion of Kalispell, and the 443rd Armored Field Artillery Battalion[43] traveled to the Limestone Hills firing range, where General Mitchell inspected their training.[44] Here, the 154th practiced with high explosives, landmines, and grenades, as well as conducting squad patrols and tactical rifle training. The 495th Ordnance Battalion fired carbines and .30 caliber tank-mounted machine guns. All units also trained with 3.5-inch rockets.[45]

Conducting live fire exercises and maneuvers in rough terrain entailed an element of danger, and injuries occasionally occurred. One such incident happened on June 16, 1955, at the firing range outside of Helena. Company A of the 163rd's 1st Battalion was engaged in rapid-fire practice with the M2 .50 caliber Browning machine gun. The particular weapon involved in this accident had been employed the previous summer. Afterward, it passed a State Maintenance Shop inspection and was placed in storage on November 30, 1954. It had not been used since, and therefore its malfunctioning on the firing range in 1955 was unexpected.[46]

Company A had just finished firing its rounds. Private Jacobsen began a routine search for links and brass lying on the ground. Finding an unfired round, Jacobsen handed it over to his tank commander, Sgt. Delbert L. Sorensen. To expend all live ammunition, as was expected, Sorensen inserted the round into the M2, but after the bolt assembly slammed forward, the round did not fire.

Uncertain as to why it had not fired, Sorensen repeated the steps, but still nothing. He tried once more, removing the cover and pushing back the bolt no more than about 1¼ inches, when the round unexpectedly exploded. Sorensen lurched back as fragments struck his eyes. He received immediate treatment for his eye injuries, as well as for a minor cut on his right foot, at the Fort Harrison Veterans Hospital.

Investigators determined the malfunction was a "cook-off." Sorensen's team had fired 1,320 rounds in less than 45 minutes. The barrel was quite hot. Investigators also learned that, while the M2 was working well prior to the accident, beforehand it had not been cleaned and oiled properly. 1st Lt. William G. DeWolf from Company C of the 3669th Ordnance interviewed Sorensen. "The base of the cartridge case was stuck in the end of the barrel extension," DeWolf reported, "and about two inches of the body of the neck of the case still remained in the breech." DeWolf concluded that the weapon "appeared to be overheated."

As Sorensen and his team fired unexpended extra rounds while waiting for the other tank crews to finish up their allotted ammunition, he did not change the overheated barrel because the spare barrel had been left in the unit supply room. DeWolf's investigative partner, Capt. James R. Bryant, Ordnance Corps, USAR at Fort Lewis, reported that Sorensen indicated he "did not remember ever having been told he could not fire the weapon in the manner he was attempting."[47]

Another accident occurred in June 1958 when captains William P. Riggert of the 154th artillery (Missoula) and Robert W. Cook, Headquarters, 443rd Armored Field Artillery (St. Ignatius), crashed a two-seat plane three miles west of Townsend during field training. While neither was seriously injured, both received cuts, bruises, and back injuries. Riggert, the pilot, hit a power line some 50 feet north of U.S. Highway 10. Perhaps most bruised, however, was their pride; the crash occurred in full view of the 154th Field Artillery Group while en route to the Limestone Hills training range that morning.[48]

Tactical field training inherently meant that sooner or later accidents would occur. The regular Army experienced its share of live-fire and training accidents as well, despite precautionary measures to prevent them. Thus, it must be expected that the National Guard would not be exempt from them either, despite careful oversight.

Armories

Preparedness meant not only proper training, but also having up-to-date armories and other facilities. The Reserve Forces Act had provided long-term funding for 1,054 new armories across the nation, which by the 1960s helped enhance the legitimacy of the guard both nationally and within individual states. In this period, the Montana National Guard endeavored to sustain a full strength of approximately 3,000 officers and enlisted personnel. The 163rd, the largest unit in the Montana organization, incorporated one regimental headquarters, three squadrons, an aviation company, and other support units.[49]

Manning units at full level strength was difficult, however, since only the largest Montana cities had population bases large enough to provide enlistment pools sufficient for filling companies of 120 men. Consequently, a number of units were split between smaller towns. This put a heavy burden on unit commanders. Col. Gerald Miller, in charge of a squadron covering much of eastern Montana, recalled a weekend "when I took a staff team, and we drove 1,100 miles to visit ten locations of our squadron units. We spent no more than an hour at a location, but there just wasn't any other way to do the job because no air transportation was available for us."[50]

Maintaining enlistment levels had continuing challenges, but relatively good progress was made in upgrading and adding armories and other facilities. In 1959, the National Guard Bureau appropriated $235,000 to "rehabilitate" Fort Harrison, and to build new armories in Dillon and Chinook, with future plans for four more armories.[51] The guard planned to begin building the new armories by early autumn 1960. Sometimes, local businesses or townspeople provided property for armories. In 1960, the Anaconda Company deeded land in Anaconda for a new armory, to be erected at an estimated $88,000 (with $66,000 coming from federal monies and the rest state funded).[52] Meanwhile, new armory construction progressed nationwide; by 1962, the National Guard Bureau reported that 70 percent of the required armory construction was completed.[53]

Still, facilities and terrain for field activities were limited in parts of Montana. Local units sometimes had to adopt innovative methods. Miller recalled that units appreciated private land owners who allowed training on their property. In Miller's Harlowton outfit, enlisted "members, and particularly officers who owned farms and ranches, were very cooperative in making training space available for unit training. The guardsmen always appreciated the opportunity to get out of the armory." The guard also took advantage of access to Bureau of Land Management and U.S. Forest Service holdings, as well as state-owned land. In these localities, "great care was extended in conducting exercises and making certain that everything was 'put right' before training ended," Miller remembered.

Unit activities on private and public property included everything from operating wheeled vehicles to practicing for small weapons qualification. Sometimes, .50-caliber machine guns were used on local ranges, but the hot slugs of this powerful long-range weapon could be a fire hazard, making guardsmen wary of this type of live-fire training. Tank and howitzer maneuvers rarely occurred at these local areas because of the disturbance it would cause to the terrain.[54]

By 1962, the State of Montana owned 15 armories—in Anaconda, Billings, Bozeman, Butte, Chinook, Dillon, Glendive, Hamilton, Helena, Kalispell, Lewistown, Miles City, Plentywood, Sidney, and Whitefish. Other facilities were leased or licensed. The two newest state armories, in Anaconda and Lewistown (the S.H. Mitchell Armory), were completed in October 1961 and January 1962 respectively at a cost of $85,012.[55] Nonetheless, Adjunct General Mitchell noted that some units still lacked proper facilities, including storage and maintenance space for track and wheeled vehicles. By June 1962, however, squadron and battalion organizations in Belgrade, Billings Chinook, Culbertson, Helena, Kalispell, and Missoula were provided with such facilities, all federally supported.[56]

Fort Harrison, as the state headquarters, had overseen the procurement, maintenance, storage, and issuance of heavy equipment and vehicles. By 1964, these responsibilities were divided among six state organizational centers, at Billings, Bozeman, Culbertson, Kalispell, Missoula, and Fort Harrison itself.[57] This disbursement and upgrade of organizational centers throughout Montana relieved much of the pressure and responsibility formerly placed on Fort Harrison personnel.

By the mid-1960s, the guard occupied 24 armories across Montana. The state-owned armories had increased to 19; other armories and facilities were leased or licensed. By 1966, Deer Lodge, Glasgow, and Malta each received new armories.[58] The value of these properties totaled about $7 million, with the state funding having been approximately $5 million. Under provisions of the Reserve Forces Act, the state and the MNG were responsible for maintenance.[59]

A concern in this period was the insufficient number of training and firing sites for the 163rd Armored Cavalry, which needed larger training areas since its reorganization in 1958–1959. The current site near Townsend had limitations, causing guard authorities to consider a new location in the Glasgow-Fort Peck region, but plans for a new training site were postponed. Adjutant General R.C. Kendall explained: "There are many obstacles to overcome before we can begin to develop a training site consistent with our needs."[60]

Disaster Preparedness

The Office of Emergency Planning, under the Executive Office of the Governor, remained well aware of the Montana guard's preparedness. "While it is quite unlikely that a nuclear attack will occur, as long as our enemies have this capability, plans must be prepared that will permit instant response conducive to the survival of our people and recovery of our resources."[61] The governor's office also noted that the guard's modern training was equally valuable in responding to earthquakes, fires, floods, and blizzards.

Indeed, in August 1959 a severe earthquake struck southwest Montana and guardsmen were deployed to protect homes and businesses from looting. In the Madison River canyon, the quake released a massive landslide killing nine vacationers in the Rock Creek Campground near Yellowstone National Park. Tremors lasted four days—the U.S. Geodetic Survey recorded 372 aftershocks—and debris blocked 75 miles of road in the western half of Yellowstone Park. In patrolling operations, the MNG assisted state patrolmen from Idaho and Wyoming[62] Ordnance units, particularly the State Maintenance Shop, provided bulldozers and trucks in clearing roads, hauling supplies, and evacuating people.

Also in 1959, an early blizzard struck Montana. The November cold snap created ice blockage and flooding on the Missouri River near Townsend, a threat to homes, ranches, and livestock. Temperatures dropped to as low as -46°, with 30 mph winds. An additional 3 inches of snow fell on top of an earlier storm that buried Helena under 21½ inches. Backwater flooding threatened a rest home housing 12 elderly persons.[63] Again, guardsmen provided assistance.

During severe drought and fire danger in 1961, the guard provided equipment and scores of men to State Forest and National Forest agencies. In the spring of 1962, the 154th Field Artillery Group was activated after a Northern Pacific passenger train wrecked near Evaro; unit members mobilized quickly to provide aid to injured passengers.[64]

Devastating springtime flooding struck Montana in June 1964, again requiring the help of guardsmen. President Lyndon Johnson declared an emergency and the government budgeted $6 million for aid.[65] The guard assisted Civil Defense personnel and highway patrolmen, collecting information on road conditions with the help of the Radio Amateur Civil Emergency Services.[66] Guardsmen provided 1,317 man-days of service during this period.[67]

In December of the same year, a blizzard struck southeast Montana, prompting the governor to call out 21 guardsmen for 7 days of state active duty to help farmers and ranchers collect and feed stranded cattle. Known as "Operation Haylift," the mission sent ten 2½-ton cargo trucks from the Billings National Guard Armory to control points in Miles City, Broadus, Ekalaka, and Baker. Other guardsmen worked as snowplow crews, hauled equipment, and operated fuel transports. Four Air National Guard aircraft flew reconnaissance missions, carrying Bureau of Public Road personnel over the area to report on road conditions and determine routes for reaching stranded livestock. During the last two days, a C-119 aircraft spotted cattle and dropped hay. Disaster relief totaled more than $235,000 in federal and state monies.[68] This work cemented community ties to the MNG in local areas.[69]

The Deer Lodge Prison Riot

The state's traditional reliance on the guard in times of civil unrest continued, though in an unusual occurrence—the 1959 Montana State Prison riot in Deer Lodge. Warden Floyd E. Powell later recalled: "The prison was a tension-ridden, overcrowded, disorganized mess, a powder keg set to explode at the slightest provocation,"[70] due to underfunding and lack of updates. Trouble began before 4 p.m. on Thursday, April 16, 1959, just as prison guards from the daytime shift ended their day. Jerry Myles, a "power-mad convict" serving his sixth burglary sentence, was the mastermind of the revolt. A habitual criminal, Myles also had served time at Alcatraz in his 25 total years of incarceration.

In the cell block, the ringleaders splashed flammable liquid on a guard and threatened to immolate him. They grabbed the guard's rifle, and then with other inmates, seized a couple more guards. Next, Myles led fellow inmates George Alton and 19-year-old Lee Smart into the front office of the deputy warden, Theodore "Ted" Rothe.[71] Armed with sharp objects and the .30 caliber rifle stolen just moments earlier. Under the impression that Myles needed medication for migraine headaches, Rothe's assistant, William Cox, left his desk and entered Rothe's office to request the pills. With the door left ajar, Myles, Smart, and Alton rushed in brandishing their weapons. Myles physically attacked Rothe. When Rothe attempted to fend him off with a file box, Smart shot Rothe through the heart, killing him instantly.[72] Before Cox could help Rothe, Myles slashed him in the arm.[73]

Forcing the injured Cox into an adjacent bathroom, the rioters waited to seize prison guards returning cell keys to Rothe's front office when going off duty. One unlucky worker, administrative assistant John K. Simonsen, wished to speak with Rothe before going off shift. Simonsen entered a trap, with Myles threatening him, and seeing Rothe lying dead on the floor. Myles also intended to take Warden Floyd Powell as a hostage and bargaining tool. He ordered Simonsen to "pick up the phone, call the warden, tell [him] there was trouble and hang up." Simonsen later explained, "if I didn't do this, they said I would get the same as Rothe."[74]

The warden, maintenance supervisor Carl Parish, and business manager Elmer Erickson rushed to the office. The convicts forced Simonsen to meet Powell at the door. Erickson and Parish, sensing something unusual, jumped back, but the warden, aware of danger a split second too late, was pulled into the office. The door slammed behind him.[75]

The escaping Erickson later described these tense moments. "We went into the main entrance, Tower 7. We let ourselves in. They grabbed the warden. I jumped back down the steps, hiding down along the building. I couldn't help. I yelled for the guard on the tower to lower the key. They [the inmates] yelled at me, 'If you don't stop and come back, we'll shoot.' I kept low. The man in the tower threw the key. I let myself out and locked the gate behind me."[76]

Having captured Powell and gathering up other hostages, the three convicts made their way into the cellblock. More rioters—some witnesses report as many as 20 altogether, others as few as 5—locked about two dozen hostages in cells. The seriously wounded Cox and a diabetic guard, Chris Pletan, were set free, and two sick, older convicts were allowed to freely walk out. As they met officers outside, one of the convicts said: "Hang-tough—it looks like things are going our way in there."[77]

The situation remained in a stalemate for the next three hours. Then, Powell was enabled to escape when the ringleaders moved elsewhere, leaving him in the hands of other rioters. Inmate Earl Jackson Howard shouted, "I will cut the throat of the first [convict] that touches the warden!" and led Powell to safety.[78]

Once outside, Powell assumed full authority over the prison guards and other alerted law enforcement officers, as well as a number of guardsmen already called up by Governor Hugo J. Aronson. The activation would include members of the Headquarters Battery, 154th Field Artillery Group; Headquarters Battery, Battery A, and the Medical Detachment of the 443rd Armored Field Artillery Battalion, Missoula; the 443rd Armored Field Artillery, Deer Lodge; Company A, 210th Engineer Battalion, Anaconda; and State Headquarters and Headquarters Detachment, Helena.[79] Highway patrol and local police officers were with the National Guard contingent as well as additional volunteers. The number of men totaled nearly 300.[80] Adjutant General Mitchell established a temporary headquarters in prison offices across the street from the cell block.[81] During the standoff, guardsmen would be housed at the Deer Lodge Armory, in motels, and local homes.[82]

A plan was developed to storm the cellblock if required. That evening, 50 guardsmen[83] were organized into teams at the Powell County High School gymnasium.[84] The assault force included seven groups of riflemen, two groups of firefighters, and medics.[85] The remaining guardsmen, along with the state patrolmen and police, stayed on the periphery of the cell block area, either occupying observation posts or patrolling outside the walls.[86]

The assignment of guardsmen in positions around the prison walls proved reassuring to the townspeople. Warden Powell later commented about this in a letter to Adjutant General Mitchell. "They worked long hours on rather tiresome positions, in some cases. They certainly are to be complimented on their devotion to duty…courtesy to everyone[,] and their conduct in general throughout this whole episode."[87]

As the crisis wore on, Powell's fear for the lives of the hostages mounted. Walter Jones, the prison sociologist, was among the men being held. Jones and riot leader Jerry Myles had previous confrontations. Jones believed that Myles was suffering from a "deep sense of insecurity" after the inmate complained to him over losing his "con-boss" status as an inmate shop supervisor. According to Jones, Myles "used this position to become a powerful 'con boss,' able to levy tribute on other prisoners until he had been fired from the job. He blamed me, along with Deputy Warden Theodore Rothe, for the demotion."[88]

Myles had threatened Jones before: "Prison is my home, and you're making it a tough place for me to live." After the warning, Jones had segregated Myles, prompting a second threat, "I warn you! Don't push me too far." Jones believed he had no choice but to keep Myles in isolation.[89]

As the face-off continued, Jones wondered if his previous actions had helped send Myles over the edge. Jones calculated that only 20 inmates were participating in the rebellion out of a prison population of 425. Many of the uninvolved inmates locked themselves in their cells.

The rioters seemed unsure of their next step. While "nervous" and "jumpy," a number of them also "seemed eager to stay on the good side of the hostages, in case the uprising failed." In total, 18 prison employees and 5 "stool pigeon" convicts were being held.[90] To confuse their besiegers, the ringleaders moved hostages from location to location in the dank cellblock.[91]

Meanwhile, the media unwittingly provided information to the rioters in radio news reports. This prompted Powell to restrict reporters to the sidelines. (Later, the warden apologized for any hard feelings, while stressing the need for silence.[92] "If the convicts had known of the planned entrance into the prison," he said, "it is believed they would have killed all hostages immediately.")

Aware of the potential for disaster, Adjutant General Mitchell and Col. Benson refined the plan to storm Cellblock One where the riot ringleaders were thought to be hiding. Col. Benson himself formerly served as acting prison warden prior to Powell's employment and, of course, he had first-hand knowledge of the prison layout.[93] The rioters were known to possess two .30 caliber rifles with nearly 20 rounds of ammunition,[94] bottles of Naphtha (a highly inflammable cleaning solution), and brooms wrapped with Naphtha-soaked rags, ready to be lit. Yelling into a loudspeaker, Myles threatened to burn the hostages with Naphtha or commit murder by other means should his demands be denied. Many hours had now elapsed since the riot began. "I hold all the aces," Myles heckled, "so you will play by my game."[95]

Myles' initial demands included a get-away car with a radio and full tank of gas, and a four-hour head start. Next, he called for a large group of reporters to enter the prison to hear his complaints. In exchange, he promised to release the remaining hostages. The warden agreed to the meeting but with the stipulation that the newsmen would report nothing about the conference until all the hostages were released.[96] Myles retorted by ordering hostage Jones to "go get the newsmen and photographers, and tell the warden that when I see a story or picture in a newspaper—any newspaper—the hostages go free."[97] Powell nevertheless prepared for a meeting inside a wire mesh cage located near the mess hall, some distance from the cells. Three reporters were chosen from a pool of newsmen for the subsequent interview.

Myles informed hostage John Simonsen that he would be the "white collar" spokesperson in future negotiations. As Simonsen later recalled, Myles "said when they got there I would know what to say. I imagine I was to be coached, but I don't know. It never got that far."[98]

Meanwhile, hostage Jones noted that some of the rioters were high on drugs stolen from the dispensary, and ringleader George Alton was incomprehensible when speaking.[99] From the best that Jones could determine, the rioters were demanding parole reform, resignation or firing of Parole Director Benjamin Wright, improved hospital facilities, and abolition of the "hole," an isolated disciplinary cell located in the basement of the 90-year-old prison. They also complained about crowded conditions and using buckets for toilets, and demanded that young, first-time offenders be segregated from the other inmates for their own safety.[100] Jones believed Myles genuinely wanted first-time offenders kept apart from others, but Myles himself had harassed and molested youngsters. Jones had been warning incoming 18 and 19 years old about Myles, which added to Myles' animosity.[101]

Late Friday afternoon, April 17, Myles released Jones, who came out with an "offer to compromise." Jones believed he was still needed inside, both as an advisor to the hostage group and as a mediator, but the warden refused to let him return. "I had to try and keep" the rioters "confidence," Jones explained, because "they were on dope and psychotic. I was afraid anything that would panic them could mean the death of all the hostages."[102] Powell thanked Jones for all he had done, but warned that "the more concessions we grant, the more they'll ask. There will never be a guarantee they will turn the hostages free. If you went back it would be just another life endangered."[103]

One "apparent concession" was the resignation of Parole Director Wright. He had officially, but not publicly, resigned a month earlier, and the warden hoped that when Myles heard this, he might free the hostages. But Myles still held out. Co-ringleader Alton, however, now felt that Myles wanted nothing but publicity and their escape attempt had failed. Alton refused to further participate in the revolt and locked himself in a cell.[104]

Nearby town residents and on-lookers could hear Myles' demands blaring over the loudspeaker, while people across the state followed events in news reports. Some contacted Governor Aronson's office giving their views. While a number were supportive of the governor's response, others were critical. One citizen, Emory M. Knapp, offered to assist. In an April 17 telegram, Knapp declared: "I have just read about the prison riot. I hereby volunteer my services and my Winchester. I am a taxpayer. If someone commits a crime and is sentenced to prison, it should be made so miserable for him that he wouldn't want to get it again. Why do you baby them?"[105]

Governor Aronson rejected the rioters' demands outright, informing the public in a press release, "I am standing firm on my original statement that I have no intention to go to Deer Lodge or talk to any of the rebellious convicts until order has been restored, all hostages released unharmed and the convicts back in their cells."[106]

Myles countered over the loudspeaker: "We're not fighting for today, but for the next guy who comes in here. The governor won't listen to us, he never will.

They give us everything on a string and then take everything away from us one at a time."[107]

In the meantime, the rioters worked on an escape tunnel, while Warden Powell suspected the inmates might be issuing demands as a delaying tactic to conceal an escape attempt.[108] They had dug an 8 to 9 foot tunnel through the corner of Cellblock One toward the prison's north side—the massive masonry wall was 4 feet wide and 20 feet high, with 6 feet of concrete underground. When the diggers' shovels hit concrete, they were forced to quit tunneling.[109] This escape effort failed.[110]

The second and final night of the siege now approached. An uninvolved prisoner got a message to Powell, informing him of Myles' decision to ignite the hostages with Naphtha by morning.[111] No longer willing to wait for a voluntary surrender, Powell turned to the guardsmen's plan, which was to separate the hostages from the rioting convicts by charging into Cellblock One under the cover of tear gas and gunfire. The assault was launched in the early hours of Saturday, April 18. At 3:45 a.m., Sgt. Maj. William L. Rose of Headquarters Battery, 154th Field Artillery Group, Missoula, fired the first of several bazooka rounds, hitting the tower of the cellblock.[112] One hostage later described the blast of the 3.5-inch rocket: "I knew something was up," he recalled, "an explosion sounded, showering glass over us. Then there was machine gun fire."[113]

Fifty guardsmen stormed the cell house, blasting off the lock on a large oak door with five shots from an M1 rifle. Floodlights came on as the teams rushed in, using tear gas to add to the rioters' confusion.[114] As the guardsmen pressed the assault,[115] two of the teams rescued hostages, while another team covered the main cellblock and another focused on the tower. A fire-fighting group followed after, in case the rioters made good on their promise to kindle the Naphtha.[116]

The inmates and hostages remaining in the cells worried about the Naphtha as well, hoisting mattresses up against the cell bars for protection. As the guardsmen raced in, they threw open the cell doors and ordered the prisoners to run for safety. Prison guards then led them out through the main cellblock and the women's quarters, and outside to the administration building.[117] Simultaneously, another team led by Capt. Raymond Dahlgren, Capt. Rueben L. Dwight, and Col. Benson arrived at the cell-house's far end. They found hostages, and radioed for a prison guard to open the doors to the last three cell units on the 6th gallery. All hostages—reports vary from 16 to 21 in number—survived, and only 29-year-old prison guard Robert Wyant was wounded.[118] The guardsmen proceeded past some 30 inmates, none of whom attempted to flee.

The assault on the main rioters also was successful. Rushing the tower, Lt. Col. Ed Ellsworth of Deer Lodge, Lt. Russell Pulliam of Missoula, and Highway Patrol Supervisor Alex B. Stephenson kicked open a tower door. Gunfire from one of the convicts wounded Pulliam, the bullet shattering on impact in his left arm and spitting fragments into his left hip.[119] Guardsmen tossed tear gas into the tower and called out for the rioters to surrender. Soon, four convicts gave up, but Myles and Smart failed to respond. After calling out to Myles but hearing no response, they fired several rounds into the tunnel area where they presumed Myles and Smart were hiding. Hearing nothing, the guardsmen moved into the tunnel, discovering two bloodied figures sprawled on the floor. Smart had shot Myles, then killed himself.[120] Two and one-quarter hours had passed since the first bazooka round was fired, and 38 hours since the riot began.

After the riot was quelled, 25 guardsmen remained at the prison to assist in restoring order and cleaning up.[121] Capt. Dwight, the guard's operations and facilities supervisor, acted as a temporary deputy warden, a position he once held at the 12th Naval District on Treasure Island, San Francisco.[122]

Lyle Gillette, later the mayor of Deer Lodge, recalled how the guardsmen helped restore order in the aftermath. "The task of inspecting each and every cell began. The National Guard was very much in evidence. The cells were stripped bare and inspected closely to assure that contraband was not present…Each inmate was stripped naked, and then given trousers, a shirt, blanket, honey-bucket…and mattress."[123]

During the Montana National Guard Association Convention later that year, Governor Aronson presented a commendation letter to the guard officers who participated in suppressing the riot. He also honored the enlisted men during summer camp. Warden Powell praised the governor for his decisive action: "Aronson did exactly as he should have in such a situation. He called out the National Guard immediately. As soon as I was released, he returned me to full command and put both the National Guard and the Highway Patrol at my full disposal."[124]

Notes

1. 1962 Decimal File #337, Folder "337 World-wide Army Info. Officer's Conference," Box 4244, RG 168, NA II, 20.
2. "Reserve Preparedness" 1957 Memorandum, National Guard Bureau Chief, Maj. Gen. Edgar C. Erickson, Decimal File 326 Gen 1957, RG 168, NA II, 3.
3. Ibid., 5.
4. Ibid., 1.
5. In 1960, there were 4 MNG graduates from Fort Knox's Armor School, 13 from Fort Olney's Ordnance School, and 4 from Fort Sill's Artillery and Missile School. Folder 352 Mont, Box 4087, RG 168, NA II.
6. *Biennial Report, 1960–1962.* In 1963, this number increased to 88 officers, 9 warrant officers, and 180 enlisted men; *Biennial Report, 1962–1964.*
7. Unpublished transcript, Col. Gerald Miller (Ret.), provided to author, February 20, 2000 [hereafter cited as Miller, unpublished transcript].
8. 1961 Decimal File 352 Gen to 357 Air Gen (Basic) Military Training Spaces, Folder 325 Gen Jan Thru Apr., Box 4082, RG 168, NA II.
9. *Biennial Report, 1960–1962.*

10. *Biennial Report, 1962–1964.*
11. Decimal File 326 Gen 1957, RG 168, NA II, 2.
12. Gerald Miller served in the Howitzer Battery, 1st Squadron, 163rd Armored Cavalry Regiment, in Harlowton. In 1955, Miller was an enlisted man on a cannon crew, then a supply sergeant until 1957. After commissioning in October 1957, he became a Reconnaissance and Survey Officer, Executive Officer (1962), and Battery Commander (1963–1967). Miller was promoted to captain in 1979, and retired a colonel in the U.S. Army Reserve. Miller, unpublished transcript.
13. *Montana Military Academy Yearbook, Class XI, 1968.* Not all of the enrollees were guardsmen; U.S. Army reservists also attended the academy. As years passed, more candidates took advantage of the academy to gain officer status:

Class	*Enrolled*	*Graduated*	*In ARNG*
1957	30	16	4
1958	24	20	3
1959	19	13	4
1960	21	14	6
1961	13	9	3
1962	24	18	4
1963	29	18	9
1964	38	19	12
1965	41	27	19
1966	24	20	19
1967	45	30	29
1968	45	30	29

14. *Biennial Report, 1960–1962.*
15. The Montana military class of 1966–1967 achieved high national honors in academics and was named the top academy among 51 OCS academies nationwide. Montana received the "Award for National Guard Academic Excellence in the National Guard State OCS Program." Students achieved an average score of 92.26. AG Richard Kendall (Montana's OCS commandant since its inception in 1957) and Arvild Christensen accepted the award at the 89th General Conference of the National Guard Association of the United States. Montana also won the Sixth U.S. Army Award that year.
16. *Biennial Report, 1960–1962.*
17. Miller, unpublished transcript.
18. "Screening of the Ready Reserve" Disposition Form, August 2, 1957, Folder 326 General, Box 3104, RG 168, NA II, 1–2.
19. 1962 Decimal File, #337, Folder "337 World-wide Army Info. Officer's Conference," Box 4244, RG 168, NA II, 20.
20. "Support by Employers for Time Off for Summer Training," Press Release, Governor John Hugo Aronson, Building T-15, Vertical File, Drawer 3, MMHM. By 1959, the Department of Defense Appropriation Act released $2.9 million toward the funding of Six-Month Active Duty Training. See also, Press Release, MNG, 2 April 1959, Building T-15, Vertical File, Drawer 3, MMHM.
21. Decimal File 326 Gen 1957, "McGowan Report," RG 168, NA II, 2. In 1958, the MNG finance officer, Lt. Peter Tyanich of the State Headquarters Detachment in Helena, stated that the payroll would total $241,000, resulting in overall pay-raises of $26,000. Nationally, payroll increases rose to more than a quarter million dollars. See also, Public Informa-

tion Office, Montana, Fort Harrison, Building T-15, Drawer 3, MNG Field Training, Press Release, June 12, 1958, MMHM.

22. *Biennial Report, 1962–1964.*
23. Miller, unpublished transcript.
24. *Biennial Report, 1964–1966.*
25. *Biennial Report, 1960–1962.*
26. Miller, unpublished transcript.
27. *Biennial Report, 1960–1962.*
28. Miller, unpublished transcript.
29. "1958 Firing Exhibitions at Summer Camp" News clipping, Drawer 3, Vertical Files, Building T-15, MMHM.
30. Miller, unpublished transcript.
31. "Colonel C.M. Snow Inspects Montana National Guard" News clipping, Drawer 3, Vertical Files, Building T-15, MMHM.
32. "3rd Battalion 163rd at Camp Irwin, CA," March 18, 1959, Press Release No. 19, Montana National Guard Public Information Office, Drawer 3, Vertical Files, Building T-15, MMHM.
33. News clipping, Drawer 3, Vertical Files, T-15 Building, MMHM.
34. Miller, unpublished transcript.
35. "MNG 1958 Field Training" Press Release, Montana National Guard Public Information Office [1958 Folder], Drawer 3, Vertical Files, Building T-15, MMHM.
36. News clipping, Drawer 3, Vertical Files, Building T-15, MMHM.
37. Press Release, Montana National Guard Public Information Office [1958 Folder], Drawer 3, Vertical Files, Building T-15, MMHM.
38. News clipping, Drawer 3, Vertical Files, Building T-15, MMHM.
39. "1958 Field Training," Press Release, Montana National Guard Public Information Office, Drawer 3, Vertical Files, Building T-15, MMHM.
40. Miller, unpublished transcript. Unexploded ordnance (UXO) imbedded on ranges in live-fire exercises in the 1940s and 1950s remains a concern to the MNG today. Investigations in the Fort Harrison area support the belief that numerous firing ranges contain UXO, and perhaps not all of the old training locations are known. Sites include the Guthrie Road/Diamond Springs area of the Helena Valley, Dempsey Creek near Deer Lodge, a site near Harlowton, the Limestone Hills training area, U.S. Forest Service land near Helmsville, and possible sites near Jefferson City and Armstead. UXO are projectiles that impacted on a target zone, but did not detonate. This can occur if a round is a dud, or is fired at extreme range or hits improperly, causing failure of the impact fuse to detonate the main explosive charge. These projectiles can remain largely undetected, and potentially could explode if disturbed. See information compiled by Dr. Clif Youmans, Environmental Building, Fort Harrison, Helena, Montana, "Unexploded Ordnance Fact Sheet," PRC Three-Ring Binder, Environmental Building, Fort Harrison, and "Draft Report: UXO Investigation, Project Diamond Springs Area, Helena," Environmental Building, Fort Harrison, January 1998.
41. Miller, unpublished transcript.
42. "1958 Firing Exhibition," News clipping, Drawer 3, Vertical Files, Building T-15, MMHM.
43. "Colonel C.M. Snow Inspects Montana National Guard," News clipping, Drawer 3, Vertical Files, Building T-15, MMHM.

44. "General Mitchell Inspects Units of 163rd Regiment" News clipping, Drawer 3, Vertical Files, Building T-15, MMHM.
45. The 210th included the Headquarters and Service Company from Livingston, A Company of Anaconda, B Company of Big Timber, and C Company of Butte. The 3rd Battalion consisted of the Headquarters Company and Tank Company of Billings, G Company of Lewistown, H Company of Miles City, I Company of Glendive, and the Howitzer Company of Billings. The 443rd Armored Field Artillery Battalion included Battery A of Deer Lodge, Battery B of Hamilton, Battery C of Thompson Falls, and a Medical Detachment, the Service Battery, and Headquarters Battery of Missoula. "General Mitchell Inspects Units of 163rd Regiment," News clipping, Drawer 3, Vertical Files, Building T-15, MMHM.
46. "1955 Malfunction of Ammo," July 14, 1959. Decimal File 1955: 471 Rhode Island to 82.2 Florida FY 1945, Folder 472 General, Box 1962, RG 168, NA II.
47. Ibid.
48. "Two National Guard Fliers Survive Crash of Their Plane West of Townsend," News clipping, Drawer 3, Vertical Files, T-15 Building, MMHM.
49. In 1959, MNG's Public Information Office informed the National Guard Bureau as to the number of units (44) and their and locations (26) in Montana:

Locations	*Units*
Great Falls (Air National Guard)	5
Helena	5
Kalispell	4
Billings	3
Bozeman	3
Missoula	3
Anaconda	2
Butte	1
Chinook	1
Culbertson	1
Deer Lodge	1
Dillon	1
Fairview	1
Glasgow	1
Glendive	1
Hamilton	1
Harlowton	1
Havre	1
Lewistown	1
Livingston	1
Malta	1
Plentywood	1
Polson	1
Shelby	1
Sidney	1
Whitefish	1

There also were 6 designated maintenance locations in the state. The Combined Support Maintenance Shop, Army Aviation Maintenance Shop, and Field Training Equipment

Concentration Site were situated in Helena. "Role of Reserve Components in National Defense," [National Guard Bureau Statement], Folder 350.001 Gen Jan Thru May, Box 4244, Records of the National Guard Bureau, RG 168, NA II, 5; "National Guard Community List," July 15 1959, Press Release, Montana National Guard Public Information Office, Drawer 3, Vertical Files, Building T-15, MMHM.

50. "An Armored Cavalry Squadron (about 900 personnel, equivalent to a battalion) had a Squadron Headquarters Troop, three Reconnaissance Troops (light tanks), one Tank Troop (heavy tanks), and one self-propelled Howitzer Battery (which required Artillery-qualified officers). A squadron also included a communications officer, chemical officer, medical officer, and a few other very specialized branches." Miller, unpublished transcript.
51. "Press Release #18," March 11, 1959, Montana National Guard Public Information Office, Drawer 3, Vertical Files, Building T-15, MMHM.
52. The unit designated to use the armory, Battery C, 1st Howitzer Battalion, 190th Artillery, was commanded by Capt. John M. Antonich and included 5 officers and 77 enlisted men. Medical Detachment, 1st Howitzer Battalion, under 1st Lt. Don B. Torgerson, also hoped to use the facilities. The detachment included Torgerson and 6 enlisted men. "Role of Reserve Components in National Defense," [National Guard Bureau Statement], Folder 350.001 Gen Jan Thru May, Box 4244, RG 168, NA II.
53. Ibid., 5.
54. Miller, unpublished transcript.
55. *Biennial Report, 1960–1962.*
56. Ibid.
57. *Biennial Report, 1964–1966.*
58. *Biennial Report, 1962–1964*; asterisks indicate armories designated as still needing work or size upgrading:

Havre*	Culbertson	Fairview*
Livingston*	Chinook	Malta
Glasgow	Plentywood	Sidney
Glendive	Miles City	Billings
Harlowton*	Lewistown	Bozeman
Butte	Whitefish	Anaconda
Ft. Missoula*	Dillon	Hamilton
Kalispell	Fort Harrison*	

59. *Biennial Report, 1962–1964.*
60. Ibid.
61. Ibid.
62. "Disaster Relief and Assistance," Book V, NGAUS Library, Washington, D.C.; "National Guardsmen Patrol Area Ravaged by Earthquake," *Daily Home News* (New Brunswick, New Jersey), August 21, 1959.
63. "New Blizzard Bears Down on Montana," *Washington Post*, November 15, 1959.
64. *Biennial Report, 1960–1962.*
65. *Biennial Report, 1964–1966.*
66. *Biennial Report, 1962–1964*, 48.
67. Ibid., 54.
68. *Biennial Report, 1964–1966*, 67. The Air Force Reserve aided in Operation Haylift.
69. Miller, unpublished transcript.
70. James R. McDonald, *History: Montana State Prison* (Deer Lodge, Montana: Powell County Museum Arts Foundation, 1979), 73.

71. Ibid.
72. Ibid.
73. Walter B. Jones (As told by Bruce Lee), "How We Broke the Montana Prison Riot," *Saturday Evening Post*, June 13, 1959.
74. "John K. Simonsen Had Right to Be Shook Up as He Walked into Knife, Rifle in Office of Slain Deputy Warden Ted Rothe," *Independent Record*, April 26, 1959, 2.
75. "Warden's Assistant Tells Inside Story of How He, Others Became Hostages," *Great Falls Tribune*, April 26, 1959, 15.
76. "Armed Convicts Riot in Montana, Kill Deputy and Hold 18 Hostages," *Washington Post*, April 17, 1959, Section C2.
77. "Rebel Convicts Free Two Men, Threaten to Make Human Torches of 21 Hostages," *Great Falls Tribune*, April 18, 1959, 1.
78. McDonald, *History: Montana State Prison*, 74. Located inside Tower 7 (the prison's main entrance), a tunnel system led to cat walks where prison guards observed the inmates in the mess hall, kitchen, and bakery. Unpublished transcript, Mayor Lyle Gillette, Deer Lodge, provided to author, February 10, 2000.
79. Montana National Guard Press Release, n.d., Building T-15, Vertical File, Drawer 3, MMHM.
80. "Task Force Ends Riot at Prison; Hostages Freed; Warden Charges Escape Attempt," *Washington Post*, April 1959, Section A-3.
81. "Deer Lodge," *Great Falls Tribune*, April 17, 1959.
82. Montana National Guard Press Release, n.d., Building T-15, Vertical Files, Drawer 3, MMHM.
83. Col. Mayhew Y. Foster, 154th Field Artillery Group, Missoula, acted as commander of the troops designated for storming the prison. Assistant commanders included Lt. Col. C. Ellsworth of the 443rd Armored Field Artillery Battalion, Deer Lodge; Lt. Col. Richard C. Kendall, 154th Field Artillery Group, Deer Lodge; and Major Hugh P. McElwain, 154th Field Artillery Group, Missoula.
84. "Troops Storm In, Free Hostages, 2 Convict Leaders Found Slain," *New York Herald Tribune*, April 19, 1959.
85. "Breaking a Rebellion, Men Armed to Teeth Plotted Attack Well," *Evening Star*, April 18, 1959.
86. "Rebel Convicts Free Two Men…," 1.
87. Memo from Warden Powell to Aronson, April 25, 1959. Governor Hugo J. Aronson Papers, MC 35, Box 155, Folder 3, MHS.
88. Jones, "How We Broke…," 72.
89. Ibid., 80
90. McDonald, *History: Montana State Prison*, 77.
91. "John K. Simonsen Had Right to be Shook Up…," 2.
92. "Newsman Describes Long, Tense Vigil at Montana Prison," *Great Falls Tribune*, April 20, 1959, 8.
93. Receiving commendations for subsequent action were Capt. Reuben L. Dwight, State Headquarters and Headquarter Detachment, Helena: 1st Lt. Wallace E. Small and capts. Raymond D. Dahlgren and Hugh G. Kidder, 154th Field Artillery Group, Missoula; capts. Horace W. Gregory Jr. and William T. Riggert, 443rd Armed Field Artillery Battalion, Missoula; capts. Earl E. Hansen and Marvin W. Trask, 443rd Field Artillery Battalion, Deer Lodge; 1st Lt. Francis R. Pulliam and 2nd Lt. Burton K. Walsh, 443rd Armed Field Artillery Battalion, Missoula; and 1st Lt. Melvin M. Ryan and 2nd Lt. Billy Flint,

Service Battery, 443rd Armed Field Artillery Battalion, Missoula. 1st Lt. James A. Girard, Deer Lodge, and 2nd Lt. Bruce L.T. Watkins, Missoula, led teams from Battery A, 443rd Armed Field Artillery Battalion. Warrant Officer Donald R. Onslow, 443rd Armed Field Artillery Battalion, Missoula, led the medical detachment, and Capt. Gerald B. Effing of the same unit established the communications set up. Other guard members later receiving commendation letters from the governor, but not team leaders or holding leadership roles, included warrant officers Otto C. Specht and Robert W. Seaman, Service Battery, 443rd Armored Field Artillery Battalion, Missoula. MNG commendation letters from Governor Hugo J. Aronson, MC35, Folder 3, Box 155, MSHS.

94. "Breaking a Rebellion..."
95. McDonald, *History: The Montana State Prison*, 74.
96. Jones, "How We Broke…," 80.
97. Ibid.
98. "John K. Simonsen Had Right to be Shook Up…," 2.
99. "I Knew I Would Never Get Out Alive, but I Thought I Might Save the Others," *Great Falls Tribune*, April 19, 1959, 15.
100. "Macabre Murder-Suicide of Ringleaders Marks Smashing of State Prison Revolt when National Guardsmen Storm Walls," *Great Falls Tribune*, April 19, 1959.
101. "I Knew I Would Never…," 15.
102. Ibid.
103. Jones, "How We Broke…," 80.
104. "Rebel Convicts Free Two Men…," 1.
105. Governor Aronson Papers, MC35, Folder 3, Box 155, MHS.
106. McDonald, *History: The Montana State Prison*, 75.
107. "Convict Spokesman Shouts Answers over Loudspeaker," *Great Falls Tribune*, April 18, 1959.
108. "Warden Starts Crackdown On Prisoners Who Rioted." *New York Herald Tribune*, April 20, 1959.
109. "Tense Situation Continues at Montana Prison," *Great Falls Tribune*, April 20, 1959.
110. "Macabre Murder-Suicide…"
111. Jones, "How We Broke…," 80.
112. Governor Aronson Papers, MC35, Folder 3, Box 155, MHS.
113. McDonald, *History: The Montana State Prison*, 75.
114. "Disaster Relief and Assistance" Book V, NGAUS Library.
115. McDonald, *History: The Montana State Prison*, 75.
116. "Disaster Relief and Assistance" Book V, NGAUS Library.
117. "Breaking a Rebellion…"
118. "Macabre Murder-Suicide…"
119. "Prison Riot Wins Citations," *Great Falls Tribune*, April 25, 1959.
120. "Breaking a Rebellion…"
121. "Guardsmen Save all 21 Hostages and End Jail Riot," *New York Times*, April 19, 1959.
122. "Troublemakers at Prison Isolated in 'Strip' Cells," *Great Falls Tribune*, April 18, 1959.
123. Unpublished transcript, Mayor Lyle Gillette, Deer Lodge, provided to author, February 10, 2000.
124. "Macabre Murder-Suicide…"

16

The Vietnam Era, 1965–1975

Dwayne A. Mack

The number of units awarded superior ratings was higher than usual and the preponderance of "Excellents" is indicative of their ability to perform tactically under any conditions.—Richard C. Kendall, Montana Adjutant General, 1966.

Originally a part of French Indochina since 1867, Vietnam had a long history of civil and ideological strife. In 1940, after Hitler's armies defeated France on the European mainland, Japan in 1940–1941 diplomatically wrested much of Southeast Asia from the Vichy French colonial government. During most of World War II, the Japanese remained in control, though allowing French Vichy officials to administer the government until the last months of the conflict. Meanwhile, Viet Minh rebels led by the fervent nationalist Ho Chi Minh (with some Allied assistance) effectively resisted the Japanese occupation, and declared Vietnam's independence after the Axis defeat.

Beginning in 1946, however, France attempted to militarily reassert hegemony over its former Southeast Asia possession. A bitter, prolonged struggle finally ended in a decisive Viet Minh victory at the Battle of Dien Bien Phu in 1954. In that year, the Geneva Accords ended French rule by partitioning Vietnam into two political and ideological zones—communist North Vietnam, and anti-communist South Vietnam. The Geneva agreement called for nationwide elections to unify the two halves, but the south refused to participate in the plebiscite, fearing the north would gain overall dominance.

Consequently, the north's intention of unifying the divided country, juxtaposed to the south's intention to remain independent, eventually resulted in guerilla warfare in South Vietnam. By the early 1960s, the United States increasingly attempted to prop up the south by sending military advisers, technicians, and equipment to assist South Vietnam's armed forces. However, the communist rebels in the south—i.e., the Viet Cong, allied with infiltrators from North Vietnam—soon were inflicting defeats on South Vietnamese troops in rural localities.

As the American role grew, a decision was reached in the spring of 1965 to send American combat units to defend South Vietnam against the threat of the North's takeover. Beginning on March 8, 1965, and in following months, approximately 44 U.S. combat battalions, and eventually Australian, South Korean, and a few other Southeast Asia Treaty Organization troops, were deployed to South Vietnam, though the effort remained vastly an American one. The Vietnam War ensued, with South Vietnam defended by increasing numbers of American troops, and the Viet Cong assisted by large influxes of North Vietnamese Army units.

By 1968–1969, more than 500,000 American servicemen were deployed in Vietnam in a conflict that was both a civil war between the north and south, and a proxy ideological conflict, juxtaposing the Soviet Union and the Communist bloc against the United States and the Free World. The hard fought struggle, essentially becoming a stalemate, continued for eight years, until a cease fire arrangement was finally reached and the last American troops were withdrawn by early 1973.[1]

More than 58,000 Americans lost their lives, while casualties were much higher for the communist side, which was willing to sacrifice an entire generation of North Vietnam's young men to achieve their aims.[2] Hundreds of thousands of civilians also were casualties in the struggle's complex mosaic of political reprisals, shifting ethnic alliances, and combat collateral damage.

Two years later, in the spring of 1975, communist forces launched a final major offensive against the South Vietnamese Army and took complete control of the south, unifying the country as the Socialist Republic of Vietnam.

President Lyndon Johnson's determination to send American combat units to Vietnam in 1965 had been a painful and fateful decision, and done with an awareness of the risks involved, particularly if China and the U.S.S.R. were directly drawn into the war. At a press conference on July 28, 1965, Johnson explained the U.S. commitment: "We had determined not to let that country fall under Communist rule as long as we could prevent it and as long as the [South] Vietnamese continued fighting for themselves. At the same time I am committed to keeping this a limited war, to prevent it from expanding to a nuclear conflict."[3] He regretted his call to deploy young Americans into a foreign country: "I do not find it easy to send the flower of our youth, our finest young men, into battle."[4]

In 1965, guardsmen across the country were well aware that they might be ordered to active duty. The White House and the Pentagon, however, decided not to call up National Guard units for several reasons. Currently, the active duty armed forces, including nearly a million U.S. Army personnel, were sufficiently strong for deployment to the combat zone. Furthermore, it was believed that increased Selective Service quotas, in addition to normal enlistment, would sustain regular Army's ranks.

Johnson also was reluctant to utilize the National Guard since a large mobilization might alarm American citizens and send an overtly aggressive message to North Vietnam and its Communist bloc allies. At the time, there yet were hopes for a negotiated settlement in Vietnam. Also, many U.S. political and military leaders believed the conflict would end quickly with direct American intervention. Few could foresee that the war would continue years into the future. Furthermore, a significant number of elected officials in Congress—many of them World War II and Korean War veterans—currently were members of the National Guard or U.S. Army Reserve. It would have been problematical if these representatives were called to active duty. And, of course, the National Guard was needed for normal domestic emergencies.[5]

The Soviet and communist Chinese threat also remained, requiring the U.S. to retain a large deployable reserve force should a second conflict erupt in Europe or the Korean Peninsula. In 1965, the Army National Guard and the U.S. Army Reserve had an action-ready force of 695,000, "organized into twenty-three divisions, eleven separate brigades, and some 8,000 units." The active U.S. Army had approximately 970,000 soldiers, with 42 percent serving overseas.[6]

In August 1965, in order to meet any potential contingencies, elements of eight Army National Guard divisions and backup units from the Army Reserve were formed into a nationwide Selected Reserve Force. This quick-response organization comprised 119,000 guardsmen and 31,000 reservists, consisting of three divisions and six separate brigades with combat and service support units. These units conducted added training and were required to maintain 100 percent strength at all times.

In the fall of 1965, Montana's adjutant general, Maj. Gen. Richard C. Kendall, announced that despite America's involvement in Southeast Asia, the nation's military leaders did "not anticipate" a reserve quota increase. He stressed, however, that the guard's primary objective was to maintain "the highest level of mobilization readiness."[7] It also was reported that Pentagon officials at the 87th General Conference of the National Guard Association, which met in Miami, Florida, informed some 3,000 guard officers, active service personnel, and other invited guests that "Vietnam was under control and looked favorable at this time."[8]

Despite the positive outlook, American war casualties increased in the following year. Across the nation, some in government and the populace now began feeling anxiety about progress in Southeast Asia. In Montana, General Kendall conveyed confidence that his units would accept any foreign and domestic challenges if called upon, but also noted that there was "no indication of a National Guard or Army Reserve call-up" in the immediate future. He reported that if the need came for "a partial mobilization," the Selected Reserve Force would respond first. Kendall again urged readiness of "the highest possible level," and asked every member of the Montana guard to "accept this task."[9]

Montana officials remained fully aware that "contingencies might arise in SE Asia or elsewhere that would require calling up some or all of the reserve components."[10] By now, however, the White House felt that mobilization of the reserves would only heighten the slowly growing opposition to the war among some elements in the American population. The Johnson administration's policy meant that large Selective Service "draft call-ups" would continue in order "to fill the expanding need for troops" in South Vietnam. (This policy would hold for the first three years of the war.) Meanwhile, in public the president somewhat downplayed the seriousness of the Vietnam conflict, hoping the situation would take a turn for the better and thus not adversely affect his administration's War on Poverty program.[11]

The Montana guard continued to maintain a high level of readiness. In March 1965, for example, the 3rd Reconnaissance Squadron, 163rd Armored Calvary, from Billings, Miles City, Lewiston, and Harlowton, was airlifted to Fort Irwin, California, for annual field training. Known as Guard Lift, the operation helped improve the rapid deployment capabilities of air crews and ground forces.[12]

Meanwhile, enlistment had increased in the National Guard and Army Reserve to full Pentagon-mandated capacity as young men faced the alternatives of either joining the guard or reserves, enlisting in the regular armed forces, being drafted, or, in a few cases, applying for conscientious objector status. For most, this decision was an obligation not taken lightly or without serious reflection regarding duty and patriotism. By joining the National Guard for six years, many enlisted men were able to finish college or other job training, continue their careers, or support their families at home, but all were fully aware that a call up to active duty might come someday.

As it became apparent that most National Guard and Army Reserve units probably would not be activated for Vietnam, accusations of the reserve services being a place for draft dodgers began circulating. Generally overlooked was the fact that a number of guard officers and senior NCOs were veterans of World War II, the Korean conflict, or inter-war active duty service. Also, some guardsmen volunteered for active duty during the Vietnam years.

On September 23, 1966, about 50 Montana army and air guard officials attended a commanders' conference in Helena. The main speaker, Major James Elliot, the National Guard Bureau's chief public affairs officer in Washington, D.C., disputed the draft-dodging appellation. Noting that serving in the guard was not a way to avoid a military obligation, Elliot pointed out: "The law of the land gives a man the right to join the Guard, so there was nothing dishonorable about joining it." Elliot further noted: "A Guardsman, when joining a unit, signs an oath to his state and country for six years, which is longer than an enlistment in the active service or longer than a man must serve under Selective Service Laws."[13]

Adjutant General Kendall also became concerned over the debate about the reservists' commitment to service as well as congressional studies and investigations regarding more equity in the Selective Service system. The general criticized some members of Congress for questioning the guardsmen's capabilities and their dedication to the national interest. "War itself [is] not fair," Kendall pointed out. He elaborated by observing if it was "equitable to send one soldier to a front line rifle company where he is exposed to enemy fire and send ten to rear echelon duty where they may never hear a shot fired in anger?"[14] The general further noted that in the guard "there is an element of fairness that does not exist" elsewhere regarding military obligation. "When a Guardsman enlists, he does so with the full knowledge that when his unit is mobilized, everyone goes. We do not defer the student or the father. That he is obligated for mobilization and immediate deployment to a combat zone is a fact that he recognizes and willingly accepts."[15]

In the midst of this controversy, the Montana guard remained focused on preparing for a potential activation, as well as providing community service on the home front. In 1966, the guard participated in national campaigns to fund research, treatment, and cures for arthritis, birth defects, and polio. An article in the May issue of the *Montana Guardsman* reminded readers, "the weapons are… microscopes and test tubes; soldiers are replaced by research chemists fighting day and night to conquer the crippling effects of heartbreaking disease." In a March of Dimes campaign, the 120th Fighter Group worked six toll stations in Great Falls for eight hours, collecting $2,315.80 for that annual campaign.[16] In Havre, Troop E, 2nd Squadron, 163rd Armored Cavalry solicited $403, while Troop G, 2nd Squadron, in Livingston raised $203.[17]

In the summer of 1966, army and air guardsmen donated more than 1,340 pints of blood during a nationwide Blood for Defense Program. As 1st Sgt. Jerry Hansen later recalled, "the blood drive was a big deal."[18] The Montana guard's effort was the largest conducted by any group in the state. Fifty-two percent of the men attending the annual field exercises were donors. The blood was earmarked for use as transfusions for injured American troops in Vietnam and as derivatives to produce vital vaccines.[19]

In 1966, the adjutant general reported to Montana Governor Tim Babcock, outlining the guard's achievements in the 1965–1966 period. Kendall cited the successful completion of two annual field training exercises, and the Sixth Army's annual inspections, noting that "the number of units awarded superior ratings was higher than usual and the preponderance of 'Excellents' is indicative of their ability to perform tactically under any conditions." The Montana guard's overall strength level was slightly above 100 percent, and its equipment was rated as adequate in a time when practically all new military equipment was being earmarked for Vietnam. The Sixth Army Inspector General also gave the guard's leadership a "superior rating."[20]

In the summer of 1966, the state experienced another severe forest fire season. Approximately 74 guardsmen assisted the Forest Service, Bureau of Land Management, and the Montana state forestry department by transporting firefighters to hot spots and providing mobile radios, meals, and water. Eleven guardsmen participated in fighting blazes in Sweet Grass County in south central Montana.[21] In the Custer National Forest of southeast Montana, more than 1,000 firefighters fought grass, brush, and timber fires engulfing more than 15,000 acres, about 30 miles south of Ashland. The guard's main duties included providing firefighters with hot meals. During the firefighters' short lunch breaks at the fire lines, guardsmen also issued C-rations and hundreds of cartons of cigarettes to the hardworking men. In this region with few natural water sources, the guard provided portable water trailers at the camps and near the burn areas.[22]

More firefighting duties arose in the following year. In August 1967, hundreds of guardsmen and their mobile field equipment, frequently from the ordnance units as usual, were assigned to eastern Idaho and across much of Montana. In nearby parts of Idaho, the guard backed up firefighters in suppressing the Trapper Peak and Sundance blazes. In Montana, assistance was provided in Glacier National Park, the Monture Creek inferno a few miles from Ovando, the Landers Fork blaze not far from Lincoln, and the Olney fire, north of Whitefish. Some 300 firefighters participated in the Monture blaze alone. At Olney, fast-spreading flames threatened the community, prompting the call up of an additional 25 guardsmen from the 143rd, 3669th, and the aviation companies to help bring the blazes under control.[23]

That summer, altogether some 4,500 firefighters were boarded at various times in Montana National Guard facilities at Fort Missoula, where transportation and medical aid also were provided. Through mid-October 1967, guard personnel and their equipment continued to assist firefighters in Glacier National Park. Overall, 361 guardsmen participated in the fire campaigns of that season.[24]

By 1967, a civil disobedience crisis had arisen across much of the nation regarding festering social and racial issues, and the growing anti-war and anti-draft movements. Young whites and Blacks, particularly college-aged students, focused their protests mainly on campuses and in major urban settings. However, violent, large-scale riots also occurred in the underprivileged, segregated sections of Detroit and Newark that year, forcing National Guard officials across the country to revise and improve methods of managing demonstrations and suppressing riots. That summer, Montana units trained in new methods of crowd control.[25] By the spring of 1968, Army officials informed Congress that the U.S. Army and the National Guard were prepared for any contingencies that might occur that summer. Secretary of the Army Stanley R. Resor and Army Chief of Staff Harold K. Johnson, a former guardsman, agreed that the National Guard, in cooperation with state and local law enforcement, could manage protests.[26]

Following the assassination of Dr. Martin Luther King Jr. in April 1968, more than 130 outbreaks of urban demonstrations, often violent, occurred in 19 states. To assist local authorities in maintaining law and order, governors and the federal government called out more than 130,000 guardsmen and regular Army soldiers.

Following the subsiding of the social upheaval, President Johnson applauded the National Guard, which provided the bulk of the troops, proclaiming it "fulfilled with distinction an assignment that was regrettable, but unavoidable."[27]

The nationwide disturbances alarmed many Montanans, and Adjutant General Kendall responded to citizens who had concerns over the guard's readiness. He stressed that there was little chance of violent protests occurring in a rural state of predominantly small towns and communities. Nevertheless, Kendall acknowledged that guardsmen were "training to improve their ability to respond to a mission of military assistance to civil authority."[28] In early autumn, Kendall again repeated this goal.[29]

Two fateful and ominous events in early 1968—North Korea's seizure of the intelligence spy ship, the USS *Pueblo*, and the enemy's Tet Offensive in Vietnam—had caused the United States to reconsider mobilizing National Guard and Reserve units. Pentagon officials announced the first call-up on January 25, 1968, just a few days after the *Pueblo*'s capture in North Korean waters. Amid suggestions that the South Korean government feared a potential communist invasion from the north, and consequently might need to withdraw its combat forces from South Vietnam, President Johnson activated approximately 14,000 Air Force and Navy reservists.[30]

Then, on January 31, nearly 70,000 North Vietnamese soldiers and Viet Cong guerillas launched a series of concerted assaults all across South Vietnam during Tet—the Vietnamese New Year holidays. Only after weeks of intense and sometimes desperate combat were U.S. and South Vietnamese forces able to regain control of the situation. Though the north's massive Tet Offensive eventually was thwarted and "viewed as a military failure," the "psychological success for the enemy [was] a major turning point in the Vietnam War."[31] The attacks disproved, or at least brought into question, the Johnson administration's claims that America was making substantial progress in winning the war. At this point, many Americans began believing that the conflict was a stalemate and could not be resolved militarily. Deep anti-war and pro-war factionalism now permeated the U.S. population.

The president's popularity accordingly declined. In the spring of 1968, this influenced Johnson to withdraw from the presidential race and to modify his strategy in Vietnam.[32] On May 13, Johnson ordered 34 Army National Guard units to active duty; 8 of them eventually served in South Vietnam. In all, 12,234 guardsmen from 17 states were called up, with 7,000 of them eventually sent to Vietnam.[33] The Montana guard was not included in the call-up;[34] rather, units in more populous states generally were among those mobilized—often heavy equipment, construction, and trucking units. Overall during the war, the Pentagon would activate 23,000 guardsmen, of which approximately 8,700 served in Vietnam.

Meanwhile in Montana, the guard remained focused on training and support, as well as renovating the state's military infrastructure. Many of the buildings at Fort William Henry Harrison were constructed during World War II as temporary training facilities and had been expected to be serviceable for only about five years. By the 1960s, many structures had deteriorated to the point where they were inadequate or even unusable. In a joint effort, the State of Montana, the Department of Defense, and the National Guard Bureau adopted a long-range plan to renovate the fort.[35] Completed in the 1966–1968 biennium with the aid of $400,000 in federal funds, the rebuilt facilities included eleven 40-man barracks, seven 200-man mess halls, five 200-man wash rooms, four headquarters buildings, and three administrative/supply buildings.

However, with the prosecution of the Vietnam War absorbing a bulk of the nation's military funding, the federal government cut off money for continuance of this refurbishing plan. In fact, inadequacies in guard facilities, equipment, and weaponry were common nationwide. Due to the demands of prosecuting the war in Southeast Asia, guard units in the mid 1960s often retained 1950s or even some World War II era weapons and equipment. As one study observed, "reservists often had to train with outmoded equipment and then read books or watch movies to learn how to use the modern equivalents."[36]

In January 1969, the political landscape changed when President Richard M. Nixon took office and Forrest H. Anderson became governor of Montana. The new governor appointed Lt. Col. John Womack as adjutant general, replacing retiring Maj. Gen. Richard C. Kendall, who had served in the military since 1942. The new adjutant general, John Womack, was a former school teacher, had served as commander of the 163rd's 2nd Reconnaissance Squadron, and, like Kendall, had a long army record dating back to 1942.[37]

As criticism of the Vietnam conflict intensified in America, Womack, along with several other adjutants general across the nation, voiced their support of the war. He criticized civil disobedience and anti-war demonstrations, arguing that the protestors were "creating a feeling of comfort in Hanoi and are leaving the enemy with the impression that these vocal and active groups represent the majority opinion within the United States."[38]

Reflecting a changing policy regarding the Vietnam War, however, President Nixon on April 20, 1970, announced a reduction of 150,000 American troops in South Vietnam. Despite this decision, ten days later Nixon ordered 20,000 American and South Vietnamese soldiers, backed by American aircraft, to attack two major North Vietnamese bases in Cambodia. The attack, which had decidedly mixed results, appeared in some measure to be a broadening and escalation of the conflict, despite the fact that the U.S. had already been surreptitiously bombing North Vietnamese supply lines and bases in the jungles of Cambodia and Laos.[39]

On many college campuses across the country, reports of the Cambodia incursion pushed protests to a higher pitch. In May 1970, tragedy occurred at Kent State University in Ohio after anti-war demonstrators stormed the Reserve

Officers Training Corps building on campus. In response, Ohio Governor James Rhodes ordered Ohio guardsmen onto the campus. On May 4, in heated circumstances fraught with confusion and emotion, some of the Ohio guardsmen fired on demonstrators, killing four and injuring others.[40] This event enflamed campus protests to the highest level of the Vietnam era.

In Montana a few days later, an anonymous letter written by a University of Montana student typified the intense feelings and extreme idealism of many college-aged demonstrators. Probably a male student, who was writing to his parents, he objected to the United States spending taxpayers' money "on wars and killing while six thousand people die every day of the year of hunger." The writer also insisted, however, that "many of us are grateful to you for not only the money you are spending on our education, but for the moral values you taught us...honesty, love of neighbor, service to mankind." He continued by saying it was "unfair to ask our young men to serve in a war, which they do not believe in, and it seems so unfair to not permit alternate service to mankind and country in the Peace Corps or Vista programs. Honesty or integrity seems to count [for] nothing to many local draft boards when conscientious objector requests are made of them."[41]

Other Americans echoed similar disillusion with the Vietnam War. The *New York Times*, for example, printed a letter from a deeply concerned American serviceman stationed in South Vietnam. The soldier insisted that the Kent State "killings have added to the tragic consequence of the Vietnam War. The frustration that prompted guard officers to order the shootings can almost be understood in the Macabre context of the deep rifts the war has driven [into] our society—yet in no way diminishes the tragedy of Kent State. The killings of unarmed students violate both simple humanity and National Guard riot procedures."[42]

On the other hand, others in America, including a number in the Montana guard, approved of continuing the war. Sgt. William Bruner later recalled that he supported the U.S. effort in Southeast Asia, but he also sympathized with civilian criticism of its conduct. At the beginning of the Asian conflict, he had witnessed strong citizen advocacy, but as the war escalated and became prolonged with uncertainty, American support waned. As dissatisfaction grew, some Americans even occasionally displayed open disrespect toward uniformed servicemen—including guardsmen.[43]

With this backdrop on the national scene, the Montana guard continued to perform emergency domestic tasks and to dutifully train, with both the army and air units conducting annual training outside of the state. Between May 29 and June 14, 1970, the 163rd's 1st and 2nd squadrons, the 46th Army Band, the 103rd Public Affairs Detachment, and the State Headquarters and Headquarters Detachment trained at Gowen Field near Boise, Idaho. Gowen's 30 square miles of desert offered the armored cavalry virtually unlimited training space.[44]

In 1971, General William Westmoreland, the former commander of American forces in Vietnam, and now Army Chief of Staff, lauded the contributions of the National Guard. Westmoreland stressed the guard's dedication to community service and domestic projects, which were significant but "not widely known." He pointed out that a guard engineering unit had built playgrounds on an Indian reservation in California, and how a guard surgical field hospital was set up in a Puerto Rico community to provide medical services to locals, only requiring that supplies be furnished by local government. Westmoreland declared that "such programs pay rich dividends. All contribute in developing trust and mutual respect so necessary between the American people and their Armed Forces."[45]

Change came with the times. On January 8, 1973, Thomas L. Judge replaced Forrest Anderson in the Montana governor's mansion. And, later that month, the United States, South Vietnam, North Vietnam, and the Provisional Revolutionary Government of the National Liberation Front (Viet Cong) finally signed a cease-fire arrangement in Paris, France, after many months of negotiations. Known as the Paris peace agreements, the treaty concluded the final withdrawal of U.S. forces, which occurred a few months later.[46]

In August 1973, Montana experienced another severe fire season. In response, Governor Judge authorized approximately 500 guardsmen to assist the Montana Division of Forestry, the Forest Service, the Bureau of Land Management, and the National Park Service.[47] Typically, guard detachments patrolled forest service roads and maintained checkpoints, operated field mess kitchens, and drove supply trucks. Closer to the fire lines, guard helicopters delivered personnel, gas, water, food, chain saws, hard hats, axes, shovels, and other supplies and equipment. The large numbers of blazes and their intensity also required guardsmen to work fire lines with other fire fighters, quelling hot spots.[48]

On August 20, Capt. James Womack commanded a 25-man detachment of guardsmen and volunteers in attacking a 900-acre fire in the Pleasant Valley area near Thompson Falls. When the guard personnel arrived to fight the sporadic fires, they received hard hats, yellow-colored safety clothing, and tools, and were given fire fighting assignments. The men were transported to the scene by helicopter. An airlift and drop strategy enabled them to control the fires faster and more efficiently than if crews had approached on the ground. They successfully contained the blaze within 36 hours. In other parts of Pleasant Valley, Lt. Jack Walsh and his men patrolled forest roads in radio-equipped jeeps and maintained checkpoints to keep onlookers out of hazardous areas. Guardsmen also operated the base camp where hard working fire crews received hot meals and could rest.[49]

Guardsmen likewise helped extinguished grass and timber fires in the Goat Creek area and other localities as well.[50] Pat Mullaney of the U.S. Forest Service later recalled the support his staff and crews received from guardsmen near Thompson Falls, citing the fact that guard vehicles could "maneuver through treacherous mountain roads" as a major contributing factor in suppressing blazes.[51]

During the 1973 forest fire season, Montana guard firefighting mishaps were minimal. The only serious accident occurred on August 22, when a 12-passenger Huey helicopter carrying firefighters crashed in a landing attempt near the Goat Creek fire, 16 miles north of the Condon River Station. The pilot, Major David Nathe of Columbia Falls and a firefighter from California were injured and hospitalized. The crash sparked another fire near the 450-acre Goat Creek blaze, but Montana guard helicopters dropped 4,200 gallons of chemical retardant, extinguishing the flames.[52] Altogether that summer in Montana, some 2,008 fires burned a total of 114,900 acres of forest and grasslands, costing the state $15,200,000. The toll would have been significantly higher if the Montana National Guard had not gone into action.[53]

In 1974, the Montana guard, always adaptable, took on unique duties during a state workers dispute. By mid-March 1974, employees at the Galen State Hospital and the Boulder River School and Hospital went on strike in an effort to force the state legislature to authorize higher wages and improve working conditions.[54] In response, Governor Judge activated several hundred guardsmen from Helena, Kalispell, Whitefish, Missoula, Hamilton, Dillon, Great Falls, and Bozeman to replace the striking workers. The governor had little precedent in making this decision because National Guard troops rarely had been used to replace public employees.[55]

Another strike occurred when about 600 union workers at the Warm Springs State Mental Hospital walked out, including a number of nurses. Non-union workers also refused to cross picket lines, leaving more than 1,000 patients in the care of administrators and a dozen physicians. Governor Judge responded immediately by calling up another 430 guardsmen.[56]

In this period, Montana guardsmen dutifully served in every department of the three institutions. The tasks included cooking, serving meals, feeding and bathing patients, dispensing medications, assisting patients to restrooms, washing linen and clothing, mopping floors, performing ordinary maintenance, and fulfilling numerous other tasks necessary to provide for the welfare of infirm, elderly, and mentally ill patients. Daily operational costs during the emergency were a burden on the state,[57] but hospital officials praised the guardsmen's efforts. As early as about March 13, a Warm Springs physician claimed: "If we had not had the National Guard, we would have had dead people."[58]

General Womack later recalled that the guard did not relish the role of strikebreaker, but "someone had to take care of the patients." The men also helped to update and renovate some of the facilities. Womack particularly praised the guardsmen's technical ability and ingenuity at the Warms Springs Hospital, where, for example, the 3669th's engineering skills enhanced the bathing facilities for the patients. "The boys in the 3669th rigged up a shower" increasing bathing capacity by 2½ times.[59]

Duty at the hospitals often left the soldiers emotionally affected. Lt. Col. Bill Willing, who served at the Boulder River School, a facility for developmentally disabled children, recalled that guardsmen had to feed, bathe, and even change some patients' diapers. Attending to the helpless youngsters, Willing observed, "brought tears to some Guardsmen's eyes." Regardless of "rank, from pilots to infantrymen," some men became so attached to particular children that they maintained contact with them for years afterward.[60] Governor Judge acknowledged the guardsmen's feeling and commitment in caring for the patients and the students by observing that "it is obvious to us all that you are skilled, highly trained, efficient and reliable men. What I find especially outstanding is the kind of concern and compassion you exhibit for our fellow Montanans."[61]

Before the end of March, workers at Boulder and Galen accepted a labor package and agreed to return to work. Shortly, strikers at Warms Spring followed suit, ending their walkout. Overall, 826 Montana army guardsmen and 16 air guard personnel had replaced some 1,100 state employees and cared for 1,700 patients at the three facilities.[62]

In December 1974, the 3669th Heavy Equipment Maintenance Company, having served at the Boulder River School during the strike and witnessing the institution and staff's needs first hand, decided to undertake improvements as one of its community action projects. The 3669th repaired a safety fence adjacent to the Boulder River, and refurbished televisions, tape recorders, electric motors, vehicle engines, and other equipment needing maintenance. The unit also sponsored a toy and clothing drive to bring Christmas joy to the young patients.[63]

In early spring 1975, a fierce three-day blizzard in northern Montana stranded cattle and sheep among high snowdrifts, preventing ranchers from feeding livestock. On April 9, Governor Judge mobilized approximately 60 guardsmen for state emergency duty in "Operation Haylift" to feed U.S. Department of Agriculture-protected livestock. Over a two-day span, the guard delivered an estimated 36 tons of hay and 43,000 pounds of grain to more than 10,000 cattle and 1,000 sheep in Glacier, Toole, and Liberty counties east of Glacier National Park.[64]

Col. A.J. Christensen, Montana's military support officer, and Maj. C. Ron Adams supervised the effort. They directed units from Troop N (Air), Headquarters and Headquarters Troop, 2nd Squadron of the 163rd Air Calvary Regiment, and State Headquarters and Headquarters Command personnel to oversee operations and to fly hay and oats to the snowbound livestock. The Montana guard arrived well-equipped for the mission with eight helicopters and four tank trucks. During the operation, a revolving roster of pilots took turns on missions to prevent fatigue during the demanding winter flights. During the loading of each helicopter, a pilot on the ground observed to ensure safety in landing zones and to direct crews in loading feed.[65]

One haylift participant, Lt. Col. Bill Willing, recalled that he was "proud to have assisted the ranchers," adding that he had "compassion for the animals, and

During a wintertime activation, guardsmen load hay on a helicopter to assist in feeding livestock stranded by snow drifts. *MMHM*

the successful operation made a positive difference in the ranchers" lives.[66] General Womack also expressed frank gratitude when informed that the mission was successful: "That's what happens when you get dedicated men—they always do a damn fine job!" Upon completion of the 48-hour operation, ranchers acknowledged that thousands of livestock, including "newborn calves were saved by the quick reaction of the governor" and the Montana National Guard.[67]

Operation Haylift was just one of a number of domestic duties that the Montana guard accomplished as the Vietnam era—the decade from 1965 to 1975—came to a close. Under the leadership of adjutant generals Richard C. Kendall and John Womack, the guard had successfully carried out its state obligations. The Montana National Guard now looked forward to playing a new and larger Pentagon-directed role in the nation's defense establishment in coming years.

Notes

1. George C. Herring. *America's Longest War: The United States and Vietnam, 1950–1975* (New York: Knopf, 1986).
2. During the height of the Vietnam War, a U.S. Marine Corps' analyst conducted a statistical study of American and Vietnamese casualties. The study revealed that with the prevailing tactics and strategy, American forces would suffer well in excess of 200,000 KIA before North Vietnam's manpower would be depleted.

3. Lyndon Baines Johnson, *The Vantage Point: Perspectives of the Presidency, 1963–1969* (New York: Holt, Rinehart and Winston, 1971), 153; *United States-Vietnam Relations, 1945–1967* (Washington: Government Printing Office, 1971), Book 4, Part IV C. 5. 31. The latter publication is better known as "The Pentagon Papers."
4. Johnson, *Vantage Point,* 153.
5. John K. Mahon, *History of the Militia and the National Guard* (New York: Macmillan, 1983), 242. Similar reason's for the president's unwillingness to send guardsmen to Vietnam are explored in David Halberstam, *The Best and the Brightest* (New York: Ballantine, 1992).
6. John D. Stuckey and Joseph H. Pistorius, "Mobilization for the Vietnam War: A Political and Military Catastrophe," *Journal of the U.S. Army War College* 15(1): 272.
7. "The Adjutant General's Message," *Montana Guardsman* (November 1965): 2. The *Montana Guardsman* was the organization's official newsletter.
8. Ibid., 4.
9. "The Adjutant General's Message," *Montana Guardsman* (February 1966): 2. For an analysis of domestic guard duty and the draft, see Lawrence M. Baskir and William Strauss, *Chance and Circumstance: The Draft and the Vietnam Generation* (New York: Knopf, 1978), 48–51.
10. "No Call-Up Seen in Near Future for National Guard or Reserve," *Montana Guardsman* (May 1966): 6.
11. Baskir and Strauss, *Chance and Circumstance,* 50.
12. *Biennial Report of the Adjutant General, State of Montana, July 1, 1964 to June 30, 1966* (Helena: State of Montana Office of the Adjutant General, 1966), 33.
13. "Draft Dodger Rumor Dispelled at Commanders Conference," *Montana Guardsman* (November 1966): 1, 8. For an analysis of "draft-dodging," see Jerry Cooper, *The Militia and the National Guard in America since Colonial Times: A Research Guide* (Westport, Connecticut: Greenwood Press 1993), 128. "The Guard's reputation suffered in particular," Cooper explained, "for while its members met their military obligation with the knowledge they would not go to Vietnam, they also served frequently in civil disorders prompted by war protesters."
14. "The Adjutant General's Message," *Montana Guardsman* (February 1967): 2.
15. Ibid.
16. "The Guard Marches for the March of Dimes," *Montana Guardsman* (May 1966): 10.
17. Ibid.
18. "Montana Guardsmen Give Generously to Blood for Defense," *Montana Guardsman* (August 1966): 1. Jerry Hansen, taped telephone interview with author, June 8, 1998. Hansen joined the Montana National Guard in 1953, and retired as a first sergeant in 1986.
19. "Montana Guardsmen Give Generously to Blood for Defense," *Montana Guardsman* (August 1966): 1, 4.
20. Richard Kendall to Tim Babcock, November 15, 1966, *Biennial Report, 1964–1966.*
21. *Biennial Report, 1966–1968,* 52.
22. "Backstage of a Forest Fire," *Billings Gazette,* July 21, 1966; "Insects Bugging Firefighters," *Billings Gazette,* July 23, 1966.
23. "Guardsmen Help Battle Forest Fires," *Montana Guardsman* (September 1967): 1, 10; "Fire Fighters Are Optimistic," *Montana Standard,* August 28, 1967.
24. *Biennial Report, 1966–1968,* 52; "Guardsmen Help Battle Forest Fires," *Montana Guardsman* (September 1967): 10.

25. "National Guard Told: Be Ready for Riots," *Billings Gazette*, August 22, 1967; "Montanans to Get New Riot Training," *Billings Gazette*, August 22, 1967. For more on domestic riots and demonstrations, see Mahon, *History of the Militia and the National Guard*, 236–41.
26. "Army Tells Congress Guard Ready for Riots," *Montana Guardsman* (May 1968): 16.
27. "68,000 Guardsmen Counter Riots: President Lauds Guard Performance," *Montana Guardsman* (May 1968): 1; Robert Weisbrot, *Freedom Bound: A History of America's Civil Rights Movement* (New York: W.W. Norton, 1991), 268–71. National Guard officials estimated that 68,600 guardsmen and 22,600 regular Army soldiers were called up, a conservative number compared to Weisbrot's estimation.
28. "The Adjutant General's Message," *Montana Guardsman* (May 1968): 2.
29. "The Adjutant General's Message," *Montana Guardsman* (September 1968): 2.
30. Martin Binkin and William W. Kaufmann, *U.S. Army Guard and Reserve: Rhetoric, Realities, Risks* (Washington, D.C.: Brookings Institution, 1989), 54; Johnson, *Vantage Point*, 385.
31. Binkin and Kaufmann, *U.S. Army Guard and Reserve*, 55.
32. George C. Herring, *L.B.J. and Vietnam: A Different Kind of War* (Austin: University of Texas Press, 1994), 148.
33. An Indiana Special Forces unit was among the few National Guard "combat" elements activated for service in Vietnam. Mahon, *History of the Militia and the National Guard*, 243.
34. *Montana Guardsman* (May 1968): 3.
35. *Biennial Report, 1966–1968*, 43.
36. Though armories were issued some modern weapons and equipment, it was not uncommon for other guard units to retain M1 rifles, .30 caliber machine guns, Browning Automatic Rifles, or other World War II period equipment. By the early 1970s, however, guard units across the nation were receiving M16s and other up-to-date weaponry. *Biennial Report, 1966–1968*, 43; Baskir and Strauss, *Chance and Circumstance*, 50.
37. "Montana's New Commander-in-Chief," *Montana Guardsman* (January 1968): 1; Gordon Dillow, "General Womack and His Tigers," *Montana Magazine* (July–August 1980): 28–31. John Womack was born and raised at Ennis, Montana. At the beginning of World War II, he was enrolled at Western Montana College in Dillon, majoring in English education. In 1942, Womack joined the horse cavalry and eventually transferred to the Army Air Corps. He also was stationed at various domestic bases, including Jefferson Barracks in Missouri. In 1945, he entered officers' candidate school, and in July earned a commission as second lieutenant in the infantry.
38. "Major General Womack Encourages Support of Nation's Policy in Vietnam," *Montana Guardsman* (December 1969): 3.
39. Stanley Karnow, *Vietnam: A History* (New York: Penguin, 1984), 608–10.
40. Ibid., 611.
41. Anonymous letter, May 7, 1970, University of Montana, Missoula, Vertical File, Montana Historical Society, Helena, Montana.
42. "Inhuman Society," *New York Times*, July 20, 1970.
43. Edward Bruner, taped telephone interview with author, October 11, 1998. Bruner retired from the Montana National Guard as a first sergeant in 1985.
44. "Annual Training Out of State this Year," *Montana Guardsman* (April 1970): 3; "Montana Army Guardsmen to Train at Boise," *Montana Guardsman* (April 1970): 1, 3, 6.

45. "General Westmoreland Speaks," *Montana Guardsman* (Spring 1971): 4. In addressing a meeting of the Association of the Adjutant General's Corps, Westmoreland discussed the increasing importance of the National Guard and Army Reserve in the nation's future military planning.
46. In January 1975, South Vietnam's final demise began with the loss of Phuoc Long Province. Initially, inland provinces first fell under North Vietnamese control, followed by the major coastal cities, with mixed resistance from South Vietnamese troops. The war effectively ended by May 1975, after North Vietnamese troops entered Saigon.
47. *Annual Report of the Department of Military Affairs* (Helena: State of Montana Office of the Adjutant General June, 1974), A-16.
48. "Guard Battle Blazes," *Montana Guardsman* (September 1973): 6.
49. Ibid.
50. Ibid.
51. Pat Mullaney, transcribed telephone interview with author, October 10, 1998.
52. "Two Fire Helicopters Crash," *Montana Standard*, August 22, 1973.
53. "Guard Battles Blazes," *Montana Guardsman* (September 1973): 6.
54. "State Workers Strike at Galen, Deer Lodge," *Montana Standard*, March 14, 1974; "Prison, Hospital Workers Strike," *Missoulian*, March 14, 1974.
55. James B. Jacobs, "The Role of Military Forces in Public Sector Labor Relations," *Industrial and Labor Relations Review* 35(3) (January 1982): 164.
56. "Warm Springs Strike Spreads," *Montana Standard*, March 19, 1974; "Warm Springs Workers Agree to 72-Hour Truce," *Missoulian*, March 21, 1974; "Nursing Staffs Praise Guardsmen," *Missoulian*, March 21, 1974.
57. "Warm Springs Says No to State Offer," *Montana Standard*, March 21, 1974; "Two Guardsmen Prove their Compassion," *Missoulian*, March 21, 1974.
58. "Guardsmen Prevented Deaths, Says Doctor," *Montana Standard*, March 14, 1974; "Prison, Hospital Workers Strike," *Missoulian*, March 21, 1974.
59. General John J. Womack (Ret.), transcribed telephone interview with author, October 10, 1998; "Guardsmen Lend Hand," *Montana Guardsman* (May 1974): 3.
60. Lieutenant Colonel William Willing, transcribed telephone interview with author, October 29, 1998. Willing entered the U.S. Army in 1969 and saw duty in Vietnam as a helicopter pilot. In 1972, he joined the Montana National Guard as CWO2 (Chief Warrant Officer 2).
61. *Montana Guardsman* (September 1974): 2.
62. *Montana Guardsman* (May 1974): 3.
63. "A Call to Community Action," *Montana Guardsman* (December 1974): 5.
64. "Operation Haylift," *Montana Guardsman* (August 1975): 5; "National Guard Aids Snowbound Cattle," *Missoulian*, April 11, 1975; "Helena Air Guard to Help Feed Cows," *Montana Standard*, April 10, 1975.
65. Ibid.
66. Willing interview.
67. "Operation Haylift," *Montana Guardsman* (August 1975), 5.

17

Total Force Policy and the Post-Vietnam Era, 1976–1990

Carol Scally Grigas

If American citizen armies, extemporized after the outbreak of war, could do as well as Washington's Continentals and as well as the citizen armies of Grant and Lee, what might they not do if organized and trained in time of peace?—John McAuley Palmer (1870–1955), citizen-soldier advocate.

A total force concept will be applied in all aspects of planning, programming, manning, equipping and employing Guard and reserve forces.—Melvin R. Laird, Secretary of Defense.

The Vietnam experience prompted the Nixon administration to reevaluate the nation's overall military policy. From this review emerged the Total Force Policy, conceptualized and articulated by Secretary of Defense Melvin R. Laird and announced on August 21, 1970. In the Total Force plan, the guard and reserve were designated as the "initial and primary source of augmentation of the active forces in any future emergency requiring a rapid and substantial expansion of active forces."[1] The program took effect in 1973.

Army Chief of Staff Creighton Abrams worked to maintain combat readiness at a time of falling budget allocations, the end of the draft, and reduced political and public support. The Total Force Policy transferred a number of combat and support units to the Army National Guard and Army Reserve, requiring additional training, equipment, and technological expertise to meet Army readiness standards. From the National Guard's standpoint, this ensured the continuation of the combat role it had first taken nearly a century earlier in the Spanish-American War.[2]

Throughout the 1970s and 1980s, Laird and other defense secretaries pursued the Total Force Policy. All service secretaries were directed to provide the manning, equipment, training, facilities, and maintenance necessary to assure that the guard and reserve could meet readiness levels and deployment deadlines required in contingency plans. The Army and the Air Force likewise adapted their thinking and force structure to accommodate the policy.

At the state level, there were challenges associated with finding the right mix of units when adopting more technologically advanced equipment and systems, but the Montana guard would receive more funding for implementation. It sent a greater number of personnel to service schools than ever before, and pay increases led to a better parity with civilian incomes, thereby promoting recruitment. Enhanced levels of competence increased the ability of Montana units to meet or surpass Army readiness tests, inspections, and assessments.[3]

Emergency Mobilizations

A well trained and full strength Guard is important both for Montana's economy and safety.—Governor Thomas L. Judge.[4]

What ever there is to do—we do it.—Adjutant General John J. Womack.[5]

Although the Total Force Policy reshaped the Montana guard's federal mission, readiness to aid citizens during natural and man-made emergencies remained its most visible public role.[6] New state and federal policies enhanced this mission, particularly the National Disaster Relief Act of 1974, making more funding available to the states and their guard units.

In 1972, a state reorganization had shifted the Division of Disaster and Emergency Services from the Executive Office of the Governor to the Department of Military Affairs. Until the state legislature modified state statutes dealing with civil defense, Adjutant General John J. Womack would direct the Civil Defense Division, rewriting the State Disaster and Emergency Plan.[7] Based on this plan, between 1976 and 1990 the guard was called out by three different governors on 40 occasions for local emergencies.

Modern disaster declarations by the governor now resulted in the deployment of a complex but effective organizational apparatus trained in emergency relief—providing equipment, personnel, and technical assistance to local authorities and residents. Federal and state budgets provided large expenditures for damage repair and disaster related costs. To meet an ever increasing responsibility for disaster relief, the division instituted ongoing training programs for emergency management personnel in state and local government.[8]

On February 22, 1976, a fire at the Montana State Prison in Deer Lodge damaged the boiler building and knocked out the electrical supply, leaving the institution without power. The next day, 27 guardsmen arrived to provide assistance and emergency support, supplying the prison with temporary cooking and power facilities.[9] The grateful warden later noted, "within 24 hours of reporting" the guard had the situation "well in hand."[10]

An emergency in late 1976 involved another state-run institution. During a recurring labor dispute between the Department of Institutions and employees at Warm Springs State Hospital, a strike began on November 11. The impasse brought on a crisis, causing Governor Thomas L. Judge to declare an emergency and activate the guard. Within four hours, guardsmen were on duty, engaged in housekeeping, security, fire watch, laundry, food preparation, transportation, administration, and other tasks.[11] For its efforts, the guard was commended by the state legislature in a joint resolution praising its performance.[12]

A winter storm in 1978 paralyzed central and eastern Montana for five days. On February 9, Governor Judge issued an emergency declaration, calling up helicopter units. Initially, guardsmen engaged in reconnaissance and evacuations, focusing especially on stranded, ill, or disabled persons.[13] During "Operation Snowbound," helicopter crews flew 13 missions on the first clear day to areas around Miles City, Glasgow, Chinook, Havre, and Lewistown. As weather permitted, the guard also transported snow removal equipment and repair parts, dropped food, clothing, and medical supplies, and provided assessments of road conditions.[14]

Though the guard's mission initially focused on helping people, attention quickly turned to livestock as well, when wind, large snowdrifts, and record low temperatures prevented ranchers from getting feed to stranded animals.[15] The guard began assisting, amid reports of significant livestock losses.[16]

Guard helicopters continued conducting fuel and food deliveries, as well as medical evacuations.[17] In one dramatic incident, a helicopter crew flying out of Glasgow airlifted an expectant mother, a two-year-old girl with a ruptured eardrum, and her ten-month-old sister.[18] The Glasgow crew alone flew more than 50 missions, including transporting a nurse to Chinook, delivering food to ranchers, replacement parts to snow crews, and checking on isolated residents.[19] In May, when spring rains created flood conditions near Hardin and Billings, a second emergency activation was needed.

In 1979, the Montana guard responded to one of its stiffest challenges—another institutional strike, this time affecting the State Prison at Deer Lodge, the Galen State Hospital, and the Boulder River School and Hospital. The emergency began when about 800 employees at the three institutions went on strike on February 5 after a breakdown in contract negotiations. The activation meant the guard would have to staff a prison, an alcoholic treatment center, and a school and hospital for the mentally disabled.[20]

Because the Montana guard had experienced similar situations in 1974 (see Chapter 16) and in 1976 at the Warm Springs State Hospital, the Military Support Section, headed by Lt. Col. James Duffy, had created "OP Plan 4," which would be instituted if the governor called for guard intervention.[21] According to Adjutant General Womack, about 500 members of the Montana Air National Guard were prepared to put the operational plan into effect. Lt. Col. Dave

Nathen, who had commanded guardsmen during the Warm Springs State Hospital incident, was ordered to head the activation.[22]

OP Plan 4 established task forces for each of the three institutions. At the two hospitals, guard personnel had met with institutional personnel prior to the strike. The early briefing and planning paid dividends because guard members quickly took up duties in security, maintenance, laundry, cooking, and housekeeping. Hospital personnel reported that many of the troops, despite putting in 12 hour days, returned after their shifts to play with the children and help in other ways.[23] The challenges were different at the Deer Lodge prison, but again, thanks to prior planning, the transition went smoothly. Air guard personnel participated in a three-hour briefing before taking up their prison assignments.[24] Ten days after the strike began they were replaced by Army guard personnel,[25] and ten-day rotation schedules between the MANG and ANG continued while the strike lasted for nearly a month.

Reflecting on her service during the Galen strike, Major Kareene F. Ostermiller, a public affairs specialist, valued her participation in the effort. "I could see the whole picture…the morale was high. It cost us some in terms of people getting out," she recalled, "but if you have some who are not committed, it's better to do with less. My job kept me hopping. I worked 10–12 hour days at Galen."

The 1980s brought more emergency mobilizations. Though the guard was active during the 1981 summer fire season, the floods of that year proved most challenging. On May 21, heavy rain caused rivers and streams to overflow in western Montana. On May 23, Governor Ted Schwinden activated the guard while declaring nine counties as disaster areas.[26] More than 150 guard personnel were involved in rescue operations and support services as flood waters threatened the Helena Valley. Helicopter crews evacuated 100 stranded people from Rimini and Colorado Gulch, areas inundated by Ten Mile Creek.[27]

Recruitment and Retention

> *If we are to continue to be ready when called, the National Guard must attract, retain, and maintain educated and motivated members. Our missions require it.*—Lt. General Emmert H. Walker Jr., Chief, National Guard Bureau.[28]

Once the draft ended in 1973 and U.S. involvement in Vietnam ceased, the usual stream of recruits diminished, reflecting a typical post-conflict challenge encountered after other wars in America's past.[29] With a low population scattered over a large area, Montana faced difficulties in maintaining unit strength as recruitment and retention dropped.

The Montana guard had been rated as "over strength," but by 1976 membership fell to a 418 deficit. Twelve units were under the required 80 percent minimum organizational strength, and only five units were at 100 percent, prompting the National Guard Bureau (NGB) to issue a warning to state headquarters.[30] The guard and the governor addressed the problem by announcing a recruiting drive focusing on retention. Faced with approximately 50 men about to complete their enlistments, one commander, Lt. James L. Hopper, interviewed these individuals, encouraging them to reenlist. Hooper felt that retention required more than just pay increases; the guard's needs had to be communicated on a one-on-one basis, because "in the past the Guard didn't always communicate with the troops."[31]

The Officers Association offered awards to units to encourage increases in enlistment. Detachment 1, Troop C, 163AC, in Malta, for example, received a check for $200 for achieving the largest unit strength increase in the last quarter of 1975.[32] Governor Judge addressed the recruitment issue at least four times in 1976. He noted that the enlisted ranks were only 84 percent of authorized strength, and urged the state legislature to approve additional benefits, such as a college tuition allowance, as other states had done in boosting enlistment.[33]

That same year, when reviewing Montana guardsmen in field training near Boise, Idaho, the governor announced a promotional campaign, which he hoped would bring the guard up to full strength. In a speech and press release, Judge called on citizens to aid in the effort, noting that not only did the guard provide emergency relief during natural and man-made emergencies, but this kind of service was indispensable in sparsely populated counties with a small infrastructure and low tax base.[34]

Judge repeated this message in a letter marking the 340th anniversary of the foundation of the state militia tradition.[35] He also personally wrote to some guard members nearing the end of their enlistments. In one typical letter, he discussed his support for enhanced benefits, which was being addressed by bills scheduled for introduction in the 1977 legislative session. Based on the results of questionnaires sent to all guard members, the governor announced that annual training would follow a new schedule more convenient for the troops and their employers. He indicated as well that more attention would be paid to unit level training.[36] Despite these vigorous efforts, Montana nationally ranked fifth from the bottom in recruiting in 1976.[37]

In 1977, bills for incentives and increased benefits were presented, both at the state and federal levels, hoping to spark enlistment and aid retention. A proposed $1,000 state income tax deduction and tuition support for troops attending college, however, was voted down by the Montana legislature as too costly.[38] Later that year, the U.S. Congress approved $5 million to test the impact of educational assistance and reenlistment bonus incentives.[39] According to the plan, reservists whose current enlistments were due to expire within one year were eligible for a bonus of up to $1,800—if they reenlisted for six years. In Montana, however, the 96th Army Reserve, and not the National Guard, was tapped to participate in the experiment.

With the incentive plan defeated in the Montana legislature, and with a shortage of 550 personnel now putting Montana at only 83 percent of authorized strength, the guard turned to its own resources. General Harry Thode announced that five full-time recruiters were being assigned to promote recruitment. Additionally, a captain was detailed to work with unit commanders and to coordinate with public high schools in an effort to sign up graduating seniors.[40]

At this time, the guard tapped into an unexpected population base for recruits—one that some senior guardsmen did not always welcome. Beginning in 1967,[41] the National Guard was authorized to recruit women, but there had been little effort to do so until after the draft was suspended in 1973 and recruitment declined. By the mid-1970s, the Army established standards regarding women and they became a welcome addition to the recruitment effort. The Civilian Acquired Skills Program consisted of a shorter version of basic training, conducted at the Women's Army Corps Center at Ft. McClellan, Alabama. By 1978, the number of females in the Army National Guard had shot up from zero in 1970 to 12,898 in eight years.[42] By 1991, women comprised 7 percent of the National Guard force in the United States, increasing to 8.6 percent in 1996.[43]

Other programs enhanced career options for women on active duty and in the reserves. Although a combat exclusion policy continued, thus closing off an important route for promotion, in 1978 women were authorized to command units in which men were assigned, attend Officer Candidate School, receive benefits for their spouses equal to those of male soldiers, and to remain on active duty when pregnant.[44] Montana women accepted the challenge; among the earliest were Major Kareene F. Ostermiller, Major Nikki S. DeWolf, and Lt. Col. Jo Ellen D. Clark.

Ostermiller, a self-described "guard brat," was the daughter of a career officer in the Air National Guard. After one year in the air reserves, she transferred to the Army National Guard in 1977 and spent two years as an administrative specialist, "learning where everyone went and what they did." In 1979, Ostermiller attended OCS in only the second class to include women cadets. After commissioning, she joined the 103rd Public Affairs Detachment (PAD) as a press, and then community relations, officer. She also served as the first female Aide-de-Camp and assistant Executive Officer for the State Area Command (STARC) Headquarters.[45]

At age 23, just after graduating from college in 1978, Major Nikki S. DeWolf began her military career by joining the U.S. Army. In 1981, she joined the Montana guard, and in 1984 attended OCS where, as the only female in her class, she was elected class president. After earning her commission in 1986, she "branched Adjutant General Corps and performed personnel duties." DeWolf next became company commander of the 210th Personnel Services Company for two years.[46]

Eventually becoming comptroller of the Montana guard, Lt. Col. Jo Ellen D. Clark enlisted in the guard in 1983 and served as an equipment parts and records specialist. When receiving her commission in 1986, she became a supply platoon leader in maintenance and then Maintenance Control Officer. Regarding the challenges she faced, Clark's opinion was similar to others. "The hardest thing was to overcome the few poor female soldiers' reputations that give all females a bad name. Once that was overcome, it was pretty easy in the Maintenance community."[47]

Attitudes changed, in part, because women in leadership positions set a high standard. When Clark took command of the Personnel Services Company in 1990, she encountered resistance. "A First Sergeant...thought women should be seen, but not heard," Clark explained. "Within three months I had him moved and replaced by someone who wanted to do the best he could for everyone...We received an Outstanding Unit Award within a one year period."[48]

Clark acknowledged, however, as have others, that despite greater opportunities for women in the military, resistance to females persists. "Since I got my LTC," Clark observed, "I have found that it's hard for senior officers that didn't 'grow up' with females to accept them into the group. Sometimes I feel I am being patronized."[49]

By 1980, Adjutant General Womack reported an increase in overall guard enrollment to 2,700, though this number yet fell 400 below full strength. The 1979 recruitment effort had gone well, however, with the enlistment of 400 personnel with no prior military service. In considering differences in guard strength across the country, Womack explained that some states were as low as 60 percent, while others, such as North Dakota, frequently exceeded full enlistment and thus were "over-strength."

Womack attributed these disparities to the branch of service assigned to state guard organizations—i.e., infantry, engineers, armored cavalry, etc. The over-strength North Dakota National Guard was an engineer outfit, and quite popular with enlistees. The training focused on heavy equipment operation and construction. Developing skills in maintaining roads, erecting structures, and undertaking other construction projects were highly valued in the civilian sphere. Essentially, the North Dakota guard provided its members with valuable crossover training for civilian work.

Womack's prescription for increased Montana guard recruitment included more effective marketing of the advantages in serving, improved and more interesting training opportunities, appeals to patriotism, and outstanding leadership.[50] After a half-decade of efforts to overcome a deficit in organizational strength, the Montana guard eventually turned the corner. A contributor to improved recruitment and reenlistment figures was the Veterans' Educational Assistance Act of 1977.[51] It expired in 1984, but new legislation extended and broadened benefits. Titled the Veterans Educational Assistance Act of 1984 (usually referred to as the

"New GI Bill"),[52] it took effect on July 1, 1985. Along with other incentives, this act developed into an effective enlistment and retention tool.[53]

Nationally, minority recruitment proved to be another important contributor to raising enlistments numbers. In 1971, Black representation was officially tallied at 1 percent, but a decade later, Blacks comprised 17 percent. In the aggregate, all minorities formed 26 percent of the National Guard.[54]

During the early 1980s, Adjutant General James W. Duffy pointed out that the approximately 3,000 members of the Montana guard were largely "weekend warriors." Its full-time technical and administrative staff numbered 528. Duffy wanted more funding for full-time staff positions. He also noted that the guard could be more selective than the regular military in accepting recruits for its ranks; only one person had joined the Montana guard in recent years classified as a Category 4 (someone who had difficulty reading). By comparison, 25 percent of those joining the regular military were designated as Category 4.[55]

In 1986, however, a budget cut threatened the recently implemented Veterans Educational Assistance Act of 1984, one of the most effective recruiting tools for the guard. As the House prepared to vote on the Reagan administration's proposal to terminate the program on October 1, Lt. Gen. Emmert H. Walker Jr. addressed a congressional subcommittee collecting information on the effectiveness of the New GI Bill. The NG Bureau Chief noted the dilemma for enlistment and retention when the thriving private business sector of the 1980s absorbed more college graduates. The benefits of the New GI Bill, however, allowed the guard to compete in the marketplace for good personnel. Moreover, the trend of modernization and use of highly complex technologies and strategies made it imperative that the guard retain its best soldiers. The bill provided the guard with a tool to attract talented recruits who wished to continue their civilian education. Also, guard members were required to perform at certain acceptable levels during their service in order to receive benefits.[56]

Budget cuts triggered by the Gramm-Rudman Act jeopardized congressional funding for the New GI Bill. The guard argued, however, that the bill was an effective recruitment tool. The numbers were equally dramatic for both the air and army guard.[57] In Montana, Adjutant General Duffy noted that since the bill went into effect, about 235 had enrolled in the program, and more than 160 of these were "directly" attributed to the availability of educational benefits. Duffy anticipated that many future recruits without prior military service also would apply for scholarships.[58] Clearly, this response demonstrated the effectiveness of the educational assistance program as a recruitment and retention incentive, and eventually the Veterans Educational Assistance Act was superseded by other similar legislation.

Federal budget cuts for fiscal years 1987–1988 and 1988–1989 presented obvious challenges for the Montana guard in implementing the increasing complex requirements necessitated by the Total Force Policy. In Montana, one result was that no authorization was received for an increase in manpower for FY 1987 or for the next two years.

Also eliminated were federal funds for deploying personnel for ten-week training programs. This was a special hardship in Montana, where many of the guard units were located in distant communities and travel costs were high. Furthermore, in-grade ceiling levels were static, meaning that even as the guard experienced success in recruiting able college-level members, the opportunity for timely promotions in rank would be stalled.[59]

Yet by late 1988—because Montana was being impacted by the Total Force Policy and under orders to reorganize by September 1989—the fiscal and manpower situation actually had improved. The regular Army's advisor to the Montana guard, Lt. Col. Robert Saxby, declared that "now is probably the best time for anyone that wants to get into the Guard."[60]

The changes included a reconfiguration from an armored cavalry regiment to a heavy armored brigade. This meant that the 163rd would now be tasked with a full combat mission rather than its earlier scouting role. To achieve this, the Montana guard was required to recruit 800 to 900 more troops. This expansion also presented more opportunities for women because many of the new slots were open to them. Although women were banned from combat roles, a separate brigade required many support positions.[61]

Effective inclusion of the brigade in the Army's Total Force Policy heightened the possibility of the unit being deployed. For both enlisted and newly recruited personnel, however, this reality added an appreciated extra dimension to their guard service. "We've technically been involved in every war in the country's history," Duffy explained. "When people join the Guard, they know that."[62] Thus, as the 1980s drew to a close, the scheduled reorganization for September 1989 was good news to the guard, strengthening both recruitment and retention efforts.

From January 1981 through January 1987, the Montana guard had experienced a dramatic increase in strength—from 84.2 percent in 1981 to a peak of 109.7 percent in 1987. As reorganization came to a conclusion, total strength stood at 3,082 personnel.[63] This number eroded somewhat in 1990, however, as the threat of conflict grew in the Persian Gulf. Recruitment numbers for September and October 1990 dropped 14 percent from the previous year. Retention was similarly affected, as the guard lost 77 members in the same time period.[64]

Facilities Development and Information Management

After the Vietnam War, the national defense policy began relegating more and more of the national mission to the National Guard...the authorized strengths... (and the facilities needed to support the training)...increased in order to modernize the fighting force.—Governor Ted Schwinden.[65]

The dollars devoted to implementing the Total Force Policy during the 1980s improved the facilities and information management systems of the Montana guard. More than $10 million was spent on new construction, adding about 154,000 square feet of space.[66] As the Reagan administration and the Department of Defense placed a renewed emphasis on upgrading military preparedness, by mid-decade the Montana state budget reflected an increased military spending of about 25 percent for projects approved by the NGB.

In 1985, foremost among the announced projects was $2 million slated for a Combined Support and Maintenance Shop at Fort Harrison.[67] The shop's expanded capability would house 64 technicians, servicing more than 900 wheeled and tracked vehicles.[68] The 30,000 square foot shop, the only one of its kind in Montana, opened in October 1987.[69] Other new construction included two new armories in Havre and Harlowton, and maintenance shops for Kalispell, Billings, Belgrade, Culbertson, Missoula, and Chinook. Additional projects undertaken between 1981 and 1988 included new multipurpose indoor range facilities at Billings, Missoula, Glendive, Helena, and Glasgow.

Maintenance was completed on 15 existing armories by replacing roofs, painting interior and exterior walls, and undertaking other interior remodeling. The training ranges at Fort Harrison and Limestone Hills also were retrofitted to better accommodate the advanced tank gunnery and weapons training being incorporated under the Total Force Policy.[70]

Prior to the early 1980s, modern electronic information management was unavailable to the National Guard, but by the end of the decade, because of the highly technical nature of the new weapons systems and due to administrative demands, computer technology became a primary focus. A Sperry 5000 mainframe computer was installed at Fort Harrison with remote terminals in Helena and Bozeman. Personal computers and access to the Intel 300 systems also became available at the unit level.[71]

Training and Equipment

> *In no other profession are the penalties for employing untrained personnel so appalling or so irrevocable as in the military.*—General Douglas MacArthur, Army Chief of Staff Annual Report, 1930.[72]

> *Are they ready?*[73]—Caspar W. Weinberg, Secretary of Defense.

Under the Army's Total Force Policy, the National Guard's role as a federal reserve force came into sharper focus, especially regarding training and equipment. In 1976, a concerted effort began to upgrade the authorized levels of modern equipment for the guard. As part of a five-year plan, units were scheduled to complete modernization by the 1980 fiscal year. Tanks, trucks, and armaments were the main focus. In March 1976, the National Guard Bureau was notified that it would receive 747 modern tanks. Other upgrades included replacement of the quarter-ton M38A1 truck with the newer quarter-ton M151A1s and the conversion of howitzers.[74]

In the late 1970s, some units trained overseas. In early 1978, Helena's 3669th Maintenance Company spent two weeks at Taylor Barracks in Mannheim, West Germany, assigned to repair and maintenance work on track and wheeled vehicles.[75] In the fall of 1981, the 3669th again deployed for annual training at Taylor Barracks, where the emphasis was to operate "under a one team concept" with that station's 51st Maintenance Battalion."[76] Combined regular Army and 3669th personnel were distributed throughout the 51st's operational area in "effective working companies."[77]

Stateside duty also emphasized the guard's integration into the regular Army training regimen. In May 1978, for example, a two-week Basic Airborne course was conducted in Montana, paralleling the training standards used by the Army at Fort Benning, Georgia. This was the first training of its type conducted nationwide by the Army National Guard. Taking part was Montana's 6th Special Forces, together with units from five other states. The course, attended by 150 troops, included mass parachute jumps from Air Force C-130 aircraft.[78]

In 1981, about 600 members of the 2nd Squadron, 163rd Armored Cavalry, participated in Border Star '81, a 15-day exercise at the Fort Bliss Military Reservation in Texas, home of Montana's parent organization, the 3rd Armored Calvary Regiment. Border Star was one of four similar exercises sponsored by USREDCOM each year that focused on the readiness of combined active-duty and reserve forces. For the Montana troops, it tested for the first time their ability to merge with a regular Army combat unit. In Border Star '81, active-duty and guard personnel were assigned the same tasks, working side by side, often with Montana NCOs serving in leadership positions. Due to the prohibitive costs of shipping their own vehicles, the Montana guard used the 3rd Regiment's equipment.

Because of its ability to meld in and train effectively with the 3rd, the 163rd won accolades for competency and proficiency. With 21,000 troops taking part,[79] the impact was summed up by Maj. Gen. Duffy: "The magnitude of the exercise was good for us." He added: "We are looking forward to staying with the Total Army Concept."[80]

A Great Falls *Tribune* profile of the 163rd Armored Calvary Regiment indicated how far the Montana guard had progressed by 1981, six years after the end of the Vietnam conflict. The article focused on members of E Troop from the 163rd's 2nd squadron, who were pictured with their M60A1 Patton tanks. The newspaper noted that the regiment had 86 tanks and also was equipped with 4.2 inch mortars, 155mm mechanized howitzers, armored personnel and

M60 main battle tank. *MMHM*

ammunition carriers, and command vehicles and helicopters. Additionally, the *Tribune* reported that the regiment was overcoming its recruitment deficit, having gained membership at the rate of about 10 percent each year, and reaching a total of 2,115 in 1981, which was 614 short of the authorized strength of 2,729 personnel. Of these, 60 women were filling non-combat roles.[81]

Training improvements continued to be emphasized in 1982. Regulations stipulated that National Guard attendance at U.S. Army Service Schools would be encouraged to enhance unit leadership positions.[82] After visiting the National Guard Bureau in Washington, D.C., Col. James D. Tutwiler, the senior Army advisor to Montana, submitted his report for the MNG, underscoring the importance of training. General Walker, the bureau chief, had informed Tutwiler that all guard units needed to improve their home training so that annual exercises could be used to "train units to work in concert."[83] As part of an NGB purchase scheduled for 1984, the Montana guard would receive the Automated Tank Target System. Other funding would be available in 1983 for range development, and preference would go to projects submitted by states that gave priority to individual and crew qualification training.[84]

The emphasis on adhering to regular Army standards included such fundamentals as using Army mess equipment during training assemblies. During inspections, Lt. Gen. David E. Grange Jr. was "surprised to find that meals were being catered." He was told that catering had been adopted for convenience, but Grange rejected the argument, indicating he was not amused that Army mess regulations were ignored. For reasons of convenience notwithstanding, General Grange expected catering to cease, or at least be used only as a last resort. "In a combat environment, an Army relies heavily on its food service operations," Grange explained. He made the point that, even in food service training, the battlefield was not the place to learn a skill, but rather the place to put it into action.[85]

The NGB remained focused on improving individual and crew weapons qualification training at the local level across the nation. The Montana guard was informed that training would be conducted with laser devices that simulated live-fire exercises, and this was approved for use in drill halls or armories. This indoor range use was intended to enhance an armory's function as a home station training facility. When training incorporated Brewster devices firing .22 caliber ammunition, local units were authorized to build outdoor mini-tank ranges. These adoptions were easily accomplished, since no additional facilities were required for laser device training, and outdoor mini-tank ranges could be quickly built. Moreover, they were funded at a 100 percent level by the Military Construction program of the Army National Guard. The NGB recommended that the Montana guard consider a combination of indoor laser training at local armories, and outdoor mini-tank ranges at selected local training sites serving several armories.[86]

In 1984, the 103rd Public Affairs Detachment was selected to attend the ninth annual Team Spirit exercises. These war games were held in South Korea each year, fielding as many as 207,000 military personnel, including 60,000 U.S. active and reserve soldiers. The 103d PAD was the first Montana unit to take part. According to Major Hal Stearns, the PAD commander, "it was a hell of a trip, the most realistic training possible for a unit."[87]

By the mid 1980s, the Blue Mountain Training Area in the Missoula locality became a special focus. The facility faced a questionable future—either make it safer or select a new training location. Because of the area's recreational attractions and complaints from local residents, it was closed in the summer of 1984 until range safety measures for controlling live fire exercises could be implemented.[88] Since 1952, the approximately 4,869 acre site had been used by the National Guard, Army Reserve, the Reserve Officer Training Corps, and state and municipal law enforcement agencies. In 1982, control of the Blue Mountain Training Area was transferred from the National Guard to the Army Reserve's 379th Engineer Battalion.[89]

To alleviate problems at the Blue Mountain Training Area, Col. James Maness, the Montana guard chief of staff, proposed scaled-down training, barbwire enclosures and the posting of warning signs, clearing of ground cover to control burns, and sweeps of impact areas to locate and remove any unexploded ordnance.[90] The guard no longer used Blue Mountain for 155mm field artillery training because of the potential danger of unexploded ordinance. The decision eliminated use of this key training area for the 2nd Squadron's Howitzer Battery (155mm) based in Missoula. The closest alternative was in Townsend, about 150 miles away. With these measures in place, the Blue Mountain Training Area was reactivated for training exercises, including the firing of .50 caliber weapons.[91] But the changes in 1985 were only temporary measures. A new site needed to be identified, acquired, and developed, a process that took until the end of the decade.

The normal patterns of annual training continued in the next couple of years. In 1988, for example, the 3669th Heavy Equipment Maintenance Company conducted training at Fort Lewis, where the personnel were housed at North Fort Lewis. The soldiers were assigned to the Department of Logistics and trained to make repairs on equipment ranging from night vision goggles to new HMMVs. Some personnel attended a course on small generators, while others participated in the Nuclear, Biological, and Chemical NCO qualification course.[92]

The following year, the new adjutant, Brig. Gen. Gary C. Blair, announced that annual training would return to locations in Montana. By June 24, 1989, about 600 soldiers had participated in training exercises at Fort Harrison. "Having our annual training in Montana…is going to be quite a boost for the state's general economy," Col. Mike Bolin predicted. General Blair added that the payroll for these 600 soldiers was about $600,000, and he judged that those billeted at Fort Harrison would spend about $60,000 on food, lodging, and fuel in the Helena area.[93]

State-of-the-art weapons upgrades accompanied the reorganizing of the 163rd Armored Cavalry Regiment into the 163rd Heavy Separate Brigade. The Montana guard received 120 M1 Abrams main battle tanks, making it the first state in the West to receive this advanced model. Considered the world's "finest battle tank," the M1s replaced 87 aging M60 Patton tanks. Retiring Adjutant General Duffy characterized the acquisition as "the most exciting and significant thing that's happened to the Montana National Guard" in his service of more than 30 years.[94]

The M1 tank, with its low profile, advanced engine, operational agility, armor, and fire-detection and suppression systems gave it great effectiveness and a higher survival rate in combat. Each tank, costing $1.8 million, weighed 62 tons, had a 1,500 horsepower engine, and was operated by a crew of four. The statistics were impressive—an M1 could accelerate from 0 to 20 mph in seven seconds, and reached a maximum speed of 45 mph. Initially, eight M1s were stationed at Fort Harrison, and 22 were located at the Limestone Hills Training Site near Townsend. Additional tanks were divided among companies in Shelby, Kalispell, Hamilton, Dillon, Great Falls, and two companies in Missoula. Sixty tanks were headquartered at Gowen Field in Boise, the annual training site.[95]

M1 "Abrams" of the 163rd Heavy Separate Brigade. Named for General Creighton Abrams, commander of U.S. forces in Vietnam (1968–1972), the M1 main battle tank entered U.S. Army and Marine Corps service in 1980. The Montana Army National Guard received the M1 by the end of the decade. *MMHM*

Another important addition to the arsenal was the TOW anti-tank missile. The TOW—an acronym for Tube launched, Optically tracked, Wire guided missile—was a three-foot-long missile launched from atop an armored personnel carrier or ITV, an Improved TOW Vehicle. Each ITV could carry up to 12 TOW missiles.[96] Each missile cost $8,000. Initially, 14 four-man crews underwent two weeks of training to learn how to operate the TOW. The first ITV was assigned to the newly formed 1-163d Infantry Battalion (Mechanized) in Billings; training officer Capt. Donald Erdmann termed the M901 "an excellent weapon system." The TOW could be fired from a distance of three kilometers, and strike targets taking evasive action.[97] The Cobra attack helicopter likewise was added to the Montana arsenal. By August 1989, the first of two were on the ground in Helena, and eventually 15 Cobras were assigned to the 189th Aviation Attack Helicopter Battalion.[98]

The 1988 Reorganization

> *The Department of Defense has changed the Montana Guard force structure many times during its 100 year tenure but none have been so challenging as the current reorganization.*—Adjutant General James W. Duffy.[99]

The 1988 transformation of the state's military infrastructure was one of the most significant events in Montana guard history. As part of the Army's Total Force structural realignment of seven armored cavalry regiments,[100] the Montana's 163rd Armored Cavalry Regiment converted into the 163rd Heavy Separate Brigade. An announcement in late December 1987 indicated that the realignment would be completed within two years—personnel would be in place by September 1988, and the state would be ready for federal recognition in September 1989.[101]

As part of this transformation, the Montana guard emerged with about 800 new personnel slots, including 90 officer positions. With the transformation, the force consisted of four battalions rather that two squadrons. Moreover, each section of the state stood to gain larger units—western Montana would be home to two tank battalions, eastern Montana emerged with a mechanized infantry battalion, and central Montana drew the support battalion. The brigade's artillery, which formed a fifth battalion, was stationed in Wyoming.[102] General Duffy noted: "We expect positive social, economic and personnel impact to expand proportionally to the number and size of units designated in the involved communities."[103]

The state also experienced an increase in the number of full-time support personnel, and opportunities for women were expected to increase as well. With a Defense Department decision in 1986, women now were allowed to serve in support battalion roles. Moreover, about 100 positions were open to women in the aviation attack helicopter battalion. With combat zone positions opening up to women, they had new avenues to higher rank, providing job training identical to that of their male counterparts.

Expansion, of course, increased the need for an additional 90 commissioned officers. Moreover, since a brigadier general commanded a brigade, that rank was added to Montana's officer positions. In all, it was estimated that the guard needed to recruit about 800 more men and women to fill its ranks. This would be accomplished without an increase in the state's military budget, since federal funds covered the reorganization. Importantly, no local community lost units. In fact, most areas gained personnel and functions.[104]

Reorganization was seen as a boon to the state with the expected addition of about $7 million to the economy. Great Falls, the state's one major urban area that lacked a guard unit, greeted the news with special interest. Great Falls now would be home to two units—a 77-member tank company and a 126-member engineer detachment. As General Duffy explained to the local chamber of commerce, this would add about $1.5 million to the local economy.[105]

Havre likewise was significantly impacted, gaining 19 full-time and 45 part-time guard personnel.[106] According to Capt. Jon Jackson, the unit commander, Havre was selected for a significant increase in troop strength because it had the population and services to provide for new recruits. Jackson noted that women also would benefit from the reorganization, because prior to 1988 women were only assigned to Helena, but now could fill positions anywhere.[107]

Ironically, while the Department of the Army reorganized the National Guard and Army, the Reagan administration reduced budget support for the military. But General Duffy remained optimistic, explaining: "Forecasted federal budget reductions in military spending do not alter or completely deny implementation of our planning."[108]

Events proved him right, and Montana's luck held in 1990 through another round of federal budget cuts. Public Affairs officer Col. Dick Mooney predicted that the possibility of a nationwide 66,000 National Guard troop cut back would not affect the Montana guard. "Not a single one is coming from here," Mooney explained, and he anticipated that Montana would be allowed to continue to fill the personnel slots allotted in the 1988 reorganization. "We still need to find about 700 more soldiers," Mooney said, echoing a welcome problem for energetic and determined recruiters.[109]

Notes

1. Melvin R. Laird, Secretary of Defense Memorandum to the Military Services, August 21, 1970.
2. Jerry Cooper, *The Militia and the National Guard in America since Colonial Times: A Research Guide* (Westport, Connecticut: Greenwood Press, 1993), 128–29.
3. Major General James W. Duffy, e-mail to author, June 1999.
4. Speech, Papers of Governor Thomas L. Judge, Montana Historical Society, Helena, Montana [hereafter cited as MHS].
5. National Guard Association of the United States [hereafter cited as NGAUS], March–April 1976, 12.
6. Cooper, 121.
7. Letter, Major General John J. Womack, Montana Adjutant General, to Crosser.
8. Transition paper, Major General James W. Duffy, Montana Adjutant General, to Governor Ted Schwinden, uncollected private papers of MG James W. Duffy (Ret.).
9. *Montana Guardsman*, March 1976, 9.
10. Letter to Governor Thomas L. Judge from Ralph E. Reiner, Prison folder, Shelf 37L, Building T-15, Ft. Harrison, Helena, Montana.
11. *Montana Guardsman*, December 1976, 7.
12. Ibid., Resolution, Montana State Legislature.
13. "Blizzard 'Disaster' in East Montana," *Independent Record* (Helena, Montana), February 9, 1978, 1.
14. "Montana Gets Relief from Storms," *Montana Standard* (Butte, Montana), February 13, 1978, 1.
15. "Cattlemen Are Facing a Winter Crisis," *Independent Record* (Helena, Montana), February 13, 1978, 2.
16. "Bitter Cold after Snow," *Independent Record* (Helena, Montana), February 13, 1978, 1.
17. "Winds Taper Off but Montana Keeps Weather Fingers Crossed," *Tribune* (Great Falls, Montana), February 14, 1978, 5.
18. "Montana Gets Relief from Storms," *Montana Standard* (Butte, Montana), February 13, 1978, 1.
19. "Cattlemen Are Facing a Winter Crisis," *Independent Record* (Helena, Montana), February 13, 1978, 2.

20. Major Kareene F. Ostermiller, e-mail response to author's questionnaire, November 1, 1999.
21. NGAUS, March–April 1979, 11.
22. "Guard Prepared to Take Over if Hospitals, Prison Struck," *Independent Record* (Helena, Montana), February 3, 1979, 3.
23. NGAUS, 3.
24. Ibid., 12.
25. "Air Guard Members to Return from State Institutions Tuesday," *Tribune* (Great Falls, Montana), February 14, 1979.
26. "Deluge Sweeps Valley," *Independent Record* (Helena, Montana), May 22, 1981, 1.
27. "Friendly Creeks Turn Cantankerous," *Independent Record* (Helena, Montana), May 23, 1981, 5A.
28. Statement, Lt. General Emmert H. Walker Jr., before the Congressional Subcommittee on Education, Training and Employment, Committee on Veterans' Affairs, November 21, 1985.
29. Cooper, 128–29.
30. "The Dying Guard," *Montana Guardsman*, May 1976, 9.
31. "Recruiting Drive," *Montana Guardsman*, March 1976, 9.
32. "Recruiting Award," *Montana Guardsman*, March 1976, 8.
33. Speech notes, Governor Thomas L. Judge Papers, MHS.
34. Press Release, Office of the Governor, Governor Thomas L. Judge Papers, April 1976, MHS.
35. Letter, Governor Thomas L. Judge Papers, October 1, 1976, MHS.
36. Letter, Governor Thomas L. Judge to Mr. Foss, December 13, 1976, MHS.
37. "Box Score," *Montana Guardsman*, December 1976, 5.
38. "House Acts: Income Tax, Retirement Bills," *Montana Guardsman*, Spring 1977, 1.
39. "$1,800 Bonus Offered Reservists, Guardsmen," Associated Press, November 14, 1977.
40. "State Reserve Units 'Want You,'" *Tribune* (Great Falls, Montana), November 16, 1977.
41. Public Law 90–130.
42. The independent Women's Army Corps was terminated in 1978. "Women in the Army National Guard," Fact Sheet, National Guard Bureau.
43. Ibid.
44. "Women in the Reserve Forces," Fact Sheet, Defense Advisory Committee on Women in the Services, March 1996.
45. Major Kareene F. Ostermiller, e-mail to author, November 11, 1999.
46. Major Nikki S. DeWolf, e-mail to author, July 23, 1999.
47. Lt. Colonel Jo Ellen D. Clark, e-mail to author, July 7, 1999.
48. Ibid.
49. Ibid.
50. "Montana Faces Fewer Problems," *Tribune* (Great Falls, Montana), September 22, 1980, 1-A.
51. Public Law 94-502 was approved on October 15, 1976.
52. Reserve components Chapter 106, USC.
53. Letter, U.S. Representative Montgomery to MG James W. Duffy, February 7, 1986.
54. Letter, President Ronald Reagan to Governor Ted Schwinden.
55. "Guard Chief Wants Bigger Share of Budget," *Independent Record* (Helena, Montana), February 21, 1982.
56. Testimony, Lt. General Emmert H. Walker Jr., Chief, National Guard Bureau, before the House Veterans' Affairs Committee, November 21, 1985.

57. Letter, U.S. Representative Montgomery to MG James W. Duffy, February 7, 1986.
58. Draft of a Letter, MG James W. Duffy to Friends of the Montana Guard, 1986.
59. Memorandum, MG James W. Duffy, February 27, 1987.
60. "The New Guard," *Independent Record* (Helena, Montana), November 1988.
61. Ibid.
62. Ibid.
63. Memorandum, MG James W. Duffy to Governor Ted Schwinden, December 1988.
64. "Guard Enlistments Plunge," *Tribune* (Great Falls, Montana), December 1, 1990.
65. Letter, Governor Ted Schwinden to Dennis Brown, January 23, 1985.
66. Memorandum, MG James W. Duffy to Governor Ted Schwinden, December 1988.
67. "Guard Details Building Plans," *Independent Record* (Helena, Montana), November 26, 1985, 1B.
68. "Work Starts on Guard Building," *Independent Record* (Helena, Montana), June 19, 1986, 1B.
69. "Guard Shows $1.8 Million Building," *Independent Record* (Helena, Montana), October 4, 1987.
70. Memorandum, MG James W. Duffy to Governor Ted Schwinden, December 1988.
71. Ibid.
72. Stephen M. Duncan, *Citizen Warriors: America's National Guard and Reserve Forces and the Politics of National Security* (Novato, California: Presidio Press, 1997), 42.
73. Ibid., 254.
74. *Montana Guardsman*, May 1976, 3.
75. "3669th Back from Tour in Germany," *Montana Guardsman*, April 1978, 1.
76. "3669th Returns to Mannheim for One Team Concept Training," *Montana Guardsman*, Fall 1981, 1.
77. Ibid., 2.
78. "Airborne Training in Missoula," *Montana Guardsman*, August 1978, 1.
79. "2nd Squadron Units Complete Readiness Training Exercises," *Montana Guardsman*, Summer 1981, 1.
80. Ibid., 5.
81. "State National Guard's armored cavalry regiment has right to be proud too," *Tribune* (Great Falls, Montana), August 30, 1981, F1.
82. Memorandum, Governor Ted Schwinden to Montana National Guard, Schools: Attendance at Service Schools, February 25, 1982.
83. Memorandum, Colonel James D. Tutwiler to Montana National Guard, August 16, 1982.
84. Ibid., 1–2.
85. Memorandum, Lt. General David E. Grange Jr., to State Adjutants General, September 24, 1982.
86. Letter, Major General Herbert R. Temple Jr. to Adjutant General James W. Duffy, September 27, 1982.
87. "Team Spirit Flexes Its Muscles," *Montana Guardsman*, Summer 1984, 10.
88. Memorandum, Colonel James Maness, Montana National Guard, Chief of Staff, to Adjutant General James W. Duffy, July 6, 1984.
89. Memorandum, Chronology of Events Montana Army National Guard (MT ARNG) Acquisition of Bearmouth Maneuver Training Area.
90. Maness memorandum.
91. "Military Again Using Blue Mountain Area," *Missoulian* (Missoula, Montana), January 26, 1985, 3.

92. "3669th Goes to Washington," *Montana Guardsman*, Summer 1988, 1.
93. "Guard 'Comes Home,'" *Independent Record* (Helena, Montana), June 3, 1989.
94. "Helena to Get 30 M1 Tanks," *Independent Record* (Helena, Montana), May 26, 1988, 1B.
95. Ibid.
96. "Guard Fires Live Anti-tank Missiles," *Independent Record* (Helena, Montana), June 16, 1989, 1A.
97. "Infantry Battalion Receives New TOW Vehicle," *Montana Guardsman*, Spring 1989, 1.
98. "Mean Machine," *Independent Record* (Helena, Montana), August 26, 1989.
99. Transition Paper, Major General James W. Duffy to Governor Ted Schwinden, December 1988.
100. The new policy implemented by the Department of the Army reorganized the Army around five corps and seven regiments. Two were to be deployed in Europe and three in the United States. Each state that served as a regimental headquarters, as Montana did, was given the responsibility to analyze the proposed changes and make recommendations on where units would be stationed. The Montana guard elected to station the brigade throughout the state. It was decided to not eliminate any community that had a unit up to the time of the 1988 reorganization, even though a specific unit's role might change.
101. Montana Army National Guard Press Release, December 16, 1987.
102. "Guard Re-organization - What Changes?" *Montana Guardsman*, Spring 1988.
103. Ibid.
104. Montana Army National Guard Press Release, December 16, 1987.
105. "Guard Revamp Boon to State," *Independent Record* (Helena, Montana), May 14, 1988; JDH collection, MHS.
106. "National Guard Units Change throughout the State," *Tribune* (Great Falls, Montana), September 2, 1988; JDH collection, MHS.
107. Ibid.
108. Montana National Guard Press Release.
109. "No Cuts for State's Guard," *Independent Record* (Helena, Montana), February 6, 1990; Holmes collection, MHS.

18

"Brave Cameras": 103rd Public Affairs Detachment, Gulf War, 1990–1991

Shirley Stephens

This victory belongs...to the regulars, to the National Guard. This victory belongs to the finest fighting force this nation has known in its history.—President George H.W. Bush, March 6, 1991.

On July 17, 1990, Saddam Hussein alleged that the Iraqi economy was suffering from collusion between the United States and the United Arab Emirates (UAE), a small but oil-rich state in the Persian Gulf. The Iraqi dictator claimed America and the UAE were "conspiring to cheat on oil production quotas previously set by the Organization of Petroleum Exporting Countries."[1]

The announcement was one of several justifications that Saddam used for an Iraqi military build-up along a disputed border with Kuwait, another small Persian Gulf country located on Iraq's southern border. In acquiring Kuwaiti oil fields, Saddam hoped to pay down his nation's foreign debt and replenish a treasury depleted by Iraq's war with Iran (1980–1988), and undertake ambitious reconstruction projects promised to his people. It also would contribute to making Iraq a leading Arab power and gaining a decisive role in world oil markets.[2] At 2 a.m. on August 2, 1990, two Iraqi Republican Guard armored divisions, a mechanized infantry division, and other forces invaded Kuwait; by 11 a.m. the Iraqis took control of Kuwait City, the capital. Baghdad Radio subsequently announced an Iraqi victory.[3]

By coincidence on the same day, President George H.W. Bush, when giving an address to a select audience at the Aspen Institute in Colorado, stated that the role of reserve forces was changing with the collapse of the Soviet Union: "The need to be prepared for a massive, short-term mobilization has diminished."[4] Although Congress currently supported a Total Force Policy in which the Army Reserve and National Guard played key roles during a mobilization, Secretary of Defense Richard Cheney and General Colin Powell, Chairman of the Joint Chiefs of Staff, advocated other ideas. They favored a comprehensive active-duty military structure known as the Base Force, which would not rely on mobilization of the reserves.[5]

This proposal, being quietly presented at the time, was a significant turnaround from the policy of the previous administration. Eight years earlier, in August 1982, Secretary of Defense Caspar Weinberger outlined the Reagan administration's Total Force Policy, which included "reserve forces as...an integral part of the total force, both within the United States and within NATO." On the other hand, the central premise of Bush's new, quietly proposed Base Force plan called for an inclusive active duty military force retaining superpower status. In the plan submitted to the White House at the end of 1990, the "active and reserve units previously assigned missions based on the threat of a short-notice global conflict would be eliminated." The events unveiling in the Persian Gulf that August, however, soon demonstrated that Bush had spoken prematurely. Retaining the Total Force concept would indeed prove essential in the war with Iraq, and it continued afterward.

Although Iraqi aggression in the Middle East appeared ominous on the international scene, many American reservists probably had little reason to believe that events in a far-off desert country would intersect with their lives.[6] Most were unaware of Washington, D.C., meetings on August 3 aimed at applying the Total Force Policy in response to events unfolding in Kuwait.[7] The National Guard Bureau chief, and the directors of the Army National Guard and Air National Guard, met to discuss options available to President Bush and the Department of Defense,[8] focusing on activating reserve units for a "partial or full mobilization."[9]

Two days later, President Bush declared that the United States was willing to use force if diplomatic efforts failed in freeing Kuwait. "This will not stand—this aggression against Kuwait."[10] Secretary Cheney met with nervous Saudi Arabian leaders on August 6 to inform them of the American resolve to halt Iraqi aggression.[11] A key component of the U.S.-Saudi relationship was a desire to protect Saudi oil fields. With Kuwait in Saddam Hussein's hands, Iraq would double its oil reserves, controlling 20 percent of the world's oil. As the Middle East scholar, Dilip Hiro, later noted, "this, and the unrivaled military power of Iraq in the region, would have made Saddam Hussein the most powerful figure in the Gulf,"[12] with the ability to "dictate the extraction rate of petroleum and thus its price, a position thus far enjoyed by Saudi Arabia, which aligned its oil policy with that of America."[13]

Previously, Cheney and Powell provided Prince Bandar, the Saudi's U.S. ambassador, with "satellite photographs to convince him that one of the three Iraqi armored divisions was advancing through Kuwait to the Saudi border."[14] To reassure Bandar that America was serious about halting Saddam Hussein and protecting the Saudi border, Powell revealed the Central Command (CENTCOM) top secret Operations Plan 90-1002, designed to protect Saudi Arabia. Headed by General Norman Schwarzkopf, CENTCOM was charged with over-seeing military intervention in the Persian Gulf area and identified Iraq as the most serious threat to regional stability. [15] The operations plan called for the deployment of 100,000 to 200,000 combat troops and three aircraft carriers to the Persian Gulf.[16]

The plan's success, however, depended upon the cooperation of the Saudi government. The United States would protect Saudi Arabia, but to do so it needed to establish military bases inside Saudi borders. Although an Iraqi patrol had, perhaps "accidentally," crossed into the Kuwaiti-Saudi Neutral Zone, the Saudis initially refused to allow the establishment of U.S. bases. While Saudi troops were placed on alert and the country's leaders accepted U.S. Air Force assistance, they did not believe at the time that their security required the presence of U.S. troops. Allowing Western soldiers into Saudi Arabia would present special problems for a regime dedicated to protecting Islam's most sacred sites—Saudi leaders feared that "accusations of defiling...holy places" would arise among their Muslim neighbors.[17]

Saudi Arabia's centrality to Islam was problematic for both Saudi and Western policymakers. Saudi Arabia was an Islamic country that prohibited "houses of worship for 'the people of the Book'—meaning Christians, Jews and Zoroastrians." Thus, the "whole...of Saudi Arabia" was considered "a mosque where two religions" could not co-exist.[18] Proselytizing by other religions was forbidden. Also, local religious police (*muttawin*) were charged with upholding Islamic practices, such as ensuring businesses closed-up during prayer times, women were modestly clothed and did not drive cars, and alcohol was not consumed in public or homes.[19] Saudi leaders feared that allowing the entry of thousands of Americans and other Westerners, especially female soldiers, might affect the country's strict religious and social order.[20]

In spite of these concerns—and Saddam Hussein's assurances that Iraq would not attack Saudi Arabia unless provoked—Cheney and Schwarzkopf on August 6 persuaded the Saudi's King Fahd to allow foreign troops inside the country's borders. The most persuasive argument came from satellite photos revealing Iraqi surface-to-air missiles in Kuwait aimed toward Saudi Arabia. Also, Iraq's warplanes could be armed with chemical agents.

With an agreement now in hand, President Bush moved rapidly, ordering General Powell "(a) to deter further Iraqi aggression, (b) defend Saudi Arabia, and (c) improve the overall defense capabilities of the Saudi" peninsula.[21] Aware that four months were needed to deploy a new minimum of 300,000 military personnel to the Persian Gulf, the Americans determined that liberating Kuwait had to wait for now, but a defensive plan for Saudi Arabia was immediately required.[22] On August 7, 48 advanced F-15 fighter jets and a brigade of 2,300 soldiers from the 82nd Airborne Division were deployed, arriving in Saudi Arabia two days later to take up defensive positions.[23] The next day, Bush announced to the world that "a line had been drawn in the sand" in Operation Desert Shield.[24]

At the same time, the Army reviewed an initial deployment list developed by the U.S. Army Forces Command and prepared a briefing paper for the Army National Guard titled "Reasons for 200K Call-Up." Key points included: (1) reserve components provided 70 percent of the Combat Support System, (2) the Gulf theater currently was "not prepared to support combat forces for long periods of time," and (3) the Total Force Policy was in effect.[25]

A day later, key Army National Guard personnel were briefed on Operation Desert Shield. Stephen Evans, the Assistant Secretary of Defense for Reserve Matters, hoped that reserve forces would be ordered to participate. "Only in that way," Evans explained, "could we bury the myth that the modern American reservist is less capable than his active-duty counterpart."[26] Indeed, on August 22, President Bush authorized the call-up of selected reserve units.[27] Although volunteers had served in Grenada in 1983 and Panama in 1989–1990, this would be the first time since 1968—the Vietnam War era—that an "American president had involuntarily activated…reservist[s] for an armed conflict."[28] On August 27, the Department of Army federalized 19 National Guard units from 13 states.[29]

Meanwhile, Saddam Hussein willingly defied UN Security Council sanctions, as well as the threat of a U.S. and allied commitment to roll back Iraqi aggression.[30] Saddam continued his plan to annex Kuwait as Iraq's "19th province." He answered Bush's November 8 order authorizing 100,000 more troops for the Gulf with his own escalation, promising to send an additional 250,000 Iraqi troops to Kuwait. Meanwhile, on November 29, the UN Security Council approved Resolution 678, authorizing the use of force to expel Iraqi troops if they were not withdrawn from Kuwait by January 15, 1991.

Preparing for the likelihood that Saddam would ignore the deadline, the United States continued to federalize reserve units. On December 5, Federal Orders No. 25, 26, and 27 authorized the activation of 27 guard units. Federal Order 26 specifically affected the Montana National Guard's 103rd Public Affairs Detachment (PAD), and outlined a timeline of service "for a period of six months unless sooner released or later extended."[31] The 13 out of 18 personnel in the 103rd PAD who eventually served in the Persian Gulf during Desert Shield/ Desert Storm included:

Major Patrick M. Hermanson
Captain Patrick J. Mohan
Captain Kareene F. Ostermiller
Captain David C. Thomas
Master Sergeant Jodie L. Yelton
Sergeant First Class David G. Sayre
Staff Sergeant Kermit M. Edmonds
Staff Sergeant Charles M. McLeod
Staff Sergeant Terrance M. Young
Sergeant Todd W. Buhmiller
Sergeant Roy A. Caldwell
Sergeant Greg A. Fox
Sergeant Andy L. Johnson

Nicknamed the "Brave Cameras," the 103rd Public Affairs Detachment was organized in the late 1950s and federally recognized on April 27, 1960.[32] In 1958, the PAD published *The Montana Militiaman*, a periodical covering National Guard news, events, and activities across the state. In 1984, 1986, 1988, and 1990, the unit traveled to South Korea for annual training in Operation Team Spirit, which included regular army, marine, navy, and air force contingents. In 1987, the 103rd PAD participated in Army exercises in Honduras and Panama to.[33]

To become a PAD member, a soldier underwent an "extra screening process." Those chosen became part of a select unit of journalism professionals. Major Patrick Hermanson, a U.S. Military Academy graduate who served as PAD's commanding officer from January 1987 to November 1993, explained that the guard had been "over strength" for years; consequently, this afforded the "luxury" of selecting highly qualified personnel with a genuine desire to be in the unit.[34] According to Sgt. Roy Caldwell, his initial interview was the hardest he ever experienced, and he had to present photography and writing samples. Joining PAD in 1989, he usually performed duties as a "46 Quebec"—an MOS acronym designating a photojournalist. Caldwell and other unit members, however, often were required to be jacks-of-all-trades. They shot and developed film, printed negatives, wrote stories, and assisted in editing and design lay-out.[35]

On December 10, 1990, Major Hermanson outlined the primary responsibilities that he expected might be assigned to the unit in Saudi Arabia.[36] PAD's Table of Organization (TOE) was divided into three sections: print journalism, community relations, and broadcasting. Hermanson believed that PAD could be used for both internal and external information functions. Internal, or command, information would go directly to soldiers in the field, providing them with a daily or weekly newspaper and relaying information about regional and world events. The external function, he explained, would provide "straight news or human interest stories...to commercial media or hometown releases."[37] Overall, the venture would give PAD a chance to showcase its journalistic expertise to a wider audience.

According to Staff Sgt. Terrance Young, PAD members had special opportunities, since the active military had relatively few public affairs photojournalists. Most units of this type were in the reserve forces.[38] Young also believed a call-up of the 103rd PAD made sense because of its mission and past experience in supporting regular Army units. For example, Capt. David Thomas, PAD's press officer, had served two 6-month active duty tours in Panama, assigned to the Southcom Public Affairs Theater Support Element. When in Korea, the unit had worked in the field, taking photographs and writing stories while living out of a rucksack. Both Sgt. Young and Capt. Thomas were confident that their training and overseas duty prepared them well.

Major Hermanson anticipated yet another role for the unit. He believed there were approximately "6,000 visas pending" from the "commercial media trying to get into Saudi Arabia,"[39] and the selected civilian media contingents would require military escorts in militarized zones. Indeed, this turn out to be one of PAD's major duties.[40]

Most in the PAD had some anxiety over how their families would cope without them—especially when leaving on such short notice. Sgt. Greg Fox expressed it this way: "It's making sure the house is ready for winter, cutting the firewood, just the dozens of little things that a person, a homeowner, and a family man always has on the back burner."[41]

There also was anxiety over the unknowns in a combat theater. Staff Sgt. Charles "Milo" McLeod observed that the period between the alert and actual mobilization was "probably one of the most difficult events I've gone through in my life and that includes a death in the family and divorce."[42] Having served in the infantry during the Vietnam War as both a rifleman and mortar man, McLeod was no stranger to danger.

Staff Sgt. Kermit Edmonds, teaching history at Hellgate High School in Missoula, explained that the veterans were especially anxious about the mobilization. Edmonds described McLeod as "a man…who has been in the thin haze of war… but he's a person who is true in what he assigns himself to do and what obligations he accepts. He of course was willing to do it."[43]

The Iraqi military's widely publicized development of chemical and biological weapons heightened concerns. Though PAD members would likely be positioned in rear areas, Sgt. Young believed there was a high probability of finding themselves interviewing and photographing soldiers in the front lines. All guard units, of course, had trained several times each year in Nuclear, Biological, and Chemical (NBC) warfare, following Mission-Oriented Protective Posture procedures. (MOPP involved familiarity with four levels of chemical/biological protective clothing and equipment). Hermanson expected their task might be difficult at times, but felt they could do the job.[44]

After PAD's mobilization on December 7, Edmonds, Thomas, and Caldwell went in advance to Fort Lewis, two days before the main group's arrival. Edmonds was chosen because of his experience as a supply sergeant; he would facilitate logistical requirements. When they arrived, the State Area Command had completed most of the necessary preparations for their transfer from National Guard to regular Army status.[45] After waving good-bye at the Helena airfield to families, friends, and fellow guard members, the remaining group members boarded a C-130 transport on December 10.

Although they expected immediate deployment overseas, 10 days were spent at Fort Lewis in refresher training, with the 525th Replacement Detachment overseeing PAD's mobilization, equipment needs, additional instruction, and briefings on Saudi culture and customs. Sgt. Fox recalled intense training in

NBC warfare. It was critical for them to become proficient in disassembling gas masks, replacing filters, and reacting to attacks quickly. PAD members also completed weapons qualifications, spending time on a firing range with the standard-issue .45 caliber pistol. "Now this had a sharp edge of immediate application," Edmonds explained.[46] A few days before leaving Fort Lewis, the group was notified of its assignment to the XVIII Airborne Corps Artillery in Saudi Arabia. Shortly, Major Hermanson communicated by telephone with the XVIII Airborne Public Affairs Office.[47]

Boarding a C-5A aircraft, they left on December 21. After a 4 hour layover at Westover AFB, Massachusetts, and a 10 hour wait in Torre de Cerredo, Spain, they arrived on December 24 at King Faud Air Base, the international airport in Dhahran, Saudi Arabia. Capt. Kareene Ostermiller, expecting a "horrible, heat filled, snake filled, scorpion infested place," was pleasantly surprised by "spring-like" weather and few insects.[48] They were picked up by members of the XVIII Airborne and trucked to a former cement factory on the outskirts of Dhahran, where a tent encampment served as a staging area.[49]

SFC David Sayre described "Cement City" as a "huge parking lot of tents and dirt and sand and filth and pestilence. And a lot of soldiers."[50] They would quickly encounter two difficulties: sand and loneliness. Trying to keep sand and dust at bay proved futile; everything was enveloped. Having arrived at Dhahran on Christmas Eve, they spent their first evening listening to carolers.[51] Thomas noted, as "Montanans, be it transplanted or not...we were basically family."[52]

Within hours of arrival, the Montana PAD received rather unwelcome news. They would be split into two cells—one serving with the 3rd Armored Cavalry Regiment (3rd ACR) from Fort Bliss, Texas, and the other with the XVIII Airborne Corps Artillery from Fort Bragg, North Carolina.[53] Still fatigued by jet lag, the unit officers responded immediately to a meeting called by Lt. Col. Ned V. Longsworth, the XVIII Airborne's public affairs officer and commander of National Guard PADs in the area. Longsworth, stationed outside of Dhahran at Dragon City—the XVIII Airborne Corps headquarters—informed the unit that they would serve as media escort rather than public affairs specialists.

The next day, Longsworth outlined a special mission for Capt. Ostermiller. She was assigned as an aide to Captain Edrington of the regular Army's 49th PAD from Fort Bragg, responsible for publication of the *Desert Dragon*. Ostermiller believed this assignment came to her both by "default" and by design. She had extensive writing experience and was the unit's only woman. As Edrington's aide, she would not move forward with the combat troops, but remain billeted in a villa with all the amenities of home. Ostermiller quickly voiced her objections to Capt. Edrington, noting that she was not his first choice anyway. Learning that Ostermiller preferred to go to the front and that Edrington had a replacement in mind, Lt. Col. Longsworth rescinded the original order, allowing Ostermiller to remain with the 103rd PAD.[54] Ostermiller requested assignment to the cell attached to the XVIII Airborne Corps Artillery.

As for the other unit members, Hermanson made assignments according to each soldier's MOS, prior service experience, and skills in photography, video tape, and broadcasting. Hermanson would lead the cell with the XVIII Airborne, while Capt. Thomas headed the 3rd ACR group.[55] Thomas' section included Capt. Patrick Mohan, SFC David Sayre, Staff Sgt. Milo McLeod, Sgt. Roy Caldwell, Sgt. Greg Fox, and Sgt. Andy Johnson—a combination that gave the cell both print and video proficiency. Major Hermanson's cell with the XVIII Airborne included Capt. Kareene Ostermiller, MSG Jodie Yelton, Staff Sgt. Kermit Edmonds, Staff Sgt. Terry Young, and Sgt. Todd Buhmiller.[56]

Dividing the unit into two components made for logistical problems—the Montana PAD had but one editing bay for broadcasting, one darkroom for making prints, and no central location for communications. Vehicles for hauling equipment also remained unavailable. Consequently, much of the equipment was stored at Dhahran.[57] In addition to logistical problems, separation was difficult. "It was kind of a frightening thing," Ostermiller later recalled.[58]

3rd Armored Cavalry Regiment

The cell assigned to the 3rd ACR deployed first, leaving Cement City on December 27. Provided with a Saudi bus, they loaded up and rode 60 miles north to Camp Foreign in Jubail. Here, they spent three days at Camp One, a former European oil workers compound occupied by the 3rd ACR. Thomas' initial contact with the commanding officers proved awkward because the 3rd ACR expected to support only two or three media personnel, not seven. Nevertheless, the 3rd assisted the cell as best it could under the circumstances.[59]

The PAD cell was not included in the 3rd ACR's supply plan. This meant they often found themselves without support items. Never issued light-colored Desert Cammies, they retained the darker Woodland Camo uniforms. After a short stay at Jubail in relatively pleasant surroundings with palm trees, prefabricated buildings, and a mess hall, the cell moved closer to the Kuwaiti border, where a tent city in the desert near Naiharia served as the 3rd ACR headquarters.

Being in a war theater, soldiers always kept gas masks close at hand; even the prefabricated shower stalls had nails for hanging gas masks during bathing. Across the border in Kuwait stood Saddam's army—the fourth largest in the world, and armed with modern Soviet equipment. In the forward American camps, everyone realized the possibility of an Iraqi Scud missile, artillery, or chemical weapons attack coming at any time.[60]

The 3rd Regimental Support Area became the home base and staging area for 2,000 troops. The encampment also included maintenance departments, refueling trucks, and a mobile hospital.[61] The 3rd Armored Cavalry officers were slow to accept the PAD cell, compounded by the fact they requested just two or three personnel and were not prepared for supporting seven. Moreover, a number of the professional soldiers were Vietnam veterans with a mistrust of the media; some also harbored skeptical views of the National Guard. The initial reception was unfriendly.[62] Despite this inauspicious start, Sgt. Fox recalled that once the cell began escorting the media, the 3rd ACR saw they could take care of themselves and the relationship improved.

Living conditions in the growing tent city were basic. All seven PAD members lived in a single general-purpose, or GP, tent. After a time, they managed to install an electric light system connected to a generator. Sgt. McLeod improved living conditions further by buying a small diesel stove for $9 on the "local economy" in a nearby town, Hafur-Al Batin. The stove heated MREs (Meals Ready to Eat) and coffee. Apples were the primary fresh food. Initially, they thought their colder climate sleeping bags would be inappropriate, but this proved not so. Desert nights often were cold; the warmer bags were welcome.[63]

They continued to be resourceful in making camp life more comfortable. While driving into Dhahran to a Saudi gas station, they managed to obtain mattresses for the cots and wood pallets for flooring. They acquired videocassette recorders and television sets; watching movies became a common nighttime activity. The cell also engaged in the soldiers' lively trade network among 3rd ACR personnel.[64]

A typical day's duty began at 5:30 a.m., and lasted 14 to 16 hours. As McLeod described it, this included "everything from drawing rations, fueling vehicles, burning shit, escorting the news media, transporting [news] product[s] from our civilian journalists…[and] transporting our commander to meetings and to the Regimental Tactical Operation Center which was about 12 miles away."[65]

At first, the PAD's escort duties were minimal because the 3rd ACR was being covered by just one civilian newsman—Bob Martin, a CBS journalist from Albuquerque, New Mexico. Martin earlier hooked up with the 3rd ACR in September at Ft. Bliss. Sgt. Roy Caldwell called Martin a "one man band," since he provided his own stand ups, sound, video, and writing.[66]

To complicate matters for the PAD, they were an awkward fit in a highly trained and mobile regimental team. McLeod described the 3rd ACR as a "lean, mean, hard charging combat arms unit. A scaled down division [with] 4,500 people in it rather than twelve to fifteen thousand, and everything about the Cavalry is geared to fight." Caldwell likewise described the 3rd as a "go, go, type of unit." Should an armored vehicle receive a hit in a combat situation, for example, other crews were trained to only briefly pause to determine if the vehicle remained operational. Dead and injured were to be left behind as other crews split up their members to get the vehicle back into action.[67]

As McLeod remembered, "it took awhile for us to win our spurs."[68] Nonetheless, most of the 3rd ACR's active regulars who interacted with the PAD came to respect the Montana men and their work. It proved beneficial that they all had prior military service, and that sergeants McLeod and David Sayre served in Vietnam, respectively as a combat infantryman and a Marine.

The lack of reliable transportation hindered the cell in providing media escort. Mostly they "hitched" rides, but occasionally were allowed a "deuce-and-a-half" truck. Eventually, after finally being assigned their own vehicles, it became considerably more convenient to transport dust-sensitive equipment into the field. By now, they were escorting two additional reporters—Lucian Perkins, a still photographer for the *Washington Post,* and Frank Bruni of the *Detroit Free Press.*[69] The morale of the frontline soldiers was boosted by knowing stories about the 3rd ACR were appearing in news reports across the United States.

While escorting civilian journalists, several PAD members found themselves near the "screen line" next to the Saudi border.[70] When CBS's Bob Martin conducted numerous interviews in late January and early February with tank and Bradley personnel, PAD members observed an Iraqi outpost with its flag flying.[71] When escorting Martin to Camp Cactus, a small R&R site,[72] McLeod had an opportunity to phone his wife, Janene Caywood, in Missoula. Just the night before, she had seen one of Martin's reports on national television. Since mail service was erratic and there were few phone centers, communicating with family back home was rare.[73]

Despite their primary mission of serving as media escort, PAD members remained committed to preparing their own news accounts, taking photos, and shooting video, though this material would largely remain unviewed until they returned to Montana.[74] They retrieved equipment from storage at the Dhahran International Hotel, and rigged a "big box container with doors in it" for the editing-bay and dark-room work.[75] They wired it, installed an exhaust fan, built tables for editing, and improvised a dark room in one section.[76]

Despite some frustration in the inability to get their own stories out, PAD members admired Martin's work and were pleased to support him. Martin had a personal interest in the 3rd ACR, sparked partly by his close association with the American Southwest—McLeod estimated that 30 to 50 percent of the cavalry unit came from Texas, New Mexico, and Arizona, with headquarters at El Paso. Although most of Martin's stories dealt with frontline infantry, tank, and helicopter personnel, he made an effort to cover support units. As a result, those watching Martin's stories on CBS affiliates or CNN saw reporting on the often unheralded but nevertheless essential work of truck drivers, fuel point operators, and water supply personnel.[77]

Later during the deployment, McLeod and Fox created considerable anxiety for the 3rd ACR's commanding officer, Col. Douglas Starr, when they filmed an Apache helicopter gunship accident. The commander's initial reaction toward McLeod and Fox was distrust for possibly "looking for sensational type stuff to sell to the media." When Capt. Thomas learned of this, he gathered up the report and film and immediately went to Col. Starr. Ultimately, the colonel appreciated the story and gained a new trust in the PAD cell's work. McLeod and Fox had shot photos and video while the helicopter's blades were fragmenting during the accident. These images later were integrated into a training film, cautioning helicopter pilots when landing or taking off in "brown out" conditions.[78]

Meanwhile on the international scene, Coalition forces in the Middle East had deployed to full strength and the standoff with Saddam Hussein finally came to a climax. When Iraq refused to comply with a mandated withdrawal from Kuwait on January 15, 1991, Coalition forces from a dozen countries—with U.S. personnel comprising 74 percent—began implementing the assault against the Iraqis. The air war began the next day, January 16; the ground attack would start in a little over five weeks. On the evening of January 15, just before the air assault began, Captain Snell of the 3rd ACR announced at a briefing: "It does not take a rocket scientist to know what is about to happen. In the morning you will be in protective suits with weapons, web gear, Kevlar helmet, body armor, and carrying your protective mask."[79]

Two hours after Operation Desert Storm began on January 16 with massive air and missile attacks against enemy installations in Iraq and Kuwait,[80] President Bush in a nationally televised address promised: "We will not fail." That same evening, the XVIII Airborne and the VII Corps formed a 120 mile long convoy on the Tapline Road west of Hafur-Al Batin, moving units and supplies in preparation for the ground war's prosecution in a few weeks.[81] In response, the Iraqis launched Scud missiles against Israel and Saudi Arabia. Saddam announced: "The great showdown has begun! The mother of all battles is under way."[82]

The PAD cell first learned about the start of the air war when Sgt. Sayre heard an announcement on Armed Forces Radio. Also, they could hear jets passing overhead.[83] McLeod felt a different reaction from what he experienced in Vietnam. In 1969 in Southeast Asia, American fatalities averaged as much as 200 a week. In the Persian Gulf, on the other hand, McLeod had confidence in the "overwhelming air superiority" and "fire power" of U.S. forces.[84] Some other PAD members, however, felt more anxious about the future.

The PAD expected to move forward with the troops,[85] and they anticipated there might be enemy ambushes and booby traps, or vehicle breakdowns, when traveling on the Tapline Road. Lacking M16 rifles, the PAD members felt vulnerable carrying only .45 caliber pistols and 21 rounds of ammunition. Eventually, they managed to obtain some M16s from the 3rd ACR.[86]

The Coalition ground offensive began on February 24, at 4 a.m., Saudi time. Security precautions in the 3rd ACR's forward area had been heightened, perimeter patrols increased, and MOPP precautions were in effect. PAD members would escort the three journalists —Bob Martin, Frank Bruni, and Lucian Perkins—across the border. Capt. Thomas and Sgt. McLeod went along with the Regimental Tactical Operations Center (RTOC), while Sgt. Johnson escorted correspondent Bob Martin, traveling with the tanks and Bradleys of the 1st Squadron. Sgt. Caldwell escorted Bruni and Perkins with the 3rd Squadron.[87]

The three squadrons attacked in a V-shaped pattern, spearheaded by the 2nd Squadron in front, and would eventually proceed 204 miles into Iraq. Traveling with the RTOC in the middle of the formation, McLeod and Thomas were three to five kilometers behind the lead tanks. McLeod recalled moving through a minefield "with artillery going off on all sides," and seeing eight Iraqis, with a Bradley's main gun trained on them, dropping their AK-47 rifles and surrendering.[88]

In the next four days, the Coalition's liberation of Kuwait proceeded swiftly on all fronts, handily routing Iraqi opposition. Having quickly advanced through Kuwait, the 3rd ACR with components of the 24th Infantry Division soon were poised to assault a main road in southern Iraq leading to the Euphrates River, along which the elite Iraqi Republican Guard was retreating. Shortly, however, the attack was called off when President Bush publicly announced a conditional cease-fire.

McLeod characterized the mood of the troops as jubilant, believing the fighting had ended. They were wrong. Iraqi soldiers fired on a helicopter crew flying to investigate a downed U.S. helicopter at an Iraqi held airfield. When the helicopter returned later in the day, the Iraqis fired again. Col. Starr was left with little choice but to order the 2nd Squadron to attack.[89] They secured the airfield after destroying a T-55, T-62, and several T-72 Soviet-built tanks. The Iraqi soldiers were aware of the cease-fire, but their commanders had given them a choice—fight or be shot. Thus, the airstrip battle was "unavoidable."[90]

When the airfield was secure, Bob Martin and Sgt. McLeod arrived on a Blackhawk helicopter to interview soldiers and photograph the knocked out enemy tanks, which the Iraqis had buried deep in sand to serve as artillery. The 3rd ACR during the next few days destroyed additional Iraqi equipment, ammunition, and about 500 AK-47s.[91]

The prisoners-of-war proved to be an unexpected spectacle; Sgt. Fox was surprised at their poor condition.[92] Many had occupied "bunkers that had been bombed," leaving them shell-shocked and seeming to "just stare off into space." They wore "torn, threadbare mismatching uniforms," and "old, beat-up loafers." Many were injured, and all were "under-fed" and "ill-equipped." They appeared relieved to be captured. Fox believed they received better treatment as prisoners than they had as soldiers in their own army. The injured were treated, and they were fed. "It was hard to believe it was an army," Fox observed. They resembled people who "had been shipwrecked for ten years."[93] These insufficiently trained and equipped soldiers were from Saddam's first line of defense, essentially ordered to perform sacrificial duty, often as enforced conscripts. His favored Republican Guard had been held back in interior positions.

Although Bob Martin hoped to be escorted to the large city of Basra in southern Iraq, the request was denied. U.S. and other Coalition forces were not allowed into that area. Meanwhile, the PAD cell's mission ended. Accordingly, they were ordered back to Saudi Arabia. Sgt. Johnson accompanied Martin, while Sgt. Caldwell escorted reporters Bruni and Perkins, on separate helicopters back to Dhahran. Thomas and McLeod drove in the one vehicle the PAD was allowed to take during the assault, and the others "hitched" rides back.[94]

The XVIII Airborne Corps Artillery

Staff Sgt. Kermit Edmonds recalled that their cell's new assignment began with something like "macabre humor." Most soldiers left Cement City in 2½ ton trucks, cut vees, or vehicles loaned by the Chrysler Corporation's Lee Iacocca or the Japanese. But Edmonds and his cell were picked up by a soldier driving a morgue truck—a large white van with a refrigerator unit on the front.

Major Ron Smith, the XVIII Corps Artillery personnel officer, greeted them at their duty station. Capt. Kareene Ostermiller was assigned to a tent with two female officers, but subsequently asked for her own tent. The request was honored. She moved into the "leakiest tent in the whole compound," but the extra space provided needed equipment storage for the cell.[95] The male personnel occupied two tents—a small GP tent shared by Major Patrick Hermanson, Master Sgt. Jodie Yelton, and Staff Sgt. Edmonds, while Staff Sgt. Terrance Young and Sgt. Todd Buhmiller occupied a decidedly unmilitary looking Bedouin tent.

Hermanson noted that regulars made a few untoward comments about their National Guard status, but he was surprised there was not more of this. The unit quickly gained credibility by becoming operational with 24 hours, rather than a week as General Nick Halley, the corps artillery commander, had predicted might happen.

Although ready to operate, the cell yet needed a facility for video editing. Capt. Scott Halacz, the XVIII Airborne's civil affairs officer, and Sgt. Akram Abuata, an interpreter, offered to introduce Ostermiller to Nasir, a local landlord renting billets to the military. En route to Nasir's residence, Ostermiller's group stopped at a local emir's home, where Ostermiller found herself surrounded by Saudi men, curious about whether she was a "normal" female. When informed that Ostermiller trained with men and handled weapons, the emir presented a baby to see if she had a "normal female response to the child."[96] The men seemed satisfied with her interaction, deciding that indeed she "was still a female."[97]

Later that day, Ostermiller and her regular Army entourage were invited to a lunchtime feast at Nasir's home. Knowing that Arab women did not eat with men, Ostermiller was surprised when they made an exception in her case. She sat to the host's right as a guest of honor. While the men ate yogurt and rice with their hands, she was allowed to use a spoon because she was a female. Ostermiller again was surprised when two Saudis showed up in camp the next day with a gift for her—a traditional Arab peasant woman's dress complete with a face veil and head covering. When she modeled the dress for the Saudis, they announced: "Now she is beautiful. Now Captain Halacz you can't look on her face any more. Now she is beautiful."[98]

Once the cell settled into their new quarters, they kept busy with the tasks at hand. Each day required performing vehicle maintenance before escorting newsmen. Digging bunkers became routine, but nevertheless General Halley expected them to produce daily stories, complete with photographs, for Fort Bragg and Fort Sill newspapers.[99]

They prepared detailed articles with photographs, but some frustration set in when their work often fell into a "black hole."[100] Frequently, photographs and undeveloped film were long delayed, came back misidentified, or never came back at all. As this mishandling of film products became repetitive and frustrating, Edmonds tried to insure accountability. He wrote his identity and unit name on an MRE ration box flap, and shot a picture of it as the first exposure on each roll of film. This proved effective. While they continued doing their job, however, little of their own work was released.

Most of the time, Major Hermanson focused on media escort, giving nightly briefings, and informing the command center about the cell's daily activities. In addition, he reviewed all media materials to ensure they met security standards before being sent out by courier to Dhahran for release. He relied on Ostermiller "to run the section" and to handle informal internal matters.[101]

The cell found that rules on media pool arrangements for Desert Shield/ Desert Storm differed substantially from previous media operations in Grenada and Panama. It was explained that more stringent control was necessary for security reasons. Journalists were "assigned" to particular units, and denied access to certain battlefield areas.[102] In the early stages of Desert Shield, Joint Information Bureau (JIB) officers escorted groups of reporters out into the field to spend a day or night. Once back at JIB, they filed their stories.[103] On January 10, a telecom from Washington, D.C., specifically outlined the types of access allowed to the media and how stories were to be reviewed before release.

A few days later, the JIB organized a "dry run of activation." According to Hermanson, it was "like an unannounced alert." Helicopters took members of the media out into the field. During this drill, Hermanson escorted three reporters from *Reuters*, the *Wall Street Journal*, and a Saudi newspaper.[104] During the second drill on January 14, as the air war was about to begin, a three-member CBS television crew, escorted by Hermanson, would remain in the field from that point on. Eventually, the Montana PAD cell also was assigned an independent photographer on contract to *Time* magazine, and a writer for the *Atlanta Constitution*. Thus, they had five newsmen to escort.

The reporters were unrelenting in their efforts to get as far forward as they could, but, due to existing media pool arrangements and restrictions, "every type of unit" already had assigned media.[105] Nevertheless, the reporters were determined to interview soldiers in units other than the XVIII Corps Artillery. Their persistence made Major Hermanson's job more difficult, since he was their primary contact, responsible for access, transportation, sleeping arrangements, and meals.[106]

In his role as liaison between the reporters and the troops, Hermanson found that most of the younger officers and soldiers welcomed a chance to talk to the media. However, he detected resistance from higher ranking XVIII Airborne officers, who yet harbored negative views regarding the media based on their Vietnam experiences. "They're still living back there in terms of how they perceived the media," Hermanson noted. They had a "paranoid feeling that somehow these media people were out to get them, to expose something or another, whatever that might be."[107] Although these commanders eventually came to know and accept the roles of the individual newsmen and the PAD cell, their general perceptions changed little. Some took advantage of their right to refuse interviews. Hermanson claimed that few commanders would "seek an opportunity to be interviewed."[108]

At 3 a.m. on January 17, a major from the XVIII Airborne's "squirrel's nest" (G-3 operations room) informed the PAD cell that U.S. ships in the Gulf had just launched missiles against Iraq—the major air assault had begun.[109] Cell members, now faced with the reality of being in an active war zone, contemplated what this meant for them. The camp remained eerily quiet, until the first Scud missile alert. Along with other personnel, the Montana guard members were ordered to don NBC suits, and, with their anti-nerve agent drugs in hand, head for the bunkers. No direct attack hit the camp. As the intensive air campaign continued in the following days, everyone remained on the alert.

Edmonds was assigned as the NCO commander for the relief guard, which stationed personnel around the camp. Finding no protective bunker near the relief personnel tent, he ordered all hands to gather and fill sandbags for an aboveground revetment. With this protection close at hand, men and women no longer need be exposed when scurrying over 100 yards to distant group shelters.

On January 20, the XVIII Airborne began deploying from central Saudi Arabia to positions just a few kilometers from the Kuwaiti border. The next day, Hermanson escorted reporters in the field artillery's forward march. Ostermiller felt the stress of their separation: "It was good-bye, have a nice war and I didn't think I'd ever see him again either."[110]

When the ground war began on February 24, the PAD cell's mission became more exposed.[111] XVIII Airborne artillery fired barrage after barrage, striking

Iraqi tanks, vehicles, and positions, as French light infantry moved out in front. The cell members at the base camp heard reports about the fighting and enemy body counts. They felt concern about the safety of Hermanson, as well as Sgt. Buhmiller, who likewise escorted reporters near the front. After troops crossed the Iraqi border at 4 a.m., Hermanson witnessed his first "fire mission," as the night sky was lit up by cannon fire and rockets from multiple launch systems.[112]

The reporters in Hermanson and Buhmiller's charge became more insistent about moving closer to the action. "They always wanted to go further up and if they could be where the eyeball to eyeball fighting was going on, that's where they wanted to be."[113] The reporters seemed fearless in their determination to move forward. Photographer Ken Jarecke, for example, insisted on taking photos of a knocked-out enemy tank, walking within 20 feet of the vehicle. It "was on fire and cooking off rounds that were dangerously close"[114] Pieces of the tank were falling off, while flames shot up 20 or 30 feet. Hermanson, meanwhile, moved his vehicle out of harm's way. Later that day, they encountered what became a familiar sight. Over 100 Iraq soldiers walked in from the desert to surrender to French troops, who were "disarming them, searching them, tying them up, putting them in back of trucks to move them out."[115]

Meanwhile, the other cell members moved north to Rafha, Saudi Arabia,[116] where the XVIII Airborne was headquartered. PAD members, however, were assigned to a camp 18 miles away in the middle of a "rock pile," making it extremely difficult to dig new bunkers. Ostermiller shared a space with Captain Colone, a Judge Advocate General officer. The two women spent the next three weeks digging in the hard ground, constructing a bunker. The wait in the desert was tedious, especially for Ostermiller, since it was inadvisable for women to venture into the nearby town due to Saudi cultural restrictions. In addition, Rafha was a border town occupied by outlaws, with weapons close at hand. They resented the military's presence since it put a damper on their gun running business.[117]

In the four day assault, the XVIII Airborne continued its artillery barrages in rain and sandstorms, and proceeded north to the major Baghdad-Basra highway. Objectives included the bluffs along the roadway, the As-Salman Airfield, the village of As-Salman, and another small town that had served as an Iraqi Army regional headquarters. By the morning of February 27, Hermanson, Buhmiller, and the reporters they were escorting had fallen back to the "headquarters element" of the corps artillery. Understanding that a conditional cease-fire was imminent, they received permission from the chief of staff to move out to the 24th Infantry Division's field of operations.[118] When the cease-fire was confirmed, they were photographing prisoners-of-war at one of the collection points.[119]

With the war over,[120] Hermanson informed the reporters that they could go back to Rafha, to Hafur-Al Batin (the public affairs center at King Kaleed Military City), or to Dhahran. Without hesitation, the five reporters requested to be taken to Kuwait City. Although not entirely clear about where Highway 8 led, PAD's two vehicles followed it, heading farther east. They saw Iraqi corpses lying along the highway among destroyed and abandoned vehicles and artillery.[121]

Passing through Coalition check points, they reached the farthest-advanced U.S. forces on the highway—the 24th Infantry Division. The brigade commander was not pleased to see Hermanson and his entourage. His soldiers had spent "four days straight prosecuting the war," and he did not want them appearing on television looking "scruffy." After instructing a lieutenant to find his "best looking soldier" for an interview, the commander himself also agreed to talk with the reporters. After the officer impressed upon Hermanson how unsafe the area was, the media group left toward Kuwait City.

By late evening, after following a circuitous route taking them past more than 150 burning oil wells sabotaged by retreating Iraqis, they approached the "highway of death," on Route 80 out off Kuwait City. Hundreds of Iraqi vehicles destroyed by Coalition air power lay in littered masses, which slowed Coalition traffic to a meandering crawl along the roadway.

Arriving in Kuwait City around 5 a.m., they found that CBS reporters had preceded them and were up-linking information in downtown Kuwait where a JIB sub-office was set up in a hotel. The reporters decided to remain here, allowing Hermanson and Buhmiller to rejoin the PAD cell. They returned to Rafha and immediately found a hotel room; Capt. Thomas joined them there the next day. As the three were cleaning their weapons the next evening, Hermanson accidentally discharged a .45 caliber pistol, striking his heel, a not uncommon injury with this sidearm in decades of use by U.S. servicemen. After surgery that evening at a field hospital, he was transported by airlift to Nuenburg, Germany.[122]

Meanwhile, during the four-day ground campaign, the other cell members—Capt. Kareene Ostermiller and sergeants Jodie Yelton, Kermit Edmonds, and Terrence Young—also had crossed the border into Iraq. Traveling 125 miles, they endured three days with little sleep while accompanying a supply convoy following engineer units clearing land mines. After the fourth day, despite the ceasefire announcement, some sporadic fighting continued. Ostermiller sent Jodie Yelton and Kermit Edmonds forward with the XVIII Corps artillery commander's group.[123] This left Ostermiller and Young with the responsibility of getting the PAD's vehicles back to Saudi Arabia.[124]

During this last mission, Edmonds photo-documented the brigadier general and his staff interviewing a captured Republican Guard commander. The Iraqi general told a half-circle of high-ranking American officers, "the people in Basra are rioting"—rebelling over Saddam's rule, and doing so in the belief that the Coalition would support the Iraqi people if they resisted their Baghdad oppressor.

With a sinking heart, Edmonds knew the Coalition had no authorization to provide direct assistance; the populace of this largely Shiite region stood alone. The subsequent retaliation by Saddam's forces, using helicopter gun ships not surrendered to Coalition forces due to deception, resulted in thousands of casualties in putting down the revolt.

Before Ostermiller and Young began the return trip, they learned of Hermanson's injury and his evacuation to Germany. Accordingly, Ostermiller took command of the PAD group. Her orders were to "regroup everyone and get them home."[125] She and Young began their trip back to the base camp in cold rain and mud. When eventually arriving at Camp Cactus, the other cell members with the 3rd ACR were located just north. Shortly, they had a "little family reunion."[126]

The rejoined group returned to Dhahran, billeting at a Saudi Arabia National Guard compound. They learned they would be going home in a week if they completed their duties. After setting up a darkroom in a laundry room and working days and night, they managed to print 1,200 pictures. Although many of the prints were for the public affairs office, some were used to compile their own scrapbooks.[127]

Meanwhile, there was a snafu in the PAD's rotation to leave Saudi Arabia.[128] Ostermiller worked tirelessly to find space on a flight, and, after a two-week wait, they finally departed. When they flew over the Statue of Liberty, "the pilot said, 'We are now in the United States of America,' the whole plane cheered." Disembarking at JFK Airport in New York City, they were greeted with a welcoming ceremony, complete with lunch. Proceeding to Fort Bragg, a National Guard liaison officer met the plane and escorted them to a welcome home party on the post. After three days of travel, the 103rd's PAD finally arrived at Fort Lewis and a greeting by the Montana National Guard's adjutant general, well wishers, welcome-home banners, and a band.[129]

In Helena on April 6, they were greeted by Governor Stan Stephens, reporters, fellow guardsmen, and, most importantly, family members. A large room was reserved in the airport for a welcome home ceremony and their dismissal from active duty. After giving an address, Governor Stephens pinned Montana National Guard Distinguished Service Medals on their uniforms.[130]

Capt. David Thomas summarized the experience and the pride that the PAD members felt on their return. "I feel that the job we did over there in keeping the American public informed on what was happening…met the needs of the nation. I think we did Montana and the Army proud."[131]

Notes

1. Stephen Duncan, *Citizen Warriors: America's National Guard and Reserve Forces and the Politics of National Security* (Novato, California: Presido Press, 1997), 5. Duncan served under presidents Reagan and Bush as the Assistant Secretary of Defense for Reserve Mat-

ters. His responsibilities included oversight of the Army National Guard, Air National Guard, Air Force Reserve, Army Reserve, Marine Corps Reserve, and the Naval Reserve.

2. Lawrence Freedman and Efraim Karsh, *The Gulf Conflict, 1990–1991: Diplomacy and War in the New World Order* (Princeton: Princeton University Press, 1993), 62.
3. Conquering Kuwait would put Saddam in a position to control one-fifth of the world's oil reserves. Leaders in Washington felt "Iraq would be able to manipulate oil prices and hold the U.S. and its allies 'at its mercy.'" The George H.W. Bush administration also feared that higher oil prices would "fuel inflation, worsening the 'already gloomy condition' of the American economy," and Secretary of Defense Cheney stated, "the marriage of Iraq's military of one million men with 20 percent of the world's oil presented 'a significant threat.'" Dilip Hiro, *Desert Shield to Desert Storm: The Second Gulf War* (New York: Routledge, 1992), 108.
4. Duncan, *Citizen Warriors*, 4.
5. It was assumed that the reserve forces role later could be reconstituted should a resurgent threat arise elsewhere in the community of nations. Ibid., 170, 181, 249.
6. Ibid., 5. Events in the Gulf region would result in the first activation of a Montana Army National Guard unit since World War II, though Montana Air Guard units were activated for stateside duty from April 1, 1951, to January 1, 1953, during the Korean War.
7. Because of Congressional support for the Total Force military structure, President Bush's remarks for the Aspen meeting were prepared quietly. Hence, military leaders meeting in Washington in early August may have been unaware of the push for adopting the Base Force policy. Ibid., 4.
8. "Army National Guard After Action Report: Operation Desert Shield, Operation Desert Storm, 2 August 1990–28 February 1991, The Army National Guard as a Strategic Force," [hereafter cited as "After Action Report"] (National Guard Bureau, June 28, 1991), 115.
9. Ibid. Congress approved legislation in 1976 establishing the Total Force Policy, giving the president authority to "involuntarily activate members of the selected reserve without congressional approval, 'to augment the active forces for any operational mission.'" Title 10, U.S. Code, Section 673b. Subsequent amendments to Section 673b authorized the president to activate 200,000 selected reservists for up to 180 days. The "selected reserve" would consist of those units and individuals in the National Guard and federal reserve components designated by their respective military services and approved by the Joint Chiefs of Staff as being essential to initial wartime missions. They held priority over other reserve forces. Duncan, *Citizen Warriors*, 250; Title 10, U.S. Code, Section 269b; "After Action Report," 115.
10. Hiro, *Desert Shield to Desert Storm*, 116.
11. "After Action Report," 116.
12. Hiro, *Desert Shield to Desert Storm*, 113.
13. Ibid.
14. Ibid., 109.
15. Freedman and Karsh, *The Gulf Conflict*, 85. CENTCOM could mobilize 400,000 troops and "exercised control over all US forces in South Asia, the Middle East and East Africa, encompassing 19 countries. Its mission was to defend US interests in the region: strategic oil reserves, shipping lanes and international waterways." Operations Plan 90-1002 evolved out of a Rapid Deployment Force plan that in 1979 "visualized fighting the Soviets or Iran in the Gulf." Hiro, *Desert Shield to Desert Storm*, 107.
16. Ibid., 109.

17. Freedman and Karsh, *The Gulf Conflict*, 87.
18. Hiro, *Desert Shield to Desert Storm*, 288.
19. Ibid.
20. Capt. Kareene Ostermiller would be the only female MNG soldier deployed to Saudi Arabia. The 103rd Public Affairs Detachment commander, Major Patrick Hermanson, noted that she "would have a harder time" because of Saudi culture, but believed that as long as Ostermiller was in uniform, American soldiers would not treat her any differently because she was a woman, and she was fully prepared for any reaction the Saudis might have. Oral History [hereafter cited as OH] 1242, Patrick Hermanson, December 10, 1990, oral history interview by John Terreo [hereafter cited as Terreo], Twentieth Century Montana Veterans Oral History Project [hereafter cited as Oral History Project], Montana Historical Society [hereafter cited as MHS] Archives, Helena, Montana, 11.
21. Hiro, *Desert Shield to Desert Storm*, 116. King Fahd insisted that an agreement with President Bush include a guarantee that U.S. military forces would leave Saudi Arabia once Iraq no longer posed a threat.
22. Ibid.
23. The 82nd Airborne Division was a subordinate unit of the XVIII Airborne Corps.
24. Duncan, *Citizen Warriors*, 15.
25. "After Action Report," 116.
26. Duncan, *Citizen Warriors*, 21; "After Action Report," 126. Combat units were deleted from the FORSCOM Force list. On November 4, however, the Department of Defense announced that it would "call-up reserve combat units," and "Congress extended the 673b call-up authority for 360 days for combat units." Ibid., 147.
27. E.O. 12727, cited in Duncan, *Citizen Warriors*, 48.
28. Ibid., 6; "After Action Report," 126.
29. Ibid., 128.
30. On August 6, the UN Security Council passed Resolution 661 imposing economic sanctions against Iraq and occupied Kuwait, including a worldwide ban of oil exports. The resolution did allow for food to be shipped into Iraq and Kuwait "in humanitarian circumstances." In addition, the council condemned the annexation of Kuwait by passing Resolution 662, "declaring Iraq's annexation of Kuwait null and void." Duncan, *Citizen Warriors*, 116–17, 504–5.
31. Order 26 dtd 041422Z DEC 90. "Permanent Orders 1-1," December 7, 1990, Personal File of Col. Raymond Read, Public Affairs Officer, Public Affairs Office (PAO), Montana National Guard Headquarters (MT-ARNG HQ), State Area Command (STARC), Helena, Montana. Staff Sgt. Charles "Milo" McLeod recalled that soon after the PAD was activated, they learned about a Presidential Order that reserves could be extended for active duty up to one year, with a one-year extension. OH 1465, Charles "Milo" McLeod, June 1, 1991, Terreo, Oral History Project, MHS Archives, Helena, Montana, 3–4.
32. The term "Brave Cameras" was coined in the early 1980s as a 103rd response to a similar term, "Brave Rifles," a motto adopted by the 3rd Armored Cavalry Regiment at Fort Bliss, Texas. The 103rd Public Affairs Detachment began calling itself "Brave Cameras" while supporting the 1981 Operation "Border Star" with the 3rd Armored Cavalry Regiment. The term stuck. In the December 4, 1992, official program for the change of command of the 103rd Public Affairs Detachment from Major Patrick Hermanson to Capt. Kareene Ostermiller, the text refers to the PAD's service in Desert Shield/Desert Storm, stating they earned the nickname "Brave Cameras." "103rd Public Affairs Detachment: 'Brave Cameras,' Change of Command," (Helena, Montana, December 4, 1993), Montana

Military History Museum [hereafter cited as MMHM], Library Archives [hereafter cited as LA], Fort William H. Harrison, Helena, Montana.

33. "Change of Command." OH 1258, Staff Sgt. Kermit Edmonds, February 13, 1992, Terreo, Oral History Project, MHS Archives, Helena, Montana, 7.
34. OH 1242, Hermanson, 8.
35. OH 1221, Roy Caldwell, December 9, 1990, Terreo, Oral History Project, MHS Archives, Helena, Montana, 2–3.
36. The 20th Century Montana Military Veterans Oral History Project includes the recollections of Montana's veterans. Interviews were conducted with veterans from World War I through the Persian Gulf War. John Terreo conducted sessions with the members of the 103rd PAD who served in Desert Shield/Desert Storm.
37. OH 1242, Hermanson, 8.
38. OH 1223, Terrance Young, December 9, 1990, Terreo, Oral History Project, MHS Archives, Helena, Montana, 8. Young was a photojournalist with the 103rd PAD, and served as the editor of *The Montana Militiaman.*
39. OH 1242, Hermanson, 10.
40. Unit Commander Major Patrick Hermanson believed that the PADs were being deployed to "get access to Captains and Majors to do media escort duties." He explained that previously the Army used a press camp headquarters with "brand new Second Lieutenants... who had not been to...the Defense Information School." They were replaced with PADs due to having little experience in dealing with the national media and having limited knowledge regarding Army personnel and equipment. OH 1469, Patrick Hermanson, August 3, 1992, Terreo, Oral History Project, MHS Archives, Helena, Montana. 10.
41. OH 1241, Greg Fox, December 9, 1990, Terreo, Oral History Project, MHS Archives, Helena Montana, 13.
42. OH 1224, Charles "Milo" McLeod, December 9, 1990, Terreo, Oral History Project, MSH Archives, Helena Montana, 11.
43. OH 1258, Edmonds, 12.
44. OH 1242, Hermanson, 14.
45. Consequently, the transfer of the 103rd PAD to regular army full-time status was quick and efficient.
46. OH 1468, Greg Fox, February 11, 1991, Terreo, Oral History Project, MHS Archives, Helena, Montana, 1–3. OH 1258, Edmonds, 22.
47. OH 1469, Patrick Hermanson, August 3, 1992, Terreo, Oral History Project, MHS Archives, Helena, Montana, 4.
48. OH 1463, Kareene Ostermiller, August 4, 1992, Terreo, Oral History Project, MHS Archives, Helena, Montana, 8.
49. OH 1468, Fox, 4–5.
50. Oh 1457, David Sayre, June 1, 1991, Terreo, Oral History Project, MHS Archives, Helena, Montana, 2.
51. Because of rigid religious restrictions imposed by Saudi authorities, traditional American holidays with religious overtones were only held on military installations, away from the Saudi public. They celebrated "Christmas with church services and turkey dinner...and bands of carol singers obliged to restrict themselves to non-religious Christmas songs like 'Jingle Bells.'" Hiro, *Desert Shield to Desert Storm,* 289. According to Edmonds, "the lack of alcohol, the lack of contact with the natives probably produced one of America's cleanest campaigns in terms of behavior with the host country." OH 1258, Edmonds, 42–44.

52. OH 1197, David C. Thomas, March 19, 1993, Terreo, Oral History Project, MHS Archives, Helena, Montana, 10.
53. The 3rd Armored Cavalry Regiment included four squadrons—a flying squadron, and three tank squadrons. The XVIII Airborne Corps Artillery consisted of a "Headquarters and Headquarters Battery for command and control and a varying arrangement of subordinate brigades, groups, battalions and batteries. In Operation Desert Shield/Desert Storm the XVIII Airborne Corps controlled the fires of the 18th, 75th, and 212th Field Artillery Brigades and the artilleries of the Corps' four divisions—a potent combination of towed 105mm and 155mm howitzers, self-propelled 155mm and 8-inch howitzers, and the Multiple Launched Rocket System (MLRS) family of weapons including the Advanced Tactical Missile System (ATACMS)." Newspaper clipping file, MMHM, LA, Fort William H. Harrison, Helena, Montana. Sgt. Roy Caldwell recalled that during their stay and training at Fort Lewis, the Sixth Army Command Headquarter advised them the unit would be tasked as a media escort unit. OH 1564, Roy Caldwell, June 24, 1991, Terreo, Oral History Project, MHS Archives, Helena, Montana, 8. Hermanson received news of the order to split the PAD on the second day in Saudi Arabia when he met with the Corps' public affairs officer. The officer briefed him on their new assignment, how they were to be organized, and how they could best support the XVIII Airborne Corps. Hermanson would have preferred to keep the unit intact. OH 1469, Hermanson, 4, 10.
54. OH 1463, Kareene Ostermiller, August 4, 1992, Terreo, Oral History Project, MHS Archives, Helena, Montana, 10–12.
55. Ibid., 12.
56. The Corps' public affairs officer recommended that Hermanson assign Ostermiller to the XVIII Airborne Corp because, "the 3rd ACR was kind of a front line maneuver fighting force." OH 1469, Hermanson, 7.
57. Equipment was left at the Joint Information Bureau in Dhahran. Ibid., 6.
58. OH 1463, Ostermiller, 17.
59. OH 1197, David C. Thomas, March 19, 1993, Terreo, Oral History Project, MHS Archives, Helena, Montana, 14.
60. Ibid., 5–7.
61. Ibid., 19.
62. OH 1468, Fox, 8.
63. Ibid, 7.
64. Ibid., 14–16.
65. OH 1465, McLeod, 8–11.
66. Sgt. Caldwell described Martin as "probably the most dedicated, most sensitive news person in the theater," who "cared about the troops [and]…about getting the soldiers' story out and he did." OH 1564, Caldwell, 19.
67. Ibid., 14–15.
68. OH 1465, McLeod, 20.
69. OH 1468, Fox, 10.
70. Troops in a "screen line" position protected the movement of a large force.
71. During Operation Desert Shield, the "regiment became part of the covering force positioned to defend Saudi Arabia against an Iraqi attack. Arrayed in front of the regiment was a thin screen of Saudi and Gulf Cooperation Council forces." Sean D. Naylor, "Home of the Brave: Desert Doesn't Scare 3d ACR," "Desert Storm After-Action Review," *Army Times*, January 27, 1992, 13. Newspaper clipping file, MML, LA, Fort William H. Harrison, Helena, Montana. Bradley Fighting Vehicles, named after famed WWII General

Omar Bradley (also a Chairman of the Joint Chiefs of Staff), are armed with a 25-mm rapid-fire cannon, a machine gun, an anti-tank missile launcher, and portals for firing light weapons.

72. After two or three weeks in the field, soldiers were given 24 hours of "rest and relaxation," allowing them to clean equipment, enjoy hot meals, do laundry, and sleep on cots.
73. OH 1465, McLeod, 14.
74. McLeod characterized their assignment in the desert as about 70 percent providing media escort, and 20 or 30 percent "historical documentation of the daily life in the Cav and the events in Iraq. And then maybe another 5 or 10 percent to actually write some stories." Ibid., 22. Caldwell described the stories that General Halley wanted as "gun bunny pictures and little short stories." According to Caldwell, Edmonds was concerned about the importance of preserving a historical record of their time in Desert Shield/Desert Storm. Caldwell explained that Edmonds wrote some "great" stories, but they did not interest the general because he thought they were too long. They did not fit his requirement for brief accounts known as "grip and grins." OH 1464, Caldwell, 20.
75. OH 1468, Fox, 11–12.
76. Ibid. Several stories that PAD members wrote during Desert Shield/Desert Storm were published afterward in the 3rd ACR's newspaper at Fort Bliss, Texas. OH 1566, Roy Caldwell, Terreo, Oral History Project, MHS Archives, Helena, Montana, 18. The situation in the desert was considerably different from former overseas training exercises. Here, the public affairs office was set up "like a press camp headquarters," which directed personnel to events it wanted covered, while also controlling transportation and facilities. Sgt. Caldwell believed the system gave local commanders too much leeway in stymieing the efforts of the press—be it civilian or National Guard. Ibid., 8.
77. Ibid., 24–25.
78. The helicopter accident occurred on February, 5, 1991. OH 1197, Thomas, 20–21.
79. Roy H. Caldwell, "A Report from Helena at the Persian Gulf," *Independent Record*, Newspaper clipping file, MML, LA, Fort William H. Harrison, Helena, Montana. The XVIII Airborne Corps assumed the Mission-Oriented Protective Posture Level I; soldiers began taking anti-nerve agent pills in readiness for combat. Kevin Don Hutchison, *Operation Desert Shield/Desert Storm: Chronology and Fact Book* (Westport: Greenwood Press, 1995), 67. CENTCOM reported 422,041 personnel, 383 attack helicopters, 1,120 support helicopters, 1,110 main battle tanks, 2,426 assorted armored fighting vehicles, 711 artillery pieces, 121 MLRS, and 18 tactical missile systems poised for battle on January 15, 1991. Ibid.
80. "From Desert Shield to Desert Storm: A Chronology," *Great Falls Tribune*, March 10, 1991, 3. Newspaper Clipping File, MML, LA, Fort William H. Harrison, Helena, Montana.
81. Hutchison, *Chronology and Fact Book*, 69.
82. "From Desert Shield to Desert Storm: A Chronology," *Great Falls Tribune*, March 10, 1991, 3.
83. OH 1465, McLeod, 18–19.
84. Ibid.
85. The 3rd Armored Cavalry' first limited ground engagement occurred after the air war began; two soldiers were wounded. Ibid., 21.
86. OH 1465, McLeod, 24; OH 1468, Fox, 19–20.
87. The XVIII Airborne and R-SENT supplied the PAD with three civilian vehicles—two Jeep Cherokees and a Nissan Patrol. As the launch of the ground war neared, Col. Douglas

Starr informed the troops that no civilian vehicles would be allowed to accompany the 3rd ACR, making it necessary for PAD members moving forward to "hitch" rides.

88. OH 1465, McLeod, 26–27.
89. President Bush ordered a cease-fire, commencing at midnight, EST, February 28. General Schwarzkopf's orders were for Coalition forces to "cease all offensive operations...Remain in current positions and assume defensive posture. Wartime rules of engagement remain in effect. Be prepared to resume offensive operations. Forces are allowed to defend themselves." Hutchison, *Chronology and Fact Book*, 135–36.
90. OH 1465, McLeod, 27–29.
91. In an article for the *Monitor* of Fort Bliss, Texas, McLeod detailed the accomplishments of the 3rd ACR between February 25 and March 1: "They captured over 500 enemy prisoners of war, thousands of tons of Iraqi equipment, (including trucks, artillery pieces, small arms and ammunition)." Charles M. McLeod, *Monitor*, March 21, 1991, Vol. XVI, No. XI, 2, 28. Newspaper clipping file, MML, LA, Fort William H, Harrison, Helena, Montana.
92. The Iraqi forces included 510,000 troops, 4,000 tanks, 2,500 armored combat vehicles, and 2,700 artillery pieces. Hiro, *Desert Shield to Desert Storm*, 292.
93. OH 1468, Fox, 32.
94. OH 1465, McLeod, 32.
95. OH 1463, Ostermiller, 19. At the Corps Artillery Headquarters, Captain Ostermiller noted that there were eight enlisted women and three female officers. In the corps artillery, which included three field artillery brigades, 75 of the 3,500 personnel were females. OH 1463, Ostermiller, 45.
96. OH 1463, Ostermiller, 21.
97. Ibid.
98. Ibid., 24. While Ostermiller was pleased by the gift, other women were not. Another female captain "thought it was absolutely disgusting. She saw it as a subjugation." Ibid., 29–31.
99. Although Major Hermanson identified General Halley as the commander of the corps artillery, he does not seem to be listed in Hutchison's chronology and fact book on Desert Shield/Desert Storm. Hutchison, *Chronology and Fact Book*, 224.
100. OH 1258, Edmonds, 35.
101. OH 1469, Hermanson, 12.
102. Caldwell believed the Pentagon misrepresented the access that the international press would have. Instead, a tight control of the press was implemented, and few journalists during the brief conflict were able to argue about the restricted arrangements. Caldwell felt that military pubic affairs offices intentionally sanitized the war, making it seem little more than a "high tech" engagement where "real" people seldom died or shed blood. "I think the American public has got a very thin, a very narrow, and a very high tech view of the whole conflict," Caldwell stated. "The great video of the smart bombs and all that other high tech jazz...[was] probably ten percent or less of the whole conflict." OH 1566, Caldwell, 29, 34, 36.
103. Central Command established two separate Joint Information Bureaus—in Riyadh and Dhahran. The Riyadh bureau was "primarily responsible for the command level briefings to the media. The Dhahran JIB was responsible for the civilian media/military public affairs interface." OH 1566, Caldwell, 3.
104. OH 1469, Hermanson, 14.

105. Although civilian journalists had the technology with them to "up-link information right from the field," the Department of Defense banned this type of unsupervised reporting, insisting that all reports be filtered through Joint Information Bureaus. The JIB set up a courier system whereby reports were picked up at designated drop-off points and taken to the military's public affairs offices at King Kaleed Military City. Ibid., 25.
106. The PAD cell was assigned a cut-vee regular Dodge pickup, and two Jeep Cherokees donated by Japan. When picking up the jeeps in Dhahran on January 15, Captain Ostermiller learned that females were no longer allowed to drive on Saudi roads, regardless of wearing a uniform or having a male escort. This restriction was put into place to avoid any incidents with local Saudis. OH 1463, Ostermiller, 29.
107. OH 1469, Hermanson, 15.
108. Ibid., 16.
109. The air war officially began with "radar-evading Stealth bombers aiming precise laser-guided Paveway bombs at key targets in Baghdad." During the first 24 hours, the USS *Wisconsin* and USS *Missouri* fired more than 100 Tomahawk cruise missiles at Iraqi command, control, and communication centers. Hiro, *Desert Shield to Desert Storm*, 321.
110. OH 1463, Ostermiller, 35.
111. The 18th Artillery Brigade followed close behind French light infantry troops in the western corridor of operations.
112. OH 1469, Hermanson, 26.
113. Ibid., 25.
114. These photos were featured in *Time* magazine and other publications. Ibid., 26.
115. Ibid., 27.
116. Ibid.
117. OH 1463, Ostermiller, 39–40.
118. The 24th Infantry Division during the early morning hours of February 27 secured the Jalibah Airfield, destroying 14 MIG fighters in the process. "At 40 MPH, Bradley and Abrams drivers move[d] down Highway 8 encountering huge logistics and ammunitions sites and scattered elements of the al-Faw, Nebuchadnezzar and Hammurabi Republican Guard Divisions." Hutchison, *Chronology and Fact Book*, 133.
119. The cease-fire, commencing at midnight, EST, February 28, required Iraq to release all allied prisoners of war and accept all UN resolutions. "After Action Report," 181.
120. President Bush announced in a public address: "Kuwait is liberated. Iraq's Army is defeated." Hutchinson, *Chronology and Fact Book*, 133. Coalition casualties included 776 injured, and 240 killed in action. U.S. forces suffered 458 wounded and 148 dead, of which almost a quarter resulted from "friendly fire." During the 26 days of the air war, an estimated 19,000 Iraqi soldiers and 1,000 civilians died while 60,000 were wounded. U.S. officials estimated an additional 10,000 Iraqi KIA during the land war. Freedman, *The Gulf Conflict*, 408. OH 1469, Hermanson, 29.
121. These Iraqi forces had been assaulted by the U.S. 24th mechanized infantry and by U.S. attack helicopters. Hiro, *Desert Shield to Desert Storm*, 390.
122. After spending four days in Germany, Hermanson was transported to the United States for treatment, arriving at Fort Lewis a few days before the Montana PAD's arrival on April 5. OH 1469, Hermanson, 38.
123. Ostermiller described Sgt. Edmonds as being an excellent chronographer and photographer, and detail-oriented. OH 11463, Ostermiller.
124. Edmonds and Yelton did not rejoin the remaining PAD members until they all regrouped in Dhahran.

125. Ostermiller was unable to establish contact with Hermanson after he was evacuated to Germany. She did not speak with him again until the PAD unit returned to Fort Lewis. OH 11463, Ostermiller, 55.
126. Edmonds and Yelton came into the camp the next day.
127. OH 1464, Young, 31.
128. They had not been put into the rotation.
129. OH 1465, McLeod, 34.
130. Ken Pekoc, "Guard Is Home," *Helena Independent Record*, April 7, 1991, 1. Thomas was diagnosed as needing surgery after arriving at Fort Lewis; he did not accompany the PAD unit's return to Helena. OH 1197, Thomas, 37.
131. OH 1197, Thomas 39.

19

Launching an Air Squadron into the Big Sky

Diane L. Krahe

The Great Falls Municipal Airport and the City meet the minimum requirements as outlined...[and the squadron] could be based here without delay.—Fritz Norby, Mayor of Great Falls, March 1946.[1]

On June 27, 1947, the federal recognition ceremony for the 186th Fighter Squadron, Montana's first Air National Guard unit, lacked U.S. government dignitaries, fighter planes, and pretension. Local and state notables attended the ceremony at the Great Falls Municipal Airport, but representatives from the U.S. Army Recognition Board failed to show-up, leaving the squadron commander scurrying to secure authorization to activate the unit himself.

At the time of its official recognition, the squadron consisted of three support aircraft. An L-5 "Sentinel" spotter plane, with a 125-hp engine, flew at a top speed of 115 mph. A bit more impressive, the squadron's pair of two-seat T-6 "Texan" trainers could fly up to 208 mph. Six fighter planes and other support aircraft, however, would arrive within two weeks. The activation ceremony for federal recognition nevertheless was a momentous occasion, the culmination of three decades of attempts to wed aviation into the Montana National Guard.[2]

Only five years after their historic flight at Kitty Hawk, North Carolina, the Wright brothers sold the world's first military flying machine to the U.S. Army in 1908.[3] That same year marked the initial involvement of a state National Guard unit in aviation. New York guardsmen first had been interested in ballooning, but they soon managed to obtain an airplane and, in 1915, established the first National Guard flying unit, the 1st Aero Company. According to historian Charles J. Gross, "The Guard was a hotbed of early interest in aviation." On the eve of World War I, guardsmen, civilian pilots, and business entrepreneurs united to form aero divisions within a number of state National Guard organizations despite the lack of state or federal financial assistance.[4]

P-51 Mustang. *Montana Air National Guard [MANG]*

The War Department, however, was not interested in supporting these fledgling guard aviation groups and disbanded them at the onset of America's involvement in World War I. Aviation personnel were encouraged—if they wanted to serve with air units—to leave the guard and volunteer with the Army Signal Corps Reserve. Many did, providing the army with "a major pool of aviators." In 1917, however, the U.S. Army's air units lagged far behind the European air forces in regard to technology, operations, and numbers. Its tiny Aviation Section within the Signal Corps was in dire need of experienced air personnel, which guardsmen helped to remedy. Growth would come relatively quickly. By the war's end, the American Expeditionary Force's air services swelled to 12,000 pilots and more than 180,000 officers and air crewmen.[5]

Not only did men from the disbanded guard aero elements volunteer to serve in aviation squadrons, but guardsmen from states without an air arm did so as well. 2nd Lt. William Belzer of the Montana guard began wartime service in France with the 163rd Infantry's machine gun company, but two months after arriving, he transferred to the U.S. Army Air Service and became an artillery observer with the 135th U.S. Aero Observation Squadron. Both Belzer and his pilot were awarded the Distinguished Service Cross for successfully completing artillery surveillance and reconnaissance missions amidst attacking enemy planes.[6]

Montana native Benjamin Harwood, who joined the Massachusetts National Guard while attending Harvard Law School, also served as an aerial observer in France. After initially entering the war with the 102nd Field Artillery, 26th Division, he transferred to the 12th U.S. Aero Squadron. Major Harwood earned a Distinguished Service Cross, Purple Heart, and Croix de Guerre for his efforts in protecting a photo reconnaissance plane from enemy fire. A future member of the Montana legislature, he won additional accolade for his administrative duties with the Air Service before his discharge in 1919. While still in the army, Harwood helped draft national legislation to establish a separate Department of Air and Aeronautics. Congress and many top military officials, however, were unwilling to see the auxiliary Air Service split from the nation's ground and sea forces, and the bill was rejected. Other Montanans, including two aerial observers, an observation pilot, and five combat pilots, are known to have served during the war.[7]

Shortly after the war, a surplus of wartime equipment and effective lobbying from guardsmen who served in Europe convinced a hesitant War Department to approve National Guard aero units. In the early 1920s, 19 National Guard observation squadrons were created to support the guard's infantry divisions. The federal government supplied the planes and paid the salaries of pilots and mechanics, while the states were required to provide airstrips and hangar facilities.[8]

The Montana guard nearly received an air unit in 1924, but by this time the War Department and Congress were losing enthusiasm for further expansion of the National Guard's role. In the spring of 1924, the commander of the 9th Corps Area, headquartered at the Presidio in San Francisco, proposed that the Oregon National Guard's fledgling 144th Air Service Observation Squadron be transferred to Helena. This proposal had the blessing of Oregon's adjutant general. Montana Adjutant General Charles L. Sheridan noted that "a large number of ex-flyers" in the Big Sky state were interested in securing a squadron, "so much so that they have volunteered to advance the money necessary for the maintenance of the unit."[9]

The War Department's Militia Bureau agreed that the transfer was a sound idea, but warned that the Secretary of War's recently modified policy on National Guard organization and Congress' appropriation constraints were blocking the formation of new Corps and Army National Guard units. Transferring an air squadron might fall under these restrictions. Even if Montana was allocated Oregon's 144th Observation Squadron, the Militia Bureau believed it was "unlikely" that funds would be available to authorize and support this reorganization. Shortly afterward, Sheridan reported, "it would hardly be worth the while to ask for its [the 144th Squadron] allocation to the State." Sheridan vowed, however, that Montana would resume lobbying for an air service unit "when appropriations permit its organization."[10]

Two years later, the Air Corps Act of 1926 launched an aircraft modernization and expansion program for the U.S. Army, but did not provide for the creation of new National Guard air units. Existing guard squadrons, however, benefited from the U.S. Army Air Corps' growth by receiving more modern "hand-me-down" aircraft in the years to come. In the interwar years, the U.S. Army Air Corps would increasingly concentrate on pursuit and bombardment missions and technology, while National Guard squadrons shouldered most of the responsibility for observation aviation, which kept the latter units firmly tied to ground support missions.[11]

Not until nine years later did Congress again consider legislation to create new National Guard squadrons. In April 1935, a House bill was introduced proposing ten additional air guard units. As the bill sat in the Military Affairs Committee for over a year, while also being mulled over by the War Department, Montana's air advocates rallied support. The state's commissioner of aeronautics, Fred Sheriff, urged Montana Adjutant General Erastus H. Williams to "find out what can be done" in securing one of the new squadrons. Sheriff saw Helena as the obvious location for an air unit. The "modern well developed" airport boasted state-of-the-art radio facilities and lighting, north and south airmail service, and an aviation school. Sheriff also noted that Montana's capital city was an "exceedingly airminded town" and the state's National Guard headquarters. The greater Helena area was home to a number of private and commercial pilots, "who could well be helped along to keep up their flying time, making out of them capable flyers instead of just having around a lot of fellows that are rusty at the game."[12]

With the "enthusiastic backing of Gov. Elmer Holt, & of all avn. [aviation] interests in Montana," Adjutant General Williams petitioned Maj. Gen. Albert H. Blanding, chief of the National Guard Bureau, and General Marlin Craig, U.S. Army chief of staff, for an air squadron. Williams pointed out that the U.S. Army already had sent air squadrons to the state for winter training and extreme cold weather experimentation. Montana also would provide military aviators with high "altitude & mountain flying."

Other leading advocates included U.S. Congressman Roy E. Ayers, Major John W. Mahan of the Montana legislature, and S.V. Stewart, associate justice of the Montana Supreme Court. Foremost, however, was Montana's Senator Burton K. Wheeler, credited by Col. E.A. Frye of the National Guard Bureau as the key legislator "carrying the ball" for the appropriations bill in the Senate. Bureau chief Albert Blanding also repeatedly assured Montana supporters that should the appropriation legislation pass, "the desires and facilities of Montana will be given every consideration."[13]

But the bill stalled in committee because, as many argued, the military establishment was reluctant once again to divert aviation resources to the National Guard. William G. Ferguson, representing the Montana Chamber of Commerce, lamented that authorities overlooked "the fact that the Guard can, and does, enlist a...higher type of individual." Ferguson hoped all of the states applying for the yet unauthorized aviation units would band together and "succeed in dynamiting this resolution out of the House Committee."

In June 1936, Public Law 785 was passed allocating funds for a larger fleet of military aircraft; however, Congress did not authorize additional National Guard air units. Montana's hopes were foiled again. Following this disappointment, Adjutant General Williams sent a curt request to the National Guard Bureau requesting, "if, and when" additional observation squadrons were authorized by Congress, that Montana be granted one.[14] Not until 1939, with hostilities mounting in Europe, did Congress finally approve funds for additional National Guard air units. The authorization was part of a legislative package committed to bolstering America's military air strength, with the War Department receiving funding to triple the armed forces aircraft inventory.[15]

Brig. Gen. Mahan, now the state adjutant general, criticized the assignment of the first two new squadrons to Mississippi and Connecticut, pointing out that Maj. Gen. George E. Leach of the National Guard Bureau, after an investigation of Montana's facilities and recruitment potential a few years before, had promised Montana "the next squadron instituted." Mahan further observed that due to the long distances between Montana communities, aviation had "advanced tremendously" with over 60 licensed pilots in the Helena area alone "eligible and anxious for commissions." Also noted was Helena High School's unique curriculum for "flying cadets...who advance to soloing in their senior year." With adequate facilities and "some of the best pilots in the United States," Mahan argued that Montana was overdue for a guard squadron. "I feel that it is being discriminated against if it does not secure and receive the same."[16]

While Congress contemplated passing appropriations for eight additional air guard units, Senator Wheeler and organizations in Montana continued to petition the War Department, recommending Butte, Great Falls, or Missoula for air unit assignment. Butte's E.J. Keeley, representing the American Legion Defense Committee, Silver Bow Post No. 1, asked that the War Department consider placing air observation and anti-aircraft units in or near Butte, a locale of "great importance as a production center of strategic minerals." Keeley discredited the concerns of factional groups in Butte, "namely, the Miner's Union," who feared that men in a new National Guard unit would only serve as strike breakers. Keeley felt that the attitudes of these "subversive elements" were hampering national defense and should not be considered.[17]

Norman Thisted, president of the Great Falls Chamber of Commerce, submitted a 30-page report to the National Guard Bureau outlining amenities that Great Falls would offer a guard squadron, including an airport and weather bureau, plus industrial and agricultural facilities, and recreational opportunities. Great Falls was the ideal location for "an air base for the protection of our territory of Alaska," the proposal claimed, as well as the midway point for "highways in the sky"—as yet undeveloped—between the Great Lakes and the Pacific Ocean, for both immediate defense purposes and longer-term commercial value.[18]

War Department officials informed these petitioners that should appropriations materialize, Montana would be given "the most careful consideration." National officials also recommended that local promoters direct their energies toward Montana's adjutant general because the 1916 National Defense Act required state, not federal, authorities to determine the assigned locations of National Guard units within a state.[19]

In May 1940, when the passage of legislation for funding eight new guard squadrons looked promising, the National Guard Bureau called for formal applications from all states interested in obtaining an air unit. Adjutant General Mahan responded immediately by direction of Governor Roy E. Ayers and with the ardent support of U.S. senators Burton Wheeler and James E. Murray. Mahan stated that Montana had been "an active applicant" for a guard air squadron for 15 years and still was "very earnest in its desire for such an allocation."

The National Guard Bureau required that state officials name a "proposed" airport that would be used for National Guard purposes. True to his previously disclosed preference, Mahan recommended the Helena Municipal Airport, noting its seven all-weather runways and "the largest and best repair shops between the Twin Cities and the Pacific Coast" that serviced planes from across the region. Also, more than 40 Montana pilots already met the bureau's minimum flight requirements as prospective officers. Realizing that Helena's population of only 12,000 might appear insufficient for supporting an air unit, Mahan stressed that 65 percent of Montana's half-million people lived within 125 miles of Helena, and the number of licensed pilots per capita in Montana was significantly higher than in most states, although he presented no numbers to prove this claim. Mahan further argued that Montana's geography provided "mountain flying in subzero weather, and other topographical conditions not available."[20]

Soon after Mahan submitted the application, he learned that C.T. Busha Jr., representing the Great Falls Chamber of Commerce, had plans to travel to Washington, D.C., and lobby for locating the air unit in his city. This was, in Mahan's view, "a purely local proposition." Mahan described Busha as "very antagonistic to the Roosevelt administration and also the present State Administration." In attempting to minimize any damage that the Great Falls independent bid might have on Montana's chances for a squadron—as well as to prevent any possible repercussions for the governor in an election year if should it become commonly known which city would receive the unit—Mahan asked the National Guard Bureau and the Secretary of War to keep Montana's application confidential.[21]

More than 30 states applied for the eight new guard squadrons. Due to this stiff competitive situation, Louis Johnson of the War Department announced that states with "available facilities for the immediate activation of these units should receive highest priorities." National Guard Bureau Chief John F. Williams regretted that "a great number of the states naturally will be disappointed." Montana would be among them.

In August 1940, Senator Wheeler received word from Secretary of War Henry L. Stimson explaining that the eight observation squadrons had been assigned to other states. Stimson added, "Please be assured" that Montana would "receive full consideration" when future legislative action allowed for additional air units. The War Department' Louis Johnson also speculated that in the near term, given the continuing expansion of the Air Corps, every state with "the facilities and the desire to organize an air squadron in the National Guard will be given an opportunity to do so."[22]

Montana fell short for a couple of reasons. In the application, Mahan stated that the Helena airport offered the guard immediate use of an 8,000-square foot-hangar, well short of the 28,800 square feet required by the bureau. Although Mahan indicated that the state was willing to construct more facilities as needed, the War Department explained that "existing" facilities were given high priority in assigning new guard squadrons to states. Helena's 12,000 population may have been a major strike against Montana's bid as well. "Experience has shown," wrote National Guard Bureau chief Williams, "that it is inadvisable to locate air squadrons in civic centers of less than 50,000 population, as it is practically impossible to maintain an air squadron to full strength in both officer and enlisted men."[23]

By now, international events intervened. Roughly 4,800 National Guard aviation personnel from 29 observation squadrons—the bulk being mechanics and ground crews, but also including over 600 pilots—were mobilized in President Franklin D. Roosevelt's military buildup prior to the U.S. entry into World War II. Guardsmen soon were serving as instructors or in other capacities directing enlistees joining the Army Air Corps. Historian Charles J. Gross claimed these efforts constituted "the most significant wartime contribution of the National Guard aviators." Many of the pilots and ground crews lost their National Guard affiliation and were assigned to other Army Air Corps units; nine guard units were disbanded altogether. The remaining guard squadrons, with their ranks substantially filled by enlistees, draftees, and regular Army pilots, were reorganized in reconnaissance, liaison, fighter, and bombardment units, usually commanded by U.S. Army, not National Guard, officers.[24]

Significant numbers of Montanans served in aviation related posts during World War II. Many hailed from Helena, which had been "the center of aviation training in Montana" since the early 1930s, with a state school of aeronautics and the high school program training airplane mechanics and pilots. Because of these opportunities, Helena Mayor John J. Haytin later proclaimed in 1946 that "a very large proportion of military personnel from this community entered the air forces during World War II." At least 40 men from the Helena locality served in aviation, with nearly half being pilots.[25]

Near the war's end, planning for a future reorganization of America's military was well underway. It eventually became apparent that a new separate branch—the U.S. Air Force—probably would be established.[26] Many top air officers, however, were skeptical of the talents and readiness of guard units. They felt that only full-time active duty servicemen could fully master the complex technologies, duties, and weaponry that a modern air force required. But late in 1944, to best guarantee the objective of forming a distinct air branch, proponents reluctantly submitted to the creation of the Air National Guard as an arm of a soon-to-be independent U.S. Air Force. Nevertheless, planners had little interest in assigning a significant mission to the National Guard, proposing instead that most of its air units be made up of antiaircraft artillery troops.[27] Fortunately, a broader role for the Air National Guard eventually prevailed.

The final postwar reorganization, approved by Secretary of War Stimson in October 1945, included the creation of the Air National Guard to serve as "the primary source for augmenting" the new federal air branch. Guard air units needed to be "capable of rapid expansion to wartime manning and full operational readiness once mobilized for federal service." The overall mission of the active duty and guard air units also would be supplemented by a new Air Force Reserve.[28] In February 1946, the National Guard Bureau announced the plan to the states.

Montana's new adjutant general, Col. S.H. Mitchell, was notified that his state finally would be allocated a long awaited air unit, "composed of a fighter squadron plus a utility Flight and maintenance detachment." For assistance in determining "the best possible location" for the new air unit, Mitchell invited officials from Montana's major cities and towns—Billings, Helena, Missoula, Glasgow, Cut Bank, Miles City, Lewistown, Great Falls, and Butte—to submit a report on their community's ability to house a squadron. Mitchell's survey focused on two primary concerns—airfield installations and personnel recruitment.

The War Department required the unit to have access to three runways and two hangars of specified dimensions, plus adequate equipment and fuel storage, and "housing, messing and drilling facilities for 300 men." A community not meeting these minimum requirements could construct new facilities in the year or so interim before the new squadron was established. No state or federal funds, however, would be provided in making these improvements.

The state would pay a "nominal" yearly rental fee to a municipal airport to compensate for the guard's use of the facilities. Also, a community would have to be "of sufficient population" to provide the necessary recruitment of aviation personnel. The squadron required 6 maintenance officers and 33 qualified single-engine pilots to serve as flight officers—these men had to be World War II veterans. Enlisted men—including qualified Air Corps technicians with at least six months of military service since 1940—must number at least 171.

Initially, Mitchell realized that only Glasgow, Lewistown, Cut Bank, and Great Falls met the War Department's minimum airfield requirements, and of these only Great Falls had a sufficient population to meet the enlistment prerequisites. However, Mitchell surveyed a larger pool of communities, seeking information about the potential for drawing air personnel from surrounding localities and to determine the local interest in upgrading runways and facilities. Construction costs could be "easily offset," Mitchell wrote, by an estimated $50,000 in earnings for local merchants providing services to the squadron.[29]

Neither Missoula nor Butte would commit to providing funds for improving runways or facilities. In Billings, S.G. Tonkin urged the adjutant general to choose a location "from a strategic standpoint," and if that should be Billings, the city would be "most anxious to co-operate in every way possible." Mayor John J. Haytin of Helena was more aggressive in his appeal. Among the "definite advantages" Helena had to offer, Haytin listed the school of aeronautics, a large number of talented pilots (a number of them World War II veterans), and the locality's superior flying weather. Haytin also outlined a Civil Aeronautics Administration and city plan to renovate Helena's municipal airport—including a new configuration of runways—to suit the squadron's needs.[30]

The Airport Commission in Cut Bank proposed dividing the new squadron into "four or five segments," with each assigned to a different community and the headquarters based at a central point. Claiming the largest airfield in Montana, Cut Bank officials expressed hope they would be chosen as one of the locations for this "dispersed" air squadron. The Cut Bank contingent appealed to other Montana towns to endorse this alternative plan. At least one other community, Miles City, agreed that the idea was worth pursuing. However, the adjutant general's original planned to choose one location for the new squadron would prevail.[31]

In March 1946, Mayor Fritz Norby and the Great Falls Chamber of Commerce submitted a strong application for acquiring the squadron. Norby noted the community's qualifications, assuring Mitchell that "the Great Falls Municipal Airport and the City meet the minimum requirements as outlined in your letter in every respect," and that the squadron "could be based here without delay for construction." The city airport, named Gore Field during World War II, had been the 7th Ferrying Group headquarters of the Army's Air Transport Command. Located here were Civil Aviation Administration communications and traffic control facilities, and a U.S. Weather Bureau station. Gore Field's manager, Thomas Dardis, and the Sletten Construction Company estimated that $78,000 would cover all needed alternations and repairs to hangers and other airport buildings to accommodate the new air unit. A yearly budget of $13,000—employing four men full time—was estimated for maintenance of the airfield for the squadron's purposes.[32]

Also noteworthy was the municipal airport's proximity to the Great Falls Army Air Base—the "gateway" for military personnel, cargo, and equipment bound for western Canada, Alaska, and the U.S.S.R. during the war. The airfield served as the largest "interior" U.S. departure point for international transport during that time, accommodated by Great Falls's average of 300 days of clear flying weather a year.[33]

Lt. Col. Willard Staples Sperry, a celebrated pilot stationed at the Great Falls Air Base in the fall of 1946, became a leading advocate for Montana's air squadron in the later stages of its inception. A pilot since he was a teenager, Sperry was an Army Air Corps flight instructor in the early days of the war. Later, he served with distinction as a bomber commander and combat pilot in the European theater. While conducting bombing missions over Nazi-occupied Hungary, the group he led shuttled between Italy and the Soviet Union. During the D-Day invasion, Sperry flew back-to-back support for Allied ground forces for three days straight. He earned a Silver Star, two Distinguished Flying Crosses, nine Air Medals, a Presidential Unit Citation, and the Croix de Guerre from the French government. After the war, Sperry served short stints at several east coast bases before being transferred to Great Falls. Impressed with the Big Sky's open spaces, the California native decided to make Montana his home, and set about helping the governor and legislature to ultimately secure the air squadron for the state.[34]

The Montana Air Guard finally took shape in 1947 as the 186th Fighter Squadron, the "reconstituted and redesignated" version of the 404th Fighter

Mustang fighters on the flight line at Gore Field. *MANG*

Squadron, 371st Fighter Group, 9th Air Force, which had been assigned to the European theater during World War II. From bases in Britain, France, Belgium, and finally, occupied parts of Germany, the 404th's P-47D "Thunderbolts" flew combat missions from March 1944 to the end of the war. The squadron had participated in the Normandy Campaign, and later received a Presidential Unit Citation "for outstanding performance of duty in action against the enemy in Germany." Immediately after returning stateside to Camp Shanks, New York, the squadron was deactivated in November 1945. In May 1946, however, the War Department allotted the unit, redesignated as the 186th Fighter Squadron, to the National Guard. Assignment of the 186th to Montana was finalized in the following year.[35]

The Great Falls Municipal Airport—Gore Field (also known as Gore Hill)—had won the bid to serve as headquarters for the 186th Fighter Squadron. The newcomer to Montana, Lt. Col. Willard Sperry, was assigned as senior air advisor and instructor, and became largely responsible for building up the new unit. Sperry launched a personalized recruiting campaign, encouraging both veterans and men without military experience to join the Montana Air Guard. He met with community civic groups to solicit enlistment, and newspaper coverage of his recruiting efforts also drew in men. On April 1, 1947, the first five members of the new unit included Capt. Robert Dardis (maintenance officer), Capt. Edmonds (supply officer), MSG Eino Kivi (inspector), Staff Sgt. Charles Van Diest, and Sgt. Don Burditt (both, aircraft mechanics). By the time of the official activation ceremony in late June, Sperry had recruited 35 officers and 39 enlistees. At the time, the unit was authorized 49 officers and 303 enlisted men.

At Great Falls on June 27, 1947, with U.S. Army officials failing to show up for the federal recognition ceremony, Sperry stepped in and officiated at the long-anticipated event. Activated were the 186th Fighter Squadron and three subordinate units—the 227th Services Group, Detachment C, directed by Major Leon Dorich; the 186th Utility Flight, led by Capt. Young; and the 186th Weather Station, Type A, under the command of Capt. Elser. Along with Idaho, Washington, and Oregon air guard squadrons, the Montana Air Guard was designated part of the 60th Fighter Wing, headquartered in Portland.[36] Although the 186th had only three aircraft on the day of its initiation—none of which were fighters—within two weeks six P-51D "Mustang" fighters and more support aircraft arrived.[37]

Major Rodger D. Young, June 1953. *MANG*

On September 18, 1947, the Air National Guard as a national entity came into being at the same time that the U.S. Air Force officially separated from the U.S. Army. By 1949, more than 500 flying and support air guard units would be established across the country, with each state assigned at least one squadron. Postwar budgetary restraints, however, forced many state air units to grow slowly.

The U.S. Air Force experienced similar financial constraints, resulting in a smaller active duty force than anticipated, leaving the National Air Guard and the Air Force Reserve to fill the void. A number of Air Force officials resented this necessary arrangement, a situation compounded by some lack of uniformity in training and operations among state air units. The most intense critics considered the guard squadrons to be little more than "state-sponsored flying clubs." Debate also swirled in the late 1940s over the demarcation lines between the Air Force and the National Guard Bureau regarding "who was in charge" of air guard units.[38]

In 1948, the Truman administration, with the support of the U.S. Air Force, proposed federalizing the National Air Guard and merging it with the Air Force Reserve, to create a single, and supposedly more efficient, reserve entity. In the backdrop of a strong National Guard Association lobbying effort, Congress rejected the plan in February 1949. Although inter-service friction remained, the new Air National Guard had secured the same state and federal status that the Army National Guard had always known.[39]

In the late 1940s, the air guard served the national interest by providing air defense for the continental United States and by acting as "a reserve component of the Air Force capable of rapid expansion to war strength" for overseas duty if needed. Like the army guard, air guard units also served their states "in the protection of life and property and the preservation of peace, order, and public safety," which often meant disaster relief.[40] For the Montana Air Guard, its part in national air defense would evolve with the escalation of the Cold War, while its responsibilities to Montana's communities and citizens would remain more constant.

Notes

1. Fritz Norby, Great Falls Mayor, to AG Mitchell, March 6, 1946; "Brief Outlining the Qualifications of Great Falls, Montana and Great Falls Municipal Airport (Gore Field) as a Base for a National Guard Air Squadron for the State of Montana," March 6, 1946, prepared by Robert M. Darling, Executive Vice President, Great Falls Chamber of Commerce, Cabinet 3, Montana Military History Museum, Fort Harrison, Helena, Montana [hereafter cited as MMHM].
2. TSgt. James Sharpe, "Fifty Years of Flying the Big Sky...," 1, Historical File 10.F, Office of James Sharpe, Wing Historian, Montana Air National Guard, Great Falls International Airport; *Montana Air National Guard: The First 50 Years* (120th Fighter Wing, Montana National Guard, 1947–1997), 68–69; *Montana Air National Guard* (10 Year Commemorative Book), 10, MMHM.

3. Charles J. Gross, *The Air National Guard and the American Military Tradition* (Washington, D.C.: Historical Services Division, National Guard Bureau, 1995). This source is relied upon throughout this chapter to provide an overview of the development of the Air National Guard at the national level.
4. Ibid., 26–27.
5. Ibid., 32–34.
6. Ibid., 35; Dennis Gordon, "Montana's Birdmen of World War I," *Montana: The Magazine of Western History* 29 (July 1979): 38–40.
7. Ibid., 36–38, 40.
8. Gross, *Air National Guard,* 36–37, 45.
9. Record of Communication Received, A.G. Mont. to Hq. 9th C.A. Calif., March 28, 1924; Edgar A. Sirmyer, Officer in Charge N.G. Affairs, Hq. Ninth Corps Area to Chief, Militia Bureau, War Department, March 28, 1924, Folder: "1924 & 1940: Plans for Formation of ANG Squadrons in MT," Army NGB, State Decimal File 1922–45, 325.4 (Air) Montana, Entry 344, Box 587, Record Group 168, National Archives, Washington, D.C. [hereafter cited as NA].
10. Maj. Gen. George C. Rickards, Chief, Militia Bureau to Commanding General, 9th Corps Area, May 8, 1924; Charles L. Sheridan, Adjutant General, to Chief, Militia Bureau, June 6, 1924, "1924 & 1940: Plans for Formation of ANG Squadrons in MT," Entry 344, Box 587, RG 168, NA.
11. Gross, *Air National Guard,* 40–41.
12. Maj. Gen. Albert H. Blanding, Chief, NGB to Sen. B.K. Wheeler, March 5, 1936, Folder: "1935–36, Rejected Proposal for New ANG Squadron," Entry 344, Box 587, RG 168, NA; Commissioner of Aeronautics Fred B. Sheriff to Col. Erastus H. Williams, Adjutant General for the State of Montana, January 2, 1935, Folder 3: "General Correspondence: Adjutant General," Box 60: General Office Correspondence: Cooney Administration: "Abstract Examiners – Barber Examiners," Montana Governors Papers, MC 35, Montana Historical Society, Helena, Montana.
13. Record of Communication, AG Montana to Gen. Marlin Craig, Chief of Staff, US Army, July 11, 1936; Col. E.A. Fry, NGB, to Joseph P. Monaghan, House of Representatives, February 25, 1935; Maj. Gen. Albert H. Blanding, Chief, NGB, to Sen. B.K. Wheeler, March 5, 1936, "1935–36, Rejected Proposal for New ANG Squadron," Entry 344, Box 587, RG 168, NA. This file contains extensive correspondence between the National Guard Bureau and advocates for a Montana air unit.
14. William G. Ferguson, Montanans, Inc., to Maj. Gen. Albert H. Blanding, Chief, NGB, March 31, 1936; Col. William E. Persons, NGB, to Maj. I.B. Summers, Office of the Chief of Staff, July 15, 1936; Col. E.H. Williams, Adjutant General, to Chief, National Guard Bureau, November 30, 1936, "1935–36, Rejected Proposal for New ANG Squadron," Entry 344, Box 587, RG 168, NA.
15. Gross, *Air National Guard,* 45.
16. Record of Communication, AG Montana, to Hon. B.K. Wheeler, U.S. Senator, October 28, 1939, "1924 & 1940: Plans for Formation of ANG Squadrons in MT," Entry 344, Box 587, RG 168, NA.
17. Harry H. Woodring, Secretary of War, to Burton K. Wheeler, U.S. Senate, January 19, 1939; Record of Communication, E.J. Keeley, Natl. Defense Comm., Butte, to Hon. Burton K. Wheeler, June 4, 1940; Record of Communication Received, E.J. Keeley to Sec. of War, July 19, 1940, "1924 & 1940: Plans for Formation of ANG Squadrons in MT," "1940: Allocation of NG Air Squadron, MT," Entry 344, Box 587, RG 168, NA.

These files contain other examples of correspondence between the National Guard Bureau and advocates for a Montana air unit from 1939 and 1940.

18. "Facts about Great Falls, Montana," prepared by the Great Falls Chamber of Commerce, October 1, 1940, Folder: "1940 Brief on Great Falls for Consideration as Location of Air Corp Unit," Entry 344, Box 587, RG 168, NA.
19. Harry H. Woodring, Secretary of War, to Burton K. Wheeler, U.S. Senate, June 4, 1940; Woodring to Wheeler, June 6, 1940; John F. Williams, Chief, National Guard Bureau, to Hon. James E. Murray, U.S. Senate, July 15, 1940, "1924 & 1940: Plans for Formation of ANG Squadrons in MT," "1940: Allocation of NG Air Squadron, MT," Entry 344, Box 587, RG 168, NA.
20. John F. Williams, Chief, National Guard Bureau, to Adjutant General of Montana, May 15, 1940; Burton K. Wheeler, U.S. Senate, to Maj. Gen. John F. Williams, Chief, National Guard Bureau, July 5, 1940; James E. Murray, U.S. Senate, to Williams, National Guard Bureau, July 5, 1940; John W. Mahan, Adjutant General (Mont.), to Chief, National Guard Bureau, May 21, 1940, "1940: Allocation of NG Air Squadron, MT," Entry 344, Box 587, RG 168, NA.
21. Memorandum for the Executive, Maj. O.P. Weyland, NGB, June 19, 1940; Record of Communication, Brig. Gen. John W. Mahan to Assistant Secretary of War, June 20, 1940, "1940: Allocation of NG Air Squadron, MT," Entry 344, Box 587, RG 168, NA.
22. Maj. Gen. John F. Williams, Chief, NGB, to Brig. Gen. John W. Mahan, Adjutant General of Montana, June 28, 1940; Louis Johnson, WD, to Mahan, July 10, 1940, Folder 8: "The Organization of National Guard Units 1940–1950," Box 1: General Correspondence, Montana Adjutant General's Office Records, RC 223, MHS; Henry L. Stimson, Secretary of War, to Hon. Burton K. Wheeler, U.S. Senate, August 12, 1940, "1940: Allocation of NG Air Squadron, MT," Entry 344, Box 587, RG 168, NA.
23. John F. Williams, Chief, National Guard Bureau, to Adjutant General of Montana, May 15, 1940; John W. Mahan, Adjutant General (Mont.), to Chief, National Guard Bureau, May 21, 1940; Williams to Mr. O.H. Bell, Chairman, Missoula County Airport Board, July 22, 1940, "1940: Allocation of NG Air Squadron, MT," Entry 344, Box 587, RG 168, NA.
24. Gross, *Air National Guard,* 53–55.
25. John J. Haytin, Helena Mayor, to Col. S.H. Mitchell, Montana Adjutant General, March 12, 1946, File: "Montana National Air Guard: Miscell.," Cabinet 3, Library Archives, MMHM.
26. Gross, *Air National Guard,* 57–58.
27. Ibid., 57–60.
28. Ibid., 61.
29. S.H. Mitchell, Adjutant General, to Mr. J.H. Bohling, Secretary-Manager, Miles City Chamber of Commerce, February 25, 1946, Folder 3: "General Correspondence, Adjutant General," Box 60: General Office Correspondence, Cooney Administration "Abstract Examiners – Barber Examiners," Montana Governors Papers, MC35, MHS; S.H. Mitchell, Colonel, FD, AUS, The Adjutant General to Dr. Harry Casebeer, Butte, February 18, 1946 (also duplicates to other community leaders); Mitchell to Mayor of Lewistown, February 26, 1946, "Montana National Air Guard: Miscell.," Cabinet 3, MMHM.
30. O.H. Bell, Chairman, Missoula County Airport Board, to S.H. Mitchell, Adjutant General, March 7, 1946; H.L. Casebeer, M.D., Butte, to Mitchell, March 4, 1946; S.G. Tonkin, Billings Airport, to Mitchell, March 7, 1946; John J. Haytin, Helena Mayor,

to Mitchell, March 12, 1946, "Montana National Air Guard: Miscell.," Cabinet 3, MMHM.

31. W.B. Lee, Mayor, Cut Bank, to Honorable Mayor, City of Great Falls, March 8, 1946; C.H. Minette, Chairman, Cut Bank Airport Commission, to Col. H.S. Mitchell, Adjutant General, March 14, 1946; Hugh J. Lemire, Deputy City Attorney, Miles City, to Hon. W.B. Lee, Cut Bank, March 15, 1946, "Montana National Air Guard: Miscell.," Cabinet 3, MMHM.
32. Fritz Norby, Great Falls Mayor, to AG Mitchell, March 6, 1946; "Brief Outlining the Qualifications of Great Falls, Montana and Great Falls Municipal Airport (Gore Field) as a Base for a National Guard Air Squadron for the State of Montana," March 6, 1946, prepared by Robert M. Darling, Executive Vice President, Great Falls Chamber of Commerce; Thomas Dardis, Airport Manager, to Adjutant General's Office, Montana National Guard, May 22, 1946; Sletten Construction Company to Airport Commission, Municipal Airport, May 20, 1946, Montana National Air Guard: Miscell.," Cabinet 3, MMHM; Richard H. Lacey, *The Montana Militia: A History of Montana's Volunteer Forces, 1967–1976* (Dillon, Montana: Dillon Tribune-Examiner Press, 1976), 84.
33. Some larger departure points existed in the nation's coastal regions during World War II. At Great Falls in the mid-1940s, adverse weather conditions prevented routine landings and takeoffs less than 3 percent of the time, year-round. "Brief in Support of Retention of the Army Air Base at Great Falls, Montana, as a Permanent Army Air Base," January 29, 1946, prepared by the Airways Committee, Great Falls Chamber of Commerce, "Montana National Air Guard: Miscell.," Cabinet 3, MMHM.
34. *Montana Air National Guard: The First 50 Years*, 4; Sharpe, "Fifty Years of Flying the Big Sky...," 1; "Biography of Lieutenant Colonel Willard Staples Sperry," Historical File 9.C, Office of James Sharpe, Wing Historian, Montana Air National Guard, Great Falls International Airport.
35. Sharpe, "Fifty Years of Flying the Big Sky...," 1; *Montana Air National Guard: The First 50 Years*, 5; "404th Fighter Sq., SE 2nd Card – 80186 – Historical Data" and Stations and movements data sheet for the 186th Fighter Squadron, SE/404th Fighter Squadron, SE, obtained May 1, 1998 from Col. Raymond Read, Montana National Guard, Helena, Montana.
36. Sharpe, "Fifty Years of Flying the Big Sky...," 1; *Montana Air National Guard: The First 50 Years*, 4–5; *Montana Air National Guard* (10 Year Commemorative Book), 10.
37. The P-51D Mustang pursuit plane, which had proven invaluable in Allied offensives during the latter stages of World War II, had a top speed of 438 mph and a range of about 1,000 miles. With a Packard-built Rolls Royce 1,490-hp engine, the Mustang was armed with six .50-caliber machine guns and had wing rails for six 2.75-inch rockets. Sharpe, "Fifty Years of Flying the Big Sky...," 1; *Montana Air National Guard: The First 50 Years*, 55.
38. Charles J. Gross, *The Air National Guard: A Short History* (Washington, D.C.: U.S. Government Printing Office, 1994), 13; Gross, *Air National Guard*, 62.
39. Ibid., 65–68.
40. Gross, *Short History*, 13; James C. Elliott, *The Modern Army and Air National Guard* (Princeton, New Jersey: D. Van Nostrand, 1965), 111–12.

A-26 Invader. *MANG*

20

Air Defense and State Service: The Montana Air National Guard, 1947–1998

Diane L. Krahe

Flight and ground personnel who had previous Air National Guard training were capable of operating almost on a par with Air Force personnel and in some cases even exceeded Air Force capability.—Major Rodger D. Young, 1954.[1]

The 186th Fighter Squadron made its public debut on July 26, 1947, with two Texan trainers and two Mustang fighters taking part in an air show at Glasgow, Montana. Difficulties with leanness in the earliest days—in terms of funding and equipment—would pale in contrast to a tragedy that befell the new organization less than three months after its creation. On September 17, 1947, the squadron's commander, Lt. Col. Willard Sperry, along with Sgt. Charles Glover, died in the crash of their A-26 "Invader" twin-engine bomber in mountainous terrain near Helena.

Sperry and Glover were flying from Great Falls to Helena, and planned to meet Montana Adjutant General A.H. Mitchell. The three men were then scheduled to travel together to Ohio for a National Guard conference. When entering a heavy snowstorm near Helena, however, Sperry radioed that the plane was icing up, then communication was lost.

"The most extensive air search in Montana history" ensued, but the wreckage remained undetected throughout the winter. In the following June, members of the 186th finally located the crash site from the air.[2]

After Sperry's death, Col. Harold E. Kofahl became the unit's senior air instructor, with Major Clifford Owen assigned as squadron commander. The first annual encampment took place at Gore Field in June 1948. For summer training the next year, the 250 men of the Montana Air Guard reported to Moses Lake Air Base in eastern Washington, joining other units of the 60th Fighter Wing from Washington, Oregon, and Idaho.

In June 1950, the 60th Fighter Wing assembled for summer training at Walla Walla, Washington, during which a flyover of 66 F-51 Mustangs presented an impressive display of air power. At this 1950 encampment, the 186th clocked a total of 839 hours flying time, practicing air-to-air and air-to-ground gunnery, ground controlled intercept missions, group formations, cargo missions, and other team-oriented operations.[3]

Monthly training at Gore Field near Great Falls enabled all air guardsmen to concentrate on their specialties and allowed the pilots to participate in formation flying exercises. Squadron leaders followed "in detail" the standardized Continental Air Command Training Directive 10-3. Unit proficiency, however, was somewhat hindered by a high pilot turnover in the late 1940s, but increased flight training in 1950 stabilized the unit's pool of pilots, each of whom needed to log 100 flight hours a year, including 20 instrument and 15 night hours. The unit's gunnery proficiency, both air-to-air and air-to-ground, was substandard due to the lack of acceptable training space in the Great Falls vicinity, although gunnery ranges in Utah and at the Walla Walla encampment provided some much-needed practice.[4]

The 186th's earliest calls to action for state emergencies were rather peculiar. In the winter of 1948, the Yellowstone River became plugged by ice jams; rising water threatened to inundate nearby residences. Air guard pilots took to their Mustangs and bombed the ice dams, clearing the river to resume its flow. In 1949, the Pondera County sheriff summoned the air guard to conduct an aerial search for robbers who had held up a Conrad bank. Four planes answered the call, but could not locate the criminals. More routine was taking part in aerial searches for missing aircraft and persons at the request of the Civil Aviation Administration and Great Falls Air Force Base.[5]

The air guard's first official state mobilization came in February 1950 after a blizzard left livestock and several hundred families snowbound on the Blackfeet Indian Reservation. With the roads impassable, Montana Air Guard cargo planes delivered more than 12,000 pounds of food and supplies at several central locations, where horse-drawn sleds distributed the provisions where needed.[6]

A few months later, an international crisis developed that deeply affected the Montana Air National Guard. On June 25, 1950, communist North Korean forces invaded South Korea and nearly overran the Korean Peninsula before reinforced American and other United Nations troops under General Douglas MacArthur finally turned the tide. By autumn 1950, UN troops had taken back all of South Korea and advanced deep into North Korea, approaching the Chinese border. In the winter of 1950–1951, however, massive Chinese divisions entered the conflict, pushing UN forces south again. Eventually, the lines stabilized and fighting continued back and forth near the 38th parallel, the original boundary between North and South Korea. A cease fire in 1953 finally ended the conflict and an uneasy truce followed.

The exigencies of the Korean War (1950–1953) resulted in an 80 percent call-up of the air reserves, mainly for stateside duty. During this time, however, numerous air guardsmen would be reassigned to serve "as fillers elsewhere in the Air Force." Thus, in respect to the Montana Air Guard, its direct contribution on the Korean Peninsula would be credited to individual servicemen, rather than to the unit.[7]

In the summer of 1950, the Montana Air Guard was ordered to send 10 of its F-51s to the U.S. Air Force in California during the buildup at the outbreak of the Korean conflict. Then, on April 1, 1951, Montana's 186th Fighter Squadron under the command of Lt. Col. Jack Blacker was federally activated. Two weeks later, 42 officers and 341 airmen with their fleet of Mustang fighters and support aircraft reported for duty at Moody Air Force Base, Georgia. Six members of the 186th's Weather Station also arrived for active service.[8]

With activation as part of the 146th Fighter Wing in Georgia, the 186th's mission shifted from the Continental Air Command to serving in the Strategic Air Command as fighter escorts. In November, the 186th was transferred to George Air Force Base, California, with a new assignment as ground support in the Tactical Air Command. While in California, Montana pilots had their first taste of flying a jet, the T-33 trainer; the airmen logged 332 hours in 2½ months.

In January 1952, the squadron participated in an Operational Readiness Test, focusing on bomber escort, ground attack, and air-to-air combat. In March and April, the 186th took part in Operation Long Horn involving many of the same exercises plus base defense, but over an extended period of time. These missions took the 186th to bases in Texas, Oklahoma, and Kentucky. After the completion of Operation Long Horn, a number of Montana aircraft and airmen served a four-month stint in Iceland.[9] Although most of the 186th would stay stateside, four Montana Air Guard pilots served in combat duty with the U.S. Air Force in Korea.

During the final months of active duty, the unit again took on a fighter-interceptor role as part of the Air Defense Command, which continued as the primary duty for the Montana Air Guard throughout the Cold War. In July 1952, the 186th began a standing runway alert at its home base, Gore Field, maintaining aircraft ready for lift off from an hour before sunup until two hours after sundown, in case of a Soviet intercontinental bomber attack from the north. On January 1, 1953, the 186th officially was deactivated and returned to state status. In nearly two years of active duty, no member of the 186th was involved in a fatal aircraft accident. Upon completion of federal service, many of the men chose to rejoin the guard.[10]

The Korean War painfully showcased some shortcomings of the country's Air National Guard—a lack of specified wartime missions, aging or obsolete aircraft, some substandard training, and general unpreparedness for combat. The causes of these difficulties were shared by both state and federal authorities.

Major Rodger D. Young, commander of Montana's squadron in 1954, reflected that during federal duty the unit's performance was hindered by other factors as well. An abrupt change to "completely unfamiliar" maintenance procedures rather confounded the unit's personnel. Also, the frequent fracturing of the unit's crews was detrimental—reassigning Montana men (often the most experienced) elsewhere, while incorporating new replacements "whose knowledge and experience were unknown." This especially drained "squadron strength at certain periods to a critical state," and the 186th's previous team training also lost much of its relevance. Yet Young defended the talents of veteran guardsmen. "Interesting to note is the fact that flight and ground personnel who had previous Air National Guard training were capable of operating almost on a par with Air Force personnel and in some cases even exceeded Air Force capability."[11]

After the difficulties of the Korean era, the U.S. Air Force formulated changes to reshape the Air National Guard into a stronger entity. Most significantly for Montana, the 186th continued to participate in the country's air defense runway alert program, and an increased number of pilot trainees attended federal instruction programs. In the mid 1950s, when all-weather flying became common for air guard units, many radar observer personnel also began receiving Air Force training.[12]

F-86A Sabre, October 1953. *MANG*

T-33 trainer, January 1957. *MANG*

At Gore Field, the air guard received its first fighter jet, an F-86A, in October 1953, which began the phasing out of the propeller-powered Mustang fighter. The 186th had the honor of being the first Air National Guard unit assigned a "Sabre." The modern Sabre jet was powered by a General Electric engine with 4,850 pounds of thrust, allowing a top speed of 650 mph and a range of 1,200 miles. In November 1953, the Montana Air Guard hosted an air show demonstrating the performance of its new fighters, while also taking Governor Hugo Aronson on a flight in a recently acquired T-33 trainer. By early 1954, the 186th possessed 10 F-86s (each named for a Montana city) and a pair of T-33s.[13]

In 1954, a $1.5-million construction project greatly enhanced the Gore Field facilities. Improvements included a new maintenance hangar, supply building, warehouse, motor pool and paint shop, crash-fire station, and mess hall. Summer training in the mid-1950s was conducted at Gowen Field in Boise, Idaho, where aerial gunnery was emphasized.[14] While settling back into state service, guardsmen returned to traditional community service projects, including participation in a Toll for Polio campaign and National Fire Prevention Week. When central Montana's Sun River flooded, unit members lent their assistance to local citizens.

The 186th experienced another aircraft conversion program in 1955, acquiring for a brief time all-weather F-94A "Starfire" fighters, which were rather unpopular with airmen because they were slower than Sabres. The F-94 soon was superseded by the two-seat F-89C, also all-weather serviceable, and armed with six 20-mm cannons. This fighter was named the "Scorpion" because of its elevated tail resembling a scorpion poised to strike. Requiring a pilot and radar observer, the Scorpions increased flying opportunities for more members of the guard.[15]

F-94B Starfire, June 1957. *MANG*

F-89C Scorpions in flight, September 1956. *MANG*

In April 1956, the Montana Air Guard was redesignated as the 120th Fighter Group and assigned to the 142nd Air Defense Wing. The 186th Fighter Interceptor Squadron retained its role as the unit's main flight element. Other units in the 120th included an Air Base Squadron, Material Squadron, and USAF Infirmary.[16]

A new insignia for the 120th, designed by Clifford Poindexter of 120th Fighter Group Headquarters, was unveiled in 1958: "The insignia's snow-capped mountains, rising sun, prairie, and river represent an adaptation of the Montana State Seal, while the rain cloud signifies the 120th's all weather capability. The same is true of the night and day portrayal separated by the conceptual fighter. The space potential of the air defense mission is shown by the stars and planets. Displayed in the lower scroll is the unit's motto, 'Seek, Contact, Destroy.'"[17]

A few years earlier, "Charlie Chicken" was adopted as the insignia for the 186th squadron. On this official Montana Air National Guard patch, Charlie, a pistol-shooting eagle (actually resembling a chicken), strode across the northern latitudes of the globe in "Montana cowboy" style guarding against a potential Russian bomber attack.

In 1956, the 550-man unit received authorization to expand to 1,000 personnel; consequently, recruiting became paramount. By 1958, the air guard's total strength rose to 683, and by 1960 it had 824 members.[18]

The Montana Air National Guard Flying Club, formed in 1957, enabled guardsmen to earn a pilot's license at about half the cost of a commercial flying school. The club's three-seat Piper Super Cruiser also was available at an affordable rate for recreational flying. Early in 1958, the club consisted of 16 members. Although women were not eligible to join the Montana Air Guard until the 1970s, wives of flying club members were granted "honorary membership," allowing them to earn a pilot's license at club rates as well. Also noteworthy in 1957, the 120th Fighter Group earned its first National Flying Safety Award.[19]

In July 1957, select members of the 186th participated in Operation Plumbbob at the Indian Springs Proving Grounds in Nevada, utilizing T-33 aircraft to take part in nuclear warfare exercises. In April of that year, security clearances also had been granted to ten Montana air guardsmen. Sent to the Nevada desert, they witnessed the firing of a MB1 "Genie," an air-to-air nuclear rocket, by an F-89J Scorpion fighter—this very plane eventually joined the Montana Air Guard's fleet a few years later.[20]

Early in 1958, the 186th Fighter Interceptor Squadron received its first F-89H, an improved Scorpion capable of carrying both missiles and 2.75 inch rockets. The Scorpion had a top speed of 636 mph and a range of 1,300 miles.

Within a few months, the 186th's fleet included 25 of the updated fighters. The Montana Air Guard's monthly newsletter, the *Scorpion,* boasted that the 186th was "one of the few ANG units in the country to be equipped with" the F-89H.[21]

On October 1, 1958, the 120th Fighter Group adopted a heightened role in the Air Defense Command by commencing a standing five-minute runway alert—for 14 hours a day, every day of the year—with a contingent of Montana air guardsmen and their armed interceptors standing ready to take to the skies throughout daylight hours. The pilots and radar observers were required to meet specific Air Defense Command qualifications before assignment to this mission. The flying crews remained on duty for up to 59 days at a time. The first crew to stand on alert included Capt. K.R. Dahlquist, the alert detachment commander, pilots Capt. H.S. Olson, 1st Lt. Roy Souder, and 2nd Lt. P.E. Jones, and radar observer Capt. Earl Morris.[22]

Escalating Cold War tensions in the late 1950s—along with expanding Russian and American nuclear arsenals, bomber forces, and long range and intercontinental missiles—necessitated a major shift in the overall U.S. armed forces strategy to a "rapid response capability." The 29th Air Division at nearby Malmstrom Air Force Base oversaw the Montana Air Guard's runway alert program. If attacking Russian planes were identified by radar in the polar regions, the 120th's interceptors were assigned as part of the American response to rapidly close with these targets before they assaulted the continental United States. This priority required more and better trained airmen and technicians, and resulted in more of an active duty atmosphere for the Montana Air Guard. (The around-the-clock shifts of Air National Guard units in the Air Defense Command strategy eventually contributed to the Pentagon's inclusion of all regular and reserve armed forces in the Total Force Policy adopted in the 1970s.) Another immediate result of the runway alert plan was heightened "respect and appreciation of Air National Guard capabilities" by the larger military establishment. For nearly 40 years, until the mid 1990s, the Montana guard's alert readiness effort would dominate its federal mission.[23]

In the 1960 biennial report, Montana's adjutant general articulated the mission of the air guard as "training to achieve an all-weather operational readiness capability that will put 50% of our aircraft and crews airborne combat ready within two hours after being alerted." The 120th maintained 20 combat ready and 10 training crews in 1960.

The 120th's summer training in 1958 and 1959 was held at Casper, Wyoming, and in 1960 at Great Falls. Facilities at Gore Field were improved and expanded in the late 1950s with the addition of a rocket storage facility, increased fuel capacity, and a new Operations and Training Building that among other purposes included a modern medical dispensary. Gore Field's main runway also was being lengthened, from 7,700 to 9,000 feet. Federal funds increasingly covered construction and operational costs for the 120th Fighter Group—not surprising, given the unit's heightened role in national air defense. The adjutant general's 1960 report noted "a ratio of over $425 federal funds for each $1 of state funds expended."[24]

The 120th underwent yet another aircraft conversion in 1960 with the F-89H being replaced by the F-89J. The newer version of the Scorpion possessed "a different fire control system and the wing tanks are all fuel as this aircraft carries a missile on the wing," noted the 120th's commander, Lt. Col. Rodger Young. "This aircraft is designed to carry a nuclear warhead missile only." The new Scorpion, with a power output of 7,200 pounds of thrust, could be armed with the AIR2A "Genie" nuclear missile.

As a result of the 120th gaining a nuclear capability, security was heightened at Gore Field and the weapons storage facilities were strengthened. One of the new interceptors was the same Scorpion that launched the nuclear missile in 1957 at Nevada's Indian Springs Proving Grounds, observed by the selected ten Montana guardsmen. (In 1970, this plane—the only Scorpion to actually launch a nuclear missile—found its final resting place as a display aircraft atop Gore Field's main gate, where it remains today.)[25] In the summer of 1961, airmen representing the 186th squadron and 120th maintenance earned a perfect score in missile firing exercises at Tyndall Air Force Base in Florida, the first Air National Guard unit to do so with the F-89J.

During the Berlin crisis in the fall of 1961, President John F. Kennedy mobilized 28 Air National Guard units. Eleven air guard fighter squadrons eventually were sent to Europe to bolster NATO forces, giving Moscow warning. Montana's 186th, already integrally involved in the nation's Air Defense Command, was not included in the call-up. While the 256 air guard fighters deployed across the Atlantic played a part "in cooling down the Communists," wrote Col. Rodger Young after a 1965 visit to Europe, the role of Montana's 120th Fighter Group in homeland defense was just as significant. "The game is the same, our battle line is here instead of Europe," he noted.[26]

The Montana Air Guard's role in national defense expanded on July 1, 1961, when the 186th squadron's daylight five-minute alert status escalated to an around-the-clock obligation to counter a potential Soviet bomber attack from the north. Anytime night and day, pilots and radar observers had to be prepared to lift off from Gore Field if ordered by Air Defense Command. The 186th was one of 25 air guard squadrons assigned to expanded 24-hour-a-day duty, a role the Air National Guard would come to monopolize. Eventually by the early 1990s, air guard squadrons constituted 100 percent of the nation's air defense interceptor force based in the continental United States. In fact, "the runway alert program was the first broad effort to integrate reserve units into the regular peacetime operating structure of the American armed forces on a continuing basis."[27]

January 25, 1962, proved to be an especially dark day for the air guard and all of Montana when a C-47 "Skytrain" from the 120th, carrying Governor Donald

Nutter, executive secretary Dennis Gorden, State Agricultural Commissioner Edward Wren, and manned by three air guardsmen—Major Clifford Hanson, Major Joseph Devine, and MSG Charles Ballard—crashed into a mountainside north of Helena. There were no survivors. The twin engine transport was en route from Helena toward Cut Bank to observe a proposed highway in the Wolf Creek area when it went down. Investigators later determined that severe turbulence ripped off the aircraft's right wing—a "structural failure in the wing due to metal fatigue." Soon after, all of the Air National Guard's C-47 "Gooney Birds" were grounded and inspected, as calls arose to replace the aging cargo carriers with turbojet aircraft.[28]

In the spring of 1962, five Montana air guardsmen—SSgt. Jack Reagor, SSgt. Eugene Charlson, TSgt. James Sutich, TSgt. Dwayne Roe, and AlC. Norbert Uhlenberg—arrived back home after a four-month tour of active duty in the South Pacific, where they had joined regular Air Force personnel conducting the U.S. military's latest round of nuclear tests, dubbed Operation Dominic. At the close of the same year, with the nation and world still reeling from the Cuban missile crisis, commander Young pleaded for guardsmen to remain in the organization. "I can think of no more direct way that any Montanan can contribute to the safety of our own people," he proclaimed. Given the nation's recent standoff with the Soviet Union in the Caribbean, Young foresaw "a strong possibility of the need to mobilize in the defense of our country...It appears that this has become a way of life for us and something we will have to live with for years to come."[29]

By the 1960s, the 186th squadron's around-the-clock runway alert under Air Defense Command included three air crews in combat-ready status at all times. "Each day's maintenance of this 24-hour vigil requires the service of nine pilots and nine officers," the *Great Falls Tribune* reported in 1963. During this period, 200 technicians—full-time civilian employees—also helped keep the 120th Fighter Group operating on a daily basis.[30]

In 1963, jet aircrews flew nearly 5,500 hours, and in 1964 accumulated 5,000 hours, consisting of "alert 'scrambles,' interceptor proficiency flights, navigational training, test and administrative flights." The 1964 decrease in flight time reflected the diversion of man hours from regular training to emergency flood operations that year. As central Montana's rivers overflowed their banks, guardsmen donated 8,000 hours of assistance in filling sandbags, boat rescues, and aerial supply transport and observation. With aid from the 120th Fighter Group, citizens of the Great Falls vicinity were able to endure the worst flood on record. Other air guard community service in the mid-1960s included blood drives and aerial transport of critical blood supplies, assistance in various aircraft emergencies involving commercial and private planes, and winter supply drops. At the same time, the air guard increased its capabilities in nuclear weapons maintenance, including the construction of additional storage facilities and in special security training.[31]

The Sun River in flood stage, 1964. *MANG*

In 1964, the National Guard Bureau reorganized the 120th Fighter Group. The 120th Combat Support Squadron replaced the 120th Air Base Squadron, and the 120th Supply Squadron was activated in place of the 120th Material Squadron. Remaining unchanged were the 120th Fighter-Group Headquarters, the 186th Fighter-Interceptor Squadron, the 120th Consolidated Aircraft Maintenance Squadron, and the 120th USAF Dispensary. Together, these components constituted "a self-sustained unit," providing "command and staff direction over assigned supply, maintenance, medical, support and combat-tactical units for executing fight-interceptor missions, identification of aircraft and destruction of enemy air craft and facilities."[32] By now, of course, the Montana Air Guard had long since lost its earlier reputation as a glorified flying club for World War II veterans.

Monetarily, too, the air guard significantly contributed to local commerce as its 20th anniversary neared. A study completed in the mid-1960s indicated that the Montana Air National Guard contributed $3.4 million annually to the Great Falls economy in the form of wages for 250 full-time technicians and 550 part-time guardsmen, plus payments for supplies, services, and the construction and maintenance of facilities. The Gore Field base was valued at $5.57 million, with the aircraft—twenty F-89 interceptors, three T-33 trainers, and one C-54 cargo plane—valued at an additional $27.5 million, and other vehicles and equipment worth approximately $2.75 million.[33]

The mid-1960s saw significant leadership changes. In 1964, Robert B. Sherman replaced Rodger D. Young as commander of Montana's 120th Fighter Group. In 1966, Young became the Montana Air Guard's first general, serving as Chief of Staff for Air at State Headquarters. Sherman's tenure as 120th commander was brief; he retired the following year for health reasons. Sherman' s successor, Emmett J. Whalen, served as group commander until 1979, with Leonard A. Gremaux filling in as acting commander in 1967 and 1968 during Whalen's temporary absence from the post.[34]

In 1966, the venerable F-89 Scorpion was replaced by the F-102A "Delta Dagger." The long, sleek, single-seat Dagger produced 17,200 pounds of thrust, with a maximum speed of 825 mph. Armament included six Hughes AIM4C/D Falcon missiles, 12 or 24 2.75 inch rockets, and one AIM26A/B. The F-102s also were equipped with improved ejection seats enabling a pilot to bail out of a crippled aircraft while traveling at high speed and altitude. This feature proved providential in 1968 when two F-102s piloted by Lt. Col. Whalen and Maj. Henry Olson brushed wing tips, throwing both planes out of control. The pilots ejected, only sustaining minor injuries from the narrow escape.

F-102A, September 1966. *MANG*

As usual, the conversion to new aircraft required months of special training for pilots and maintenance crews. After a year, the Montana Air Guard passed the Air Force evaluation for combat readiness in October 1967. The F-102 fighter jets were not designed to carry nuclear weaponry, as did the retired F-89J Scorpion. Consequently, 35 full-time nuclear weapons specialists within the Montana Air Guard's security, weapons, and fire departments were eliminated. The 120th's nuclear era, 1960–1967, was relatively short-lived.[35]

Although Montana remained mostly unaffected by the urban and college unrest sweeping much of America by the late 1960s, the Montana Air Guard was not entirely immune from the abrupt generational changes of that era. General Young lamented that "new recruits were often of the 'different breed,' and some were almost hippies,"[36] yet in 1967 he also defended his part-time guardsmen against charges of draft dodging. "This organization is an essential part of the defense of the country and [citizens] are dependent upon it to fulfill its mission when needed. Any Guardsman with the right attitude does not have to excuse himself to anyone or accept accusation of being a draft dodger. If you know that you are doing a good job as a Guardsman, then let no one criticize you. You are meeting your military obligation damn well."[37]

In 1968, President Johnson mobilized more than 10,000 Air National Guardsmen in two phases while responding to escalating tension in Southeast Asia following North Korea's capture of the intelligence ship U.S.S. *Pueblo* and the enemy's massive Tet Offensive in South Vietnam. Four tactical fighter squadrons (from Colorado, New Mexico, Iowa, and New York) were deployed to Vietnam. Also included were medical airlift squadrons for transporting wounded soldiers. Montana guardsmen were not included in the president's limited call-up. Johnson avoided activating extensive numbers of reservists for Vietnam duty, partially because he wished not to further arouse anti-war critics. This decision, however, only contributed to the perception among some elements in the population that reservist organizations—the Air National Guard included—served "as draft havens for relatively affluent young white men."

The air guard units called into service were combat ready and performed well, a vast improvement over the Korean mobilizations. By this time, of course, relations between the U.S. Air Force and the Air National Guard were increasingly cooperative, with guard units trading some of their autonomy for vastly increased federal dollars.[38]

In the midst of the 1968 mobilizations, Brig. Gen. Rodger Young and group commander Leonard Gremaux reminded Montana guardsmen that although a call-up of any portion of the 120th was unlikely, the unit needed to be vigilant in respect to such a possibility. "We cannot afford to be unprepared, either in our personal affairs or our operational capability assuming that we won't be called. If we do, we have failed in our obligation."

Meanwhile, the Montana Air Guard's assistance to the effort in Southeast Asia took other forms. In March 1968, an air guard C-54 cargo plane transported 5,000 pounds of soap to South Vietnam to be distributed to civilian hospitals and orphanages. The soap was collected by the Montana Jaycees under the direction of air guardsman Art Galliger of Lewistown. In 1971, 22 members of the 120th USAF Dispensary aided wounded servicemen at Travis Air Force Base in California, offering medical expertise in postoperative wards, pharmacies, labs, supply and X-ray centers, and the Air Evacuation Central Staging Unit.[39] Also during the late 1960s, two of Montana's F-102 pilots volunteered for tours of duty with the U.S. Air Force in Southeast Asia. Major Harold Juedeman flew 43 combat missions, and Capt. Gary Blair served in 72 combat missions. Both received the prestigious Air Medal.[40]

The changing times in America, with frequent protests and demonstrations in urban areas and on college campuses, affected air guard training. During the summer of 1968, 150 airmen practiced riot and crowd control, but civil unrest never erupted locally. For summer training in 1970, the 120th Fighter Group was sent to Gulfport, Mississippi—the first time in years that the organization held an encampment outside its home region.[41] In this period, officers reported that hair and uniform standards were becoming more difficult to uphold, given the pervasive fashion trends among most young men in America. By the early 1970s, the National Guard Association formed a Committee on Grooming Standards to survey state guard units regarding the impact of strict grooming standards on recruitment. Lt. Col. Francis Murphy of the Montana Air Guard responded that approximately 15 percent of potential recruits opted not to join because they considered the short haircut requirement too severe, and 15 percent of air guardsmen failed to reenlist for the same reason. Murphy believed that the "relaxation of the fullness of hair styles to accommodate present moderate styles would help" bolster recruitment numbers, but he opposed "any relaxation in the length [because it] would result in an unkept, slovenly appearance." In 1974, new Air National Guard regulations permitted long-haired guardsmen to conceal their hair by wearing "short hair wigs of good quality" when serving for a month or less. The wig policy resulted in "some pretty bizarre looking guardsmen and a sometimes almost comical cat and mouse game" between enlisted personnel and their superiors.[42]

Jody Lee Nichols. *MANG*

Effective on July 1, 1968, the U.S. Air Force allowed Air National Guard units to recruit women. The 120th, with 750 personnel, was authorized to accept women to fill 3 officer, 12 enlisted, and 10 registered nurse positions. In 1971, Jody Lee Nichols became the first female enlistee to join Montana's 120th. After completing basic training, this licensed practical nurse was assigned to the 120th USAF Dispensary. Soon after, army veterans Connie Wilcox and Maggie Coomes also joined the Montana Air Guard, with both serving as administrative specialists. The following year, Lt. Gwendolyn Leidmann was hired as the base communications officer, the first woman to hold a major managerial post within the Montana Air Guard. Meanwhile, SSgt.

Christine Ruff became the organization's first female recruiter. Although integrating women into the guard culture was hardly a flawless transition, this new policy held advantages for the organization, as it "effectively doubled the pool of prospective recruits available to fill ever increasing unit vacancies." By the end of 1975, 39 women were assigned to the 120th, "many of them in what traditionally [were] male-oriented jobs."[43]

At the close of the Vietnam era, the Pentagon's new Total Force Policy governed policies pertaining to the Air National Guard and other reserve organizations. The plan intended "to strengthen and rebuild public confidence in the reserves while saving money by reducing the size of the active-duty force." Reserve units no longer took a backseat to the regular armed forces, but assumed a greater role, receiving a larger percentage of the defense budget. Since 1952, Montana's air defense runway alert program, of course, already was filling a crucial, full-time role in national defense.[44]

In 1972, the Montana Air Guard experienced another aircraft conversion. The transition from the F-102 to the F-106 "Delta Dart" constituted "one of the biggest challenges the 120th Fighter Group has faced in its history," reported the monthly *Montana Air Guardsman.* Montana was the first guard unit selected to receive this state-of-the-art fighter interceptor, a highly complex aircraft with an equally complicated weapons system. Slightly longer and lighter than the F-102, the F-106 housed a Pratt & Whitney J75P17 engine capable of 24,500 pounds of thrust and a top speed of 1,525 mph, almost twice as fast as its predecessor. It could carry four AIM4F/G missiles and one AIM2A "Genie" rocket.[45]

F-106 Delta Dart. *MANG*

In the spring of 1972, four pilots—Lt. Don Stevlingson, Maj. Jerry Cooper, Maj. J.K. Olson, and Capt. Wayne Finney—received intensive training on the new aircraft at Tyndall Air Force Base, Florida. Upon returning to Great Falls, they joined U.S. Air Force personnel in instructing guard pilots on the intricacies of these "electronic nightmares." Facilities makeovers and special training—especially regarding maintenance—was a huge undertaking for the 120th Fighter Group. Only two months elapsed, however, between suspension of the F-102 runway alerts and the full resumption of 24-hour duty with the new F-106s on July 1, 1972.

In the years following the conversion, members of the 120th—redesignated as the 120th Fighter Interceptor Group in October 1972—were exceedingly proud of their fleet of F-106s. "Montana's airplanes were almost a legend throughout the Air National Guard and the U.S. Air Force with respect to their appearance and reliability," later boasted the organization's in-house history. Yet in the 1970s, a number of F-106 mishaps resulted in some jets being destroyed. There were no serious pilot injuries, until 1977 when Lt. David L. Denning was killed in Alberta during North American Air Defense Command exercises.[46]

The 1970s nevertheless proved to be a golden decade for the 120th, which racked up a multitude of performance awards. In the fall of 1973, the unit earned an "Outstanding" evaluation from an Air Defense Command Headquarters team after a combined General and Capability Inspection. "It was a great day for the 120th," the *Montana Air Guardsman* announced, "as the report compliments a great number of functional areas from Command and Management down to the individual member, his grooming and military courtesy." In June 1975, the 120th Fighter Interceptor Group for the first time earned a long-coveted "Outstanding" evaluation during an eight-day Operational Readiness Inspection, which was conducted by an Air Defense Command team every 18 months.[47]

The 120th also took its impressive show on the road. In October 1974, the Montana Air Guard was represented by a team of pilots, weapons loaders, and ground support crewmen at the William Tell Fighter Interceptor Weapons Meet held at Tyndall Air Force Base, Florida. The 120th was one of only two air guard units earning berths at this contest, which included the best interceptor teams from the United States and Canada. The competition tested the combat skills of the teams in a simulated continental bomber attack. In the prestigious event, the 120th won first place in the F-106 category. Lt. Col. Albert Cooper, Capt. David Harding, Capt. Frederick Herre, Capt. Joseph Comeau, and Lt. Warren Roach were awarded the "Firebee" killer plaque for their missile strikes on the smallest, most elusive targets in the competition. TSgt. Bill Brosz, TSgt. Paul Heppner, TSgt. Lowell Olson, TSgt. Scott Pering, SSgt. Kenneth Larson, SSgt. Stephen Lyczewski, and SSgt. Joseph Skaggs of the loading team were awarded the Air Force Commendation Medal in December for their winning performance at the competition. In the spring of 1975, all 42 members of the first-place William Tell team received Air Force Commendation Medals for their "outstanding professional skill, job knowledge and ability."[48]

In August 1975, the 120th's weapons team returned to Tyndall Air Force Base to participate in the "Loadeo" competition against 20 other units. TSgt. Michael Miller joined Olson, Pering, and Brosz on this squad. Montana's load team earned perfect marks—a first in the history of the competition—in its second loading exercise. At the end of the competition, it emerged with first-place team honors.

In November 1976, the 120th returned to the bi-annual William Tell competition to successfully defend its reign as the top F-106 Delta Dart fighter interceptor unit in North America. Consequently, it became the first air guard unit to win the meet two consecutive times. Montana pilots Capt. Rex Tanberg and Capt. Joel Rude scored perfect marks in several attack simulations, and at the competition's conclusion, the 120th accumulated 19,335 points out of a possible 21,300, winning the meet.[49]

Montana's 120th returned to Tyndall's William Tell competitions several more times, placing "2nd" twice and "3rd" once. The 120th's missile loading team competed eight times, bringing home the "1st" place trophy in their division four times, and placing a respectable "2nd" on four occasions. In both 1974 and 1975, the 120th was ranked "1st" among all Air National Guard flying units by the National Guard Association and the American Fighter Pilots Association, winning the Spaatz Trophy and the Winston P. Wilson Award, respectively, for this top billing. The unit won a number of other annual accolades in the 1970s

William Tell loaders. *MANG*

William Tell pilots, 1978. *MANG*

and 1980s, including eight Distinguished Flying Unit Awards, five Air Force Outstanding Unit Awards, the U.S. Air Force Supply Effectiveness Award, the U.S. Air Force Maintenance Award, and the Aerospace Defense Command "A" Award.

In 1985, the 120th Fighter Interceptor Group won the ultimate honor with the Hughes Trophy, acknowledging the best fighter interceptor group in the Air Force. In this competition, air guard units competed with a full range of regular U.S. Air Force units from Europe, the Pacific, Alaska, the 1st Air Force, the Tactical Air Command, and the Air Reserve. Judging was based on a variety of criteria, from a unit's inspection results to operational readiness, deployments, and community relations. The 120th was only the second air guard unit to be honored with the Hughes award in the competition's 33-year history.[50]

In the 1970s, there were no shortages of state and local emergencies. In November 1971, members of the 120th were instrumental in helping bring an international skyjacking incident to a nonviolent conclusion. An Air Canada DC8, flying from Toronto with 188 passengers and a crew of 6, was skyjacked by a Canadian who forced the plane to land at the Great Falls airport twice, first to collect ransom money and later to release passengers. Airborne a third time, the crew finally managed to subdue the hijacker and regain control of the airliner, landing safely in Calgary. Among other tasks, air guardsmen provided open lines of communication, ground transportation, food, refueling services, and special airport lighting during this crisis.[51]

In the 1970s, air guard personnel assisted in keeping state medical and prison facilities operational during employee walk outs, with the longest strike extending 37 days in February and March 1979. Alternating on ten-day assignments with army guardsmen, members of the 120th performed patient and inmate care at the Boulder River School and Hospital, the Galen Hospital, and the Montana State Prison in Deer Lodge. Other state mobilizations included fighting fires in western Montana in August 1973, and providing flood relief for Cascade County residents in June 1975 when the Missouri and Sun rivers overflowed their banks. In the flood's aftermath, air guardsmen refurbished the water-damaged Girl Scout camp, "Scoutana," near Augusta, restoring the facility in time for the girls' summer activities. In 1976, the 120th attended to exploding commercial propane tanks touched off by a train derailment in Belt.[52]

Other achievements included raising $15,000 for the March of Dimes by organizing a walk-a-thon in 1975, presenting statewide flyovers and participating in Operation Patriotism to celebrate the nation's 1976 bicentennial, and hosting Vice President Walter Mondale and several cabinet members arriving in Air Force Two at Gore Field in 1978. Also in 1978, Philip W. Strope was promoted to general when serving as Chief of Staff for Air at Montana Air Guard Headquarters, only the second Montana air guardsman to achieve this high of rank. In 1979, Lt. Col. Paul Maxwell took the reins as group commander from Col. Emmett Whalen, who subsequently became Assistant Adjutant General for Air in Helena.[53]

But the decade closed on a somber note. In September 1979 during a flyover at a Dillon parade, Capt. Joel Rude's F-106 crashed in the downtown area after a wing clipped the top of a grain elevator. A 17,000-gallon fuel tank, and eventually the grain elevator as well, were ignited by the crash's flaming debris. Rude, an experienced, award-winning pilot, unfortunately did not survive. Luckily, no parade-goers or residents died, although 16 people sustained injuries. As a result of the tragedy, flyovers were banned from almost all Montana events, as the 120th became more reflective about these kinds of demonstrations.[54]

Captain Joel Rude, March 1976. *MANG*

In 1980, the 120th lent a hand when deployed to Springfield, Illinois, to help build a firing range for the Illinois air and army guard, and to Phoenix to remodel an Arizona Air Guard building. When the 84th Fighter Interceptor Squadron at Castle Air Force Base in California was gradually deactivated that year, seven Montana air guardsmen with two F-106s served runway alert duty at the airfield.[55]

In 1981, the 120th hosted President Ronald Reagan and Air Force One, providing security for the presidential aircraft while Reagan spoke at C.M. Russell High School in Great Falls. In 1982, air guardsmen assisted in the Montana Special Olympics in Butte. In 1983, the unit held its 14th Fire Service Training Academy, the largest ever, drawing participants from Malmstrom Air Force Base, Montana cities, and from other states in the region. In 1984, the 120th contributed to Great Falls' centennial celebration by providing a 50 x 30 foot American flag in Outlook Park, a joint project with the Great Falls Realtor Association.

Also in 1984, a portion of the Montana guard's runway alert team was transferred to the nation's southern border. Under Maj. Dick Trebescha, a permanent detachment of 15 personnel and three F-106s was assigned to Davis-Monthan Air Force Base near Tucson. By 1990, the 120th's Detachment 1 in Arizona had proven its effectiveness, winning the Tactical Air Command's award for Best Detachment Facility. Also in 1990, the detachment's TSgt. Melodee McClusky was selected as the Air Force Air National Guard NCO of the Year.[56]

By 1985, the air guard's membership boasted a record 1,003 personnel, including about 350 full-time technicians and active guard reservists. The 120th's commander, Paul Maxwell, was promoted to brigadier general, becoming Assistant Adjutant General for Air at State Headquarters. Lt. Col. Gary Blair took Maxwell's place as group commander and served in this role until 1989.

Also in 1985, the 120th was the first air guard unit to take part in "Red Flag" exercises at Nellis Air Force Base in Nevada, a two-week gathering of aircraft and maintenance specialists from the U.S. Air Force, U.S. Navy, and the French Air Force to simulate war games scenarios involving different aircraft types. The 120th also began participating in temporary deployments of aircraft and technicians to airfields around the state and in Canada to better prepare guardsmen for operations at other regional sites if necessary.[57]

In 1986, the 120th began converting from F-106s to the F-16A/B "Fighting Falcon," with the usual intensive transition and procedural training. The Falcon, with a 30-foot wingspan and nearly 50 feet in length, was compact and lightweight. Pilots could land and depart from practically any improved airstrip. The Pratt & Whitney F100PW200 engine had 23,500 pounds of thrust, allowing a top speed of 1,466 mph, qualifying as Mach 2. Armaments included two

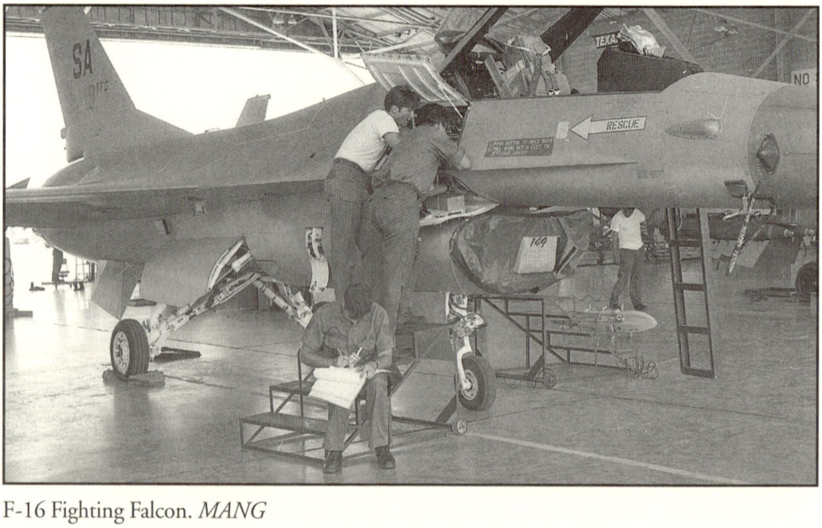

F-16 Fighting Falcon. *MANG*

AIM120, two AIM7, and one AIM9 air-to-air missiles, and a 20-mm Gatling gun.

As usual, Montana's "new" F-16s were hand-me-downs from the U.S. Air Force and in various stages of repair or readiness. In addition to becoming familiarized with the new jets, the 120th's technicians also had the responsibility of restoring the fighters to top working order. In the spring of 1987, the 120th's runway alert duties were suspended for three months while the conversion was completed. Gore's alert status was up and running again on July 1. At this time, the group's C-131 support plane was replaced by a C-130A "Hercules," the unit's first propjet aircraft.[58]

C-130A Hercules, winter 1986. *MANG*

The only state mobilization of the Montana Air Guard in the 1980s occurred in September and October 1988 at the end of an especially hot, dry summer. Up to this time, air guardsmen already had helped to control a number of forest and grassland fires in western and central Montana. Once the unit was activated, the largest fire fighting efforts that the airmen participated in included the Lick Creek, Elk Creek, and Canyon Creek fires.[59]

In the late 1980s, the 120th continued to take part in various deployments, both near and far, including air defense exercises at Canadian and Alaskan bases and repeat performances at Nellis Air Force Base in Nevada. In addition, 120th firefighters participated in Team Spirit 89 at Kadena Air Force Base in Japan. In 1989, 40 members of the 120th Civil Engineering Flight spent two weeks in Honduras constructing facilities for U.S. training forces, as well as providing concrete slabs for a new school as part of a humanitarian civic action program. In January 1989, Group Commander Gary Blair was promoted to brigadier general and appointed Adjutant General of Montana, the first air officer named to that office. Lt. Col. Donald Stevlingson succeeded Blair as the 120th's commander.[60]

In the spring of 1990, the National Guard Bureau announced that the five-minute, 24-hour runway alert system in the northern tier of states would end on September 1 of that year. Termination of the program was first proposed in 1988, with arguments that given the shift of radar surveillance far north in Canada, keeping interceptors and their crews at instant readiness within the United States was ineffective. Also, by 1990 the Soviet Union's disintegration appeared to be bringing the Cold War to an end, and the alert program was unnecessary. This entailed the loss of part-time pilots (adding up to 7 full-time positions altogether) and 14 full-time technicians. Some guardsmen protested the program's demise, but to no avail. On September 30, 1990, Gore Field's runway alert stood down for good, ending a 38-year tradition.[61]

In the last month of alert duties, an extensive overhaul of the F-16 fleet began, which "enhanced operational capabilities" and readied the aircraft for future missions. The Air Defense Fighter program was installed in the fighters, which among other improvements included an Identification Friend-or-Foe system, a Combined Altitude Radar Altimeter and updated radar, a harness for a Global Positioning System, and a Continuous Wave Illuminator, permitting the on board fitting of the AIM7 missile.[62]

Following the end of its alert commitment, the 120th's first overseas deployment included a contingent of F-16s and personnel participating in Sentry Nighthawk, an illegal drug interdiction program executed from Howard Air Force Base in Panama. After this month-long deployment in the fall of 1990, the 120th returned to Panama several other times from 1991 to 1994 to participate in Sentry Nighthawk. Participation in another drug interdiction effort, Coronet Buccaneer, occurred in Puerto Rico in March 1992.[63]

During the first Iraq war—Operation Desert Shield and Operation Desert Storm—72 members of the 120th were federally activated from mid-December 1990 to mid-June 1991, serving as replacements at various stateside U.S. Air Force bases, including Mountain Home, Luke, Holloman, and Nellis. Twenty-six guardsmen of the 120th clinic operated the 842nd Strategic Hospital at Grand Forks Air Force Base in North Dakota from February to April 1991. Thirteen activated 120th security police were kept at home, providing heightened security at Gore Field. The 120th Fighter Interceptor Group, having been assigned to federal continental air defense for nearly four decades, was not prepared and had not been trained to operate in the Persian Gulf combat zones, with the threats from surface-to-air missiles and chemical attacks.[64]

However, relieved of the ready alert mandate, the unit was enabled to participate in increased training deployments. In June 1991, 6 F-16s and 100 support personnel were deployed to Ellison Air Force Base in Alaska for a week of Dissimilar Air Combat Tactics training with Ellison's F-15s. The same year, 50 members of the 120th Civil Engineering Squadron and the 120th Services Flight constructed buildings for the Belize Self Defense Force. In 1993 and 1994, civil engineering personnel were again deployed overseas to work on various construction projects in Great Britain and South Korea. In June 1992, several 120th aircraft and a support team of technicians flew to Newfoundland to engage in NORAD exercises.

Later that year, five pilots and 49 ground personnel returned to the William Tell Competition at Tyndall Air Force Base in Florida, after a 10-year absence. The 120th won first place among participating air guard units and placed sixth overall. In August 1993, 20 members of the 120th Communications Flight participated in exercises with the Royal Air Force at Mindenhall, England. Two years later, they were sent to Anderson Air Force Base on Guam. In 1996, the 120th's military police were deployed to Atlanta, Georgia, to help bolster the city's security during the Summer Olympic Games.[65]

Closer to home, the Montana Air Guard was mobilized on a state level several times in the 1990s. In April 1991, 124 members of the 120th provided patient care and basic maintenance services at the Montana Developmental Center in Boulder during a brief state employee strike. That fall, activated air guardsmen also fought forest fires near Lewistown. More fires during the summer of 1994 demanded state activation, with 160 airmen mobilized to assist U.S. Forest Service fire crews at a number of major blazes.[66]

The Montana Air Guard experienced a number of structural changes in the 1990s. In 1991, James Higgins became the group commander. Although there was talk in 1992 of converting the 120th from a fighter role to a transport group—exchanging the F-16 fleet for one consisting mostly of C-130s—the conversion never materialized, to the relief of many 120th members. Yet the group was happy to see its C-130B "Hercules" replaced with a C-26B support plane, coming directly from the manufacturer and only the second new aircraft ever

C-26 support plane, 1992 (in foreground). *MANG*

assigned to the Montana Air Guard. In April 1992, the 120th Fighter Interceptor Group was redesignated as the 120th Fighter Group under the Air Combat Command.

Throughout this transitional period, the unit continued to earn performance awards. For example, in early 1992 the 120th's recruiters won the Highest Net Gain Award, the Zero Basic Military Training Elimination Rate Award, and the Highest Overall Manned State Award for air guard units. In the 1993 Operational Readiness Inspection, major ground attack exercises were added for the first time, in addition to regular operations in regard to nuclear fallout scenarios. Training in "Ability to Survive and Operate"—i.e., readiness for countering terrorist and small unit ground attacks—also became part of the 120th's repertoire.

In early 1995, Washington, D.C., announced that the 120th would transition into a General Purpose unit. Although this change was to be accompanied by an aircraft conversion—with a lesser number of F-16 C and D models replacing Montana's F-16 A and B versions—ultimately the 120th's preference to retain its existing larger fleet prevailed. On October 1, 1995, the 120th Fighter Group was redesignated as the 120th Fighter Wing.[67]

In 1996, to better prepare the Montana Air Guard for its new multipurpose mission, large numbers of personnel from nearly all elements of the 120th were deployed to Fargo, North Dakota, home of the 119th Fighter Wing. They participated in Joint Field Training Exercises, which simulated chemical, biological, and radiological attacks. The same year, most of the civil engineering unit was split from the 120th Fighter Wing to establish the Red Horse Squadron (Rapid Engineering Deployable Heavy Operational Repair Squadron Engineering) at Malmstrom Air Force Base. The mission of this joint active duty and air guard squadron was rapid deployment worldwide to build necessary structures, even in the most primitive locations, preparatory to troop arrivals. With the formation of the Red Horse Squadron, Montana now had two major air guard units. In 1998, the Red Horse Squadron deployed to Honduras for its two-week annual training and constructed foundations for three schools in Jesus De Otoro.[68]

In June 1997, the Montana Air Guard celebrated its 50th anniversary with official ceremonies. In September, aircraft displays, retiree ceremonies, an open house, and an evening social event were organized to commemorate this milestone. The Montana legislature issued a resolution recognizing 1997 as a "year of commemoration for the 120th Fighter Wing."[69]

In February 1998, the U.S. Air Force announced that the Montana Air Guard officially would be retired from a role in air defense in the following October, adopting instead a combined offensive and defensive federal mission. This meant that the 120th's pilots, support personnel, and F-16s would be available for peacekeeping and military actions anywhere in the world. With this shift came the end of the 120th's permanent detachment at Davis-Monthan Air Base in Arizona, in operation since 1984 guarding the southern border and tracking drug smugglers. With the layoff of 18 full-time personnel in Arizona, the change left the Montana Air Guard with about 340 full-time employees and 1,050 part-time guard members.

As the end of the 20th century approached, the 120th in addition to its continued mission of intercepting enemy planes would specialize in air-to-ground capabilities—"bombing or strafing ground targets." A conversion of aircraft was not imminent, though the F-16A fighters were nearing 20 years in age, with "their frames...edging closer to the 3,750-hour threshold when they [could not] be flown anymore as a safety precaution."[70]

In a few short years after its creation in 1947, the Montana Air Guard had settled into its federal role as an integral part of the Air Defense Command, eventually assuming a 24-hour runway alert status in the early 1960s. The unit stood at-the-ready to intercept a potential Soviet attack across North America's vast polar region. Fortunately for the United States, Canada, Europe, and indeed the world, that need did not arise. By remaining prepared and highly capable, however, the Montana Air Guard played an invaluable role in the Air Defense Command as a deterrent to the Soviet Union, thus helping to maintain a tenuous peace.

Nearly four decades of runway alert duty—by flight and ground crews alike—also had honed the Montana Air Guard's skills in air defense to award-winning precision. Countless hours of training in the vast Big Sky airspace and at Gore Field paid off in competitions against other Air National Guard, Air Reserve, U.S. Air Force, and U.S. Navy units across the country. Just as the Montana guard's frequent conversions to new aircraft were challenges to the airmen's talents and tenacity, the transition to a general defensive/offensive federal mission in the 1990s posed yet another demand on the organization's ability to change with the times.

The Montana Air Guard's obligation to the state for providing community service and assisting in times of difficulty also remained strong. During natural and man-made emergencies, air guardsmen remained on constant alert to aid the welfare and needs of Montana's citizens.

Notes

1. Maj. Rodger D. Young, ANG Commander, to Chief, National Guard Bureau, July 13, 1954, "Korean War – Mobilization Data, ANG," Box TF AS-1, National Guard Memorial Library, Washington, D.C. [hereafter cited as NGML].
2. *Montana Air National Guard: The First 50 Years* (120th Fighter Wing – Montana National Guard, 1947–1997), 4–6.
3. Major Clifford Owen was succeeded by Capt. Robert L. Dardis and Lt. Col. Floyd Robberson in the early 1950s. Ibid., 6–7; "A Brief History of the 120th FIGp and 186th

FISq," Historical File 9.C, Office of James Sharpe, Wing Historian, Montana Air National Guard, Great Falls International Airport; *Biennial Report of the Adjutant General, State of Montana, 1948–1950*, 32–33, 34, Montana State Library, Helena, Montana.

4. Ibid., 32.
5. Ibid., 34; *Montana Air National Guard*, 6.
6. "120th Fighter Group, Table of Federal and State Missions and Mobilizations," Historical File 9.C, Office of James Sharpe; *Biennial Report, 1948–1950*, 34; "Operations Get Under Way for Relief of Blackfeet," *Great Falls Tribune*, February 3, 1950.
7. Charles J. Gross, *The Air National Guard: A Short History* (Washington, D.C.: U.S. Government Printing Office, 1994), 13–14.
8. *Montana Air National Guard*, 7; *Biennial Report, 1950–1952*, 30–39; "Data Concerning Air National Guard Units Called into Active Military Service," Folder: "ANG Mobilization – Korea," Box TF AS-1, NGML; *Montana Air National Guard* (10-year Commemorative Booklet), 16, in Montana Military History Museum, Fort Harrison, Helena, Montana.
9. *Montana Air National Guard*, 7–8; Maj. Rodger D. Young, ANG Commander, to Chief, National Guard Bureau, July 13, 1954, Folder: "Korean War – Mobilization Data, ANG," Box TF AS-1, NGML; *Montana Air National Guard* (10-year Commemorative Booklet), 16.
10. *Montana Air National Guard*, 8; *Montana Air National Guard* (10-year Commemorative Booklet), 22.
11. Gross, *Short History*, 13; Maj. Rodger D. Young, ANG Commander, to Chief, National Guard Bureau, July 13, 1954, "Korean War – Mobilization Data, ANG," Box TF AS-1, NGML.
12. Gross, *Short History*, 16; *Biennial Report, 1956–1958*, 48; *Biennial Report, 1958–1960*, 44.
13. *Montana Air National Guard*, 8–9, 57.
14. Ibid., 9–10.
15. Ibid., 10, 59, 61; "A Brief History," Historical File 9.C, Office of James Sharpe.
16. Action Data Sheet for the 120th Fighter Group (Air Defense) HQ – Montana, obtained May 1, 1998 from Col. Raymond Read, Montana National Guard, Helena, Montana.
17. *Montana Air National Guard*, 10.
18. Ibid., *Biennial Report, 1956–1958*, 50; *Biennial Report, 1958–1960*, 43.
19. *Montana Air National Guard*, 10; "MANG Flying Club," *Scorpion* (January 1958): 2.
20. The ten men receiving the Nevada security clearances included capts. Robert Sherman and Emmett Whalen, CWO Rex Tanberg, Lt. Lippert, and sgts. G. Roadhouse, G. Schmidt, R. Nevins, R. Rutz, R. Vian, and N. Fritz. Memo by Col. R.W. Finn, USAF, April 2, 1957; Col. Jack D. Blanchard, USAF, to Commander, 1950th Test Group (Nuclear), April 5, 1957; Maj. Gen. Winston P. Wilson, USAF, to Adjutant General, State of Ohio, August 7, 1957, Folders "Operation Pilgrim" and "Operation PLUMBBOB," NGB Decimal File 1957 (354.2), Box 3173, Record Group 168, National Archives, Washington, D.C.; Larry G. Barton, "F-89J Scorpion," *Montana Air Guardsman* (September 1970): 4.
21. *Biennial Report, 1956–1958*, 48; *Montana Air National Guard*, 61; "New Scorpions – F-89H," *Scorpion* (June 1958): 6.
22. "Montana Air Guard on Runway Alert," *Scorpion* (October 1958), 1.
23. *Biennial Report, 1956–1958*, 49.
24. *Biennial Report, 1958–1960*, 43–44.

25. Roger D. Young, "Commander's Message," *Scorpion* (March 1960): 1; *Montana Air National Guard*, 11, 61; "F-89 Is Mounted; It's Been a Long Wait!" *Montana Air Guardsman* (November 1970): 1.
26. "Air and Ground Crews Set Perfect Record at Tyndall," *Scorpion* (September 1961): 1; Rodger D. Young, Colonel, Montana ANG, Chief of Staff, "A Look at Europe," *Scorpion* (May 1965): 3.
27. *Biennial Report, 1960–1962*, "Operations"; Charles J. Gross, *The Air National Guard and the American Military Tradition* (Washington, D.C.: Historical Services Division, National Guard Bureau, 1995), 87.
28. *Montana Air National Guard*, 11–12, 71; "In Memoriam," *Scorpion* (February 1962): 1.
29. "Guardsmen Return from Active Duty," *Scorpion* (July 1962): 3; Commander Rodger D. Young, "To All Guardsmen," *Scorpion* (December 1962).
30. "'Minutemen' of the Montana Air National Guard," *Great Falls Tribune*, May 5, 1963. The feature article focused on the 750 air Montanans and their one weekend a month training and two week summer encampment.
31. *Biennial Report, 1962–1964*, 19–20; *Montana Air National Guard*, 13; *Montana Air National Guard—Seek, Contact and Destroy, 1947–1967* (20-year Commemorative Booklet), Montana Military History Museum.
32. *Biennial Report, 1964–1966*, 10–11.
33. *Montana Air National Guard*, 13; *Biennial Report, 1964–1966*, 15.
34. "Group Command Changes," *Scorpion* (October 1965): 1; *Montana Air National Guard*, xi, 14.
35. Ibid., 13–15, 63; "F-102 Facts," *Montana Air Guardsman* (May 1967): 2; *Biennial Report, 1966–1968*, 14.
36. *Montana Air National Guard*, 15.
37. Rodger D. Young, Brig. Gen., Mont. ANG, Chief of Staff for Air, "What Is a Guardsman?" *Montana Air Guardsman* (February 1967): 1.
38. Gross, *Air National Guard*, 96–102; Charles J. Gross, *Mobility Milestones: An Air National Guard Chronology* (Washington, D.C.: National Guard Bureau, Historical Services Division, 1996), 5.
39. Rodger D. Young and Leonard A. Gremaux, "To All Guardsmen," *Montana Air Guardsman* (February 1968): 1; "Soap to Vietnam," *Montana Air Guardsman* (March 1968): 2; *Montana Air National Guard*, 16.
40. Ibid., 15–16.
41. Ibid.
42. Ibid., 15, 20; Francis J. Murphy, Lt. Col., MT ANG, Air Administrative Officer/State to NGAUS, Washington, D.C., January 11, 1974, "NGAUS Committee on Grooming Standards," Folder: "Grooming Standards #2," Box TF-U2, NGML.
43. *Montana Air National Guard*, 15–17; "First WAF Enlisted into MONT ANG," *Montana Air Guardsman* (May 1971): 1; "Lady Airman," *Big Sky Flyer* (October 1975): 2.
44. Gross, *Air National Guard*, 113–15.
45. "Official: F-106 to Come," *Montana Air Guardsman* (April 1972): 2; *Montana Air National Guard*, 65.
46. "First '6' Pilot" and 'Eyeballin' the Cockpit," *Montana Air Guardsman* (June 1972): 1; "The 59 Day Caper," *Montana Air Guardsman* (August 1971): 1; *Montana Air National Guard*, 18–20, 23–24.
47. Ibid., 16, 22, 24; "Best Inspection Ever," *Montana Air Guardsman* (December 1973): 1; "120th Is Outstanding," *Montana Air Guardsman* (June 1975): 1.

48. "History of the 120th Fighter Wing, 186th Fighter Squadron, Montana Air National Guard," Historical File 9.C, Office of James Sharpe; "We're Number One," *Montana Air Guardsman* (November/December 1974): 1; "Seven Get Medals," *Montana Air Guardsman* (January 1975): 1; "42 Awarded AFCM," *Montana Air Guardsman* (March 1975-II): 1.
49. *Montana Air National Guard,* 20–23.
50. "History of the 120th Fighter Wing, 186th Fighter Squadron, Montana Air National Guard," Historical File 9.C, Office of James Sharpe; "'A' Award Presented," *Big Sky Flyer* (November/December 1975): 1; "120th FIGp Wins Hughes Trophy: We Are Number One," *Big Sky Flyer* (April 1986): 1–2.
51. *Montana Air National Guard,* 16; "Skyjacking," *Montana Air Guardsman* (November 1971): 9.
52. *Montana Air National Guard,* 19, 21, 23–25; "120th Fighter Group, Table of Federal and State Missions and Mobilizations," Historical File 9.C, Office of James Sharpe; "Guard Helps Flood Victims" and "Summer Fun Rescued," *Montana Air Guardsman* (July/August 1975): 1.
53. *Montana Air National Guard,* 21, 23–25.
54. Ibid., 26.
55. Ibid., 26–27.
56. Ibid., 27–28, 32.
57. Ibid., 28.
58. Ibid., 28–30, 67, 79; "Sleek Aircraft to Arrive in 1986," *Big Sky Flyer* (July 1986): 1.
59. "120th Fighter Group, Table of Federal and State Missions and Mobilizations," Historical File 9.C, Office of James Sharpe; *Montana Air National Guard,* 32.
60. Ibid., 31–32; "U.S. Forces Receive Assist," *Big Sky Flyer* (March 1989), 4.
61. *Montana Air National Guard,* 31, 33.
62. Ibid., 33.
63. Ibid., 34–35, 37.
64. "120th Fighter Group, Table of Federal and State Missions and Mobilizations," Historical File 9.C, Office of James Sharpe; *Montana Air National Guard,* 34–35; "ANG Support of 'Desert Storm' Unit Mobilization Status by State," Folder: "ANG Desert Shield/Desert Storm III," Box: "Guard, Desert Shield/Desert Storm," National Guard Association Library, Washington, D.C.
65. *Montana Air National Guard,* 35–38.
66. "120th Fighter Group, Table of Federal and State Missions and Mobilizations," Historical File 9.C, Office of James Sharpe; *Montana Air National Guard,* 35, 37.
67. Ibid., xii, 35–38.
68. Ibid., 39; Sgt. 1st Class Donald R. Dunn II, "New Horizons '98 Kicks Off – Reserve, Guard Troops Hard at Work," *Tropic Times* (February 6, 1998): 3.
69. *Montana Air National Guard,* 39–40; "House Joint Resolution No. 17," 55th Legislature, Office of Col. Raymond Read, Montana National Guard, Helena, Montana.
70. Peter Johnson, "Air Force Gives New Role to Montana Air National Guard," *Great Falls Tribune*, February 11, 1998.

Epilogue

Operation Big Sky: Reorganization in the Modern Era

Colonel Raymond K. Read, USA (Retired)
Montana Military History Museum, Director

Background: 1947–1988

Montana's 163rd Infantry Regiment was called to active duty on September 16, 1940, for a one-year period of training as part of the nation's first mobilization in response to fascist aggression in Europe and Asia. The one-year training period was extended in late 1941, and then the regiment served for the duration of World War II after the Japanese attacked Pearl Harbor. The 163rd remained assigned to the 41st Infantry "Sunset" Division, which achieved fame as the "fighting Jungleers." The regiment received recognition a number of times for exemplary service in the Pacific Theater. Deactivation officially occurred on January 1, 1946.

Due to the 163rd being federalized in 1940, Montana did not have National Guard units for seven years. In the autumn of 1946, Spencer H. Mitchell, destined to be Montana's longest serving adjutant general (1943–1962), took on the challenge of reorganizing the Montana National Guard. After months of negotiations between Congress, the War Department, the U.S. Army, and the National Guard Bureau, the Montana regiment was reconstituted in October 1947 as the 163rd Regimental Combat Team.

The newly organized regiment consisted of the 443rd Field Artillery Battalion headquartered in Missoula (with companies in Kalispell, Missoula, and Deer Lodge), the 210th Engineer Combat Company stationed at Bozeman, and the 3669th Ordnance Company in Helena. In eastern Montana, the 163rd Armored Cavalry Regiment was headquartered in Bozeman, with the 1st Battalion headquartered in Culbertson, the 2nd Battalion in Bozeman, and the 3rd Battalion in Billings. The creation of the Montana Air National Guard in 1947 was of special significance, as part of a revised Department of Defense establishment under President Harry Truman. The Montana Air National Guard was stationed at Gore Hill in Great Falls, now the International Airport, but formerly the home of the famed 7th Ferrying Service during World War II. These major revamps provided Montana with a diverse military structure, setting the stage for the guard's evolution in the Post World War II era.

By 1953, the 210th Engineer Company was made into the 210th Engineer Battalion. In 1954, the 443rd Field Artillery expanded to include the 639th Field Artillery Battalion in Kalispell.

In 1959, the 443rd again reorganized with additional units in Hamilton and Thompson Falls, plus the 639th Field Artillery, headquartered in Kalispell, as the 2nd Battalion to the 190th Field Artillery. This restructuring was in response to the ever-evolving world situation during the Cold War.

In 1963, change came again with the reorganization of the 1st Battalion, 190th Field Artillery, as Company C, 19th Special Forces Group, in Missoula. The 2nd Battalion, 190th Field Artillery, remained in Kalispell with units in Whitefish, Kalispell, and Polson.

Reorganization came again in 1967, when the 2nd Battalion, 190th Field Artillery, was reclassified as the 2nd Squadron of the 163rd Armored Cavalry. For the first time since World War II, the Montana Army Guard for the most part was again under the direction of one regiment.

Later directives divided the 163rd into three squadrons, with the 1st Squadron located in Kalispell and the 2nd in Billings, and the 3rd out-of-state in Nevada. The State Headquarters and separate unit organizations, including aviation, were located in Helena.

Background: 1988–1993

In 1987, the guard's mission took a turn again when the Department of the Army recommended transforming the 163rd Armored Cavalry into a Heavy Separate Armored Brigade—the 163rd Armored Brigade. This was accomplished in 1988–1989, bringing two new battalion headquarters, to Havre and Butte. Previous organizations at these two locations were cavalry troops with approximately 75 personnel.

The 163rd Armored Brigade Separate configuration included the Brigade Headquarters, Bozeman, 1-163rd (Mechanized) Inf., Billings, the 1-163rd Armored Cavalry, Butte, the 2-163rd Armored Cavalry, Kalispell, and the 495th Support Battalion, Havre. All total there were 27 locations associated with the new organization.

As soon as the brigade became operational, however, world events again affected military missions and the structure of the Army. With the demise of the Soviet Union, the United States began downsizing the military. (This downsizing continues today, and the current reorganization of the Montana Army National Guard is a result of this restructuring.)

In 1991, Maj. Gen. Blair, Montana's adjutant general, received word that the 163rd Armored Brigade would be inactivated as early as September 1994. Associated with this inactivation, there was no offer of replacement units. Potentially, the state would reduce its force structure by nearly 83 percent, causing the closing of armories throughout Montana and only leaving the Army National Guard organization in Helena, and the Air National Guard in Great Falls. Through the diligent efforts of the State of Montana, the congressional delegation, and the Montana Army National Guard, the deadline was extended through Fiscal Year 1995.

However, new developments in the nation's armed forces structuring was just around the corner, which further integrated the National Guard and Reserves into key roles in national defense.

Operation Big Sky: 1993 to the Present

On December 10, 1993, a momentous change was announced in the nation's military structure as it affected reserve components. This Army Guard and Reserve restructuring, as agreed to in the Off Site Agreement, redefined missions and announced the new strength of the Army Guard and Reserve. There were three key parts to the plan.

First, there were overall reductions. By Fiscal Year 1999 (October 1, 1998), the Army National Guard would be reduced to 367,000 personnel and the Army Reserve, 208,000. (The strengths at the end of FY93 were: Army National Guard 422,700, and Army Reserve 279,600.)

Second, the Army National Guard would focus on both a wartime combat mission and a peacetime domestic emergency mission. Therefore, some force structure currently in the Army Reserve would be transferred to the Army National Guard. The guard would gain artillery, aviation, mechanized infantry, armor, and Special Forces units.

Third, the Army Reserve would focus on providing combat service support missions during wartime. Some force structure currently in the Army Guard would be transferred to the Army Reserve. The Army Reserve would retain such units as needed for medical, signal, military police, and transportation missions. Overall, the restructuring would be implemented in ways to protect personnel and enhance readiness.

In December 1993, Maj. Gen. John E. "Gene" Prendergast in Montana received notification from the National Guard Bureau of the proposed Army Guard and Reserve restructuring. This was shortly followed by a formal notification when Prendergast attended the Adjutant Generals Association Meeting in Washington, D.C. Upon returning to Montana, Prendergast formed an initial group to plan and coordinate the force structure initiative.

In May 1994, the National Guard Bureau notified Prendergast about the type of units included in the new Montana Army National Guard Force Structure. Prendergast quickly established a committee to fully develop reorganization concept plans for his review. In October, he selected the best of the three proposed courses of action for the stationing of Montana guard units, as well as setting up a provisional headquarters to develop implementation directives.

Consequently, the provisional headquarters identified the specific tasks of reorganization in Operations Order 1-94, "Operation Big Sky." Prendergast and key staff visited Fort Lewis to develop a Memorandum of Understanding for the transfer of the Infantry Battalion from Oregon to Montana. He also briefed the National Guard Bureau leadership on the proposed plan to transfer the unit, which the bureau approved.

Because of the fluid situation, Prendergast reformed the reorganization team to review and complete tasks identified in OPLAN "Big Sky." During December's Inactive Duty Training period, the team briefed Prendergast, the National Guard leadership, and key personnel, ordering implementation of Operation Big Sky to begin, effective February 1, 1995. The completion date for reorganization was October 1, 1997.

With Operation Big Sky in place, reorganization quickly commenced in a three phase program. A year later, a press release issued on February 14, 1996, to the public and media presented a comprehensive outline of the restructuring:

> MONTANA ARMY NATIONAL GUARD REORGANIZATION UPDATE (#1) HELENA, Mont.
>
> -- OPERATION BIG SKY, the directed reorganization of the Montana Army National Guard, has reached another milestone with the completion of Phase I.
>
> Operation Big Sky was developed by a team appointed by Major General John E. "Gene" Prendergast, Montana's Adjutant General and Commander of the Montana National Guard.
>
> The team charter was to review the National Guard Bureau (NGB) directed mission of reorganization, develop tasks and time lines, and make recommendations for implementation of reorganization plans.
>
> General Prendergast approved the Team's recommendations and implementation began February, 1995. Transition activities for all affected units are scheduled to be completed by October, 1997.
>
> No armory facilities are closing as the Montana Guard takes on a new face. The authorized strength of the Guard will be 3,520 at the completion of reorganization. The current strength of the Montana Army Guard is 2,789.
>
> PHASE I (February 1 - September 30, 1995) is complete with the following organizational changes:
>
> In Helena, a new unit, the 3669 General Support Maintenance Company (-), was activated on September 1, 1995. (The unit symbol (-) means part of the unit is detached elsewhere.) The authorized strength is 139 personnel. Det 1 3669 was activated in Missoula with an authorized strength of 116. Combined authorized strength for both locations is 255 personnel and includes gender neutral positions, meaning that either men or women may be assigned.
>
> Detachment 2, Headquarters and Headquarters Company and Detachment 1, Company A, 2-137th Aviation Battalion inactivated in Helena on

October 1, 1995. Activated in their place are Companies B and C, 1-112th Light Utility Helicopter Battalion. The units are located at the new Aviation Unit Armory on the northern side of Helena Regional Airport.

Each LUH company is authorized a strength of 97, for a total of 194 positions. These two organizations are gender neutral to include aviator positions. Their primary aircraft is the UH-1H "Huey" Helicopter.

Finally under PHASE I, Detachment 1, 1214th Medical Company (Air Ambulance) converted to Detachment 1, 1085th Medical Company (Air Ambulance), effective October 1, 1995. The strength is 35 personnel to include gender neutral positions. The unit's primary aircraft is the UH-IV "Huey" Helicopter (Air Ambulance Configuration).

PHASE II started October 1, 1995 and continued through September 30, 1996.

This phase has seen the activation of the new Mechanized Infantry Battalion, the 1-163rd Infantry (Mechanized Bradley Fighting Vehicle) of the 116th Cavalry Brigade, 4th Infantry Division.

The 116th Cavalry, headquartered in Boise, Idaho, is one of the 15 Enhanced Readiness Brigades within the Army National Guard Force Structure.

An Enhanced Brigade is organized and resourced to enable it to mobilize, train, and be available for deployment within 90 days after a Presidential call-up. The 1-163rd Mechanized Infantry, as part of that Brigade, will be able to directly deploy into fast evolving regional conflicts, or to reinforce active component combat units.

The 1-163rd Infantry Battalion was activated in Bozeman, Livingston, Butte, Billings, Missoula, Great Falls, and Lewistown. The total strength is 759 personnel, plus an authorized overstrength of 64 for a total of 823.

Located at the Infantry Battalion Headquarters in Bozeman is a Company Fire Support Element with an authorized strength of 5 personnel.

In addition to the Infantry Battalion's activation, the following units will be reorganized during Phase II:

Second Battalion, 163rd Armor Brigade is reorganizing to become 2-163rd Armor Battalion (Cavalry), a battalion of California's 40th Armor Division. The Battalion Hqs, located in Kalispell, has units in Libby, Deer Lodge, Havre, Missoula, Hamilton, Helena, Shelby, and Whitefish. The total authorized strength is 575 personnel.

Located with the Battalion Hqs in Kalispell is a Company Fire Support Team of 32 personnel, plus a Battalion Fire Support Element from the 40th Armor Division with an authorized strength of 37. A food service augmentation team of 10 brings the strength of the Battalion to 654.

In June, 1996, a Medical Support Detachment, Detachment 3, Hqs State Area Command (STARC) will activate in Billings. Members of this Detachment may be attached to various Guard units throughout the state. With an authorized strength of 60 gender neutral positions, this unit is made up of physicians, nurses and medical support personnel.

During Phase II the 1-189th Attack Helicopter Battalion Headquarters converted to the 1-189th Combat Support Aviation Battalion. Its Hqs, with Company A, is located at the new Aviation Unit Armory at the Helena Regional Airport complex. The remaining companies of this new Battalion are located in Idaho, Utah, and Arizona. Their primary aircraft is the UH-60 Black Hawk helicopter.

A support airlift detachment of eight personnel are located with the Battalion. This detachment operates the C-12R Fixed Wing Aircraft in support of state and federal missions in Montana.

PHASE III (October 1, 1996 - September 30, 1997) will conclude all activities concerning the Montana Army National Guard Reorganization: The 210th Personnel Services Company of Helena will be inactivated. In its place will be a Personnel Services Detachment with an authorized strength of 48 personnel.

A new organization, the 1-190th Field Artillery Battalion of Wyoming's 115th Artillery Brigade, will complete activation by September 1, 1996. With its Headquarters in Billings, the Battalion will include companies and detachments located in Malta, Miles City, Chinook, Glendive, Glasgow, Sidney, Plentywood and Culbertson with an authorized strength of 579.

In addition, several other units will be activated, including a B495th General Maintenance Company to be located in Havre, Harlowton and Billings with an authorized strength of 222 gender neutral positions.

The 1063rd Engineer Company, that specializes in paving roads, is currently being activated in Dillon and Anaconda with a total strength of 172 with gender neutral positions.

During this time period, a series of inactivations will occur. The primary inactivation will be of Bozeman's 163rd Armored Brigade (Separate) and its five subordinate Battalions, four of which are located in Montana and one in Wyoming.

The Montana Guard's 163rd lineage and honors will be retained with the 1st Battalion of the 163rd Mechanized Infantry.

The results of the Reorganization will be three combat battalions and numerous separate units, all under the control of the 95th Troop Command, a part of HQ STARC. They will oversee the operational and administrative functions of the Montana units.

General Prendergast's primary goal is to effectively reorganize the Montana Army National Guard with as little turbulence as possible for soldiers and their families. Maintaining opportunities for careers and advancement throughout the Guard is a major goal. OPERATION BIG SKY is designed to maximize these goals of the Montana Army National Guard.

The new Montana units, in addition to being able to conduct their assigned federal missions, will remain in all of their current community locations and will continue to effectively respond to state and community missions.

In effect the Montana Army Guard continues its proud heritage of nearly 130 years of federal, state and community service as it enters the 21st Century.

FY 1998 (1997–1998)

The Montana Army National Guard (MTARNG) successfully concluded the Operation Big Sky reorganization and also executed a $62 million building program in Fiscal Year 1998. The construction projects included an Army Aviation Support Facility at the Helena Regional Airport, the Fort Harrison Training Site Support Facility at Fort William Henry Harrison, and a Basic Officer/Enlisted Quarters at Fort Harrison, which increased the fort's capacity to nearly 800 soldiers. The Armed Forces Reserve Center in Billings was also initiated.

The 1049th Engineer Battalion (Fire Fighters) mobilized in July 1997 for Operation Joint Guard in Hungary, returning in the spring of 1998.

MTARNG began moving toward a statewide Distance Learning Initiative in partnership with a number of federal and state agencies, with a projected authorized funding of $4.6 million in FY99.

More than 600 MTARNG soldiers participated in Operation Desert Avenger at the National Training Center, Fort Irwin, California—this was an additional benefit of having Montana's Troop E, 163rd ACR as a separate armored cavalry troop, to stand up as a roundout unit to the 11th Armored Cavalry Regiment "Black Horse."

Montana guard personnel also conducted medical missions to Kyrgyzstan under Partnership for Peace, and to Bolivia under SOUTHCOM directive.

FY 1999 (1998–1999)

The Montana Army National Guard continued to fulfill its federal mission, meeting the challenge of deployment to El Salvador, Honduras, Germany, Kazakhstan, Kyrgyzstan, and Japan. Montana stood up new units—such as Troop E, 163rd Cavalry, part of the NTC OPFOR 11th Armored Cavalry "Black Horse" Regiment. Montana also began fielding new Army Division Redesign Strategy units with relevant and immediate real world missions.

The MTARNG led the National Guard in new military construction during FY99, with over $31 million for ongoing construction at several key facilities, including the Billings Armed Forces Reserve Center, the Helena Armed Forces Reserve Center, and the Pistol and Rifle Qualification Ranges and Simulation Center. Additionally, the MTARNG provided $4.6 million for the Distance Learning Initiative and $41.9 million for the Youth ChalleNGe Program in the state. The MTARNG successfully launched the Youth ChalleNGe Program by recruiting 124 students in its first year.

The MTARNG strengthened its presence in 28 local communities in FY99 through ongoing recruiting and counter drug programs. Successful community action projects included Christmas at Our House, American Cancer Society's Relay for Life, Race for the Cure, Kaleidoscope Food Drive, and the Disabled American Veterans Homeless Stand Down.

FY 2000 (1999–2000)

MTARNG established itself as a national leader in its military training facilities, and the Department of Defense's Partnership for Peace program. Montana units performed missions in El Salvador and supported contingency operations in Kuwait.

Montana's fire season was the worst in modern history. After close to 1 million acres burned, the MTARNG stepped forward. Over 1,600 soldiers served on state active duty to combat the blazes, distinguishing themselves nationally as the only troops to commit to fire-line duty in addition to traditional support missions.

Military construction projects exceeded $9.7 million after completion of the 130,000 sq. ft. Billings Armed Forces Reserve Center (AFRC), a state-of-the-art simulation training center, upgraded weapons firing ranges, a new modern lodging facility, and groundbreaking of the Helena AFRC. Fort Harrison was a regionally recognized, high quality training center for all military services and components.

Based at Western Montana College, Montana's Youth ChalleNGe program graduated 134 students from its first two classes.

The Guard's 49 units—located in 22 communities statewide—had an annual $148 million economic impact, remaining integral to the state's resource infrastructure, economic base, and social fabric.

The Montana Army National Guard received adequate funding during FY00. Early in the first quarter, shortages were identified in Communications Services, Administrative Support, Technician Training, and Travel programs. Montana reprogrammed the existing Annual Funding Program (AFP) to make up these shortages. Wildfires in July and August severely impacted the fourth quarter allocation of training dollars. As a result, Montana turned in excess National Guard Pay and Allowance AFP to the National Guard Bureau prior to the fiscal year's end. Overall, the MTARNG was able to fund all training requirements and execute funding in accordance with FY00 spending priorities.

FY 2001 (2000–2001)

The Montana guard maintained its status as a national leader in military training facilities and as the home of some of the nation's best-rated forces. Upon completing nation-building missions in El Salvador, contingency operations in Kuwait, and dropping 2.3 million gallons of water during 4,483 accident-free sorties in the fire season, the 1-189th CSAB was selected as the top Army National Guard aviation unit for 2000, receiving the Army Aviation Association's Outstanding Aviation Unit award.

Montana's Blackhorse unit, TRP E 163rd CAV, conducted full-scale OPFOR training with the 11th ACR for the first time since placement in the state. They won all engagements and provided outstanding training for the U.S. Army's 3rd Infantry Division.

Unique training accomplishments included airlifting a Brontosaurus skull—the largest dinosaur skull ever found in the world. The MTARNG also planned and conducted its largest community-support activity in state history, when 3,000 citizens joined Montana's governor, the congressional delegation, and author Stephen Ambrose in a "Salute to the Greatest Generation," honoring World War II and all armed forces veterans.

Montana's 43 Army Guard units had an annual $61 million economic impact in the state.

The MTARNG received sufficient funding during FY01, but, as in past years, the trend of shortages in Communications Services and Technician Pay continued. Montana reprogrammed existing AFP from other Operations and Maintenance programs in order to makeup the shortages and fund additional technician positions authorized by Congress. A new strategy for execution of NGPA funding was introduced to significantly reduce "de-obligation" or "grow-back" of FY02 funds. Overall, the MTARNG was able to fund all training requirements and execute funding in accordance with FY01 spending priorities.

FY 2002 (2001–2002)

The MTARNG took on unprecedented, critical new missions as part of America's heightened security efforts following the 9/11 World Trade Center attack in New York. The Montana guard's Installation Security mission began immediately on September 12, 2001 (and continues today). Over 30 Army guard personnel would provide 24-hour security at Fort Harrison.

Montana's 1-189th CSAB was designated as command and control for Department of Defense units supporting Salt Lake City's 2002 Winter Olympics. In Operation Airport Guardian, the Montana guard staffed 14 airports with up to 126 security personnel for over six months. Guard members received many compliments from air travelers about their reassuring presence in airports. The Montana guard also provided security on the border with Canada, assisting U.S. Border Patrol agents at 19 border-crossings. The MTARNG also continued its commitment in the Innovative Readiness Training program. Guard members conducted 10 separate IRT exercises in FY02.

Montana was involved in international objectives as well, supporting SFOR 11. Three units deployed to Bosnia for six months to support the peacekeeping mission.

The MTARNG received sufficient funding in NGPA and actually grew in OMNG funds during FY02. For the first time ever, states were allowed to align their OMNG funding at the start of the fiscal year to make up shortages in programs, such as Technician Pay or Communication Services. Montana continued to use locally developed automated programs to assist with the review of unliquidated obligations, specifically unpaid orders, which significantly reduced the "growback" of the current and prior years' NGPA funds. Overall, the MTARNG was able to fund all training requirements and execute funding in accordance with FY02 spending priorities.

Members of the 1-190th Field Artillery conducted annual training in Suffield, Alberta, at the British Army Training Unit Suffield. The terrain provided the soldiers with an extremely realistic and challenging training experience. The Montana guard also soon fielded new equipment, most notably, the first CH-47 "Chinook" helicopter.

FY 2003 (2002–2003)

Montana guard members took on a significant additional mission in wildfire fighting, creating an aerial initial attack. Air crews established helibases along with state fire-fighting entities, putting out fires before they grew too large. This measure saved the State of Montana thousands of dollars in fire-fighting costs. The MTARNG also continued its commitment to its citizens through the Innovative Readiness Training program, conducting eight separate medical exercises.

The MTARNG again received adequate funding in National Guard Personnel, Army, and Operations and Maintenance funding. Montana continued to lead the way in having less than 1 percent "growback" of prior year funds. The MTARNG interest penalties were .0001 percent, significantly under the allowable authorized. Montana deployed over 200 soldiers in FY03, and another 200 soldiers were activated to assist in fighting fires. Overall, the MTARNG was able to fund all training requirements and execute funding in accordance with FY03 spending priorities.

FY 2004 (2003–2004)

An increase in deployments occurred in support of Operation Enduring Freedom (typically, Afghanistan) and Operation Iraqi Freedom. At one point in the year, 55 percent of MTARNG service members were mobilized or alerted. MTARNG combat support and combat service support units continued to operate in these overseas theaters, while combat arms units at mobilization stations prepared for overseas deployments in FY05.

The MTARNG expanded its role as a leader in the State Partnership Program. A large delegation from Montana, including educators, civic leaders, and officials from state government and the guard traveled to Kyrgyzstan for a historic visit. Adjutant General Prendergast received the Kyrgyz Medal of Glory, in appreciation of the MTARNG providing humanitarian assistance to the Republic of Kyrgyzstan.

In a formal ceremony in September 2004, Maj. Gen. John E. "Gene" Prendergast retired as adjutant general. Randy Mosley took the reins of the MTARNG and was promoted to major general in the same ceremony. Prendergast retired with 46 years of military service—12 while serving as Montana's adjutant general.

For the first time ever, the MTARNG received more National Guard Personnel, Army (NGPA), and Operations and Maintenance funds than it could execute (largely due to an over 50 percent deployment rate). Loss of funding flexibility at the state level severely impacted MTARNG's ability to move funding where requirements existed. Montana continued to use locally developed automated programs to assist with review of unliquidated obligations, specifically unpaid orders, which significantly reduced "growback" of current and prior year NGPA funds; this earned recognition from National Guard Bureau for excellent business practices. Overall, the MTARNG was able to fund all training requirements and execute funding in accordance with FY04 spending priorities.

FY 2005 (2004–2005)

The MTARNG began FY05 with over half of its assigned strength deployed in support of Enduring Freedom, Iraqi Freedom, and Noble Eagle (securing North American skies); and ended FY05 with the deployment of 130 soldiers supporting Hurricane Katrina relief efforts.

In January, Governor Brian Schweitzer announced his appointment of Maj. Gen. Randall D. Mosley as Montana Adjutant General and head of the Department of Military Affairs for the State of Montana.

The MTARNG continued its strong support of the State Partnership Program in Kyrgyzstan. Because of political unrest in Kyrgyzstan, however, only two of the seventeen planned events were supported. Major General Mosley visited Kyrgyzstan, demonstrating Montana's continued support of the program and ties to that country.

In support of its state response mission, the MTARNG established a continuity of operations and a wide-area wireless network between the Joint Force Headquarters and the Montana Air National Guard Headquarters, ensuring continuous operations in case either of the locations became non-operational. Also, the 83rd Civil Support Team, one of the Phase 5 teams, began establishing its operations during FY05.

The MTARNG's National Guard Personnel, Army Appropriation accounts were reduced by almost 24 percent, and the Operations and Maintenance, Army National Guard Appropriation accounts were reduced by almost 22 percent. Because of rigorous and effective funds management, however, the MTARNG's funds execution allowed the state to maintain full readiness and to continue support of transformation requirements. Overall, the MTARNG met its requirements and executed funds in accordance with ARNG financial constraints.

FY 2006 (2005–2006)

The MTARNG began FY06 with a strength of 2,518 and ended the year at 2,616. This increase was due to the Global War on Terrorism's impact on recruitment and the fact that over 60 percent of MTARNG's assigned strength returned from deployments in support of Enduring Freedom, Iraqi Freedom, and Noble Eagle. Successful retention was also a factor.

After two intensive years dedicated to personnel selections, significant schooling requirements, and sustainment training, the 83rd Civil Support Team (CST) successfully passed all 15 external certification requirements. After receiving its certification from the Secretary of Defense, the CST provided support to Montana's civil authorities.

The Montana guard celebrated other significant accomplishments. The 1049th Firefighters Unit was the first in the Army to field new tactical firefighting trucks. Over 25 percent of students in Montana schools were taught the importance of the Lewis and Clark Expedition in American history. The MTARNG conducted eight medical innovative readiness trainings in support of the Native American population. The Joint Headquarters staff was validated to perform joint homeland security operations. And, the MTARNG provided support in Hurricane Katrina relief and wildland fire-fighting missions.

The Montana Army National Guard began FY06 under a continuing readiness resolution extending into February 2006; through diligent resource management, the MTARNG met its readiness requirements. Restrictions in Active Guard Reserve (AGR) travel, caused by transformation, required more AGR permanent change of station moves than anticipated. School requirements exceeded initial funding, but funding was increased to meet requirements. FY06 ended short in technician pay, but the National Guard Bureau provided the needed funding.